FOURTH EDITION

BUSINESS FORECASTING

JOHN E. HANKE
ARTHUR G. REITSCH
Eastern Washington University

ALLYN AND BACON
Boston   London   Sydney   Toronto   Tokyo   Singapore

Dedicated to Harry, Gerry, Jack, and Irene (who don't need to read it);
Judy and Judy (who will and probably won't, respectively);
Jill, Amy, Julie, Katrina, and Kevin (who might);
and all of our students (who better).

Executive Editor: Richard Wohl
Series Editorial Assistant: Cheryl Ten Eick
Editorial–Production Service: Raeia Maes
Composition and Manufacturing Buyer: Megan Cochran
Cover Administrator: Linda Dickinson

Copyright © 1992, 1989, 1986, 1981 by Allyn and Bacon
A Division of Simon & Schuster, Inc.
160 Gould Street
Needham Heights, MA 02194

Library of Congress Cataloging-in-Publication Data

Hanke, John E., 1940–
    Business forecasting / John E. Hanke, Arthur G. Reitsch.—4th
ed.
      p.   cm.
    Includes bibliographical references and index.
    ISBN 0-205-13349-5
    1. Business forecasting.   I. Reitsch, Arthur G., 1938–
II. Title.
HD30.27.H37 1991
338.5'44—dc20   91-32555
                                            CIP

Printed in the United States of America

10 9 8 7 6 5 4 3 2 1   96 95 94 93 92 91

CONTENTS

10 THE BOX-JENKINS (ARIMA) METHODOLOGY   381

11 JUDGMENTAL ELEMENTS IN FORECASTING   451

PREFACE

The goal of the fourth edition of *Business Forecasting* remains the same as that of the previous editions: to present the basic statistical techniques that are useful for preparing individual business forecasts and long-range plans. This book is written in a simple straightforward style and makes extensive use of practical business examples. Twenty-five cases appear at the end of the chapters to provide the students with the necessary link between theoretical concepts presented in the text and their real-world applications. The emphasis is on the application of techniques by management for decision making. Students are assumed to have taken an introductory course in both statistics and computer usage.

ORGANIZATION

All chapters have been revised to enhance the clarity of the writing and to increase teaching and learning effectiveness. The content has been organized into six sections.

The first section (Chapters 1 and 2) serves as background and lays the groundwork. The nature of forecasting and a quick review of basic statistical concepts set the stage for the coverage of techniques that begin in the second section.

The second section (Chapters 3 and 4) emphasizes data collection methods, the exploration of data patterns, and the choosing of a forecasting technique.

The third section (Chapter 5) covers averaging and smoothing techniques. The fourth section (Chapters 6 and 7) emphasizes causal forecasting techniques, such as correlation, regression, and multiple regression analysis. The fifth section (Chapters 8 through 10) looks at techniques involving time series analysis. The book concludes with a final chapter (Chapter 11) on technological and judgemental forecasting techniques, along with a discussion of managing and monitoring the forecasting process.

CHANGES IN THE FOURTH EDITION

The following changes are new in this edition:

- A new chapter (four) on exploring data patterns and choosing a forecasting technique.
- Several examples of how to use Minitab have been added throughout all chapters.
- Most of the exercises are new in Chapters 4 through 9.
- Seven new data sets have been added to Appendix E.
- New discussions of double moving averages and double exponential smoothing have been added to old Chapter 4, which is now new Chapter 5.
- A comprehensive case has been added to Chapter 11.
- A new discussion on tracking and monitoring forecasts has been added to Chapter 11.
- A new discussion of macroeconomic forecasting has been added to Chapter 1.

FEATURES OF THIS TEXT

The following features have proven to be effective, and are included in this edition:

- A wealth of real world cases—both solved and unsolved—included in every chapter.
- Helpful learning aids—included in each chapter are applications to management, glossary, key formulas, problems, and case studies.
- Computer output from different computer packages are provided at the end of each chapter. They familiarize students with a range of software packages used in the business world and teach them how to read the output.
- A unique chapter (9) on econometric topics, including coverage of the regression of time series data that makes these difficult concepts understandable to students.
- A unique chapter (10) that explains autocorrelation analysis and the use of Box-Jenkins techniques in understandable terms.
- A chapter (11) emphasizing judgmental forecasting techniques, an important but often overlooked set of techniques.

THE ROLE OF THE COMPUTER

In the first three editions, the computer was recognized as a powerful tool in forecasting. The computer is even more important now, with modern managers taking advantage of the ease and availability of sophisticated forecasting afforded by desk-top microcomputers.

The authors have spent several sleepless nights deciding what to do about the computer. Two nationwide research studies conducted by the authors to determine what faculty do about using computers for teaching forecasting showed that (1) most forecasting faculty attempt to provide students with hands-on experience in using the computer, and (2) several mainframe statistical packages and specific personal computer forecasting packages were mentioned in the survey. The packages mentioned most frequently were Minitab, SAS, SPSS^X, SPSSpc, Sibyl/Runner, TSP, and Lotus 1-2-3.

The authors decided to use the following approaches to help faculty and students use the computer for forecasting:

1. Minitab instructions are presented throughout all chapters of the book.
2. A brief look at computer forecasting packages in general has been placed at the end of Chapter 1.
3. Examples of different computer outputs are placed throughout the text.
4. Examples of four computer packages are provided at the end of various chapters: packages include Minitab, SAS, SPSS^X, and TSP.

SUPPLEMENTS

The Instructor's Manual includes answers to chapter-end problems, comments on the case studies that appear at the end of most chapters, and multiple choice questions.

A Student Edition of Forecast Plus by Walonick Associates, a popular forecasting package for microcomputers, can be purchased at a special discount when packaged with the textbook.

A Data Disk is available to qualified adopters upon request. The disk contains numerous data sets to be used for student practice.

ACKNOWLEDGMENTS

The authors are indebted to the many instructors around the world who have used the first three editions and have provided invaluable suggestions for improving the book. Special thanks go to Professor Frank Forst (Marquette University), Professor William Darrow (Towson State University), Professor William C. Struning (Seton Hall University), Professor Mark Craze (Eastern Washington University), and Professor Shik Chun Young (Eastern Washington University); to Marilyn Love, Judy Johnson, Dorothy

Mercer, Vicki LaBlanc, and Paul Nosbisch (Decision Science Associates) for providing cases; and to Jennifer Dahl for constructing the index.

The authors sincerely appreciate the time taken by J. Scott Armstrong, Judy Johnson, and Essam Muhoud who provided useful materials. Also, portions of this text, particularly several data sets, are adapted from those that appeared in our *Understanding Business Statistics* text published by Richard D. Irwin, Inc., whom we here credit for this reuse.

We also thank reviewers Benito Flores, Texas A & M; Harriet Hinck, Trenton State College; Leo Mahoney, Bryant College; David R. McKenna, Boston College; Ahman Sorabian, Cal State Polytech; and Richard Withycombe, University of Montana, for their very constructive comments in the revision of the book. If we were talented enough to accomplish everything our reviewers suggested, this book would be improved 100 percent. As is, we did our best.

Finally, we thank our computers and wonder how we ever wrote a textbook without one. We, not the computers, are responsible for any errors. We also sincerely thank Ruth Kembel who recently retired. *Business Forecasting* would have never made the first edition without her.

J. E. H.
A. G. R.

Introduction to Forecasting

T his book is concerned with the process of business forecasting. This process involves the study of historical data to discover their underlying tendencies and patterns and the use of this knowledge to project the data into future time periods as forecasts. As the world of business has become more complex, the need to assess the future on some rational basis has grown, and forecasting has assumed a prominent position in the business administration process.

HISTORY OF FORECASTING

Many of the forecasting techniques used today and discussed in this book were developed in the nineteenth century; regression analysis procedures are an example. By contrast, some of the topics in this book were developed and have received attention only recently. The Box–Jenkins procedures fall into this category.

With the development of more sophisticated forecasting techniques, along with the advent of the electronic computer, forecasting has achieved more and more attention during recent years. This statement is especially true since the proliferation of the small, personal computer. Every manager now has the ability to utilize very sophisticated data analysis techniques for forecasting purposes, and an understanding of these techniques is now essential for business managers.

New techniques for forecasting continue to be developed as management attention to the forecasting process continues to grow. A particular focus of this attention is on the errors that are an inherent part of any forecasting procedure. Predictions as to future outcomes rarely are precisely on the mark; the forecaster can only endeavor to make the inevitable errors small.

NEED FOR FORECASTING

In view of inherent inaccuracies in the process, why is forecasting necessary? The answer is that all organizations operate in an atmosphere of uncertainty and that, in spite of this fact, decisions must be made that affect the future of the organization. Educated guesses about the future are more valuable to organization managers than are uneducated guesses. This book discusses various ways of making forecasts that rely on logical methods of manipulating the data that have been generated by historical events.

This is not to say that intuitive forecasting is bad. On the contrary, the "gut" feelings of persons who manage organizations are often the best forecasts available. This text discusses forecasting techniques that can be used to supplement the common sense and management ability of decision makers. A decision maker is better off understanding quantitative forecasting techniques and using them wisely than being forced to plan for the future without the benefit of valuable supplemental information.

The role of judgmental forecasting appears to have changed during recent years. Before the advent of modern forecasting techniques and the power of the computer, the manager's judgment was the only forecasting tool available. There is now evidence that forecasts using judgment only are not as accurate as those involving judicious application of quantitative techniques:

> Humans possess unique knowledge and inside information not available to quantitative methods. Surprisingly, however, empirical studies and laboratory experiments have shown that their forecasts are not more accurate than those of quantitative methods. Humans tend to be optimistic and underestimate future uncertainty. In addition, the cost of forecasting with judgmental methods is often considerably higher than when quantitative methods are used.[1]

It is our view that the most effective forecaster is able to formulate a skillful mix of quantitative forecasting techniques and good judgment and to avoid the extremes of total reliance on either. At the one extreme we find the executive who, through ignorance and fear of quantitative techniques and computers, relies solely on intuition and feel. At the other extreme is the forecaster skilled in the latest sophisticated data manipulation techniques who is unable or unwilling to relate the forecasting process to the needs of the organization and its decision makers. We view the quantitative forecasting techniques discussed in this book to be only the starting point in the effective forecasting of outcomes important to the organization: analysis, judgment, common sense, and business experience must be brought to bear at the point where these important techniques have generated their results.

Since the world in which organizations operate has always been changing, forecasts have always been necessary. However, recent years

---

[1] S. Makridakis, "The Art and Science of Forecasting," *International Journal of Forecasting*, Vol. 2 (1986), p. 17.

have brought about increased reliance on techniques which involve sophisticated data manipulation techniques. New technology and new disciplines have sprung up overnight; government activity at all levels has intensified; competition in many areas has become more keen; international trade has stepped up in almost all industries; social help and service agencies have been created and have grown. These factors have combined to create an organizational climate that is more complex, more fast-paced, and more competitive than ever before. Organizations that cannot react quickly to changing conditions and that cannot foresee the future with any degree of accuracy are doomed to extinction.

Electronic computers, along with the quantitative techniques they make possible, have become more than a convenience for modern organizations: they have become essential. The complexities discussed above generate tremendous amounts of data and an overwhelming need to extract useful information from these data. The modern tools of forecasting, along with the capabilities of the electronic computer, have become indispensable for organizations operating in the modern world.

Who needs forecasts? Almost every organization, large and small, private and public, uses forecasting either explicitly or implicitly, because almost every organization must plan to meet the conditions of the future for which it has imperfect knowledge. In addition, the need for forecasts cuts across all functional lines as well as across all types of organizations. Forecasts are needed in finance, marketing, personnel, and production areas; in government and profit-making organizations; in small social clubs and in national political parties. Consider the following questions that suggest the need for some forecasting procedures.

- If we increase our advertising budget by 10%, how will sales be affected?
- What revenue might the state government expect over the next two-year period?
- How many units might we sell in an effort to recover our fixed investment in production equipment?
- What factors can we identify that will help explain the variability in monthly unit sales?
- What is a year-by-year prediction for the total loan balance of our bank over the next ten years?
- Will there be a recession? If so, when will it begin, how severe will it be, and when will it end?

TYPES OF FORECASTS

When organization managers are faced with the need to make decisions in an atmosphere of uncertainty, what types of forecasts are available to them?

Forecasting procedures might first be classified as long-term or short-term. Long-term predictions are necessary to set the general course of an organization for the long run; they thus become the particular focus of top management. Short-term forecasts are used to design immediate strategies and are used by mid-management and first-line management to meet the needs of the immediate future.

Forecasts might also be classified in terms of their position on a micro-macro continuum, that is, on the extent to which they involve small details vs. large summary values. For example, a plant manager might be interested in forecasting the number of workers needed for the next several months (a micro-forecast), while the federal government is forecasting the total number of people employed in the entire country (a macro-forecast). Again, different levels of management in an organization tend to focus on different levels of the micro-macro continuum. Top management would be interested in forecasting the sales of the entire company, for example, while individual salespersons would be much more interested in forecasting their own sales volumes.

Forecasting procedures can also be classified according to whether they tend to be more quantitative or qualitative. At one extreme, a purely qualitative technique is one requiring no overt manipulation of data. Only the "judgment" of the forecaster is used. Even here, of course, the forecaster's "judgment" is actually a result of the mental manipulation of past historical data. At the other extreme, purely quantitative techniques need no input of judgment; they are mechanical procedures that produce quantitative results. Some quantitative procedures require a much more sophisticated manipulation of data than do others, of course. This book emphasizes the quantitative forecasting techniques because a broader understanding of these very useful procedures is needed in the effective management of modern organizations. However, we must emphasize again that judgment and common sense must be used along with the mechanical and data manipulative procedures discussed here. Only in this way can intelligent forecasting take place.

MACROECONOMIC FORECASTING

We usually think of forecasting in terms of predicting important variables for an individual company or perhaps one component of a company. Monthly company sales, unit sales for one of a company's stores, and absent hours per employee per month in a factory are examples.

By contrast, there is growing interest in forecasting important variables for the entire economy of a country. Much work has been done in evaluating methods for doing this kind of overall economic forecasting, called *macroeconomic forecasting*. Examples of interest to the federal government of the United States are unemployment rate, gross national product, and the prime interest rate.

Economic policy is based, in part, on projections of important economic indicators such as the three just mentioned. For this reason, there is great interest in improving forecasting methods that focus on such overall measures of a country's economic performance. Currently, forecasting methods can be generally divided into two approaches: methods that use traditional time series analysis approaches, and less structured methods that focus on the statistical properties of historical measurements. Both these approaches are described in this book.

One of the chief difficulties in developing accurate forecasts of overall economic activity is an unexpected and significant shift in a key economic factor. Among such factors are significant changes in oil prices, inflation surges, and broad policy changes by another country's government that affect the U.S. economy.

The possibility of such significant shifts in the economic scene has raised a key question in macroeconomic forecasting: Should the forecasts generated by the forecasting model be modified using the forecaster's judgment? Current work on forecasting methodology often involves this question.

Much work, both theoretical and practical, continues on the subject of macroeconomic forecasting. A recent issue of the *International Journal of Forecasting* is devoted to this subject (Volume 6, Number 3, October 1990). Considering the importance of accurate economic forecasting to economic policy formulation in this country and others, continuing attention to this kind of forecasting in the future can be expected.

CHOOSING A FORECASTING METHOD

The above discussion suggests several factors to be considered in choosing a forecasting method. The level of detail must be considered. Are forecasts of specific details needed (a micro-forecast)? Or, is the future status of some overall or summary factor needed (a macro-forecast)? Is the forecast needed for some point in the near future (a short-term forecast), or for a point in the distant future (a long-term forecast)? And, to what extent are qualitative (judgment) and quantitative (data manipulative) methods appropriate?

The overriding consideration in choosing a forecasting method is that the results must facilitate the decision-making process of the organization's managers. The essential requirement, then, is not that the forecasting method involve a complicated mathematical process or that it be the latest sophisticated method. Rather, the method chosen should produce a forecast which is accurate, timely, and understood by management so that the forecast can help produce better decisions. As well, the use of the forecasting procedure must produce a benefit that is in excess of the cost associated with its use.

FORECASTING STEPS

All formal forecasting procedures involve extending the experiences of the past into the uncertain future. They thus involve the assumption that the conditions that generated past data are indistinguishable from the conditions of the future except for those variables explicitly recognized by the forecasting model. If one is forecasting job performance ratings of employees using only the company entrance examination score as a predictor, for example, it is being assumed that each person's job performance rating is affected only by the entrance examination score. To the extent that this assumption of indistinguishable past and future is not met, inaccurate forecasts result unless they are modified by the judgment of the forecaster.

The recognition that forecasting techniques operate on the data generated by past historical events leads to the identification of the following steps in the forecasting process:

> Data collection
> Data reduction or condensation
> Model building
> Model extrapolation (the actual forecast)

Step 1 suggests the importance of getting the proper data and making sure they are correct. This step is often the most challenging part of the entire forecasting process, and often the most difficult to monitor since subsequent steps can be performed on data whether relevant to the problem at hand or not. Collection and quality control problems usually abound whenever it becomes necessary to obtain pertinent data in an organization.

Step 2, data reduction, is often involved since it is possible to have too much data in the forecasting process as well as too little. Some data may not be relevant to the problem and may reduce forecasting accuracy. Other data may be appropriate but only in certain historical periods. For example, in forecasting the sales of small cars one may wish to use only car sales data since the oil embargo of the 1970s rather than data over the past 50 years.

Step 3, model building, involves fitting the collected data into a forecasting model that is appropriate in terms of minimizing the forecasting error. As well, the simpler the model, the better it is in terms of gaining acceptance of the forecasting process by managers who must make the firm's decisions. Often a balance must be struck between a sophisticated forecasting approach which offers slightly more accuracy and a simple approach that is easily understood and gains the support of—and hence is actively used by—the company's decision makers. Obviously, judgment is involved in this selection process. Since this book discusses numerous forecasting models and their applicability, it is our hope that the reader's ability to exercise good judgment in the choice and use of appropriate forecasting models will increase after studying this material.

Once the appropriate data have been collected and possibly reduced, and an appropriate forecasting model has been chosen, the actual forecasting model extrapolation occurs (step 4). Often the accuracy of the process is checked by forecasting for recent periods in which the actual historical values are known. The forecasting errors are then observed and summarized in some way. Some forecasting procedures sum the absolute values of the errors and may report this sum, or divide it by the number of forecast attempts to produce the average forecast error. Other procedures produce the sum of squared errors, which is then compared with similar figures from alternative forecasting methods. Some procedures also track and report the magnitude of the error terms over the forecasting period. Examination of error patterns often leads the analyst to a modification of the forecasting procedure which then generates more accurate forecasts. Several specific methods of measuring forecasting errors are discussed near the end of Chapter 4.

MANAGING THE FORECASTING PROCESS

The discussion in this chapter serves to underline our belief that management ability and common sense must be involved in the forecasting process. The forecaster should be thought of as an advisor to the manager rather than as the monitor of an automatic decision-making device. Unfortunately, the latter is sometimes the case in practice, especially when the aura of the computer is present. Again, quantitative techniques in the forecasting process must be regarded as what they really are, namely, tools to be used by the manager in arriving at better decisions.

> The usefulness and utility of forecasting can be improved if management adopts a more realistic attitude. Forecasting should not be viewed as a substitute for prophecy but rather as the best way of identifying and extrapolating established patterns or relationships in order to forecast. If such an attitude is accepted, forecasting errors must be considered inevitable and the circumstances that cause them investigated.[2]

With the preceding in mind several key questions should always be raised if management of the forecasting process is to be properly conducted.

- Why is a forecast needed?

---

[2] Ibid., p. 33.

- Who will use the forecast, and what are their specific requirements?
- What level of detail or aggregation is required, and what is the proper time horizon?
- What data are available, and will the data be sufficient to generate the needed forecast?
- What will the forecast cost?
- How accurate can we expect the forecast to be?
- Will the forecast be made in time to help the decision-making process?
- Does the forecaster clearly understand how the forecast will be used in the organization?
- Is a feedback process available to evaluate the forecast after it is made and adjust the forecasting process accordingly?

COMPUTER FORECASTING PACKAGES

The area that has had the greatest impact on forecasting in the past decade is the development of computer software packages specifically designed to deal directly with various forecasting methods. Two types of computer packages are of interest to forecasters: (1) statistical packages that include regression analysis and other techniques used frequently by forecasters, and (2) forecasting packages that are specifically designed for forecasting applications.

Hundreds of statistical and forecasting packages have been developed for both mainframes and microcomputers (personal computers, frequently referred to as PCs). Managers with PCs on their desks and a knowledge of forecasting techniques are no longer dependent on other people for their forecasts. Modern managers are taking advantage of the ease and availability of sophisticated forecasting afforded by personal computers.

In this section, some of the more commonly used statistical and forecasting computer packages will be mentioned. The authors are not recommending one software package over another. Instead, an attempt is made to create an awareness of what packages exist for forecasters. Statistical packages that run on mainframe computers and include subparts that deal directly with various forecasting methods have been used frequently in the past. Three of the most popular packages are Minitab (see examples of output throughout the text), the Statistical Package for the Social Sciences (SPSS[X]) (see an example of output at the end of Chapter 6), and Statistical Analysis System (SAS) (see an example of output at the end of Chapter 6). A very useful summary of 48 mainframe statistical packages has been compiled by Mahmoud, Rice, McGee, and Beaumont.[3] Unfortunately, these

---

[3] E. Mahmoud, G. Rice, V. E. McGee, and C. Beaumont, "Mainframe Multipurpose Forecasting Software: A Survey," *Journal of Forecasting*, Vol. 5 (1986), pp. 127–137.

forecasting subroutines require knowledge of the total package and a fairly sophisticated analyst for their application.

During recent years, a new type of mainframe forecasting package specifically aimed at the needs of managers has been developed. Sibyl/Runner, owned and supported by Applied Decision Systems, has gained widespread acceptance over the past several years. It has been used successfully by both companies and academic institutions. A new package called Futurcast: The Total Forecasting System, developed by Spyros Makridakis and Robert Carbone, is another good example of an interactive forecasting package designed for managers. This package is marketed by Futurion Associates, Inc. TSP (see an example of output at the end of Chapter 9) and Shazam are two packages that have found widespread usage by economic forecasters. A very useful summary of 37 mainframe forecasting packages has been compiled by Mahmoud, Rice, McGee, and Beaumont.[4]

Minitab, SPSS, TSP (see an example of output at the end of Chapter 9), and Sibyl/Runner have recently created versions that run on personal computers. Statpro, StatPac, Daisy, Decision Support Modeling, VisiTrend/Plot, Graph N' Calc, Expert Choice, Nuametrics, and Xtrapolastor are packages similar to Minitab that contain several forecasting methods and can be run on personal computers.

Several forecasting packages have been developed that are specifically designed to run on microcomputers. A few of the many forecasting software packages designed for micros currently being marketed are Autobox Plus by Automatic Forecasting Systems, Inc.; Autocast II by Levenbach Associates, Business and Economic Forecasting; Decision Support System Software by John Wiley & Sons; Economics Software Program (ESP) by Chase Econometrics; Express Easycast by Management Decision Systems, Inc.; Forecast Master by Scientific Systems, Inc.; Forecast Plus by Walonick Associates; 4 Cast by Scientific Systems, Inc.; Forecasting by Hewlett-Packard; Forecast Pro by Business Forecast Systems Inc.; Micranal by Gwilym Jenkins & Partners Ltd.; Micro-BJ by Stratix; MTS (The Multiple Time Series Program) by Automatic Forecasting Systems; Pro*Cast by Fleming Software; +Forecast by Computer Software Consultants, Inc.; RATS by Var Econometrics; Smartforecasts II by Smart Software, Inc.; SORITEC by Sorites Group; Timestat by Timestat, Inc.; The Forecaster by Wadsworth Electronic Publishing Company; and Trends II by SPSS, Inc.

A very useful analysis of several of these micro packages can be found in the March 14, 1989, copy of *PC Magazine*.[5] And a very useful summary of 94 personal computer forecasting packages has been compiled

---

[4] E. Mahmoud, G. Rice, V. E. McGee, and C. Beaumont, "Mainframe Specific Purpose Forecasting Software: A Survey," *Journal of Forecasting*, Vol. 5 (1986), pp. 75–83.

[5] "Statistical Analysis: Forecasting," *PC Magazine*, Vol. 8(5) (March 1989), pp. 225–241.

by Beaumont, Mahmoud, and McGee[6] (1985) and can be found in an article entitled "Microcomputer Forecasting Software: A Survey" in the *Journal of Forecasting.*

It should also be mentioned that integrated packages such as Lotus 1-2-3, Framework, Symphony, Visi On, Lisa 7/7 Office System, and similar software can be used to forecast. None of these integrated packages (with the possible exception of Lisa 7/7) performs forecasting all by itself, but each of them may be easily modified for forecasting. Lotus 1-2-3 add-ons include ForeCalc from Business Forecast Systems, Forecast! for 1-2-3 from Intex Solutions, Add a Stat and Multifit both from Abacus Scientific Software Company, Stat-Packets from Walonick Associates, and The Spreadsheet Forecaster from Levenbach Associates.

For an excellent discussion of business forecasting software, consult "Choosing and Using Business Forecasting Software" in the January 1985 issue of *Creative Computing.*[7]

In summary, the purpose of a forecast is to reduce the range of uncertainty within which management judgments must be made. This purpose suggests two primary rules to which the forecasting process must adhere:

1. The forecast must be technically correct and produce accurate forecasts.
2. The forecasting procedure and its results must be effectively presented to management so that the forecasts are utilized in the decision-making process to the firm's advantage; results must also be justified on a cost–benefit basis.

The latter consideration is often misunderstood and can be frustrating to professional forecasters. Yet, if forecasts are to be used to the firm's benefit, they must be utilized by those in decision-making authority. This fact raises the question of what might be called the "politics" of forecasting. Substantial and sometimes major expenditures and resource allocations within the firm often rest on management's view of the course of future events. As the movement of resources and power within an organization is often based on the perceived direction of the future (forecasts), it is not surprising to find a certain amount of political intrigue surrounding the forecasting process. This consideration underlines the importance of point 2 above: the forecasts which are generated within the firm must be understood and appreciated by its decision makers so that they find their way into management of the firm.

---

[6] C. Beaumont, E. Mahmoud, and V. E. McGee, "Microcomputer Forecasting Software: A Survey," *Journal of Forecasting,* Vol. 4 (1985), pp. 305–311.

[7] K. Keating, "Choosing and Using Business Forecasting Software," *Creative Computing,* 11(1) (January 1985), pp. 119–135.

The remainder of this book discusses various forecasting models and procedures. First, a review of basic statistical concepts appears, followed by a discussion of regression analysis procedures. Forecasting time series data is then discussed, followed by more advanced forecasting techniques in the following chapters. The final chapter in this book discusses the forecasting process as it relates to the decision makers of the firm.

CHAPTER **1**

SELECTED BIBLIOGRAPHY

Adams, F. G. *The Business Forecasting Revolution.* New York: Oxford University Press, 1986.

Beaumont, C., Mahmoud, E., and McGee, V. E. "Microcomputer Forecasting Software: A Survey." *Journal of Forecasting* 4 (1985): 305–311.

Georgoff, D. M., and Mardick, R. G. "Manager's Guide to Forecasting." *Harvard Business Review* 1 (1986): 110–120.

Hogarth, R. M., and Makridakis, S. "Forecasting and Planning: An Evaluation." *Management Science* 27 (2) (1981): 115–138.

Keating, K. "Choosing and Using Business Forecasting Software." *Creative Computing* 11 (1) (1985): 119–135.

Mahmoud, E., Rice, G., McGee, V. E., and Beaumont, C. "Mainframe Multipurpose Forecasting Software: A Survey." *Journal of Forecasting* 5 (1986): 127–137.

Mahmoud, E., Rice, G., McGee, V. E., and Beaumont, C. "Mainframe Specific Purpose Forecasting Software: A Survey." *Journal of Forecasting* 5 (1986): 75–83.

Makridakis, S. "The Art and Science of Forecasting." *International Journal of Forecasting* 2 (1986): 15–39.

Reid, R. A. "The Forecasting Process: Guidelines for the MIS Manager." *Journal of Systems Management* (November 1986): 33–37.

Wright, G., and Ayton, P., eds. *Judgemental Forecasting.* New York: John Wiley & Sons, 1987.

2

A Review of Basic Statistical Concepts

Most forecasting techniques are based on fundamental statistical concepts that are the subject of business statistics textbooks and introductory statistics courses. This chapter reviews some of these basic concepts that will serve as a foundation for much of the material in the remainder of the text.

Most statistical procedures make inferences about the items of interest, called the *population,* after selecting and measuring a subgroup of these items, called the *sample.* Careful selection of a representative sample and the use of a sufficiently large sample size are important components of a statistical inference process that has an acceptably low degree of risk.

Along with statistical inference, *descriptive statistics* constitutes the other major subdivision of statistics. Descriptive statistical procedures are employed to briefly summarize or describe data collections so that their essential components become obvious and can be used in the decision-making process.

DESCRIPTIVE STATISTICS

The purpose of descriptive statistical procedures is to briefly describe a large collection of measurements with a few key summary values. The most common way of doing this is by averaging the values. In statistics the process of averaging is usually accomplished by computing the *mean,* which involves adding all values and dividing by the number of values. Since both the population and the sample taken from it possess a mean, there are two formulas for computing means. The appropriate formula depends on whether the values collected constitute all the values of interest (the population) or a partial collection of them (a sample).

> *Descriptive statistics* involves describing data collections with a few key summary values.

Population values or parameters are usually identified using Greek letters, and the symbol chosen for the population mean is the Greek letter μ (mu). The formula for the population mean is[1]

$$\mu = \frac{\Sigma X}{N} \tag{2.1}$$

where

ΣX represents the sum of all the values of the population
N represents the population size

The symbol for the sample mean is $\bar{X}$ (X-bar) and is found as

$$\bar{X} = \frac{\Sigma X}{n} \tag{2.2}$$

where

ΣX represents the sum of all the values of the sample
n represents the sample size

In addition to measuring the central tendency of a group of values by computing the mean, the extent to which the values are dispersed around the mean is usually of interest. For this purpose the *standard deviation* of either group can be computed. The standard deviation can be thought of as the typical difference between the group values and their mean. Following are the formulas for the standard deviations of the population (σ) and the sample (s):

$$\sigma = \sqrt{\frac{\Sigma (X - \mu)^2}{N}} = \sqrt{\frac{\Sigma X^2 - \frac{(\Sigma X)^2}{N}}{N}} \tag{2.3}$$

$$s = \sqrt{\frac{\Sigma (X - \bar{X})^2}{n - 1}} = \sqrt{\frac{\Sigma X^2 - \frac{(\Sigma X)^2}{n}}{n - 1}} \tag{2.4}$$

where the numerators represent the sum of squared differences between the measured values and their means.

---

[1] Throughout this text a simplified summation notation is used. The notation ΣX means to sum all the X values. Some texts use a more formal and complete notation such as

$$\sum_{i=1}^{n} X_i$$

which means to sum the Xs beginning with X_1 (the lower value of i) and to increment the X subscript by one until n (the upper value of i) is reached.

Finally, many statistical procedures make use of the population or sample *variance*. The variance of a collection of measurements is the standard deviation squared. Thus, the population variance (σ^2) and the sample variance (s^2) are computed as

$$\sigma^2 = \frac{\Sigma (X - \mu)^2}{N} = \frac{\Sigma X^2 - \dfrac{(\Sigma X)^2}{N}}{N} \qquad\qquad (2.5)$$

$$s^2 = \frac{\Sigma (X - \bar{X})^2}{n - 1} = \frac{\Sigma X^2 - \dfrac{(\Sigma X)^2}{n}}{n - 1} \qquad\qquad (2.6)$$

EXAMPLE 2.1

■ Consider the following collection of people's ages, where the values are considered to be a sample from the population rather than the population itself:

23, 38, 42, 25, 60, 55, 50, 42, 32, 35

For this sample,

$$\bar{X} = \frac{\Sigma X}{n} = \frac{402}{10} = 40.2$$

As shown in Table 2.1, the sample mean is 40.2 years, the sample variance is 148.84, and the sample standard deviation is 12.2 years. Had the original collection of values been identified as a population rather than a sample, the calculations would have

TABLE 2.1 Calculation of s ($\bar{X} = 40.2$).

X	$X - \bar{X}$	$(X - \bar{X})^2$
23	−17.2	295.84
38	−2.2	4.84
42	1.8	3.24
25	−15.2	231.04
60	19.8	392.04
55	14.8	219.04
50	9.8	96.04
42	1.8	3.24
32	−8.2	67.24
35	−5.2	27.04
		$\Sigma = 1,339.60$

$$s^2 = \frac{1,339.6}{10 - 1} = 148.84$$

$$s = \sqrt{148.84} = 12.2$$

been the same except that the denominator used in calculating variance and standard deviation would have been 10 (N) instead of 9 ($n - 1$). The term $n - 1$ is known as the degrees of freedom. ■

The term *degrees of freedom* is used to indicate the number of data items that are free of each other in the sense that they cannot be deduced from each other and can therefore carry unique pieces of information. For example, suppose the following four statements are made:

I am thinking of the number 5. I am thinking of the number 7. The sum of the two numbers I am thinking of is 12.

At first glance there are three pieces of information presented here. However, if any two of these statements are known, the other one can be deduced. It could be said that there are only two unique pieces of information in the three statements above or, to use the statistical term, there are only two degrees of freedom.

In the example presented in Table 2.1, the ages of ten people constitute a sample with 10 degrees of freedom. Anyone's age could have been included in the sample, and, therefore, each of the ages is free to vary. When the mean is calculated, all ten ages are used to account for a total mean age equal to 40.2 years.

The computation of the sample standard deviation differs. When the sample standard deviation is calculated, an estimate of the population mean is used (the sample mean $\bar{X}$). A bias is introduced because the value $\Sigma (X - \bar{X})^2$ for a given distribution is a minimum value. If any value other than 40.2 were subtracted from every item in the distribution and these differences were squared and summed, the total sum of squares would be larger than 1,339.6. By using the sample mean as an estimate of the population mean in the computation, a standard deviation that is smaller than the population standard deviation will usually be obtained. However, this bias can be corrected by dividing the value $\Sigma (X - \bar{X})^2$ by the appropriate degrees of freedom. Since the sample mean was used as an estimate of the population mean in the computation of the sample standard deviation, only nine of the ages are free to vary. If nine of the ages are known, the tenth can be accounted for because $\Sigma (X - \bar{X})$ must equal zero. Only nine ages are required to account for the totality of information. In general, whenever a sample statistic is used as an estimate of a population parameter in a computation, one degree of freedom is lost.

> *Degrees of freedom* in a data collection indicate the number of data items that are independent of one another and that can carry unique pieces of information.

TABLE 2.2 Population and Sample Characteristics.

Characteristic	Population	Sample
Mean	μ	$\overline{X}$
Variance	σ^2	s^2
Standard deviation	σ	s

In summary, in a statistical investigation there are two groups of values, the population and the sample, each of which has the characteristics shown in Table 2.2.

PROBABILITY DISTRIBUTIONS

A *random variable* is the name given to a quantity that is capable of taking on different values from trial to trial in an experiment, the exact outcome being a chance or random event. If only certain specified values are possible, the random variable is called a *discrete variable.* Examples include the number of rooms in a house, the number of people arriving at a supermarket checkout stand in an hour, and the number of defective units in a batch of electronic parts. If any value of the random variable is possible within some range, it is called a *continuous variable.* Examples of this type of variable are the weights of people, the length of a manufactured part, and the time between car arrivals at a toll bridge.

A *discrete random variable* can assume only certain specified values, usually the integers; a *continuous random variable* can assume any numerical value within some range.

If a discrete random variable is considered, its *probability distribution* lists all possible values that the variable can take on, along with the probability of each.

EXAMPLE 2.2

■ The number of no-sales days for a salesperson during a month might be described by the probability distribution shown in Table 2.3. These values are based on the salesperson's past experience. The X column lists all values (no-sales days) that are possible, while the $P(X)$ column lists the corresponding probabilities. Note that since all possible values of X are listed, the probabilities sum to 1.00, or 100%. This is true for all probability distributions, disregarding rounding errors. ■

TABLE 2.3 Probability Distribution.

X	P(X)
1	.10
2	.20
3	.25
4	.15
5	.30

The *expected value* of a random variable is the average value that the variable assumes over many trials. The expected value for a discrete probability distribution can be found by multiplying each possible X value by its probability and then summing these products. Formula 2.7 shows this calculation:

$$E(X) = \Sigma [X \cdot P(X)] \tag{2.7}$$

For the probability distribution given in Table 2.3, the expected value is found as follows:

$$E(X) = (1)(.10) + (2)(.20) + (3)(.25) + (4)(.15) + (5)(.30)$$
$$= 3.35$$

Thus, if this salesperson were observed for a very large number of months and the number of no-sales days were recorded, the average would be 3.35.

> The *expected value* of a random variable is the average value of the variable over many trials or observations.

For a continuous distribution the probability of obtaining a specific value approaches zero. For instance, the probability of anyone weighing 150 pounds may be considered zero since this would mean that this weight is exactly 150.000 . . . no matter how accurate a scale is used. Continuous distributions are dealt with by finding the probability that a value will fall in some interval when randomly drawn from the distribution. The probability that a person's weight falls in the interval 140 pounds to 150 pounds might be computed, for example.

Some theoretical distributions occur over and over again in practical statistical applications, and for this reason it is important to examine their properties and applications. One of these important distributions is the *binomial distribution*, often used to represent a discrete random variable. The requirements for a binomial experiment are as follows:

1. There are n identical trials, each of which results in one of two possible outcomes.
2. The probability of success on each outcome remains fixed from trial to trial.
3. The trials are independent.

The interest is in finding the probability of X successful occurrences in the n trials, where a successful occurrence is arbitrarily defined to be one of the two possible outcomes. The various values of X along with their probabilities form the binomial distribution. These probabilities can be found from the following binomial formula:

$$P(X) = C_X^n \pi^X (1 - \pi)^{n-X} \qquad \text{for } X = 0, 1, 2, \ldots, n \qquad (2.8)$$

where

C_X^n = the number of combinations of n things taken X at a time

π = the probability of success on each trial

X = the particular number of successes of interest

n = the number of trials

An easier way to find binomial probabilities is to refer to a binomial distribution table such as found in Appendix C, Table C.1. The probabilities are grouped by blocks representing n and have columns headed by p (or π) and rows indicated by x.

EXAMPLE 2.3

■ Suppose eight items are randomly drawn from a production line that is known to produce defective parts 5% of the time. What is the probability of getting exactly zero defectives? The answer, from the binomial table in Appendix C, is .6634 (here, $n = 8$, $\pi = .05$, $X = 0$). ■

An important continuous distribution of interest, because many useful populations can be approximated by it, is the *normal distribution,* specified by knowing its two parameters, the mean and the standard deviation. A normal curve is symmetrical and bell-shaped, as shown in Figure 2.1. This distribution represents many real-life variables that are measured on a continuous scale.

Probabilities of values drawn from a normal distribution falling into various intervals can be found by first converting all intervals to standard units called *Z-scores.* The Z-score of any X value is the number of standard deviations from the central value of the curve (μ) to that value. Thus, the formula for Z is

$$Z = \frac{X - \mu}{\sigma} \qquad (2.9)$$

FIGURE 2.1 Normal Distribution.

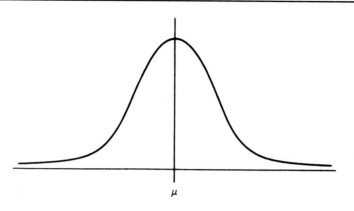

μ

where

$X =$ the particular value of interest
$\mu =$ the mean
$\sigma =$ the standard deviation

After the Z-score has been computed, the normal curve table can be consulted to find the area under the curve between the center of the curve (μ) and the value of interest (X).

EXAMPLE 2.4

■ A population of part weights made by a certain machine is normally distributed with mean 10 pounds and standard deviation 2 pounds. What is the probability that a part drawn at random from the machine falls between 9 and 12 pounds? The normal curve with the appropriate area shaded is shown in Figure 2.2.

Since normal curve tables are designed to give areas from the center of the curve to some point, two separate areas must be found, one on each side of the mean, and these areas added together. This process will produce the probability of a value falling in this interval. The two Z-scores are

$$Z_1 = \frac{9 - 10}{2} = -.50$$

$$Z_2 = \frac{12 - 10}{2} = 1.00$$

The negative sign on the first Z-score is disregarded since it simply indicates that the X value of interest (9) is less than the mean of the curve (10). These two Z-scores can be taken to the normal curve table in Appendix C, Table C.1, to yield the two areas, which are then added together:

$$Z_1 = -.50 \rightarrow .1915$$

$$Z_2 = 1.00 \rightarrow \underline{.3413}$$

$$.5328$$

FIGURE 2.2 Normal Curve Area.
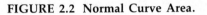

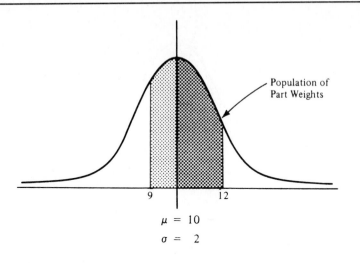

The conclusion is that there is about a 53% chance that a part randomly drawn from this population of parts will weigh between 9 and 12 pounds. ■

Finally, the *t distribution* is frequently used in statistical tests when small sample sizes are used and where it can be assumed that the populations being investigated are normally distributed. Appendix C, Table C.3, shows values taken from the *t* distribution. Note that only one value need be specified before referring to the table, namely, the degrees of freedom (abbreviated *df*). Once the degrees of freedom are known, the *t* values that exclude desired percentages of the curve can be found. For example, if the *t* distribution of interest has 14 degrees of freedom, then a *t* value of 2.145 on each side of the curve center will include 95% of the curve and exclude 5% of it. An example using the *t* distribution will be presented later in this chapter.

SAMPLING DISTRIBUTIONS

In most statistical applications a random sample is taken from the population under investigation, a statistic is computed from the sample data, and conclusions are drawn about the population on the basis of this sample. A *sampling distribution* is the distribution of all possible values of the sample statistic that can be obtained from the population for a given sample size. For instance, a random sample of 100 persons might be taken from a population and weighed and then their mean weight computed. This sample mean, $\bar{X}$, can be thought of as having been drawn from the distribution of all possible sample means of sample size 100 that could be

FIGURE 2.3 Sampling Distribution of $\bar{X}$.

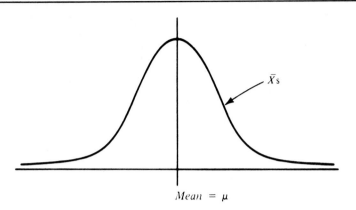

$\bar{X}$s

Mean $= \mu$

taken from the population. Similarly, each sample statistic that can be computed from sample data can be considered as having been drawn from some sampling distribution.

> A *sampling distribution* is the array of all possible sample statistics that can be drawn from a population for a given sample size.

The *central limit theorem* states that as the sample size becomes larger the sampling distribution of sample means tends toward the normal distribution, and that the mean of this normal distribution is μ, the population mean, and that the standard deviation is $\sigma/\sqrt{n}$ (this value is known as the *standard error of the sampling distribution*). This sampling distribution will tend toward normality regardless of the shape of the population distribution from which the sampled items were drawn. Figure 2.3 demonstrates how such a sampling distribution might appear.

The central limit theorem is of particular importance in statistics since it allows the analyst to compute the probability of various sample results through a knowledge of normal curve probabilities.

EXAMPLE 2.5

■ What is the probability that the mean of a random sample of 100 weights drawn from a population will be within 2 pounds of the true population mean weight if the standard deviation of the population is estimated to be 15 pounds? Figure 2.4 illustrates the appropriate sampling distribution.

FIGURE 2.4 Sampling Distribution Area.

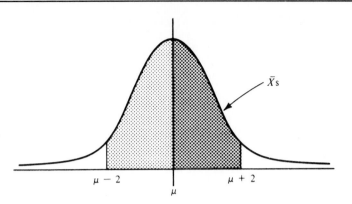

The standard error is $\sigma/\sqrt{n} = 15/\sqrt{100} = 1.5$. Then $z = 2/1.5 = 1.33$, yielding an area from the normal curve table of .4082. Doubling this area to account for both sides of the mean results in a total area of .8164.

Chances are about 82% that the sample mean will be within 2 pounds of the true mean, reflecting the sample size of 100 and the estimated variability of the population, $\sigma = 15$. As will be seen, this ability to calculate probabilities of sample results will enable an analyst to arrive at useful results in estimation and in hypothesis testing. ■

ESTIMATION

A *point estimate* of a population parameter is a single value calculated from the sample data that estimates the unknown population value. Table 2.4 contains a list of several population parameters and the sample statistics that provide point estimates of them.

An *interval estimate* or *confidence interval* is an interval within which the population parameter of interest probably lies. It is found by forming an interval around the point estimate and is computed using either the normal distribution or the *t* distribution.

TABLE 2.4 Population and Sample Values.

Population Parameter	Sample Statistic (Estimate)
Mean (μ)	$\bar{X}$, the sample mean
Standard deviation (σ)	s, the sample standard deviation
Variance (σ^2)	s^2, the sample variance
Percentage (π)	p, the sample percentage

EXAMPLE 2.6

■ An interval estimate for a population mean is desired. The sample size is 400, the sample mean (the point estimate) is 105 pounds, and the sample standard deviation (an estimate of σ) is 10 pounds. Within what interval is it 95% likely that μ lies? The interval can be found by forming an interval around $\bar{X}$ using 1.96 standard deviations from the $\bar{X}$ sampling distribution (1.96 standard deviations on each side of the mean of any normal curve will include approximately 95% of the values). The calculations are

$$\bar{X} \pm Z \frac{s}{\sqrt{n}} \qquad\qquad (2.10)$$

$$105 \pm 1.96 \frac{10}{\sqrt{400}}$$

$$105 \pm .98$$

$$104.02 \text{ to } 105.98$$

Thus, it is 95% likely that the sample mean was chosen from the sampling distribution such that the true population mean is somewhere in the interval 104.02 to 105.98.

Likewise, confidence intervals can be formed around point estimates of the population percentage using the following formula.

$$p \pm Z \sqrt{\frac{\pi(1 - \pi)}{n}} \qquad\qquad (2.11) \ \blacksquare$$

In practice, π, the population percentage, is usually estimated with p, the sample percentage, in computing the standard error of the sampling distribution.

EXAMPLE 2.7

■ A 99% confidence interval for the true percentage, π, of the population that is familiar with a product can be formed around the point estimate, $p = .23$, with $n = 150$:

$$.23 \pm 2.58 \sqrt{\frac{(.23)(.77)}{150}}$$

$$.23 \pm .089$$

$$.141 \text{ to } .319$$

In this example the point estimate of π is .23. Given the sample size of 150, it is 99% likely that the sample was drawn in such a way that the true value of π is somewhere in the interval .141 to .319. ■

> A *point estimate* is a single-valued estimate of a population
> parameter; an *interval estimate* is a numerical interval within
> which it is likely that the population parameter lies.

HYPOTHESIS TESTING

In many statistical situations the interest is in testing some claim about the
population rather than estimating one of its parameters. This procedure is
called *hypothesis testing* and involves the following steps:

Step 1 State the hypothesis being tested (called the null hypothesis, symbol
H_0) and state the alternative hypothesis (the one accepted if H_0 is
rejected, symbol H_1).

Step 2 Collect a random sample of items from the population, measure
them, and compute the appropriate sample statistic.

Step 3 Assume the null hypothesis is true and consult the sampling distribution from which the sample statistic was drawn under this
assumption.

Step 4 Compute the probability that such a sample statistic could have been
drawn from this sampling distribution.

Step 5 If this probability is high, do not reject the null hypothesis; if this
probability is low, the null hypothesis can be rejected with low
chance of error.

When the above series of steps is followed, two types of error can
occur, as shown in Table 2.5. It is always hoped that the correct decision
concerning the null hypothesis will be reached after examining sample
evidence, but there is always a possibility of rejecting a true H_0 and failing
to reject a false H_0. The probabilities of these events are known as alpha (α)
and beta (β), respectively. Alpha is also known as the *significance level* of
the test.

TABLE 2.5 Results of Hypothesis Test.

		Do Not Reject H_0	**Reject H_0**
State of Nature	H_0 **True**	Correct decision	Type I error probability: α
	H_0 **False**	Type II error probability: β	Correct decision

EXAMPLE 2.8

■ It is desired to test the hypothesis that the average weight of parts produced by a certain machine is still 50 pounds, the average weight of the parts in past years. A random sample of 100 parts is taken. It is assumed that the standard deviation of part weights is 5 pounds regardless of the mean weight since this value has remained constant in past studies of parts. If the null hypothesis is assumed true (the null hypothesis states that the mean part weight is 50 pounds), the appropriate sampling distribution is the normal distribution in accordance with the central limit theorem. The test is demonstrated in Figure 2.5.

The decision rule for this test can now be formed as follows:

1. Take a random sample of 100 items from the population under investigation and compute the sample mean weight.
2. If this sample mean weight is between 49.02 pounds and 50.98 pounds, do not reject the null hypothesis. If it is outside this interval, reject the null hypothesis. ■

In stating the decision rule in this way, the probability of rejecting the null hypothesis when it is true, that is, committing a type I error, is 5% ($\alpha = .05$). This can be seen on the curve in Figure 2.5 that shows an area of .025 on each end of the sampling distribution.

FIGURE 2.5 Hypothesis Test—Example 2.8.

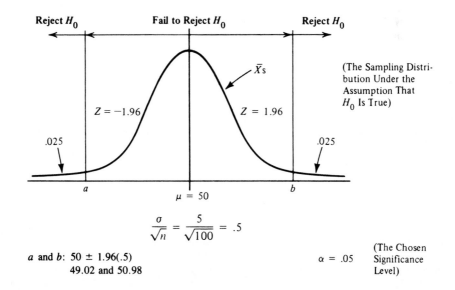

H_0: $\mu = 50$ pounds (the Null Hypothesis)

H_1: $\mu \neq 50$ pounds (the Alternative Hypothesis)

Reject H_0 Fail to Reject H_0 Reject H_0

$\bar{X}$s

$Z = -1.96$ $Z = 1.96$

.025   .025

(The Sampling Distribution Under the Assumption That H_0 Is True)

a b

$\mu = 50$

$$\frac{\sigma}{\sqrt{n}} = \frac{5}{\sqrt{100}} = .5$$

a and b: $50 \pm 1.96(.5)$

49.02 and 50.98

$\alpha = .05$

(The Chosen Significance Level)

TABLE 2.6 Summary of Hypothesis Tests.

H_0	Sample Statistic	Sampling Distribution	Parameters of Sampling Distribution
$\mu = 50^*$	$\bar{X}$	Normal	μ and $\dfrac{\sigma}{\sqrt{n}}$
$\pi = .30^*$	p	Normal	π and $\sqrt{\dfrac{\pi(1-\pi)}{n}}$
$\mu_1 - \mu_2 = 0$	$\bar{X}_1 - \bar{X}_2$	Normal	$\mu_1 - \mu_2$ and $\sqrt{\dfrac{\sigma_1^2}{n_1} + \dfrac{\sigma_2^2}{n_2}}$
$\pi_1 - \pi_2 = 0$	$p_1 - p_2$	Normal	$\pi_1 - \pi_2$ and $\sqrt{\pi(1-\pi)\left(\dfrac{1}{n_1} + \dfrac{1}{n_2}\right)}$

* Example values.

To complete Example 2.8, if the sample mean turns out to be 50.4, we would not reject the null hypothesis and conclude that the population still has a mean weight of 50 pounds. On the other hand, if the sample mean was 48.1 pounds, we would conclude that the mean of the population had dropped below 50 pounds.

Table 2.6 summarizes the four most widely used statistical hypothesis tests. In each of these tests the indicated sample statistic is computed, the appropriate sampling distribution is consulted after assuming the null hypothesis is true, a decision rule is formed that specifies the range within which the statistic will most likely be, and a decision to reject or not reject the null hypothesis is reached.

The first hypothesis test in Table 2.6 is illustrated in Figure 2.5. Figures 2.6 through 2.8 are examples to illustrate the use of the other three hypothesis tests summarized in Table 2.6.

EXAMPLE 2.9

■ For several years, 30% of the population has had a favorable impression of our product. Recent events lead us to suspect that this percentage may have dropped. To test the hypothesis that the percentage is still 30%, a random sample of 50 persons is taken, and it is found that 27% of them have a favorable impression of our product. On the basis of the evidence shown in Figure 2.6, what is the conclusion?

Decision Rule. If $p < .17$, reject H_0.

Conclusion. Since $p = .27$, do not reject H_0. Based on this sample evidence, the hypothesis that the population percentage is .30 cannot be rejected at the 2% level of significance. There is not enough sample evidence to say that the percentage of people favoring our product has decreased. ■

FIGURE 2.6 Hypothesis Test—Example 2.9.

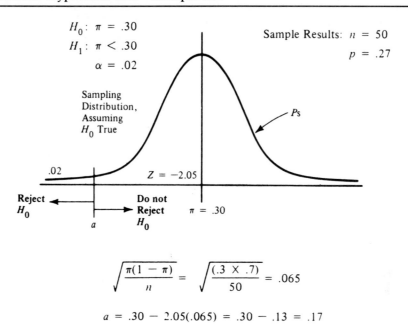

$$\sqrt{\frac{\pi(1 - \pi)}{n}} = \sqrt{\frac{(.3 \times .7)}{50}} = .065$$

$$a = .30 - 2.05(.065) = .30 - .13 = .17$$

FIGURE 2.7 Hypothesis Test—Example 2.10.

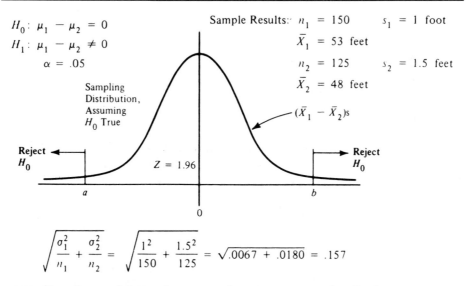

$$\sqrt{\frac{\sigma_1^2}{n_1} + \frac{\sigma_2^2}{n_2}} = \sqrt{\frac{1^2}{150} + \frac{1.5^2}{125}} = \sqrt{.0067 + .0180} = .157$$

NOTE: Since the population variances are unknown, we use sample estimates.

a and b: $0 \pm 1.96(.157) = 0 \pm .31$

FIGURE 2.8 Hypothesis Test—Example 2.11.

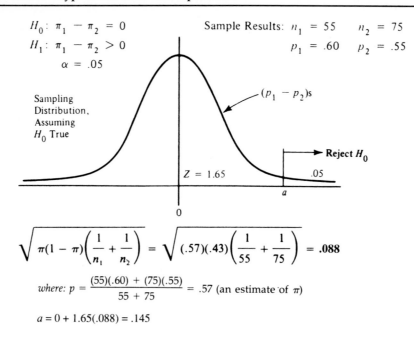

$$H_0: \pi_1 - \pi_2 = 0 \qquad \text{Sample Results: } n_1 = 55 \quad n_2 = 75$$
$$H_1: \pi_1 - \pi_2 > 0 \qquad\qquad\qquad\qquad\quad p_1 = .60 \quad p_2 = .55$$
$$\alpha = .05$$

Sampling
Distribution,
Assuming
H_0 True

$(p_1 - p_2)s$

Reject H_0

$Z = 1.65$ .05

a

0

$$\sqrt{\pi(1-\pi)\left(\frac{1}{n_1}+\frac{1}{n_2}\right)} = \sqrt{(.57)(.43)\left(\frac{1}{55}+\frac{1}{75}\right)} = \textbf{.088}$$

$$\text{where: } p = \frac{(55)(.60) + (75)(.55)}{55 + 75} = .57 \text{ (an estimate of } \pi)$$

$$a = 0 + 1.65(.088) = .145$$

EXAMPLE 2.10

■ Can it be concluded that two cable-manufacturing machines produce cables of different average lengths? The sample evidence appears in Figure 2.7.

Decision Rule. If $\bar{X}_1 - \bar{X}_2$ is within .31 of 0, do not reject H_0.

Conclusion. Since $\bar{X}_1 - \bar{X}_2 = 5$ feet, reject H_0. Based on the sample evidence, the hypothesis that the two population means are equal can be rejected at the 5% level of significance. It appears that the average lengths of cables produced by the two machines are different. ■

EXAMPLE 2.11

■ It is desired to determine if the percentage of students that work part time at two universities are the same, or if the percentage is higher at university 1. Based on the sample evidence in Figure 2.8, what is the conclusion?

Decision Rule. If $p_1 - p_2 > .145$, reject H_0.

Conclusion. Since $p_1 - p_2 = .05$, do not reject H_0. Based on the sample evidence, the hypothesis that the population percentages are equal cannot be rejected at the 5% level of significance. The evidence does not support the notion that a higher percentage of students work part time at university 1 than at university 2. ■

EXAMPLE 2.12

■ Consider a hypothesis test where the sample size is small and for which the t distribution is the appropriate sampling distribution. Suppose it is desired to test the hypothesis that the mean score of students on a national examination is 500 against the alternative hypothesis that it is less than 500. A random sample of 15 students is taken from the population, which produces a sample mean of 475. The standard deviation of the population is estimated by the standard deviation of the 15 sampled items, which is 35. It is assumed that the population of examination scores follows a normal distribution.

The t distribution is the appropriate sampling distribution when n is small (as a rule of thumb, under 30), σ is unknown (and is being estimated by s), and the population can be assumed to be approximately normally distributed. The correct degrees of freedom for this test is $n - 1$. The test statistic is $(\bar{X} - \mu)/(s/\sqrt{n})$. The test is demonstrated in Figure 2.9, assuming a significance level of .05.

Decision Rule.   If $(\bar{X} - \mu)/(s/\sqrt{n}) < -1.761$, reject H_0.

Conclusion.   Since $(\bar{X} - \mu)/(s/\sqrt{n}) = -2.77$, reject H_0. The sample evidence supports rejection of the hypothesis that the population mean is 500 at the 5% level of significance. It is concluded that the mean score of students on the national examination has decreased. ■

FIGURE 2.9 Hypothesis Test—Example 2.12.

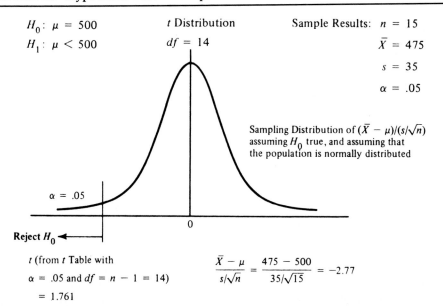

$H_0: \mu = 500$

$H_1: \mu < 500$

t Distribution

$df = 14$

Sample Results: $n = 15$

$\bar{X} = 475$

$s = 35$

$\alpha = .05$

Sampling Distribution of $(\bar{X} - \mu)/(s/\sqrt{n})$ assuming H_0 true, and assuming that the population is normally distributed

$\alpha = .05$

0

Reject H_0

t (from t Table with $\alpha = .05$ and $df = n - 1 = 14$) $= 1.761$

$$\frac{\bar{X} - \mu}{s/\sqrt{n}} = \frac{475 - 500}{35/\sqrt{15}} = -2.77$$

GOODNESS-OF-FIT TEST

It is often of interest to determine whether or not a sample of data fits some known, suspected, or theoretical distribution. A sample is drawn from the population of interest, and the categories into which these items fall are observed. If the observed frequencies are quite close to what would theoretically be seen under the hypothetical population distribution, the hypothetical formulation of the population is accepted; if great differences are observed, this formulation is rejected.

EXAMPLE 2.13

■ Suppose it is hypothesized that people have no brand preference regarding the four brands of milk they may purchase at the supermarket. If this hypothesis is true, then in a sample of buyers exactly one-fourth of them may be expected, on average, to choose each brand. If a sample of 100 buyers is randomly chosen, 25 of them would be expected to purchase each of the four brands. Suppose the random sample is actually taken and reveals the preference information shown in Table 2.7.

One-fourth of the buyers obviously did not choose each brand; however, only a small sample of buyers has been examined, not all buyers. The question becomes, "Is there enough sample evidence to reject the null hypothesis?" The hypothesis under test is

H_0:   The population from which this sample was drawn is uniformly distributed.

Under this hypothesis an equal number of persons in the population prefer each brand. The sample evidence may or may not be strong enough to reject this notion. It is not apparent from the evidence whether preference exists for one brand or another in the population, or whether the differences observed in the sample are due to random sampling error. ■

Suppose the actual observations are arrayed with the frequencies expected if the null hypothesis were true, as shown in Table 2.8. The goodness of the fit between observed and expected frequencies can now be observed. A statistic can be calculated from the comparisons of Table 2.8; it is known to follow the chi-square distribution. Formula 2.12 shows the computation:

TABLE 2.7 Brand Preference—Example 2.13.

	A	B	C	D	Total
Number buying	20	35	18	27	100

TABLE 2.8 Brand Preference—Null Hypothesis True.

	A	B	C	D	Total
Actual (observed)	20	35	18	27	100
Theoretical (expected)	25	25	25	25	100

$$\chi^2 = \sum_{\text{all categories}} \frac{(f_o - f_e)^2}{f_e} \tag{2.12}$$

where

f_o = observed frequency
f_e = expected frequency

Formula 2.12 can be used to compute the chi-square statistic for Example 2.13. Table 2.9 shows the calculations resulting in a chi-square statistic of 7.12.

The computed chi-square value using Formula 2.12 is now compared with the table value of chi-square from the chi-square table. If the calculated value is less than this table value, a good fit is indicated, and the hypothesis about the underlying population is accepted. If the computed chi-square value is larger than the table value, a poor fit is indicated, and the null hypothesis is rejected.

To obtain a tabulated value from the chi-square table, it is necessary to know the number of degrees of freedom. For Example 2.13 one degree of freedom is lost since the expected frequencies must total 100, the number of original data points. Thus, $df = k - 1 = 4 - 1 = 3$ (k = number of categories). From the chi-square table,

$$\chi^2_{.05} = 7.81473$$

$$\chi^2_{.025} = 9.34840 \qquad \text{for } df = 3$$

$$\chi^2_{.01} = 11.3449$$

TABLE 2.9 χ^2 Calculations.

f_o	f_e	$f_o - f_e$	$(f_o - f_e)^2$	$(f_o - f_e)^2/f_e$
20	25	−5	25	1.00
35	25	10	100	4.00
18	25	−7	49	1.96
27	25	2	4	.16
				7.12 = χ^2

Since the computed chi-square value is smaller than any of the tabulated values, even at the .05 significance level, it is not possible to reject the null hypothesis at these levels. As usual in statistical tests, this result does not prove that the null hypothesis is true; it merely states that there is not enough sample evidence to reject it. It is concluded that no population brand preference is indicated by the sample, using any of the indicated significance levels.

EXAMPLE 2.14

■ As another example of a goodness-of-fit test, consider the data in Table 2.10. These data reveal the number of errors in a random sample of 200 accounts taken from a firm's accounting records. The firm wishes to run a simulation of the accounting process and wants to use the Poisson distribution to describe the incidence of error. On the basis of the collected data, does this seem reasonable?

If the data in Table 2.10 are regarded as the observed frequencies, the expected frequencies can then be computed under the assumption that the data were drawn from a population that is Poisson distributed. A goodness-of-fit chi-square statistic can then be computed using Formula 2.12, and a conclusion can be reached. First, the sample mean number of errors can be computed as shown in Table 2.11.

Thus, the mean or expected value of the distribution is approximately 1.5. A Poisson table is now consulted to find the probabilities of different numbers of errors for a Poisson distribution whose mean is estimated to be 1.5 (see second column of Table 2.12). These probabilities are then multiplied by 200 (the number of sample observations) to get the expected frequencies of each cell (see column 3 of Table 2.12). The chi-square value is then computed using Formula 2.12. The calculations are shown in Table 2.12, where the last two categories are combined due to fewer than five expected observations in the five-and-over category.

The chi-square value of Table 2.12 is 4.3452, representing the fit between the observed frequencies in each cell and the frequencies expected if the sample was drawn from a Poisson distribution. The appropriate degrees of freedom are $k - 2$, where k is the number of categories. Two degrees of freedom are lost because the cells must total 200 and because one population parameter (μ) is being estimated

TABLE 2.10 Account Errors.

Number of Errors	Number of Accounts Having These Errors
0	50
1	69
2	39
3	25
4	13
5 or more	4
	$n = 200$

TABLE 2.11 Mean Account Error Calculation.

Number of Errors	Probability	Errors × Probability
0	50/200	.000
1	69/200	.345
2	39/200	.390
3	25/200	.375
4	13/200	.260
5 or more	4/200	.100
		Total = 1.470

with sample data. In general, the degrees of freedom in a goodness-of-fit test are computed as follows:

$$df = k - 1 - c \qquad (2.13)$$

where

k = number of data categories
c = number of population parameters estimated by sample statistics

In this case,

$$df = k - 2 = 3 \quad \text{for} \quad \begin{matrix} \alpha = .01 & \chi^2 = 11.3 \\ \alpha = .05 & \chi^2 = 7.8 \end{matrix}$$

Since the computed chi-square value (4.3452) is less than the chi-square tabulated value for either the .05 or .01 significance levels, the hypothesis that the sample data were drawn from a Poisson distribution is not rejected at either of these significance levels. The firm is justified in using the Poisson distribution to simulate the incidence of error in its accounting process. ∎

TABLE 2.12 Computation of χ^2 Value.

Number of Errors	Probability (for $\mu = 1.5$)	Prob. × 200 f_e	f_o	$(f_o - f_e)^2/f_e$
0	.2231	44.62	50	.6487
1	.3347	66.94	69	.0634
2	.2510	50.20	39	2.4988
3	.1255	25.10	25	.0004
4 or more	.0657	13.14	17	1.1339
				$\chi^2 = 4.3452$

In summary, observed distributions can be compared to theoretical distributions by use of the goodness-of-fit test. The distribution of expected frequencies from the theoretical population must be computed and compared with the sample values. If large differences exist across categories, a large chi-square value will be computed, and the hypothesis regarding the population will be rejected. If the actual frequencies are quite close to the expected values across categories, a small chi-square value will be computed, and the hypothesis regarding the distribution of the population cannot be rejected.

> The *goodness-of-fit* test determines whether sampled items may be assumed to have been drawn from a population that follows a specified distribution.

Many different population distributions may be hypothesized in a goodness-of-fit test. The test is often performed against a normal population distribution since many statistical tests assume such a population distribution. The goodness-of-fit can also be tested using current data against the distribution of a previous time period, or against an industry norm or desired target figures. In all such tests, nonnumerical or categorical data are used.

Data measured on a continuous scale must first be converted to categories before the test is conducted. A distribution of part weights, for example, could be placed into weight categories to generate the observed frequencies.

CORRELATION ANALYSIS

A common objective in statistical applications is to examine the relationship that exists between two numerical variables. This subject is reviewed here, while its extension, regression analysis, is discussed in Chapters 6 and 7. In addition, special cases of correlation and regression are considered in Chapters 9 and 10.

This emphasis on correlation and regression is justified in view of the widespread use of these techniques in all sorts of statistical applications, including forecasting. In addition, extensions of the basic regression and correlation concepts into more complex areas account for many additional forecasting procedures.

It is assumed that the variables under investigation are numerical measurements; that is, they are measured by a device or process that generates real numbers rather than categories (interval or ratio-scaled data are being used).

Scatter Diagrams

A study of the relationship of variables begins with the simplest case, that of the relationship existing between two variables. Suppose two measurements have been taken on each of several objects. An analyst wishes to determine whether one of these measurable variables, called Y, tends to increase or decrease as the other variable, called X, changes. For instance, suppose both age and income have been measured for several individuals, as shown in Table 2.13. What can be said about the relationship between X and Y?

From Table 2.13 it appears that Y and X have a definite relationship. As X rises, Y tends to rise also. By observing this sample of five persons, it might be tempting to conclude that the older a person becomes, the more money that person makes. Of course, it is dangerous to reach conclusions on the basis of an inadequate sample size, a subject to be pursued later on. Yet on the basis of the observations ($n = 5$), a definite relationship appears to exist between Y and X.

These five data points can be plotted on a two-dimensional scale, with values of X along the horizontal axis and values of Y along the vertical axis. Such a plot is called a *scatter diagram* and appears in Figure 2.10.

A scatter diagram plots X–Y data points on a two-dimensional graph.

The scatter diagram helps to illustrate what intuition suggested when the raw data were first observed, namely, the appearance of a relationship between Y and X. This relationship is called a *positive* relationship because as X increases, so does Y.

In other situations involving two variables, different scatter diagram patterns might emerge. Consider the plots in Figure 2.11.

Diagram (a) of Figure 2.11 suggests what is called a *perfect, positive, linear relationship*. As X increases, Y increases also, and in a perfectly

TABLE 2.13 Income and Age Measurements.

Person Number	Y, Income	X, Age
1	$ 7,800	22
2	8,500	23
3	10,000	26
4	15,000	27
5	16,400	35

FIGURE 2.10 Scatter Diagram for Age and Income.

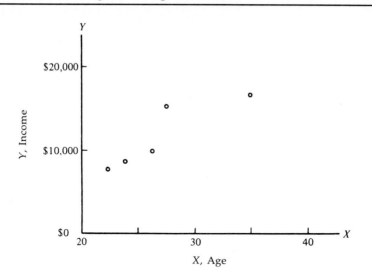

predictable way. That is, the X and Y data points appear to lie on a straight line. Diagram (b) suggests a *perfect, negative, linear relationship.* As X increases, Y decreases in a perfectly predictable way.

Figures 2.11(c) and (d) illustrate *imperfect, positive* and *negative, linear relationships.* As X increases in these scatter diagrams, Y increases (c) or decreases (d), but not in a perfectly predictable way. Thus Y might be slightly higher or lower than "expected." That is, the X–Y points do not lie on a straight line.

Scatter diagrams in Figures 2.11(a) through (d) illustrate what are called *linear relationships.* The X–Y relationship, be it perfect or imperfect, can be summarized by a straight-line. In comparison, a *curved* relationship appears in diagram (e).

Finally, diagram (f) of Figure 2.11 suggests that no relationship of any kind exists between variables X and Y. As X increases, Y does not appear either to increase or decrease in any predictable way. On the basis of the sample evidence that appears in diagram (f), it might be concluded that in the world containing *all* the X–Y data points, there exists no relationship, linear or otherwise, between variables X and Y.

Now consider the two scatter diagrams in Figure 2.12. Both scatter diagrams suggest imperfect, positive, linear relationships between Y and X. The difference is that this relationship appears quite strong in Figure 2.12(a) because the data points are all quite close to the straight line that passes through them. In Figure 2.12(b) a weaker relationship is suggested. The data points are farther away from the straight line that passes through them, suggesting that X and Y are less linearly related. Later in this chapter

FIGURE 2.11 Patterns for *X–Y* Data Plots.

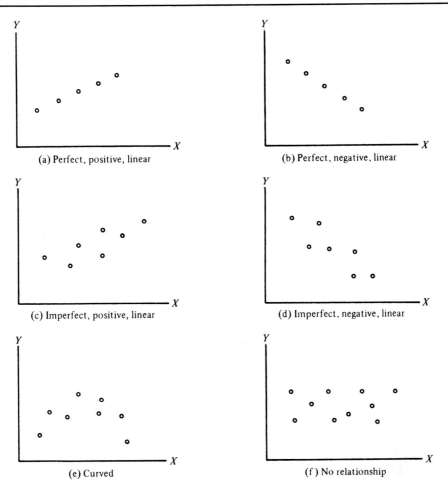

(a) Perfect, positive, linear

(b) Perfect, negative, linear

(c) Imperfect, positive, linear

(d) Imperfect, negative, linear

(e) Curved

(f) No relationship

it will be shown how to measure the strength of the relationship that exists between two variables.

As the two scatter diagrams in Figure 2.12 suggest, it is frequently desirable to summarize the relationship between two variables by fitting a straight line through the data points. You will learn how to do so later, but at the moment it can be said that a straight line can be fitted to the points in a scatter diagram so that a "good" fit results. The question now suggested is, How rapidly does this straight line rise or fall?

Answering this question requires the calculation of the slope of the line. The *slope* of any straight line is defined as the change in *Y* associated with a change in *X*. Line slope is demonstrated in Figure 2.13.

FIGURE 2.12 Strong and Weak *X*–*Y* Data Plots.

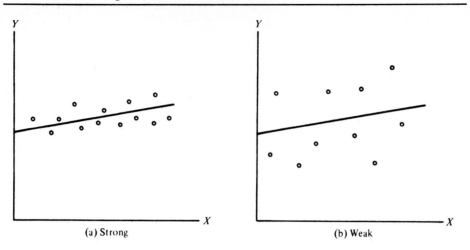

(a) Strong   (b) Weak

In Figure 2.13(a) the change in *Y* between the two data points is 1, while the change in *X* is 2. Therefore the slope of the line is $\frac{1}{2}$. In Figure 2.13(b) the line has a negative slope. As *X* increases by 1, *Y* *decreases* by 1.2. Therefore the slope is −1.2.

To summarize, in investigating a relationship between two variables, one must first know whether the relationship is linear (a straight line) or curved. If it is linear one wishes to know whether the relationship is positive or negative and how sharply the line that fits the data points rises or falls. Finally, the *degree* of the relationship is needed, that is, how close the data points are to the line that best fits them.

FIGURE 2.13 Line Slope.

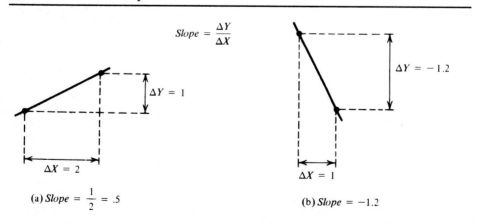

$$Slope = \frac{\Delta Y}{\Delta X}$$

$\Delta Y = 1$

$\Delta X = 2$

(a) *Slope* $= \frac{1}{2} = .5$

$\Delta Y = -1.2$

$\Delta X = 1$

(b) *Slope* $= -1.2$

Correlation Coefficient

A way of measuring the amount of linear relationship that exists between the two variables of interest is needed. To use the correct terminology, a measurement of the *correlation* that exists between the two variables is desired. The commonly used measurement of this relationship is the *coefficient* of *correlation*. Two variables with a perfect negative relationship have a correlation coefficient equal to -1. At the other extreme, two variables with a perfect positive relationship have a correlation coefficient equal to $+1$. Thus the correlation coefficient varies between -1 and $+1$ inclusive, depending on the amount of correlation between the two variables being measured.

> The *correlation coefficient* measures the extent to which two variables are linearly related to each other.

Scatter diagram (a) of Figure 2.11 illustrates a situation that would produce a correlation coefficient of $+1$. Scatter diagram (b) has a correlation coefficient of -1. Diagrams (e) and (f) plot two variables that are not linearly related. The correlation coefficients for these relationships are equal to 0; that is, no linear relationships are present.

It is also important to distinguish between two groups of data points with which the forecaster is concerned. In the *population* containing all the $X–Y$ data points of interest, there is a correlation coefficient whose symbol is ρ, the Greek letter rho. If a random *sample* of these $X–Y$ data points is drawn, the correlation coefficient for these sample data is called r. A summary of important characteristics of ρ and r is given in Table 2.14.

EXAMPLE 2.15

■ Consider a specific set of $X–Y$ values, and assume that these points constitute the entire population of such data points. In the data array of Table 2.15, X represents the number of sales-training courses taken, and Y represents the number of no-sales days per month for the five salespeople on a company's staff.

TABLE 2.14 Population and Sample Correlation.

Population	Sample
Correlation coefficient: ρ $(-1 \leq \rho \leq 1)$	Correlation coefficient: r $(-1 \leq r \leq 1)$
$\rho = -1$: perfect negative correlation	$r = -1$: perfect negative correlation
$\rho = 0$: no correlation	$r = 0$: no correlation
$\rho = 1$: perfect positive correlation	$r = 1$: perfect positive correlation

TABLE 2.15 Data for Example 2.15: Courses and No-Sales Days.

Salesperson	Y No-Sales Days	X Courses
1	3	7
2	4	6
3	5	5
4	6	4
5	7	3

A negative relationship is apparent from the data because as X moves in one direction (down), Y moves precisely in the other direction (up). Thus for this population of data points it is expected that ρ will be approximately -1.

Frequently, X and Y are measured in different units, such as pounds and dollars, sales units and sales dollars, unemployment rate and GNP dollars. In spite of these differing methods of measuring X and Y, it is still important to measure the extent to which X and Y relate. This measurement is done by first converting the sample data measurements to standard units.

The X–Y measurements are converted to Z-scores. The Z-scores for each X–Y measurement are multiplied, providing cross products for each item or person. These cross products are of interest because the mean of these values is the correlation coefficient. Formula 2.14 shows that the mean of the cross products of Z-scores for two variables is the correlation coefficient.

$$\rho = \frac{\Sigma Z_y Z_x}{N} \tag{2.14}$$

The calculation of the correlation coefficient ρ by using the cross product of Z-scores will always produce the correct value, but in most cases there is an easier way to perform the computations. Formula 2.15 is equivalent to finding ρ by calculating the mean cross product of the Z-scores.

$$\rho = \frac{\Sigma Z_y Z_x}{N} = \frac{N \Sigma XY - (\Sigma X)(\Sigma Y)}{\sqrt{N \Sigma X^2 - (\Sigma X)^2} \sqrt{N \Sigma Y^2 - (\Sigma Y)^2}} \tag{2.15}$$

(See Appendix A for a proof of this relationship.)

To calculate ρ by using this formula, a table of values is needed. For Example 2.15 the computations are illustrated in Table 2.16.

All the values needed to solve Formula 2.15 are now calculated. The substitution and computations are

$$\rho = \frac{(5)(115) - (25)(25)}{\sqrt{(5)(135) - 25^2} \sqrt{(5)(135) - 25^2}} = \frac{575 - 625}{\sqrt{50} \sqrt{50}}$$

$$= \frac{-50}{\sqrt{50^2}} = \frac{-50}{50} = -1 \qquad\blacksquare$$

TABLE 2.16 Calculations Needed for Use of Formula 2.14 for Data of Example 2.15.

	Y	X	Y^2	X^2	XY
	3	7	9	49	21
	4	6	16	36	24
	5	5	25	25	25
	6	4	36	16	24
	7	3	49	9	21
Sums	$\overline{25}$	$\overline{25}$	$\overline{135}$	$\overline{135}$	$\overline{115}$

In examining a collection of data points, judgment must be used in deciding when the value for ρ becomes large enough to consider the two variables highly linearly correlated. In most cases involving a collection of X–Y population points, however, Equation (2.15) can be used to find the correlation coefficient that measures the extent to which the two measured variables move together in a linear fashion.

It is usually the case that a sample of data points has been randomly drawn from the population under investigation. In this case Equation 2.15 is used after replacing N, the population size, by n, the sample size. The formula for the sample correlation coefficient thus becomes[2]

$$r = \frac{n \; \Sigma \; XY - (\Sigma \; X)(\Sigma \; Y)}{\sqrt{n \; \Sigma \; X^2 - (\Sigma \; X)^2} \; \sqrt{n \; \Sigma \; Y^2 - (\Sigma \; Y)^2}} \qquad (2.16)$$

EXAMPLE 2.16

■ If the relationship between age and income is being studied (Table 2.13), it might be of interest to know the value of r for these data. The required computations appear in Table 2.17.

From the table it can be seen that the sample correlation coefficient confirms what was observed in Table 2.13 and Figure 2.10. The value for r is positive, suggesting a positive linear relationship between age and income. Also, on a scale of 0 to 1, the value of r is fairly high (.89). This result suggests a strong linear relationship rather than a weak one. The remaining question is whether or not the combination of sample size and correlation coefficient is strong enough to make meaningful statements about the population from which the data values were drawn. ■

---

[2] This coefficient, which deals with numerical data values, is known as the *Pearson correlation coefficient* for the sample.

TABLE 2.17 Computations for Example 2.16 for the Correlation of Age and Income.

	Y	X	Y^2	X^2	XY
	7,800	22	60,840,000	484	171,600
	8,500	23	72,250,000	529	195,500
	10,000	26	100,000,000	676	260,000
	15,000	27	225,000,000	729	405,000
	16,400	35	268,960,000	1,225	574,000
Sums	57,700	133	727,050,000	3,643	1,606,100

$$r = \frac{(5)(1,606,100) - (133)(57,700)}{\sqrt{(5)(3,643) - (133)^2}\sqrt{(5)(727,050,000) - (57,700)^2}}$$

$$= \frac{8,030,500 - 7,674,100}{(22.93)(17,491.71)} = \frac{356,400}{401,084.90}$$

$$= .89$$

Two important points in the discussion of correlation should now be made.

First, it must always be kept in mind that *correlation,* not *causation,* is being measured. It may be perfectly valid to say that two variables are correlated on the basis of a high correlation coefficient. It may or may not be valid to say that one variable is *causing* the movement of the other; that is a question for the analyst's judgment. For instance, it may be true that the sales volume of a country store in a lightly populated area is highly correlated with the average stock market price in New York City. It might be concluded after examining a large sample of these two variables that such a high correlation exists. It is probably not true that one of these variables is causing the movement of the other. In fact, the movements of both these variables are probably caused by a third factor, the general state of the economy. The error of assuming causation on the basis of correlation is frequently made by politicians, advertisers, and others.

Second, note that the correlation coefficient is measuring a *linear* relationship between two variables. In the case where the correlation coefficient is low, it can be concluded that the two variables are not closely related in a linear way. It may be that they are closely related in a nonlinear or curved fashion. Thus a low correlation coefficient does not mean that the two variables are not related, only that a linear or straight-line relationship does not appear to exist.

APPLICATION TO MANAGEMENT

Many of the concepts in this review chapter may be considered background material necessary for understanding of the more advanced forecasting techniques found throughout the remainder of this book. However, the concepts of this chapter also have value in many statistical applications by themselves. While some of these applications might not logically fall under the heading "forecasting," they nonetheless involve using collected data to answer questions about the uncertainties of the business operation, especially the uncertain outcomes of the future.

The descriptive statistical procedures mentioned early in the chapter are widely used wherever large amounts of data must be described so that they may be assimilated and used in the decision-making process. It would be nearly impossible to think of a single area involving numerical measurements where data collections are not routinely summarized using descriptive statistics. This fact applies particularly to the mean, commonly referred to as the "average," and—to a somewhat lesser extent—to the standard deviation. Averaging data collections is understood by everyone and has been used for many years to provide central measurements of data arrays. Measures of dispersion, such as standard deviation, are gaining increasing use as the value of such measures becomes more widely understood.

The binomial and normal distributions are good examples of theoretical distributions that are good models of many real-life situations. As such, their use is widespread in many applications, including forecasting. The prediction of the percentage of defects in a lot of parts, for example, might be found through use of the binomial distribution.

Estimation and hypothesis testing are the two mainstays of basic statistical applications. Forecasting, or estimating, population values of interest through measurement of a random sample is widespread wherever the constraints of time and money force reliance on sample results for decision-making information. Sampling has become especially widespread in the accounting auditing process. Hypothesis testing is widely used to compare past time-period population values with present values, to compare the parameter values of two different branches or business locations, and to detect the changes in key measurements of production processes. This latter application is known as production control.

The goodness-of-fit test is often used to check the validity of assumptions regarding underlying population distributions. This process is especially important when using certain simulation models that require, for example, the assumption of Poisson processes in order for the model results to be valid. Such simulations are used to model real situations and, after validation, for forecasting the results of system changes on output results.

Correlation is widely used to examine the relationships between pairs of numerical variables. As will be seen in later chapters, these relationships are of great importance in forecasting, since forecasting a variable often involves the attempt to find related variables. Both regression analysis and multiple regression rely on correlation coefficients in this process.

CHAPTER 2

GLOSSARY

Continuous random variable   A continuous random variable can assume any numerical value within some range.

Correlation coefficient   A measurement that indicates the extent to which two numerical variables are linearly related to each other.

Degrees of freedom   Degrees of freedom in a data collection indicate the number of data items that are independent of one another and that can carry unique pieces of information.

Descriptive statistics   Methods used to describe data collections with a few key summary values.

Discrete random variable   A discrete random variable can assume only certain specified values, usually the integers.

Expected value   The expected value of a random variable is the average value of the variable over many trials or observations.

Goodness-of-fit test   The goodness-of-fit test determines whether sampled items may be assumed to have been drawn from a population that follows a specified distribution.

Interval estimate   An interval estimate is a numerical interval within which it is likely that the population parameter lies.

Point estimate   A point estimate is a single-valued estimate of a population parameter.

Sampling distribution   A sampling distribution is the array of all possible sample statistics that can be drawn from a population for a given sample size.

Scatter diagram   A plot of X–Y data points in two-dimensional space.

KEY FORMULAS

Population mean $\mu = \dfrac{\Sigma X}{N}$ (2.1)

Sample mean $\bar{X} = \dfrac{\Sigma X}{n}$ (2.2)

Population standard deviation $\sigma = \sqrt{\dfrac{\Sigma (X - \mu)^2}{N}} = \sqrt{\dfrac{\Sigma X^2 - \dfrac{(\Sigma X)^2}{N}}{N}}$ (2.3)

Sample standard deviation $s = \sqrt{\dfrac{\Sigma (X - \bar{X})^2}{n - 1}} = \sqrt{\dfrac{\Sigma X^2 - \dfrac{(\Sigma X)^2}{n}}{n - 1}}$ (2.4)

Population variance $\quad \sigma^2 = \dfrac{\Sigma\,(X - \mu)^2}{N} = \dfrac{\Sigma\,X^2 - \dfrac{(\Sigma\,X)^2}{N}}{N}$ (2.5)

Sample variance $\quad s^2 = \dfrac{\Sigma\,(X - \bar{X})^2}{n - 1} = \dfrac{\Sigma\,X^2 - \dfrac{(\Sigma\,X)^2}{n}}{n - 1}$ (2.6)

Expected value $\quad E(X) = \Sigma\,[X \cdot P(X)]$ (2.7)

Binomial formula $\quad P(X) = C_X^n\,\pi^X(1 - \pi)^{n - X}$ (2.8)

Z-score formula $\quad Z = \dfrac{X - \mu}{\sigma}$ (2.9)

Confidence interval for a mean $\quad \bar{X} \pm Z\,\dfrac{s}{\sqrt{n}}$ (2.10)

Confidence interval for a proportion $\quad p \pm Z\sqrt{\dfrac{\pi(1 - \pi)}{n}}$ (2.11)

Chi-square formula $\quad \chi^2 = \displaystyle\sum_{\text{all categories}} \dfrac{(f_o - f_e)^2}{f_e}$ (2.12)

Degrees of freedom for the goodness-of-fit test $\quad df = k - 1 - c$ (2.13)

Correlation coefficient for a population

$\rho = \dfrac{\Sigma\,Z_y Z_x}{N}$ (2.14)

$\rho = \dfrac{\Sigma\,Z_y Z_x}{N} = \dfrac{N\,\Sigma\,XY - (\Sigma\,X)(\Sigma\,Y)}{\sqrt{N\,\Sigma\,X^2 - (\Sigma\,X)^2}\,\sqrt{N\,\Sigma\,Y^2 - (\Sigma\,Y)^2}}$ (2.15)

Correlation coefficient for a sample

$r = \dfrac{n\,\Sigma\,XY - (\Sigma\,X)(\Sigma\,Y)}{\sqrt{n\,\Sigma\,X^2 - (\Sigma\,X)^2}\,\sqrt{n\,\Sigma\,Y^2 - (\Sigma\,Y)^2}}$ (2.16)

PROBLEMS

1. Do the same percentage of students work full time at University A and University B? The sample evidence is

$$n_A = 100 \qquad n_B = 125$$
$$p_A = .25 \qquad p_B = .28$$

2. If no more than 5% of the electronics parts in a boxcar are defective, we wish to accept the entire shipment. To decide on acceptance, we randomly sample 100 parts and find that 7 of them are defective. Should the shipment be accepted?

3. A teacher claims that a new method of teaching mathematics will raise the average standard mathematics score of sixth-grade students. The average test score is now 75 with a standard deviation of 10. A random sample of 30 students will be taught with the new method next fall.
   a. State the null and alternative hypotheses.
   b. Sketch the appropriate sampling distribution.
   c. State the decision rule for the test (assume some significance level).

4. $\quad H_0: \mu = 5\,\text{lb} \qquad n = 10$

   $\quad H_1: \mu \neq 5\,\text{lb} \qquad \bar{X} = 6.5\,\text{lb}$

   $\quad$ Reject H_0? $\qquad s = 1.5\,\text{lb}$

5. A salesman claims that his company can deliver light bulbs that have a higher average lifetime than the ones we currently use. We sample some of his bulbs to find out their average lifetime and do the same for our current brand of bulbs. Should we buy from the new supplier after observing the following sample results?

Old	New
$\bar{X} = 200\,\text{h}$	$\bar{X} = 210\,\text{h}$
$s = 20\,\text{h}$	$s = 15\,\text{h}$
$n = 35$	$n = 18$

6. Consider the population of 200 family sizes presented in the accompanying table. Ten years ago the average family size was 2.9. Randomly select a sample of 30 sizes and test the hypothesis that the average family size has not changed in the last ten years. (*Hint:* Make sure your sample is *randomly*

drawn from the population. Consult your instructor if you do not know how to do this.)

(1) 3	(35) 1	(69) 2	(102) 1	(135) 5	(168) 6
(2) 2	(36) 2	(70) 4	(103) 2	(136) 2	(169) 3
(3) 7	(37) 4	(71) 3	(104) 5	(137) 1	(170) 2
(4) 3	(38) 1	(72) 7	(105) 3	(138) 4	(171) 3
(5) 4	(39) 4	(73) 2	(106) 2	(139) 2	(172) 4
(6) 2	(40) 2	(74) 6	(107) 1	(140) 4	(173) 2
(7) 3	(41) 1	(75) 2	(108) 2	(141) 1	(174) 2
(8) 1	(42) 3	(76) 7	(109) 2	(142) 2	(175) 1
(9) 5	(43) 5	(77) 3	(110) 1	(143) 4	(176) 5
(10) 3	(44) 2	(78) 6	(111) 4	(144) 1	(177) 3
(11) 2	(45) 1	(79) 4	(112) 1	(145) 2	(178) 2
(12) 3	(46) 4	(80) 2	(113) 1	(146) 2	(179) 4
(13) 4	(47) 3	(81) 3	(114) 2	(147) 5	(180) 3
(14) 1	(48) 5	(82) 5	(115) 2	(148) 3	(181) 5
(15) 2	(49) 2	(83) 2	(116) 1	(149) 1	(182) 3
(16) 2	(50) 4	(84) 1	(117) 4	(150) 2	(183) 1
(17) 4	(51) 1	(85) 3	(118) 2	(151) 6	(184) 2
(18) 4	(52) 6	(86) 3	(119) 1	(152) 2	(185) 4
(19) 3	(53) 2	(87) 2	(120) 3	(153) 5	(186) 3
(20) 2	(54) 5	(88) 4	(121) 5	(154) 1	(187) 2
(21) 1	(55) 4	(89) 1	(122) 1	(155) 2	(188) 5
(22) 5	(56) 1	(90) 2	(123) 2	(156) 1	(189) 3
(23) 2	(57) 2	(91) 3	(124) 3	(157) 4	(190) 4
(24) 1	(58) 1	(92) 3	(125) 4	(158) 2	(191) 3
(25) 4	(59) 5	(93) 2	(126) 3	(159) 2	(192) 2
(26) 3	(60) 2	(94) 4	(127) 2	(160) 7	(193) 3
(27) 2	(61) 7	(95) 1	(128) 1	(161) 4	(194) 2
(28) 3	(62) 1	(96) 2	(129) 6	(162) 2	(195) 5
(29) 6	(63) 2	(97) 4	(130) 1	(163) 1	(196) 3
(30) 1	(64) 6	(98) 3	(131) 2	(164) 7	(197) 3
(31) 2	(65) 4	(99) 2	(132) 5	(165) 2	(198) 2
(32) 4	(66) 1	(100) 6	(133) 2	(166) 7	(199) 5
(33) 3	(67) 2	(101) 4	(134) 1	(167) 4	(200) 1
(34) 2	(68) 1				

7. In a survey at a supermarket the following numbers of people were observed purchasing five brands of coffee:

	Coffee			
A	B	C	D	E
74	53	81	70	82

Do these data support the notion that the population of coffee buyers prefers each of the five brands equally? Use $\alpha = .05$. (*Hint:* Could the data have been drawn from a uniform distribution?)

8. A computer program that is supposed to generate random numbers is tested. Specifically, the program is supposed to generate random numbers between zero and one. To test the program, 10,000 numbers are generated with the following results:

Interval	Number Observed
0.0 to 0.1	950
0.1 to 0.2	1,069
0.2 to 0.3	992
0.3 to 0.4	966
0.4 to 0.5	980
0.5 to 0.6	1,051
0.6 to 0.7	1,012
0.7 to 0.8	952
0.8 to 0.9	960
0.9 to 1.0	1,068

Do these data support the notion of a random generator?

9. Can it be assumed that the ounces of fill has dropped below the 25-ounce minimum needed for a "25-ounce" can of tomato juice? The machine that fills the cans has been suspected of slowly reducing the average fill volume during the past two months. A random sample of 200 cans is selected from the machine during a typical week and their contents measured. The results indicate an average fill volume of 24.5 ounces with a standard deviation of .35 ounce.

10. A candidate for county commissioner has just begun running a new series of TV ads that strongly attack her opponent for office. She decides to take a market survey to measure the impact of the new campaign. Before the new campaign began running, she was polling about 38% of the voter preference. In a random sample of 350 voters conducted after the new campaign was aired, 144 indicated they intended to vote for her. Has the new TV campaign made any difference?

11. A company about to enter the light beer market wants to know if consumers can distinguish among currently available brands in a blind taste test. One hundred beer drinkers are offered five different beers in identical containers and asked to indicate their favorite. On the basis of the following preference evidence collected during this test, what can be said about light beer preference among all beer drinkers?

Favorite Beer

A	B	C	D	E
18	22	29	15	16

12. A large manufacturer of motorcycles is attempting to model its production process with a computerized simulation. The simulation model it wishes to use assumes that the arrival of units at the paint shop follows a Poisson process. To check on this assumption, the time-between-arrivals for a number of units is recorded during a three-week period along with the frequencies expected from a Poisson distribution.

Interarrival Time (Minutes)

	0–5	5–10	10–15	15–20	20+
f_e	23	39	28	17	11
f_e	20	42	22	19	15

Is the company justified in assuming a Poisson process for interarrival times at the paint shop?

13. A company wants to determine whether or not two of its retail outlets have the same average sales amount per customer transaction. Random sampling methods are determined for both outlets, and the samples are taken with the following results:

Store 1	Store 2
$\bar{X} = \$138.50$	$\bar{X} = \$165.40$
$s = \$23.50$	$s = \$42.91$
$n = 85$	$n = 75$

Choose a significance level and determine whether or not the above sample evidence supports a rejection of the null hypothesis of equal population means.

14. A politician wants to determine if the unemployment rates are the same or different in two key cities. Since official figures are not available, it is necessary to randomly sample residents of the two cities so that a comparison can be made. Random samples are taken from each city with these results:

City 1: $n = 450, \quad p = .058$
City 2: $n = 725, \quad p = .074$

Do these data support the notion that City 2 has an unemployment rate different from City 1?

15. A quality control campaign has focused on reducing the percentage of new cars sold by a major manufacturer that are returned for major repairs. Prior to this campaign this percentage stood at 12%. After six months of the improvement campaign, the company randomly selects several of its dealers and determines how many cars they sold and the number that are returned for major repair. A total of 1,542 cars was delivered by these dealers during the sample period with 123 of them returned. Does this evidence indicate that the quality control campaign has been successful?

16. A seller of toothpaste in the western United States wants to increase its market share from the current level of 23%. A new advertising campaign is instituted, and after a trial period of one month with this campaign, shoppers are randomly selected to determine their brand preference. The ad agency points with pride to the fact that 28% of a sample of 1,000 shoppers uses the company's product. Does the evidence support the ad agency's position that its campaign has increased market share?

17. A large hospital is concerned that the average number of days in the hospital per patient has declined during the past year and decides to randomly sample a number of patient records to see if a drop has actually taken place. A sampling method is determined, and 150 patient files are pulled and hospital stay times recorded. The average stay for the sampled patients was 3.4 days with a standard deviation of .85 day. A study done two years ago indicated an average stay of 4.9 days. Using correct statistical procedures, find whether there has been a reduction in average stay length.

18. Suppose $n = 500$ and $r = -.98$. Explain why the following statement is incorrect:
"Movement of X is causing Y to move in the opposite direction." Correctly interpret the sample results above.

19. In a correlation problem, does $r = \rho$? Why? Explain the difference between r and ρ.

For Problems 20–24, proceed as follows:
a. Construct a scatter diagram of the data given in the accompanying tables.
b. State whether or not the variables appear to be correlated.
c. Compute the sample correlation coefficient.

20. Y is transportation time, in days, for goods ordered for our firm from various suppliers, and X is the distance, in miles:

Supplier	Y	X	Supplier	Y	X
1	10	983	5	8	416
2	2	426	6	3	283
3	10	1,015	7	3	124
4	11	1,763	8	5	674

21. Y is starting salary after college, in dollars, and X is age:

Y	X
9,800	23
10,000	24
10,200	22
12,400	30
11,000	28
9,780	25

22. Y is average monthly sales of company salespeople, and X is hours spent in formal sales-training courses:

Y	X	Y	X
5,583	100	2,420	85
7,420	83	18,960	0
12,340	70	25,862	50
4,260	90	14,920	40
17,960	25	11,360	50
10,400	35	9,840	55
12,360	40		

23. Y is the average price, in dollars, of selected stocks over randomly selected months, and X is the earnings per share for the quarter in which the selected month falls:

Y	X	Y	X
54	6.25	40	10.13
75	7.33	33	3.14
103	8.16	28	2.98
83	14.24	76	5.18
50	24.23		

24. Y is the monthly sales for our organization, and X is the previous month's total advertising budget:

Y	X
50,500	1,400
55,710	1,400
63,800	1,000
45,200	1,200
56,000	1,500
75,800	1,500
93,850	2,000

25. The sales aptitude examination scores for $n = 10$ life insurance salespeople and their annual sales (in millions of dollars of insurance) are provided in the accompanying table.
   a. Calculate the correlation coefficient for the data.
   b. Do you think that the 10 salespeople illustrate that the aptitude examination scores are related to annual sales?

Sales-person	Sales, Y	Score, X	Sales-person	Sales, Y	Score, X
Rich	1.1	85	Jones	2.7	93
Hank	1.2	72	Smith	2.4	100
Johns	1.6	81	Booker	.7	76
White	.7	64	Zipp	.6	68
Green	2.1	84	Johnson	.9	59

26. Is annual rate of return related to the total amount invested? The portfolios listed in the accompanying table were randomly selected to help answer this question. What is your conclusion? Use acceptable statistical procedures.

Total Investment (1000)	Rate of Return (%)	Total Investment (1000)	Rate of Return (%)
500	10	742	6
120	8	40	8
5	7	76	10
75	12	124	9
40	11	853	9
321	15	325	18
78	20	320	10
480	8	710	12
794	7	850	11

Table for Problem 27.

Obs.	Y	X	Obs.	Y	X	Obs.	Y	X	Obs.	Y	X
(1)	50	37	(51)	54	86	(101)	22	43	(151)	79	85
(2)	90	77	(52)	76	48	(102)	32	5	(152)	79	27
(3)	46	55	(53)	55	48	(103)	24	13	(153)	48	61
(4)	47	27	(54)	12	15	(104)	63	3	(154)	5	7
(5)	12	49	(55)	5	70	(105)	16	58	(155)	24	79
(6)	23	23	(56)	2	9	(106)	4	13	(156)	47	49
(7)	65	18	(57)	77	52	(107)	79	18	(157)	65	71
(8)	37	1	(58)	6	71	(108)	5	5	(158)	56	27
(9)	87	41	(59)	67	38	(109)	59	26	(159)	52	15
(10)	83	73	(60)	30	69	(110)	99	9	(160)	17	88
(11)	87	61	(61)	3	13	(111)	76	96	(161)	45	38
(12)	39	85	(62)	6	63	(112)	15	94	(162)	45	31
(13)	28	16	(63)	70	65	(113)	10	30	(163)	90	35
(14)	97	46	(64)	33	87	(114)	20	41	(164)	69	78
(15)	69	88	(65)	13	18	(115)	37	1	(165)	62	93
(16)	87	87	(66)	10	4	(116)	56	27	(166)	0	51
(17)	52	82	(67)	21	29	(117)	6	73	(167)	8	68
(18)	52	56	(68)	56	21	(118)	86	19	(168)	47	30
(19)	15	22	(69)	74	9	(119)	27	94	(169)	7	81
(20)	85	49	(70)	47	8	(120)	67	5	(170)	48	30
(21)	41	44	(71)	34	18	(121)	22	31	(171)	59	46
(22)	82	33	(72)	38	84	(122)	32	13	(172)	76	99
(23)	98	77	(73)	75	64	(123)	90	11	(173)	54	98
(24)	99	87	(74)	0	81	(124)	88	50	(174)	95	11
(25)	23	54	(75)	51	98	(125)	35	40	(175)	7	6
(26)	77	8	(76)	47	55	(126)	57	80	(176)	24	83
(27)	42	64	(77)	63	40	(127)	73	44	(177)	55	49
(28)	60	24	(78)	7	14	(128)	13	63	(178)	41	39
(29)	22	29	(79)	6	11	(129)	18	74	(179)	14	16
(30)	91	40	(80)	68	42	(130)	70	40	(180)	24	13
(31)	68	35	(81)	72	43	(131)	9	53	(181)	36	31
(32)	36	37	(82)	95	73	(132)	93	79	(182)	62	44
(33)	22	28	(83)	82	45	(133)	41	9	(183)	77	11
(34)	92	56	(84)	91	16	(134)	17	52	(184)	32	60
(35)	34	33	(85)	83	21	(135)	10	82	(185)	12	82
(36)	34	82	(86)	27	85	(136)	69	37	(186)	85	7
(37)	63	89	(87)	13	37	(137)	5	57	(187)	90	68
(38)	30	78	(88)	6	89	(138)	18	62	(188)	78	10
(39)	31	24	(89)	76	76	(139)	88	21	(189)	60	27
(40)	84	53	(90)	55	71	(140)	99	94	(190)	96	90
(41)	56	61	(91)	13	53	(141)	86	99	(191)	51	6
(42)	48	18	(92)	50	13	(142)	95	45	(192)	9	62
(43)	0	45	(93)	60	12	(143)	78	19	(193)	93	78
(44)	58	4	(94)	61	30	(144)	3	76	(194)	61	22
(45)	27	23	(95)	73	57	(145)	38	81	(195)	5	99
(46)	78	68	(96)	20	66	(146)	57	95	(196)	88	51
(47)	78	79	(97)	36	27	(147)	77	30	(197)	45	44
(48)	72	66	(98)	85	41	(148)	25	59	(198)	34	86
(49)	21	80	(99)	49	20	(149)	99	93	(199)	28	47
(50)	73	99	(100)	83	66	(150)	9	28	(200)	44	49

Table for Problem 28.

Obs.	Y	X	Obs.	Y	X	Obs.	Y	X
(1)	1.0	10	(48)	2.2	180	(95)	2.0	330
(2)	0.9	10	(49)	2.4	180	(96)	2.4	340
(3)	0.8	10	(50)	1.6	180	(97)	2.2	340
(4)	1.3	20	(51)	1.8	190	(98)	2.0	340
(5)	0.9	20	(52)	4.1	190	(99)	2.5	350
(6)	0.6	30	(53)	2.0	190	(100)	2.8	350
(7)	1.1	30	(54)	1.5	200	(101)	2.3	350
(8)	1.0	30	(55)	2.1	200	(102)	2.7	350
(9)	1.4	40	(56)	2.5	200	(103)	2.8	360
(10)	1.4	40	(57)	1.7	220	(104)	3.1	360
(11)	1.2	40	(58)	2.0	220	(105)	2.5	370
(12)	1.7	50	(59)	2.3	220	(106)	2.9	370
(13)	0.9	50	(60)	1.8	220	(107)	2.6	370
(14)	1.2	50	(61)	1.3	230	(108)	3.0	380
(15)	1.3	50	(62)	1.6	230	(109)	3.2	380
(16)	0.7	60	(63)	2.8	230	(110)	2.9	390
(17)	1.0	60	(64)	2.2	230	(111)	2.6	390
(18)	1.3	70	(65)	2.6	230	(112)	2.5	390
(19)	1.5	70	(66)	1.4	240	(113)	2.7	400
(20)	2.0	70	(67)	1.6	240	(114)	3.1	400
(21)	0.8	80	(68)	1.7	240	(115)	2.4	400
(22)	0.6	80	(69)	1.5	250	(116)	3.0	400
(23)	1.8	80	(70)	2.2	250	(117)	3.4	420
(24)	1.0	90	(71)	2.5	250	(118)	3.5	420
(25)	2.0	100	(72)	2.4	260	(119)	3.1	420
(26)	0.5	100	(73)	2.0	260	(120)	2.9	420
(27)	1.5	100	(74)	2.7	260	(121)	2.8	430
(28)	1.3	110	(75)	2.0	270	(122)	3.3	430
(29)	1.7	110	(76)	2.2	270	(123)	2.5	440
(30)	1.2	110	(77)	2.4	270	(124)	2.8	440
(31)	0.8	110	(78)	1.8	280	(125)	2.4	450
(32)	1.0	120	(79)	2.8	290	(126)	2.6	450
(33)	1.8	120	(80)	2.2	290	(127)	3.0	450
(34)	2.1	120	(81)	2.4	290	(128)	3.4	460
(35)	1.5	130	(82)	2.1	290	(129)	3.0	460
(36)	1.9	130	(83)	1.9	290	(130)	3.3	470
(37)	1.7	140	(84)	2.4	300	(131)	3.4	470
(38)	1.2	150	(85)	2.5	300	(132)	3.1	470
(39)	1.4	150	(86)	2.9	300	(133)	3.6	480
(40)	2.1	150	(87)	2.0	300	(134)	3.0	480
(41)	0.9	160	(88)	1.9	310	(135)	2.9	480
(42)	1.1	160	(89)	2.5	310	(136)	3.2	480
(43)	1.7	160	(90)	2.6	310	(137)	2.6	490
(44)	2.0	160	(91)	3.2	320	(138)	3.8	490
(45)	1.6	170	(92)	2.8	320	(139)	3.3	490
(46)	1.9	170	(93)	2.4	320	(140)	2.9	500
(47)	1.7	170	(94)	2.5	320			

27. Consider the population of 200 weekly observations that are presented in the accompanying table. The independent variable X is the average weekly temperature of Spokane, Washington. The dependent variable Y is the number of shares of Sunshine Mining Stock traded on the Spokane exchange in a week. Randomly select data for 16 weeks, and compute the coefficient of correlation. Test the hypothesis that the relationship between temperature and the number of shares traded is not significant. (*Hint:* make sure your sample is *randomly* drawn from the population. Consult your instructor if you do not know how to draw a random sample.)

28. Consider the population of 140 observations that are presented on page 54. The Marshall Printing Company wishes to estimate the relationship between the number of copies produced by an offset-printing technique (X) and the associated direct labor cost (Y). Select a random sample of 20 observations, and determine whether a significant relationship exists between number of copies and total direct labor cost.

CASE STUDY **2.1**

ALCAM ELECTRONICS

David Branch recently received a degree in business administration from a small university and went to work for Alcam Electronics, a manufacturer of various electronics components for industry. After a few weeks on the job he was called into the office of Alcam's owner and manager, Alice Cameron, who asked him to investigate two questions regarding a certain transistor manufactured by Alcam because a large TV company was interested in a major purchase.

First, Alice wanted to know what percent of the transistors currently in stock were defective. The potential buyer desired information on the quality of units received, and Alice thought the percent defective in current inventory would be a good answer to that question. Second, she wanted information on the estimated lifetimes of the transistors. The potential buyer had great interest in this question since its current supplier guaranteed an average lifetime of 5,000 hours.

David decided to take a random sample of the transistors in question and formulated a plan to accomplish this task. He numbered the storage bins holding the transistors, drew random numbers, and sampled all transistors in each selected bin for the sample. Since each bin contained about 20 transistors, he selected 10 random numbers, which gave him a final sample size of 205 transistors. Since he had selected 10 of 55 bins, he thought he had a good representative sample and could use the results of this sample to generalize to the entire population of transistors in inventory, as well as to units yet to be manufactured by the same process.

David next had each of the 205 units subjected to laboratory tests to determine which were operating properly. After the lab results had been completed, it was found that 6 of the units did not function in accordance with specifications. Using a 95% confidence level, David then performed the following calculations to arrive at point and interval estimates for the percentage of all transistors made by the plant that were defective:

$$p = \frac{6}{205} = .029$$

$$.029 \pm 1.96\sqrt{\frac{(.029)(.971)}{205}}$$

$$.029 \pm .023$$

$$.006 \rightarrow .052$$

On the basis of these calculations, David intended to include the following information in his final report to Alice:

1. It is estimated that approximately 3% of the transistors manufactured by the current process are defective.
2. There is a 95% chance that the following statement is true: between .6% and 5.2% of the transistors are defective.

David next moved on to the question of the average lifetime of the units. Because these lifetimes can extend to several years, he realized that none of the sampled units could be tested if a timely answer was desired. He therefore decided to contact several users of this component to determine if any lifetime records were available. Fortunately, he found three companies that had used the transistor in the past and that had limited records on component lifetimes. In total, he received data on 38 transistors whose failure times were known. Since these transistors were manufactured using the same process as was currently being used, he reasoned that the results of this sample could be inferred to the units in inventory and those yet to be produced.

Following are the results of the computations David performed on the lifetime data of his sample:

$n = 38$

Average lifetime $= \bar{X} = 4{,}805$ hours

Standard deviation of lifetimes $= s = 675$ hours

After finding that the sample average lifetime was only 4,805 hours, David was concerned because he knew the current supplier of components was guaranteeing an average lifetime of 5,000 hours. Although his sample average was a bit below 5,000 hours, he realized that the sample size was only 38 and that this did not constitute positive proof that Alcam's quality was inferior to that of the other supplier. He decided to test the hypothesis that the average lifetime of all transistors was 5,000 hours against the alternative that it was less. Following are the calculations he performed:

$$H_0: \mu = 5{,}000 \qquad \alpha = .01$$

$$H_1: \mu < 5{,}000 \qquad s = 675$$

Decision Rule Point. $5{,}000 - 2.33\dfrac{675}{\sqrt{38}} = 4{,}744.9.$

Decision Rule.   If $\bar{X} < 4{,}744.9$, reject H_0.

Since the sample mean (4,805) was not below the decision rule point for rejection (4,744.9), David failed to reject the hypothesis that the mean lifetime of all components was equal to 5,000 hours. He thought this would be good news to Alice Cameron and included a summary of his findings in his final report. A few days after he gave his written and verbal report to her, Alice called him into her office to compliment him on a good job and to share a concern she had regarding his findings. She said, "I am concerned about the very low significance level of your hypothesis test. You took only a 1% chance of rejecting the null hypothesis if it is true. This strikes me as very conservative. I am concerned that we will enter into a contract and then find that our quality level does not meet the desired 5,000-hour specification."

QUESTION

How would you respond to Alice Cameron's comment?

CASE STUDY **2.2**

GREAT CITY BANK

As a recently hired employee of Great City bank you have been asked by the Vice-President for Operations to check into a concern recently expressed by the bank president. This concern involves a suspicion that recent unfavorable economic conditions have reduced the average savings account balance of the bank's customers. Alternatively, several bank executives believe these conditions may have raised the average account balance.

When given this assignment, you decide to randomly sample savings accounts and record the balance of each. You choose a three-day period in the middle of the month to do your sampling so that end-of-the-month withdrawals and deposits will not affect the account balances. You write a brief computer program that selects every 25th account in a run through the computerized listing of savings accounts. This process generates a random sample of 128 savings accounts that yield the following statistics:

$$\bar{X} = \$1,674.93$$

$$s = \$428.79$$

From a similar sampling that was done 18 months ago, you learn that the average savings account balance at that time was $1,794.25. Although it is apparent that your sample average is below this figure, you are not sure that it has dropped sufficiently to support the conclusion that the average of all customer savings accounts has changed.

QUESTION

Using the sample data given above, what conclusion can be reached and reported to bank management?

ALUMINUM PRODUCTS

Ms. Emry is the personnel manager for a large branch of a national company that produces aluminum products. Recently, shift foremen have complained that older hourly workers are not producing the output expected of them, and this condition has been given as the reason for an overall drop in the plant's output.

Top management in the branch believes this reason is just an excuse used to hide a general lack of management leadership on the floor. The branch manager calls Emry in one morning and says, "I know what I'm being told is bunk. Go get me some data that show the older workers are doing just as well as the younger ones."

Emry decides to concentrate on the production of aluminum engine blocks used in small gasoline engines since this product currently constitutes a large percentage of the plant's output. These blocks are finished and prepared for delivery by individual workers after the rough castings are made and stored in a central factory location. Records are kept of the daily output of each worker, but to Emry's knowledge, this information has never been used by management in any way.

Emry goes to the personnel file cabinet and pulls every twentieth file. After removing those persons not currently engaged in making engine blocks, she finds she has a random sample of 38 hourly workers. She records the names of these persons and calculates their ages from the birthdays noted in their files.

She then goes to the production records and finds the output levels for these 38 people. She decides to compute the average daily number of units produced over the past year as an indication of output level. She feels that the records are quite accurate after talking with the three shift foremen and learning that the records have been carefully kept on a daily basis over this period of time.

She then records both the age and average number of units produced for each of the 38 workers chosen for the sample. These data appear in Table 2.18. She believes that after she has computed the correlation coefficient between these two variables and tested the hypothesis that the population correlation coefficient is zero, she will be in a position to give the branch manager some useful information.

TABLE 2.18 Emry's Sample Data.

Person	Age	Output	Person	Age	Output	Person	Age	Output
1	25	3	14	53	2	27	25	3
2	53	5	15	31	8	28	32	8
3	48	1	16	29	7	29	46	7
4	31	2	17	42	6	30	21	4
5	26	7	18	33	7	31	34	9
6	36	4	19	27	6	32	47	4
7	41	2	20	51	5	33	22	5
8	27	3	21	35	8	34	38	3
9	50	6	22	26	6	35	46	7
10	52	7	23	39	4	36	24	6
11	39	6	24	45	5	37	33	3
12	28	5	25	58	7	38	42	4
13	43	9	26	55	4			

QUESTIONS

1. How would you conduct the analysis suggested by Emry?

2. Prepare a memo to the branch manager summarizing the results of your analysis.

BANK CUSTOMERS

Betty Blume, the manager of marketing for a medium-sized bank, is interested in determining those factors that define a profitable bank customer. She decides that the size of a customer's outstanding loan balance is a good measurement of profitability and decides to randomly select 150 customer files and record the average loan balance during the past six months.

She next turns her attention to variables that might be strongly related to average loan balance and thus profitability. She initially hopes to find factors that are easy to measure and selects two possible related variables: customer age and estimated total asset value. Both these variables are recorded on loan application forms that are included in the customer file.

After randomly choosing 150 customer files and recording the three desired values, she uses a computer program available on one of the bank's minicomputers to compute the correlation coefficients between loan balance and each of the two potential predictor variables. Using X_1 to represent customer age and X_2 to represent total asset value, she finds the following correlation coefficients:

For X_1: $r = -.45$

For X_2: $r = .82$

Betty is surprised at first to find a rather low correlation between customer profitability and age $(-.45)$. She is also surprised to find that this correlation is negative. The negative sign suggests that older customers are less profitable than younger ones. After giving these results some thought, she decides that perhaps customers in their late twenties and early thirties may be quite profitable, that people in their forties and fifties may have lower loan balances, and that retired persons have almost no outstanding loans. Although she finds that her sample size has produced a significant correlation on age, she decides to eliminate age as a determinant of customer profitability.

Betty is more pleased with the results on total asset value $(r = .82)$. She tests the null hypothesis of no population correlation and rejects it. Apparently total asset value is a good determinant of average loan balance and thus profit to the bank. However, this result becomes less satisfying the more she thinks about it. In terms of marketing the bank's services and producing higher profits, she feels that she has really made no progress. She reasons that a wealthier person would naturally carry a larger loan balance than a less wealthy person; her data have only verified an obvious fact. As she thinks about this situation, she begins to consider how to go about reaching a more useful definition of a profitable customer. The information contained in the customer files offers no help to her, and she begins considering sending a written questionnaire to a sample of bank customers. Perhaps certain information that customers could provide might help define those characteristics that generate higher profits for the bank.

QUESTION

If Betty were to send out a questionnaire to a sample of bank customers, what sorts of questions should be asked in an attempt to formulate a usable definition of profitability?

UNIT LIFETIMES

Joe Worth has just joined a company that is located in a farming area and whose activities involve freezing vegetables for a large national frozen food company. One of his first jobs is to look into the recent failure of several large engine transmissions that connect diesel engines to the conveyor belts used throughout the operation.

There have been eight failures during the past year, and records on the failed units are available. Joe finds it is possible to obtain two measurements on the failed components that he thinks might be related: total lifetime of failed transmission in months and time since last major overhaul in months. He records these two variables on the failed components as follows:

Lifetime	Time Since Last Overhaul
458	18
129	37
94	94
718	25
516	129
813	105
259	110
312	27

Joe believes that if he can show a positive connection between overhauls and part lifetimes, he will be in a position to determine the cost of major overhauls against the cost of transmission replacement. He suspects that a good correlation will lead to a more careful maintenance policy and fewer breakdowns.

QUESTIONS

1. What is the correlation between transmission lifetime and time since last overhaul?
2. Given the small sample size, can it be concluded that there is a correlation between the two variables for the entire population of transmissions?
3. Should Joe continue his investigation by costing out transmission overhauls and part failures?

MINITAB EXAMPLE

Many statistical software packages are available on mainframe computers and smaller computers, including PCs. Many of these perform basic statistical operations, and many others are designed exclusively for forecasting.

One of the more popular software packages used for both statistical analysis and forecasting is Minitab. This package is available for both large and small computers, and is one of the computer packages referred to throughout this book. You will find Minitab instructions for many tasks as you learn about the forecasting techniques covered in the following chapters.

For the following Minitab example, it is assumed that Minitab is available on your computer and that it has been called up. The MTB > prompt appears on the screen when the callup has been successful. In the following example, two data sets are keyed into the computer, the sets are printed, some basic statistics are computed, and finally a test is conducted to test the null hypothesis that the population mean of the second variable is exactly 25.

```
MTB > SET C1   *1
DATA > 4 6 5 8 7 6 3 5 4 2   *2
MTB > END   *3
MTB > SET C2   *4
DATA > 24 35 18 36 24 28 26 10 20 31
MTB > END
MTB > PRINT C1 C2   *5

  ROW    C1    C2

   1      4     24
   2      6     35
   3      5     18
   4      8     36
   5      7     24
   6      6     28
   7      3     26
   8      5     10
   9      4     20
  10      2     31

MTB > DESCRIBE C1 C2   *6

              N      MEAN    MEDIAN    TRMEAN    STDEV    SEMEAN
C1           10     5.000     5.000     5.000    1.826     0.577
C2           10     25.20     25.00     25.75     7.94      2.51

             MIN       MAX        Q1        Q3
C1         2.000     8.000     3.750     6.250
C2         10.00     36.00     19.50     32.00

MTB > TTEST [MU=25]C2   *7
```

continues

Continued

```
TEST OF MU = 25.000 VS MU N.E. 25.000

           N      MEAN     STDEV    SE MEAN       T   *8  P VALUE  *9
C2        10     25.200    7.941     2.511      0.08       0.94

MTB > STOP  *10
```

---

*1 Command **SET** to enter data into C1
*2 Data values are keyed in separated by spaces. A return can be
    used at any time if multiple lines are needed.
*3 Command to **END** data entry
*4 Command **SET** to enter data into C2
*5 Command **PRINT** is used to show what is in columns C1 and C2
*6 Command **DESCRIBE** is used to compute statistics such as the mean
    and standard deviation for C1
*7 Command **TTEST** performs a null hypothesis that the population mean
    value of variable C2 is exactly 25
*8 The t value for the above test is t = .08.
*9 The p value is .94.
*10 Command **STOP** returns the computer to the main promt

CHAPTER 2

SELECTED BIBLIOGRAPHY

Carpenter, J., Deloria, D., and Morganstein, D. "Statistical Software for Microcompu-
    ters." *BYTE* (April 1984): 234–264.

Groebner, D., and Shannon, P. *Business Statistics. A Decision-Making Approach*, 2nd
    ed. Columbus, Ohio: Charles E. Merrill Publishing Company, 1985.

Hanke, J., and Reitsch, A. *Understanding Business Statistics*. Homewood, Ill.: Richard
    D. Irwin, Inc., 1991.

Keating, B. "Choosing and Using Business Forecasting Software." *Creative Comput-
    ing* (January 1985): 119–135.

Lachenbruch, P. A. "Statistical Programs for Microcomputers." *BYTE* (November
    1983): 560–570.

Mahmoud, E. "Accuracy in Forecasting." *Journal of Forecasting* 3 (2) (1984): 140–159.

McClave, J., and Benson, P. *Statistics for Business and Economics*. San Francisco:
    Dellen Publishing Company, 1982.

Neffendorf, H. "Statistical Packages for Microcomputers: A Listing." *The American
    Statistician* 37 (1) (1983): 83–86.

Olson, C., and Picconi, M. *Statistics for Business Decision Making*. Glenview, Ill.:
    Scott, Foresman and Company, 1983.

Seitz, N. *Business Forecasting Concepts and Microcomputer Applications*. Reston, Va.:
    Reston Publishing Company, 1984.

Sincich, T. *Business Statistics by Example*. San Francisco: Dellen Publishing Company,
    1982.

3

Data Sources

O ne of the most time-consuming and difficult parts of forecasting is the collection of valid and reliable data. Data-processing personnel are fond of using the expression "garbage in, garbage out" (GIGO). This expression also applies to the forecasting area. A forecast can be no more accurate than the data on which it is based. The most sophisticated forecasting model will fail if it is applied to unreliable data.

The advent of the computer has helped generate an incredible accumulation of data on almost all subjects. The difficult task facing most forecasters is how to find relevant data that will help solve their specific decision-making problems.

Four criteria can be applied to the determination of whether data will be useful:

1. Data should be reliable and accurate. Proper care must be taken that data are collected from a reliable source with proper attention given to accuracy.
2. Data should be relevant. The data must be representative of the circumstances for which they are being used. Data that are supposed to represent economic activity should show upswings and downswings in accordance with past historical business cycle fluctuations.
3. Data should be consistent. When definitions concerning how data are collected change, adjustments need to be made in order to retain consistency in historical patterns.
4. Data should be timely. Data collected, summarized, and published on a timely basis will be of greatest value to the forecaster.

DATA TYPES

Generally, two types of data are of interest to the forecaster. The first is data that are collected at a single point in time, be it a day, a week, or a month. The objective is to examine such data and then to extrapolate or extend the revealed relationships to the larger population.

By contrast, many data values of interest to a business are collected every day, month, quarter, or year. In such instances, *time series data* have been collected. Time series are analyzed to discover past patterns of growth and change that can be used to predict future patterns along with needs for business operations. Time series analysis does not provide the answer to what the future holds, but it is valuable in the forecasting process and helps to reduce errors in forecasts.

> A *time series* is a chronologically arranged sequence of observations on a particular variable.

Publications such as the *Statistical Abstract of the United States,* the *Survey of Current Business,* the *Monthly Labor Review,* the *Federal Reserve Bulletin,* and the annual reports of corporations contain time series of all types. Data—typically reported on a monthly, quarterly, or annual basis and covering prices, production, sales, employment, unemployment, hours worked, fuel used, energy produced, earnings, and so on—fill the pages of these and other business economic publications.

It is important that managers understand the past and use historical data and sound judgment to make intelligent plans to meet the demands of the future. Forecasts are made to assist management in determining alternative strategies.

Long-term forecasts are usually 5-, 10-, and even 20-year predictions into the future. Long-range predictions are essential to allow sufficient time for the procurement, manufacturing, sales, finance, and other departments of a company to develop plans for possible new plants, financing, development of new products, and new methods of assembly.

Business organizations in the United States must forecast the level of sales, both short-term and long-term. Competition for the consumer's dollar, stress on earning a profit for the stockholders, and a desire to produce a larger and larger share of the market are some of the prime motivating forces in business. Thus a statement of the expectations of management, called *forecasts,* is considered necessary in order to have the raw materials, production facilities, and staff available to meet the projected demand.

The alternative, of course, is not to plan ahead. In a dynamic business environment, however, this lack of planning might be disastrous. An electronics firm that ignored the trend to color television and solid-state circuitry would have lost all of its market share by now.

Subjective considerations are extremely important in time series analysis, since a satisfactory probability approach to such analysis has not yet been found. But subjective evaluations would be necessary in making forecasts even if a suitable probability approach to time series analysis were available. Whenever the past is examined to obtain clues about the future, it is relevant only to the extent that causal conditions previously in effect continue to hold in the period ahead. In economic and business activity, causal conditions seldom remain constant. The multitude of causal factors at work tends to be constantly shifting, so the connection between the past, the present, and the future must be continually reevaluated.

While the techniques of time series analysis do not eliminate subjective evaluations, they do make a useful contribution by providing a conceptual approach to forecasting. Forecasts are made with the aid of a set of specific formal procedures, and judgments are indicated explicitly.

DATA SOURCES

Sources of data may be classified as either primary or secondary. *Primary data sources* involve all methods of original data collection. This type of data is often collected using sampling procedures, panel surveys, or a complete census of the items of interest. Even more common is the recording of key company variables each week, month, quarter, or year. Such *time series* variables are often the focus of a great deal of management attention.

> *Primary data sources* involve all methods of original data collection.

Secondary data sources are already published data collected for purposes other than the specific forecasting or research needs at hand. This type of data can be classified as coming from internal sources, originating within the organization, or from external sources, originating outside the organization. Publications that are based on census data are good examples of secondary external sources. Accounting records are frequently used as secondary internal data sources.

> *Secondary data sources* are already published data collected for purposes other than the specific forecasting or research needs at hand.

Secondary Data Sources

The significance of the distinction between primary and secondary sources involves the fact that a primary source is likely to contain more complete and accurate data than may be found in a secondary source. Primary data also tend to be more expensive than secondary data.

External Sources

In recent years, there has been a tremendous increase in the quantity of published data sources available to forecasters. The computer has been mentioned as being partially responsible for this increase in available data. The realization of business and government managers that more and better information increases the effectiveness of planning and decision making has also contributed to this increase. The libraries are filled with billions of pieces of historical data on every topic imaginable. Government sources, computerized services, and nonprofit organizations issue an enormous quantity of statistical data that can be used as relevant input to the forecasting process. Several secondary data sources are listed below.

The U.S. government is the largest publisher and collector of data in the world. Every large city in the United States has at least one library designated as a U.S. government depository. These libraries have extensive collections of data accumulated by the government. There are two governmental sources that are used frequently by business forecasters. The *Survey of Current Business,* published monthly, presents detailed data on economic activity. The *Statistical Abstract of the United States,* published annually, is a general source of statistics on many topics.

Another source of governmental data used by forecasters is the census. Each census provides detailed information by geographical area on many demographic characteristics. Demographic characteristics are variables such as gender, age, income, marital status, and educational level. These data can be extremely valuable for those companies concerned with forecasting time series that depend on such demographic characteristics. Census data are also valuable for forecasters conducting feasibility studies. Will a particular geographical area support a proposed shopping center? Will the geographical area surrounding the shopping center support a proposed athletic club? Census data are frequently used to answer these kinds of questions.

Other important governmental sources of data include the *American Statistics Index,* which provides a guide to the various sources of government statistics; the *Business Conditions Digest,* which is a primary source of data on leading economic indicators; the *CIS/Index to Publications of the United States Government,* which represents the most complete and timely listing of publications of the U.S. Congress; the *County and City Data Book,* which is published every four years and contains economic and population data broken down by city and county; the *Economic Report of the President,* which includes a statistical appendix concerning the labor force, inflation, and economic activity; *Employment and Earnings,* which is published monthly and is a primary source of labor force and unemployment data; the

Federal Reserve Bulletin, which contains statistical series on banks and financial markets as well as incidental material on inflation and economic activity; the *Handbook of Labor Statistics,* which contains historical data for many of the series in *Employment and Earnings;* and the *Statistics of Income,* which is published by the Internal Revenue Service and contains information on categories of income and expenses.[1]

The National Bureau of Economic Research (NBER) (261 Madison Avenue, New York, N.Y. 10016) is another useful source of data for organizations doing long-range planning. This bureau provides data on several different business cycle indicators. These include leading, coincidental, and lagging series that can be used as the basis for predicting turning points in the economy. Business indicators are discussed more completely in Chapter 8.

Private organizations frequently produce inexpensive forecasts of demographic and economic measures. *Business Forecasting in the 1980s* is a selected annotated bibliography of books and articles providing general forecasts as well as the sources of forecasts on specific subjects.[2] Examples of such services are *Forecasting Studies,* which covers trends and key indicators; the *Guide to Consumer Markets,* which provides statistics and graphs on consumer behavior in the marketplace; the *National and Regional Economic Projection Series,* which analyzes and projects population, personal income, and personal consumption expenditures for the United States, the individual states, and SMSAs (Standard Metropolitical Statistical Areas); and the *Survey of Buying Power,* which contains short-range projections and growth rates for population, households, effective buying income, and retail sales for states, counties, and SMSAs.[3]

Commercial organizations also publish statistics that can serve as source data in many forecasting applications. Financial data such as bond yields, company earnings ratios, dividends, stock prices, and trading volumes can be obtained from Dun and Bradstreet, Inc., Moody's Investors Service, Standard and Poor's Corporation Statistical Service, *The Fortune Directory* by Time Inc., and *Value Line Investment Survey* by Arnold Berhard and Company.[1,3]

Many types of data discussed above can also be accessed from computerized databases such as Compuserve, Inc., Dow-Jones' News Retrieval Service, Standard and Poor's Compustat, The Source, and Value Line.[3]

---

[1] W. G. Zikmund, *Business Research Methods,* 3rd Ed. (New York: The Dryden Press, 1984), pp. 129–137.

[2] A selected annotated bibliography compiled by Lorna Daniells of Baker Library at Harvard Business School, Boston.

[3] R. P. Vichas, *Complete Handbook of Profitable Marketing Research Techniques* (Englewood Cliffs, N.J.: Prentice-Hall, 1982), pp. 36–45.

Several market research firms sell data on a subscription basis. Most of this market research is based on a sampling of the population. The use of private firms to supply an organization with forecasting data can spread the cost of primary data collection so that the individual organization is provided with very reliable data at much lower cost. Examples of prominent firms providing data for retail store audits and product tracking services are A. C. Nielsen Company, and Audits and Surveys, Inc. Firms providing data from consumer panels and mail surveys include Market Facts, Inc., Market Research Corporation of America, National Family Opinion, NPD Research, Inc., and the J. Walter Thompson Company. Another valuable source is Predicasts, Inc., which in addition to its own forecasts provides summaries and bibliographies of forecasts prepared by others.[4]

Private Data

In addition to data collected from public sources, forecasters need to use data from internal sources within their organizations. There has been a tremendous increase in the establishment of databases in the last few years. When an organization develops a database, data are collected on a number of different variables and stored on a computerized system so that they will be widely available when needed. Three types of data that are important for forecasters to store in database are: (1) data needed for existing operations, (2) data that are available but not currently required, (3) data that will be needed in the future but not presently available. While the particular data in the database vary according to specific needs, there are guidelines that should be followed in the establishment of any database used for forecasting:

- There should be a forecasting plan, and only needed data should be collected. (Following this guideline assures that the necessary data will be available when needed and avoids the expense and confusion of excess data.)
- Publicly available data should be used whenever possible because they can be obtained quickly and economically.
- Data should be stored in their original form so that they can be used for several different purposes.
- Data must be verified and documented before being used.
- Database systems must be designed to allow for expansion.

---

[4] T. C. Kinnear and J. R. Taylor, *Marketing Research: An Applied Approach* (New York: McGraw-Hill, 1983), pp. 146–156.

Primary Data Sources

Survey Data

Survey respondents are a major source of primary data for a firm. Respondents might include customers, the general public, suppliers, or employees. The purpose of the data collection effort is to find out what the selected persons think about key issues of management concern. The data collection might involve a one-time effort or might be repeated on a periodic basis to generate time series variables, which are then analyzed and projected into the future (forecasting).

When researchers are confronted with the need to gather an extensive amount of data from a large number of people, they turn to some form of survey. The first phase in this process is determining what specific survey method should be used to collect the required information. The three most commonly used interviewing methods are mail, personal, and telephone.

The mail questionnaire has the advantage of reaching a large number of widely dispersed people with less cost per contact than the other two methods. In addition, analysts can be sure that the questions are posed in the same manner to everyone, thus reducing interview bias. Further, the respondents can answer the questions at their leisure. Finally, the mail questionnaire can reach hard-to-interview respondents such as doctors and other professional people who keep irregular schedules.

On the other hand, because of the slowness of the mail and the tendency of respondents to procrastinate in filling out the questionnaire, mail surveys take much longer to complete than do telephone or personal surveys. Thus if speed is necessary, mail surveys are less desirable. Furthermore, only a portion of the people contacted actually respond to mail surveys. Past studies have shown a typical return rate of between 10% and 50%, depending on the nature of the study. This factor may bias the results if people who do not answer the questionnaire differ from respondents in important areas. Finally, few questions can be asked in a mail study because people will not expend much effort reading questions and supplying answers. Thus although this technique is inexpensive per contact, it is both expensive per returned form and time-consuming.

The personal interview approach offers the advantage of ensuring good sampling techniques since interviewers can carefully select respondents. This method can yield the greatest amount of information because respondents tend to be more open and more willing to spend time answering questions. Furthermore, this approach offers the greatest flexibility due to its personal nature. However, personal interviews have the highest potential for interviewer bias, greater costs per contact, and greater staff control problems.

In recent years the telephone interview has offered increasing advantages to the analyst as a data collection technique. While it cannot achieve a completely representative sample of the population, since certain people do not have phones or cannot be reached at certain times, it does come close to being representative for many projects. The cost per contact is lower than the cost for the personal interview, and the results can be obtained very quickly. Further, this method allows greater interviewer control. The disadvantage of the telephone is that only short, easy to answer questions can be used. Also, many people consider this type of data collection an invasion of their privacy and will not respond. Such nonresponse introduces a bias into the research results.

Survey Sampling Design

This section provides a brief overview of the decisions the forecaster must make in selecting respondents or sample units for inclusion in the research process. At the beginning the forecaster must answer the following questions:

1. Whom do I want to respond to my survey and why?
2. How many people should be included in the survey (sample size)?
3. How should I select people to be included in the survey? (This question determines reliability.)

The answer to the first question is not always as clear-cut as might be expected. For instance, consider the case in which an intermediate-size cosmetics manufacturer contacted 120 males in an effort to determine purchase and use habits of after-shave lotions. The manufacturer was faced with the question of determining what the demographic characteristics of the people should be who were to be included in the sample. Should the sample unit consist of husbands, wives, relatives, a specific age group, or some combination of these people? The manufacturer chose to question males only when, in fact, females should have been included since they actually make the purchase of after-shave lotions in many cases. As a further example of the difficulties in selecting the correct sample unit, consider the situation confronting industrial researchers when conducting research. Should they contact the buyer who is responsible for purchasing, the engineer or production manager who gives the specifications and uses of the product, or the executive who is often the decision maker? The point is that when users, buyers, and decision makers are not the same person, the forecaster must determine who is most likely to have the information desired.

Next the forecaster or analyst must decide on the sample size. This depends on the type of research being conducted and how reliable the results must be. For instance, in exploratory research where ideas are being sought rather than conclusions, fewer than 30 in-depth interviews will usually be sufficient to cover the gamut of problem areas. At the same time, the forecaster is not concerned with being able to say, "I am 95% confident my answers are correct within plus or minus 2%." Later research into specific areas will achieve this goal using a larger sample size.

When conclusive research is being conducted to find specific answers to specific questions, large samples must be used. However, it is not necessary to sample the entire population or even a major portion of it to achieve accurate results. Just as a wine taster can judge a whole bottle of wine from the initial taste, a researcher can analyze a large market from a small sample. The exceptions to this rule are as follows: (1) If the sample is biased (as in the cosmetics survey), then larger samples do not improve reliability; they just lead one further astray. (2) Small samples that are selected and measured very carefully can be more reliable than large samples using less exacting standards.

In general, while large samples yield more accurate results than small samples, it should also be remembered that large samples cost more in terms of both time and money. For example, doubling the size of a sample may require doubling the cost as well as delaying the decision time. Thus the forecaster should attempt to evaluate the value of increased information versus increased costs and a longer data collection period.

Interestingly, doubling the size of a sample does not double its accuracy and in some cases may add very little information. The goal of sampling is to select the minimum sample size necessary to provide the amount of information needed to make a good decision, given fiscal constraints, time constraints, and the degree of accuracy desired.

The third question the forecaster must face, determining a method of data collection, is addressed in the following section.

Simple Random Sampling

The last question to be answered in designing a data collection effort is, How should people be selected for the sample? Once again the answer to this question will depend on the type of research being done and its objectives.

In the case of exploratory research, sample selection is not too critical. In most cases it is possible for the researcher to use good judgment in selecting the sample, keeping these characteristics in mind: the sampled persons should have relevant knowledge regarding the problem, be fairly easy to contact and talk with, and be willing to discuss the problem.

In conclusive research, if the forecaster wishes to make precise estimates of population characteristics and use them to predict the future, a random sample should be drawn, or a near approximation of one. Unfortunately, random sampling is usually more expensive than nonrandom sampling. The expense arises from (1) trying to find a list of all members of the sample unit (e.g., women between the ages of 18 and 35), (2) selecting a sample from this list in a random manner, (3) having to send interviewers or survey forms to all parts of a city or state, and (4) having to recontact respondents who are not available on the first try. Most of these costs are not incurred in nonrandom sampling.

Random-sampling techniques ensure that each unit in the population of interest has an equal chance of being included in the sample.

How is a random sample actually selected? One technique that can be used is *simple random sampling*. In this approach the researcher must have a complete list of all the population items (e.g., people's names). Then a computer random number generator or a random number table is used to select the sample.

Suppose, for example, that a wholesaler carries 9,000 items and wants to select 250 of them to monitor for testing a new inventory control system. It would be possible to use the process of assigning all items a number, putting the numbers on cards, putting the cards in a hopper, and drawing 250 cards randomly. However, this procedure is time-consuming and expensive. A random number generator or a random number table simplifies this procedure. First, each item is assigned a number from 1 to 9,000. Next, 250 five-digit random numbers that are less than 9,000 are generated by a computer random number generator or selected from a random number table (see Table C.5). Finally, the 250 items that correspond to the 250 five-digit random numbers are included in the sample.

Unfortunately, in the majority of cases it is difficult, costly, or even impossible to select a simple random sample. So the researcher must fall back on some other method. Several of the most common methods are briefly described in the next section.

Other Random Sampling Techniques

Because of the difficulties involved in selecting a simple random sample, researchers and forecasters have developed other sampling techniques that are widely used. The most common are (1) systematic sampling, (2) stratified sampling, and (3) cluster sampling. Like simple random sampling, these techniques are true random sampling techniques, and therefore the forecaster can use established statistical techniques in analyzing and projecting results.

A *systematic sample* is very useful when the analyst has a complete list of the sample units and the sample units are listed in a random manner. In this technique, the analyst selects a random starting point in the list. Then every *n*th unit is selected until the desired number is obtained.

A common variation of this technique is used to select names from a telephone book. First, a page is randomly drawn from the front pages of the directory. Next, a column is randomly selected from the page, and, finally, a name is selected from the column. Suppose, for example, that the analyst needs 200 names and the directory has 450 pages. Suppose further that the analyst initially selects page 4, column 2, and the seventh name down. Then the analyst might proceed in the following manner: choose every other page and select the name in column 2, row 7 until 200 names are listed. This procedure is much easier, faster, and cheaper than selecting a simple random sample.

Stratified-sampling techniques are used when the forecaster knows that important subgroups (or strata) can be identified in the population, subgroups that are homogeneous within the group but heterogeneous between groups. In this situation a stratified sample is statistically more efficient as well as cheaper than a simple random sample. Selection of units from each substratum is done on a random basis; the proportion of the total sample represented by each substratum is determined by using statistical techniques designed to reflect the importance and variability of each substratum.

This technique is used, for example, in selecting test stores for the testing of new products. A manufacturer wishing to test a new product in grocery stores might use the fact that while large supermarkets make up only about 20% of all retail grocery stores, they account for about 80% of total sales. Therefore the firm might select 70%–80% of its test stores from supermarkets and only 20%–30% from small convenience stores.

Cluster sampling involves grouping the population into clusters and then randomly selecting clusters, or groups, rather than single items. A particularly useful variation of this technique is area sampling. Suppose a forecaster wants to draw a random sample of people living in the city of Indianapolis. Since there are no directories available that list all people living in this city (telephone books do not list all people having telephones and completely miss people without telephones), some other technique is needed. So an area sample is drawn by randomly selecting blocks from a map of the city. Then a predetermined number of people are interviewed from each block. This technique is both simple and economical. Cost savings accrue because interviewers can be sent to clusters of selected persons rather than to extremely divergent locations.

Nonrandom Samples

When the analyst, rather than chance, determines which items will be included in the sample, the selection process is nonrandom. The purpose of nonrandom sampling is to yield quick, inexpensive, and easy-to-select samples; however, they may or may not be representative of the population being studied. Two of the most common nonrandom techniques used are convenience or quota samples, and judgment samples.

The only major criterion used in selecting *convenience samples* is that of ease of selection for the analyst. An example is the use of students by professors in collecting data for their research projects. Similarly, a company may test the taste of a new product by placing the product in a booth at a shopping mall and asking people to try the product. This method is frequently used when quick, inexpensive exploratory studies are needed, such as in the pretesting of a questionnaire. This method is sometimes called *quota sampling* because the sampling continues until the desired sample size is reached.

Judgment samples are selected by analysts who use their judgment about the items to include in the sample. Some analysts claim that they can actually reduce sampling error and costs by using effective judgmental techniques to reduce "extreme" sample units, or outliers. This procedure is acceptable as long as the analyst can develop a truly representative sample of the population. However, there is no way to statistically test the extent to which the sample is representative. Once again, this technique is primarily used in exploratory research.

Test Markets

Test marketing is becoming a popular management tool. The market researcher or forecaster arranges for the placement of a new product or brand in cities believed to be representative of the firm's geographical target market, and then observes the product's sales behavior in the test market over a period of time. This sales behavior is frequently compared to sales in control markets, where a different product or brand is being offered. The objective is to observe the product's sales in a small-scale setting, and the basic assumption is that behavior in this setting will forecast that of the larger marketplace.

Test market results provide management the data it needs to evaluate potential profit opportunities. Some of the information that can be obtained in a good market test include:

> Potential market share of the new product
> Who is buying the product, how frequently, and for what purpose
> Where purchases are usually made
> Any changes in strategy made by the competition
> The effect of the new product on already established brands

The market test allows the forecaster an opportunity to test all the variables in a real-world environment.

In summary, one of the most time-consuming and difficult aspects of forecasting is the collection of valid and reliable data. This chapter has discussed the difficult task facing most forecasters of how to find the relevant data that will help them solve their application problems. Sources of data may be classified as either primary or secondary. Primary data sources involve all methods of original data collection. Secondary data sources are already published data collected for purposes other than the specific forecasting or research needs at hand. The significance to forecasters of the distinction between primary and secondary sources involves the fact that a primary source is likely to contain more complete and accurate data than may be found in a secondary source. On the other hand, such data are usually more expensive to obtain.

In recent years, there has been a tremendous increase in the quantity of published data sources (secondary data) available to forecasters. Libraries, government sources, computerized services, and nonprofit organizations provide enormous quantities of statistical data that can be used in forecasting.

Primary data collection involves selecting items to be included in the sample. Several methods of doing this were discussed in this chapter: simple random sampling, systematic sampling, cluster and stratified sampling, judgment sampling, and convenience or quota sampling. If the selected items are people, there are many ways of approaching them to determine their characteristics and opinions. Mail questionnaires, telephone surveys, and personal interviews are primary data collection methods that were discussed in this chapter.

APPLICATION TO MANAGEMENT

The decisions faced by managers in all organizations usually require some manipulation or analysis of data. Such analyses require that appropriate data be available, and this chapter is concerned with the gathering of such relevant data. Since almost all important business decisions require data analysis, the gathering of data that are relevant to the decision at hand is extremely important.

Many business decisions can be made after examining data that already exist, that is, with secondary data. It is important for every manager to be familiar with the sources of secondary data, both within the company and in outside agencies such as the government, libraries, and universities. Many decision situations are greatly aided by the simple and inexpensive collection of existing data from such sources.

Even more prevalent in business decision making is the necessity of gathering data specifically designed for the problem at hand. The collection of such primary data is discussed in this chapter; business managers need to be familiar with these techniques both to design their own research studies and to effectively evaluate the efforts of others. It is important in any decision-making situation to know if the data that were collected and analyzed are relevant to the problem and represent the best possible data for the situation.

Following are a number of questions that might be addressed by business managers in a variety of circumstances. Answering each question would involve collecting data, either primary or secondary, and performing an appropriate analysis on them. An understanding of the material presented in this chapter is essential for each of these questions if relevant data are to be identified and collected.

- Has market share increased as a result of our new ad campaign?
- What is our audience's opinion of our new television news anchor team?
- What is a normal cash balance for companies similar to ours?
- What are the opinions of the persons in our service area regarding our hospital, its doctors, and its staff?
- What do our credit union members think of our services? What improvements can they suggest?
- What is the opinion of our nonunionized work force toward current efforts to organize them?
- How do our stockholders view the effectiveness of the company's management team?
- What economic trends are evident in our industry based on past history?
- How do our monthly sales relate to important regional economic indicators?
- What factors can be identified that affect the absenteeism of our hourly work force?
- What is the opinion of area shoppers about our store, especially when compared with our major competitors?
- What are the attitudes of various departments toward the company's computer support group?
- What effect does shelf position have on a shopper's food item selection?
- What is the market for a hand-operated winch designed for four-wheel-drive vehicles?
- What are the opinions of visitors to our city regarding shopping, restaurants, hotels and motels, and entertainment?
- How can the Civic Theater increase its membership and revenues?
- What qualities are desired by area employers in the persons they hire for entry-level positions in their computer departments?

GLOSSARY

Primary data sources   Primary data sources involve all methods of original data collection.

Random sampling   Random-sampling techniques ensure that each sample unit in the population of interest has an equal chance of being included in the sample.

Secondary data sources   Secondary data sources are already published data collected for purposes other than the specific forecasting or research needs at hand.

PROBLEMS

1. What is the role of secondary data in the forecasting process? What is the role of primary data?

2. What are the advantages of primary data relative to secondary data?

3. Suggest some examples of secondary data useful to forecasters.

4. What would be the advantages of using each of the following methods to reach students at your university to conduct a survey?
   a. Mail
   b. Telephone
   c. Personal interviews

5. What is wrong with each of the following questions?
   a. Do you prefer tall, blonde friends or short, dark, friends?
   b. Do you exercise regularly?
   c. What is your company's sales level?
      $0–$100,000
      $100,000–$500,000
      $500,000–$1,000,000
      $1,000,000 or over
   d. Do you prefer Coke or some other brand of cola?
   e. Do you hire minorities or women?

6. How would you randomly select 30 students from the university/college student directory? How did you accomplish this selection?

7. Develop a sampling plan for brainstorming new-product ideas for Kodak. Whom would you include? How would they be selected?

8. Develop a sampling plan for inspecting accounts receivable at a retail hardware store. What information would you need to know and how would you select specific items?

9. Develop a questionnaire for use in evaluating your university's business program.

ARGYL FOOD PRODUCTS

Rob Arabicaf, a junior-level economics major at Premier State College, was delighted to be accepted into a summer intern program with the Argyl Food Products Company. Argyl had recently bought out a competitor whose product line included several coffee items. The coffee items were assigned to Argyl's Beverage Division, headed by Sue Maxwell. Coffee was new to Argyl, and Sue felt that she needed to know which way the coffee market was headed. She thought that this would provide a useful project for Rob, Argyl's neophyte economist.

Sue's request for Rob's services was granted. Rob, who didn't even drink coffee, was suddenly confronted with making a forecast on which Argyl would base a key decision. If the demand for coffee in the United States were expanding, Sue would allocate sizable funds to capture a larger market share. But, if the potential for coffee appeared to be contracting, Sue would consider selling off Argyl's coffee products to a company more specialized in that field.

Rob thought that he would have a better chance of providing a realistic and reliable forecast if he learned a little more about coffee. He had already taken courses that had provided familiarity with techniques for making forecasts. He decided to conduct a preliminary, or situation, analysis so that his ultimate forecast would be more understandable and useful to management.

Rob contacted several key people in the coffee group inherited by Argyl. They were most helpful in that their backgrounds in technical aspects of coffee were extensive. But they really did not know very much about broad patterns of coffee consumption. So Rob realized that he would have to examine publications on the subject of coffee, particularly those related to coffee consumption in the United States.

A decade or so ago, a literature search would have required numerous hours of examining card indexes of library publications as well as searching through guides to periodicals. But Rob remembered that the university library could conduct a computer search of available publications. The librarian helped Rob log on to a service called Dialog (Dialog Information Services Inc.). Dialog is one of several large information vendors that offers data and text via computer (on-line). The Dialog offerings consist of more than 100 data banks, each created, updated, and serviced by an organization specializing in information for that particular field. Rob was pleased to learn that one of the Dialog databases, Coffeeline, is accessed through Dialog, although it is maintained and serviced by the International Coffee Organization in London, England. When Rob logged on, a record was kept of his contact time and the amount of data obtained, which formed the basis for the amount that he was charged.

Rob found that there were many entries on coffee consumption in the United States. He selected a printout that included a brief summary of each article as well as its bibliographic reference. He would have to obtain the original source to read the complete text of a given article. A number of firms work through Dialog to provide full text printouts. Unfortunately, that service is not available for Coffeeline.

This case was contributed by William C. Struning of the General Foods Corporation, New York, New York.

However, reading the summaries provided many insights into his area of interest, and he was able to locate full texts of several pertinent articles by directly contacting the respective publishers.

Rob then decided to see if there was a previously published forecast of coffee consumption in the United States. If such a forecast were available, he might be able to use it without spending time and other resources in making his own forecast. This time he selected another Dialog database, PTS Forecasts Abstracts. The creators of this database, Predicasts, specialize in abstracting whatever forecasts they can find in published literature and in making summaries of these forecasts available to Dialog subscribers. Searching under coffee in the United States, Rob found an overall consumption projection that had been originally prepared and published by a government agency. But he would still have to do his own forecast, because the figures at hand gave no breakdown (by age, income, etc.), although they provided good aggregate consumption benchmarks with which to compare his own work.

Rob was beginning to get a feel for the U.S. coffee market. He decided to try his hand at a preliminary forecast. Using historical data on coffee consumption obtained from the International Coffee Organization (which he learned about from Coffeeline), he first performed a preliminary statistical analysis on a microcomputer using a popular spreadsheet program together with a supplementary statistical add-in package. The results provided insights into the general characteristics of the data, such as averages, variability, and overall trends. Graphs produced by the package were particularly helpful. Data that were well out of the general range (outliers) were also detected.

From what he had learned so far, Rob thought that the amount of coffee consumed could be related to outside influences and, therefore, could be forecasted by projecting those influences. Disposable personal income, the average price of coffee at retail, and the average price of tea at retail were some of the influences that came to his mind. He remembered from his basic statistics course that he could measure relationships between those variables on one hand and coffee consumption on the other by correlation/regression techniques. That analysis would be relatively easy to do on a computer. The bulk of the work would be in locating, copying, and entering into his computer the data series required. He wondered if there was a shortcut.

A chance meeting at lunch with another Argyl employee led to the discovery that Argyl was a subscriber to DRI (Data Resources Inc., a division of McGraw-Hill Co., Inc.). DRI is a major supplier of statistical data series, mostly of an economic/financial nature. Since statistical data series are usually obtained for use in further analysis, DRI also makes available state-of-the-art software as well as facilities for storing data provided by the client. Those facilities enabled Rob to perform analyses directly on his computer in a DRI work space. On the other hand, Rob could have elected to download several DRI data series into a work space on his own computer. Using a packaged statistical analysis program (or a routine of his own programming) and adding whatever other data series he chose, Rob could have made his analysis off-line with respect to DRI.

Rob found several DRI data series of interest: price per pound of roasted/ground coffee in one-pound vacuum cans (U.S. Bureau of Labor Statistics), personal income (U.S. Department of Commerce), and population by age group (U.S. Department of Commerce), among others. He created a data series using coffee consumption figures obtained from Coffeeline and entered it in a DRI work space. From DRI data banks he obtained several series in which he was interested and entered those series in the same work space. He then selected a tool for analysis from the many stored for client use by DRI, in this case, regression. The resulting printout yielded results that, while showing promise, were inconclusive. Rob realized that his assignment would be challenging and would require much more effort.

Rob felt that his preliminary analysis had been extremely useful in designing his formal forecasting project. He now had a clear objective, a basic background in coffee, and a number of ideas on what produced changes in the consumption of coffee. Also, he could now provide his boss, Sue Maxwell, with estimates of how long it would take to complete his project and how much it would cost. Of help in making those estimates was a project management software package for personal computers that Sue Maxwell bought for him so that he could sharpen his plans and estimates as well as maintain control over the project as it progressed.

QUESTIONS

1. What are the purposes of conducting a preliminary analysis? Is a preliminary analysis always necessary? Can you justify the time/cost of conducting a preliminary analysis?

2. What other alternatives could Rob have utilized in conducting a preliminary analysis?

3. What other databases within Dialog could have provided Rob with information on coffee? What data vendors other than Dialog are available?

4. What other vendors of numerical or statistical data could Rob have utilized—if he paid the proper fees?

CASE STUDY **3.2**

SOLOMON'S JEWELRY

Solomon's is a leading jewelry store located in one of the most prestigious shopping centers in Houston. Over the years it has developed an excellent reputation for carrying fine products, selected to appeal to people desiring a quality product. Ms. Solomon, the company's president, feels that her store has a loyal, upper-income clientele, who are for the most part satisfied with the service they receive at Solomon's. The only major problem Solomon sees on the near-term horizon is that a major new competitor is planning to open a store in the same shopping center in two months. While the competitor is a chain store merchandiser, it tends to emphasize higher-quality merchandise. However, Solomon feels sure that her firm can compete effectively by emphasizing the distinctive product line it carries, its long-term commitment to customers, and its high quality of service.

Mr. Wind, recently hired as vice-president of marketing, is responsible for seeing that the store's marketing efforts are designed to complement past marketing practices as well as offset the effects of the new competitor's marketing efforts. Wind, who had been a college professor at a local university as well as a longtime consultant to the retail jewelry industry, is generally pleased by what he sees at Solomon's. The marketing plan is well designed and coordinated, products are well suited for the target market, prices are high but consistent with the product's quality, salespeople are knowledgeable and courteous, and promotional efforts seem effective.

After a few weeks at his new job, Wind decides to visit one of the new competitor's existing stores in Dallas to try and assess the impact it might have on Solomon's operations. A careful evaluation of the competitor's store seems to indicate that it too appeals to upper-income clientele and provides friendly, courteous service. However, its product line, while a little less distinctive, is also about 20% less expensive.

Upon returning to Houston, Wind suggests to Solomon that she conduct a survey to learn more about the potential problems her firm may face when the new store opens. She agrees to this plan. Thus if you were Wind, how would you answer the following questions?

QUESTIONS

1. Whom should he contact?
2. How should they be contacted?
3. When should they be contacted?
4. What questions should be asked?
5. What type of sample should be selected?

CASE STUDY **3.3**

MARKET FEASIBILITY STUDY

The McMillan Development Corporation asked a local research firm to conduct a market feasibility study to determine market factors that would affect the success of an athletic club in the Northwood Shopping Center in Peyton, Wisconsin. The research involved an analysis of demographic data, traffic flow data, perceived image of competitors, and potential area growth. When the study was completed, Mark Craze, research analyst for the research firm, prepared the following report.

OBJECTIVES

The objectives of this study were to determine:

Whether the population (especially 18- to 54-year-olds) of the Northwood area is large enough to produce enough members to support a new club

Whether area residents are interested in joining an athletic club

Whether area residents can afford to join the proposed athletic club

Whether an athletic club with a modern atmosphere has the potential to draw from the memberships of existing clubs

METHODOLOGY

The research methodologies used to complete this study included

An analysis of demographic data for the Northwood primary market area, including an investigation of potential growth

A statistical comparison of demographic data for the Northwood primary
market area and the primary market area for the Westwood Athletic Club of
Cadott, Wisconsin

An analysis of traffic flow for the Northwood site, using secondary research
sources and personal interviews

Investigation of the perceived image of area competitors, using personal
interviews with competitor's members

An analysis of the proposed site through personal observation

ANALYSIS

The Site

The proposed development is to be located on a 39,600-square-foot tract of land at
the southwest end of the Northwood Shopping Center. The Northwood Shopping
Center is located on West Salnave Road north of the Peyton city limits just west of
Main Street and occupies almost the entire block across Salnave Road from Northwest High School.

Accessibility

Northwood Shopping Center is approximately one-half mile from Main Street,
which is the most frequently used north-south arterial in the city of Peyton. Most of
the population north of the center travels close to Northwood on trips into Peyton.
The shopping center is also bordered by Walnut Street, which provides easy access
for residents living to the south and southwest.

Surrounding Environment

The Northwood Shopping Center consists of approximately 120,000 square feet of
leasable space presently being used by 27 tenants. There are more than 900 parking
spaces available.

The site location is in a highly affluent suburban neighborhood north of the
city of Peyton. The closest available shopping for this neighborhood is approximately three miles south on Main Street or 15 minutes north of the center in
Dayton, Wisconsin.

Area Development

All indications are that the sustained growth pattern to the north of the city of
Peyton will continue. Professional buildings have been constructed along Main
Street, and business development along this major north-south arterial continues to
move northward. The Peyton County Real Estate Research Report published in the
Fall of 1983 indicates

1. The number of mortgage recordings in Peyton County in the second and
   third quarters of 1983 were up substantially over respective quarters of 1982.
2. The number of new lots platted has been high in the northwest part of
   Peyton County and City for 1982 and 1983.

3. A large number of condominium units were filed in the northeast part of Peyton County for 1983.
4. Recent data show the number of residential sales in Peyton County has increased over the last two quarters and the average sales price in the third quarter of 1983 appears to be rising.
5. Unemployment in Peyton County is declining significantly.

Traffic Flow

The traffic flow in the Northwood area seems to generally run north-south. A marketing survey completed at the Northwood Shopping Center by a Whitewater University marketing class showed that most shoppers came because of Safeway, some to Giant-T, and others for specific purposes. Almost all of the shoppers came from nearby, primarily north, and primarily for convenience rather than store preference. Evidently, people prefer to travel south toward downtown Peyton for most of their major shopping needs.

The Competition

Northtown Racquet Club

The Northtown Racquet Club is located approximately one mile north of Metro on Main (N4532). The facility has six tennis courts, five racquetball courts, an outdoor swimming pool, lounge area, saunas, a weight room, and a Jacuzzi bath. The club plans on converting one of the tennis courts into an indoor swimming pool by next year. It has approximately 1,000 members, approximately 900 of whom come from the Northwood market area. Initiation fee for a tennis club family is $300 with monthly dues of $35 and court fees of $3 an hour. Initiation fee for a tennis club single is $200 with monthly dues of $25 and an hourly court fee of $3. While the fee schedule indicates hourly court fees, interviews with club members indicated that these fees had been dropped. The advantages and disadvantages of this club are as follows.

Advantages

1. The club is well established and has a reputation for indoor tennis.
2. The club is conveniently located on a major arterial.
3. Court time is plentiful during the day.

Disadvantages

1. The parking area is inadequate.
2. The club has a reputation for being poorly managed.
3. The club atmosphere is comfortable but not especially appealing to upper-income families and individuals.

Eagles Lodge

The Eagles Lodge is located three blocks east of Main on Metro. The facility has five racquetball courts, an indoor swimming pool (25 by 50 feet), lounge area, a sauna, a Jacuzzi, and men's and women's weight rooms. The lodge has 10,800 male members. Somewhere between 5,000 and 6,000 of these members come from zip codes on the north side of Peyton. It is estimated that approximately 2,000 to 2,500 of them come from the Northwood market area. Most of these people come from census tracts east of Main Street. Membership dues are $40 a year for the Eagles Lodge. There is a racquetball court fee of $2 an hour.

Advantages

1. The lodge is well established and has a reputation as the largest Eagles Lodge in the country.
2. The lodge is conveniently located on a major arterial.
3. The lodge provides social as well as health club facilities.
4. The lodge is extremely inexpensive.
5. Court time is plentiful during the day.

Disadvantages

1. Because of the inexpensive cost of the lodge, it tends to draw members from lower-income groups.
2. The club atmosphere is comfortable but not especially appealing to middle- and upper-income families and individuals.
3. The facilities are sometimes crowded in the evening.

Whitewater University Aquatic Center

Another factor that could potentially affect this situation is the Whitewater University Aquatic Center. The first stage (indoor swimming pool) will be completed for use in the fall and will be open to the public. Subsequent stages will involve racquetball, spa, etc. This facility will not be luxurious but will probably be competitive with Northtown and better than the Eagles Lodge.

Summary of Interviews with Competitors' Members

The interviewees felt that business and professional people were the real market. They indicated that the Northtown Racquet Club was thought to be a midrange facility. They considered the Peyton Club to have superior facilities. The Eagles Lodge was considered a lower-class facility appealing to a lower-price population segment. It was felt that if a facility was located on the north side, it would probably draw only from around the shopping center and that this would be an inadequate population base.

Demographic Data

The primary market area for the proposed athletic club includes census tracts 103.01, 103.02, 105.01, 105.02, 106, 107, 108, 109, 110, 111, 112.01, and 112.02 and tract 8, which is within the Peyton city limits. The population reported in the 1980 census for each census tract is presented in Table 3.1. Approximately 30% of the primary market area population lives to the north of Northwood. A total of 5,337 people, or 11% of the population, live in the Northwood area (census tract 105.01). The remaining 59% of the population live south or southeast of the Northwood area.

A summary of demographic data for the primary market area is presented in Table 3.2. The data show that 64.5% of the people who were employed were white-

TABLE 3.1 Population for the Primary Market Area.

Census Tract	Population
103.01	2,568
103.02	6,742
105.01	5,337
105.02	4,830
106	4,104
107	804
108	3,815
109	1,141
110	4,129
111	4,848
112.01	2,465
112.02	2,966
Tract 8	5,139
Total	48,888

TABLE 3.2 Demographics for the Primary Market Target Area.

Population	1988 projection		54,999
	1983 estimate		50,990
	1980 census		48,888
	1970 census		38,862
	Percent change, 1970–1980		25.8%
	Percent change, 1980–1983		4.3%
Population by age	0–17		31.4%
	18–34		26.5%
	35–54		25.3%
	55–64		9.3%
	65+		7.5%
	Median age total population		29.8
	Median age adult population		40.7
Occupation	Mgr./prof.	5,447	
	Tech./admin.	4,581	
	Sales	3,428	
	Total white collar		13,456
	Prod./craft/repair	2,091	
	Mach. operators	729	
	Laborers/trans./etc.	1,771	
	Total blue collar		4,591
	Farm/forest/fish		279

continues

TABLE 3.2 Continued

	Service	2,529
	Total employed	20,855
	Total unemployed	1,706
	Total labor force	22,561
Education	High school graduates (only)	64.0%
	College graduates	22.9%
	Median school years completed	12.93
Households	1988 projection	18,272
	1983 estimate	16,510
	1980 census	15,517
	1970 census	10,456
	Percent change, 1970–1980	48.4%
	Percent change, 1980–1983	6.4%
Population	Household population	46,242
	Households w/children under 18	7,436
	Households w/persons 65+	2,543
	Family population	41,790
	Nonfamily population	4,452
	Group quarters	1,040
	Average household size	2.98
	Average family size	3.34
	Family household	12,512
	Nonfamily households	3,005
Household income*	$ 0–$ 7,499	8.9%
	$ 7,500–$ 9,999	4.0%
	$10,000–$14,999	7.7%
	$15,000–$24,999	25.0%
	$25,000–$34,999	24.2%
	$35,000–$49,999	21.0%
	$50,000–$74,999	6.9%
	$75,000+	2.3%
	Median HH income (1988 proj.)	$33,207
	Median HH income (1983 est.)	$26,383
	Median HH income (1980 census)	$22,245
	Per capita income (1980 census)	$ 8,402
	Average HH income (1980 census)	$25,036
	Housing units	17,182
	Condominiums	1,097
Units at address	1 unit	$13,805
	2–5 units	727
	5+ units	1,796
	Mobile homes	854
	Median home value	$61,536
	Median monthly rent	$ 232
	Average condo value	$67,711

* 1983 est.

collar workers. Over one-fourth of the people who were employed were classified as either managers or professionals. Almost 52% of the population were between the ages of 18 and 54 years. Over one-half of the households had incomes over $25,000. The median household income was $22,689. Finally, the population of the market area has increased on an average of over 2% per year since 1970, while the number of households has increased on an average of approximately 4% per year.

Table 3.3 attempts to summarize the most important demographic information.

Table 3.4 is designed to compare the primary market area with the market area served by the Westwood Athletic Club of Cadott, Wisconsin. After studying Westwood's membership roster, it was decided that approximately 95% of Westwood's members come from either Cadott, Howard, Howard Lake, or Rockford. Therefore, demographic data for these areas were compared to the primary market target area.

The Northwood market area has a larger population, approximately 41.4% more people, than the Westwood area. The Northwood area also has approximately 45.7% more 18- to 54-year-olds. Household median income was also 39.6% higher in the Northwood area.

A feasibility study done for the Westwood Athletic Club used the following formula to determine whether the Cadott area can support a new facility:

$$\frac{\text{Active membership}}{(\% \text{ Pop. 18–49 years} \times \text{County pop.}) - \text{University students}}$$

TABLE 3.3 Demographic Summary.

Year	Total Population	Total Households	Household Population	Average HH size	Median HH Income
1980	48,888	15,517	46,242	2.98	$22,245
1983	50,990	16,510	48,209	2.92	$26,383

TABLE 3.4 Primary Market Area Compared to Westwood's Market Area.

	Northwood	Westwood
Population	48,888	28,649
Population (18–54)	25,324	13,751
Households	15,517	11,227
Families	12,512	7,609
University students	1,200	1,600
Median income households	$22,245	$13,705
Membership in modern court clubs	3,250	3,028
Court club membership as % of nonuniversity population 18–54	13.5%	24.9%

Since county population is not relevant in the Northwood decision, a more precise formula would be

$$\frac{\text{Active membership}}{\text{Market area pop. 18--54 years} - \text{University students}}$$

It should be noted that the active membership values are strictly estimates based on best information. The estimate for the Westwood market area was based on 1,953 membership for the Westwood Athletic Club and a 1,575 estimate used in 1982 for its competitors. It is important to realize that many of the people may belong to both clubs or may have switched to the Westwood Club. For this reason, the estimate for the Westwood market area was computed as $1,953 + 1,575 - 500 = 3,028$.

The estimate for Northwood is based on 900 Northtown members, 2,500 Eagles Lodge members, and 100 Peyton Club members who reside in the market area.

CONCLUSIONS

1. The population base of 18- to 54-year-olds in the Northwood market area would seem to be large enough to support the proposed athletic club.
2. The large number of managers, professionals, and white-collar workers would seem to provide a good market for a modern high-class athletic club.
3. The average household income would seem to provide a good market for a modern high-class athletic club.
4. The only direct competition would come from the Northtown Racquet Club, which presently has 1,000 members.
5. Most people who shop at the Northwood Shopping Center come from the immediate vicinity. A strong marketing strategy would be needed to widen the primary market area to the boundaries included in this study. People will travel the five to eight miles necessary to participate at a modern athletic club; however, they will have to be sold on the idea.

QUESTIONS

1. What secondary data sources did Mark Craze use to complete this study?
2. What primary data sources did Mark Craze use to complete his study?
3. What other data sources could have been used to complete this research?
4. Do you agree with the results?

MINITAB EXAMPLE

Minitab will be used to demonstrate how easy it is to generate random numbers using a statistical software package.

THE PROBLEM

The table for Problem 6 in Chapter 2 provided a population of 200 family sizes, and the problem asked you to select a sample of 30 sizes and test the hypothesis that the average family size had not changed from 2.9 people in the last ten years.

THE MINITAB SOLUTION

The Minitab commands to generate random numbers are

```
MTB > RANDOM 30 C1;
SUBC > INTEGER 1 200.
```

The Minitab command to print the data is

```
MTB > PRINT C1
C1
    55    75    70    53    33     9   141    40   146   136
   132   134   160   143   173   163   148   102   179   135
    22    91   146   128   148   182    62    81    60   197
MTB > STOP
```

CHAPTER 3

SELECTED BIBLIOGRAPHY

Alreck, P. L., and Settle, R. B. *The Survey Research Handbook*. Homewood, Ill.: Richard D. Irwin, Inc., 1985.

Daniells, L. M. *Business Forecasting for the 1980s—And Beyond*. Boston: Baker Library, Harvard Business School, 1980.

Davidson, T. A., and Ayers, J. L. "Selecting and Using External Data Sources." In *Handbook of Forecasting*, S. Makridakis and S. C. Wheelwright, eds. New York: John Wiley & Sons, 1982.

Kinnear, T. C., and Taylor, J. R. *Marketing Research: An Applied Approach*. New York: McGraw-Hill, 1983.

Vichas, R. P. *Complete Handbook of Profitable Marketing Research Techniques*. Englewood Cliffs, N.J.: Prentice Hall, 1982.

Zikmund, W. G. *Exploring Marketing Research*. New York: The Dryden Press, 1986.

Zikmund, W. G. *Business Research Methods,* 3rd ed. New York: The Dryden Press, 1991.

4

Exploring Data Patterns and Choosing a Forecasting Technique

T wo basic considerations are involved in producing an accurate and useful forecast. The first is to collect data that are relevant to the forecasting task and that contain the information that can yield accurate forecasts. Chapter 3 discussed this important task. The second key factor is to choose a forecasting technique that will utilize the information contained in the data and its patterns to the fullest.

The first step in the forecasting process discussed in Chapter 1 was data collection. After collection, the forecaster must then review past attempts to forecast the variable of interest. A literature search and discussions with company colleagues may help to assess past successes and/or failures of alternative approaches. After conducting this initial research, the forecaster is in a better position to reduce the data (step 2).

With good data in hand, a forecaster can start the important task of exploring data patterns. This step involves looking at the data, understanding what the data are suggesting, and using various display methods to gain insights into the process that generated the data. The construction of a time series graph is often helpful if the data are collected over time. Figure 4.2 (p. 99) shows an example of this type of graph. This examination of the data leads to step 3 in the forecasting process (choosing a forecasting technique), the final subject of this chapter.

Two basic forecasting methods can be employed. *Qualitative* forecasting techniques rely on human judgment and intuition more than on manipulation of past historical data. Common qualitative techniques include the Delphi method, growth curves, scenario writing, market research, and focus groups. These techniques are often of importance in the overall forecasting picture and are discussed in some detail in Chapter 11.

Quantitative forecasting techniques are used when sufficient historical data are available and when these data values are judged to be representative of the unknown future. This judgment is an important step in the forecasting process, since all quantitative techniques rest on the assumption that the past can be extended into the future in some meaningful manner to provide accurate forecasts. Quantitative techniques are frequently classified into two categories: statistical and deterministic.

Statistical techniques focus entirely on patterns, pattern changes, and disturbances caused by random influences. This book discusses many of these, such as moving averages and exponential smoothing (Chapter 5), time series decomposition and trend projections (Chapter 8), and Box–Jenkins methodology (Chapter 10).

Statistical forecasting techniques use basically two approaches. One is based on the assumption that the data can be decomposed into components such as trend, cycle, seasonality, and irregularity. A forecast is made by combining the projections for each of these individual components.

A second approach is associated with econometric time series modeling and Box–Jenkins methodologies. Their theoretical foundations are based primarily in statistical concepts and do not assume that the data are represented by separate components.

Deterministic (causal) techniques involve the identification and determination of relationships between the variable to be forecast and other influencing variables. These techniques include regression and multiple regression models (Chapters 6 and 7), leading indicators (Chapter 8), econometric models (Chapter 9), and anticipation surveys and input–output models (not discussed in this book).

The next two sections deal briefly with the key elements of data patterns that are important for understanding the forecasting techniques that follow in later chapters. A discussion of the components often explicitly recognized in time series data appears first, followed by an introduction to the basics of autocorrelation analysis that underlie many sophisticated forecasting procedures. The chapter ends with a section devoted to a most important question: Once the general patterns have been identified in the historical data, what forecasting techniques should be chosen?

TIME SERIES COMPONENTS

As discussed in Chapter 3, observations of data are frequently made over time. Any variable that consists of data that are collected, recorded, or observed over successive increments of time is called a *time series.*

> A *time series* consists of data that are collected, recorded, or observed over successive increments of time.

An immediate temptation in the analysis of time series data is to try to explain or account for the behavior of the series. To avoid wasted effort, what is needed is a systematic approach to analyzing the series. Classical decomposition is a method based on the assumption that the data can be decomposed into components such as trend, cycle, seasonality, and irregularity. A forecast is made by combining the projections for each of these individual components. The classical decomposition technique is discussed in Chapter 8. Another approach, called autocorrelation analysis, can also be used to identify components and data patterns. This technique is discussed in a later section of this chapter.

Many macroeconomic variables, such as the U.S. Gross National Product (GNP), employment, and industrial production are dominated by a strong trend. The *trend* of a time series is the long-term component that represents the growth or decline in the series over an extended period of time. The basic forces that affect and help explain the trend of a series are population growth, price inflation, technological change, and productivity increases.

> The *trend* is the long-term component that represents the growth or decline in the time series over an extended period of time.

The *cyclical component* is the wavelike fluctuation around the trend usually affected by general economic conditions. Cyclical patterns tend to repeat in the data roughly every two, three, or more years. Cyclical fluctuations are usually influenced by changes in economic expansions and contractions, commonly referred to as the business cycle.

> The *cyclical component* is the wavelike fluctuation around the trend.

The *seasonal component* refers to a pattern of change that repeats itself year after year. For a monthly series, the seasonal component measures the variability of the series each January, each February, and so on. For a quarterly series, there are four seasonal elements, one for each quarter. Seasonal variation may reflect weather conditions, holidays, or length of calendar months.

> The *seasonal component* is a pattern of change that repeats itself year after year.

The *irregular component* measures the variability of the time series after the other components have been removed. It accounts for the random variability in a time series caused by unanticipated and nonrecurring factors. Most of the irregular component is made up of random variability. However, sometimes unpredictable events such as strikes, weather changes (droughts, floods, or earthquakes), elections, armed conflicts, or the passage of legislative bills cause irregularities in a variable.

> The *irregular component* measures the variability of the time series after the other components have been removed.

EXPLORING DATA PATTERNS WITH AUTOCORRELATION ANALYSIS

When a variable is measured over time, it is frequently correlated with itself when lagged one or more periods. This correlation is measured using the *autocorrelation* coefficient.

> *Autocorrelation* is the correlation between a variable, lagged one or more periods, and itself.

Data patterns, including components such as trend, seasonality, and irregularity, can be studied using the autocorrelation analysis approach. Autocorrelation coefficients for different time lags of a variable are used to identify time series data patterns.

　　The concept of autocorrelation is illustrated by the data presented in Table 4.1. Note that variables y_{t-1} and y_{t-2} are actually the Y values that have been lagged by one and two periods, respectively. The values for March, which are shown on the row for time period 3, are March sales, $y_t = 125$; February sales, $y_{t-1} = 130$; and January sales, $y_{t-2} = 123$.

　　Equation 4.1 is commonly used to compute the first-order autocorrelation coefficient (r_1), or the correlation between y_t and y_{t-1}.

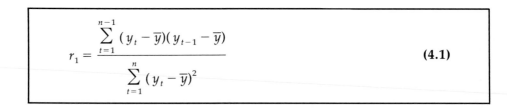

$$r_1 = \frac{\sum_{t=1}^{n-1}(y_t - \bar{y})(y_{t-1} - \bar{y})}{\sum_{t=1}^{n}(y_t - \bar{y})^2} \qquad (4.1)$$

TABLE 4.1 Autocorrelated Data.

Time, t	Month	Original Data, y_t	Y Lagged One Period, y_{t-1}	Y Lagged Two Periods, y_{t-2}
1	January	123		
2	February	130	123	
3	March	125	130	123
4	April	138	125	130
5	May	145	138	125
6	June	142	145	138
7	July	141	142	145
8	August	146	141	142
9	September	147	146	141
10	October	157	147	146
11	November	150	157	147
12	December	160	150	157

where

r_1 = first-order autocorrelation coefficient

$\bar{y}$ = mean of the values of the series

y_t = observation at time period t

y_{t-1} = observation one time period earlier or at time period $t-1$

Equation 4.2 is the formula for computing the order k autocorrelation coefficient (r_k) between observations that are k periods apart: y_t and y_{t-k}.

$$r_k = \frac{\sum\limits_{t=1}^{n-k} (y_t - \bar{y})(y_{t-k} - \bar{y})}{\sum\limits_{t=1}^{n} (y_t - \bar{y})^2} \qquad (4.2)$$

where

r_k = autocorrelation coefficient for a lag of k periods

$\bar{y}$ = mean of the values of the series

y_t = observation at time period t

y_{t-k} = observation k time periods earlier or at time period $t-k$

EXAMPLE 4.1

■ Harry Vernon has collected data on the number of VCRs sold last year for Vernon's Music Store. The data were presented in Table 4.1. Table 4.2 shows the computations that lead to the use of Equation 4.1.

The first-order autocorrelation coefficient (r_1), or the correlation between y_t and y_{t-1}, is computed using the summations from Table 4.2 in Equation 4.1.

$$r_1 = \frac{\sum_{t=1}^{n-1} (y_t - \bar{y})(y_{t-1} - \bar{y})}{\sum_{t=1}^{n} (y_t - \bar{y})^2}$$

$$= \frac{843}{1,474} = .572$$

It appears that some autocorrelation exists in this time series lagged one time period. The correlation between y_t and y_{t-1}, or the autocorrelation for lag 1, is .572. This means that the successive monthly sales of VCRs are somewhat correlated with each other. This information may give Harry valuable insights about his time series, may help him prepare to use an advanced forecasting method, and can warn him

TABLE 4.2 Computation of the First Sample Autocorrelation Coefficient for the Data Presented in Table 4.1.

Time, t	y_t	y_{t-1}	$(y_t - \bar{y})$	$(y_{t-1} - \bar{y})$	$(y_t - \bar{y})^2$	$(y_t - \bar{y})(y_{t-1} - \bar{y})$
1	123	—	−19	—	361	—
2	130	123	−12	−19	144	228
3	125	130	−17	−12	289	204
4	138	125	−4	−17	16	68
5	145	138	3	−4	9	−12
6	142	145	0	3	0	0
7	141	142	−1	0	1	0
8	146	141	4	−1	16	−4
9	147	146	5	4	25	20
10	157	147	15	5	225	75
11	150	157	8	15	64	120
12	160	150	18	8	324	144
Sums	1,704		0	−18	1,474	843

$$\text{Mean } \bar{y} = \frac{1,704}{12} = 142$$

$$r_1 = \frac{843}{1,474} = .572$$

about using regression analysis with his data. This latter situation will be discussed in Chapter 9.

The second-order autocorrelation coefficient (r_2), or the correlation between y_t and y_{t-2} for Harry's data, is computed using Equation 4.2.

$$r_2 = \frac{\sum_{t=1}^{n-2} (y_t - \overline{y})(y_{t-2} - \overline{y})}{\sum_{t=1}^{n} (y_t - \overline{y})^2}$$

$$= \frac{682}{1474} = .463$$

It appears that moderate autocorrelation exists in this time series lagged two time periods. The correlation between y_t and y_{t-2}, or the autocorrelation for lag 2, is .463. Notice that the autocorrelation coefficient at lag 2 (.463) is less than the autocorrelation coefficient at lag 1 (.572). The denominator is the same for both computations; however, one less term is included in the numerator when the autocorrelation for lag 2 is computed. Generally, as the number of time lags, k, increases, the size of the autocorrelation coefficients decrease. ■

Figure 4.1 shows a correlogram for the Harry Vernon data used in Example 4.1. The *correlogram* is a useful graphical tool for displaying the autocorrelations for various lags of a time series. The vertical scale on the left shows the number of lagged time periods of interest. The vertical scale on the right shows the autocorrelation coefficients, the correlations between y_t and y_{t-k}, for the appropriate number of lagged periods shown on the left. The horizontal scale at the bottom shows the possible range for an auto-correlation coefficient, -1 to $+1$. The autocorrelation coefficient for a particular time lag corresponds to this horizontal scale. A vertical line is placed above zero in the middle of the correlogram. Patterns in a correlogram are used to analyze key patterns in the data. This concept is demonstrated in the next section.

FIGURE 4.1 Correlogram for the Data in Table 4.1.

```
TIME LAG                                                    AUTOCORRELATION
    6                 .          * I              .            -0.10
    5                 .           *I              .            -0.03
    4                 .            *              .             0.02
    3                 .            I *            .             0.11
    2                 .            I        *     .             0.46
    1                 .            I          *.                0.57
          I.I.I.I.I.I.I.I.I.I.I.I.I.I.I.I.I.I.I.I.I.I.I
              -1                  0               +1
```

> The *correlogram* is a graphical tool for displaying the autocorrelations for various lags of a time series.

The Minitab computer package can be used to compute autocorrelations and develop correlograms. The Minitab commands to solve Example 4.1 are as follows:

```
MTB > SET C1 *1
DATA> 123 130 125 138 145 142 141 146 147 157 150 160
DATA> END *2
MTB > ACF C1 *3
                -1.0 -0.8 -0.6 -0.4 -0.2  0.0  0.2  0.4  0.6  0.8  1.0
                 +----+----+----+----+----+----+----+----+----+----+
   1    0.572 ┐                          XXXXXXXXXXXXXXX
   2    0.463 │                          XXXXXXXXXXXXX
   3    0.111 │                          XXXX
   4    0.016 │                          X
   5   -0.033 │ *4                      XX
   6   -0.102 │                       XXXX
   7   -0.250 │                    XXXXXXX
   8   -0.328 │                  XXXXXXXX
   9   -0.466 │              XXXXXXXXXXXXX
  10   -0.250 │                    XXXXXX
  11   -0.232 ┘                    XXXXXXX

MTB > STOP
```

---

*1 Command **set** to enter data into c1
*2 Command to **end** data entry
*3 **Acf** command to compute autocorrelation coefficients for c1
*4 Autocorrelation coefficients for first 11 time lags

Note that the Minitab correlogram is different from Figure 4.1. The autocorrelation scale is shown on the top of the graph instead of at the bottom. The number of lags and their autocorrelation coefficients are both shown on the left. With such a display, the data patterns, including trend, seasonality, and irregularity, can be studied using the autocorrelation analysis approach. Autocorrelation coefficients for different time lags of a variable can be used to identify the following about a time series data collection:

1. Are the data random?
2. Do the data have a trend (nonstationary)?
3. Are the data stationary?
4. Are the data seasonal?

If a series is random, the correlation between y_t and y_{t-1} is close to zero, and the successive values of a time series are not related to each other.

If a series has a trend, y_t and y_{t-1} are highly correlated, and the autocorrelation coefficients are typically significantly different from zero for the first several time lags and then gradually drop toward zero as the number of periods increases. The autocorrelation coefficient for time lag 1 is typically very large (close to 1). The autocorrelation coefficient for time lag 2 will also be large. However, it will not be as large as for time lag 1 because one less term is used to calculate its numerator.

If a series has a seasonal pattern, a significant autocorrelation coefficient will occur at the appropriate time lag: four for quarterly data or twelve for monthly data.

Table 4.3 shows a time series of 30 three-digit random numbers selected from a random number table. Figure 4.2 shows a time series graph of the data. The autocorrelations computed from these data should theoretically be equal to zero. Of course, the 30 values in Table 4.3 are only one set of a large number of possible samples of size 30. Each sample will produce different autocorrelations. Most of these samples will produce autocorrelation coefficients that are close to zero. However, it is possible that a sample will produce an autocorrelation coefficient that is significantly different from zero just by chance.

How does an analyst determine whether an autocorrelation coefficient is significantly different from zero for the data of Table 4.3? A sampling distribution of autocorrelation coefficients could theoretically be developed by taking an infinite number of samples of 30 random numbers.

Quenouille[1] and others have demonstrated that the autocorrelation

TABLE 4.3 Time Series with 30 Selected Random Numbers.

Period t	y_t	Period t	y_t	Period t	y_t
1	646	11	707	21	173
2	477	12	709	22	145
3	560	13	39	23	674
4	688	14	164	24	533
5	892	15	30	25	67
6	386	16	708	26	296
7	747	17	379	27	838
8	533	18	458	28	242
9	127	19	590	29	717
10	54	20	766	30	196

[1] M. H. Quenouille, "The Joint Distribution of Serial Correlation Coefficients," *Annuals of Mathematical Statistics*, Vol. 20 (1949), pp. 561–571.

FIGURE 4.2 Graph for a Random Series.

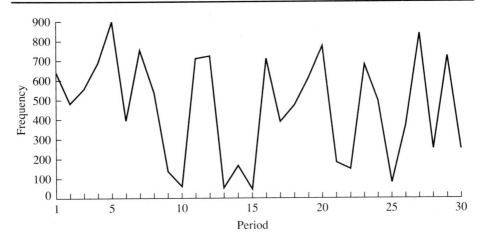

coefficients of random data have a sampling distribution that can be approximated by a normal curve with mean zero and standard deviation $1/\sqrt{n}$. Knowing this, the analyst can compare the sample autocorrelation coefficients with this theoretical sampling distribution and determine whether they come from a population whose mean is zero at particular time lags.

Actually, the autocorrelation coefficients for all time lags can be tested simultaneously. If the series is truly random, most of the sample autocorrelation coefficients should lie within a range specified by 0, plus or minus a certain number of standard errors. At a specified confidence level, a series can be considered random if the calculated autocorrelation coefficients are all within the interval produced by Equation 4.3.

$$0 \pm z \frac{1}{\sqrt{n}} \qquad\qquad (4.3)$$

where

        z = standard normal value for a given confidence level
        n = number of observations in the data series

This procedure is illustrated in Example 4.2.

EXAMPLE 4.2

■ A hypothesis test is developed to determine whether the series presented in Table 4.3 is random. The null and alternative hypotheses to test whether the autocorrelation coefficient for a particular time lag is significantly different from zero are

$$H_0: \quad \rho_k = 0$$

$$H_1: \quad \rho_k \neq 0$$

Since $n = 30$, the standard error (standard deviation of the sampling distribution of autocorrelation coefficients) is $1/\sqrt{30} = .18$. If the null hypothesis is tested at the .05 significance level, the correct standard normal z value is 1.96 and the critical value is $1.96(.18) = .353$. The decision rule is as follows:

> If an autocorrelation coefficient is less than $-.353$ or greater than .353, reject the null hypothesis; otherwise, accept it (reject H_0 if $r_k < -.353$ or $r_k > .353$).

The autocorrelation coefficients for the data of Table 4.3 are graphed on a correlogram in Figure 4.3. The two dotted lines parallel to the vertical axis are the 95% confidence limits ($-.353$ and $.353$). Fifteen time lags are checked, and all the autocorrelation coefficients lie within these limits. The analyst concludes that this series is a random walk; that is, the series was generated by a random process.

The Minitab computer package can also be used to solve Example 4.2. The Minitab commands are as follows:

```
MTB > RANDOM 30 C1;   *1
SUBC> INTEGER 1 999.  *2
MTB > PRINT C1

C1
    646    477    560    688    892    386    747    533    127     54    707
    709     39    164     30    708    379    458    590    766    173    145
    674    533     67    296    838    242    717    196

MTB > ACF C1  *3
ACF of C1

              -1.0 -0.8 -0.6 -0.4 -0.2  0.0  0.2  0.4  0.6  0.8  1.0 +----+
                ---+----+----+----+----+----+----+----+
   1  -0.027┐                        XX
   2  -0.217│                     XXXXXX
   3  -0.018│                        X
   4   0.284│                        XXXXXXXX
   5  -0.116│                      XXXX
   6  -0.156│                     XXXXX
   7   0.083│*4                      XXX
   8   0.016│                        X
   9  -0.070│                       XXX
  10  -0.311│                 XXXXXXXXX
  11   0.117│                        XXXX
  12   0.101│                        XXXX
  13   0.032│                        XX
  14  -0.312│                 XXXXXXXXX
  15   0.219┘                        XXXXX

MTB > STOP
```

*1   Command **random** generates 30 random numbers and enters
      them into c1
*2   Subcommand **integer** indicates that the 30 generated random
      numbers are to be between 1 and 999
*3   **Acf** command to compute autocorrelation coefficients for
      c1
*4   Autocorrelation coefficients for first 15 time lags

At the 95% confidence level, the series can be considered random since all the calculated autocorrelation coefficients are within the interval produced by Equation 4.3 ($-.353 > r_k < .353$). ∎

If a series has a trend, a significant relationship exists between successive time series values. The autocorrelation coefficients are typically significantly different from zero for the first several time lags and then gradually drop toward zero as the number of periods increases.

Some advanced forecasting models, such as the Box–Jenkins models, are designed for use with stationary time series. A *stationary* series is one whose basic statistical properties, such as the mean and variance, remain constant over time. A series that contains no growth or decline is said to be stationary. A series that contains a trend is said to be nonstationary. The autocorrelation coefficients of stationary data drop to zero after the second or third time lag, while for a nonstationary series they are significantly different from zero for several time periods. In such a series, the trend must be removed before any further analysis, such as use with the Box–Jenkins procedures.

FIGURE 4.3 Autocorrelations for Random Data in Table 4.3.

```
TIME LAG                                            AUTOCORRELATION
   15                  .       I   *   .                 0.22
   14                .*        I       .                -0.31
   13                .         I*      .                 0.03
   12                .         I   *   .                 0.10
   11                .         I   *   .                 0.12
   10                .*        I       .                -0.31
    9                .       * I       .                -0.07
    8                .         I*      .                 0.02
    7                .         I   *   .                 0.08
    6                .       * I       .                -0.16
    5                .       * I       .                -0.12
    4                .         I     *.                  0.28
    3                .        *I       .                -0.02
    2                .       * I       .                -0.22
    1                .        *I       .                -0.03
          I.I.I.I.I.I.I.I.I.I.I.I.I.I.I.I.I.I.I.I
          -1                   0                   +1
```

> A *stationary series* is one whose average value is not changing over time.

A method called differencing is used to remove the trend from a nonstationary series. y_t is subtracted from y_{t-1}, y_{t-1} is subtracted from y_{t-2}, and so forth, to create a new series. This process is demonstrated using the Minitab computer package. The series in C1 has been transformed into a new differenced form in C2. In this new form the mean and variance remain constant over time, and the series is stationary.

The Minitab commands to difference an example data series are as follows:

```
MTB > SET C1 *1
DATA> 221 224 230 237 235 240 247 248 250 255 262 271
DATA> END
MTB > DIFFERENCES 1 FOR C1, STORE IN C2 *2
MTB > PRINT C1-C2 *3

 ROW      C1    C2

   1      221    *
   2      224    3
   3      230    6
   4      237    7
   5      235   -2
   6      240    5  *4
   7      247    7
   8      248    1
   9      250    2
  10      255    5
  11      262    7
  12      271    9

MTB > STOP
```

*1   Command **set** to enter data into c1
*2   Command **differences takes the first** difference of the
     data in c1 and stores the differences in c2
*3   **print c1-c2** shows what is stored in columns c1 and c2
*4   First differences of c1

EXAMPLE 4.3

■ Maggie Trymane, an analyst for Sears, is assigned the task of forecasting sales for 1986. She gathers the data for the years 1955–1985 shown in Table 4.4. The data are

TABLE 4.4 Yearly Sales for Sears Roebuck & Co., 1955–1985.

Year	Sears Sales y_t
1955	3,307
1956	3,556
1957	3,601
1958	3,721
1959	4,036
1960	4,134
1961	4,268
1962	4,578
1963	5,093
1964	5,716
1965	6,357
1966	6,769
1967	7,296
1968	8,178
1969	8,844
1970	9,251
1971	10,006
1972	10,991
1973	12,306
1974	13,101
1975	13,639
1976	14,950
1977	17,224
1978	17,946
1979	17,514
1980	25,195
1981	27,357
1982	30,020
1983	35,883
1984	38,828
1985	40,715

Source: *Industry Surveys,*
1987.

plotted on the time series graph shown in Figure 4.4. First, Maggie computes a 95% confidence interval for the autocorrelation coefficients:

$$0 + 1.96 \; \frac{1}{\sqrt{31}}$$

$$0 + .352$$

FIGURE 4.4 Graph for a Trended Series: Sears Data for Example 4.3.

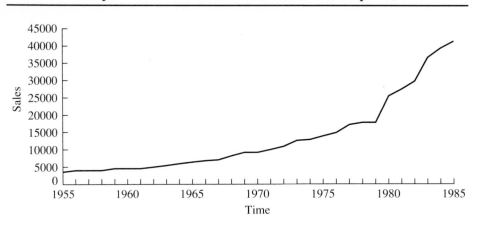

Next, she uses the following Minitab commands to compute the autocorrelation coefficients:

```
MTB > READ 'SEARS.DAT' INTO C1  *1
    31 ROWS READ

C1
    3307      3556      3601      3721      .    .    .

MTB > ACF C1  *2

ACF of C1

            -1.0 -0.8 -0.6 -0.4 -0.2  0.0  0.2  0.4  0.6  0.8  1.0
             +----+----+----+----+----+----+----+----+----+----+
     1   0.865                         XXXXXXXXXXXXXXXXXXXXXXX
     2   0.725                         XXXXXXXXXXXXXXXXXXX
     3   0.591                         XXXXXXXXXXXXXXXX
     4   0.477                         XXXXXXXXXXXXX
     5   0.371                         XXXXXXXXXX
     6   0.271                         XXXXXXXX
     7   0.220           *3            XXXXXXX
     8   0.158                         XXXXX
     9   0.094                         XXX
    10   0.041                         XX
    11  -0.005                         X
    12  -0.053                        XX
    13  -0.100                       XXXX
    14  -0.140                       XXXX
    15  -0.174                       XXXXX

MTB> STOP
```

---

*1   Command **read** to enter a file called sears.dat into c1
*2   **Acf** command to compute autocorrelation coefficients for
     c1
*3   Autocorrelation coefficients for first 15 time lags

Maggie examines the above correlogram and notices that the autocorrelations for the first five time lags are significantly different from zero (greater than .352): .865, .725, .591, .477, and .371. The values then drop gradually toward zero rather than dropping to zero exponentially. She decides that a trend exists in the data. Maggie discovers that the advanced forecasting model she wants to experiment with requires that the series be stationary. She uses Minitab to difference the data and compute the autocorrelation coefficients for the differenced data.

```
MTB > DIFFERENCES 1 C1, STORE C2  *1
MTB > ACF C2  *2

ACF of C2

             -1.0 -0.8 -0.6 -0.4 -0.2  0.0  0.2  0.4  0.6  0.8  1.0
             +----+----+----+----+----+----+----+----+----+----+
   1    0.275⌐                       XXXXXXXX
   2    0.248│                       XXXXXXX
   3    0.529│                       XXXXXXXXXXXXXX
   4    0.177│                       XXXXX
   5    0.055│                       XX
   6    0.069│                       XXX
   7    0.080│*3                     XXX
   8    0.024│                       XX
   9    0.007│                       X
  10   -0.020│                       X
  11   -0.027│                      XX
  12   -0.025│                      XX
  13   -0.072│                     XXX
  14   -0.087│                     XXX
  15   -0.076⌐                     XXX

MTB > STOP
```

_____

*1 Command **differences takes the first** difference of the data in c1 and stores the differences in c2
*2 **Acf** command to compute autocorrelation coefficients for c2
*3 Autocorrelation coefficients for first 15 time lags

Maggie is pleased because the autocorrelations for the differenced data are stationary and show that some pattern might exist (the third autocorrelation coefficient equals .529; then they trail off to zero). She can now attempt to use an appropriate advanced forecasting procedure. ∎

If a series is seasonal, a pattern repeats itself regularly during a particular interval of time (usually a year), and a significant autocorrelation coefficient will occur at the appropriate time lag. If quarterly data are analyzed, a significant autocorrelation coefficient will appear at time lag 4. If monthly data are analyzed, a significant autocorrelation coefficient will appear at time lag 12. That is, January will correlate with other Januarys, February will correlate with other Februarys, and so on. Example 4.4 illustrates a series that is seasonal.

EXAMPLE 4.4

■ Perkin Kendell is an analyst for the Outboard Marine Corporation. He has always felt that sales were seasonal, but the absorption of six boat builders by his company between 1986 and 1988 has made him question this assumption. Perkin gathers the data shown in Table 4.5 for the quarterly sales of the Outboard Marine Corporation from 1984 to 1990 and plots them on the time series graph shown in Figure 4.5. Next, he computes a 95% confidence interval for the autocorrelation coefficients.

$$0 + 1.96 \; \frac{1}{\sqrt{28}}$$

$$0 + .37$$

TABLE 4.5 Quarterly Sales for Outboard Marine, 1984–1990

Fiscal Year Ends	Dec. 31	Mar 31	June 30	Sept. 30
1984	147.6	251.8	273.1	249.1
1985	139.3	221.2	260.2	259.5
1986	140.5	245.5	298.8	287.0
1987	168.8	322.6	393.5	404.3
1988	259.7	401.1	464.6	479.7
1989	264.4	402.6	411.3	385.9
1990	232.7	309.2	318.1*	310.0*

Source: *The Value Line Investment Survey* (New York: Value Line, 1988, 1990), p. 1766.

* Value Line estimates.

FIGURE 4.5 Graph for a Seasonal Series: Outboard Marine Data from Example 4.4.

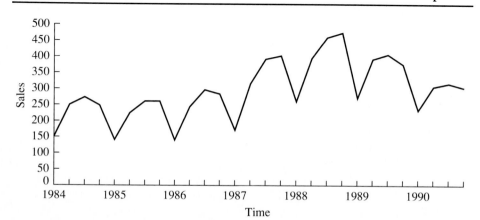

Next, he uses the following Minitab commands to compute the autocorrelation coefficients.

```
MTB > READ 'OUTBOARD.DAT' INTO C1  *1
      28 ROWS READ

C1
   147.6    251.8    273.1    249.1    .    .    .

MTB > ACF C1  *2

ACF of C1
```

```
            -1.0 -0.8 -0.6 -0.4 -0.2  0.0  0.2  0.4  0.6  0.8  1.0
             +----+----+----+----+----+----+----+----+----+----+
    1    0.440 ┐                          XXXXXXXXXXXX
    2    0.219 │                          XXXXXX
    3    0.334 │                          XXXXXXXXX
    4    0.734 │                          XXXXXXXXXXXXXXXXXXX
    5    0.193 │                          XXXXXX
    6   -0.065 │              *3          XXX
    7   -0.009 │    *3                    X
    8    0.307 │                          XXXXXXXXX
    9   -0.122 │                       XXXX
   10   -0.325 │                 XXXXXXXXX
   11   -0.253 │                  XXXXXX
   12    0.028 │                          XX
   13   -0.273 │                 XXXXXXXX
   14   -0.385 │               XXXXXXXXXXX
   15   -0.303 ┘                XXXXXXXXX

MTB > STOP
```

---

*1   Command **read** to enter a file called outboard.dat into c1
*2   **Acf** command to compute autocorrelation coefficients for
     c1
*3   Autocorrelation coefficients for first 15 time lags

Perkin notes that the autocorrelation coefficient at time lag 4 is significantly different from zero (.734 > .37). He concludes that Outboard Marine sales are seasonal on a quarterly basis. ■

CHOOSING A FORECASTING TECHNIQUE

This text is mostly devoted to explaining various forecasting techniques and showing their usefulness. But, first, the important job of choosing the best forecasting techniques is addressed.

Some of the questions that must be considered before deciding on the most appropriate forecasting technique for a particular problem are the following:

- Why is a forecast needed?
- Who will use the forecast?
- What are the characteristics of the available data?
- What time period is to be forecast?
- What are the minimum data requirements?
- How much accuracy is desired?
- What will the forecast cost?

To select the appropriate forecasting technique properly, the forecaster must be able to:

- Define the nature of the forecasting problem.
- Explain the nature of the data under investigation.
- Describe the capabilities and limitations of potentially useful forecasting techniques.
- Develop some predetermined criteria on which the selection decision can be made.

A major factor influencing the selection of a forecasting technique is the identification and understanding of historical patterns in the data. If trend, cyclical, or seasonal patterns can be recognized, then techniques that are capable of effectively using these patterns can be selected.

Forecasting Techniques for Stationary Data

A *stationary series* was defined earlier as one whose average value is not changing over time. Such situations arise when the demand patterns influencing the series are relatively stable. In its simplest form, forecasting a stationary series involves using the available history of the series to estimate its average value, which then becomes the forecast for future values. More sophisticated techniques involve updating the estimate as new information becomes available. These techniques are useful when initial estimates are unreliable or when the stability of the average is in question. In addition, updating techniques provide some degree of responsiveness to changes in the underlying structure of the series.

Stationary forecasting techniques are used in the following situations:

- Whenever the forces generating a series have stabilized and the environment in which the series exists is relatively unchanging. Examples are the number of breakdowns per week on an assembly line having a uniform production rate, the unit sales of a product or service in the maturation stage of its life cycle, and the number of sales resulting from a constant level of effort.

- Whenever a very simple model is needed because of a lack of data or for ease of explanation or implementation. An example is when a business or organization is new and very little past historical data are available.
- Whenever stability may be obtained by making simple corrections for factors such as population growth or inflation. Examples are changing income to per capita income or changing dollar sales to constant dollar amounts.
- Whenever the series may be transformed into a stable one. Examples are transforming a series by taking logarithms, square roots, or differences.
- Whenever the series is a set of forecast errors from a forecasting technique that is considered adequate. An example is Example 4.6.

Several techniques that should be considered when forecasting stationary series include naive methods, simple averaging methods, moving averages, simple exponential smoothing, and Box–Jenkins methods.

Forecasting Techniques for Data with a Trend

A *trended* series was defined earlier as a time series that contains a long-term component that represents the growth or decline in the series over an extended period of time. In other words, a time series is said to have a trend if its expected value changes over time so that it is expected to increase or decrease during the period for which forecasts are desired. It is common for economic time series to contain a trend.

Forecasting techniques for trended data are used in the following situations:

- Whenever increased productivity and new technology lead to changes in life style. Examples are the demand for electronic components, which increased with the advent of the computer, and railroad usage, which decreased with the advent of the airplane.
- Whenever increasing population causes increases in demand for goods and services. Examples are the sales revenues of consumer goods, demand for energy consumption, and use of raw materials.
- Whenever the purchasing power of the dollar affects economic variables due to inflation. Examples are salaries, production costs, and prices.
- Whenever market acceptance increases. An example is the growth period in the life cycle of a new product.

Techniques that should be considered when forecasting trended series include linear moving average, Brown's linear exponential smoothing, Holt's linear exponential smoothing, Brown's quadratic exponential smoothing, simple regression, Gompertz model, growth curves, and exponential models.

Forecasting Techniques for Data with Seasonality

A *seasonal* series was defined earlier as a time series with a pattern of change that repeats itself year after year. Developing a seasonal forecasting technique usually involves selecting either a multiplicative or additive method and then estimating seasonal indexes from the history of the series. These indexes are then used to include seasonality in forecasts or to remove such effects from the observed values. The latter process is referred to as seasonally adjusting the data and is discussed in Chapter 8.

Forecasting techniques for seasonal data are used in the following situations:

- Whenever weather influences the variable of interest. Examples are electrical consumption, summer and winter activities (sports like skiing), clothing, and agricultural growing seasons.
- Whenever the annual calendar influences the variable of interest. Examples are retail sales influenced by holidays, three-day weekends, and school calendars.

Techniques that should be considered when forecasting seasonal series include classical decomposition, Census II, Winter's exponential smoothing, time series multiple regression, and Box–Jenkins methods.

Forecasting Techniques for Cyclical Series

The *cyclical* effect was defined earlier as the wavelike fluctuation around the trend. Cyclical patterns tend to repeat in the data every two, three, or more years. Cyclical patterns are difficult to model because their patterns are not stable. The up–down wavelike fluctuations around the trend rarely repeat at fixed intervals of time, and the magnitude of the fluctuations also usually varies. Decomposition methods (Chapter 8) can be extended to analyze cyclical data. However, because of the irregular behavior of cycles, analyzing the cyclical component of a series often requires finding coincidental or leading economic indicators.

Forecasting techniques for cyclical data are used in the following situations:

- Whenever the business cycle influences the variable of interest. Examples are economic, market, and competition factors.
- Whenever shifts in popular tastes occur. Examples are fashions, music, and food.

- Whenever shifts in population occur. Examples are wars, famines, epidemics, and natural disasters.
- Whenever shifts in the product life cycle occur. Examples are introduction, growth, maturation and market saturation, and decline.

Techniques that should be considered when forecasting cyclical series include classical decomposition, economic indicators, econometric models, multiple regression, and Box–Jenkins methods.

Other Factors to Consider When Choosing a Forecasting Technique

The time horizon for a forecast has a direct bearing on the selection of a forecasting technique. For short- and intermediate-term forecasts, a variety of quantitative techniques can be applied. As the forecasting horizon increases, however, a number of these techniques become less applicable. For instance, moving averages, exponential smoothing, and Box–Jenkins models are poor predictors of economic turning points, whereas econometric models are more useful. Regression models are appropriate for the short, intermediate, and long terms. Means, moving averages, classical decomposition, and trend projections are quantitative techniques that are appropriate for the short and intermediate time horizons. The more complex Box–Jenkins and econometric techniques are also appropriate for short- and intermediate-term forecasts. Qualitative methods are frequently used for longer time horizons (see Chapter 11).

The applicability of forecasting techniques is generally something a forecaster bases on experience. Managers frequently need forecasts in a relatively short time. Exponential smoothing, trend projection, regression models, and classical decomposition methods have an advantage in this situation.

Ultimately, a forecast will be presented to management executives for approval and use in the decision-making process. Therefore, ease of understanding and in interpreting the results is an important consideration. Regression models, trend projections, classical decomposition, and exponential smoothing techniques all rate highly on this criterion.

Computer costs are no longer a significant part of technique selection. Desk-top computers (microprocessors) and forecasting software packages are becoming commonplace for many organizations. Due to these developments, other criteria will likely overshadow computer cost considerations in the future.

As part of the final selection, each technique must be evaluated by the forecaster in terms of its reliability and applicability to the problem at hand, its value in terms of effectiveness as compared to other appropriate techniques, its accuracy level, its cost, and its acceptance by management.

TABLE 4.6 Choosing a Forecasting Technique.

Method	Pattern of Data	Time Horizon	Type of Model	Minimum Data Requirements	
				Nonseasonal	Seasonal
Naive	ST, T, S	S	TS	1	
Simple averages	ST	S	TS	30	
Moving averages	ST	S	TS	4–20	
Exponential smoothing	ST	S	TS	2	
Linear exponential smoothing	T	S	TS	3	
Quadratic exponential smoothing	T	S	TS	4	
Seasonal exponential smoothing	S	S	TS		2*L
Adaptive filtering	S	S	TS		5*L
Simple regression	T	I	C	10	
Multiple regression	C, S	I	C	10*V	
Classical decomposition	S	S	TS		5*L
Exponential trend models	T	I, L	TS	10	
S-curve fitting	T	I, L	TS	10	
Gompertz models	T	I, L	TS	10	
Growth curves	T	I, L	TS	10	
Census II	S	S	TS		6*L
Box–Jenkins	ST, T, C, S	S	TS	24	3*L
Leading indicators	C	S	C	24	
Econometric models	C	S	C	30	
Time series multiple regression	T, S	I, L	C		6*L

Pattern of the data: ST, stationary; T, trended; S, seasonal; C, cyclical.

Time horizon: S, short term (less than 3 months); I, intermediate; L, long term.

Type of model: TS, time series; C, causal.

Seasonal: L, length of seasonality.

Table 4.6 summarizes which forecasting techniques should be used with particular data patterns.

MEASURING FORECASTING ERROR

Since quantitative forecasting techniques usually involve time series data, a mathematical notation is developed to refer to each specific time period. The letter y will be used to denote a time series variable unless there is more than one variable involved. The time period associated with an observation is shown as a subscript. Thus, y_t refers to the value of the time series at time period t. The quarterly data for the Outboard Marine Corporation presented in Example 4.4 would be denoted $y_1 = 147.6$, $y_2 = 251.8$, $y_3 = 273.1, \ldots, y_{28} = 310$.

Mathematical notation must also be developed for distinguishing between an actual value of a time series and the forecast value. A ˆ (hat) will be placed above a value to indicate that it is being forecast. The forecast value for y_t is $\hat{y}_t$. The accuracy of a forecasting technique is frequently judged by comparing the original series $y_1, y_2, \ldots$ to the series of forecast values $\hat{y}_1, \hat{y}_2, \ldots$.

Basic forecasting notation is summarized as follows:

Basic Forecasting Notation

y_t = value of a time series at period t

$\hat{y}_t$ = forecast value of y_t

$e_t = y_t - \hat{y}_t$ = residual or forecast error

Several methods have been devised to summarize the errors generated by a particular forecasting technique. Most of these measures involve averaging some function of the difference between an actual value and its forecast value. These differences between observed values and forecast values are often referred to as *residuals*.

A *residual* is the difference between an actual value and its forecast value.

Equation 4.4 is used to compute the error or residual for each forecast period.

$$e_t = y_t - \hat{y}_t \qquad\qquad (4.4)$$

where

e_t = forecast error in time period t

y_t = actual value in time period t

$\hat{y}_t$ = forecast value for time period t

One method for evaluating a forecasting technique uses the summation of the absolute errors. The mean absolute deviation (MAD) measures forecast accuracy by averaging the magnitudes of the forecast errors (absolute values of each error). MAD is most useful when the analyst wants to measure forecast error in the same units as the original series. Equation 4.5 shows how MAD is computed.

$$MAD = \frac{\sum_{t=1}^{n} (y_t - \hat{y}_t)}{n} \qquad (4.5)$$

The mean squared error (MSE) is an alternative method for evaluating a forecasting technique. Each error or residual is squared; these are then summed and divided by the number of observations. This approach provides a penalty for large forecasting errors because it squares each. This is important since a technique that produces moderate errors may well be preferable to one that usually has smaller errors but occasionally yields extremely large ones. Equation 4.6 shows how MSE is computed.

$$MSE = \frac{\sum_{t=1}^{n} (y_t - \hat{y}_t)^2}{n} \qquad (4.6)$$

Sometimes it is more useful to compute the forecasting errors in terms of percentages rather than amounts. The mean absolute percentage error (MAPE) is computed by finding the absolute error in each period, dividing this by the actual observed value for that period, and then averaging these absolute percentage errors. This approach is useful when the size or magnitude of the forecast variable is important in evaluating the accuracy of the forecast. MAPE provides an indication of how large the forecast errors are in comparison to the actual values of the series. MAPE can also be used to compare the accuracy of the same or different techniques on two entirely different series. Equation 4.7 shows how MAPE is computed.

$$MAPE = \frac{\sum_{t=1}^{n} \frac{|y_t - \hat{y}_t|}{y_t}}{n} \qquad (4.7)$$

Sometimes it is necessary to determine whether a forecasting method is biased (consistently forecasting low or high). The mean percentage error (MPE) is used in these cases. It is computed by finding the error in each period, dividing this by the actual value for that period, and then averaging these percentage errors. If the forecasting approach is unbiased, Equation 4.8 will produce a percentage that is close to zero. If the result is a large negative percentage, the forecasting method is consistently overestimating.

If the result is a large positive percentage, the forecasting method is consistently underestimating.

$$\text{MPE} = \frac{\sum_{t=1}^{n} \dfrac{(y_t - \hat{y}_t)}{y_t}}{n} \qquad\qquad\qquad \textbf{(4.8)}$$

Part of the decision to use a particular forecasting technique involves the determination of whether the technique will produce forecast errors that are judged to be sufficiently small. It is certainly realistic to expect a technique to produce relatively small forecast errors on a consistent basis.

The four measures of forecast accuracy just described are used in the following ways:

- The comparison of the accuracy of two different techniques.
- The measurement of a technique's usefulness or reliability.
- The search for an optimal technique.

Example 4.5 will illustrate how each of these error measurements is computed.

EXAMPLE 4.5

■ Table 4.7 shows the data for the daily number of customers requiring repair work, y_t, and a forecast of these data, $\hat{y}_t$, for Gary's Chevron Station. The forecasting technique used the number of customers serviced in the previous period as the

TABLE 4.7 Computations for Forecasting Evaluation Methods for Example 4.5.

Time, t	Data, y_t Customers	Forecast, $\hat{y}_t$	e_t	$\lvert e_t \rvert$	e_t^2	$\lvert e_t \rvert / y_t,$ %	$e_t / y_t,$ %
1	58	—	—	—	—	—	—
2	54	58	−4	4	16	7.4	−7.4
3	60	54	6	6	36	10.0	10.0
4	55	60	−5	5	25	9.1	−9.1
5	62	55	7	7	49	11.3	11.3
6	62	62	0	0	0	0.0	0.0
7	65	62	3	3	9	4.6	4.6
8	63	65	−2	2	4	3.2	−3.2
9	70	63	7	7	49	10.0	10.0
		Sums	$\overline{12}$	$\overline{34}$	$\overline{188}$	$\overline{55.6}$	$\overline{16.2}$

forecast for the current period. This simple technique will be discussed in Chapter 5. The computations for evaluating this model using MAD, MSE, MAPE, and MPE are demonstrated in Table 4.7.

$$\text{MAD} = \frac{\sum\limits_{t=1}^{n} |y_t - \hat{y}_t|}{n} = \frac{34}{8} = 4.3$$

$$\text{MSE} = \frac{\sum\limits_{t=1}^{n} (y_t - \hat{y}_t)^2}{n} = \frac{188}{8} = 23.5$$

$$\text{MAPE} = \frac{\sum\limits_{t=1}^{n} \dfrac{|y_t - \hat{y}_t|}{y_t}}{n} = \frac{55.6\%}{8} = 6.95\%$$

$$\text{MPE} = \frac{\sum\limits_{t=1}^{n} \dfrac{(y_t - \hat{y}_t)}{y_t}}{n} = \frac{16.2\%}{8} = 2.03\%$$

MAD indicates that each forecast deviated by an average of 4.3 customers. The MSE of 23.5 and the MAPE of 6.95% would be compared to the MSE and MAPE for any other method used to forecast these data. Finally, the small MPE of 2.03% indicates that the technique is not biased: since the value is close to zero, the technique does not consistently over- or underestimate the number of customers serviced daily. ■

DETERMINING THE ADEQUACY OF A FORECASTING TECHNIQUE

Before forecasting with a selected technique, the adequacy of the choice should be evaluated. The forecaster should answer the following questions:

- Are the autocorrelation coefficients of the residuals indicative of a random series? This question can be answered by examining the autocorrelation coefficients for the residual plot, such as the one demonstrated in Example 4.6.
- Are the residuals approximately normally distributed? This question can be answered by analyzing a histogram of the residuals.
- Do all parameter estimates have significant t ratios? The t distribution was reviewed in Chapter 2 and applications of t ratios are demonstrated in Chapter 6.
- Is the technique simple to use and easy to understand for decision makers?

The basic requirement that the residual pattern is random is verified by examining the autocorrelation coefficients of the residuals. There should be no significant autocorrelation coefficients. Equation 4.3 provided a criteria for testing the significance of autocorrelation coefficients. Example 4.2 illustrated how a correlogram can be used to determine whether a series is random. Example 4.6 illustrates this procedure.

EXAMPLE 4.6

■ Perkin Kendell, the analyst for the Outboard Marine Corporation, has been asked to forecast quarterly sales for 1991. The data are shown in Table 4.5 for 1984 to 1990. Since Perkin determined that the data are seasonal in Example 4.4, he tries one of the seasonal forecasting techniques available on his computer. The autocorrelation coefficients for the series of residuals, the differences between the actual values and their forecast values, are shown in Figure 4.6. An examination of these autocorrelation coefficients indicates that four are significantly different from zero, $r_1 = .39$, $r_3 = .40$, $r_4 = .51$, and $r_8 = .37$. Significant autocorrelation coefficients indicate some

FIGURE 4.6 Autocorrelations for the Residuals for an Inadequate Model for the Outboard Marine Data of Example 4.6.

```
TIME LAG                                              AUTOCORRELATION
  12                    .       I *    .                   0.10
  11                    .    *  I     .                   -0.11
  10                    .      *I     .                   -0.07
   9                    .       I   * .                    0.27
   8                    .       I      *                   0.37
   7                    .    *  I     .                   -0.08
   6                    .       I  *  .                    0.16
   5                    .       I *   .                    0.12
   4                    .       I   .  *                   0.51
   3                    .       I   .*                     0.40
   2                    .       I  * .                     0.22
   1                    .       I   .*                     0.39
       I.I.I.I.I.I.I.I.I.I.I.I.I.I.I.I.I.I.I.I.I
      -1                       0              +1
```

FIGURE 4.7 Autocorrelations for the Residuals for an Adequate Model for the Outboard Marine Data of Example 4.6.

```
TIME LAG                                              AUTOCORRELATION
  12                    .       *      .                   0.00
  11                    .      *I      .                  -0.05
  10                    .   *   I      .                  -0.13
   9                    .      *I      .                  -0.06
   8                    .       I  *   .                   0.13
   7                    .   *   I      .                  -0.21
   6                    .   *   I      .                  -0.14
   5                    .    *  I      .                  -0.09
   4                    .   *   I      .                  -0.17
   3                    .       I*     .                   0.04
   2                    .       I *    .                   0.11
   1                    .       I   *  .                   0.18
       I.I.I.I.I.I.I.I.I.I.I.I.I.I.I.I.I.I.I.I.I
      -1                       0              +1
```

pattern in the residuals. One basic requirement for an adequate forecasting technique is that it provide a residual pattern that is random. Perkin judges the forecasting technique that generated these residuals to be inadequate.

Perkin now tries a different forecasting technique. The autocorrelation coefficients for the series of residuals when this forecasting technique is used are shown in Figure 4.7. An examination of these autocorrelation coefficients indicates that none of them are significantly different from zero. The new forecasting technique appears to be adequate, and Perkin decides to use this technique in forecasting the future quarterly sales of Outboard Marine. ■

APPLICATION TO MANAGEMENT

The concepts in this chapter constitute the basis for selection of the proper forecasting technique in a given situation. Many of the most important forecasting techniques are discussed and applied to forecasting situations in the chapters that follow.

The following are a few examples of situations constantly arising in the business world for which a sound forecasting technique would help the decision-making process. The material in this chapter, along with the data collection discussions of Chapter 3, applies to these examples since, for each, the two vital components of a useful forecast are present: collecting appropriate data and choosing the right forecasting method.

A soft drink company wants to project the demand for its major product over the next two years, by month.

A major telecommunications company wants to forecast the quarterly dividend payments of its chief rival for the next three years.

A university needs to forecast student credit hours by quarter for the next four years in order to develop budget projections for the state legislature.

A public accounting firm needs monthly forecasts of dollar billings so it can plan for additional accounting positions and begin recruiting.

The quality control manager of a factory that makes aluminum ingots needs a weekly forecast of production defects for top management of the company.

A banker wants to see the projected monthly revenue of a small bicycle manufacturer that is seeking a large loan to triple its output capacity.

A federal government agency needs annual projections of average miles per gallon of American-made cars over the next 10 years in order to make regulatory recommendations.

A personnel manager needs a monthly forecast of absent days for the company workforce in order to plan overtime expenditures.

A savings and loan company needs a forecast of delinquent loans over the next two years in an attempt to avoid bankruptcy.

A company that makes computer chips needs an industry forecast for the number of personal computers sold over the next five years in order to plan its research and development budget.

GLOSSARY

Autocorrelation Autocorrelation is the correlation between a variable, lagged one or more periods, and itself.

Correlogram The *correlogram* is a graphical tool for displaying the autocorrelations for various lags of a time series.

Cyclical component The cyclical component is the wavelike fluctuation around the trend.

Irregular component The irregular component measures the variability of the time series after the other components have been removed.

Residual A residual is the difference between an actual observed value and its forecast value.

Seasonal component The seasonal component is a pattern of change that repeats itself year after year.

Stationary series A *stationary series* is one whose average value is not changing over time.

Time series A time series consists of data that are collected, recorded, or observed over successive increments of time.

Trend The trend is the long-term component that represents the growth or decline in the time series over an extended period of time.

KEY FORMULAS

First sample autocorrelation coefficient

$$r_1 = \frac{\sum\limits_{t=1}^{n-1} (y_t - \overline{y})(y_{t-1} - \overline{y})}{\sum\limits_{t=1}^{n} (y_t - \overline{y})^2} \tag{4.1}$$

kth sample autocorrelation coefficient

$$r_k = \frac{\sum\limits_{t=1}^{n-k} (y_t - \overline{y})(y_{t-k} - \overline{y})}{\sum\limits_{t=1}^{n} (y_t - \overline{y})^2} \tag{4.2}$$

Autocorrelation coefficient confidence intervals

$$0 + z \frac{1}{\sqrt{n}} \tag{4.3}$$

Forecast error or residual

$$e_t = y_t - \hat{y}_t \tag{4.4}$$

Mean absolute deviation

$$\text{MAD} = \frac{\sum_{t=1}^{n} |y_t - \hat{y}_t|}{n} \tag{4.5}$$

Mean squared error

$$\text{MSE} = \frac{\sum_{t=1}^{n} (y_t - \hat{y}_t)^2}{n} \tag{4.6}$$

Mean absolute percentage error

$$\text{MAPE} = \frac{\sum_{t=1}^{n} \dfrac{|y_t - \hat{y}_t|}{y_t}}{n} \tag{4.7}$$

Mean percentage error

$$\text{MPE} = \frac{\sum_{t=1}^{n} \dfrac{(y_t - \hat{y}_t)}{y_t}}{n} \tag{4.8}$$

CHAPTER **4**

PROBLEMS

1. Explain the differences between qualitative forecasting techniques and quantitative techniques.

2. What is a time series?

3. Describe each of the four components in a time series.

4. What is autocorrelation?

5. What does an autocorrelation coefficient measure?

6. Describe how correlograms are used to analyze autocorrelations for various lags of a time series.

7. Each of the following statements describes either a stationary or nonstationary series. Indicate which.
   a. A series that has a trend.
   b. A series that has no trend but is very cyclical.
   c. A series whose mean and variance remain constant over time.
   d. A series whose average value is changing over time.
   e. A series that contains no growth or decline.

8. Descriptions are provided for several types of series: random, stationary, have a trend, or are seasonal. Identify each type of series.
   a. A series that has basic statistical properties, such as the mean and variance, that remain constant over time.
   b. The successive values of a time series are not related to each other.
   c. A high relationship exists between each successive value of a series.
   d. A significant autocorrelation coefficient appears at time lag 4.
   e. A series that contains no growth or decline.
   f. The autocorrelation coefficients are typically significantly different from zero for the first several time lags and then gradually drop to zero as the number of periods increases.

9. List some of the forecasting techniques that should be considered when forecasting a stationary series. Give examples of situations where these techniques would be applicable.

10. List some of the forecasting techniques that should be considered when forecasting a trended series. Give examples of situations where these techniques would be applicable.

11. List some of the forecasting techniques that should be considered when forecasting a seasonal series. Give examples of situations where these techniques would be applicable.

12. List some of the forecasting techniques that should be considered when forecasting a cyclical series. Give examples of situations where these techniques would be applicable.

13. The number of marriages in the United States is given below. Compute the first differences for these data.

Year	Marriages in Thousands
1985	2,425.0
1986	2,400.0
1987	2,421.0

Source: *Statistical Abstract of the United States,* 1988, 1989.

14. Compute the 95% confidence interval for the autocorrelation coefficients for a series that contains 80 items.

15. Compute the 90% confidence interval for the autocorrelation coefficients for a series that contains 60 items.

16. Which method for evaluating a forecasting technique should be used in each of the following situations?
    a. The analyst needs to determine whether a forecasting method is biased.
    b. The analyst feels that the size or magnitude of the forecasted variable is important in evaluating the accuracy of the forecast.
    c. The analyst needs to penalize large forecasting errors.

17. Which of the following statements are true concerning the methods used to evaluate forecasts?
    a. The MAPE takes into consideration the magnitude of the values being forecasted.
    b. The MSE penalizes large errors.
    c. The MPE is used to determine whether a model is systematically predicting too high or too low.
    d. The advantage of the MAD method is that it relates the size of error to the actual observation.

18. Allie White, the chief loan officer for the Dominion Bank, would like to analyze the bank's loan portfolio for the years 1984 to 1989. The data are as follows:

Quarterly Loans for Dominion Bank, 1984–1987 ($ million).

Calendar	Mar. 31	June 30	Sept. 30	Dec. 31
1984	2313	2495	2609	2792
1985	2860	3099	3202	3161
1986	3399	3471	3545	3851
1987	4458	4850	5093	5318
1988	5756	6013	6158	6289
1989	6369	6568	6646	6861

Source: *The Value Line Investment Survey* (New York: Value Line, 1990), p. 2018.

a. Compute the autocorrelations for time lags 1 and 2. Test to determine whether these autocorrelation coefficients are significantly different from zero at the .05 significance level.
b. Use a computer program to determine whether these data are stationary.

19. This question refers to Problem 18. First difference the quarterly loan data for Dominion Bank.
    a. Compute the autocorrelation coefficient for time lag 1 using the first differenced data.
    b. Use a computer program to determine whether these differenced data are stationary.

20. Analyze the autocorrelation coefficients for the series shown in Figures 4.8 through 4.11. Briefly describe each series.

FIGURE 4.8 Autocorrelation Coefficients for Problem 20.

```
TIME LAG                                        AUTOCORRELATION
   12              .       I*    .                   0.04
   11              .       *     .                  -0.02
   10              .    *  I     .                  -0.09
    9              .      *I     .                  -0.04
    8              .       I  *  .                   0.15
    7              .       I*    .                   0.05
    6              .    *  I     .                  -0.11
    5              .       I *   .                   0.08
    4              .       I*    .                   0.04
    3              .    *  I     .                  -0.13
    2              .       *     .                  -0.01
    1              .       I   . *                   0.54
       I.I.I.I.I.I.I.I.I.I.I.I.I.I.I.I.I.I.I.I.I
      -1                   0                +1
```

FIGURE 4.9 Autocorrelation Coefficients for Problem 20.

```
   12              .       I    .*                   0.32
   11              .       I  * .                    0.16
   10              .  *    I     .                  -0.16
    9              .       I *   .                   0.08
    8              .       I    .  *                 0.44
    7              .       I  * .                    0.16
    6              .  *    I     .                  -0.15
    5              .       *     .                   0.02
    4              .       I    . *                  0.51
    3              .      *I     .                  -0.07
    2              .       I *   .                   0.12
    1              .       I  *. .                   0.21
       I.I.I.I.I.I.I.I.I.I.I.I.I.I.I.I.I.I.I.I.I
      -1                   0                +1
```

FIGURE 4.10 Autocorrelation Coefficients for Problem 20.

```
TIME LAG                                        AUTOCORRELATION
   12              .    *  I        .               -0.22
   11              .    *  I        .               -0.16
   10              .     * I        .               -0.10
    9              .    *  I        .               -0.13
    8              .     * I        .               -0.09
    7              .       *        .                0.00
    6              .       I *      .                0.10
    5              .       I   *  . .                0.24
    4              .       I      .*                 0.43
    3              .       I      . *                0.59
    2              .       I      .   *              0.71
    1              .       I      .     *            0.74
       I.I.I.I.I.I.I.I.I.I.I.I.I.I.I.I.I.I.I.I.I
      -1                   0                +1
```

FIGURE 4.11 Autocorrelation Coefficients for Problem 20.

```
TIME LAG                                             AUTOCORRELATION
   12                    .      I*    .                    0.04
   11                    .      *     .                   -0.02
   10                    .   *  I     .                   -0.09
    9                    .     *I     .                   -0.04
    8                    .      I   * .                    0.15
    7                    .      I*    .                    0.05
    6                    .   *  I     .                   -0.11
    5                    .      I  *  .                    0.08
    4                    .      I*    .                    0.04
    3                    .   *  I     .                   -0.13
    2                    .      *     .                   -0.01
    1                    .   *  I     .                   -0.15
          I.I.I.I.I.I.I.I.I.I.I.I.I.I.I.I.I.I.I.I.I
          -1                   0                  +1
```

21. An analyst would like to determine whether there is a pattern to earnings per share for the Price Company, which operates a wholesale/retail cash and carry business in several states under the name Price Club. The data are as follows:

Quarterly Earnings per Share for Price Club, 1986–1990.

Calendar	Period			
	December	March	June	August
1986	.40	.29	.24	.32
1987	.47	.34	.30	.39
1988	.63	.43	.38	.49
1989	.76	.51	.42	.61
1990	.86	.51		

Source: *The Value Line Investment Survey* (New York: Value Line, 1990), p. 1652.

Describe any patterns that exist in these data.
a. Find the forecast value of the quarterly earnings per share for Price Club for each quarter by using the naive approach (the forecast for June 1990 is whatever it was for March 1990, .51).
b. Evaluate using MAD.
c. Evaluate using MSE.
d. Evaluate using MAPE.
e. Evaluate using MPE.
f. Write a memo summarizing your findings.

MURPHY BROTHERS FURNITURE

In 1958 the Murphy brothers established a furniture store in downtown Dallas. Over the years they were quite successful and extended their retail coverage throughout the West and Midwest. By 1990, their chain of furniture stores had become well established in 36 states.

Julie Murphy, the daughter of one of the founders, recently completed her business studies and joined the firm. Here father and uncle were sophisticated in many ways, but not in the area of quantitative skills. In particular, they both felt that they could not accurately forecast the future sales of Murphy Brothers using modern computer techniques. For this reason, they appealed to Julie for help as part of her new job.

Julie had studied forecasting in her business program and ordered a forecasting software package, along with Minitab, to use on her office computer. She first considered using Murphy sales dollars as her variable, but found that several years of history were missing. She asked her father about this and he told her that at the time he "didn't think it was that important."

Julie decided that Murphy sales were probably closely related to national sales figures and decided to search for an appropriate variable in one of the many federal publications. After looking through a recent copy of the *Survey of Current Business,* she found the history on monthly sales for all retail stores in the United States and decided to use this variable as a substitute for her variable of interest, Murphy Brothers sales dollars. She reasoned that if she could establish accurate forecasts for national sales she could relate these forecasts to Murphy's own sales and come up with the forecasts she wanted.

Table 4.8 shows the data that Julie collected, and Figure 4.12 shows a data plot provided by Julie's computer program. Julie began her analysis by using

TABLE 4.8 Monthly Sales (Billions) for All Retail Stores, January 1980 to August 1990.

Year:	1980	1981	1982	1983	1984	1985	1986	1987	1988	1989	1990
Jan.	69.4	77.4	76.6	81.3	93.1	98.8	105.6	106.4	113.6	122.5	132.6
Feb.	69.6	73.7	75.7	78.9	93.7	95.6	99.7	105.8	115.0	118.9	127.3
Mar.	74.9	83.9	86.1	93.8	104.3	110.2	114.2	120.4	131.6	141.3	148.3
Apr.	74.2	85.2	87.5	93.8	103.9	113.1	115.7	125.4	130.9	139.8	145.0
May	78.2	86.9	90.3	97.8	111.8	120.3	125.4	129.1	136.0	150.3	154.1
Jun.	76.4	87.3	88.4	100.6	112.3	115.0	120.4	129.0	137.5	149.0	153.5
Jul.	78.9	88.2	90.6	99.4	106.9	115.5	120.7	129.3	134.1	144.6	148.9
Aug.	80.8	89.0	89.1	100.1	111.2	121.1	124.1	131.5	138.7	153.0	156.4
Sept.	76.7	85.5	87.8	97.9	104.0	113.8	124.4	124.5	131.9	144.1	
Oct.	83.0	88.8	90.9	100.7	109.6	115.8	123.8	128.3	133.8	142.3	
Nov.	82.8	87.3	94.0	103.9	113.5	118.1	121.4	126.9	140.2	148.8	
Dec.	99.6	106.1	113.2	125.8	132.3	138.6	152.1	157.2	171.0	176.5	

Source: *Survey of Current Business,* various years.

FIGURE 4.12 Estimated Monthly Sales (Billions) for All U.S. Retail Stores, 1980–1990.

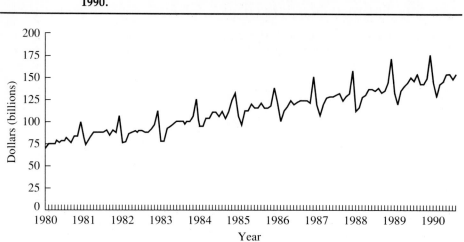

Minitab to compute the autocorrelation coefficients for her data. Following are the Minitab commands she used along with the results.

```
MTB > READ 'RETAIL.DAT' INTO C1
      128 ROWS READ

C1
   69.4     69.6     74.9     74.2     .    .    .

MTB > ACF C1

ACF of C1

               -1.0 -0.8 -0.6 -0.4 -0.2  0.0  0.2  0.4  0.6  0.8  1.0
                 +----+----+----+----+----+----+----+----+----+----+
    1   0.820                             XXXXXXXXXXXXXXXXXXXXXX
    2   0.755                             XXXXXXXXXXXXXXXXXXXXX
    3   0.765                             XXXXXXXXXXXXXXXXXXXXX
    4   0.754                             XXXXXXXXXXXXXXXXXXXXX
    5   0.750                             XXXXXXXXXXXXXXXXXXXXX
    6   0.722                             XXXXXXXXXXXXXXXXXXXX
    7   0.716                             XXXXXXXXXXXXXXXXXXXX
    8   0.698                             XXXXXXXXXXXXXXXXXXX
    9   0.647                             XXXXXXXXXXXXXXXXXX
   10   0.596                             XXXXXXXXXXXXXXXX
   11   0.618                             XXXXXXXXXXXXXXXXX
   12   0.746                             XXXXXXXXXXXXXXXXXXXXX
   13   0.583                             XXXXXXXXXXXXXXXX
   14   0.520                             XXXXXXXXXXXXXX
   15   0.525                             XXXXXXXXXXXXXX
   16   0.512                             XXXXXXXXXXXXXX
   17   0.511                             XXXXXXXXXXXXXX
   18   0.485                             XXXXXXXXXXXXX
   19   0.481                             XXXXXXXXXXXXX
   20   0.469                             XXXXXXXXXXXXX
   21   0.418                             XXXXXXXXXXX
```

After examining the above correlogram, it was obvious to Julie that her data contained a trend. The early autocorrelation coefficients are very large, and they gradually drop toward zero with time. To make the series stationary, so that various forecasting methods could be considered, Julie decided to first difference her data to see if the trend could be removed. Following are the Minitab commands she used, along with the results.

```
MTB > DIFFERENCES 1 FOR C1, STORE IN C2
MTB > ACF C2

ACF of C2

           -1.0 -0.8 -0.6 -0.4 -0.2  0.0  0.2  0.4  0.6  0.8  1.0
            +----+----+----+----+----+----+----+----+----+----+
    1 -0.360                    XXXXXXXXXX
    2 -0.244                      XXXXXXX
    3  0.064                          XXX
    4  0.002                          X
    5  0.063                          XXX
    6 -0.030                         XX
    7  0.033                          XX
    8  0.017                          X
    9  0.056                          XX
   10 -0.224                      XXXXXXX
   11 -0.315                     XXXXXXXXX
   12  0.880                          XXXXXXXXXXXXXXXXXXXXXXX
   13 -0.320                     XXXXXXXXX
   14 -0.206                      XXXXXX
   15  0.054                          XX
   16 -0.020                         XX
   17  0.080                          XXX
   18 -0.032                         XX
   19  0.020                          XX
   20  0.027                          XX
   21  0.037                          XX

MTB > STOP
```

Julie concluded that her series was now stationary, since a pattern of large autocorrelation coefficients gradually approaching zero did not exist. However, she noted the large autocorrelation coefficient (.880) at time period 12. Since she used monthly data, this coefficient strongly suggested the presence of a monthly seasonal effect.

On the basis of her analysis of the data, Julie believed she had made good progress. Since she had identified both a trend and a 12-month seasonal effect in her data, she strongly considered either Winter's exponential smoothing or classical decomposition for her forecasts. She also remembered that the Box–Jenkins procedures are a possibility, although she realized this technique would be much more difficult to explain to her father and uncle. However, since all these techniques were included on her forecasting software, she decided to try them and see which produced the most accurate forecasts.

Moving Averages and Smoothing Methods

A tremendous emphasis is being placed on the improvement of decision making in both business and governmental organizations. Since we exist in an environment influenced by time, it has become a common goal to allocate available time among competing resources in some optimal manner. This goal can be accomplished, in part, through accurate forecasting. Twenty years ago managers made their decisions largely based on their own feelings and intuition about the industry and economy. Now they are supplementing this "feel" for the industry or economy with both simple and sophisticated forecasting techniques. The increase in the usage of microcomputers continues to strengthen this trend.

This chapter will describe three types of forecasting techniques: naive, averaging, and smoothing. *Naive* methods are used to develop simple models that assume that recent periods are the best predictors of the future. *Averaging* methods are developed based on an average of weighted observations. *Smoothing* methods are based on averaging past values of a series in a decreasing (exponential) manner.

Figure 5.1 shows an outline of the forecasting procedure for the methods discussed in this chapter. Visualize yourself on a time scale. You are at point t in Figure 5.1 and can look backward over past observations of the variable of interest (y_t) or forward into the future. Once a forecasting technique has been selected, it is adjusted to the known data, and forecast values ($\hat{y}_t$) are obtained. Once forecast values are available, they can be compared to the known observations, and the forecast error (e) can be calculated.

A typical strategy for evaluating the forecasting methods discussed in this chapter involves the following steps. (1) A forecasting method is chosen based on the analyst's intuition about the pattern of the data. (2) The data set is divided into two sections—an initialization part and a test part. (3) The chosen forecasting technique is used to develop fitted values for the initialization part of the data. (4) The technique is used to forecast the test part of the data, and the forecasting error is determined and evaluated (refer to Chapter 4 for a review of measures of forecasting accuracy). (5) A decision is made. The decision might be to use the

FIGURE 5.1 Forecasting Outline.

You Are Here

Past Data	t	Periods to be Forecast

$y_{t-3}, y_{t-2}, y_{t-1}, y_t, \hat{y}_{t+1}, \hat{y}_{t+2}, \hat{y}_{t+3},$

where y_t is the most recent observation of a variable
$\hat{y}_{t+1}$ is the forecast for one period in the future

technique in its present form, to modify the technique, or to develop a forecast using another technique and compare the results.

NAIVE MODELS

The simplest naive techniques assume that recent periods are the best predictors of the future. The simplest model is

$$\hat{y}_{t+1} = y_t \qquad\qquad\qquad (5.1)$$

where $\hat{y}_{t+1}$ is the forecast made in time t for time $t + 1$.

EXAMPLE 5.1

■ Figure 5.2 shows the quarterly sales of saws for the Acme Tool Company. The naive technique is used to forecast sales for the next quarter to be the same as the previous quarter. Table 5.1 shows the data from 1985 to 1991. If the data from 1985 to

FIGURE 5.2 Sales of Saws for the Acme Tool Co., 1985–1991.

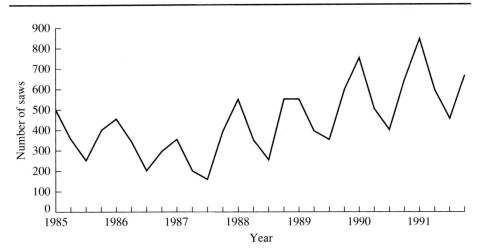

TABLE 5.1 Sales of Saws for the Acme Tool Company (1985–1991).

Year	Quarter	t	Sales
1985	1	1	500
	2	2	350
	3	3	250
	4	4	400
1986	1	5	450
	2	6	350
	3	7	200
	4	8	300
1987	1	9	350
	2	10	200
	3	11	150
	4	12	400
1988	1	13	550
	2	14	350
	3	15	250
	4	16	550
1989	1	17	550
	2	18	400
	3	19	350
	4	20	600
1990	1	21	750
	2	22	500
	3	23	400
	4	24	650
1991	1	25	850
	2	26	600
	3	27	450
	4	28	700

1990 are used as the initialization part and 1991 as the test part, the forecast for first quarter of 1991 is

$$\hat{y}_{t+1} = y_t$$
$$y_{25} = 650$$

The forecasting error is determined using Equation 4.4. The error for period 25 is

$$e_{25} = y_{25} - \hat{y}_{25} = 850 - 650 = 200$$

The forecast for period 26 is 850 with an error of -250. Figure 5.2 shows that these data are trended, so a decision is made to modify the model. ■

Examination of the data in Example 5.1 leads the analyst to conclude that they are increasing over time. When data values increase over time, they are said to be *nonstationary* in level or to have a *trend*. If Equation 5.1 is used, the projections are consistently low. The technique can be adjusted to take this trend into consideration by adding the difference between this period and the last period. The model is

$$\hat{y}_{t+1} = y_t + (y_t - y_{t-1}) \tag{5.2}$$

Equation 5.2 takes into account the amount of change that occurred between quarters. The forecast for the first quarter of 1991 is

$$\hat{y}_{24+1} = y_{24} + (y_{24} - y_{24-1})$$

$$\hat{y}_{25} = y_{24} + (y_{24} - y_{23})$$

$$\hat{y}_{25} = 650 + (650 - 400)$$

$$\hat{y}_{25} = 650 + 250$$

$$\hat{y}_{25} = 900$$

The forecast error with this model is

$$e_{25} = y_{25} - \hat{y}_{25}$$

$$e_{25} = 850 - 900$$

$$e_{25} = -50$$

For some purposes, the rate of change might be more appropriate than the absolute amount of change, and then the model is

$$\hat{y}_{t+1} = y_t \, \frac{y_t}{y_{t-1}} \tag{5.3}$$

The forecast for the first quarter of 1991 using this model is

$$\hat{y}_{24+1} = y_{24} \cdot \frac{y_{24}}{y_{24-1}}$$

$$\hat{y}_{25} = y_{24} \cdot \frac{y_{24}}{y_{23}}$$

$$\hat{y}_{25} = 650 \cdot \frac{650}{400}$$

$$\hat{y}_{25} = 1{,}056$$

It would probably be better if the forecaster used an *average* of past absolute changes or rates of change in preparing the forecast.

Visual inspection of the data in Table 5.1 indicates that seasonal variation seems to exist. Sales in the fourth quarter are typically larger than those in any of the other quarters. If the seasonal pattern is strong, then the appropriate model might be

$$\hat{y}_{t+1} = y_{t-3} \qquad\qquad (5.4)$$

Equation 5.4 states that next quarter the variable will take on the same value it did in the corresponding quarter one year ago. The forecast for the first quarter of 1991 is

$$\hat{y}_{24+1} = y_{24-3}$$
$$\hat{y}_{25} = y_{21}$$
$$\hat{y}_{25} = 750$$

The major weakness of this approach is that it ignores everything that has occurred since last year and also any trend pattern. There are several ways of introducing more recent information. For example, the analyst can combine approaches and take into consideration both seasonal and trend variations. One possible model is

$$\hat{y}_{t+1} = y_{t-3} + \frac{(y_t - y_{t-1}) + \cdots + (y_{t-3} - y_{t-4})}{4} \qquad (5.5)$$

where the y_{t-3} term forecasts the seasonal patterns and the remaining term averages the amount of change for the past four quarters (trend). The forecast for the first quarter of 1991 using this model is

$$\hat{y}_{24+1} = y_{24-3} + \frac{(y_{24} - y_{24-1}) + \cdots + (y_{24-3} - y_{24-4})}{4}$$

$$\hat{y}_{25} = y_{21} + \frac{(y_{24} - y_{23}) + (y_{23} - y_{22}) + (y_{22} - y_{21}) + (y_{21} - y_{20})}{4}$$

$$\hat{y}_{25} = 750 + \frac{(650 - 400) + (400 - 500) + (500 - 750) + (750 - 600)}{4}$$

$$\hat{y}_{25} = 750 + 12.5$$

$$\hat{y}_{25} = 762.5$$

It is apparent that the number and complexity of possible naive models are limited only by the ingenuity of the analyst, but use of these techniques should be guided by sound judgment.

AVERAGING METHODS

Frequently, management faces the situation where forecasts need to be updated daily, weekly, or monthly for inventories containing hundreds or thousands of items. Often it is not possible to develop sophisticated forecasting techniques for each item. Instead, some quick, inexpensive, very simple short-term forecasting tools are needed to accomplish this task.

A manager facing such a situation is likely to use an averaging or smoothing technique. These types of techniques use a form of weighted average of past observations to smooth short-term fluctuations. The assumption underlying these techniques is that the fluctuations in past values represent random departures from some smooth curve. Once this curve is identified, it can be projected into the future to produce a forecast.

Simple Averages

Historical data can be smoothed in many ways. The objective is to use past data to develop a forecasting model for future periods. In this section the method of simple averages is considered. As with the naive methods, a decision is made to use the first t data points as the initialization part and the rest as a test part. Next, Equation 5.6 is used to average (compute the mean of) the initialization part of the data and to forecast the next period.

$$\hat{y}_{t+1} = \overline{y} = \frac{\sum\limits_{t=1}^{n} y_t}{n} \tag{5.6}$$

Finally, the forecast errors are determined, and a decision is made about the appropriateness of the forecasting technique.

A *simple average* is obtained by finding the mean for all the relevant values and then using this mean to forecast the next period.

EXAMPLE 5.2

■ The method of simple averages is demonstrated using the quarterly sales of saws for the Acme Tool Company presented in Table 5.1. The forecast for first quarter 1991 is

$$\hat{y}_{24+1} = \overline{y} = \sum\limits_{t=1}^{n} \frac{y_t}{n}$$

$$\hat{y}_{25} = \frac{9{,}800}{24}$$

$$\hat{y}_{25} = 408.33$$

The forecasting error is

$$e_{25} = y_{25} - \hat{y}_{25}$$

$$e_{25} = 850 - 408.33$$

$$e_{25} = 441.67$$

The forecast for second quarter 1991 includes one more data point added to the past history initialization part (850). The forecast is

$$\hat{y}_{25+1} = \frac{10{,}650}{25}$$

$$\hat{y}_{26} = 426$$ ∎

The simple average method does not seem appropriate for this data. This method should be used when the data are stationary; has no trend, seasonality, or other systematic patterns.

Moving Averages

The simple average method uses the mean of all the data to forecast. What if the analyst is more concerned with recent observations? A constant number of data points can be specified at the outset and a mean computed for the most recent observations. The term *moving average* is used to describe this approach. As each new observation becomes available, a new mean can be computed by dropping the oldest value and including the newest one. This moving average is then used to forecast the next period. Equation 5.7 sets forth the simple moving-average model.

$$M_t = \hat{y}_{t+1} = \frac{(y_t + y_{t-1} + y_{t-2} + \cdots + y_{t-n+1})}{n} \tag{5.7}$$

where

M_t = moving average at time t

$\hat{y}_{t+1}$ = forecasted value for next period

y_t = actual value at period t

n = number of terms in the moving average

The moving average for time period t is the arithmetic mean of the n most recent observations.

Note that equal weights are assigned to each observation. As it becomes available, each new data point is included in the average, and the earliest data point is discarded. The rate of response to changes in the underlying data pattern depends on the number of periods, n, included in the moving average.

Note that the moving-average technique deals only with the latest n periods of known data; the number of data points in each average does not change as time continues. The moving-average model works best with stationary data. It does not handle trend or seasonality very well, although it does better than the simple average method.

The analyst must choose the number of periods n in a moving average. A moving average of order 1 would take the last observation, y_t, and use it to forecast the next period. This is simply the naive forecasting approach of Equation 5.1. For quarterly data, a 4-quarter moving average yields an average of the 4 quarters, and for monthly data, a 12-month moving average eliminates or averages out seasonal effects. Moving averages are frequently used with quarterly or monthly data to help examine the components within a time series, as shown in Chapter 8. The larger the order of the moving average, the greater the smoothing effect. Used as a forecast, the large moving average pays very little attention to fluctuations in the data series.

A *moving average* is obtained by finding the mean for a specified set of values and then using it to forecast the next period.

EXAMPLE 5.3

■ Table 5.2 demonstrates the moving average forecasting technique with Acme Tool Company data. The moving average forecast for the first quarter of 1990 is

TABLE 5.2 Four-Quarter Moving Average for Acme Tool Company.

Year	Quarter	t	Sales, y_t	Moving Total	Moving Average Forecast, $\hat{y}_{t+1}$	e_t
1989	1	17	550			
	2	18	400			
	3	19	350			
	4	20	600	1,900		
1990	1	21	750	2,100	475	+275
	2	22	500	2,200	525	−25
	3	23	400	2,250	550	−150
	4	24	650	2,300	562.5	+87.5
1991	1	25	850	2,400	575	+275
	2	26	600	2,500	600	0
	3	27	450	2,550	625	−175
	4	28	700	2,600	637.5	+62.5
1992	1	29			650	

$$M_{20} = \hat{y}_{20+1} = \frac{y_{20} + y_{20-1} + y_{20-2} + y_{20-4+1}}{4}$$

$$\hat{y}_{21} = \frac{y_{20} + y_{19} + y_{18} + y_{17}}{4}$$

$$\hat{y}_{21} = \frac{550 + 400 + 350 + 600}{4} = \frac{1,900}{4} = 475$$

When the actual first-quarter 1990 value is known, the forecast error is calculated:

$$e_{21} = y_{21} - \hat{y}_{21} = 750 - 475 = 275$$

The forecast for the first quarter of 1992 is

$$M_{28} = \hat{y}_{28+1} = \frac{y_{28} + y_{28-1} + y_{28-2} + y_{28-4+1}}{4}$$

$$\hat{y}_{29} = \frac{y_{28} + y_{27} + y_{26} + y_{25}}{4}$$

$$\hat{y}_{29} = \frac{700 + 450 + 600 + 850}{4} = \frac{2,600}{4} = 650$$ ∎

The analyst must use judgment when determining how many weeks, months, or quarters on which to base the moving average. The smaller the number, the more weight is given to recent periods. Conversely, the greater

TABLE 5.3 Weekly Rentals for the Movie Video Store: Example 5.4.

t	Weekly Units Rented y_t	Three-week Moving Total	Three-week Moving Average	e_t
1	654	—	—	
2	658	—	—	
3	665	—	—	
4	672	1977	659	13
5	673	1995	665	8
6	671	2010	670	1
7	693	2016	672	21
8	694	2037	679	15
9	701	2058	686	15
10	703	2088	696	7
11	702	2098	699	3
12	710	2106	702	8
13	712	2115	705	7
14	711	2124	708	3
15	728	2133	711	17
16	—	2151	717	

MSE = 133.

the number, the less weight is given to more recent periods. A small number is most desirable when there are sudden shifts in the level of the series. A small number places heavy weight on recent history, which enables the forecasts to catch up more rapidly to the current level. A large number is desirable when there are wide, infrequent fluctuations in the series.

Note that an assumption of the moving average is that the data are stationary. Example 5.4 shows what happens when the moving average technique is used with trended data. Examination of the error column in Table 5.3 shows that every entry is positive, signifying that the forecasts do not catch up to the trend. The double moving average technique, which is designed to handle trended data, is introduced in the next section.

Double Moving Average

One way of forecasting time series data that have a linear trend is by using the double moving average technique. The method does what the name implies: one set of moving averages is computed, and then a second set is computed as a moving average of the first set.

Figure 5.3 shows the weekly rentals for the Movie Video Store. The three-week moving average and the double moving average for these data are also shown on the graph. Note how the three-week moving averages lag behind the actual values for comparable periods. This illustrates what happens when the moving average technique is used with trended data. Note also that the double moving averages lag behind the first set about as much as the first set lags behind the actual values. This difference between the two sets of moving averages is used to help calculate the forecast. This

FIGURE 5.3 Double Moving Averages: Movie Video Store.

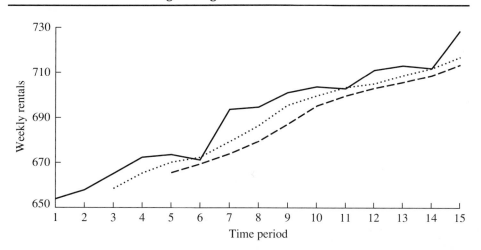

difference is added to the three-week moving average to forecast the actual values.

The double moving average technique is summarized using Equations 5.8 through 5.11.

First, Equation 5.7 is used to compute the moving average.

$$\hat{y}_{t+1} = \frac{y_t + y_{t-1} + y_{t-2} + \cdots + y_{t-n+1}}{n}$$

Let $M_t = \hat{y}_{t+1}$. Then Equation 5.8 is used to compute the second moving average.

$$M_t' = \frac{M_t + M_{t-1} + M_{t-2} + \cdots + M_{t-n+1}}{n} \tag{5.8}$$

Equation 5.9 is used to compute the difference between the two moving averages.

$$a_t = 2M_t - M_t' \tag{5.9}$$

Equation 5.10 is an additional adjustment factor, which is similar to a slope measure that can change over the series.

$$b_t = \frac{2}{n-1}(M_t - M_t') \tag{5.10}$$

Finally, Equation 5.11 is used to make the forecast m periods into the future.

$$\hat{y}_{t+p} = a_t + b_{tp} \tag{5.11}$$

where

n = number of periods in the moving average

y_t = actual series value at time period t

p = number of periods ahead to be forecast

EXAMPLE 5.4

■ The Movie Video Store operates several videotape rental outlets in Denver, Colorado. The company is growing and needs to expand its inventory to accommodate the increasing demand for its services. The president of the company assigns Jill Ottenbreit to forecast rentals for the next month. Rental data for the last 15 weeks are available and are presented in Table 5.4. At first, Jill attempts to develop a forecast using a three-week moving average. The MSE for this model is 133. Since the data are obviously trended, she finds that her forecasts are consistently underestimating actual rentals. For this reason, she decides to try the double moving average. The results are presented in Table 5.4. To understand the forecast for week 16, the computations are presented next. Equation 5.7 is used to compute the three-week moving average (column 3).

TABLE 5.4 Double Moving Average Forecast for Movie Video Store: Example 5.4.

(1)	(2)	(3) Three-week Moving Average (2)	(4) Three-week Moving Average (3)	(5)	(6)	(7) Forecast $a + bp$	(8)
Time t	Weekly Sales y_t	M_t	M'_t	Value of a	Value of b	($p = 1$)	e_t
1	654	—	—	—	—	—	—
2	658	—	—	—	—	—	—
3	665	659	—	—	—	—	—
4	672	665	—	—	—	—	—
5	673	670	665	675	5	—	—
6	671	672	669	675	3	680	−9
7	693	679	674	684	5	678	15
8	694	686	679	693	7	689	5
9	701	696	687	705	9	700	1
10	703	699	694	704	5	714	−11
11	702	702	699	705	3	709	−7
12	710	705	702	708	3	708	2
13	712	708	705	711	3	711	1
14	711	711	708	714	3	714	−3
15	728	717	712	722	5	717	11
16	—	—	—	—		727	

MSE = 63.7.

$$\hat{y}_{15+1} = \frac{y_{15} + y_{15-1} + \cdots + y_{15-3+1}}{3}$$

$$\hat{y}_{16} = \frac{728 + 711 + 712}{3} = 717$$

Let $M_t = 717$. Then Equation 5.8 is used to compute the second three-week moving average (column 4).

$$M'_{15} = \frac{M_{15} + M_{15-1} + \cdots + M_{15-3+1}}{3}$$

$$= \frac{717 + 711 + 708}{3} = 712$$

Equation 5.9 is used to compute the difference between the two moving averages (column 5).

$$a_{15} = 2M_{15} - M'_{15} = 2(717) - 712 = 722$$

Equation 5.10 adjusts the slope (column 6).

$$b_{15} = \frac{2}{3-1}(M_{15} - M'_{15}) = \frac{2}{2}(717 - 712) = 5$$

Equation 5.11 is used to make the forecast one period into the future (column 7).

$$\hat{y}_{15+1} = a_{15} + b_{15}(1) = 722 + 5 = 727$$

The forecast four weeks into the future is

$$\hat{y}_{15+4} = a_{15} + b_{15}(4) = 722 + 5(4) = 742$$

Note that the MSE has been reduced from 133 to 63.7. ∎

It seems reasonable that more recent observations are likely to contain more important information. A technique is introduced in the next section that gives more emphasis to the most recent observations.

EXPONENTIAL-SMOOTHING METHODS

Exponential smoothing is a procedure for continually revising an estimate in the light of more recent experiences. This method is based on averaging (smoothing) past values of a series in a decreasing (exponential) manner. The observations are weighted, with more weight being given to the more recent observations. The weights used are α for the most recent observation, $\alpha(1 - \alpha)$ for the next most recent, $\alpha(1 - \alpha)^2$ for the next, and so forth.

In smoothed form, the new forecast (for time $t + 1$) may be thought of as a weighted average of the new observation (at time t) and the old forecast (for time t). The weight α is given to the newly observed value, and weight $1 - \alpha$ is given to the old forecast, assuming that $0 < \alpha < 1$. Thus

New forecast = $\alpha \times$ (new observation) + $(1 - \alpha) \times$ (old forecast)

More formally, the exponential smoothing equation is

$$\hat{y}_{t+1} = \alpha y_t + (1 - \alpha)\hat{y}_t \qquad \textbf{(5.12)}$$

where

$\hat{y}_{t+1}$ = new smoothed value or the forecast value for next period
α = smoothing constant $(0 < \alpha < 1)$
y_t = new observation or actual value of series in period t
$\hat{y}_t$ = old smoothed value or average experience of series smoothed to period $t - 1$

In an effort to better interpret alpha, Equation 5.12 is written as

$$\begin{aligned}
\hat{y}_{t+1} &= \alpha y_t + (1 - \alpha)\hat{y}_t \\
&= \alpha y_t + \hat{y}_t - \alpha\hat{y}_t \\
&= \hat{y}_t + \alpha(y_t - \hat{y}_t)
\end{aligned}$$

TABLE 5.5 Comparison of Smoothing Constants.

Time Period	$\alpha = .1$ Calculations	Weight	$\alpha = .6$ Calculations	Weight
t		.100		.600
$t-1$	$.9 \times .1$	.090	$.4 \times .6$	.240
$t-2$	$.9 \times .9 \times .1$	.081	$.4 \times .4 \times .6$	.096
$t-3$	$.9 \times .9 \times .9 \times .1$	.073	$.4 \times .4 \times .4 \times .6$	.038
$t-4$	$.9 \times .9 \times .9 \times .9 \times .1$	.066	$.4 \times .4 \times .4 \times .4 \times .6$	.015
All others		.590		.011
	Totals	1.000		1.000

Exponential smoothing is simply the old forecast ($\hat{y}_t$) plus alpha times the error ($y_t - \hat{y}_t$) in the old forecast.

> *Exponential smoothing* is a procedure for continually revising a forecast in the light of more recent experience.

The smoothing constant α serves as the weighting factor. The actual value of α determines the extent to which the most current observation is to influence the forecast value. When α is close to 1, the new forecast will include a substantial adjustment for any error that occurred in the preceding forecast. Conversely, when α is close to 0, the new forecast will be very similar to the old one. Think of $\hat{y}_t$ as a weighted average of all past observations with weights that decrease exponentially with the age of the data. The speed at which past values lose their importance depends on the value of α as demonstrated in Table 5.5.

The value assigned α is the key to the analysis. If it is desired that predictions be stable and random variations smoothed, a small α is required. If a rapid response to a real change in the pattern of observations is desired, a larger value of α is appropriate. One method of estimating α is an iterative procedure that minimizes the mean square error (MSE) calculated in Equation 4.6. Forecasts are computed for α equal to .1, .2, ..., .9, and the sum of the squared forecast errors is computed for each. The value of α producing the smallest error is chosen for use in generating future forecasts.

EXAMPLE 5.5

■ The exponential-smoothing technique is demonstrated in Table 5.6 for the Acme Tool Company for the years 1985 to 1990, using smoothing constants of .1 and .6. The data for 1991 will be used as the test part to help evaluate which model performs better. The exponentially smoothed series is computed by initially setting $\hat{y}_1$ equal to 500. If earlier data are available, it might be possible to use them to develop a

TABLE 5.6 Exponentially Smoothed Values for Example 5.5: Acme Tool Company Sales.

Time Period	Actual Value, y_t	Smoothed Value, $\hat{y}_t(\alpha = .1)$		Forecast Error, e_t		Smoothed Value, $\hat{y}_t(\alpha = .6)$	Forecast Error, e_t
1	500	500		—			—
2	350	500		−150		500	−150
3	250	485	(1)	−235	(3)	410	−160
4	400	462	(2)	−62		314	+86
5	450	455		−5		366	+84
6	350	455		−105		416	−66
7	200	444		−244		376	−176
8	300	420		−120		270	+30
9	350	408		−58		288	+62
10	200	402		−202		325	−125
11	150	382		−232		250	−100
12	400	359		+41		190	+210
13	550	363		+187		316	+234
14	350	382		−32		456	−106
15	250	378		−128		392	−142
16	550	366		+184		307	+243
17	550	384		+166		453	+97
18	400	401		−1		511	−121
19	350	401		−51		444	−96
20	600	395		+205		388	+212
21	750	416		+334		515	+235
22	500	449		+51		656	−156
23	400	454		−54		562	−12
24	650	449		+201		465	+185
25		469	(4)			576	(4)

The numbers in parentheses refer to the steps given in the text.

smoothed series up to 1985 and use this experience as the initial value for the smoothed series. The computations leading to the forecast for period 3 are demonstrated below.[1]

Step 1 $\hat{y}_{t+1} = \alpha y_t + (1 - \alpha)\hat{y}_t$

$\hat{y}_{2+1} = \alpha y_2 + (1 - \alpha)\hat{y}_2$

$\hat{y}_3 = .1(350) + (1 - .1)500 = 485$

Step 2 The forecast for period 4 is

$\hat{y}_4 = .1(250) + .9(485) = 462$

---

[1] Steps 1 to 4 are shown by the numbers in parentheses in Table 5.6.

Step 3 The error in this forecast is

$$e_3 = 250 - 485 = -235$$

Step 4 The forecast sales for the first quarter of 1991 using smoothing constants of .1 and .6 are 469 and 576, respectively. ∎

Note how stable the smoothed values are for the .1 smoothing constant. On the basis of minimizing the mean square error (MSE), the .6 smoothing constant is better. If the mean absolute percentage error (MAPE) is compared, the .6 smoothing constant is also better. When the forecasts for each smoothing constant are compared to actual sales for first quarter 1991, the .6 smoothing constant also appears to do a better job.

$$\alpha = .1 \qquad MSE = 25{,}317 \qquad MAPE = 40.61\% \qquad MPE = -20.81\%$$
$$\alpha = .6 \qquad MSE = 23{,}216 \qquad MAPE = 38.14\% \qquad MPE = -10.33\%$$
$$\alpha = .34 \qquad MSE = 21{,}421 \qquad MAPE = 35.41\% \qquad MPE = -11.50\%$$

When a computer program that chooses the smoothing constant automatically is used, α equals .34. The MSE is reduced to 21,421, and the MAPE equals 35.41%. The mean percentage error (MPE), sometimes referred to as *bias,* is -11.50% for this model, which means that the predictions based on this model are consistently too large. The possibility of a trend or seasonal variation in the data needs to be investigated.

Another factor that affects the value of subsequent forecasts is the choice of the initial value of $\hat{y}_t$. Table 5.6 shows that y_t was used as the initial value of $\hat{y}_t$ in Example 5.5:

$$\hat{y}_t = y_t$$
$$\hat{y}_1 = 500$$

This choice tends to give y_1 too much weight in later forecasts. Fortunately, the influence of the initial forecast diminishes greatly as t increases.

Another approach to initializing y_t is to average the first n observations. The smoothing column then begins with

$$\hat{y}_t = \bar{y} = \frac{\sum\limits_{t=1}^{n} y_t}{n}$$

If n is chosen to equal 4, then the initial value for Example 5.5 is

$$\hat{y}_t = \bar{y} = \frac{\sum\limits_{t=1}^{4} y_t}{n} = \frac{500 + 350 + 250 + 400}{4} = 375$$

Tracking

Since exponential smoothing assumes the continuation of some historical pattern into the future, it is useful to develop a measure that can be used to determine when the basic pattern has changed. A *tracking signal* is the most common such measure. A tracking signal involves computing some measure of the error over time and setting limits so that, when the error goes outside those limits, the forecaster is alerted.

> A *tracking signal* involves computing some measure of the error over time and setting limits so that, when the cumulative error goes outside those limits, the forecaster is alerted.

For example, a tracking signal can be used to determine when the size of alpha used in an exponential smoothing technique should be changed. Since a large number of items are usually being forecast, common practice is to continue with the same alpha size for many periods before attempting to determine if a revision is necessary. Unfortunately, the simplicity of using an established exponential smoothing model is a strong motivator for not making a change. But at some point it is necessary to update alpha. When the model produces forecasts containing a great deal of error, a change is appropriate.

A tracking system provides a method of monitoring the need for change. Such a system contains a range of permissible variations of the forecast from actual values. As long as a forecast falls within this range, no change in alpha is necessary. However, if a forecast falls outside the range, the system signals a need to update alpha.

For instance, if things are going well, the forecasting technique should over- and underestimate equally often. A tracking signal based on this rationale can be developed.

Let U equal the number of underestimates out of the last n forecasts. In other words, U is the number of errors out of the last n that are positive. If the process is in control, the expected value of U is $n/2$; but sampling variability is involved, so values close to $n/2$ would not be unusual. On the other hand, values that are not close to $n/2$ would indicate that the technique is producing biased forecasts.

EXAMPLE 5.5

■ Suppose that the Acme Tool Company has decided to use the exponential smoothing technique with alpha equal to .1, as shown in Example 5.4. If the process is in control and the analyst decides to monitor the last 10 error values, U has an expected value of 5. Actually, values of 2, 3, 4, 6, 7, or 8 would not be unduly alarming. However, values of 0, 1, 9, or 10 would be of concern since the probability of obtaining such values by chance alone would be .024 (binomial distribution).

If $2 \leq U \leq 8$, then the process is in control.
If $U < 2$ or $U > 8$, then the process is out of control.

Assume that out of the next ten forecasts using this technique only one has a positive error. Since the probability of obtaining only one positive error out of ten is quite low, .011, the process is considered to be out of control (overestimating), and the value of alpha should be changed. ∎

Another way of tracking a forecasting technique is to determine a range that should contain the forecasting errors. This can be accomplished by utilizing the MSE that was established when the optimal-size alpha was determined. If the exponential smoothing technique is reasonably accurate, the forecast error should be normally distributed about a mean of zero. Under this condition, there is a 95% chance that the actual observation will fall within approximately two standard deviations of the forecast. The setting of a 95% confidence interval for tracking systems is generally sufficient. Example 5.6 illustrates this approach.

EXAMPLE 5.6

∎ In the Acme Tool Company example, the optimal alpha was determined to be $\alpha = .34$ with MSE = 21,421. The standard deviation of the forecast error equals $\sqrt{\text{MSE}}$, or $\sqrt{21,421} = 146.4$. The forecast error should be normally distributed about a mean of zero. Under this condition, there is a 95% chance that the actual observation will fall within approximately two standard deviations of the forecast or

$$\pm 1.96\sqrt{\text{MSE}} = \pm 1.96\sqrt{21,421} = \pm 1.96(146.4) = \pm 286.9$$

For the example, therefore, the permissible variation is 286.9. If for any future forecast the error is greater than 286.9, there is reason to believe that a new optimal alpha should be calculated. ∎

The preceding discussion on tracking signals also applies to the smoothing methods yet to be discussed in the rest of the chapter.

Note that an assumption of the single exponential smoothing technique is that the data are stationary. Example 5.7 shows what happens when the exponential smoothing technique is used with trended data. Whenever a significant trend exists, single exponential smoothing will lag behind the actual time series forecast values over time. Examination of the error column in Table 5.7 shows that every entry is positive, signifying that the forecasts do not catch up to the trend. The double exponential smoothing technique, which is designed to handle trended data, is introduced next.

TABLE 5.7 Weekly Rentals for the Movie Video Store: Example 5.7.

	Weekly Units Rented		
t	y_t	y_{t+1}	e_t
1	654	654	—
2	658	654	4.0
3	665	655.6	9.4
4	672	659.4	12.6
5	673	664.4	8.6
6	671	667.8	3.2
7	693	669.1	23.9
8	694	678.7	15.3
9	701	684.8	16.2
10	703	691.3	11.7
11	702	696.0	6.0
12	710	698.4	11.6
13	712	703.0	9.0
14	711	706.6	4.4
15	728	708.4	19.6
16	—	716.2	

MSE = 147.3.

Double Exponential Smoothing

The double exponential smoothing technique, often referred to as *Brown's method,* is used for forecasting time series data that have a linear trend. The basic concepts are similar to those of double moving averages. The double exponential smoothing technique is summarized using Equations 5.13 through 5.17.

Because the smoothed series values themselves are not the forecasts, the updating equations are easier to understand if the following notation is adopted.

A_t = exponentially smoothed value of y_t at time t

A_t' = double exponentially smoothed value of y_t at time t

The simple exponentially smoothed value is now computed using Equation 5.13.

$$A_t = \alpha y_t + (1 - \alpha) A_{t-1} \tag{5.13}$$

Equation 5.14 is used to compute the double exponentially smoothed value.

$$A'_t = \alpha A_t + (1 - \alpha) A'_{t-1} \qquad \qquad \textbf{(5.14)}$$

Equation 5.15 is used to compute the difference between the exponentially smoothed values.

$$a_t = 2A_t - A'_t \qquad \qquad \textbf{(5.15)}$$

Equation 5.16 is an additional adjustment factor, which is similar to a slope measurement that can change over the series

$$b_t = \frac{\alpha}{1 - \alpha} (A_t - A'_t) \qquad \qquad \textbf{(5.16)}$$

Finally, Equation 5.17 is used to make the forecast p periods into the future.

$$\hat{y}_{t+p} = a_t + b_t p \qquad \qquad \textbf{(5.17)}$$

where

α = smoothing constant

y_t = actual series value at time period t

p = the number of periods ahead to be forecast

EXAMPLE 5.7

■ This example refers to Example 5.4, where the Movie Video Store was attempting to forecast rentals for the next month. The rental data for the last 15 weeks were presented in Table 5.4. Jill has attempted to develop a forecast using a three-week moving average and a double moving average. Now she has decided to try exponential smoothing. She uses a smoothing constant of .4. The results are presented in Table 5.7. Since the data are obviously trended, Jill finds that her forecasts are always underestimating actual rentals. For this reason, she decides to try double exponential smoothing. The computer program that she uses chooses the best smoothing constant automatically by minimizing MSE. The results are presented in Table 5.8 for an alpha of .4. For us to understand the forecast for week 16, the computations are presented next.

Equation 5.13 is used to compute the simple exponentially smoothed value (column 3).

$$\begin{aligned} A_{15} &= \alpha y_{15} + (1 - \alpha) A_{15-1} \\ &= .4(728) + (1 - .4)(708.4) = 716.2 \end{aligned}$$

Equation 5.14 is used to compute the double exponential smoothing value (column 4).

$$\begin{aligned} A'_{15} &= A_{15} + (1 - \alpha) A'_{15-1} \\ &= .4(716.2) + (1 - .4)(703.7) = 708.7 \end{aligned}$$

TABLE 5.8 Double Exponential Smoothing Forecast for Movie Video Store, Brown's Technique: Example 5.7.

(1) Time t	(2) Weekly Sales y_t	(3) A_t	(4) A'_t	(5) Value of a	(6) Value of b	(7) Forecast $a + bp$ ($p=1$)	(8) e_t
1	654	654	654	654	0	654	—
2	658	655.6	654.6	656.6	.7	654	4.0
3	665	659.4	656.5	662.3	1.9	657.3	7.7
4	672	664.4	659.7	669.1	3.1	664.2	7.8
5	673	667.8	662.9	672.7	3.3	672.2	0.8
6	671	669.1	665.4	672.8	2.5	676.0	−5.0
7	693	678.7	670.7	686.7	5.3	675.3	17.7
8	694	684.8	676.3	693.3	5.7	692.0	2.0
9	701	691.3	682.3	700.3	6.0	699.0	2.0
10	703	696.0	687.8	704.2	5.5	706.3	−3.3
11	702	698.4	692.0	704.8	4.3	709.7	−7.7
12	710	703.0	696.4	709.6	4.4	709.1	0.9
13	712	706.6	700.5	712.7	4.1	714.0	−2.0
14	711	708.4	703.7	713.1	3.1	716.8	−5.8
15	728	716.2	708.7	723.7	5.0	716.2	11.8
16	—	—	—	—		728.7	

MSE = 39.82.

Equation 5.15 is used to compute the difference between the exponentially smoothed values (column 5).

$$a_{15} = 2A_{15} - A'_{15}$$
$$= 2(716.2) - 708.7 = 723.7$$

Equation 5.16 is an additional adjustment factor, which is similar to a slope measure that can change over the series (column 6).

$$b_{15} = \frac{\alpha}{1-\alpha}(A_{15} - A'_{15})$$
$$= \frac{.4}{.6}(716.2 - 708.7) = 5.0$$

Finally, Equation 5.17 is used to make the forecast one period into the future (column 7).

$$\hat{y}_{15+1} = a_{15} + b_{15}(1) = 723.7 + 5.0(1) = 728.7$$

The forecast four weeks into the future is

$$\hat{y}_{15+4} = a_{15} + b_{15}(4) = 723.7 + 5(4) = 743.7$$

Jill thinks that she has found a good forecasting technique. The MSE has been reduced to 39.82. As a final check, she decides to compute the autocorrelation coefficients for the residuals and test to determine whether any of them are significantly different from zero. The null and alternative hypotheses to test whether the autocorrelation coefficient for a particular time lag is significantly different from zero are

$$H_0: \quad \rho_k = 0$$

$$H_1: \quad \rho_k \neq 0$$

Since $n = 14$, the standard error (standard deviation of the sampling distribution of autocorrelation coefficients) is $1/\sqrt{14} = .267$. If the null hypothesis is tested at the .05 significance level, the correct standard normal z value is 1.96 and the critical value is $1.96(.267) = .524$. The decision rule is as follows:

If an autocorrelation coefficient is less than $-.524$ or greater than .524, reject the null hypothesis; otherwise, accept it (reject H_0 if $r_k < -.524$ or $r_k > .524$).

The MINITAB commands to run the autocorrelations for the residuals of Table 5.8 are as follows:

```
MTB > SET C1
DATA> 4.0 7.7 7.8 .8 -5 17.7 2 2 -3.3 -7.7 .9 -2 -5.8 11.8
DATA> END
MTB > ACF C1
```

```
ACF of C1

          -1.0 -0.8 -0.6 -0.4 -0.2  0.0  0.2  0.4  0.6  0.8  1.0 +---
            -+----+----+----+----+----+----+----+----+----+----+
    1  -0.062                           XXX
    2  -0.059                            XX
    3   0.080                           XXX
    4  -0.139                          XXXX
    5   0.051                            XX
    6  -0.112                          XXXX
    7  -0.271                      XXXXXXXX
    8   0.212                            XXXXXX
    9  -0.160                         XXXXX
   10  -0.126                         XXXX
   11   0.003                            X
   12   0.058                            XX
```

```
MTB > STOP
```

Twelve time lags are checked, and all the autocorrelation coefficients lie within the appropriate limits. Jill concludes that this series of residuals is random. ■

As with single exponential smoothing, choosing alpha is a problem. Alpha is selected by minimizing the MSE between the actual values and forecasts of these values utilizing the model. Some computer programs determine this value automatically. Otherwise, the process becomes one of trial and error.

A problem when using double exponential smoothing is the determination of the initial values for the smoothed series and the trend adjustment. In Example 5.7, the initial actual value of the series was used for A_t and A_t'. The problem is that this procedure assumes that there is no trend present and will result in error. It will tend to underestimate a positive trend.

The initial values for the trend's slope and intercept can be computed using the least-squares procedure, which will be discussed in Chapter 6. The estimates generated for period $t = 0$ are $a_0 = 650.3$ and $b_0 = 4.9$. The initial values are established using Equations 5.18 and 5.19.

$$A_0 = a_0 - \frac{1 - \alpha}{\alpha} b_0 \tag{5.18}$$

$$A_0' = a_0 - 2 \frac{1 - \alpha}{\alpha} b_0 \tag{5.19}$$

EXAMPLE 5.8

■ Jill computed the appropriate initial values for Example 5.7 using Equations 5.18 and 5.19.

$$A_0 = a_0 - \frac{1 - \alpha}{\alpha} b_0 = 650.3 - \frac{.6}{.4} 4.9 = 642.9$$

$$A_0' = a_0 - 2 \frac{1 - \alpha}{\alpha} b_0 = 650.3 - 2 \frac{.6}{.4} 4.9 = 635.6$$

Jill begins the smoothing using these values. Column 3 is

$$A_1 = \alpha y_1 + (1 - \alpha) A_{1-1}$$
$$= .4(654) + (1 - .4)(642.9) = 647.3$$

Column 4 is

$$A_1' = \alpha A_1 + (1 - \alpha) A_{1-1}'$$
$$= .4(647.3) + (1 - .4)(635.6) = 640.3$$

Column 5 is

$$a_1 = 2A_1 - A_1'$$
$$= 2(647.3) - 640.3 = 654.3$$

Column 6 is

$$b_1 = \frac{\alpha}{1-\alpha}(A_1 - A_1')$$

$$= \frac{.4}{.6}(647.3 - 640.3) = 4.7$$

Column 7 is

$$y_{1+1} = a_1 + b_1(1) = 654.3 + 4.7(1) = 659 \qquad \blacksquare$$

Exponential Smoothing Adjusted for Trend: Holt's Method

Another technique frequently used to handle a linear trend is called *Holt's two-parameter method*. Holt's technique smooths the trend and slope directly by using different smoothing constants for each. In Brown's approach, only one smoothing constant is used, and the estimated trend values are very sensitive to random influences. Holt's technique gives more flexibility in selecting the rates at which the trend and slope are tracked.

The three equations used in this technique are as follows:

1. The exponentially smoothed series:

$$A_t = \alpha y_t + (1 - \alpha)(A_{t-1} + T_{t-1}) \qquad (5.20)$$

2. The trend estimate:

$$T_t = \beta(A_t - A_{t-1}) + (1 - \beta)T_{t-1} \qquad (5.21)$$

3. Forecast p periods into the future:

$$\hat{y}_{t+p} = A_t + pT_t \qquad (5.22)$$

where

A_t = new smoothed value

α = smoothing constant for the data $(0 \leqslant \alpha \leqslant 1)$

y_t = new observation or actual value of series in period t

β = smoothing constant for trend estimate $(0 \leqslant \beta \leqslant 1)$

T_t = trend estimate

p = periods to be forecast into future

$\hat{y}_{t+p}$ = forecast for p periods into the future

The first equation, 5.20, is very similar to the original, single exponential smoothing equation 5.12, except that a term has been added for the trend (T_t). The trend estimate is calculated by taking the difference between two successive exponential smoothing values $(A_t - A_{t-1})$. Since the successive values have been smoothed for randomness, their difference constitutes an estimate of the trend in the data.

A second smoothing constant, β, is used to smooth the trend estimate. Equation 5.21 shows that the estimate of the trend $(A_t - A_{t-1})$ is multiplied by β and then added to the old estimate of the trend (T_t), multiplied by $(1 - \beta)$. Equation 5.21 is similar to Equation 5.20, except that the smoothing is done for the trend rather than the actual data. The result of Equation 5.21 is a smoothed trend excluding any randomness.

Equation 5.22 shows the forecast for p periods into the future. The trend estimate (T_t) is multiplied by the number of periods to be forecast (p), and then the product is added to the current level of the data-smoothed A_t to eliminate randomness.

EXAMPLE 5.9

■ Table 5.9 illustrates exponential smoothing adjusted for trend for the Acme Tool Company data. To begin the computations, two estimated initial values are needed, namely, the initial smoothed value and the initial trend value. The initial smoothed value is usually estimated by averaging a few past observations of the series. The initial trend value is estimated by using the slope of the trend equation obtained from past data. If past data are not available, zero is used as the initial estimate.

The value for α is similar to the one for the smoothing model (Equation 5.23), and it smooths the data to eliminate randomness. The smoothing constant β is like α except that it smooths the trend in the data. Both smoothing constants remove randomness by weighting past values.

The technique is demonstrated in Table 5.9 for $\alpha = .3$ and $\beta = .1$. The computations leading to the forecast for period 3 are shown next.

Step 1 Update the exponentially smoothed series:

$$A_t = \alpha y_t + (1 - \alpha)(A_{t-1} + T_{t-1})$$
$$A_2 = .3y_2 + (1 - .3)(A_{2-1} + T_{2-1})$$
$$= .3(350) + .7(500 + 0) = 455$$

Step 2 Update the trend estimate:

$$T_t = \beta(A_t - A_{t-1}) + (1 - \beta)T_{t-1}$$
$$T_2 = .1(A_2 - A_{2-1}) + (1 - .1)T_{2-1}$$
$$= .1(455 - 500) + .9(0) = -4.5$$

Step 3 Forecast one period into the future:

$$\hat{y}_{t+p} = A_t + pT_t$$
$$\hat{y}_{2+1} = A_2 + pT_2$$
$$\hat{y}_3 = 455 + (-4.5) = 450.5$$

TABLE 5.9 Exponentially Smoothed Forecast for Acme Tool Company Sales, Holt's Technique: Example 5.9.

(1) t	(2) y_t	(3) A_t	(4) T_t	(5) $\hat{y}_t$	(6) e_t
1	500	500.0	0	500	0
2	350	455.0	−4.5	500	−150
3	250	390.4	−10.5	450.5	−200.5
4	400	385.9	−9.9	379.8	20.2
5	450	398.2	−7.7	376.0	74.0
6	350	378.3	−8.9	390.5	−40.5
7	200	318.6	−14.0	369.4	−169.4
8	300	303.2	−14.1	304.6	−4.6
9	350	307.4	−12.3	289.1	60.9
10	200	266.6	−15.2	295.1	−95.0
11	150	221.0	−18.2	251.4	−101.4
12	400	262.0	−12.3	202.8	197.2
13	550	339.8	−3.3	249.7	300.3
14	350	340.6	−2.9	336.5	13.5
15	250	311.4	−5.5	337.7	−87.7
16	550	379.1	1.8	305.9	244.1
17	550	431.7	6.9	381.0	169.0
18	400	427.0	5.7	438.6	−38.6
19	350	407.9	3.3	432.7	−82.7
20	600	467.8	8.9	411.2	188.8
21	750	558.7	17.1	476.8	273.2
22	500	553.1	14.8	575.9	−75.9
23	400	517.6	9.8	567.9	−167.9
24	650	564.2	13.5	527.4	122.6
25				577.7	

MSE = 21,448.3.

Step 4 Determine the forecast error:

$$e_t = y_t - \hat{y}_t$$
$$e_3 = y_3 - \hat{y}_3 = 250 - 450.5 = -200.5$$

The forecast for period 25 is computed:

Step 1 Update the exponentially smoothed series:

$$A_{24} = .3y_{24} + (1 - .3)(A_{24-1} + T_{24-1})$$
$$A_2 = .3(650) + .7(517.6 + 9.8) = 564.2$$

Step 2 Update the trend estimate:

$$T_{24} = .1(A_{24} - A_{24-1}) + (1 - .1)T_{24-1}$$
$$= .1(564.2 - 517.6) + .9(9.8) = 13.5$$

Step 3 Forecast one period into the future:

$$\hat{y}_{24+1} = A_{24} + pT_{24}$$

$$\hat{y}_{25} = 564.2 + (13.5) = 577.7$$ ■

On the basis of minimizing the mean square error (MSE), this model is not better than the simple smoothing model that used a smoothing constant of .34. If the mean absolute percentage errors (MAPEs) are compared, the Holt model is better. When the forecasts for the actual sales for first quarter 1991 are compared, the Holt model appears to do a better job. The mean percentage error (MPE) also is smaller for the Holt model.

$\alpha = .34$ $\text{MSE} = 21{,}421$ $\text{MAPE} = 35.41\%$ $\text{MPE} = -11.50\%$

$\left.\begin{array}{l}\alpha = .30\\ \beta = .10\end{array}\right\}$ $\text{MSE} = 22{,}380$ $\text{MAPE} = 33.48\%$ $\text{MPE} = -6.65\%$

$\left.\begin{array}{l}\alpha = .30\\ \beta = .20\end{array}\right\}$ $\text{MSE} = 22{,}349$ $\text{MAPE} = 33.74\%$ $\text{MPE} = -6.22\%$

When a computer program that chooses the smoothing constants automatically is used, α equals .3 and β equals .2. The MSE is reduced slightly to 22,349, and the MAPE is about the same, 33.74%. The mean percentage error (MPE) is -6.22%, which means that the predictions based on this model are still consistently large. The possibility of seasonal variation in the data needs to be investigated.

Exponential Smoothing Adjusted for Trend and Seasonal Variation: Winter's Model

Examination of the data for Acme Tool Company in Table 5.1 indicates that sales are consistently higher during the first and fourth quarters and lower during the third quarter. A seasonal pattern appears to exist. Winter's three-parameter linear and seasonal exponential-smoothing model, an extension of Holt's model, might reduce forecast error. One additional equation is used to estimate seasonality. This seasonality estimate is given as a seasonal index, and it is calculated with Equation 5.25. Equation 5.25 shows that the estimate of the seasonal index (y_t/A_t) is multiplied by γ and then added to the old seasonal estimate (S_{t-L}), multiplied by $(1 - \gamma)$. The reason y_t is divided by A_t is to express the value as an index rather than in absolute terms, so that it can be averaged with the seasonal index smoothed to period $t - 1$.

The four equations used in Winter's model are as follows:

1. The exponentially smoothed series:

$$A_t = \alpha \, \frac{y_t}{S_{t-L}} + (1 - \alpha)(A_{t-1} + T_{t-1}) \qquad \textbf{(5.23)}$$

2. The trend estimate:

$$T_t = \beta(A_t - A_{t-1}) + (1 - \beta)T_{t-1} \tag{5.24}$$

3. The seasonality estimate:

$$S_t = \gamma \frac{y_t}{A_t} + (1 - \gamma)S_{t-L} \tag{5.25}$$

4. Forecast p periods into the future:

$$\hat{y}_{t+p} = (A_t + pT_t)S_{t-L+p} \tag{5.26}$$

where

A_t = new smoothed value

α = smoothing constant $(0 < \alpha < 1)$

y_t = new observation or actual value of series in period t

β = smoothing constant for trend estimate $(0 < \beta < 1)$

T_t = trend estimate

γ = smoothing constant for seasonality estimate $(0 < \gamma < 1)$

S_t = seasonal estimate

p = periods to be forecast into future

L = length of seasonality

$\hat{y}_{t+p}$ = forecast for p periods into the future

Equation 5.23 updates the smoothed series. A slight difference in this equation distinguishes it from the corresponding one in Holt's model, equation 5.20. In equation 5.23, y_t is divided by S_{t-L}, which adjusts y_t for seasonality, thus removing the seasonal effects that might exist in the original data y_t.

After the seasonality estimate and trend estimate have been smoothed in equations 5.24 and 5.25, a forecast is obtained with equation 5.26. It is almost the same as the corresponding formula, equation 5.22, used to obtain a forecast in Holt's model. The difference is that this estimate for future period, $t + p$, is multiplied by S_{t-L+p}. This seasonal index is the last one available and is therefore used to adjust the forecast for seasonality.

EXAMPLE 5.10

■ Table 5.10 illustrates exponential smoothing adjusted for trend and seasonality for the Acme Tool Company data. To begin the computations, initial value estimates are needed for the initial smoothed value, the initial trend estimate, and each of the four seasonality estimates. The initial smoothed value can be estimated by averaging a few past values of the series. The initial trend value can be estimated by using the slope of the trend equation obtained from past data. The seasonality estimates can be computed for past data using time series decomposition (Chapter 8).

TABLE 5.10 Exponentially Smoothed Forecast for Acme Tool Company Sales, Winter's Technique: Example 5.10.

(1)	(2)	(3)	(4)	(5)	(6)	(7)
t	y_t	A_t	T_t	S_t	$\hat{y}_{t+p}$	e_t
1	500	500.0	0.0	1.00	500.0	0.0
2	350	440.0	−6.0	0.94	500.0	−150.0
3	250	360.4	−13.4	0.91	500.0	−250.0
4	400	368.2	−11.2	1.03	500.0	−100.0
5	450	394.2	−7.5	1.04	357.0	93.0
6	350	381.2	−8.1	0.93	362.9	−12.9
7	200	311.9	−14.2	0.83	338.8	−138.8
8	300	295.6	−14.4	1.02	305.5	−5.5
9	350	303.0	−12.2	1.08	293.2	56.8
10	200	260.3	−15.3	0.88	271.2	−71.2
11	150	219.5	−17.8	0.78	202.9	−52.9
12	400	277.5	−10.2	1.15	206.2	193.8
13	550	364.7	−0.5	1.21	287.6	262.4
14	350	377.0	0.8	0.90	321.7	28.3
15	250	354.1	−1.6	0.76	296.5	−46.5
16	550	403.1	3.5	1.21	404.9	145.1
17	550	426.4	5.5	1.23	490.3	59.7
18	400	437.5	6.0	0.90	387.3	12.7
19	350	450.1	6.7	0.77	337.6	12.4
20	600	471.9	8.2	1.23	554.1	45.9
21	750	531.8	13.4	1.28	591.0	159.0
22	500	548.8	13.7	0.90	491.7	8.3
23	400	546.4	12.1	0.76	430.9	−30.9
24	650	546.4	10.9	1.22	687.3	−37.3
25					751.9	
26					546.2	
27					449.6	
28					718.8	

MSE = 12,431.5.

The value for α is similar to the one for the simple smoothing model (Equation 5.23), and it smooths the data to eliminate randomness. The smoothing constant β is like alpha except that it smooths the trend in the data. The smoothing constant γ is like alpha and beta except that it smooths the seasonality in the data.

The Winter's technique is demonstrated in Table 5.10 for $\alpha = .4$, $\beta = .1$, $\gamma = .3$. Since no past data are available, 500 is used as the initial smoothed value, 0 is used as the initial trend estimate, and 1.0 is used as the initial seasonality estimate. The computations leading to the updated smoothed values for period 2 are shown next.

Step 1 The exponentially smoothed series:

$$A_t = \alpha \, \frac{y_t}{S_{t-L}} + (1 - \alpha)(A_{t-1} + T_{t-1})$$

$$A_2 = .4 \frac{y_2}{1.0} + (1 - .4)(A_{2-1} + T_{2-1})$$

$$= .4 \frac{350}{1.0} + (1 - .4)(500 + 0) = 140 + 300 = 440$$

Step 2 The trend estimate:

$$T_t = \beta(A_t - A_{t-1}) + (1 - \beta)T_{t-1}$$
$$T_2 = .1(A_2 - A_{2-1}) + (1 - .1)T_{2-1}$$
$$= .1(440 - 500) + (1 - .1)0 = -6 + 0 = -6$$

Step 3 The seasonality estimate:

$$S_t = \gamma \frac{y_t}{A_t} + (1 - \gamma)S_{t-L}$$

$$S_2 = .3 \frac{y_2}{A_2} + (1 - .3)1.0$$

$$= .3 \frac{350}{440} + (1 - .3)1.0 = .2386 + .7 = .9386$$

The computations leading to the forecast for period 6 are shown next.

Step 1 The exponentially smoothed series:

$$A_5 = .4 \frac{y_5}{S_{5-1}} + (1 - .4)(A_{5-1} + T_{5-1})$$

$$= .4 \frac{450}{1.0} + .6[368.4 + (-11.2)] = 394.189$$

Step 2 The trend estimate:

$$T_5 = .1(A_5 - A_{5-1}) + (1 - .1)T_{5-1}$$
$$= .1(394.189 - 368.2) + .9(-11.2) = -7.5$$

Step 3 The seasonality estimate:

$$S_5 = .3 \frac{y_5}{A_5} + (1 - .3)S_{5-4}$$

$$= .3 \frac{450}{394.2} + .7(1.0) = .3425 + .7 = 1.0425$$

Step 4 Forecast one period into the future:

$$\hat{y}_{t+p} = (A_t + pT_t)S_{t-L+p}$$
$$\hat{y}_{5+1} = (A_5 + pT_5)S_{5-4+1}$$
$$\hat{y}_6 = [394.2 + 1(-7.5)](.9386) = 362.9$$

On the basis of minimizing the MSE, the Winter's technique is better than both of the previous models. When the forecasts for the actual sales for the first quarter of 1991 are compared, the Winter's technique also appears to do a better job. The use of a computer program that automatically selects the best smoothing constants should decrease the MSE even further. ■

Exponential smoothing is a popular technique for short-run forecasting. Its major advantages are low cost and simplicity. When forecasts are needed for inventory systems containing thousands of items, smoothing methods are often the only acceptable approach.

Simple moving averages and exponential smoothing base forecasts on weighted averages of past measurements. The rationale is that past values contain information about what will occur in the future. Since past values include random fluctuations as well as information concerning the underlying pattern of a variable, an attempt is made to smooth these values. This approach assumes that extreme fluctuations represent randomness in a series of historical observations.

Moving averages involve computing the mean of a certain number of values of a variable. This average now becomes the forecast for the next period; then the process is repeated until a forecast is made for the desired future period. This approach assigns an equal weight to each past value. However, a convincing argument can be made for emphasizing the most recent values. Exponential smoothing is utilized because decreasing weight is assigned to the older observations. Both approaches involve a rule or set of rules that determine the weights.

APPLICATION TO MANAGEMENT

Forecasts are one of the most important inputs managers develop to aid them in the decision-making process. Virtually every important operating decision depends to some extent on a forecast. Inventory accumulation is based on forecast of expected demand; the production department has to schedule employment needs and raw material orders for the next month or two; the finance department must arrange short-term financing for the next quarter; the personnel department must determine hiring and layoff requirements. The list of forecasting applications is quite lengthy.

Executives are keenly aware of the importance of forecasting. Indeed, a great deal of time is spent studying trends in economic and political affairs and how events might affect demand for products and/or services. One issue of interest is the importance executives place on quantitative forecasting methods versus their own opinions. This issue is especially sensitive when events that have a significant impact on demand are involved. One problem with quantitative forecasting methods is that they depend on historical data. For this reason they are probably least effective in calling the turn that often results in sharply higher or lower demand. The computer has aided managers in automating sensitivity to sharp changes in demand through adaptive systems and causal models.

The naive methods are useful because of their relative simplicity. These simple methods tend to be less costly, easier to implement, and easier to understand. Frequently, the cost and complexity of more sophisticated models outweigh any gains in accuracy. For these reasons, small businesses find naive methods practical. Businesses without computers and/or personnel capable of handling statistical models also turn to naive methods. Business managers frequently face the need to prepare short-term forecasts for a number of different items. A typical example is the manager who must schedule production on the basis of some forecast of demand for several hundred different products in a product line. Finally, new businesses without lengthy historical databases find these approaches helpful.

The moving-average method does a good job of adjusting to shifts in patterns. It is economical to update, and it does not require much data storage. Because these advantages are somewhat offset by higher start-up costs, the moving-average methods are most frequently used when repeated forecasts are necessary.

Exponential smoothing is a popular technique whose strength lies in good short-term accuracy combined with quick low-cost updating. The technique is widely used when regular monthly or weekly forecasts are needed for a large number of items. Exponential smoothing is used when forecasts are needed for inventory systems containing thousands of items.

CHAPTER 5

GLOSSARY

Exponential smoothing   Exponential smoothing is a procedure for continually revising a forecast in the light of more recent experience.

Moving average   A moving average is obtained by finding the mean for a specified set of values and then using it to forecast the next period.

Simple average   A simple average is obtained by finding the mean for all the relevant values and then using this mean to forecast the next period.

Tracking signal   A tracking signal involves computing some measure of the error over time and setting limits so that, when the cumulative error goes outside those limits, the forecaster is alerted.

CHAPTER 5

KEY FORMULAS

Naive model $\hat{y}_{t+1} = y_t$ (5.1)

Naive trend model $\hat{y}_{t+1} = y_t + (y_t - y_{t-1})$ (5.2)

Naive rate of change model $\quad \hat{y}_{t+1} = y_t \dfrac{y_t}{y_{t-1}}$ $\qquad$ (5.3)

Naive seasonal model $\quad \hat{y}_{t+1} = y_{t-3}$ $\qquad$ (5.4)

Naive trend and seasonal model

$$\hat{y}_{t+1} = y_{t-3} + \frac{(y_t - y_{t-1}) + \cdots + (y_{t-3} - y_{t-4})}{4} \qquad (5.5)$$

Simple average $\quad \hat{y}_{t+1} = \dfrac{\displaystyle\sum_{t=1}^{n} y_t}{n}$ $\qquad$ (5.6)

Moving average

$$\hat{y}_{t+1} = \frac{y_t + y_{t-1} + y_{t-2} + \cdots + y_{t-n+1}}{n} \qquad (5.7)$$

Double moving average

$$M'_t = \frac{M_t + M_{t-1} + M_{t-2} + \cdots + M_{t-n+1}}{n} \qquad (5.8)$$

$$a_t = 2M_t - M'_t \qquad (5.9)$$

$$b_t = \frac{2}{n-1}(M_t - M'_t) \qquad (5.10)$$

$$\hat{y}_{t+p} = a_t + b_t p \qquad (5.11)$$

Exponential smoothing $\quad \hat{y}_{t+1} = \alpha y_t + (1-\alpha)\hat{y}_t$ $\qquad$ (5.12)

Double exponential smoothing

$$A_t = \alpha y_t + (1-\alpha)A_{t-1} \qquad (5.13)$$

$$A'_t = \alpha A_t + (1-\alpha)A'_{t-1} \qquad (5.14)$$

$$a_t = 2A_t - A'_t \qquad (5.15)$$

$$b_t = \frac{\alpha}{1-\alpha}(A_t - A'_t) \qquad (5.16)$$

$$\hat{y}_{t+p} = a_t + b_t p \qquad (5.17)$$

Double exponential smoothing initial values

$$A_0 = a_0 - \frac{1-\alpha}{\alpha}b_0 \qquad (5.18)$$

$$A'_0 = a_0 - 2\frac{1-\alpha}{\alpha}b_0 \qquad (5.19)$$

Holt's model

$$A_t = \alpha y_t + (1-\alpha)(A_{t-1} + T_{t-1}) \qquad (5.20)$$

$$T_t = \beta(A_t - A_{t-1}) + (1-\beta)T_{t-1} \qquad (5.21)$$

$$\hat{y}_{t+p} = A_t + pT_t \qquad (5.22)$$

Winter's model

$$A_t = \alpha \frac{y_t}{S_{t-L}} + (1 - \alpha)(A_{t-1} + T_{t-1}) \tag{5.23}$$

$$T_t = \beta(A_t - A_{t-1}) + (1 - \beta)T_{t-1} \tag{5.24}$$

$$S_t = \gamma \frac{y_t}{A_t} + (1 - \gamma)S_{t-L} \tag{5.25}$$

$$\hat{y}_{t+p} = (A_t + pT_t)S_{t-L+p} \tag{5.26}$$

CHAPTER 5

PROBLEMS

1. Which forecasting technique continually revises an estimate in the light of more recent experiences?
2. Which forecasting technique uses the value for the current period as the forecast for the next period?
3. Which technique assigns equal weights to each observation?
4. Which technique should be used if the data are trended?
5. Which technique should be used if the data are seasonal?
6. Apex Mutual Fund invests primarily in technology stocks. The net asset values of the fund at the end of each month for the 12 months of 1991 are as follows:

Month	Mutual Fund Price
Jan	19.39
Feb	18.96
Mar	18.20
Apr	17.89
May	18.43
Jun	19.98
Jul	19.51
Aug	20.63
Sep	19.78
Oct	21.25
Nov	21.18
Dec	22.14

a. Find the forecast value of the mutual fund for each month by using a naive model. The value for December 1990 was 19.00.
b. Evaluate this forecasting method using MAD.
c. Evaluate this forecasting method using MSE.
d. Evaluate this forecasting method using MAPE.

e. Evaluate this forecasting method using MPE.

f. Forecast the mutual fund price for January 1992.

g. Write a memo summarizing your findings.

7. This question refers to Problem 6. Use a three-month moving average to forecast the mutual fund price for January 1992. Is this forecast better than the forecast made using the naive model? Explain.

8. Given the following series:

Time Period	y_t	$\hat{y}_t$	e_t
1	200	100	—
2	210		
3	215		
4	216		
5	219		
6	220		
7	225		
8	226		

a. What is the forecast for period 8 using a five-month moving average?

b. If a smoothing constant of .4 is used, what is the exponentially smoothed forecast for period 4?

c. In part b, what is the forecast error for time period 3?

9. The yield on a general obligation bond for the city of Davenport fluctuates with the market. The monthly quotations for 1991 are as follows:

Month	Yield
Jan	9.29
Feb	9.99
Mar	10.16
Apr	10.25
May	10.61
Jun	11.07
Jul	11.52
Aug	11.09
Sep	10.80
Oct	10.50
Nov	10.86
Dec	9.97

a. Find the forecast value of the yield for the obligation bonds for each month, starting with April, by using a three-month moving average.

b. Find the forecast value of the yield for the obligation bonds for each month, starting with June, by using a five-month moving average.

c. Evaluate these forecasting methods using MAD.

d. Evaluate these forecasting methods using MSE.

    e. Evaluate these forecasting methods using MAPE.

    f. Evaluate these forecasting methods using MPE.

    g. Forecast the yield for January 1992 using the best technique.

    h. Write a memo summarizing your findings.

10. This question refers to Problem 9. Use exponential smoothing with a smoothing constant of .2 and an initial value of 9.29 to forecast the yield for January 1992. Is this forecast better than the forecast made using the moving average model? Explain.

11. The Hughes Supply Company uses an inventory management method to determine the monthly demands for various products. The demand values for the last 12 months of each product have been recorded and are available for future forecasting. The demand values for the past 12 months of 1991 for one electrical fixture are presented next:

Month	Demand
Jan	205
Feb	251
Mar	304
Apr	284
May	352
Jun	300
Jul	241
Aug	284
Sep	312
Oct	289
Nov	385
Dec	256

Source: Hughes Supply Company records.

Use exponential smoothing with a smoothing constant of .5 and an initial value of 205 to forecast the demand for January 1992.

12. General American Investors Co., a closed-end regulated investment management company, invests primarily in medium- and high-quality stocks. Jim Campbell is studying the asset value per share for this company and would like to forecast this variable for 1990. The data are as follows:

Quarter:	1	2	3	4
1985	16.98	18.47	17.63	20.63
1986	21.95	23.85	20.44	19.29
1987	22.75	23.94	24.84	16.70
1988	18.04	19.19	18.97	17.03
1989	18.23	19.80	22.89	21.41

Source: *The Value Line Investment Survey* (New York: Value Line, 1990), p. 2097.

Evaluate the asset value per share variable using the following forecasting methods: naive, moving average, and exponential smoothing. When you compare techniques, take into consideration that the actual asset value per share for the first quarter of 1990 was 21.50. Write a report for Jim indicating which method he should use and why.

13. Southdown, Inc., the nation's third largest cement producer, is pushing ahead with a waste-fuel burning program. The cost for Southdown will total about $37 million. For this reason, it is extremely important for the company to have an accurate forecast of second quarter revenues for 1990. The data are as follows:

Quarter:	1	2	3	4
1986	77.4	88.8	92.1	79.8
1987	77.5	89.1	92.4	80.1
1988	74.7	185.2	162.4	178.1
1989	129.1	158.4	160.6	138.7
1990	127.2			

Source: *The Value Line Investment Survey* (New York: Value Line, 1990), p. 902.

a. Use exponential smoothing with a smoothing constant of .4 and an initial value of 77.4 to forecast the earnings per share for the second quarter of 1990.

b. Now use a smoothing constant of .6 and an initial value of 77.4 to forecast the earnings per share for the second quarter of 1990.

c. Estimate the smoothing constant that will provide the best forecast.

14. The Triton Energy Corporation explores for and produces oil and gas. Company president, Gail Freeman, wants to have her company analyst forecast the company's sales per share for 1990. This will be an important forecast since Triton's restructuring plans have hit a snag. The data are as follows:

Triton Sales per Share, 1974–1989.

Year	Sales per Share	Year	Sales per Share
1974	.93	1982	5.54
1975	1.35	1983	7.16
1976	1.48	1984	1.93
1977	2.36	1985	5.17
1978	2.45	1986	7.72
1979	2.52	1987	5.33
1980	2.81	1988	8.12
1981	3.82	1989	10.65

Source: *The Value Line Investment Survey* (New York: Value Line, 1990), p. 1843.

Use both Brown's double moving average and Holt's technique to forecast for 1990. Compare the results using the appropriate measures. How does your forecast compare with the *Value Line* forecast of 11.95?

15. The Consolidated Edison Company sells electricity (82% of revenues), gas (13%), and steam (5%) in New York City and Westchester County. Bart Thomas, company forecaster, is assigned the task of forecasting the company's quarter revenues for 1990. He collects the following data:

Quarterly Revenues for Consolidated Edison ($ millions), 1985–1989.

Year	Mar. 31	June 30	Sept. 30	Dec. 31
1985	1441	1209	1526	1321
1986	1414	1187	1411	1185
1987	1284	1125	1493	1192
1988	1327	1102	1469	1213
1989	1387	1218	1575	1371

Source: *The Value Line Investment Survey* (New York: Value Line, various years).

Determine the best technique and forecast for 1990.

THE SOLAR ALTERNATIVE COMPANY

The Solar Alternative Company is about to enter its third year of operation. The company was founded by Bob and Mary Johnson, who both teach science in the local high school. The Johnsons founded the Solar Alternative Company to provide a supplement to their teaching income. Based on their research into solar energy systems, they were able to put together a solar system for heating domestic hot water. The system consists of a 100-gallon fiberglass storage tank, two 3 × 6 foot solar panels, electronic controls, PVC pipe, and miscellaneous fittings.

The payback period on the system is ten years. While this situation does not present an attractive investment opportunity from a financial point of view, there is sufficient interest in the novelty of the concept to provide a moderate level of sales. The Johnsons clear about $75.00 on the $2,000.00 cost of an installed system, after costs and expenses. Material and equipment costs account for 75% of the installed system cost. An advantage that helps to offset the low profit margin is that the product is not profitable enough for there to be any significant competition from heating contractors. The Johnsons operate the business out of their home. There is an office in the basement, and their one-car garage is used exclusively to store the system components and materials. As a result, overhead is at a minimum. The Johnsons enjoy a modest supplemental income from the company's operation. The business also provides a number of tax advantages.

This case was contributed by William P. Darrow of the Towson State University, Towson, Maryland.

Bob and Mary are pleased with the growth of the business. Although sales vary from month to month, overall the second year had been much better than the first. Many of the second-year customers are neighbors of people who had purchased the system in the first year. Apparently after seeing the system operate successfully for a year, others were willing to try the solar concept. Sales occur throughout the year. Demand for the system is greatest in late summer and early fall, when homeowners typically make plans to winterize their homes for the upcoming heating season.

With the anticipated growth in the business, the Johnsons felt that they needed a sales forecast to manage effectively in the coming year. It usually takes 60 to 90 days to receive storage tanks after placing the order. The solar panels are available off the shelf most of the year. However, in the late summer and throughout the fall, the lead time can be as great as 90 to 100 days. While there is limited competition, lost sales are nevertheless a real possibility if the potential customer is asked to wait several months for installation. Perhaps more important is the need to make accurate sales projections to take advantage of quantity discount buying. These factors, when combined with the high cost of system components and the limited storage space available in the garage, make it necessary to develop a reliable forecast. The sales history for the company's first two years is given in the accompanying table.

Month	1990	1991	Month	1990	1991
Jan.	5	17	July	23	44
Feb.	6	14	Aug.	26	41
Mar.	10	20	Sept.	21	33
Apr.	13	23	Oct.	15	23
May	18	30	Nov.	12	26
June	15	38	Dec.	14	17

QUESTIONS

1. Identify which model Bob and Mary should use as the basis for their business planning in 1992, and discuss why this model was selected.
2. Forecast sales for 1992.

CASE STUDY **5.2**

FIVE-YEAR REVENUE PROJECTION FOR DOWNTOWN RADIOLOGY

Downtown Radiology is developing a medical imaging center more complete and technologically advanced than any currently located in the Inland Empire. The equipment planned for the center will equal or surpass the imaging facilities of all medical centers in the region. The center will contain a 9800 series CT scanner and nuclear magnetic resonance imaging (MRI) equipment. The center will also include ultrasound, nuclear medicine, digital subtraction angiography (DSA), mammography equipment, and conventional radiology and fluoroscopy equipment. Ownership interest will be offered in some type of public offering, and Downtown desires an independent evaluation of the market. Downtown Radiology asked Professional Marketing Associates, Inc. to evaluate the market and complete a five-year projection of revenue.

STATEMENT OF THE PROBLEM

The purpose of this study is to forecast for the next five years for the proposed medical imaging center.

OBJECTIVES

The objectives of this study are to

> Identify market areas for each type of procedure to be offered by the new facility
>
> Gather and analyze existing data on market area revenue for each type of procedure to be offered by the new facility
>
> Identify trends in the health care industry that will positively or negatively affect revenue of procedures to be provided by the proposed facility
>
> Identify factors in the business, marketing, or facilities planning of the new venture that would positively or negatively impact revenue projections
>
> Analyze past procedures of Downtown Radiology as a database for the forecasting model to be developed
>
> Utilize the appropriate quantitative forecasting model to arrive at five-year revenue projections for the proposed center

METHODOLOGY

Procedures

The following steps were implemented in order to complete the five-year projection of revenue. An analysis of the past number of procedures was performed. The appropriate forecasting model was developed and used to determine a starting point for the projection of each procedure.

1. The market area was determined for each type of procedure, and population forecasts were obtained for 1986 and 1990.
2. Doctor referral patterns were studied to determine the percentage of doctors who refer to Downtown Radiology and the average number of referrals per doctor.
3. National rates were acquired from the National Center for Health Statistics. These rates were compared with actual numbers obtained from the Hospital Commission.

4. Downtown Radiology's market share was calculated based on actual CT scans in the market area. (Market share for other procedures was determined based on Downtown Radiology's share compared to rates provided by the National Center for Health Statistics.)

Assumptions

Certain assumptions were necessary in order to develop a quantitative forecast. The following assumptions were made:

- The new imaging center will be operational, with all equipment functional except the MRI, on January 1, 1985.
- The nuclear magnetic resonance imaging equipment will be functional in April 1985.
- The offering of the limited partnership will be successfully marketed to at least 50 physicians in the service area.
- Physicians who have a financial interest in the new imaging center will increase their referrals to the center.
- There will be no other MRIs in the market area before 1987.
- The new imaging center will offer services at lower prices than the competition.
- An effective marketing effort will take place, especially concentrating on large employers, insurance groups, and unions.
- The MRI will replace approximately 60% of the head scans that are presently done with the CT scanner during the first six months of operation, and 70% during the next 12 months.
- The general public will continue to pressure the health care industry to hold down costs.
- Costs of outlays in the health care industry rose 13.2% annually from 1971 to 1981. The Health Care Financing Administration estimates that the average annual rate of increase will be reduced to approximately 11%–12% between 1981 and 1990 (*Industry Surveys,* April 1984).
- Insurance firms will reimburse patients for at least 80% and as much as 100% of the cost of magnetic resonance imaging (*Imaging News,* February 1984).

Models

A forecast was developed for each procedure based on past experience, industry rates, and reasonable assumptions. Since the models were developed based on the assumptions listed above, if the assumptions are not valid, the models will not be accurate.

ANALYSIS OF PAST DATA

Office X-Rays

The number of X-ray procedures performed were analyzed from July 1981 to May 1984. The data included diagnostic X-rays, gastrointestinal X-rays, breast imaging,

FIGURE 5.4 Office X-Rays by Month, July 1981–May 1984.

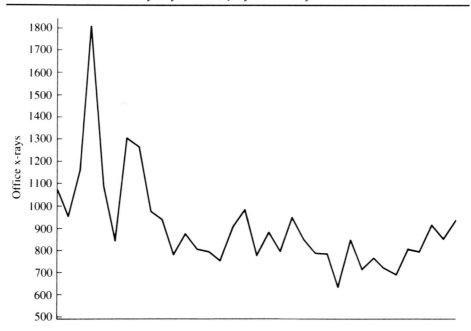

injections, and special procedures. The data are presented in Figure 5.4. Examination of these data indicates that no trend or seasonal or cyclical pattern is present. For this reason exponential smoothing was chosen as the appropriate forecasting method. Various smoothing factors were examined, and a smoothing constant of .3 was found to provide the best model. This value means that the most recent historical observation was given a weight of .3 and the rest of the historical series a weight of .7. This model is presented in Table 5.11. The forecast for June 1984 is 855 X-ray procedures.

Office Ultrasound

The numbers of ultrasound procedures performed were analyzed from July 1981 to May 1984. Figure 5.5 shows the data pattern. Again, no trend or seasonal or cyclical pattern was present. Exponential smoothing with a smoothing factor of .3 was again determined to provide the best model. Table 5.12 shows that the forecast for June 1984 is 118 ultrasound procedures.

The numbers of ultrasound procedures performed by the two mobile units owned by Downtown Radiology were analyzed from July 1981 to May 1984. Figure 5.6 shows the data pattern. An increasing trend is apparent and can be modeled using Holt's two-parameter linear exponential smoothing method. Smoothing constants of $\alpha = .37$ and $\beta = .18$ are used, and the forecast for June 1984 is 226.

TABLE 5.11 Exponential Smoothing.

| | Smoothed Data: Office X-Rays | | Smoothing Factor = .3 | | |
Procedure	Office X-Ray	Smoothed Value	Procedure	Office X-Ray	Smoothed Value
1	1,072.00	1,072.00	19	882.00	863.94
2	953.00	1,036.30	20	794.00	842.96
3	1,157.00	1,072.51	21	946.00	873.87
4	1,800.00	1,290.76	22	848.00	866.11
5	1,085.00	1,229.03	23	785.00	841.78
6	837.00	1,111.42	24	779.00	822.94
7	1,301.00	1,168.29	25	636.00	766.85
8	1,262.00	1,196.41	26	846.00	790.60
9	977.00	1,130.58	27	712.00	767.02
10	937.00	1,072.51	28	767.00	767.02
11	780.00	984.76	29	719.00	752.61
12	873.00	951.23	30	689.00	733.53
13	808.00	908.26	31	804.00	754.67
14	796.00	874.58	32	796.00	767.07
15	752.00	837.81	33	910.00	809.95
16	901.00	856.77	34	849.00	821.66
17	978.00	893.14	35	932.00	854.76
18	770.00	856.20			

FIGURE 5.5 Office Ultrasound by Month, July 1981–May 1984.

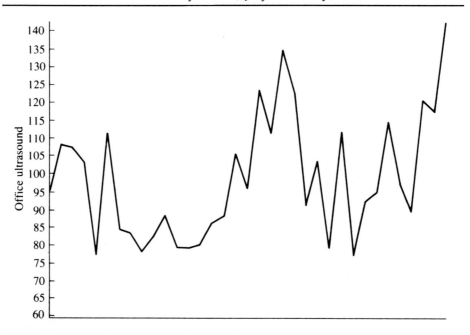

TABLE 5.12 Exponential Smoothing.

	Smoothed Data: Office Ultrasound		Smoothing Factor = .3		
Procedure	Office Procedure	Smoothed Value	Procedure	Office Procedure	Smoothed Value
1	94.00	94.00	19	123.00	101.50
2	108.00	98.20	20	111.00	104.35
3	107.00	100.84	21	134.00	113.24
4	103.00	101.49	22	122.00	115.87
5	77.00	94.14	23	91.00	108.41
6	111.00	99.20	24	103.00	106.79
7	84.00	94.64	25	79.00	98.45
8	83.00	91.15	26	111.00	102.22
9	78.00	87.20	27	77.00	94.65
10	82.00	85.64	28	92.00	93.86
11	88.00	86.35	29	95.00	94.20
12	79.00	84.14	30	114.00	100.14
13	79.00	82.60	31	97.00	99.20
14	80.00	81.82	32	89.00	96.14
15	86.00	83.07	33	120.00	103.30
16	88.00	84.55	34	117.00	107.41
17	105.00	90.69	35	142.00	117.79
18	96.00	92.28			

FIGURE 5.6 Nonoffice Ultrasound by Month, July 1981–May 1984.

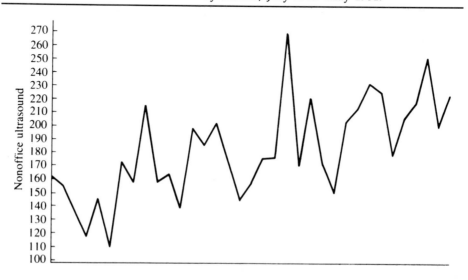

Nuclear Medicine Procedures

The numbers of nuclear medicine procedures performed by the two mobile units owned by Downtown Radiology were analyzed from August 1982 to May 1984. Figure 5.7 shows the data pattern. The data were not seasonal and had no trend or cyclical pattern. For this reason exponential smoothing was chosen as the appropriate forecasting method. A smoothing factor of .3 was found to provide the best model. This model is presented in Table 5.13. The forecast for June 1984 is 44 nuclear medicine procedures.

FIGURE 5.7 Nonoffice Nuclear Medicine by Month, August 1982–May 1984.

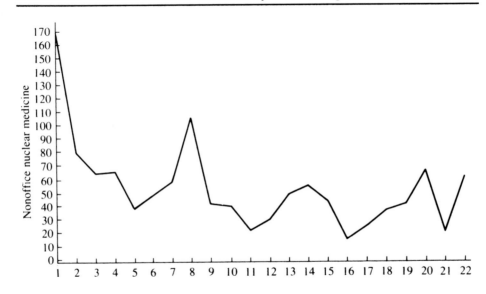

TABLE 5.13 Exponential Smoothing.

| | Smoothed Data: Nuclear Medicine | | Smoothing Factor = .3 | | |
Procedure	Nonoffice Procedure	Smoothed Value	Procedure	Nonoffice Procedure	Smoothed Value
14	167.00	167.00	25	29.00	41.95
15	78.00	140.30	26	49.00	44.06
16	64.00	117.41	27	56.00	47.64
17	65.00	101.69	28	44.00	46.55
18	37.00	82.28	29	14.00	36.79
19	48.00	72.00	30	24.00	32.95
20	58.00	67.80	31	36.00	33.87
21	104.00	78.66	32	41.00	36.01
22	41.00	67.36	33	65.00	44.70
23	39.00	58.85	34	19.00	36.99
24	21.00	47.50	35	61.00	44.19

FIGURE 5.8 Office CT Scans by Month, July 1981–May 1984.

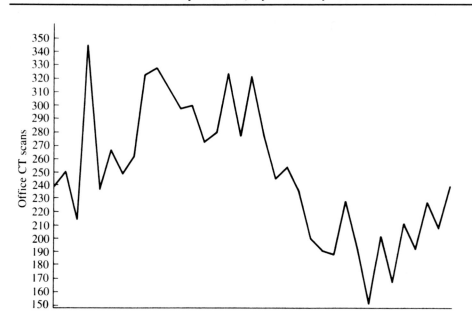

TABLE 5.14 Exponential Smoothing.

	Smoothed Data: Office CT Scans		Smoothing Factor = .5		
Procedure	Office CT Scan	Smoothed Value	Procedure	Office CT Scan	Smoothed Value
1	238.00	238.00	19	277.00	290.80
2	250.00	244.00	20	244.00	267.40
3	214.00	229.00	21	253.00	260.20
4	344.00	286.50	22	234.00	247.10
5	236.00	261.25	23	199.00	223.05
6	266.00	263.63	24	190.00	206.53
7	248.00	255.81	25	187.00	196.76
8	261.00	258.41	26	226.00	211.38
9	322.00	290.20	27	190.00	200.69
10	327.00	308.60	28	151.00	175.85
11	312.00	310.30	29	201.00	188.42
12	297.00	303.65	30	166.00	177.21
13	299.00	301.33	31	210.00	193.61
14	272.00	286.66	32	191.00	192.30
15	279.00	282.83	33	226.00	209.15
16	322.00	302.42	34	207.00	208.08
17	276.00	289.21	35	238.00	223.04
18	320.00	304.60			

Office CT Scans

The numbers of CT scans performed were also analyzed from July 1981 to May 1984. The data are presented in Figure 5.8. Seasonality was not found, and the number of CT scans did not seem to have a trend. However, a cyclical pattern seemed to be present. Knowledge of how many scans were performed last month would be important in the forecast of what is going to happen this month. An autoregressive model (see Chapters 9 and 10) was examined and compared to an exponential-smoothing model with a smoothing constant of .5. The larger smoothing constant gives the most recent observation more weight in the forecast. This model was determined best, and Table 5.14 shows the projection of the number of CT scans for June 1984 to be 223.

MARKET AREA ANALYSIS

Market areas were determined for procedures currently done by Downtown Radiology by examining patient records and doctor referral patterns. Market areas were determined for procedures not currently done by Downtown by investigating the competition and analyzing the geographical areas they served.

CT Scanner Market Area

The market area for CT scanning for the proposed medical imaging center includes Spokane, Whitman, Adams, Lincoln, Stevens, and Pend Oreille Counties in Washington and Bonner, Boundary, Kootenai, Benewah, and Shoshone Counties in Idaho. Based on the appropriate percentage projections, the CT scanning market area will have a population of 630,655 in 1985 and 696,018 in 1990.

Quantitative Estimates

To project revenue, it is necessary to determine certain quantitative estimates. The most important estimate involves the number of doctors who will participate in the limited partnership. The estimate used in future computations is that at least 8% of the doctor population of Spokane County will participate.

The next uncertainty that must be quantified involves the determination of how the referral pattern will be affected by the participation of 50 doctors in the limited partnership. It is assumed that 30 of the doctors who presently refer to Downtown will join the limited partnership. Of the 30 who join, it is assumed that 10 will not increase their referrals and the other 20 will double their referrals. It is also assumed that 20 doctors who had never referred to Downtown will join the limited partnership and will begin to refer at least half of their work to Downtown Radiology.

The quantification of additional doctor referrals should be clarified with some qualitative observations. The estimate of 50 doctors joining the proposed limited partnership is conservative. There is a strong possibility that doctors from areas outside of Spokane County may join. Traditionally, the doctor referral pattern changes very slowly. However, the sudden competitive nature of the marketplace will probably have an impact on doctor referrals. If the limited partnership is marketed to doctors in specialties with high radiology referral potential, the number of referrals should increase more than projected. The variability in the number of doctor referrals per procedure is extremely large. A few doctors referred an extremely large percentage of the procedures done by Downtown Radiology. If a few new large-referral doctors are recruited, they can have a major effect on the total number of procedures done for any individual service provided by Downtown.

Finally, the effect that a new imaging center will have on Downtown Radiology's market share must be estimated. The new imaging center will have the best equipment and will be prepared to do the total spectrum of procedures at a lower cost. The number of new doctors referring should increase on the basis of word of mouth from the new investing doctors. If insurance companies, large employers, and/or unions enter into agreements with the new imaging center, Downtown should be able to increase its share of the market by at least 4% in 1985, 2% in 1986, and 1% in 1987 and retain this market share in 1988 and 1989. This market share increase will be referred to as the *total imaging effect* in the rest of this report.

Revenue Projections

Revenue projections were completed for every procedure. Only the projections for the CT scanner are shown in this case.

CT Scan Projections

Based on the exponential smoothing model and what has already taken place in the first five months of 1984, the forecast of CT scans for 1984 (January 1984 to January 1985) is 2,600.

The National Center for Health Statistics reports a rate of 261 CT scans per 100,000 population per month. Using the population of 630,655 projected for the CT scan market area, the market should be for 19,752 procedures in 1985. The actual number of CT scans performed in the market area during 1983 was estimated to be 21,600. This estimate was based on actual known procedures for Downtown Radiology (2,260), Sacred Heart (4,970), Deaconess (3,850), Valley (2,300), and Kootenai (1,820) and estimates for Radiation Therapy (2,400) and Northwest Imaging (4,000). If the estimates are accurate, Downtown Radiology had a market share of approximately 10.5% in 1983. The actual values were also analyzed for 1982, and Downtown was projected to have approximately 15.5% of the CT scan market during that year. Therefore Downtown Radiology is forecasted to average about 13% of the market.

Based on the increased referrals from doctors belonging to the limited partnership and an analysis of the average number of referrals of CT scans, an increase of 320 CT scans is projected for 1985 from this source. If actual values for 1983 are used, the rate for the Inland Empire CT scan market area is 3,568 (21,600/6.054) per 100,000 population. If this pattern continues, the number of CT scans in the market area will increase to 22,514 (3,568 × 6.31) in 1985. Therefore, Downtown Radiology's market share is projected to be 13% (2,920/22,514). When the 4% increase in market share based on total imaging is added, Downtown Radiology's market share increases to 17.0%, and their projected number of CT scans is 3,827 (22,514 × .17).

TABLE 5.15 Five-Year Projected Revenue for CT Scans.

Year	Procedures	Revenue
1985	3,138	$1,129,680
1986	2,531	1,012,400
1987	2,716	1,205,904
1988	2,482	1,223,626
1989	2,529	1,383,363

However, research seems to indicate that the MRI will eventually replace a large number of CT head scans (*Applied Radiology,* May/June 1983, and *Diagnostic Imaging,* February 1984). The National Center for Health Statistics indicated that 60% of all CT scans were of the head. Downtown Radiology records showed that 59% of their CT scans in 1982 were head scans, and 54% in 1983. If 60% of Downtown's CT scans are of the head and the MRI approach replaces approximately 60% of them, new projections for CT scans in 1985 are necessary. Since the MRI will operate for only half the year, a reduction of 689 ($3,827/2 \times .60 \times .60$) CT scans is forecasted.

The projected number of CT scans for 1985 is 3,138. The average cost of a CT scan is $360, and the projected revenue from CT scans is $1,129,680. Table 5.15 shows the projected revenue from CT scans for the next five years. The cost of procedures is estimated to increase approximately 11% per year.

Without the effect of the MRI the projection for CT scans in 1986 is estimated to be 4,363 ($6.31 \times 1.02 \times 3,568 \times .19$). However, if 60% are CT head scans and the MRI replaces 70% of the head scans, the projected number of CT scans should drop to 2,531 [$4,363 - (4,363 \times .60 \times .70)$].

The projection of CT scans without the MRI effect for 1987 is 4,683 ($6.31 \times 1.04 \times 3,568 \times .20$). The forecast with the MRI effect is 2,716 [$4,683 - (4,683 \times .60 \times .70)$].

The projection of CT scans without the MRI effect for 1988 is 4,773 ($6.31 \times 1.06 \times 3,568 \times .20$). The forecast with the MRI effect is 2,482 [$4,773 - (4,773 \times .60 \times .8)$].

The projection of CT scans without the MRI effect for 1989 is 4,863 ($6.31 \times 1.08 \times 3,568 \times .20$). The forecast with the MRI effect is 2,529 [$4,863 - (4,863 \times .60 \times .8)$].

QUESTION

Downtown Radiology's accountant projected that revenue would be considerably higher. Since ownership interest will be offered in some type of public offering, Downtown Radiology's management must make a decision concerning the accuracy of Professional Marketing Associates' projections. You are asked to analyze the report. What recommendations would you make?

SELECTED BIBLIOGRAPHY

Aaker, D. A., and Jacobson, R. "The Sophistication of 'Naive' Modeling." *International Journal of Forecasting* 3 (314) (1987): 449–452.

Dalrymple, D. J., and King, B. E. "Selecting Parameters for Short-Term Forecasting Techniques." *Decision Sciences* 12 (1981): 661–669.

Gardner, E. S., Jr., and Dannenbring, D. G. "Forecasting with Exponential Smoothing: Some Guidelines for Model Selection." *Decision Sciences* 11 (1980): 370–383.

Harrison, P. J. "Exponential Smoothing and Short-Term Sales Forecasting." *Management Science* 13 (11) (1967): 821–842.

Holt, C. C. "Forecasting Seasonal and Trends by Exponentially Weighted Moving Averages." Office of Naval Research, Memorandum no. 52 (1957).

Ledolter, J., and Abraham, B. "Some Comments on the Initialization of Exponential Smoothing." *Journal of Forecasting* 3 (1) (1984): 79–84.

Makridakis S., and Wheelwright, S. C. *Interactive Forecasting*. Palo Alto, Calif.: Scientific Press, 1977, pp. 145–152.

McKenzie, E., "An Analysis of General Exponential Smoothing." *Operations Research* 24 (1976): 131–140.

Thiel, H., and Wage, S. "Some Observations on Adaptive Filtering." *Management Science* 10 (2) (1964): 198–224.

Winters, P. R. "Forecasting Sales by Exponentially Weighted Moving Averages." *Management Science* 6 (1960): 324–342.

6

Regression Analysis

I n Chapter 2, the linear relationship between two numerical variables (correlation) was discussed. Once a linear relationship is established, knowledge of the independent variable can be used to forecast the dependent variable. The simplest graphical model for relating a dependent variable to a single independent variable is a straight line. In this chapter, simple linear regression (straight-line) models are discussed along with how to fit them to a set of data points using the method of least squares. Since there are a great many calculations necessary in regression analysis, computer applications for the techniques discussed are emphasized.

To extend the analysis of the relationship between two variables reviewed in Chapter 2, consider the following example.

EXAMPLE 6.1

■ Suppose Mr. Bump observes the selling price and sales volume of milk gallons for 10 randomly selected weeks. The data he has collected are presented in Table 6.1.

TABLE 6.1 Data for Example 6.1: Milk Gallons.

Week	Weekly Sales Level, Y (Thousand of Gallons)	Selling Price, X
1	10	$1.30
2	6	2.00
3	5	1.70
4	12	1.50
5	10	1.60
6	15	1.20
7	5	1.60
8	12	1.40
9	17	1.00
10	20	1.10

He first decides to construct a scatter diagram of the data, which is shown in Figure 6.1. It appears from this scatter diagram that a negative linear relationship exists between Y, the number of milk gallons sold, and X, the price of each gallon. It seems that as price goes up, volume goes down.

Bump now wishes to measure the degree of this apparent relationship. The computations he needs are presented in Table 6.2.

From Equation 2.16 the correlation coefficient of this sample data is calculated as follows:

$$r = \frac{n \sum XY - (\sum X)(\sum Y)}{\sqrt{n \sum X^2 - (\sum X)^2} \cdot \sqrt{n \sum Y^2 - (\sum Y)^2}}$$

$$= \frac{(10)(149.3) - (14.4)(112)}{\sqrt{(10)(21.56) - 14.4^2} \cdot \sqrt{(10)(1{,}488) - 112^2}}$$

$$= \frac{1493 - 1612.8}{\sqrt{215.6 - 207.36} \cdot \sqrt{14{,}880 - 12{,}544}}$$

$$= \frac{-119.8}{\sqrt{8.24} \cdot \sqrt{2{,}336}}$$

$$= \frac{-119.8}{(2.87)(48.33)} = \frac{-119.8}{138.7}$$

$$= -.86 \, .$$

The sample of 10 data points has revealed a sample correlation coefficient of $-.86$, a fairly strong negative linear relationship between Y and X. Thus Bump may tentatively conclude that as the price of a gallon of milk goes up, the number of gallons sold goes down.

The question that may occur next is, How much does the volume drop as price is raised? This question suggests drawing a straight line through the data

FIGURE 6.1 Scatter Diagram for Example 6.1.

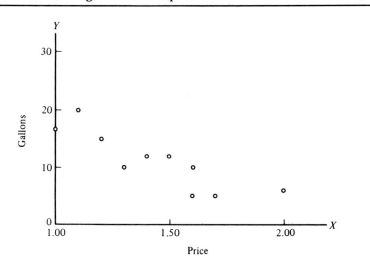

TABLE 6.2 Computations Needed for Example 6.1.

	Y	X	XY	X^2	Y^2
$n = 10$	10	1.30	13.0	1.69	100
	6	2.00	12.0	4.00	36
	5	1.70	8.5	2.89	25
	12	1.50	18.0	2.25	144
	10	1.60	16.0	2.56	100
	15	1.20	18.0	1.44	225
	5	1.60	8.0	2.56	25
	12	1.40	16.8	1.96	144
	17	1.00	17.0	1.00	289
	20	1.10	22.0	1.21	400
Totals	112	14.4	149.3	21.56	1,488

points displayed on the scatter diagram. After this line has been drawn, the slope of the line will show the average decrease in Y for each dollar increase in X. ■

REGRESSION LINE

Mr. Bump might actually draw a straight line through the data points, attempting to fit the line to the points as closely as possible. However, a better procedure is to find the equation of the line that best fits the points. This straight line is of the form $Y_R = b_0 + bX$. The first term in this equation, b_0, is called the *Y intercept* since it is the value that Y takes on when X is equal to zero. The second term, b, is called the *slope* of the straight line since it represents the amount of change in Y when X increases by one unit (recall the discussion of line slope in Chapter 2). What Bump wishes to do, then, is to compute the values for b_0 and b.

But first it is necessary to define precisely what is meant by a line that "best" fits the collected data points. Many definitions are possible, but the definition almost universally used in regression analysis is as follows:

> The *line that best fits* a collection of X–Y data points is that line minimizing the sum of the squared distances from the points to the line as measured in the vertical, or Y, direction. This line is known as the *regression line,* and its equation is called a *regression equation.*

The method that finds values for b_0 and b under this definition is called the *method of least squares.* Finding the equations for b_0 and b requires the use of calculus. The derivation of these two equations appears in Appendix A, with the following results:

$$b = \frac{n \sum XY - \sum X \sum Y}{n \sum X^2 - (\sum X)^2} \tag{6.1}$$

$$b_0 = \frac{\sum Y}{n} - \frac{b \sum X}{n} \tag{6.2}$$

EXAMPLE 6.2

■ The computations for the data presented in Table 6.2 are

$$b = \frac{(10)(149.3) - (14.4)(112)}{(10)(21.56) - (14.4)^2} = \frac{-119.8}{8.24} = -14.54$$

$$b_0 = \frac{112}{10} - (-14.54)\left(\frac{14.4}{10}\right) = 11.2 + 14.54(1.44) = 32.14$$

Thus the equation of the straight line that best fits the collected data points, under the method of least squares, is

$$Y_R = b_0 + bX \tag{6.3}$$
$$= 32.14 - 14.54X$$

This equation is called the *sample regression equation*.

Mr. Bump may now wish to interpret the values in this equation. The Y intercept, b_0, is the value of Y when X is equal to zero. A strict interpretation would suggest that the average number of gallons sold when $X = 0$ (that is, if the price of a gallon of milk were zero) is 32,140 gallons. This interpretation does not agree with common sense since one would expect more milk to be "sold" if it were free. The problem illustrated here involves predicting a value for Y based on an X value about which no sample evidence has been collected. That is, none of the sample points has an X value at or near zero. In this case, as in many regression analysis cases, a useful interpretation of the Y intercept is not possible. In more general terms, it is not wise to predict Y values for any X beyond the range of the Xs collected in the sample data.

The slope value, b, may be interpreted as the average change in Y that occurs when X increases by 1. In this example Y decreases by an average of 14.54 (that is, 14,540 fewer gallons are sold) when X increases by 1 (the cost of a gallon of milk is raised by \$1). Each dollar increase in a gallon of milk reduces the quantity purchased by an average of 14,540 gallons. Or, to put this statement in more meaningful units, the sample evidence indicates that each increase of 1 cent in a gallon of milk reduces the quantity purchased by an average of 145.4 gallons.

The X–Y relationship can be illustrated by drawing the straight line that best fits the data points of the scatter diagram, as shown in Figure 6.2. Notice that the vertical distances from the points to the line have been shown as dotted lines. If these distances were squared and added, this sum would be the lowest possible for any line that could be drawn through the points. Any other line that might be drawn through the points would have a higher sum of squared distances. In

FIGURE 6.2 Regression Line for Bump's Data.

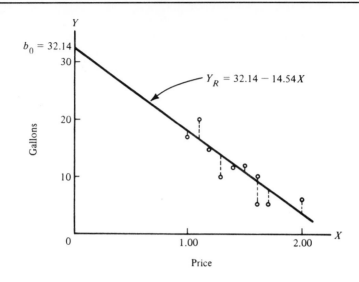

accordance with the least squares procedure, then, this line represents the best possible fit to the 10 sample data points. ■

At this point it should be noted that the regression line calculated is correctly termed the *sample* regression line because it is the line that best fits a *sample* of data points randomly drawn from the population of all such data points. As usual in statistical procedures, statisticians distinguish between the population of data values and a sample of data values. To keep these two groups clearly separated, different notation is used to describe the X–Y relationships that exist, as shown in Table 6.3.

The population and sample correlation coefficients listed in Table 6.3 were discussed in Chapter 2. The sample regression equation is the equation of the straight line that best fits the observed sample data points. Underlying the X–Y relationship revealed by the sample data values is the X–Y relationship of the entire population, represented by the population regression model. This model suggests that each value of Y in the population is equal to an intercept value β_0 (Greek letter beta), plus a constant β times its X value, plus an error term ε (Greek letter epsilon). The error terms

TABLE 6.3 Notation for Population and Sample.

Population	Sample
Correlation coefficient = ρ	Correlation coefficient = r
Population regression model:	Sample regression equation:
$Y = \beta_0 + \beta X + \varepsilon$	$Y_R = b_0 + bX$

are thus the differences between the actual population Y values and the values represented by the population regression equation, or $\varepsilon = Y - (\beta_0 + \beta X)$. In a sample these differences, or errors, are known as *residuals*.

Many computer software packages perform correlation and regression analysis. One of the most popular is the Minitab package. Following are the Minitab regression commands and the resulting computer output for the data presented in Table 6.1.

The Minitab commands to plot a scatter diagram follow.

```
MTB > SET C1  *1
DATA > 10 6 5 12 10 15 5 12 17 20
MTB > END
MTB > SET C2  *2
DATA > 1.30 2.00 1.70 1.50 1.60 1.20 1.60 1.40 1.00 1.10
MTB > END
MTB > NAME C1 'SALES' C2 'PRICE'  *3
MTB > PLOT C1 VS C2  *4
```

```
    20.0+           *
        -
SALES   -
        -         *
    15.0+             *
        -
        -                     *      *
        -
    10.0+                 *              *
        -
        -
        -
        -                                              *
     5.0+                             *      *
        -
        ----+---------+---------+---------+---------+---------+--PRICE
          1.00      1.20      1.40      1.60      1.80      2.00
```

---

*1 Command set enters the sales data into c1
*2 Command set enters the price data into c2
*3 Command name is used to name the variables in each column
*4 Command plot develops a scatter diagram with **c1** on the Y axis and **c2** on the X axis

The Minitab command to compute a correlation coefficient is

```
MTB > CORR C1-C2  *1

Correlation of SALES and PRICE = -0.863
```

---

*1 Command **corr** computes the correlation between **c1** and **c2**

The Minitab command to compute the regression analysis is

```
MTB > REGRESS C1 1 PREDICTOR C2 *1

The regression equation is
SALES = 32.1 - 14.5 PRICE

   Predictor        Coef       Stdev     t-ratio         p
   Constant       32.136       4.409        7.29     0.000
   PRICE         -14.539       3.002       -4.84     0.000

   s = 2.725       R-sq = 74.6%      R-sq(adj) = 71.4%

Analysis of Variance

   SOURCE          DF          SS          MS         F         p
   Regression       1      174.18      174.18     23.45     0.000
   Error            8       59.42        7.43
   Total            9      233.60
```

---

[1] Command regress for **c1** as the dependent variable with 1 independent variable **c2**

The Minitab commands to compute a prediction interval are

```
MTB > REGRESS C1 1 PREDICTOR C2;
SUBC > PREDICT 1.63.   *1

  Fit   Stdev.Fit          95% C.I.            95% P.I.
8.438        1.034   (  6.054, 10.822)   (  1.714, 15.161)
```

---

[1] Subcommand **predict** computes a 95% confidence interval in this case for an X value of 1.63

The Minitab commands to compute residuals are

```
MTB > REGRESS C1 1 PREDICTOR C2, DHATS IN C3, RES IN C4 *1
MTB > PRINT C1-C4 *2

   ROW   SALES   PRICE          C3           C4

     1      10     1.3     13.2354     -1.26820
     2       6     2.0      3.0583      1.49764
     3       5     1.7      7.4199     -0.98173
     4      12     1.5     10.3277      0.64836
     5      10     1.6      8.8738      0.44329
     6      15     1.2     14.6893      0.12512
     7       5     1.6      8.8738     -1.52477
     8      12     1.4     11.7816      0.08458
     9      17     1.0     17.5971     -0.26864
    10      20     1.1     16.1432      1.62355
```

*1 Subcommand **dhats** computes the etimates of Y and stores them
   in **c3**.   Subcommand res computes the residuals and stores them
   in **c4**.
*2 Command **print** prints out the contents of **c1** through **c4**

STANDARD ERROR OF ESTIMATE

Having computed the sample regression line equation, Mr. Bump might
next be interested in measuring the extent to which the sample data points
are dispersed around the sample regression line. In particular, he might
wish to compute the typical distance from a data point to the regression line
as measured in the Y direction. This concept of measuring dispersion is
similar to the notion of standard deviation used to measure the dispersion
of data values around their mean. In regression analysis the measurement is
called the *standard error of estimate* and is represented by the symbol $s_{y.x}$.
The standard error of estimate is

$$s_{y.x} = \sqrt{\frac{\Sigma\,(Y - Y_R)^2}{n - 2}} \qquad\qquad (6.4)$$

The *standard error of estimate* measures the typical amount by
which the actual Y values differ from the estimated values
(Y_R).[1]

Note the similarity between the formula of Equation 6.4 and the
sample standard deviation formula in simple descriptive statistics. In the
numerator are the measurements between the actual data values (Y) and
the "average" or "expected" value of the variable (Y_R) as determined by the
sample regression line. These distances are squared and added and are
divided by degrees of freedom, and the square root is taken. (Note that two
degrees of freedom are lost because two population parameters are being
estimated by sample data values, namely, b_0 and b.) The standard error thus
measures the standard or typical distance from a data point to the sample
regression line. A regression analysis that has a small standard error
involves data points very close to the regression line, and one with a large
standard error involves data points widely dispersed around the line.

---

[1] The standard error of estimate is also defined as an estimate of the standard deviation of the
assumed normal distributions of Y for any given X.

For computation purposes, Equation 6.14 can be converted to

$$s_{y.x} = \sqrt{\frac{\Sigma\,Y^2 - b_0\,\Sigma\,Y - b\,\Sigma\,XY}{n - 2}} \qquad\qquad \textbf{(6.5)}$$

For the Bump example, the standard error is

$$S_{y'x} = \sqrt{\frac{1{,}488 - (32.14)(112) + (14.54)(149.3)}{8}}$$

$$= \sqrt{\frac{59.14}{8}} = \sqrt{7.39}$$

$$= 2.72$$

The standard error is a measurement of the typical vertical distance from the sample data points to the sample regression line. It can be used to compare the dispersion of data points around the regression line in this situation with the dispersion of data points in other situations. It is used by experienced analysts to judge the extent to which the sample data points may be summarized by the best-fit regression line. Also, if it is assumed that the population of data points is normally distributed around the population regression line, $s_{y.x}$ can be used as an estimate of the standard deviation of that normal distribution. The importance of making such a normality assumption is discussed later in this chapter.

PREDICTING Y

The next task is to estimate the value of Y for a given value of X. To obtain a *point prediction,* the regression equation is used. The value of X is substituted in the equation and the predicted value of Y found.

EXAMPLE 6.3

■ Suppose Mr. Bump wished to forecast the quantity of milk sold if the price were set at $1.63. From Equation 6.3:

$$Y_R = 32.14 - 14.54X$$

$$= 32.14 - 14.54(1.63)$$

$$= 8.440 \quad \text{or} \quad 8{,}440 \text{ gallons}$$

Note that this estimate is the value of Y_R; that is, it represents the point on the regression line where $X = 1.63$. ■

Of course, Bump realizes that the data points that generated the regression line are dispersed around that line, as measured by $s_{y.x}$. To make an *interval prediction* of Y when $X = 1.63$, this dispersion must be taken into account. In addition, a second factor must be considered before making such a prediction.

It was stated earlier that the calculated regression line was a sample regression line since it was computed from a random sample of ten data points, not from all data points in the population. Other random samples of ten would produce different sample regression lines, similar to the case where many samples drawn from a population have different means. So to make an interval prediction for Y, both the dispersion of sample data points around the sample regression line and the dispersion of many sample regression lines around the true population regression line must be considered.

The *standard error of the forecast* measures the variability of predicted values of Y around the true value of Y for a given value of X. It takes into account both of the factors mentioned. The standard error of the forecast is

$$s_f = s_{y.x} \sqrt{1 + \frac{1}{n} + \frac{(X - \bar{X})^2}{\Sigma (X - \bar{X})^2}} \tag{6.6}$$

Note that $s_{y.x}$ is one term in this standard error since the first term under the radical sign is 1. The other factors are measuring the variability of sample regression lines around the true regression line. Also, note that the particular value of X being used appears in Equation 6.6. In other words, the forecast error *depends on* the value of X for which a forecast is desired. The lowest possible forecast error is for $X = \bar{X}$ since the third term under the radical then equals zero, $(X - \bar{X})^2 = 0$. The farther X is from $\bar{X}$, the larger the forecast error.

EXAMPLE 6.4

■ Pictorially, Mr. Bump's 95% prediction interval for various values of X would look similar to Figure 6.3.

More specifically, the standard error of the forecast is calculated as follows for $X = 1.63$:

$$s_f = 2.72 \sqrt{1 + \frac{1}{10} + \frac{(1.63 - 1.44)^2}{.8240}}$$
$$= 2.72(1.066) = 2.90$$

Note: In this calculation $\Sigma (X - \bar{X})^2$ was determined as shown in Table 6.4. ■

A 95% prediction interval for Y and $X = 1.63$ is calculated by using Equation 6.7. This equation can be used as long as the sample size is sufficiently large ($n \geq 30$).

$$Y_R \pm Z s_f \tag{6.7}$$

FIGURE 6.3 Prediction Interval for Bump's Data.

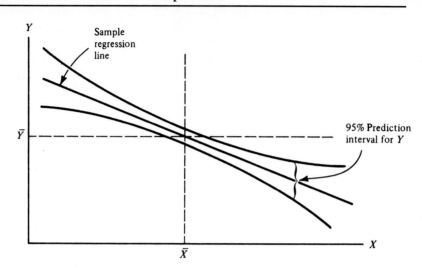

Important assumptions are made when an interval prediction is computed. In fact, the entire regression analysis procedure rests on the following basic assumptions.

1. *The population of Y values is normally distributed about the population regression line.* This condition is shown in Figure 6.4. In practice, reasonably accurate results are obtained as long as the Y values are approximately normally distributed.

TABLE 6.4 Calculation of $\Sigma (X - \bar{X})^2$ for Example 6.4.

X	$(X - \bar{X})^2$
1.30	.0196
2.00	.3136
1.70	.0676
1.50	.0036
1.60	.0256
1.20	.0576
1.60	.0256
1.40	.0016
1.00	.1936
1.10	.1156
$\Sigma (X - \bar{X})^2 =$	.8240

FIGURE 6.4 Normality Assumption.

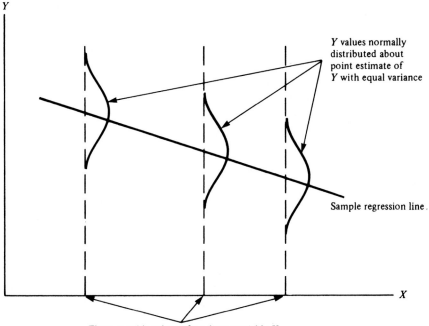

Three possible values of predictor variable X

2. *The dispersion of population data points around the population regression line remains constant everywhere along the line.* That is, the population variance does not become larger or smaller as the X value of the data points increases. A violation of this assumption is called *heteroscedasticity* and is discussed in detail in Chapter 7; an example of this condition and its cure appear in Chapter 9.

3. *The error terms (ε) are independent of each other.* This assumption implies a random sample of X–Y data points. A violation of this assumption is called *autocorrelation* and frequently occurs when the X–Y data values are measured over time. Chapter 9 is devoted to the identification and solution of this problem.

4. *A linear relationship exists between X and Y in the population.* Nonlinear regression lines constitute an extension of the linear case discussed in this chapter. There are techniques for dealing with X–Y relationships that are nonlinear; some of these are discussed later in this chapter.

Actually, the interval prediction given by Equation 6.7 is only approximately correct for Bump's example. For correct use of the Z value from the normal curve table, the sample size cannot be small. As a rule of thumb, a sample size of at least 30 is required to use the normal table. For small sample sizes it is appropriate to compute an interval prediction by using the t distribution. The interval in this case becomes

$$Y_R \pm ts_f \tag{6.8}$$

(For the t table, $df = n - 2$.)

For Bump's data, a collection of 10 data points, the t distribution formula is appropriate. The interval is thus

$$Y_R \pm ts_f$$

$$8.44 \pm 2.306(2.90)$$

$$8.44 \pm 6.69$$

1.75 to 15.13   or   1,750 gallons to 15,130 gallons

The formula in Equation 6.8 produces a somewhat wider interval than that produced if the normal curve were used, reflecting the presence of a small sample size. Notice the extreme width of the computed confidence interval. It is so wide as to be virtually worthless in predicting Y. While this inaccuracy is quite apparent in the interval width, it is not apparent in the point estimate computed from the regression equation. This implied degree of accuracy is the major benefit of the interval estimate.

Another important point to remember is that it is unwise to predict beyond the range of observed data. Thus Bump is justified in trying to predict Y when $X = 1.63$ because some of the original X values are near 1.63. On the other hand, he would not be wise to predict Y when $X = 3.00$. No data have been collected for X values nearly this large, and for this reason any prediction involving such an X value would be highly suspect. To estimate quantity sold when price per unit is $3, Bump has to assume that the linear model is still valid. He may have good reason to make this assumption, but he has no direct evidence to support it.

COEFFICIENT OF DETERMINATION

Next, a useful statistic called the *coefficient of determination* is discussed.

Consider Figure 6.5, which shows Bump's sample regression line along with a hypothetical data point. In considering the single data point that lies below the regression line, he would first "expect" that its Y value would be equal to the average of all Y values, namely, $\bar{Y}$. The vertical distance between Y and $\bar{Y}$ shown in Figure 6.5 thus becomes the total difference or deviation that must be explained.

Part of this vertical distance is readily explainable. The Y value would be expected to equal $\bar{Y}$ only if the X value of the observation were equal to

FIGURE 6.5 Explained and Unexplained Variation for Bump's Data.

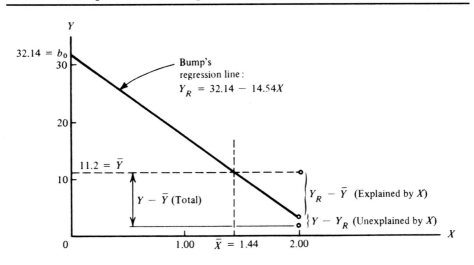

$\overline{X}$. However, this is not the case. The X value of this observation is considerably higher than $\overline{X}$. Thus it is understandable why the Y value of this observation might have moved from $\overline{Y}$ down to Y_R: the X value of the observation is greater than $\overline{X}$, and it is known that X and Y have a fairly strong negative correlation ($r = -.86$). The vertical distance $Y_R - \overline{Y}$ is, therefore, "explained" by the movement in X, while the vertical distance $Y - Y_R$ is "unexplained" by the movement in X.

EXAMPLE 6.5

■ For Bump's data, consider the data point with a large X value ($X = 1.70$, $Y = 5$). For this data point,

$$Y_R = 32.14 - 14.54(1.70)$$
$$= 32.14 - 24.72 = 7.422$$

Thus

$$\overline{Y} = 11.2$$
$$Y_R = 7.422$$
$$Y = 5$$

These values appear in Figure 6.6.

In this case the distance from $\overline{Y}$ to Y_R is explained by the movement of X from $\overline{X}$ (1.44) to its actual value (1.70), as expected from knowledge of the relationship between Y and X ($r = -.86$). In other words, the movement of X from 1.44 to 1.70 has explained the movement of Y from 11.2 to 7.422, but it has *not* explained its movement from 7.422 to 5.00. ■

FIGURE 6.6 Predicting Y for Example 6.5.

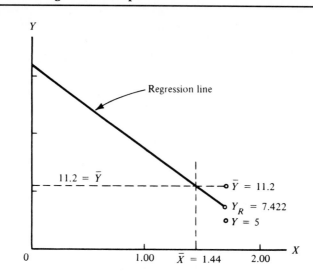

To find the portion of the total deviation that is explained by X for any observation, the explained deviation must be divided by the total deviation, as follows:

$$\text{Percent of total deviation explained by } X \text{ is } \frac{Y_R - \bar{Y}}{Y - \bar{Y}}$$

and

$$\text{Percent of total deviation unexplained by } X \text{ is } \frac{Y - Y_R}{Y - \bar{Y}}$$

Of course, all the data points must be considered, not just one. Also, the calculation for all the data points is made with squared differences. This calculation is done so that the final result will have a useful interpretation.

The symbol for the sample coefficient of determination is r^2, and this value is defined as

$$r^2 = \frac{\text{Explained deviation}}{\text{Total deviation}} = \frac{\Sigma (Y_R - \bar{Y})^2}{\Sigma (Y - \bar{Y})^2}$$

or

$$r^2 = 1 - \frac{\text{Unexplained deviation}}{\text{Total deviation}} = 1 - \frac{\Sigma (Y - Y_R)^2}{\Sigma (Y - \bar{Y})^2} \tag{6.9}$$

> The *coefficient of determination* measures the percentage of the variability in Y that can be explained through knowledge of the independent variable X.

Equation 6.9 is the usual form for defining r^2, and it states that the percentage of the variability in Y that is explained by the variability in X is 100% minus the percentage unexplained by X. The value r^2 is a most important value in any regression analysis since it shows the extent to which the variability of Y and X are related.

In practice, r^2 can be calculated by using the following equivalent computational formula:

$$r^2 = \frac{b_0 \, \Sigma \, Y + b \, \Sigma \, XY - n\bar{Y}^2}{\Sigma \, Y^2 - n\bar{Y}^2} \tag{6.10}$$

EXAMPLE 6.6

■ For Bump's data r^2 is calculated using Equation 6.10.

$$r^2 = \frac{(32.14)(112) - (14.54)(149.3) - (10)(11.2)^2}{1{,}488 - (10)(11.2)^2}$$

$$= \frac{3{,}599.68 - 2{,}170.82 - 1{,}254}{1{,}488 - 1{,}254} = \frac{174.9}{234} = .747$$

On the basis of this r^2 value, the following statements are made:

1. Of the variability in the quantity of milk sold, 75% can be explained by the variability in milk price.
2. Of the variability in the quantity of milk sold, 25% *cannot* be explained by the variability in milk price. This portion of the variability in milk volume must be explained by factors that have not been identified in this regression analysis (e.g., weather, amount of advertising, availability of substitute products). ■

Note that r^2 is the square of r, the coefficient of correlation (disregarding rounding errors). That is,

Coefficient of determination = (Coefficient of correlation)^2

$$r^2 = (r)^2$$

Thus

$$.75 = (-.86)^2$$

$$.75 = .75$$

FIGURE 6.7 Extreme Values of r^2.

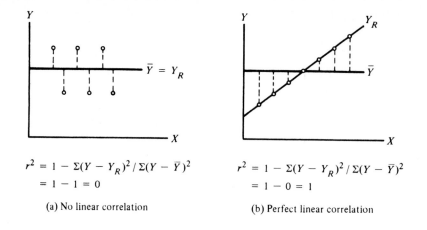

$r^2 = 1 - \Sigma(Y - Y_R)^2 / \Sigma(Y - \bar{Y})^2$

$\quad = 1 - 1 = 0$

(a) No linear correlation

$r^2 = 1 - \Sigma(Y - Y_R)^2 / \Sigma(Y - \bar{Y})^2$

$\quad = 1 - 0 = 1$

(b) Perfect linear correlation

Then why is it necessary to identify both values in a regression analysis? The answer is that each has an advantage over the other.

The advantage of the coefficient of correlation (r) is that both positive and negative relationships are revealed. In the case of the data that Bump has collected, a negative relationship exists ($r = -.86$). In other cases a positive relationship might be revealed by the value for r. As will be seen in the next chapter, it is important to identify relationships that exist between certain pairs of variables when confronted with a large collection of variables, and it is necessary to know whether positive or negative relationships exist. Note that when the coefficient of correlation is squared, the value is always positive, and so the nature of the relationship is lost.

The advantage of the coefficient of determination (r^2) is that it has a very useful interpretation. The value for r^2 measures the percentage of the variability in Y that is explained by the variability in X. This interpretation is most useful, making r^2 one of the most frequently consulted statistics in regression analysis.

Figure 6.7 illustrates the two extreme cases for r^2, where it is equal to zero and where it is equal to one. In the former case, *none* of Y's variability is explained by X: the scatter diagram suggests no correlation between X and Y. When r-squared $= 1$, *all* of Y's variability is explained away when X is known: the sample data points all lie on the regression line.

RESIDUALS

Mr. Bump's analysis began with knowledge of only ten weekly sales volume quantities (the Y variable). If no further information were available, Bump might employ the mean $\bar{Y}$ of Y as the predictor for each weekly sales volume. If he does, he will generate certain errors, one for each prediction made. These errors are called residuals, as discussed earlier in this chapter. By estimating the Y values with $\bar{Y}$, Bump minimizes estimation errors over a long period of time, since the mean sales volume, 11,200 gallons, is used as the best estimator of each week's sales volume. The errors sum to zero because the mean is the mathematical center of the distribution of Y. The ten predictions and the ten residuals appear as shown in Table 6.5.

In addition to presenting residuals, Table 6.5 also shows the sum of squared residuals. This calculation is done so that the total amount of error can be measured; because there are both positive and negative residuals, the sum of the actual residuals is always zero. The summed value is called the *sum of the squared residuals,* and it represents the total variability of Y values around their mean. It is this total variability (233.60) that Bump wishes to reduce by introducing knowledge of a related variable, X. The formula for the sum of the squared residuals around the mean of Y or the total sum of squares is

$$\Sigma \, (Y - \bar{Y})^2 \tag{6.11}$$

The sum of the squared residuals can be changed to a variance by dividing it by the appropriate degrees of freedom. Since one population parameter (μ) is being estimated by a sample statistic ($\bar{Y}$), one degree of freedom is lost. The appropriate degree of freedom is thus $n - 1$. So the total variance of Y around its mean is

$$s_y^2 = \frac{\Sigma \, (Y - \bar{Y})^2}{n - 1} \tag{6.12}$$

Note: The square root of this variance is the standard deviation of Y.

TABLE 6.5 Residuals for Bump's Data.

Actual Y	Predicted Y $(\bar{Y})$	Residual $(Y - \bar{Y})$	$(Y - \bar{Y})^2$
10	11.2	−1.2	1.44
6	11.2	−5.2	27.04
5	11.2	−6.2	38.44
12	11.2	.8	.64
10	11.2	−1.2	1.44
15	11.2	3.8	14.44
5	11.2	−6.2	38.44
12	11.2	.8	.64
17	11.2	5.8	33.64
20	11.2	8.8	77.44
		Sums 0.0	233.60

EXAMPLE 6.7

■ For Bump's data,

$$s_y^2 = \frac{233.6}{9} = 25.96$$

Note the following important point: this variance of Y values has been computed by using $\overline{Y}$ as the best estimator for each week's Y value. That is, no information about the related variable X has been used. When Mr. Bump brings in information about X, a lower variance of Y should result because X is correlated with Y, and more accurate predictions should be possible using the regression equation. ■

Now suppose that Bump uses the calculated regression equation to predict Y. Since he has established a relationship between X and Y on the basis of the sample data points ($r = -.86$), the regression line should generate more accurate predictions for Y than are generated when $\overline{Y}$ is used to predict the Y values. If Bump predicts Y values by using this regression equation, residuals will still exist, but he expects them to be smaller. Likewise, both the sum of the squared residuals and the variance of Y values around the regression line should be smaller. It follows that r^2 will be larger. Table 6.6 presents this analysis of residuals.

From Table 6.6 it can be seen that the sum of the squared residuals is reduced from 233.6 to 59.41; the reduction occurs because the residuals now involve the variability of the Y values around the regression line instead of around $\overline{Y}$. In other words, knowledge of the related variable X reduces the prediction error, just as Bump might expect through his knowledge of the

TABLE 6.6 Analysis of Residuals for Bump's Data.

X	Y	Predicted Y (Y_R) Using $Y_R = 32.14 - 14.54X$	Residual $(Y - Y_R)$	$(Y - Y_R)^2$
1.30	10	13.238	−3.238	10.48
2.00	6	3.060	2.940	8.64
1.70	5	7.422	−2.422	5.87
1.50	12	10.330	1.670	2.79
1.60	10	8.876	1.124	1.26
1.20	15	14.692	.308	.09
1.60	5	8.876	−3.876	15.02
1.40	12	11.784	.216	.05
1.00	17	17.600	− .600	.36
1.10	20	16.146	3.854	14.85
		Sums	0.000	59.41

sample correlation coefficient between X and Y. The sum of the squared residuals is

$$\Sigma (Y - Y_R)^2 \qquad\qquad (6.13)$$

The variance of Y around the predicted values is

$$s_{y.x}^2 = \frac{\Sigma (Y - Y_R)^2}{n - 2} \qquad\qquad (6.14)$$

EXAMPLE 6.8

■ For Bump's data,

$$s_{y.x}^2 = \frac{59.41}{8} = 7.43$$

Note that this result is the square of the standard error of estimate, $s_{y.x}$.

Of the original error, what percentage has Bump been able to explain through knowledge of the related variable X? This value is the coefficient of determination r^2.

$$r^2 = 1 - \frac{\Sigma (Y - Y_R)^2}{\Sigma (Y - \bar{Y})^2}$$

$$= 1 - \frac{59.41}{233.6} = 1 - .254 = .746$$

This answer, of course, is the same r^2 value obtained earlier, and it indicates that knowledge of X allows Bump to explain 74.6% of the variability of Y around its mean. Also, 25.4% of the variability in Y is not explained by knowledge of X. ■

The relationship between total deviation, explained deviation, and unexplained deviation is

Total deviation = explained deviation + unexplained deviation

$\Sigma (Y - \bar{Y})^2$	$=$	$\Sigma (Y_R - \bar{Y})^2$	$+$	$\Sigma (Y - Y_R)^2$
233.6	$=$	174.2	$+$	59.4
233.6	$=$	233.6		

HYPOTHESIS TESTING

In Chapter 2, it was noted that the sample coefficient of correlation r has a counterpart in the population, namely ρ (rho). Likewise, the population of all X–Y data points possesses a coefficient of determination, ρ^2. As always, it must be kept in mind that the sample information produces sample statistics that allow the forecaster to make inferences about the relationship that exists between X and Y among all the population data points. A statistical test that might be considered is

$$H_0: \quad \beta = 0$$

where β is the slope of the true population regression line. Failing to reject this null hypothesis means that in spite of the fact the sample evidence has produced a nonzero value for b, the evidence is not strong enough to reject the notion that in the population of all data points the regression line is flat (horizontal). Note that such a statement is equivalent to stating that $\rho = 0$. A population of data points that has a flat regression line would also have a zero correlation coefficient.

How could β be zero while b is nonzero? Consider Figure 6.8, where a population of data points is shown from which a sample of five has been taken (sampled data points are indicated by $\times$). As this scatter diagram suggests, if enough sample data points are taken, it will become obvious that the population of data points has a regression line with a flat slope. That is, both β and ρ are zero. However, in the random sample of five data points, points were selected that lie fairly close to an upward-trending regression line. It might be erroneously concluded from this evidence that X and Y are related in a positive linear way. However, if the hypothesis that $\beta = 0$ is tested, the forecaster will probably not be able to reject it.

FIGURE 6.8 Population and Sample Data Points.

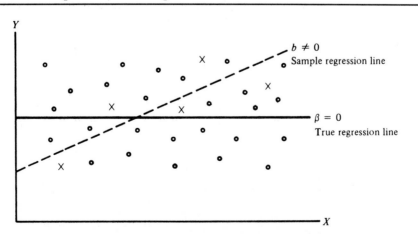

EXAMPLE 6.9

■ For Bump's data, the test appears as shown in Table 6.7.
From the t table for $n - 2$ degrees of freedom,

$t_{.01,(df=8)} = 3.355$

$t_{.05,(df=8)} = 2.306$

Therefore, Bump is able to reject the following null hypothesis: the population regression line has a flat slope ($\beta = 0$). ■

Now consider two special situations that illustrate the importance of testing a hypothesis regarding the population as well as considering the value of r^2.

Situation

Suppose $n = 1000$ and $r^2 = .10$. The following hypothesis is rejected: $H_0: \beta = 0$. However, the regression is not considered useful.

Reason. The extremely large sample size produces a very accurate estimate of ρ^2, the population coefficient of determination. The notion that this coefficient is equal to zero can be rejected. However, the relationship between X and Y, while the forecaster is confident it exists, is very weak ($r^2 = .10$). Therefore it has been established, with small chance of error, that a weak relationship exists in the population between X and Y, and thus the forecaster cannot use the regression analysis.

Situation

Suppose $n = 3$ and $r^2 = .95$. The following hypothesis cannot be rejected: $H_0: \beta = 0$.

TABLE 6.7 Hypotheses Test for Slope.

$$H_0: \quad \beta = 0$$

$$s_b = \frac{s_{y.x}}{\sqrt{\Sigma (X - \bar{X})^2}} \qquad (6.15)$$

$$t = \frac{b - \beta}{s_b} \qquad (6.16)$$

$$t = \frac{-14.54 - 0}{2.72 / \sqrt{.824}} = \frac{-14.54}{3.00}$$

$$= -4.8$$

Note: The values used in the calculations were all computed earlier in this chapter. The term s_b is the standard error of the regression coefficient.

Reason. The three data points lie nearly on a straight line. However, there is an extremely small sample size, not constituting enough evidence to make a positive statement about the population of all data points. The null hypothesis cannot be rejected even though the value for r^2 is quite high. More sample evidence needs to be collected before meaningful statements about the population can be made.

Some computer packages do not contain the t statistic. Instead, they use the variance ratio test, or F statistic. To test the hypothesis that a particular model is a good one, an unbiased estimate of the variance explained by the model is divided by the unbiased estimate of the un-explained or error variance for the model. Equation 6.17 is used to compute the F statistic.

$$F = \frac{\text{variance accounted for}}{\text{total variance}}$$

$$= \frac{(r_F^2 - r_R^2)/(K_F - K_R)}{(1 - r_F^2)/(n - K_F)} \tag{6.17}$$

where

$r_F^2 = r^2$ for full model

$r_R^2 = r^2$ for restricted model

K_F = number of linearly independent parameters to be estimated in full model

K_R = number of linearly independent parameters to be estimated in restricted model

n = sample size

$r_F^2 - r_R^2$ = percent of total variance explained by variable(s) in full model but not in the restricted model

$1 - r_F^2$ = percent of total variance not explained by full model

The full model is the model that the analyst is interested in testing. The restricted model is formed by using the mean of the Y variable ($\bar{Y}$) as the predictor or independent variable. r_F^2 is the percent of variance explained when X is used to predict Y. r_R^2 is zero because using the mean of Y to predict Y does not explain any Y variable variance.

To determine the appropriate F value from Table C.6, the analyst needs to know two parameters: the degrees of freedom for both the numerator ($K_F - K_R$) and the denominator ($n - K_F$).

EXAMPLE 6.10

■ The null hypothesis for testing Bump's equation is the following: the model using price to predict sales is not a good one or knowledge of the movement of the price variable does not explain a significant percent of the sales variable variance. Equation 6.17 is used to compute the appropriate F statistic.

$$F = \frac{(r_F^2 - r_R^2)/(K_F - K_R)}{(1 - r_F^2)/(n - K_F)}$$

$$= \frac{(.746 - 0)/(2 - 1)}{(1 - .746)/(10 - 2)}$$

$$= \frac{.746}{.03175} = 23.5$$

Since the computed F statistic (23.5) is greater than the tabulated F value for 1 and 8 degrees of freedom at both the .05 (5.32) and .01 significance levels (11.26), the null hypothesis is rejected at either significance level. Mr. Bump concludes that the model is a good one and explains a significant percent of the dependent variable variance. ∎

COMPUTER OUTPUT

Mr. Bump's regression analysis problem (data from Table 6.1) is run on a computer regression program to produce the output presented in Table 6.8.

TABLE 6.8 Computer Output for Bump's Regression Problem.

VARIABLE NO.	MEAN	STANDARD DEVIATION	CORRELATION X VS Y	REGRESSION COEFFICIENT	STD. ERROR OF REG.COEF	COMPUTED T VALUE
2	1.44000	0.30258	-0.86 (1)	-14.54 (2)	3.00 (3)	-4.84 (4)
DEPENDENT						
1	11.20000	5.09466				

INTERCEPT	32.14 (5)	MULTIPLE CORRELATION 0.86 (7)
STD. ERROR OF ESTIMATE	2.725 (6)	R SQUARED 0.746 (8)
		CORRECTED R SQUARED 0.714 (9)

ANALYSIS OF VARIANCE FOR THE REGRESSION (14)

SOURCES OF VARIATION	DEGREES OF FREEDOM	SUM OF SQUARES	MEAN SQUARES	F VALUE
ATTRIBUTABLE TO REGRESSION	1	174.175	174.175	23.448
DEVIATION FROM REGRESSION	8	59.425 (10)	7.428	
TOTAL	9	233.600 (11)		

CORRELATION MATRIX: 2 BY 2 (13)

VAR.	1	2
1	1.000	-0.863
2	-0.863	1.000

TABLE OF RESIDUALS

CASE NO.	Y VALUE	Y ESTIMATE	RESIDUAL
1	10.00000	13.23543	-3.23543 (12)
2	6.00000	3.05824	2.94176
3	5.00000	7.41989	-2.41989
4	12.00000	10.32765	1.67235
5	10.00000	8.87376	1.12624
6	15.00000	14.68932	0.31068
7	5.00000	8.87376	-3.87376
8	12.00000	11.78154	0.21846
9	17.00000	17.59706	-0.59706
10	20.00000	16.14317	3.85683

The software that was used produces an output that is typical of those generated by other regression analysis programs. While there is not a standardized format for presenting the results of a regression analysis, the output shown in Table 6.8 contains the values displayed by almost all regression analysis programs. To explain the terminology used in the computer output, definitions and computations are presented in the list below. These definitions and calculations are keyed to Table 6.8.

1. *Correlation X vs Y = −.86.* The sample correlation coefficient (r) indicates the relationship between X and Y, or price and sales, respectively.

2. *Regression coefficient = −14.54.* This value is the ratio of change in Y (sales) when X (price) increases by one unit (b). When price increases $1, sales decrease by 14,450 units.

3. *Std. error of reg. coef. (standard error of regression coefficient) = 3.0.* This value is the standard deviation of the sampling distribution of the regression coefficient value (b).

$$s_b = \frac{s_{y.x}}{\sqrt{\Sigma\,(X - \overline{X})^2}} = \frac{2.72}{\sqrt{.824}} = \frac{2.72}{.908} = 3.00$$

4. *Computed t value = −4.84.* The computed t value is used to test whether the population regression coefficient β is significantly different from zero.

$$t = \frac{b - \beta}{s_b} = \frac{-14.54}{s_b}$$

$$s_b = \frac{s_{y.x}}{\sqrt{\Sigma\,(X - \overline{X})^2}} = \frac{2.725}{\sqrt{.8240}} = 3.00$$

$$t = \frac{-14.54}{3.00} = -4.85 \text{ (rounding error)}$$

5. *Intercept = 32.14.* This value is the y intercept (b_0). Therefore the entire regression equation is

$$Y_R = 32.14 - 14.54X$$

6. *Std. error of estimate = 2.725.* The standard error of the estimate indicates that the Y values fall typically about 2.725 units from the regression line.

$$s_{y.x} = \sqrt{\frac{\Sigma\,(Y - Y_R)^2}{n - 2}} = \sqrt{\frac{59.425}{10 - 2}} = \sqrt{7.428} = 2.725$$

7. *Multiple correlation = .86.* The multiple correlation coefficient is the positive square root of r^2 and indicates the degree of relationship between X and Y but not the kind of relationship.

$$r^2 = .74$$
$$\sqrt{r^2} = \sqrt{.74}$$
$$r = .86$$

8. *r squared = .746.* The regression line explains 74.6% of the sales volume variance.

$$r^2 = 1 - \frac{\Sigma (Y - Y_R)^2}{\Sigma (Y - \bar{Y})^2} = 1 - \frac{59.4}{233.6}$$

$$= 1 - .254 = .746$$

9. *Corrected r squared = .714.* The r^2 is adjusted for the appropriate degrees of freedom.

$$r_c^2 = 1 - \frac{\Sigma (Y - Y_R)^2/(n - 2)}{\Sigma (Y - \bar{Y})^2/(n - 1)} = 1 - \frac{59.425/8}{233.6/9}$$

$$= 1 - \frac{7.428}{25.956} = 1 - .286 = .714$$

10. *Sum of squares deviation from regression = 59.425.* The sum of squared residuals is the difference between the actual Y and the predicted $Y(Y_R)$, squared and summed (sometimes referred to as the *error sum of squares*).

$$\Sigma (Y - Y_R)^2 = 59.425$$

11. *Sum of squares total = 233.6.* This value is the sum of the squared deviations from the mean.

$$\Sigma (Y - \bar{Y})^2 = 233.6$$

12. *Table of residuals.* Residuals measure the difference between what Y actually is and what it is predicted to be when using the regression equation. For example,

Case 1: $Y - Y_R = 10 - 13.23543 = -3.23543$

Case 2: $Y - Y_R = 6 - 3.05824 = 2.94176$

13. *Correlation matrix.* This matrix gives the correlation among all variables in the analysis. Since only two variables are involved, there is only one correlation coefficient ($-.863$).

14. *Analysis of variance.* The F value (23.448) in this ANOVA (analysis of variance) table tests the null hypothesis that the regression is not significant; that is, the reduction in the error sum of squares from 233.6 to 59.425 is due to chance. A high F value will allow rejection of this hypothesis, suggesting a *significant* regression. The F value ($23.448 = 174.175/7.428$) becomes larger as a larger portion of the total sum of squared residuals is explained by the regression. In this case the tabulated F value ($df_n = 1$, $df_d = 8$, $\alpha = .01$) is 11.26. Thus the hypothesis of no significant regression is rejected at the 1% significance level since $23.448 > 11.26$. The appropriate degrees of freedom in any regression analysis are $k - 1$, $n - k$, and $n - 1$ for attributable to regression, deviation from regression, and total, respectively, where k is the number of regression coefficients computed from the sample data (all bs).

Variable Transformations

The techniques of this chapter rest on the assumption that a *linear* relationship exists between the dependent variable (Y) and the predictor variable (X). With multiple predictors, as discussed in Chapter 7, this linear relationship between Y and the predictors is also assumed.

Sometimes data of interest do not exhibit a linear relationship. If the X–Y relationship is close to linear, the straight line relationship discussed in this chapter may provide sufficient accuracy. When this is not the case, some way must be found to deal with a relationship that cannot be approximated with a linear model.

There are two basic approaches for dealing with nonlinear relationships. The first is to fit the data with a curved line or model and use the established relationship for forecasting purposes. This approach constitutes an extension of the linear model discussed in this book and is the subject of more advanced treatments of regression analysis.

The second approach is to convert one or more variables to another form so that the resulting relationship with Y is linear. Four of the most common transformations that are used to generate new predictor variables are the log of X, the square root of X, X squared, and the reciprocal of X. When these variables are each plotted against Y, the hope is that, whereas the X–Y relationship itself is nonlinear, one of the transformations will yield a linear relationship. If so, Y and this new variable can be treated using the linear model discussed in this chapter, including calculation of the correlation coefficient and the regression equation.

In the following example, Minitab is used to plot a simple X–Y relationship that appears to be nonlinear. The program is then instructed to calculate the four transformations described above. These variables are then each plotted against Y to produce the data plots shown.

Note: The numbers preceded by asterisks are keyed to the box below where the Minitab commands are explained.

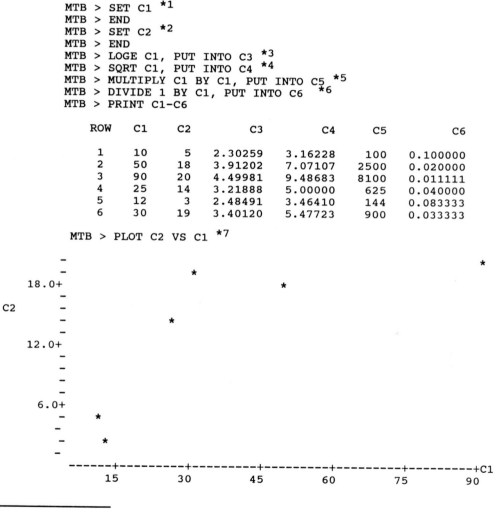

```
MTB > SET C1 *1
MTB > END
MTB > SET C2 *2
MTB > END
MTB > LOGE C1, PUT INTO C3 *3
MTB > SQRT C1, PUT INTO C4 *4
MTB > MULTIPLY C1 BY C1, PUT INTO C5 *5
MTB > DIVIDE 1 BY C1, PUT INTO C6 *6
MTB > PRINT C1-C6

    ROW    C1    C2       C3         C4      C5        C6

     1     10     5    2.30259    3.16228    100    0.100000
     2     50    18    3.91202    7.07107   2500    0.020000
     3     90    20    4.49981    9.48683   8100    0.011111
     4     25    14    3.21888    5.00000    625    0.040000
     5     12     3    2.48491    3.46410    144    0.083333
     6     30    19    3.40120    5.47723    900    0.033333

   MTB > PLOT C2 VS C1 *7
```

```
         -                                                             *
         -              *
   18.0+                              *
         -
C2       -
         -          *
         -
   12.0+
         -
         -
         -
         -
    6.0+
         -    *
         -
         -    *
         -
         ------+---------+---------+---------+---------+---------+C1
             15        30        45        60        75        90
```

---

*1 Command **set** enters the data into c1
*2 Command **set** enters the data into c2

continues

Continued

> *3 Command **loge** computes the logs of the values in c1 and stores the results in c3
> *4 Command **sqrt** computes the square roots of the values in c1 and stores the results in c4
> *5 The squares of the values in c1 are computed and the results are stored in c5
> *6 The reciprocals of the values in c1 are computed and the results are stored in c6
> *7 A plot of the values in c1 is generated with c2 values on the vertical axis and c1 values on the horizontal axis

MTB > PLOT C2 VS C3

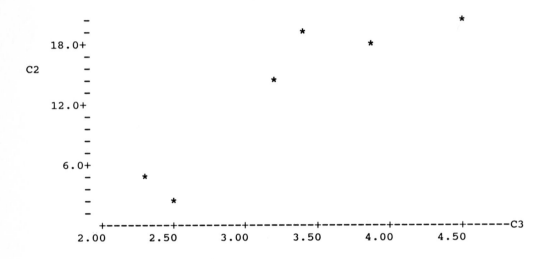

MTB > PLOT C2 VS C4

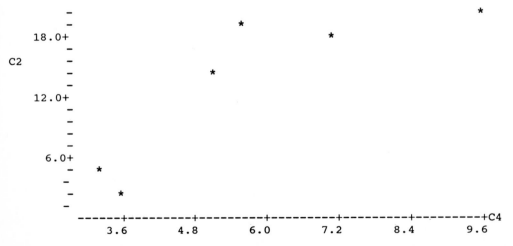

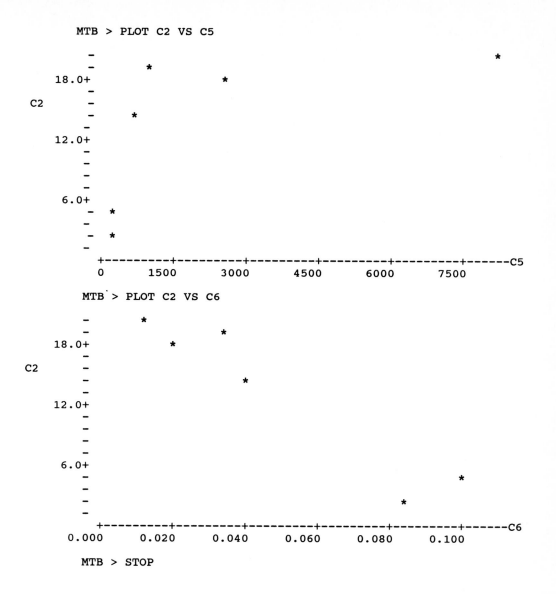

```
        MTB > PLOT C2 VS C5

              -                                                              *
              -          *
        18.0+                        *
              -
  C2          -
              -       *
              -
        12.0+
              -
              -
              -
              -
         6.0+
              -    *
              -
              -    *
              -
              +---------+---------+---------+---------+---------+------C5
              0        1500      3000      4500      6000      7500

        MTB > PLOT C2 VS C6

              -       *
              -                   *
        18.0+             *
              -
  C2          -
              -                        *
              -
        12.0+
              -
              -
              -
              -
         6.0+
              -                                                   *
              -
              -                                             *
              -
              +---------+---------+---------+---------+---------+------C6
           0.000     0.020     0.040     0.060     0.080     0.100

        MTB > STOP
```

Notice that the first data plot above (X versus Y) produces a plot that is nonlinear. A straight line fitted through these data points would probably introduce an undesirable degree of error into the analysis and subsequent forecasts.

By contrast, the second plot (Y versus the log of X) and the fifth plot (Y versus the reciprocal of X) both show promise for the linear model. The linear methods of this chapter and Chapter 7 could be used with these two predictors in an attempt to find a prediction equation with an acceptable degree of accuracy.

APPLICATION TO MANAGEMENT

Regression analysis is probably the most widely used statistical tool employed by management when there is a need to evaluate the impact of a single independent variable on a dependent variable. Regression analysis, along with correlation analysis, helps the forecaster characterize the relationships among variables. The forecaster can determine both the importance and the direction of the relationship between variables.

Most problems utilizing regression analysis involve the more sophisticated version called *multiple regression analysis* (to be described in the next chapter), because most relationships involve the study of more than just one independent variable. Nevertheless, simple regression and correlation analysis is sometimes used, and a few examples of its use are the following:

- *Product consumption.* A manufacturer might try to predict how much beer a person drinks per week from looking at variables such as income, age, education, or social class.
- *Sales.* A retailer might try to predict the sales of a product for one store versus another on the basis of price differentials, the relative income of the surrounding community, the relative friendliness of store personnel, or the number and strength of competitors in each market.
- *Stock prices.* A stock analyst for a regional brokerage firm might try to predict the price of a new issue for a local firm on the basis of the regional economy, income, population, or visibility of the firm.
- *Bad debts.* An accountant might try to predict the bad debt a firm might expect to encounter in the next fiscal quarter on the basis of number of people unemployed, outstanding credit, interest rates, or expected sales.
- *Employment needs.* A personnel director of a large manufacturing firm might try to predict the coming year's staffing requirements from the average age of its employees, its wage scale compared with that of the surrounding community, expected new sales contracts, or the availability of competitive jobs.
- *Shopping center demand.* The manager of a new shopping center might try to anticipate demand by analyzing the income of the surrounding community, the size of the population, or the proximity and size of competitive shopping centers.

Once the relationships between the independent and the dependent variables are determined, management can, in some cases, try to control the dependent variable with this knowledge. For instance, suppose that a marketing manager determines that there is a significant positive relationship between advertising expenditures and sales. The regression equation might be

Sales = \$43,000 + .3 (advertising expenditure)

From this equation the marketing manager can try to control sales by increasing or decreasing advertising by the amount that would maximize profits. Whenever the manager has control over the independent variable, there is the opportunity for possible partial control of the dependent variable. Thus the regression equation and the coefficient of determination help management determine if such control is worthwhile.

CHAPTER **6**

GLOSSARY

Regression line   A regression line is the line that best fits a collection of X–Y data points. It minimizes the sum of the squared distances from the points to the line as measured in the vertical, or Y, direction.

Standard error of estimate   The standard error of estimate measures the typical amount by which the actual Y values differ from the estimated values (Y_R).

CHAPTER **6**

KEY FORMULAS

Method of least squares: slope formula $b = \dfrac{n \, \Sigma \, XY - \Sigma \, X \, \Sigma \, Y}{n \, \Sigma \, X^2 - (\Sigma \, X)^2}$

(6.1)

Method of least squares: Y intercept formula $b_0 = \dfrac{\Sigma \, Y}{n} - \dfrac{b \, \Sigma \, X}{n}$

(6.2)

Regression equation $Y_R = b_0 + bX$

(6.3)

Standard error of estimate: definitional formula $s_{y.x} = \sqrt{\dfrac{\Sigma \, (Y - Y_R)^2}{n - 2}}$

(6.4)

Standard error of estimate: computational formula

$$s_{y.x} = \sqrt{\dfrac{\Sigma \, Y^2 - b_0 \, \Sigma \, Y - b \, \Sigma \, XY}{n - 2}}$$

(6.5)

Standard error of the forecast $s_f = s_{y.x} \sqrt{1 + \dfrac{1}{n} + \dfrac{(X - \bar{X})^2}{\Sigma \, (X - \bar{X})^2}}$

(6.6)

Prediction interval: large sample $Y_R \pm Z s_f$

(6.7)

Prediction interval: small sample $Y_R \pm t s_f$

(6.8)

Coefficient of determination $r^2 = 1 - \dfrac{\Sigma \, (Y - Y_R)^2}{\Sigma \, (Y - \bar{Y})^2}$

(6.9)

Coefficient of determination: computational formula

$$r^2 = \dfrac{b_0 \, \Sigma \, Y + b \, \Sigma \, XY - n\bar{Y}^2}{\Sigma \, Y^2 - n\bar{Y}^2}$$

(6.10)

Total sum of squares $\quad \Sigma (Y - \bar{Y})^2$ (6.11)

Total variance of Y around its mean $\quad s_y^2 = \dfrac{\Sigma (Y - \bar{Y})^2}{n - 1}$ (6.12)

Sum of squared residuals $\quad \Sigma (Y - Y_R)^2$ (6.13)

Total variance of Y around the predicted values $\quad s_{y.x}^2 = \dfrac{\Sigma (Y - Y_R)^2}{n - 2}$ (6.14)

Standard error of the regression coefficient $\quad s_b = \dfrac{s_{y.x}}{\sqrt{\Sigma (X - \bar{X})^2}}$ (6.15)

t statistic for regression coefficient $\quad t = \dfrac{b - \beta}{s_b}$ (6.16)

Variance ratio test or F statistic $\quad F = \dfrac{(r_F^2 - r_R^2)/(K_F - K_R)}{(1 - r_F^2)/(n - K_F)}$ (6.17)

CHAPTER **6**

PROBLEMS

1. Consider the data in the accompanying table, where X = weekly advertising expenditures and Y = weekly sales.

Y	X	Y	X
$1,250	$41	$1,300	$46
1,380	54	1,400	62
1,425	63	1,510	61
1,425	54	1,575	64
1,450	48	1,650	71

   a. Does a significant relationship exist between advertising expenditures and sales?
   b. State the prediction equation.
   c. Predict sales for an advertising expenditure of $50.
   d. What percentage of the variance can be explained with the prediction equation?
   e. State the amount of unexplained variance.
   f. State the amount of total variance.

2. The times required to check out customers in a supermarket and the corresponding values of purchases are shown in the accompanying table. Answer parts a, b, e, and f of Problem 1 by using these data. Give a point and a 99% confidence interval estimate for Y if $X = 3.0$.

Time Required for Checkout (Minutes)	Value of Purchase (Dollars)	Time Required for Checkout (Minutes)	Value of Purchase (Dollars)
3.6	30.6	1.8	6.2
4.1	30.5	4.3	40.1
.8	2.4	.2	2.0
5.7	42.2	2.6	15.5
3.4	21.8	1.3	6.5

3. A study to show the relationship of income to education produced the results in the accompanying table. Determine whether the linear relationship is significant between income and years of education. Compute the sample regression equation. Compute r^2 and interpret its value.

Group	Average Number of Years of Education, X	Average Annual Income (Thousands of Dollars), Y	Group	Average Number of Years of Education, X	Average Annual Income (Thousands of Dollars), Y
1	3	3	7	11	13
2	4	4	8	12	20
3	5	5	9	16	35
4	7	7	10	15	40
5	6	9	11	21	50
6	9	11			

4. A farming cooperative has undertaken an investigation to determine the nature of the relationship between yield per acre of a particular crop and the intensity of application of a fertilizer compound. The results are shown in the accompanying table.

Tract	Yield Per Acre (Thousands of Bushels), Y	Tons of Fertilizer, X	Tract	Yield Per Acre (Thousands of Bushels), Y	Tons of Fertilizer, X
A	7	11	E	9	30
B	8	21	F	10	36
C	10	24	G	15	41
D	12	31	H	13	50

a. Calculate the regression equation.
b. Predict yield when 25 tons of fertilizer are used.
c. Test $H_0: \beta = 0$.
d. Compute r^2.

5. Information supplied by a mail-order business for 12 cities is shown in the accompanying table.

City	Number of Mail Orders Received (Thousands), Y	Number of Catalogs Distributed (Thousands), X	City	Number of Mail Orders Received (Thousands), Y	Number of Catalogs Distributed (Thousands), X
A	24	6	G	38	15
B	16	2	H	18	3
C	23	5	I	35	11
D	15	1	J	34	13
E	32	10	K	15	2
F	25	7	L	32	12

a. Determine whether a significant linear relationship exists between these two variables. (Test at the .05 significance level.)
b. Determine the regression line.
c. Calculate the standard error of estimate.
d. What percentage of the mail-order variable variance is explained by the catalogs distributed variable?
e. Predict the number of mail orders received when 10,000 catalogs are distributed.
f. Test to determine whether the regression coefficient is significantly different from zero. (Use the .01 significance level.)
g. Calculate the explained variance for the Y variable.

6. In a regression of investment on the interest rate, the results in the accompanying table were observed during 10 years.

Yearly Investment (Thousands of Dollars)	Average Interest Rate (Percent)	Yearly Investment (Thousands of Dollars)	Average Interest Rate (Percent)
1,060	4.8	2,050	3.8
940	5.1	2,070	3.7
920	5.9	2,030	4.5
1,110	5.1	1,780	4.9
1,590	4.8	1,420	6.2

a. Is the relationship between these variables significant?
b. Can an effective prediction equation be developed?
c. If the average interest rate is 4% five years from now, can we forecast yearly investment?
d. Calculate and interpret r^2.
e. Discuss correlation and causation in this example.

7. The personnel manager of a company wants to find a measure that can be used to forecast weekly sales. As an experimental project, six of the regular salespeople were asked to complete the Norse Sales Aptitude Test. The

manager reasoned that if the relationship between the test scores and weekly sales were high, the test might be used to select new salespeople. The test scores and the weekly sales of the six people are shown in the accompanying table. Use appropriate statistical procedures to prepare a recommendation for the personnel manager.

Salesperson	Weekly Sales (Thousands)	Norse Test Score
M. N.	10	6.2
A. D.	15	10.1
O. I.	8	2.9
S. B.	7	3.2
N. D.	12	8.5
J. J.	5	2.4

8. Some investors feel that since AT&T (American Telephone and Telegraph) is such a large utility, its earning per common share (EPS) should be related to GNP (gross national product), using the latter as a predictor of the former. From the data in the accompanying table, can the EPS of AT&T be forecast by GNP? What is the prediction equation? Present an interval estimate for Y when $X = 800$. Test $H_0: \beta = 0$. Summarize the investigation in a report to investors.

Year	GNP (Billions of Current Dollars)	AT&T Earnings per Share (Dollars)
1961	520.1	.82
1962	560.3	.86
1963	590.5	.88
1964	632.4	1.02
1965	684.9	1.08
1966	747.6	1.18
1967	789.7	1.22

9. The ABC Investment Company is in the business of making bids on investments offered by various firms that desire additional financing. ABC has tabulated its bid on the last 25 issues bid on in terms of the bid's percentage of par value. The bid of ABC's major competitor, as a percentage of par value, is also tabulated on these issues. ABC now wonders if it is using the same rationale in preparing bids as its competitor. In other words, could ABC's bid be used to forecast the competitor's bid? If not, then the competitor must be evaluating issues differently. The data are given in the accompanying table.

Issue	ABC Bid	Competitor Bid	Issue	ABC Bid	Competitor Bid
1	99.035	100.104	14	100.542	99.936
2	104.358	105.032	15	96.842	95.834
3	99.435	99.517	16	99.200	99.863
4	96.932	95.808	17	101.614	102.010
5	98.904	98.835	18	99.501	99.432
6	101.635	101.563	19	100.898	99.965
7	100.001	101.237	20	97.001	96.838
8	98.234	99.123	21	100.025	100.804
9	93.849	94.803	22	103.014	104.300
10	99.412	100.063	23	98.702	99.010
11	99.949	99.564	24	101.834	100.936
12	104.012	103.889	25	102.903	103.834
13	99.473	99.348			

    a. To what extent are the two firms using the same rationale in preparing their bids?

    b. Forecast the competitor's bid if ABC bids 101% of par value. Give both a point and an interval prediction under the assumption that the given data constitute the entire *population* of bid data.

    c. Under part b, what is the probability of ABC winning this particular bid (lowest bid wins)?

    d. If the given data constitute a random *sample* of bid data rather than the entire population, what changes would be necessary in parts b and c? Answer the question in part c, assuming that the data are from a random sample.

10. Evaluate the following statements:

    a. "A high r^2 means a significant regression."

    b. "A very large sample size in a regression problem will always produce useful results."

11. Many analysts consider a scatter diagram to be an important first step in analyzing an $X-Y$ relationship. Explain why this belief might be true.

12. A large computer firm is considering the possibility that computer sales could be closely correlated with gross private domestic investment. What conclusion would you reach after examining the 16 years' data given in the accompanying table?

Year	Gross Private Domestic Investment (Billions of Dollars)	Computer Sales (Millions)	Year	Gross Private Domestic Investment (Billions of Dollars)	Computer Sales (Millions)
1960	74.8	13.2	1968	126.3	42.8
1961	69.0	14.4	1969	139.6	52.1
1962	83.0	15.9	1970	140.8	56.7
1963	87.1	18.3	1971	160.0	51.7
1964	93.0	27.3	1972	188.3	61.1
1965	112.0	29.6	1973	220.0	73.6
1966	121.3	41.6	1974	215.0	91.2
1967	116.0	46.8	1975	183.7	85.8

13. Consider the population of observations on temperature and shares traded presented in Chapter 2, Problem 27. Draw a random sample of 30 data pairs.
   a. Construct a scatter diagram.
   b. Compute the sample correlation coefficient.
   c. Determine the sample regression line equation.
   d. Plot the regression line on the scatter diagram.
   e. Compute the standard error of estimate.
   f. Compute the standard error of forecast for $X = 20$.
   g. Compute the sample coefficient of determination and interpret its value.
   h. Test the hypothesis that the slope of the regression line that passes through the entire population of data is zero.

14. Consider the population of observations on number of copies and direct labor cost presented in Chapter 2, Problem 28. Draw a random sample of 20 data pairs and perform the analysis indicated in Problem 13 for parts a through h (exclude f). Also, make a point and a 90% confidence interval estimate for the direct labor cost if the project involves 250 copies.

CASE STUDY 6.1

TIGER TRANSPORT

Tiger Transport Company is a trucking firm that moves household goods locally and across the country. Its current concern involves the price charged for moving small loads over long distances. It has rates it is happy with for full truckloads; these rates are based on the variable costs of driver, fuel, and maintenance, plus overhead and profit. When a truck is less than fully loaded, however, there is some question about the proper rate to be charged on goods needed to fill the truck.

Tiger feels that the only additional cost incurred if extra cargo is added to the truck is the cost of additional fuel since the miles per gallon of the truck would then be lowered. As one of the factors used to determine rates for small loads, it would like to know its out-of-pocket cost associated with additional cargo fuel costs.

You are a recent business school graduate working in the cost accounting department, and you are assigned the job of investigating this matter and advising top management on the considerations necessary for a sound rate decision. You begin by assuming that all trucks are the same; in fact, they are nearly identical in terms of size, gross-weight capacity, and engine size. You also assume that every driver will get the same truck mileage over a long trip. Tiger's chief accountant feels that these assumptions are reasonable.

You are then left with only one variable that might affect the miles per gallon of long-haul trucks: cargo weight. You find that the accounting department has records for every trip made by a Tiger truck over the past several years. These records include the total cargo weight, the distance covered, and the number of gallons of diesel fuel used. A ratio of these last two figures is the miles per gallon for the trip.

You select trips made over the past four years as your population; there are a total of 5,428 trips. You then select 40 random numbers from a random number table, and since the trips are recorded one after another, you assign the number 1 to the first recorded trip, 2 to the second, and so on. Your 40 random numbers thus produce a random selection of 40 trips to be examined. The cargo weight and miles per gallon for these trips are recorded and appear in Table 6.9.

Since Tiger has a computer with a regression analysis package, you then run the data of Table 6.9 through this program. The resulting printout appears in Table 6.10.

In studying the printout of Table 6.10, you decide that the sample data have produced a useful regression equation. This conclusion is based on a relatively high r^2 (76%), a high t value (-10.9), and a high F value (119). You then formulate the regression equation from the printout.

TABLE 6.9 Data for Tiger Transport: Trip Cargo Weight (Thousands of Pounds) and Miles Per Gallon.

Weight	Miles per Gallon	Weight	Miles per Gallon	Weight	Miles per Gallon	Weight	Miles per Gallon
60	5.3	58	4.9	63	5.0	63	5.0
55	5.0	60	5.1	65	4.9	62	4.9
80	4.0	74	4.5	72	4.6	77	4.6
72	4.2	80	4.3	81	4.0	76	4.5
75	4.5	53	5.9	64	5.3	51	5.7
63	5.1	61	5.5	78	4.4	74	4.2
48	7.2	80	3.5	62	4.9	78	4.3
79	3.9	68	4.1	83	3.8	50	6.1
82	3.8	76	4.5	79	4.1	79	4.3
72	4.4	75	4.4	61	4.8	55	4.7

TABLE 6.10 Regression Analysis Output for Tiger Transport.

VARIABLE NO.	MEAN	STANDARD DEVIATION	CORRELATION X VS Y	REGRESSION COEFFICIENT	STD. ERROR OF REG.COEF.	COMPUTED T VALUE
1	68.59999	10.21763	-0.87055	-0.06040	0.00554	-10.90562

DEPENDENT

2	4.70499	0.70890				

INTERCEPT	8.84833			
MULT. CORR	0.87055		R-SQUARE	0.75786
STD. ERR.	0.35339		CORR-RSQUARE	0.75786

ANALYSIS OF VARIANCE FOR THE REGRESSION

SOURCE OF VARIATION	DEGREES OF FREEDOM	SUM OF SQUARES	MEAN SQUARES	F VALUE
ATTRIBUTABLE TO REGRESSION	1	14.85315	14.85315	118.93246
DEVIATION FROM REGRESSION	38	4.74572	0.12489	
TOTAL	39	19.59886		

$$Y_R = 8.84833 - .06040X$$

where Y is measured in miles per gallon and X is measured in thousands of pounds.

The slope of the regression equation ($-.06040$) is interpreted as follows: *each additional 1,000 pounds of cargo reduces the mileage of a truck by .06040 mile per gallon.*

Tiger is currently paying approximately $1.25 per gallon for diesel fuel. You can therefore calculate the cost of hauling an additional 1,000 pounds of cargo 100 miles, as follows:

Average miles per gallon from Table 6.10 = 4.7 (mean of variable 2)

Cost of 100 miles,

$$\frac{100(1.25)}{4.7} = \$26.60$$

Cost of same trip with an additional 1,000 pounds,

$$\frac{100(1.25)}{(4.7 - .0604)} = \$26.94$$

Thus

Incremental cost of 1000 pounds carried 100 miles = $.34

You now believe you have completed part of your assignment, namely, determination of the out-of-pocket costs associated with adding cargo weight to a less-than-full truck. You realize, of course, that other factors bear on a rate decision for small loads.

ASSIGNMENT

Prepare a memo for Tiger's Top management that summarizes the analysis.

BUTCHER PRODUCTS, INC.

Gene Butcher is owner and president of Butcher Products, Inc., a small company that makes fiberglass ducting for electrical cable installations. Gene has been studying the number of duct units manufactured per day over the past two and a half years and is concerned about the wide variability in this figure.

Based on his experience with the company, Gene is unable to come up with any reason for the variability in output until he begins thinking about weather conditions. His reasoning is that the outside temperature may have something to do with the productivity of his work force and the daily output achieved.

He randomly selects several days from his records and records the number of ducting units produced for each of these days. He then goes to the local weather bureau and, for each of the selected days, records the high temperature for the day. He is then ready to run a correlation study between these two figures when he realizes that output would probably be related to deviation from an ideal temperature rather than the temperature itself. That is, he thinks that a day that is either too hot or too cold would have a negative effect on production when compared with a day that has an ideal temperature. He decides to convert his temperature readings to deviations from 65 degrees Fahrenheit, a temperature he understands is ideal in terms of generating high worker output. His data appear as follows; Y represents the number of units produced, while X represents the absolute difference (negative signs eliminated) between the day's high temperature and 65 degrees:

Y	X	Y	X
485	12	327	15
512	10	308	25
625	3	603	8
585	4	321	35
318	27	426	5
405	10	410	12
379	18	515	2
497	12	498	7
316	27	357	17
351	20	429	8
535	4	401	12
395	11		

Gene performs a regression analysis using his company's computer and the Minitab software program. He keys the following into the program after Minitab has been called up:

```
MTB > SET C1
DATA > 12 10 3 4 27 10 18 12 27 20 4 11
DATA > 15 25 8 35 5 12 2 7 17 8 12
DATA > END
MTB > SET C2
DATA > 485 512 625 585 318 405 379 497 316
DATA > 351 525 395 327 308 603 321 426 410
DATA > 515 498 357 429 401
DATA > END
MTB > NAME C1 'TEMP' C2 'UNITS'
MTB > REGRESS C2 ON 1 PREDICTOR C1

The regression equation is
UNITS = 552 - 8.91 TEMP
```

Predictor	Coef	Stdev	t-ratio	p
Constant	552.04	22.85	24.16	0.000
TEMP	-8.911	1.453	-6.13	0.000

s = 59.41   R-sq = 64.2%   R-sq(adj) = 62.5%

Analysis of Variance

SOURCE	DF	SS	MS	F	p
Regression	1	132758	132758	37.62	0.000
Error	21	74109	3529		
Total	22	206866			

Unusual Observations

Obs.	TEMP	UNITS	Fit	Stdev.Fit	Residual	St.Resid
15	8.0	603.0	480.8	14.5	122.2	2.12R
16	35.0	321.0	240.2	34.0	80.8	1.66 X

```
MTB > STOP
```

Gene is pleased to see the results of his regression analysis as presented above. The *t* values are high, indicating that both the values in the sample regression equation (552 and −8.9) are significant: for both, the significance level is near zero, as indicated by the *p* values for the *t* test. The *F* value is high (37.62), so the sample regression equation can be used in the population of all production days.

Turning to *Y*-squared, Gene is somewhat disappointed to find that this value, while satisfactory, is not as high as he had hoped (64.2%). However, he decides that it is high enough to begin thinking about ways to increase daily production levels.

QUESTIONS

1. How many units would you predict for a day in which the high temperature is 89 degrees?

2. How many units would you predict for a day in which the high temperature is 41 degrees?

3. Based on the results of the regression analysis as shown above, what action would you advise Gene to take in order to increase daily output?

ACE PERSONNEL DEPARTMENT

The Ace Manufacturing Company employs several thousand people in the manufacture of keyboards, equipment cases, and cables for the small-computer industry. The president of Ace has recently become concerned with the absentee rate among the company's employees and has asked the Personnel Department to look into this matter.

Bill McGone, the personnel director, decides to take a look at a few personnel folders in an attempt to size up the problem. He decides to randomly select 15 folders and record the number of absent days during the past fiscal year along with employee age. After reading an article in a recent personnel journal, he believes that age may have a significant effect on absenteeism. If he finds that age and absent days show a good correlation in his small sample, he intends to take a sample of 200 or 300 folders and formulate a good prediction equation.

Following are the data values collected in the initial sample. Number of absent days during the past fiscal year is represented by Y, while X represents employee age.

Y	X	Y	X
3	25	9	56
4	36	12	60
7	41	8	51
4	27	5	33
3	35	6	37
3	31	2	31
5	35	2	29
7	41		

QUESTIONS

1. How well are absent days and age correlated? Can this correlation be generalized to the entire work force?

2. What is the prediction equation for absent days using age as a predictor variable?

3. What percent of the variability in absent days can be explained through knowledge of age?

4. How good a prediction equation has resulted? In answering this question, use proper statistical procedures to support your answer.

5. Suppose a newly hired person is 24 yeas old. How many absent days would you predict for this person during the coming fiscal year?

6. Should Bill McGone proceed to take a large sample of company employees based on the preliminary results of his sample?

SPSS EXAMPLE

One popular data analysis program currently available is the Statistical Package for the Social Sciences (SPSS). A version is available for mainframe computers (SPSS^X) and for personal computers (SPSS-PC). Recent modifications in this package are designed specifically for forecasting. An example SPSS problem is given next, both with the analysis commands and the output.

THE PROBLEM

In Chapter 2, Problem 28, the Marshall Printing Company wanted to estimate the relationship between the number of copies produced by an offset-printing technique and the associated direct labor cost. Twenty observations were randomly selected and the number of copies and direct labor cost variables correlated.

THE SPSS^X SOLUTION

Twenty random numbers between 1 and 140 were drawn from Table C.5 in Appendix C (note that a random number computer program could have been used, as was illustrated at the end of Chapter 3). The random numbers and the corresponding X–Y values from the Marshall Printing data are

Obs.	Cost	# Copies	Obs.	Cost	# Copies
38	1.2	150	111	2.6	390
102	2.7	350	137	2.6	490
67	1.6	240	134	3.0	480
136	3.2	480	139	3.3	490
17	1.0	60	68	1.7	240
1	1.0	10	35	1.5	130
52	4.1	190	41	0.9	160
8	1.0	30	56	2.5	200
88	1.9	310	55	2.1	200
85	2.5	300	64	2.2	230

To run the problem on the SPSS^X system, the data are entered into a data file (MARSHALL.DAT), and then a command file is submitted that gives specific instructions to the program.

The command file to run the data of Problem 2.28 (see your instructor about the information you need to run SPSS^X on your particular computer system) is

```
TITLE MARSHALL
FILE HANDLE MARSHALL / NAME = 'MARSHALL.DAT'
DATA LIST FILE = MARSHALL /
         COST 1-2 COPIES 3-5
VARIABLE LABELS
         COST      'COST'
         COPIES    'COPIES'
SCATTERGRAM COST COPIES
OPTIONS 4
STATISTICS 1 3
FINISH
```

FIGURE 6.9 Marshall Printing Output.

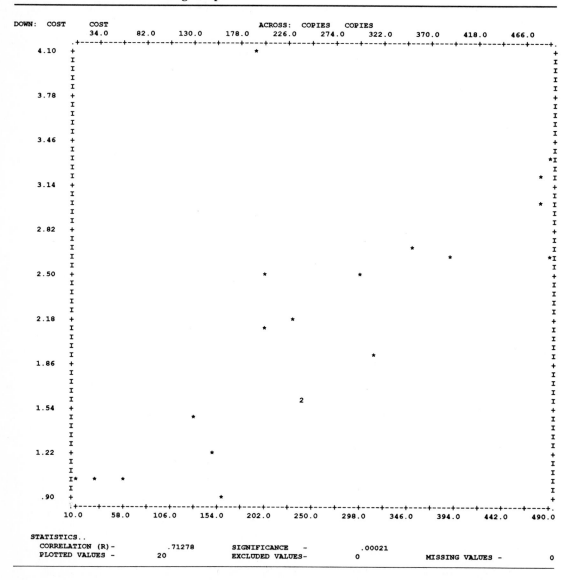

The options 4 command suppresses grid lines in the scatter diagram. Statistics 1 and 3 provide the correlation coefficient and its significance.

A scatter diagram and the results for the SPSS^X run are shown in Figure 6.9.

SAS EXAMPLE

A popular statistical package that runs on mainframe computers is the Statistical Analysis System (SAS). SAS allows the analyst to run many techniques commonly used in forecasting.

SAS will be demonstrated in this section to illustrate the use of statistical software packages for solving regression analysis problems.

THE PROBLEM

In Case Study 6.1, a computer regression package is used to run the data shown in Table 6.9. The computer output is presented in Table 6.10. The SAS commands illustrated below show how to run the data of Table 6.9. The SAS output for this problem is also presented and can be compared to the output of Table 6.10.

THE SAS SOLUTION

The SAS command file to run the data of Table 6.9 (see your instructor about the information you need to run SAS on your particular computer system) is

```
DATA;
      INPUT MPG 1-3 WEIGHT 5-6;
CARDS;
5.3 60
5.0 55
4.0 80
4.2 72
4.5 75
    .
    .
    .
4.3 79
4.7 55
RUN;
PROC REG;
    MODEL MPG = WEIGHT;
    TITLE 'TIGER TRANSPORT REGRESSION';
RUN;
```

The resulting regression output is

```
DEP VARIABLE: MPG
                      SUM OF           MEAN
   SOURCE      DF    SQUARES         SQUARE     F VALUE    PROB>F
   MODEL        1   14.853288      14.853288    118.934    0.0001
   ERROR       38    4.745712       0.124887
   C TOTAL     39   19.599000

   ROOT MSE        0.353394     R-SQUARE        0.7579
   DEP MEAN        4.705000     ADJ R-SQ        0.7515
   C.V.            7.511026

                      PARAMETER      STANDARD     T FOR HO:
   VARIABLE    DF     ESTIMATE          ERROR  PARAMETER=0    PROB>  T
   INTERCEP     1     8.848362       0.384014       23.042    0.0001
   WEIGHT       1    -0.060399  0.005538298      -10.906      0.0001
```

CHAPTER 6

SELECTED BIBLIOGRAPHY

Draper, N., and Smith, H. *Applied Regression Analysis.* New York: John Wiley & Sons, 1966.

Kleinbaum, D., and Kupper, K. *Applied Regression Analysis and Other Multivariable Methods.* North Scituate, Mass.: Duxbury Press, 1978.

Neter, J., Wasserman, W., and Kutner, M. *Applied Linear Regression Models.* Homewood, Ill.: Richard D. Irwin, Inc. 1983.

7

Multiple Regression

I n simple regression the relationship between an independent variable and a dependent variable is investigated. The relationship between two variables oftentimes allows a person to predict accurately the dependent variable from knowledge of the independent variable. Unfortunately, most real-life situations are not so simple. More than one independent variable is usually necessary in order to predict a dependent variable accurately. When more than one independent or predictor variable is used, the problem becomes one for multiple regression analysis. The basic concepts remain the same, but more than one independent variable is used to predict the dependent variable.

> *Multiple regression* involves the use of more than one independent variable to predict a dependent variable.

PREDICTOR VARIABLES

As an example, return to the problem in which sales volume of gallons of milk is forecast from knowledge of price per gallon. Mr. Bump is faced with the problem of making a prediction that is not entirely accurate. He can explain almost 75% of the total variance of the sales volume of gallons of milk sold by using one independent variable. Thus 25% $(1 - r^2)$ of the total variation is unexplained. In other words, from the sample evidence Bump knows 75% of what he must know to forecast sales volume perfectly. To do a more accurate job of forecasting, he needs to find another predictor variable that will enable him to explain more of the total variance. If Bump can reduce the unexplained variation, his forecast will involve less error and more accuracy.

A search must be conducted for another independent variable that is related to sales volume of gallons of milk. However, this new independent, or predictor, variable cannot relate too highly with the independent variable (price per gallon) already in use. If the two independent variables are highly related to each other, they will explain the same variation, and the addition of the second variable will not improve the forecast. In fields such as econometrics and applied statistics, there is a great deal of concern with this problem of intercorrelation among independent variables, often referred to as *collinearity*. The simple solution to the problem of two highly related independent variables is merely *not* to use both of them together. The collinearity problem will be discussed later in this chapter.

> To summarize, the attributes of a *good predictor variable* are:
>
> A good predictor variable is related to the dependent variable.
>
> A good predictor variable is not highly related to any other independent variable.

CORRELATION MATRIX

Mr. Bump decides that advertising expense might help improve his forecast of weekly sales volume. He investigates the relationships among advertising expense, sales volume, and price per gallon by examining a correlation matrix. The *correlation matrix* is constructed by computing the simple correlation coefficients for each combination of pairs of variables.

An example of a correlation matrix is illustrated in Table 7.1. The correlation coefficient that indicates the relationship between variables 1 and 2 is represented as r_{12}. Note that the first subscript ($r_{\textcircled{1}2}$) refers to the row and the second subscript ($r_{1\textcircled{2}}$) refers to the column. This standardized approach allows one to determine, at a glance, the relationship between any two variables. Of course, the relationship between variables 1 and 2 (r_{12}) is exactly the same as for variables 2 and 1 (r_{21}). Therefore only half the matrix is necessary. Also, the primary diagonal will always contain ones since it always relates a variable with itself (r_{11}, r_{22}, r_{33}).

Bump runs his data on the computer, and the correlation matrix shown in Table 7.2 results. (Most multiple regression computer programs

TABLE 7.1 Correlation Matrix.

		Variables	
Variables	1	2	3
1	r_{11}	r_{12}	r_{13}
2	r_{21}	r_{22}	r_{23}
3	r_{31}	r_{32}	r_{33}

TABLE 7.2 Computer Correlation Matrix for Bump's Data.

Variables	Variables Sales, 1	Price, 2	Advertising, 3
Sales, 1	1.00	−.86	.89
Price, 2		1.00	−.65
Advertising, 3			1.00

provide a correlation matrix.) An investigation of the relationships among advertising expense, sales volume, and price per gallon indicates that the new independent variable should contribute to improved prediction. The correlation matrix shows that advertising expense has a high positive relationship ($r_{13} = .89$) to the dependent variable, sales volume, and a moderate negative relationship ($r_{23} = -.65$) to the independent variable, price per gallon. This combination of relationships should permit advertising expenses to explain some of the total variance of sales volume that is not already being explained by price per gallon. As will be seen, when both price per gallon and advertising expense are used to estimate sales volume, R^2 increases to 93.2%.

The analysis of the correlation matrix is an important initial step in the solution of any problem involving multiple independent variables.

MULTIPLE REGRESSION EQUATION

In simple regression the dependent variable can be represented by Y and the independent variable by X. In multiple regression analysis Xs with subscripts are used to represent the independent variables. The dependent variable is still represented by Y, and the independent variables are represented by $X_2, X_3, \ldots, X_n$. In this system of notation Mr. Bump's new regression equation is written

$$Y_R = b_0 + b_2 X_2 + b_3 X_3 \qquad (7.1)$$

where

Y_R = volume of gallons sold estimated by the regression equation

b_2, b_3 = net regression coefficients (the best set of weights for the two independent variables in order to achieve maximum prediction)

X_2 = price per gallon

X_3 = advertising expense (hundreds of dollars)

b_0 = constant, or Y intercept

The analysis uses the method of least squares to obtain the best-fitting, three-variable, linear regression equation. Whereas in the two-variable problem the least squares method produced the best-fitting straight line, in this three-variable problem the method is used to obtain the best-fitting plane (see Figure 7.1). The points are plotted in three dimensions along the Y, X_2, and X_3 axes. The points fall above and below the plane in such a way that $\Sigma (Y - Y_R)^2$ is a minimum. The b_2 and b_3 values are derived as the best set of weights that minimize the sum of the squared distances between the data points and the multiple regression plane.

In Chapter 6 the example involved two variables, and two equations resulted from the minimization process. Now three equations must be solved in order to determine the values of b_2, b_3, and b_0.[1] These equations are

FIGURE 7.1 Multiple Regression Plane for Bump's Data.

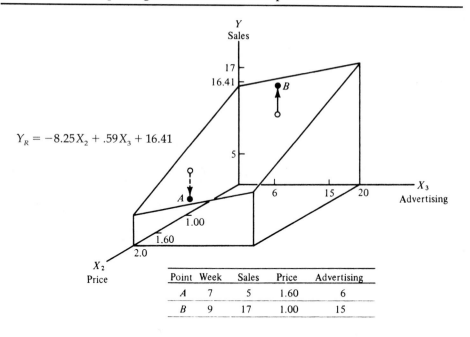

$$Y_R = -8.25X_2 + .59X_3 + 16.41$$

Point	Week	Sales	Price	Advertising
A	7	5	1.60	6
B	9	17	1.00	15

---

[1] As illustrated in Appendix A, a function of the form

$$F(b_2, b_3, b_0) = \Sigma (Y - b_0 - b_2X_2 - b_3X_3)^2$$

is minimized by the calculus method of taking partial derivatives with respect to b_0, b_2, and b_3 and equating these derivatives.

$$\Sigma\,Y = nb_0 + b_2\,\Sigma\,X_2 + b_3\,\Sigma\,X_3$$

$$\Sigma\,X_2Y = b_0\,\Sigma\,X_2 + b_2\,\Sigma\,X_2^2 + b_3\,\Sigma\,X_2X_3 \qquad (7.2)$$

$$\Sigma\,X_3Y = b_0\,\Sigma\,X_3 + b_2\,\Sigma\,X_2X_3 + b_3\,\Sigma\,X_3^2$$

EXAMPLE 7.1

■ The computations for the required summations for Bump's problem are shown in Table 7.3. Substituting into Equation 7.2 gives

$$112 = 10b_0 + 14.4b_2 + 114b_3$$

$$149.3 = 14.4b_0 + 21.56b_2 + 155.3b_3$$

$$1{,}480 = 114b_0 + 115.3b_2 + 1{,}522b_3$$

These three equations, often called *normal equations,* can be solved simultaneously by using matrix methods. This approach is discussed by Younger and by Neter and Wasserman, texts you may wish to refer to if you are interested in the mathematics of the procedure.

In this example a computer program was used to obtain

$$b_2 = -8.2476$$

$$b_3 = .5851$$

$$b_0 = 16.4064$$

TABLE 7.3 Computations for the Linear Multiple Regression Analysis for Bump's Data.

Week	Sales (Thousands), Y	Price per Gallon, X_2	Advertising (Hundreds of Dollars), X_3	X_2Y	X_3Y	X_2X_3	Y^2	X_2^2	X_3^2
1	10	$1.30	9	13	90	11.7	100	1.69	81
2	6	2.00	7	12	42	14.0	36	4.00	49
3	5	1.70	5	8.5	25	8.5	25	2.89	25
4	12	1.50	14	18	168	21.0	144	2.25	196
5	10	1.60	15	16	150	24.0	100	2.56	225
6	15	1.20	12	18	180	14.4	225	1.44	144
7	5	1.60	6	8	30	9.6	25	2.56	36
8	12	1.40	10	16.8	120	14.0	144	1.96	100
9	17	1.00	15	17	255	15.0	289	1.00	225
10	20	1.10	21	22	420	23.1	400	1.21	441
Totals	112	14.40	114	149.3	1,480	155.3	1,488	21.56	1,522
Means	11.2	1.44	11.4						

By substituting in Equation 7.1, the multiple regression equation is now written as

$$Y_R = 16.41 - 8.25X_2 + .59X_3$$

This equation is useful for the forecast of next week's sales. If plans call for a price per unit of $1.50 and advertising expenditures of $1,000, the forecast is 9,930 gallons; that is,

$$Y_R = 16.41 - 8.25X_2 + .59X_3$$
$$= 16.41 - 8.25(1.5) + .59(10)$$
$$= 9.93 \text{ (thousands of gallons)}$$ ■

The analysis for the example in Chapter 6 for two variables can be performed on a hand calculator. With more than two variables, however, the analysis becomes increasingly complicated since the number of equations to be solved increases with each new independent variable. The best approach is to use one of the numerous multiple regression computer programs that are available.

REGRESSION COEFFICIENTS

In Chapter 6 the interpretation of b_0 and b in the regression equation was discussed. Now consider the interpretation of b_0, b_2, and b_3 in the multiple regression equation. The value b_0 is again the Y intercept. However, now it is interpreted as the value of Y_R when both X_2 and X_3 are equal to zero. The b_2 and b_3 values are referred to as *net regression coefficients*. Each measures the average change in Y per unit change in the relevant independent variable. However, since the simultaneous influence of all independent variables on Y is being measured, the net effect of X_2 (or any other X) must be measured apart from any influence of other variables. Therefore it is said that b_2 measures the average change in Y per unit change in X_2, holding the other independent variables constant.

The *net regression coefficient* measures the average change in the dependent variable per unit change in the relevant independent variable, holding the other independent variables constant.

In the present example the b_2 value of -8.25 indicates that each increase of 1 cent in a gallon of milk when advertising expenditures are held *constant* reduces the quantity purchased by an average of 82.5 gallons.

Similarly, the b_3 value of .59 means that if advertising expenditures are increased by \$100 when price per gallon is held constant, then sales volume will increase an average of 590 gallons.

EXAMPLE 7.2

■ To illustrate these influences, an example where price is to be \$1.00 per gallon and \$1,000 is to be spent on advertising is considered. Then

$$Y_R = 16.41 - 8.25X_2 + .59X_3$$
$$= 16.41 - 8.25(1.00) + .59(10)$$
$$= 16.41 - 8.25 + 5.9 = 14.06 \quad \text{or} \quad 14{,}060 \text{ gallons}$$

Sales are forecast to be 14,060 gallons of milk.
What is the effect on sales of a 1-cent price increase if \$1,000 is still spent on advertising?

$$Y_R = 16.41 - 8.25(1.01) + .50(10)$$
$$= 16.41 - 8.3325 + 5.9 = 13.9775$$

Note that sales decrease by 82.5 gallons $(14.06 - 13.9775 = .0825)$.
What is the effect on sales of a \$100 increase in advertising if price remains constant at \$1.00?

$$Y_R = 16.41 - 8.25(1.00) + .59(11)$$
$$= 16.41 - 8.25 + 6.49 = 14.65$$

Note that sales increase by 590 gallons $(14.65 - 14.06 = .59)$. ■

STATISTICAL INFERENCE IN MULTIPLE REGRESSION

When the measures used in developing a multiple regression equation each represent a probability sample from some specific population, it is possible to make statistical inferences about parameters in the population on the basis of the following multiple regression equation:

$$Y = \beta_0 + \beta_2 X_2 + \beta_3 X_3 + \varepsilon \tag{7.3}$$

For instance, sample data can be used to develop a sample multiple regression equation in the form

$$Y_R = b_0 + b_2 X_2 + b_3 X_3$$

where b_0, b_2, and b_3 are efficient, linear, unbiased estimates of the corresponding population parameters β_0, β_2, and β_3. Since sample data are generally used, the analyst is usually interested in making inferences about population parameters.

Certain assumptions that underlie this inference procedure were discussed in Chapter 6 and are summarized below:

---

1. The Y values are normally distributed about the multiple regression plane.
2. The dispersion of points around the regression plane remains constant everywhere on the plane.
3. The error terms (ε) are independent of each other.
4. A linear relationship exists between each X and Y in the population.

RESIDUALS

As discussed in Chapter 6, a residual is the difference between what is actually observed and what is forecast by the regression equation ($Y - Y_R$). Thus Bump's multiple regression equation for each past weekly sales volume is

$$Y = b_0 + b_2 X_2 + b_3 X_3 + e \qquad (7.4)$$

where

Y = actual weekly sales volume, in gallons

b_2, b_3 = net regression coefficients

X_2 = price per gallon

X_3 = advertising expense, in hundreds of dollars

b_0 = constant

e = residual [difference between actual Y value and forecast of $Y(Y_R)$]

If Y_R is substituted for $b_0 + b_2 X_2 + b_2 X_3$ in Equation 7.4,

$$Y = Y_R + e$$

or

$$e = Y - Y_R$$

EXAMPLE 7.3

■ If Bump substitutes the data for the first week into Equation 7.1, a forecast for that week's sales of 10,950 gallons of milk is obtained.

$$Y_R = 16.4064 - 8.2476X_2 + .5851X_3$$
$$= 16.4064 - 8.2476(1.30) + .5851(9) = 10.9504$$

However, he already knows that sales were 10,000 gallons during that week. His forecast missed by 950 gallons. In other words, the residual from this forecast is 950 gallons.

$$e = Y - Y_R$$
$$= 10.000 - 10.950 = -.950$$ ■

Table 7.4 illustrates the concept of the residual for each of the ten data points. The b_2 and b_3 values are derived as the best set of weights that minimize the sum of the squared distances between the data points and the multiple regression plane. When the residuals are summed $[\Sigma (Y - Y_R)]$ for all ten data points, the column sums to zero $\Sigma (Y - Y_R) = 0$. When the errors are squared and summed $[\Sigma (Y - Y_R)^2]$, the sum of squares is a minimum value, $\Sigma (Y - Y_R)^2 = 15.901$. No other b values can be found for these data points that will produce a sum of squared residuals that is less than 15.901.

When Bump used only price per gallon to estimate quantity of gallons sold, the sum of the squared residuals, $\Sigma (Y - Y_R)^2$, was 59.4. When price per gallon and advertising expense are used as predictor variables, the sum of the squared residuals is reduced to 15.9. So Bump can now explain 93.2% of the sales volume variance through his knowledge of the relationships between price per gallon, advertising expense, and quantity sold.[2]

TABLE 7.4 Residuals from the Full Model for Bump's Data.

X_2	X_3	Y	Predicted $Y(Y_R)$, Using $Y_R = 16.4064$ $-8.2476X_2 + .5851X_3$	Residual, $(Y - Y_R)$	$(Y - Y_R)^2$
1.30	9	10	10.9504	-.95041	.903279
2.00	7	6	4.0069	1.99311	3.972487
1.70	5	5	5.3110	-.31097	.096702
1.50	14	12	12.2264	-.22639	.051252
1.60	15	10	11.9867	-1.98673	3.947095
1.20	12	15	13.5305	1.46953	2.159518
1.60	6	5	6.7208	-1.72083	2.961256
1.40	10	12	10.7108	1.28925	1.662166
1.00	15	17	16.9353	.06471	.004187
1.10	21	20	19.6211	.37888	.143550
			Sums	.00000	15.901493

---

[2] Deviations are used here to simplify the example. If the deviations are divided by the appropriate degrees of freedom, variances result.

TABLE 7.5 Summary of the Analysis of Bump's Data.

Variables Used to Explain Variance of Y	R^2	$\Sigma (Y - Y_R)^2$
None	.00	233.6
Price	.75	59.4
Price and advertising expense	.93	15.9

Total deviation = Explained deviation + Unexplained deviation

$$\Sigma (Y - \bar{Y})^2 = \Sigma (Y_R - \bar{Y})^2 + \Sigma (Y - Y_R)^2$$

$$233.6 = 217.7 + 15.9$$

$$R^2 = \frac{\Sigma (Y_R - \bar{Y})^2}{\Sigma (Y - \bar{Y})^2} = \frac{217.7}{233.6} = .932 \quad \text{or} \quad 93.2\%$$

Also,

$$R^2 = 1 - \frac{\Sigma (Y - Y_R)^2}{\Sigma (Y - \bar{Y})^2} = 1 - \frac{15.9}{233.6} = 1 - .068 = .932$$

The information derived up to this point is summarized in Table 7.5.

STANDARD ERROR OF ESTIMATE

Just as in simple regression, the standard error of estimate is the standard deviation of the residuals. It measures the typical scatter of Y values around the regression plane. The standard error of estimate is written

$$s_{y.x_2x_3} = \sqrt{\frac{\Sigma (Y - Y_R)^2}{n - k}} \tag{7.5}$$

where

$s_{y.x_2x_3}$ = standard error of estimate of dependent variable Y regressed against two independent variables X_2 and X_3

Y = actual weekly sales volume, in gallons

Y_R = volume of gallons estimated sold from regression equation

n = number of observations

k = number of linearly independent parameters to be estimated in multiple regression equation (b's)

> The *standard error of the estimate* measures the typical amount that the actual values (Y) differ from the estimated values (Y_R).

EXAMPLE 7.4

■ For Bump's data the standard error is

$$s_{y.x_2x_3} = \sqrt{\frac{15.901493}{10-3}} = \sqrt{2.27} = 1.51$$

The typical amount that the actual value of volume of milk sold differs from what is forecast using the multiple regression equation is 1,510 gallons. ■

COMPUTER OUTPUT

The computer output for Bump's problem is presented in Table 7.6. Examination of this output leads to the following observations (explanations are keyed to Table 7.6).

1. The regression coefficients are -8.2476 for price and $.5851$ for advertising expense. The regression equation is $Y_R = 16.4064 - 8.2476X_2 + .5851X_3$.
2. The regression equation explains 93.2% of the sales volume variance.
3. The standard error of estimate is 1.507 gallons. This value is the typical amount the actual values differ from the forecast values.
4. In Chapter 6 the regression coefficient was tested to determine whether it was different from zero. Both regression coefficients in this equation are significant, as indicated by the computed t values of -3.76 and 4.38 (since, from Appendix Table C.3 for 7 degrees of freedom, $t_{.01} = 3.499$).
5. The correlation matrix was demonstrated in Table 7.2.
6. The computation for the sum of squares deviation from regression (15.901) was demonstrated in Table 7.4. This term is called the sum of the squared residuals $[\Sigma (Y - Y_R)^2]$.
7. The computation for the sum of squares attributable to regression (217.699) was discussed in the residual section. This term is called the explained sum of the squares $[\Sigma (\bar{Y} - Y_R)^2]$.
8. The computation for the sum of squares total (233.6) was demonstrated in Table 6.5. This term is called the total sum of squares $[\Sigma (Y - \bar{Y})^2]$ and can be computed by summing the sum of the squared residuals and the explained sum of squares.
9. The residual column was demonstrated in Table 7.4.

TABLE 7.6 Computer Output for Bump's Multiple Regression Problem.

VARIABLE	MEAN	STANDARD DEVIATION	CORRELATION X VS Y	REGRESSION COEFFICIENT	STD. ERROR OF REG.COEF.	COMPUTED T VALUE
2	1.44000	0.30258	-0.86349	-8.24760 (1)	2.19605	-3.75565 (4)
3	11.40000	4.97103	0.89150	0.58510 (1)	0.13367	4.37716 (4)

DEPENDENT

| 1 | 11.20000 | 5.09466 | | | | |

INTERCEPT		16.40639 (1)		MULTIPLE CORRELATION		0.96536
STD. ERROR OF ESTIMATE		1.50719 (3)		R SQUARED		0.93193 (2)
				CORRECTED R SQUARED		0.91248

ANALYSIS OF VARIANCE FOR THE REGRESSION

SOURCES OF VARIATION	DEGREES OF FREEDOM	SUM OF SQUARES	MEAN SQUARES	F VALUE
ATTRIBUTABLE TO REGRESSION	2	217.699 (7)	108.849	47.917 (10)
DEVIATION FROM REGRESSION	7	15.901 (6)	2.272	
TOTAL	9	233.600 (8)		

CORRELATION MATRIX: 3 BY 3

VAR.	1	2	3 (5)
1	1.000	-0.863	0.891
2	-0.863	1.000	-0.654
3	0.891	-0.654	1.000

TABLE OF RESIDUALS

CASE NO.	Y VALUE	Y ESTIMATE	(9) RESIDUAL
1	10.00000	10.95041	-0.95041
2	6.00000	4.00689	1.99311
3	5.00000	5.31097	-0.31097
4	12.00000	12.22639	-0.22639
5	10.00000	11.98673	-1.98673
6	15.00000	13.53047	1.46953
7	5.00000	6.72083	-1.72083
8	12.00000	10.71075	1.28925
9	17.00000	16.93529	0.06471
10	20.00000	19.62112	0.37888

10. The computed F value (47.917) is used to test whether the multiple regression equation ($Y_R = 16.4064 - 8.2476X + .5851X$) is explaining a significant percent of the Y variable variance. The computation for the F value is

$$F = \frac{(.93193 - 0)/(3 - 1)}{(1 - .93193)/(10 - 3)} = 47.917$$

Since the F value from Table C.6 for 2 and 7 degrees of freedom is 9.55 at the .01 significance level, it can be concluded that the multiple regression equation is explaining a significant percent of the Y variable variance.

11. The computation for the corrected or adjusted R^2 is

$$R_c^2 = 1 - \frac{\dfrac{\Sigma (Y - Y_R)^2}{n - k}}{\dfrac{\Sigma (Y - \overline{Y})^2}{n - 1}} = \frac{\dfrac{15.9}{10 - 3}}{\dfrac{233.6}{10 - 1}} = .91248$$

DUMMY VARIABLES

This discussion is opened by looking at an example.

EXAMPLE 7.5

■ Suppose an analyst wishes to investigate how well a particular aptitude test predicts job performance. Eight women and seven men have taken the test, which measures manual dexterity in using the hands with tiny objects. Each subject then went through a month of intensive training as electronics assemblers, followed by a month at actual assembly, during which their productivity was evaluated by an index having values ranging from 0 to 10 (0 means unproductive).

The data are shown in Table 7.7. A scatter diagram is presented in Figure 7.2. Each female worker is represented by a 0 and each male by a 1.

FIGURE 7.2 Scatter Diagram for Data of Example 7.5.

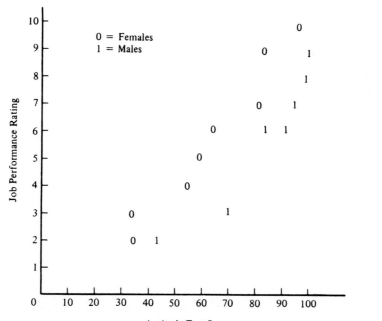

TABLE 7.7 Data for Example 7.5: Electronics Assemblers Dummy Variable.

Subject	Job Performance Rating, Y	Aptitude Test Score, X_2	Gender, X_3
1	5	60	0 (F)
2	4	55	0 (F)
3	3	35	0 (F)
4	10	96	0 (F)
5	2	35	0 (F)
6	7	81	0 (F)
7	6	65	0 (F)
8	9	85	0 (F)
9	9	99	1 (M)
10	2	43	1 (M)
11	8	98	1 (M)
12	6	91	1 (M)
13	7	95	1 (M)
14	3	70	1 (M)
15	6	85	1 (M)
	87	1,093	

$\overline{Y}_F$ = mean female job performance rating = 5.75

$\overline{Y}_M$ = mean male job performance rating = 5.86

$\overline{X}_F$ = mean female aptitude test score = 64

$\overline{X}_M$ = mean male aptitude test score = 83

It is immediately evident that the relationship of this aptitude test to job performance follows two distinct patterns, one applying to women and the other to men. ∎

It is sometimes necessary to determine how a dependent variable is related to an independent variable when a *qualitative* factor is influencing the situation. This relationship is accomplished by creating a *dummy variable*. There are many ways to identify quantitatively the classes of a qualitative variable. The values 0 and 1 are used in this text.

Dummy, or indicator, *variables* are used to determine the relationship between qualitative independent variables and a dependent variable.

The dummy variable technique is illustrated in Figure 7.3. The data points for females are shown as 0; the 1s represent males. Two parallel lines

FIGURE 7.3 Regression Lines for Dummy Variables of Example 7.5.

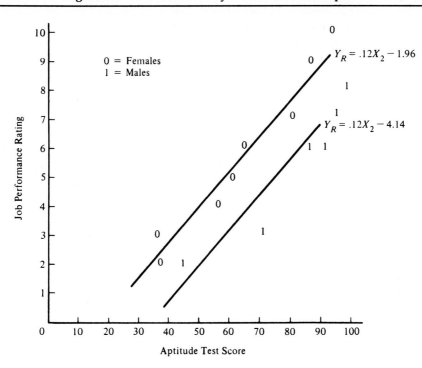

are constructed for the scatter diagram. The top one fits the data for females; the bottom line fits the male data points.

Each of these lines was obtained through the solution of the multiple regression Equation, 7.1.

$$Y_R = b_0 + b_2 X_2 + b_3 X_3$$

where

X_2 = test score

$X_3 = \begin{cases} 0 \text{ for females} \\ 1 \text{ for males} \end{cases}$ dummy variable

The single equation is equivalent to the following two equations:

$$Y_R = b_0 + b_2 X_2 \qquad \text{for females}$$

$$Y_R = b_0 + b_2 X_2 + b_3 \qquad \text{for males}$$

Note that b_3 represents the effect of a male on job performance and that b_2 represents the effect of aptitude test score differences (the b_2 value is assumed to be the same for males and females). The important point is that one multiple regression equation will yield the two estimated lines shown in Figure 7.3. The top line is the estimate for females, and the lower line is the estimate for males. One might envisage X_3 as a "switching" variable that is "on" when an observation is made for a male and "off" for a female.

The Minitab commands to run the data of Example 7.5 are

```
MTB > SET C1  *1
DATA > 5 4 3 10 2 7 6 9 9 2 8 6 7 3 6
MTB > END
MTB > SET C2  *2
DATA > 60 55 35 96 35 81 65 85 99 43 98 91 95 70 85
MTB > END
MTB > SET C3  *3
DATA > 0 0 0 0 0 0 0 0 1 1 1 1 1 1 1
MTB > END
MTB > NAME C1 'JOB' C2 'TEST' C3 'GENDER'  *4
MTB > REGRESS C1 ON 2 PREDICTORS C2 C3  *5

The regression equation is
JOB = - 1.96 + 0.120 TEST - 2.18 GENDER

Predictor        Coef       Stdev     t-ratio          p
Constant      -1.9565      0.7068       -2.77      0.017
TEST          0.12041     0.01015       11.86      0.000
GENDER        -2.1807      0.4503       -4.84      0.000

s = 0.7863      R-sq = 92.1%      R-sq(adj) = 90.8%

Analysis of Variance

SOURCE          DF           SS          MS          F          p
Regression       2       86.981      43.491      70.35      0.000
Error           12        7.419       0.618
Total           14       94.400

SOURCE          DF       SEQ SS
TEST             1       72.486
GENDER           1       14.496

MTB > CORR C1-C3

              JOB       TEST
TEST        0.876
GENDER      0.021      0.428

MTB > STOP
```

---

*1 Command **set** enters the job performance data into c1
*2 Command **set** enters the test score data into c2
*3 Command **set** enters the gender variable into c3
*4 Command **name** is used to name the variables in each column
*5 Command **regress** for **c1** as the dependent variable with 2 independent variables **c2 c3**

EXAMPLE 7.6

■ The estimated multiple regression equation for the data of Example 7.5 is shown in the Minitab computer output. It is

$$Y_R = -1.96 + .12X_2 - 2.18X_3$$

For the two values (0 and 1) of X_3, the equation provides

$$Y_R = -1.96 + .12X_2 - 2.18(0) = -1.96 + .12X_2 \qquad \text{for females}$$

and

$$Y_R = -1.96 + .12X_2 - 2.18(1) = -4.14 + .12X_2 \qquad \text{for males}$$

These equations may be interpreted in the following way. The regression coefficient value $b_2 = .12$, which is the slope of each of the lines, is the estimated average increase in performance rating for each 1-unit increase in aptitude test score. This coefficient applies to both males and females.

The other regression coefficient, $b_3 = -2.18$, applies only to males. If a male has taken the test, the estimated job performance rating is lowered by 2.18 units when the aptitude score is held constant.

An examination of the means of the Y and X_2 variables, classified by gender, helps one understand this result. Table 7.7 shows that the mean job performance ratings for males, 5.86, and females, 5.75, were approximately equal. However, the males scored significantly higher (83) on the aptitude test than did the females (64). Therefore if two applicants, one male and one female, took the aptitude test and both scored 70, the female's estimated job performance rating would be 2.18 points higher than the male's, as shown:

$$\text{Female:} \quad Y_R = -1.96 + .12X_2 = -1.96 + .12(70) = 6.44$$

$$\text{Male:} \quad Y_R = -4.14 + .12X_2 = -4.14 + .12(70) = 4.26$$

A look at the correlation matrix in the Minitab output provides some interesting insights. A high linear relationship exists between job performance and the aptitude test, $r_{12} = .88$. Through one's knowledge of this relationship 77% of the variance of the job-performance-rating variable ($.88^2 = .77$) can be explained.

The correlation coefficient $r_{13} = .02$ indicates virtually no relationship between gender and job performance. This conclusion is also evident when the fact that the mean performance ratings for males and females are nearly equal (5.86 versus 5.75) is considered. At first glance, one might conclude that knowledge of whether an applicant is male or female is not useful information. However, the moderate relationship, $r_{23} = .43$, between gender and aptitude test score indicates that the test might discriminate between sexes. Males seem to do better on the test than do females (83 versus 64). Perhaps some element of strength is required on the test that is not required on the job.

When both test results and gender are used to forecast job performance, 92% of the variance is explained. This result suggests that both variables make a valuable contribution to predicting performance. The aptitude test explains 77% of the variance, and gender used in conjunction with the aptitude test results adds another 15%. If the computed t values are tested, 11.86 and -4.84, both variables will be included in the final equation. ■

VALIDATION OF THE MODEL

So far the validity of the underlying assumptions of the regression model has not been checked. It is time to discuss those situations in which the assumptions are violated and to investigate the proper corrective techniques.

The assumptions are listed in the box in the section "Statistical Inference in Multiple Regression" given earlier in this chapter. The first assumption of normality is needed to perform t and F tests and was discussed in Chapter 6. Actually, when the sample size is sufficiently large (30 or greater), the central limit theorem provides a rationale for using these statistical tests without the normality assumption.

The second assumption concerns the dispersion of population data points around the population plane. The analyst assumes that the dispersion of data points remains constant everywhere along the plane. If a situation does not have constant variance, it has *heteroscedasticity*. The concept of heteroscedasticity is discussed in the next section.

The third assumption implies a random sample of $X–Y$ data points. But economic data ordered in a time series, for example, cannot always be regarded as random. That is, an observation on price in a given time period is usually correlated with the value in the previous time period. The term *serial correlation* is used to describe this situation. This concept will be discussed extensively in Chapter 9.

The fourth assumption indicates a linear relationship; this assumption that the model is correctly specified is an important one. Plotting the data in a scatter diagram is an invaluable first step in avoiding misspecification. A pronounced curvature often shows up in the plot of $X–Y$ data points. Data transformations are sometimes used on curvilinear data so that the transformed data will be linear. This technique was demonstrated in Chapter 6.

Heteroscedasticity

Heteroscedasticity occurs because of changes in the background conditions not recognized in the specification of the model. Changes that alter the underlying structure of the economy and changes in laws or government policies often cause heteroscedasticity. The change in the accuracy of measurement with regard to time series data is a common reason for this condition.

FIGURE 7.4 Constant and Heteroscedastic Variance.

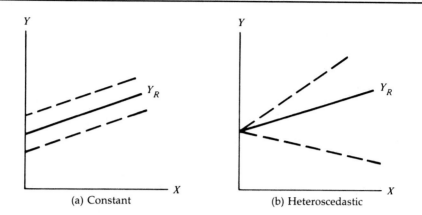

(a) Constant   (b) Heteroscedastic

> *Heteroscedasticity* exists when the errors or residuals do not have a constant variance across an entire range of values.

Figure 7.4 illustrates the effect of heteroscedasticity. Figure 7.4(a) shows constant variance. The observations of Y given X fall within a constant band around the regression line. Thus variance is not dependent on the X value specified. In Figure 7.4(b) the variance increases as X increases. If the regression equation is used to forecast Y, the confidence intervals will be less likely to contain the true value of the Y variable for large values of the X variable. This condition is specifically addressed in Chapter 9.

Collinearity

Whenever more than one independent variable appears in a regression equation, it is possible that these variables are related to each other. This situation is referred to as *collinearity*.

> *Collinearity* is the situation in which independent variables in a multiple regression equation are highly intercorrelated.

Collinearity causes problems with respect to the following aspects of an analysis:

1. A regression coefficient that is positive in sign in a two-variable regression equation may change to a negative sign in a multiple regression equation containing other independent variables with which it is highly interrelated. (The change can also be reversed, negative to positive.)
2. Estimates of the regression coefficients fluctuate markedly from sample to sample.
3. Multiple regression is often used as an interpretative tool to evaluate the relative importance of various independent variables. When predictor variables are intercorrelated, they explain the same variance in the estimation of the dependent variable. For this reason it is extremely difficult to separate the individual influences of each of the independent variables.

These problems are explored in the following example.

EXAMPLE 7.7

■ A multiple regression equation is developed from the data presented in Table 7.8. Food expenditure is forecast from a knowledge of its relationship with the variables income and family size. A quick examination of the correlation matrix for these three variables given in Table 7.9 leads to the following conclusions:

1. Both income and family size are positively related to food expenditures and have potential as good predictor variables ($r_{12} = .88$ and $r_{13} = .74$).
2. Income and family size are highly interrelated and will probably be explaining the same portion of food expenditure variance ($r_{23} = .87$).

TABLE 7.8 Data for Example 7.7.

Family	Yearly Food Expenditures (Hundreds of Dollars), Y	Yearly Income (Thousands of Dollars), X_2	Family Size, X_3
A	24	11	6
B	8	3	2
C	16	4	1
D	18	7	3
E	24	9	5
F	23	8	4
G	11	5	2
H	15	7	2
I	21	8	3
J	20	7	2

TABLE 7.9 Computer Output for Example 7.7.

VARIABLE NO.	MEAN	STANDARD DEVIATION	CORRELATION X VS Y	REGRESSION COEFFICIENT	STD ERROR OF REG.COEF.	COMPUTED T VALUE
2	6.9	2.38	.884	2.28	0.81261	2.80
3	3.0	1.56	.737	-0.41	1.23603	-0.33

DEPENDENT						
1	18.0	5.5				

INTERCEPT		3.52		MULTIPLE CORRELATION		.886
STD. ERROR OF ESTIMATE		2.89		R SQUARED		0.785
				CORRECTED R SQUARE		0.723

CORRELATION MATRIX

	EXPENDITURES	INCOME	SIZE
EXPENDITURES	1.00	.88	.74
INCOME		1.00	.87
SIZE			1.00

The multiple regression equation for this example is

$$Y_R = 3.52 + 2.28X_2 - .41X_3$$

Note the negative regression coefficient, $-.41$, for the family size (X_3) variable. This coefficient suggests that an increase of one person in a family when yearly income is held constant *decreases* estimated yearly food expenditures by $41, regardless of whether the family earns $10,000 or $20,000. This result is not logical, especially when one observes in the correlation matrix that the family size and food consumption are *positively* related, $r_{13} = .74$.

Note also that when income alone is used to estimate food expenditures, 78.1% ($.884^2$) of the variance is explained. When family size is added, R^2 increases to only 78.5%. Evidently, family size is explaining the same variance as income. ∎

When extreme collinearity exists, no acceptable way is available to perform a multiple regression analysis by using the given set of independent variables. Two suggested solutions are (1) to use only one of the highly interrelated variables in the final equation or (2) to create and use a new variable that is a combination of the two highly intercorrelated variables.

SELECTING THE BEST REGRESSION EQUATION

How does one develop the best multiple regression equation to forecast a variable of interest? The *first step* involves the selection of a complete set of potential independent predictor variables. Any variable that might add to the accuracy of the forecast is included. In the selection of a final equation one is usually faced with the dilemma of providing the most accurate forecast for the smallest cost. In other words, when choosing predictor variables to include in the final equation, the analyst must evaluate them by using the following two *opposed* criteria:

1. The analyst wants the equation to include as many predictor variables as possible. Whenever a new predictor variable is added to a multiple regression equation, R^2 either remains unchanged or increases. As long as the sample is sufficiently large—a sample size n of 10 for every independent variable used in the equation is recommended—every new predictor variable has the potential of improving the forecast.
2. Since it costs money to obtain and monitor information on a large number of Xs, the equation should include as few predictors as possible. The simplest equation is usually the best equation.

The selection of the best regression equation usually involves a compromise between these extremes. Since no unique statistical procedure exists for developing this compromise, personal judgment will be a necessary part of any solution.

After a lengthy list of potential predictors has been compiled, the *second step* is to screen out the independent variables that do not seem appropriate. An independent variable (1) may not be fundamental to the problem (there should be some plausible causality between the dependent variable and an independent variable), (2) may be subject to large measurement errors, (3) may duplicate other independent variables (collinearity), or (4) may be difficult to measure accurately (accurate data are unavailable or costly).

The *third step* is to shorten the list of predictors so as to obtain a "best" selection of independent variables. In the next section techniques currently in use are discussed. None of the search procedures can be said to yield the "best" set of independent variables. Indeed, there is often no unique "best" set. To add to the confusion, the various techniques do not all necessarily lead to the same final prediction equation. The entire variable selection process is extremely subjective. For this reason the correlation matrix should be analyzed as a first step before any automatic procedure is used. The primary advantage of automatic-search procedures is that analysts can focus their judgments on the pivotal areas of the problem.

To demonstrate various search procedures, a simple example is presented that has five potential independent variables.

EXAMPLE 7.8

■ The personnel manager of the Zurenko Pharmaceutical Company is interested in forecasting whether a particular applicant will become a good salesperson. She decides to use the first month's sales as the dependent variable (Y), and she chooses to analyze the following independent variables:

X_2 = selling aptitude test

X_3 = age, in years

X_4 = anxiety test score

X_5 = experience, in years

X_6 = high school GPA (grade point average)

The personnel manager collects the data shown in Table 7.10, and she assigns

TABLE 7.10 Data for Example 7.8: Zurenko Pharmaceutical Company.

One Month's Sales (Units)	Aptitude Test Score	Age (Years)	Anxiety Test Score	Experience (Years)	High School GPA
44	10	22.1	4.9	0	2.4
47	19	22.5	3.0	1	2.6
60	27	23.1	1.5	0	2.8
71	31	24.0	.6	3	2.7
61	64	22.6	1.8	2	2.0
60	81	21.7	3.3	1	2.5
58	42	23.8	3.2	0	2.5
56	67	22.0	2.1	0	2.3
66	48	22.4	6.0	1	2.8
61	64	22.6	1.8	1	3.4
51	57	21.1	3.8	0	3.0
47	10	22.5	4.5	1	2.7
53	48	22.2	4.5	0	2.8
74	96	24.8	.1	3	3.8
65	75	22.6	.9	0	3.7
33	12	20.5	4.8	0	2.1
54	47	21.9	2.3	1	1.8
39	20	20.5	3.0	2	1.5
52	73	20.8	.3	2	1.9
30	4	20.0	2.7	0	2.2
58	9	23.3	4.4	1	2.8
59	98	21.3	3.9	1	2.9
52	27	22.9	1.4	2	3.2
56	59	22.3	2.7	1	2.7
49	23	22.6	2.7	1	2.4
63	90	22.4	2.2	2	2.6
61	34	23.8	.7	1	3.4
39	16	20.6	3.1	1	2.3
62	32	24.4	.6	3	4.0
78	94	25.0	4.6	5	3.6

TABLE 7.11 Correlation Matrix for Example 7.8.

	(1) Sales	(2) Test	(3) Age	(4) Anxiety	(5) Experience	(6) GPA
(1) Sales	1.000	.676	.798	−.296	.550	.622
(2) Test		1.000	.228	−.222	.350	.318
(3) Age			1.000	−.287	.540	.695
(4) Anxiety				1.000	−.279	−.244
(5) Experience					1.000	.312
(6) GPA						1.000

the task of obtaining the "best" set of independent variables for forecasting sales ability to her analyst.

The first step is to obtain a correlation matrix for all the variables from a computer program. This matrix will provide essential knowledge about the basic relationships among the variables.

Examination of the correlation matrix in Table 7.11 reveals that the selling aptitude test, age, experience, and GPA are positively related to sales ability and have potential as good predictor variables. The anxiety test score shows a low negative correlation with sales, and it is probably not an important predictor. Further analysis indicates that GPA and age, and experience and age, are intercorrelated. It is the presence of these interrelationships that must be dealt with in attempting to find the best possible set of explanatory variables. ∎

Two procedures are demonstrated: all possible regressions and stepwise regression.

All Possible Regressions

This procedure calls for the investigation of all possible regression equations that involve the potential independent variables. The analyst starts with an equation containing no independent variables and analyzes every possible combination in order to select the best set of predictors.

Different criteria for comparing the various regression equations may be used with the all possible regressions approach. Only the R^2 technique, which involves four steps, is discussed here.

The procedure first requires the fitting of every possible regression model that involves the dependent variable and any number of independent variables. Each independent variable can either be, or not be, in the equation (two possible outcomes), and this fact is true for every independent variable. Thus altogether there are 2^i equations (where i equals the number of independent variables). So if there are eight independent variables to consider ($i = 8$), then $2^i = 256$ equations must be examined.

The second step in the procedure is to divide the equations into sets according to the number of parameters to be estimated.

EXAMPLE 7.9

■ The results from the all possible regression runs for the Zurenko Pharmaceutical Company example are presented in Table 7.12. Notice that Table 7.12 is divided into six sets of regression equation outcomes. This breakdown coincides with the number of parameters contained in each equation. ■

TABLE 7.12 R^2 **Values for All Possible Regressions for Zurenko Pharmaceutical.**

Independent Variables Used	Number of Parameters	Degrees of Freedom	R^2
None	1	29	0
X_2	2	28	.457
X_3	2	28	.637
X_4	2	28	.088
X_5	2	28	.302
X_6	2	28	.387
X_2, X_3	3	27	.8948
X_2, X_4	3	27	.479
X_2, X_5	3	27	.569
X_2, X_6	3	27	.641
X_3, X_4	3	27	.642
X_3, X_5	3	27	.657
X_3, X_6	3	27	.646
X_4, X_5	3	27	.324
X_4, X_6	3	27	.409
X_5, X_6	3	27	.527
X_2, X_3, X_4	4	26	.8951
X_2, X_3, X_5	4	26	.8948
X_2, X_3, X_6	4	26	.8953
X_2, X_4, X_5	4	26	.575
X_2, X_4, X_6	4	26	.646
X_2, X_5, X_6	4	26	.701
X_3, X_4, X_5	4	26	.659
X_3, X_4, X_6	4	26	.650
X_3, X_5, X_6	4	26	.669
X_4, X_5, X_6	4	26	.531
X_2, X_3, X_4, X_5	5	25	.8951
X_2, X_3, X_4, X_6	5	25	.8955
X_2, X_3, X_5, X_6	5	25	.8953
X_2, X_4, X_5, X_6	5	25	.701
X_3, X_4, X_5, X_6	5	25	.671
X_2, X_3, X_4, X_5, X_6	6	24	.8955

TABLE 7.13 Best Regression Equations for Zurenko Pharmaceutical.

Number of Parameters	Independent Variables	Degrees of Freedom	R^2	F
1	None	29	0	49.09
2	X_3	28	.637	66.220
3	X_2, X_3	27	.8948	.124
4	X_2, X_3, X_6	26	.8953	.054
5	X_2, X_3, X_4, X_6	25	.8955	.000
6	X_2, X_3, X_4, X_5, X_6	24	.8955	

The third step involves the selection of the best independent variable (or variables) for each parameter grouping. The equation with the highest R^2 is considered best. The best equation from each set listed in Table 7.12 is presented in Table 7.13.

The fourth step involves making the subjective decision "Which equation is the best?" On the one hand, the analyst desires the highest R^2 possible; on the other hand, he or she wants the simplest equation possible. It should also be noted that a sample size of $n = 10$ for each independent variable used is desirable but not essential. The all possible regressions approach assumes that n exceeds the number of parameters.

EXAMPLE 7.10

■ The analyst is attempting to find the point where adding additional independent variables for the Zurenko Pharmaceutical problem is not worthwhile because it leads to a very small increase in R^2. The results in Table 7.13 clearly indicate that adding variables after test (X_2) and age (X_3) is not necessary. Therefore, the final equation is

$$Y_R = b_0 + b_2 X_2 + b_3 X_3$$

and it explains 89.48% of Y's variance. ■

The all possible regressions procedure is best summed up by Draper and Smith[3]:

> In general the analysis of all regressions is quite unwarranted. While it means that the statistician has looked at all possibilities it also means he has examined a large number of regression equations which intelligent thought would often reject out of hand. The amount of computer time used is wasteful and the sheer physical effort of examining all the computer printouts is enormous when more than a few variables are being examined. Some sort of selection procedure which shortens this task is preferable.

[3] N. R. Draper and H. Smith, *Applied Regression Analysis* (New York: Wiley, 1966), p. 167.

Stepwise Regression

The stepwise regression procedure adds one independent variable at a time to the model, one step at a time. A large number of independent variables can be handled on the computer in one run when using this procedure.

Essentially, this approach computes a sequence of regression equations, at each step adding or deleting an independent variable. In other words, the computer program enters variables in single steps from best to worst provided that they meet the statistical criteria established.

The independent variable that explains the greatest amount of variance in the dependent variable will enter first. The next variable to enter explains the greatest amount of variance in conjunction with the first, and so on. The variable that explains the greatest amount of variance unexplained by the variables already in the model enters the equation at each step.

It should be pointed out that some stepwise programs allow an independent variable, entered into the equation at an early stage, to be eliminated subsequently because of the relationships between it and other variables added to the model at later stages. As a check on this step, the partial F statistic for each variable in the regression equation at any stage of computation is evaluated and compared with a predetermined critical point chosen from the appropriate F distribution. This comparison provides a check on the contribution made by each variable as though it were the most recent variable entered, irrespective of when it actually entered the equation. Any variable that does not contribute is removed from the model.

The partial F test value is similar to the F test value computed in Chapter 6 (Equation 6.17). The partial F is computed to determine whether the variable added to the equation at any particular step is making an important contribution to explaining the dependent variable variance. The formula for the partial F value is similar to Equation 6.17.

$$F = \frac{(R_F^2 - R_R^2)/(K_F - K_R)}{(1 - R_F^2)/(n - K_F)} \tag{7.6}$$

where

$R_F^2 = R^2$ for the model containing the new variable added to the model

$R_R^2 = R^2$ for the restricted model that does not contain the new model

$K_F =$ number of linearly independent parameters to be estimated in full model

$K_R =$ number of linearly independent parameters to be estimated in restricted model

$n =$ sample size

$R_F^2 - R_R^2 =$ percent of total variance explained by adding the new variable

$1 - R_F^2 =$ percent of total variance not explained by full model

EXAMPLE 7.11

■ Now the Zurenko problem is solved, step by step, as a stepwise regression program might operate.

1. Examine the correlation matrix in Table 7.11. Which variable is most highly related with the dependent variable "sales"? "Age" shows a high relationship ($r_{13} = .798$). This variable explains the greatest percentage of variance, $R^2 = .798^2 = .6368$, in the dependent variable and will be entered first.

2. Compare the model using age with the model using no independent variables. (The mean of Y is the predictor.) The analysis is as follows:

$$Y_R = b_0 + b_3 X_3 \qquad R_F^2 = .6368 \qquad K_F = 2$$

$$Y_R = b_0 \quad \text{where } b_0 = \bar{Y} \qquad R_R^2 = .0000 \qquad K_R = 1$$

$$F = \frac{(R_F^2 - R_R^2)/(K_F - K_R)}{(1 - R_F^2)/(N - K_F)} = \frac{(.6368 - 0)/(2 - 1)}{(1 - .6368)/(30 - 2)} = 49.09$$

Therefore the "age" variable is making a contribution to the prediction of sales.

3. Enter the variable "test" into the equation next because it is highly related to sales, $r_{12} = .676$, and not related to age, $r_{23} = .228$. The R^2 increases to .8948.

4. Compare the model using age and test with the model using only age:

$$Y_R = b_0 + b_2 X_2 + b_3 X_3 \qquad R_F^2 = .8948 \qquad K_F = 3$$

$$Y_R = b_0 + b_3 X_3 \qquad R_R^2 = .6368 \qquad K_R = 2$$

$$F = \frac{(.8948 - .6368)/(3 - 2)}{(1 - .8948)/(30 - 3)} = \frac{.2580}{.003896} = 66.22$$

Therefore the "test" variable in conjunction with "age" is making a contribution to the prediction of sales.

5. Enter the variable "GPA" into the equation next because it is highly related to sales, $r_{16} = .622$. However, GPA is also highly related to age, $r_{36} = .695$, and will probably explain the same dependent variable variance. The R^2 increases to only .8953.

6. Compare the model using age, test, and GPA with the model using only age and test:

$$Y_R = b_0 + b_2 X_2 + b_3 X_3 + b_6 X_6 \qquad R_F^2 = .8953 \qquad K_F = 4$$

$$Y_R = b_0 + b_2 X_2 + b_3 X_3 \qquad R_R^2 = .8948 \qquad K_R = 3$$

$$F = \frac{(.8953 - .8948)/(4 - 3)}{(1 - .8953)/(30 - 4)} = \frac{.0005}{.004027} = .124$$

(The critical value of F at the $\alpha = .05$ level is $F_{1,26} = 4.22$.) Therefore the "GPA" variable in conjunction with the "age" and "test" variables is not making a sufficient contribution to the prediction of sales.

The analysis is ended at this point. Table 7.14 shows a summary of the completed stepwise regression analysis. Note that the same conclusion was arrived at as with the all possible regressions procedure. ■

TABLE 7.14 Summary Table of Stepwise Regression for Zurenko Pharmaceutical.

Independent Variables	Degrees of Freedom	R^2	Increase in R^2	Partial F
None	29	0	0	
X_3	28	.6368	.6368	49.09
X_2, X_3	27	.8948	.2580	66.22
X_2, X_3, X_6	26	.8953	.0005	.124
X_2, X_3, X_4, X_6	25	.8955	.0002	.054

Stepwise regression is generally the best procedure when the analyst's task is to develop the best prediction equation. It is easy to use because the computer program does almost all of the work. Unfortunately, this technique is easily abused by amateur statisticians because it is relatively automatic. Sensible judgment is sometimes not used in the initial selection of variables and/or the critical examination of the residuals. That is, the completion of a stepwise regression run implies a best set of independent variables. However, if the initial list of explanatory variables includes none that are highly related to the dependent variable, this "best set" will be virtually useless.

The Minitab commands to do the stepwise regression are

```
MTB > READ 'ZURENKO.DAT' C1-C6  *1
      30 ROWS READ

ROW    C1    C2     C3     C4    C5    C6

 1     44    10    22.1    4.9    0    2.4
 2     47    19    22.5    3.0    1    2.6
 3     60    27    23.1    1.5    0    2.8
 4     71    31    24.0    0.6    3    2.7
 .  .  .

MTB > NAME C1 'SALES' C2 'APTITUDE' C3 'AGE' C4 'ANXIETY'
MTB > NAME C5 'EXP' C6 'GPA'  *2
MTB > STEP C1 USING PREDICTORS C2-C6  *3
```

STEPWISE REGRESSION OF SALES ON 5 PREDICTORS, WITH N = 30

	1 *4	2 *5
STEP	1	2
CONSTANT	−100.85	−86.79
AGE	6.97	5.93
T−RATIO	7.01	10.60
APTITUDE		0.200
T−RATIO		8.13
S	6.85	3.75
R−SQ	63.70	89.48

continues

Continued
_____

*1 Command **read** enters the data from the Zurenko.dat file into
    c1 through **c6**
*2 Command **name** is used to name the variables in each column
*3 Command **step** develops a stepwise regression using **c1** as the
    dependent variable and **c2** through **c6** as independent variables
*4 The output for step 1.   The regression equation is
    Y_R = -100.85 + 6.97(AGE) and it explains 63.7% of the
    variance.
*5 The output for step 2.   The regression equation is
    Y_R = -86.79 + 5.93(AGE) + .20(APTITUDE) and it explains
    89.48% of the variance.

USING REGRESSION TO FORECAST SEASONAL DATA

In Chapter 8, a *multiplicative* time series model will be introduced in which the seasonal fluctuation will be proportional to the trend level for each observation. This section introduces an *additive* time series model in which a constant amount is added to the time series trend estimate corresponding to the expected increase in the value of the dependent variable due to seasonal factors. In the multiplicative model the trend estimate is multiplied by a fixed percentage. In the additive model a constant amount is *added* to the trend estimate. Equation 7.7 is used to regress quarterly data using this method.

$$\hat{y}_t = b_0 + b_2 S_2 + b_3 S_3 + b_4 S_4 \qquad\qquad (7.7)$$

where

$\hat{y}_t$ = the forecast y value for time period t

S_2 = 1 if quarter t is the first quarter of the year; 0, otherwise

S_3 = 1 if quarter t is the second quarter of the year; 0, otherwise

S_4 = 1 if quarter t is the third quarter of the year; 0, otherwise

b_0 = constant

b_2, b_3, b_4 = regression coefficients

The variables S_2, S_3, and S_4 are dummy variables representing the first, second, and third quarter, respectively. Note that the four levels of the qualitative variable have been described with only three dummy variables. This is because the mean of the fourth quarter will be accounted for by the intercept b_0. If S_2, S_3, and S_4 are all equal to 0, the fourth quarter is represented by b_0.

EXAMPLE 7.12

■ James Brown, forecaster for the Washington Water Power Company, is trying to forecast electrical usage for residential customers for 1992. He knows that the data are seasonal and decides to use Equation 7.7 to develop a seasonal regression model. He gathers quarterly data from 1980 through 1990. The data for electrical usage measured in millions of kilowatt hours are shown in Table 7.15.

James creates dummy variables S_2, S_3, and S_4, representing the first, second, and third quarters, respectively. The data for the four quarters of 1980 are

y_t	S_2	S_3	S_4
1071	1	0	0
648	0	1	0
480	0	0	1
746	0	0	0

TABLE 7.15 Electrical Usage Data for Washington Water Power Company, 1980–1990, for Example 7.12.

Year	Quarter	Kilowatts (Millions)	Year	Quarter	Kilowatts (Millions)
1980	1	1071	1986	1	975
	2	648		2	623
	3	480		3	496
	4	746		4	728
1981	1	965	1987	1	933
	2	661		2	582
	3	501		3	490
	4	768		4	708
1982	1	1065	1988	1	953
	2	667		2	604
	3	486		3	508
	4	780		4	708
1983	1	926	1989	1	1036
	2	618		2	612
	3	483		3	503
	4	757		4	710
1984	1	1047	1990	1	952
	2	667		2	628
	3	495		3	534
	4	794		4	733
1985	1	1068			
	2	625			
	3	499			
	4	850			

Source: Washington Water Power Annual Report, various years.

James inputs all the data of Table 7.15 into a data file and uses Minitab for the analysis.

The Minitab commands to run the seasonal analysis are as follows:

```
MTB > READ 'USAGE.DAT' C1-C4  *1
      44 ROWS READ

  ROW      C1    C2    C3    C4

    1    1071     1     0     0
    2     648     0     1     0
    3     480     0     0     1
    4     746     0     0     0
    .     .     .

MTB > REGRESS C1 3 PREDICTORS C2-C4;  *2
SUBC> PREDICT 1 0 0;  *3
SUBC> PREDICT 0 1 0;
SUBC> PREDICT 0 0 1;
SUBC> PREDICT 0 0 0.
```

```
The regression equation is          *4
C1 = 753 + 246 C2 - 122 C3 - 255 C4
```

```
Predictor        Coef       Stdev     t-ratio         p
Constant       752.91       11.92       63.17     0.000
C2             246.27       16.85       14.61     0.000
C3            -122.45       16.85       -7.27     0.000
C4            -255.18       16.85      -15.14     0.000

s = 39.53      R-sq = 96.0%      R-sq(adj) = 95.7%
```

Analysis of Variance

```
SOURCE        DF          SS          MS        F         p
Regression     3     1500939      500313   320.22     0.000
Error         40       62495        1562
Total         43     1563435

SOURCE        DF      SEQ SS
C2             1     1142598
C3             1         193
C4             1      358148
```

```
    Fit   Stdev.Fit         95% C.I.              95% P.I.
 999.18       11.92   ( 975.09,1023.27)   ( 915.72,1082.64)

 630.45       11.92   ( 606.36, 654.55)   ( 547.00, 713.91)

 497.73       11.92   ( 473.63, 521.82)   ( 414.27, 581.19)

 752.91       11.92   ( 728.82, 777.00)   ( 669.45, 836.37)

MTB > STOP
```

*1 Command **read** enters the data from the Usage.dat file into **c1** through **c4**
*2 Command **regress** develops a regression using **c1** as the dependent variable and **c2** through **c4** as independent variables
*3 Command **predict** uses the regression equation to estimate usage for 1 0 0 which is the first quarter
*4 The regression equation is Y_R = C1 = 753 + 246 C2 - 122 C3 - 255 C4

The seasonal regression model is:

$$\hat{y}_t = b_0 + b_2 S_2 + b_3 S_3 + b_4 S_4$$
$$\hat{y}_t = 753 + 246 S_2 - 122 S_3 - 255 S_4$$

James notes that this model explains 96% of the dependent variable variance. His forecasts for each quarter of 1991 are as follows:

First quarter: $\hat{y}_t = 753 + 246(1) - 122(0) - 255(0)$
$= 999$

Second quarter: $\hat{y}_t = 753 + 246(0) - 122(1) - 255(0)$
$= 631$

Third quarter: $\hat{y}_t = 753 + 246(0) - 122(0) - 255(1)$
$= 498$

Fourth quarter: $\hat{y}_t = 753 + 246(0) - 122(0) - 255(0)$
$= 753$

Note that the constant, 753, is the forecast for the fourth quarter. This value is also the average or mean of fourth-quarter electrical usage. ■

ECONOMETRIC FORECASTING

In this chapter and Chapter 6, regression analysis used knowledge of one or more independent variables to forecast the variable of interest. The use of an independent variable allows the analyst to forecast the value of a dependent variable whenever there is a significant linear relationship between the dependent and the independent variable. When the dependent variable is in a time series, the regression analysis is known as an *econometric model.*

For the regression equation to be useful in forecasting a future value of a variable, such as retail sales, the analyst must obtain an estimate of the value of the independent variable for the same period in the future. As a linear regression model is developed, the analyst must be aware that to forecast some future value of the dependent variable the value of the independent variable(s) must be known if the regression equation is to be useful. For example, if GNP is used to forecast retail sales, the value for GNP must be estimated. If the GNP variable cannot be estimated for next year, it cannot be used to forecast retail sales for next year.

The essence of econometric model building using regression analysis is the identification and specification of causative factors to be used in a regression equation. However, recall from the discussion in Chapter 6 that the use of statistical analysis does not allow the analyst to claim cause and effect. In econometric model building, the analyst is developing a model from the theory that the independent variables influence the behavior of the dependent variable in ways that can be explained on a commonsense basis.

Large-scale econometric models are being used today to model specific firms within an industry, selected industries within the economy, and the total economy. Econometric models include any number of simultaneous multiple linear regression equations. Thus, econometric models are systems of simultaneous equations involving several independent variables.

EXAMPLE 7.13

■ An economist for a national appliance company must develop a regression equation that will be used for forecasting the monthly sales of microwave ovens. The economist decides to use as independent variables disposable personal income, the typical price of a microwave oven, and the number of housing starts lagged three months. Her rationale for including the latter variable is that microwave ovens are one of the last items added to the house, so there is a three-month lag between a housing start and a microwave oven purchase. The regression equation she develops is

$$\hat{y}_t = b_0 + b_2 X_2 + b_3 X_3 + b_4 X_4$$

where

$\hat{y}_t$ = forecast of sales of microwave ovens for next month

X_2 = estimate of disposable personal income for next month

X_3 = housing starts three months ago

X_4 = price of a typical microwave oven this month

If the analyst is forecasting microwave oven sales for January 1992, she must obtain the following information: an estimate of disposable personal income for January, usually supplied by government agencies; the number of housing starts that occurred during October 1991; and the price charged during the present month (December 1991). The analyst has the potential for developing a good model. She will only have to estimate one of the independent variables, disposable personal income. She will have actual data for both the price of a typical microwave oven during December and the number of housing starts that occurred during October. ■

OVERFITTING

Overfitting involves the selection of a model that matches the eccentricities of the sample data under analysis. When such a model is applied to new sets of data selected from the same population, it does not perform in nearly the same manner.

Overfitting is more likely to occur when the sample size is small, especially if a large number of independent variables is included in the model. Experience has indicated that sample size should be an n of 10 for each independent variable. (If there are 4 independent variables, a sample size of at least 40 is needed).

One way to guard against overfitting is to develop the model from one part of the data and then to apply the results to another segment. If the model takes into account primarily the eccentricities of the particular sample from which it has been developed, this result should show up when the estimating errors from the two sets are compared. If a comparable measure of the mean squared error $[\Sigma (Y - Y_R)^2]/(n)$ is substantially larger from the set that used the model to estimate new observations, overfitting has occurred.

APPLICATION TO MANAGEMENT

Multiple regression analysis was initially devised by statisticians and mathematical economists (econometricians) to aid in forecasting the economic activity of the various segments of the economy. This use is still one of its primary applications. Many of the reports and forecasts about the future of our economy that appear in *The Wall Street Journal, Fortune, Business Week,* and other similar journals are based on econometric models. The U.S. government makes wide use of regression analysis in predicting future revenues, expenditures, income levels, interest rates, birth rates, unemployment, Social Security benefit requirements, as well as a multitude of other events. In fact, almost every major department in the U.S. government makes use of the tools described in this chapter.

Similarly, business entities have adopted and, where necessary, modified regression analysis to help in the forecasting of future events. Few firms can survive in today's environment without a fairly accurate forecast of tomorrow's sales, expenditures, capital requirements, and cash flows. While small or less sophisticated firms may be able to get by with intuitive forecasts, larger and/or more sophisticated firms have turned to regression analysis to permit them to study the relationships among multiple independent variables and how these variables will affect the future.

Unfortunately, the very notoriety that regression analysis receives for its usefulness as a tool in predicting the future tends to overshadow an equally important asset: its ability to help evaluate and control the present. Since the regression analysis equation provides the researcher with both *strength* and *direction* information, management can evaluate and change current strategies.

Suppose, for example, a manufacturer of jams wants to know whom to concentrate its marketing efforts on in introducing a new flavor. Regression analysis can be used to help determine the profile of heavy users of jams. For instance, a company might try to predict the number of flavors of jam a household might have at any one time on the basis of a number of independent variables, such as the following:

Number of children living at home
Age of children
Gender of children
Home ownership versus rental
Time spent shopping
Income

Even a superficial reflection on the jam example quickly leads the researcher to realize that regression analysis has numerous possibilities for use in market segmentation studies. In fact, many companies do use it to study market segments to determine which variables seem to have impact on market share, purchase frequency, product ownership, product and brand loyalty, as well as many other areas.

Agricultural scientists use regression analysis to explore the relationship between product yield (e.g., number of bushels of corn per acre) and fertilizer type and amount, rainfall, temperature, days of sun, and insect infestation. Modern farms are equipped with mini- and microcomputers complete with software packages to help them in this process.

Medical researchers use regression analysis to seek links between blood pressure and independent variables such as age, social class, weight, smoking habits, and race. Doctors explore the impact of communications, number of contacts, and age of patient on patient satisfaction with service.

Personnel directors explore the relationship of employee salary levels to geographic location, unemployment rates, industry growth, union membership, industry type, or competitive salaries. Financial analysts look for causes of high stock prices by analyzing dividend yields, earnings per share, stock splits, consumer expectation of interest rates, savings levels, and inflation rates.

Advertising managers frequently try to study the impact of advertising budgets, media selection, message copy, advertising frequency, or spokesperson choice on consumer attitude change. Similarly, marketers attempt to determine sales from advertising expenditures, price levels, competitive marketing expenditures, consumer disposable income, as well as a wide variety of other variables.

A final example further illustrates the versatility of regression analysis. Real estate site location analysts have found that regression analysis can be very helpful in pinpointing geographic areas of over- and underpenetration of specific types of retail stores. For instance, a hardware store chain might look for a potential city to locate a new store in by developing a regression model designed to predict hardware sales in any given city.

Researchers could concentrate their efforts on those cities where the model predicted higher sales than actually achieved (as can be determined by many sources). The hypothesis is that sales of hardware are not up to potential in these cities.

In summary, regression analysis has provided management with a powerful and versatile tool for studying the relationships between a dependent variable and multiple independent variables. The goal is to better understand and control present events as well as to better predict future events.

CHAPTER **7**

GLOSSARY

Collinearity Collinearity is the situation in which independent variables in a multiple regression equation are highly intercorrelated.

Dummy variables Dummy variables are used to determine the relationships between qualitative independent variables and a dependent variable.

Heteroscedasticity Heteroscedasticity exists when the errors or residuals do not have a constant variance across an entire range of values.

Multiple regression Multiple regression involves the use of more than one independent variable to predict a dependent variable.

Net regression coefficient Net regression coefficients measure the average change in the dependent variable per unit change in the relevant independent variable, holding the other independent variables constant.

Standard error of estimate The standard error of estimate measures the typical amount that the actual Y values differ from the estimated values (Y_R).

CHAPTER **7**

KEY FORMULAS

Multiple regression prediction equation $Y_R = b_0 + b_2 X_2 + b_3 X_3$ $\qquad$ (7.1)

Population multiple regression equation $Y = \beta_0 + \beta_2 X_2 + \beta_3 X_3 + \varepsilon$ $\qquad$ (7.3)

Sample multiple regression equation $Y = b_0 + b_2 X_2 + b_3 X_3 + e$ $\qquad$ (7.4)

Standard error of estimate $s_{y.x_2 x_3} = \sqrt{\dfrac{\Sigma (Y - Y_R)^2}{n - k}}$ $\qquad$ (7.5)

Partial F statistic $F = \dfrac{(R_F^2 - R_R^2)/(K_F - K_R)}{(1 - R_F^2)/(n - K_F)}$ $\qquad$ (7.6)

Seasonal regression $\hat{y}_t = b_0 + b_2 S_2 + b_3 S_3 + b_4 S_4$ $\qquad$ (7.7)

PROBLEMS

1. What are the characteristics of a good predictor variable?
2. What are the assumptions of the multiple regression technique?
3. What does the net regression coefficient measure in multiple regression?
4. What does the standard error of estimate measure in multiple regression?
5. Your multiple regression equation is $Y_r = 7.52 + 3X_2 - 12.2X_3$. Make a point estimate given $X_2 = 20$ and $X_3 = 7$.
6. Explain each of the following concepts.
   a. Correlation matrix
   b. R^2
   c. Multicollinearity
   d. Residual
   e. Dummy variable
   f. Stepwise regression
7. Most computer solutions for multiple regression begin with a correlation matrix. This matrix should be the first step when analyzing a problem that involves more than one independent variable. Answer the following questions concerning the correlation matrix given in the accompanying table.

Variable Number	Variable Number					
	1	2	3	4	5	6
1	1.00	.55	.20	-.51	.79	.70
2		1.00	.27	.09	.39	.45
3			1.00	.04	.17	.21
4				1.00	-.44	-.14
5					1.00	.69
6						1.00

   a. Why are all the entries on the primary diagonal equal to 1?
   b. Why is the bottom half of the matrix below the primary diagonal blank?
   c. If variable 1 is the dependent variable, which independent variables have the highest degree of relationship with variable 1?
   d. What kind of relationship exists between variables 1 and 4?
   e. Does this correlation matrix show any evidence of collinearity?
   f. In your opinion, which variable or variables will be included in the best forecasting model? Explain why.
   g. If the problem is run on a stepwise program, which variable will be entered first?

8. Jennifer Dahl, supervisor of the Circle O discount chain, would like to forecast the time it takes to check out a customer. She decides to use the following independent variables: the amount a person purchases and the number of purchased items. She collects data for a sample of 18 customers:

Customer	Checkout Time (minutes) Y	Amount (dollars) X_2	Number of Items X_3
1	3.0	36	9
2	1.3	13	5
3	.5	3	2
4	7.4	81	14
5	5.9	78	13
6	8.4	103	16
7	5.0	64	12
8	8.1	67	11
9	1.9	25	7
10	6.2	55	11
11	.7	13	3
12	1.4	21	8
13	9.1	121	21
14	.9	10	6
15	5.4	60	13
16	3.3	32	11
17	4.5	51	15
18	2.4	28	10

a. Determine the best regression equation.
b. When an additional item is purchased, what is the average increase in the checkout time?
c. Compute the residual for customer 18.
d. Compute the standard error of estimate.
e. Interpret part d in terms of the variables used in this problem.
f. Compute a point estimate of the checkout time if a customer purchases 14 items that amount to $70.
g. Compute a 95% interval estimate for your prediction in part f.
h. What should Jennifer conclude?

9. Beer sales at the Shapiro One-Stop Store are analyzed by using temperature and number of people (21 or over) on the street as independent variables. A regression is run, using the following variables:

$Y =$ number of six-packs of beer sold each day

$X_2 =$ high temperature

$X_3 =$ traffic count

A random sample of 20 days is selected. The partial computer output yields the following results.

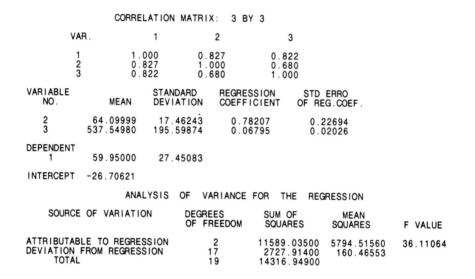

```
                CORRELATION MATRIX:  3 BY 3

        VAR.          1           2           3

          1        1.000       0.827       0.822
          2        0.827       1.000       0.680
          3        0.822       0.680       1.000

VARIABLE                  STANDARD     REGRESSION      STD ERRO
   NO.         MEAN       DEVIATION    COEFFICIENT   OF REG.COEF.

    2        64.09999     17.46243      0.78207       0.22694
    3       537.54980    195.59874      0.06795       0.02026

DEPENDENT
    1        59.95000     27.45083

INTERCEPT  -26.70621

                ANALYSIS  OF  VARIANCE FOR  THE  REGRESSION

   SOURCE OF VARIATION          DEGREES      SUM OF       MEAN
                              OF FREEDOM     SQUARES     SQUARES    F VALUE

ATTRIBUTABLE TO REGRESSION         2       11589.03500  5794.51560  36.11064
DEVIATION FROM REGRESSION         17        2727.91400   160.46553
        TOTAL                     19       14316.94900
```

a. Analyze the correlation matrix.
b. Test the significance of the net regression coefficients at the .01 significance level.
c. Forecast the volume of beer sold if the high temperature is 60 degrees and the traffic count is 500 people.
d. Calculate the R^2, and interpret its meaning in terms of this problem.
e. Calculate the standard error of estimate.
f. Explain how beer sales are affected by an increase of 1 degree in the high temperature.
g. State your conclusions for this analysis concerning the accuracy of the forecasting equation and also the contributions of the independent variables.

10. The sales manager of a large automotive parts distributor, Hartman Auto Supplies, wants to develop a model to forecast as early as May the total annual sales of a region. If regional sales can be forecast, then the total sales for the company can be forecast. The number of retail outlets in the region stocking the company's parts and the number of automobiles registered for each region as of May 1 are the two independent variables investigated. The data appear in the accompanying table.

Region	Annual Sales (Millions), Y	Number of Retail Outlets, X_2	Number of Automobiles Registered (Millions), X_3
1	52.3	2,011	24.6
2	26.0	2,850	22.1
3	20.2	650	7.9
4	16.0	480	12.5
5	30.0	1,694	9.0
6	46.2	2,302	11.5
7	35.0	2,214	20.5
8	3.5	125	4.1
9	33.1	1,840	8.9
10	25.2	1,233	6.1
11	38.2	1,699	9.5

a. Analyze the correlation matrix.
b. How much error is involved in the prediction for region 1?
c. Forecast the annual sales for region 12, given 2,500 retail outlets and 20.2 million automobiles registered.
d. Discuss the accuracy of the forecast made in part c.
e. Show how the standard error of estimate was computed.
f. Give an interpretation of the net regression coefficients. Are these regression coefficients valid?
g. How can this regression equation be improved?

11. The sales manager of Hartman Auto Supplies decides to investigate a new independent variable, personal income by region. The data for this new variable are presented in the accompanying table.

Region	Personal Income (Billions)	Region	Personal Income (Billions)
1	98.5	7	67.6
2	31.1	8	19.7
3	34.8	9	67.9
4	32.7	10	61.4
5	68.8	11	85.6
6	94.7		

a. Does personal income by region make a contribution to the forecasting of sales?
b. Forecast annual sales for region 12 for personal income of $40 billion, using all three independent variables.

    c. Discuss the accuracy of the forecast made in part b.

    d. Which independent variables would you include in your final forecast model? Why?

12. The Nelson Corporation decides to develop a multiple regression equation to forecast sales performance. A random sample of 14 salespeople is interviewed and given an aptitude test. Also, an index of effort expended is calculated for each salesperson on the basis of a ratio of the mileage on his or her company car to the total mileage projected for adequate coverage of territory. Regression analysis yields the following results:

$$Y_R = 16.57 + .65\,X_2 + (20.6X_3$$
$$\quad\quad\quad\;\; (.05) \quad\;\; (1.69)$$

The quantities in parentheses are the standard errors of the net regression coefficients. The standard error of estimate is 3.56. The standard deviation of the sales variable is $s_y = 16.57$. The variables are

    Y = sales performance, in thousands

    X_2 = aptitude test score

    X_3 = effort index

    a. Are the net regression coefficients significantly different from zero, at the .01 significance level?

    b. Interpret the net regression coefficient for the effort index.

    c. Forecast the sales performance for a salesperson who has an aptitude test score of 75 and an effort index of .5.

    d. Calculate the sum of the squared residuals, $\Sigma\,(Y - Y_R)^2$.

    e. Calculate the total sum of squares, $\Sigma\,(Y - \bar{Y})^2$.

    f. Calculate R^2 and interpret what it means in terms of this problem.

    g. Calculate a corrected R_C^2.

13. Mr. Palmer, the owner of a mobile home sales lot, wishes to forecast gross sales. He randomly selects data for 40 months on the following four variables:

    X_2 = number of salespeople employed

    X_3 = average monthly temperatures

    X_4 = Number of different mobile lines in inventory during the month

    X_5 = advertising expenditures

The data are presented in the table on page 267.

    a. Run a correlation matrix on a multiple regression program and analyze it.

Table for Problem 13.

Gross Sales (Thousands), Y	Number of Salespeople, X_2	Average Temperatures, X_3	Number of Lines, X_4	Advertising, X_5
$54.3	5	16.3	6	$ 716
79.9	7	26.1	9	792
57.1	5	35.9	8	492
89.3	7	46.2	8	650
115.0	11	57.4	15	865
126.0	12	65.2	16	1,293
76.5	10	67.4	7	790
81.1	7	67.1	7	802
56.7	6	59.8	8	484
138.8	11	43.7	16	1,501
47.9	7	36.3	5	326
42.5	7	29.4	4	202
39.4	5	25.9	5	215
68.9	5	36.3	10	609
60.3	7	37.0	10	600
87.7	8	41.6	13	764
46.9	6	54.9	6	304
44.2	6	66.2	8	252
84.4	8	72.5	5	746
64.1	5	70.2	8	629
115.3	11	54.2	8	1,044
40.7	5	44.9	4	158
79.2	5	36.0	7	716
39.5	4	27.9	5	176
14.7	4	31.8	6	102
24.1	5	33.6	4	209
117.3	10	35.2	11	1,501
67.9	7	45.3	9	631
73.2	10	56.3	11	692
63.7	10	58.2	6	618
36.1	7	69.7	5	140
58.6	5	74.1	6	544
97.2	7	55.2	11	901
41.8	5	44.2	4	100
93.9	6	35.4	9	862
21.8	5	25.8	2	175
17.3	3	22.6	4	111
65.9	6	30.7	7	594
32.4	4	41.4	7	131
61.1	6	42.0	9	589

b. Discuss the importance of each independent variable.

c. Which regression equation should Mr. Palmer use to forecast gross sales if he wishes to include all of the statistically significant independent variables? Use the .01 significance level.

d. Which regression equation would you advise Mr. Palmer to use? Why?

e. Is collinearity a problem in the equation chosen in part c, and if so, what effects might it have?

f. Forecast gross sales, given the following:

There are 4 salespeople employed.
The average temperature is 40° for the month.
There are 5 different mobile lines in inventory.
The advertising expenditures are $750. (*Note:* Use the equation you selected in part d.)

g. Discuss the accuracy of this forecast.

14. Ms. Haight, a real estate broker, wishes to forecast the importance of four factors in determining the prices of lots. She accumulates data on price, area, elevation, and slope, and rates the view for 50 lots. She runs the data on a correlation program and obtains the correlation matrix given in the accompanying table. Ms. Haight runs the data on a stepwise multiple regression program.

			Variable		
Variable	Price	Area	Elevation	Slope	View
Price	1.00	.59	.66	.68	.88
Area		1.00	.04	.64	.41
Elevation			1.00	.13	.76
Slope				1.00	.63
View					1.00

a. Determine which variable would enter the model first, second, third, and last.

b. Which variable or variables will be included in the best prediction equation?

15. National Presto is a manufacturer of small electrical appliances and housewares, including pressure cookers, heaters, canners, fry pans, griddles, roaster ovens, deep fryers, corn poppers, can openers, coffee makers, slicers, hand mixers, and portable ranges. Their quarterly sales dollars in millions are shown on page 269. Presto's is mainly a Christmas business, so there is a strong seasonal effect. Develop a multiple regression model using dummy variables to forecast sales for the second, third, and fourth quarters of 1990. Write a report summarizing your results.

Quarter:	1	2	3	4
1985	16.3	17.7	28.1	34.3
1986	17.3	16.7	32.2	42.3
1987	17.4	16.9	30.9	36.5
1988	17.5	16.5	28.6	45.5
1989	24.3	24.2	33.8	45.2
1990	20.6			

Source: *The Value Line Investment Survey* (New York: Value Line, 1990), p. 135.

CASE STUDY **7.1**

THE BOND MARKET

Early in 1982 Judy Johnson, Vice-President of Finance of a large, private, investor-owned utility in the Northwest, was faced with a financing problem. The company needed money both to pay off short-term debts coming due and to continue construction of a coal-fired plant.

Judy's main concern was estimating the 10- or 30-year bond market; the company needed to decide whether to use equity financing or long-term debt. To make this decision, the utility needed a reliable forecast of the interest rate it would pay at the time of bond issuance.

Judy called a meeting of her financial staff to discuss the bond market problem. One member of her staff, Ron Peterson, a recent MBA graduate, said he thought a multiple regression model could be developed to forecast the bond rates. Since the vice-president was not familiar with multiple regression, she steered the discussion in another direction. After an hour of unproductive interaction, Judy then asked Ron to have a report on her desk the following Monday.

Ron knew that the key to the development of a good forecasting model is the identification of independent variables that relate to the interest rate paid by utilities at the time of bond issuance. After discussing the problem with various people at the utility, Ron decided to investigate the following variables: a utility's bond rating (Moody's), a utility's ratio of earnings to fixed charges, Treasury bond rates, bond maturity (10 or 30 years), and the prime lending rate at time of issuance.

Ron gathered data he believed might correlate with bond interest rates for utility bond issuances during 1980 and 1981. At first he was uncertain how to handle the utility bond rating. He finally decided to consider only utilities with the same or a slightly higher rating than that of his company. This decision provided him with a sample of 93 issuances to analyze. But he was still worried about the validity of using the bond ratings as interval data. So he called his former statistics professor and learned that dummy variables would solve the problem. Thus he coded the bond ratings in the following way:

The data for this case study were provided by an Eastern Washington University MBA student, Dorothy Mercer. The analysis was done by MBA students Tak Fu, Ron Hand, Dorothy Mercer, Mary Lou Redmond, and Harold Wilson.

$X_2 = 1$ if the utility bond rating is A; 0 otherwise

$X_3 = 1$ if the utility bond rating is AA; 0 otherwise

If the utility bond rating is BAA, both X_2 and X_3 are 0.

The next step was for Ron to select a multiple regression program from the computer library and input the data. The following variables were included in the full-model equation:

Variable 1: Y = interest rate paid by utility at the time of bond issuance

Variable 2: X_2 = 1 if utility's bond rating is A

Variable 3: X_3 = 1 if utility's bond rating is AA

Variable 4: X_4 = utility's ratio of earnings to fixed charges

Variable 5: X_5 = U.S. Treasury bond rates (for 10 and 30 years) at the time of bond issuance

Variable 6: X_6 = bond maturity (10 or 30 years)

Variable 7: X_7 = prime lending rate at the time of issuance

The actual data are presented in Appendix D.

Ron decided to analyze the correlation matrix shown in Table 7.16. He was not surprised to find a high positive relationship between the interest rate paid by the utility at the time of bond issuance and the Treasury bond rate, $r_{15} = .883$. He also expected a fairly high positive relationship between the dependent variable and the prime lending rate ($r_{17} = .596$). He was not too surprised to discover that these two predictor variables were also related to each other (collinearity, $r_{57} = .713$). The negative relationship between the dependent variable and length of bond maturity (10 or 30 years), $r_{16} = -.221$, was also a result that made sense to Ron.

Next, Ron ran a full model containing all the predictor variables. Examination of the computed t values, which are presented in Table 7.17, indicated that the ratio of earnings to fixed charges, variable 4, and the prime interest rate, variable 7, were not making a contribution to the forecast of the dependent variable.

Ron concluded that variable 4 was not related to the dependent variable ($r_{14} = .097$) and that variable 7 was collinear with variable 5. He decided to eliminate

TABLE 7.16 Correlation Matrix for Bond Market Study.

				Variable			
Variable	1	2	3	4	5	6	7
1	1.000	−.347	.173	.097	.883	−.221	.596
2	−.347	1.000	−.399	.037	−.256	.278	−.152
3	.173	−.399	1.000	.577	.291	.010	.342
4	.097	.037	.577	1.000	.253	.094	.255
5	.883	−.256	.291	.253	1.000	−.477	.713
6	−.221	.278	.010	.094	−.477	1.000	−.314
7	.596	−.152	.342	.255	.713	−.314	1.000

TABLE 7.17 Full-Model Run for Bond Market Study.

VARIABLE NO.	MEAN	STANDARD DEVIATION	CORRELATION X VS Y	REGRESSION COEFFICIENT	STD ERROR OF REG.COEF.	COMPUTED T VALUE
2	0.47312	0.50198	-0.34654	-0.82853	0.13423	-6.17266
3	0.15054	0.35954	0.17257	-0.88937	0.22474	-3.95737
4	2.59053	0.64437	0.09701	-0.24165	0.11352	-2.12877
5	12.63572	1.45429	0.88303	1.25751	0.05964	21.08649
6	21.18279	9.98356	-0.22122	0.06284	0.00659	9.53710
7	16.78168	2.94729	0.59627	-0.00313	0.02720	-0.11502

DEPENDENT
1   14.99006   1.69549

INTERCEPT   -1.02621

MULT. CORR	0.95441	R SQUARED	0.91090
STD. ERROR	0.52344	CORRECTED R SQUARED	0.90578

ANALYSIS OF VARIANCE FOR THE REGRESSION

SOURCE OF VARIATION	DEGREES OF FREEDOM	SUM OF SQUARES	MEAN SQUARES	F VALUE
ATTRIBUTABLE TO REGRESSION	6	240.90656	40.15109	146.54047
DEVIATION FROM REGRESSION	86	23.56342	0.27399	
TOTAL	92	264.46997		

both variables 4 and 7. The results of the computer run for this model are shown in Table 7.18. The computed t values were significant for each of the independent variables.

Ron's report to Judy included the following comments:

1. The appropriate multiple regression model, $Y_R = -1.276 - .929X_2 - 1.175X_3 + 1.233X_5 + .061X_6$, explained 90.6% of the dependent variable variance.

TABLE 7.18 Final Model for Bond Market Study.

VARIABLE NO.	MEAN	STANDARD DEVIATION	CORRELATION X VS Y	REGRESSION COEFFICIENT	STD ERROR OF REG.COEF.	COMPUTED T VALUE
2	0.47312	0.50198	-0.34654	-0.92932	0.12637	-7.35422
3	0.15054	0.35954	0.17257	-1.17506	0.17810	-6.59793
5	12.63572	1.45429	0.88303	1.23307	0.04599	26.80913
6	21.18279	9.98356	-0.22122	0.06147	0.00665	9.24634

DEPENDENT
1   14.99006   1.69549

INTERCEPT   -1.27627

MULT. CORR	0.95195	R SQUARED	0.90621
STD. ERROR	0.53093	CORRECTED R SQUARED	0.90304

ANALYSIS OF VARIANCE FOR THE REGRESSION

SOURCE OF VARIATION	DEGREES OF FREEDOM	SUM OF SQUARES	MEAN SQUARES	F VALUE
ATTRIBUTABLE TO REGRESSION	4	239.66434	59.91608	212.55716
DEVIATION FROM REGRESSION	88	24.80563	0.28188	
TOTAL	92	264.46997		

2. The standard error of the estimate, which is the typical or average error when using the model for forecasting, is .53. Thus about 95% of the actual dependent variable values would lie within 1.06 of a given forecast.
3. The regression coefficients are valid and reliable.

Ron was very pleased with his effort and felt that Judy would also be pleased.

QUESTION

What questions do you think Judy will have for Ron?

CASE STUDY **7.2**

RESTAURANT SALES

Jim Price, who was working on his MBA degree, worked at a small restaurant near Marquette University in Milwaukee, Wisconsin. One day the restaurant manager asked Jim to report to her office. She indicated that she was very interested in forecasting weekly sales and wanted to know whether Jim would help. Since Jim had just taken an advanced statistics course, he said that he would enjoy the challenge.

Jim asked the restaurant manager to provide him with whatever historical records she had available. She indicated that the restaurant compiled the previous week's sales every Monday morning. Jim began his analysis by obtaining weekly sales data from the week ending Sunday, January 4, 1981 through the week ending Sunday, December 26, 1982—a total of 104 observations.

The mean weekly sales for the 104 weeks turned out to be $4,862. Figure 7.5 is a graph of the weekly sales over time. The graph indicates that weekly sales were quite volatile, ranging from $1,870 to $7,548, with very little trend. Since Jim had recently completed a course on regression analysis, he decided to use weekly sales as the dependent variable and see if he could find some useful independent or predictor variables.

Jim tested three predictors. The first predictor was time. The second predictor was a dummy variable indicating whether or not Marquette University was in full session that week (0 = not in full session, 1 = in full session). Examination of the sales data in Figure 7.5 revealed that weekly sales always dropped when Marquette was not in full session, namely, during the Christmas break, the spring break, and the summer break. Jim was not surprised, since the restaurant is located near Marquette's campus and most of its customers are members of the Marquette community. The third predictor Jim tried was sales lagged one week, since examination of Figure 7.5 indicated sales for two adjacent weeks were frequently similar.

Using Minitab, Jim computed the simple correlations among the three potential predictors and the dependent variable, weekly sales. The results are presented in the correlation matrix shown in Table 7.19. As Jim expected, there was almost no trend in the weekly sales as indicated by the correlation coefficient of .049.

This case was contributed by Frank G. Forst, Marquette University, Milwaukee, Wis.

FIGURE 7.5 Restaurant Sales, January 1981–December 1982.

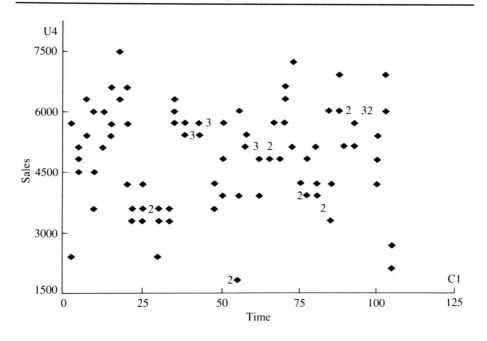

However, the dummy variable was strongly correlated with current sales, $r = .772$; in other words, whether or not Marquette University is in full session has good potential as a predictor of the current week's sales. The current week's sales were moderately related, $r = .58$, to sales lagged one week. However, Jim also noticed that the dummy variable was moderately related, $r = .49$, to sales lagged one week.

Again, with the aid of the Minitab computer package, Jim experimented with several regression models. The results of the various regression models are presented in Table 7.20. Since the sales data manifest almost no trend, the predictor "time" adds very little predictive power to the regression model. Note that model 4 has only a slightly higher R^2 than model 2 and that both models possess a significant amount of autocorrelation (autocorrelation will be discussed more fully in Chapter 9). Furthermore, models 3 and 5 have the same R^2, while model 7 has only a

TABLE 7.19 Restaurant Sales Correlation Matrix.

	Current Sales	Time	Dummy Variable	Sales Lagged One Week
Current Sales	1.000	.049	.772	.580
Time		1.000	−.048	.120
Dummy Variable			1.000	.490
Lagged Sales				1.000

TABLE 7.20 Restaurant Regression Models.

Model Predictor(s)	R^2	Durbin-Watson Statistic	Autocorrelation Significant at .05 Level?	Amount of Collinearity
1. Time	.0024	.81	Yes	None
2. Dummy	.596	1.30	Yes	None
3. Lagged sales	.336	1.89	No	None
4. Time and dummy	.603	1.32	Yes	Very little
5. Time and lagged sales	.336	1.89	No	Little
6. Dummy and lagged sales	.649	1.74	No	Some
7. Time, dummy, and lagged sales	.651	1.73	No	Moderate

slightly higher R^2 than model 6. On the other hand, the predictor "lagged sales" adds a fair amount of predictive power to a regression model. Model 6 has a significantly higher R^2 than model 2, without a significant amount of autocorrelation.

Jim decided to select regression model 6 to forecast weekly sales for the following reasons:

1. Model 6 had the second largest R^2, only .002 below that of model 7.
2. The parameters of model 6 were each significantly different from zero at the .01 level.
3. Model 6 did not exhibit a significant amount of autocorrelation.
4. Model 6 is simpler than model 7 and does not have as much collinearity.

The regression model that Jim used was $Y_R = 2,614.3 + 1,610.7$ (dummy variable) + .2605 (lagged sales). $R^2 = .649$ means 64.9% of the variation in weekly sales can be explained by whether or not Marquette was in full session and by the previous week's sales. The regression equation implies that weekly sales average is about $1,611 higher when Marquette is in full session, holding the previous week's sales constant.

Jim was pleased with his effort but wondered if another type of forecasting model might not be more effective. For this reason he decided to take a forecasting course.

QUESTIONS

1. Was Jim's use of a dummy variable correct?
2. Was it correct for Jim to use lagged sales as a predictor variable?
3. Do you agree with Jim's conclusions?
4. Would another type of forecasting model be more effective for forecasting weekly sales?

SELECTED BIBLIOGRAPHY

Belsley, D. A. "Collinearity and Forecasting." *Journal of Forecasting* 3 (1984): 183–196.

Draper, N. R., and Smith, H. *Applied Regression Analysis.* New York: John Wiley & Sons, 1966, p. 167.

Larsen, W. A., and McCleary, S. J. "The Use of Partial Residual Plots in Regression Analysis." *Technometrics* 14 (1972): 781–790.

Levenbach, H., and Cleary, J. P. *The Professional Forecaster.* Belmont, Calif.: Lifetime Learning Publications, 1982.

Neter, J., and Wasserman, W. *Applied Linear Statistical Models.* Homewood, Ill.: Richard D. Irwin, 1985.

Younger, M. S. *A Handbook for Linear Regression.* North Scituate, Mass.: Duxbury Press, 1979.

Time Series Analysis

R egression and correlation analyses are concerned with the linear relationship between two or more variables. Knowledge of the independent variable X is used to predict the dependent variable Y. In time series analysis the independent variable is time. The variable under study (Y) takes on different values over time. Thus any variable classified chronologically is a time series. The time periods may be years, quarters, months, weeks, and, in some cases, days or hours. Time series are analyzed to discover past patterns of growth and change that can be used to predict future patterns and needs for business operations. Time series analysis does not provide the answer to what the future holds, but it is valuable in the forecasting process and helps to reduce errors in forecasts.

Publications such as the *Statistical Abstract of the United States,* the *Survey of Current Business,* the *Monthly Labor Review,* the *Federal Reserve Bulletin,* and the annual reports of corporations contain time series of all types. Data—typically reported on a monthly, quarterly, or annual basis and covering prices, production, sales, employment, unemployment, hours worked, fuel used, energy produced, earnings, and so on—fill the pages of these and other business economic publications.

It is important that managers understand the past and use historical data and sound judgment to make intelligent plans to meet the demands of the future. Forecasts are made to assist management in determining alternative strategies.

Long-term forecasts are usually 5-, 10-, and even 20-year forecasts into the future. Long-range forecasts are essential to allow sufficient time for the procurement, manufacturing, sales, finance, and other departments of a company to develop plans for possible new plants, financing, development of new products, and new methods of assembly.

Business organizations in the United States must forecast the level of sales, both short-term and long-term. Competition for the consumer's dollar, stress on earning a profit for the stockholders, and a desire to produce a larger and larger share of the market are some of the prime motivating forces in business. Thus a statement of the expectations of management, called *forecasts,* is considered necessary in order to have the raw materials, production facilities, and staff available to meet the projected demand.

The alternative, of course, is not to plan ahead. In a dynamic business environment, however, this lack of planning might be disastrous. An electronics firm that ignored the trend to color television and solid-state circuitry would have lost all of its market share by now.

Subjective considerations are extremely important in time series analysis, since a satisfactory probability approach to such analysis has not yet been found. But subjective evaluations would be necessary in making forecasts even if a suitable probability approach to time series analysis were available. Whenever the past is examined to obtain clues about the future, it is relevant only to the extent that causal conditions previously in effect continue to hold in the period ahead. In economic and business activity, causal conditions seldom remain constant. The multitude of causal factors at work tends to be constantly shifting, so the connection between the past, the present, and the future must be continually reevaluated.

While the techniques of time series analysis do not eliminate subjective evaluations, they do make a useful contribution by providing a conceptual approach to forecasting. Forecasts are made with the aid of a set of specific formal procedures, and judgments are indicated explicitly.

DECOMPOSITION

One approach to the analysis of time series data involves an attempt to identify the component factors that influence each of the periodic values in a series. This identification procedure is called *decomposition*. Each component is identified so that the time series can be projected into the future and used for both short-run and long-run forecasting.

The four components found in a time series analysis were introduced in Chapter 4. They are trend, cyclical variations, seasonal variations, and irregular fluctuations.

1. *Trend.* The trend is the long-term component that underlies the growth (or decline) in a time series. The basic forces producing or affecting the trend of a series are population change, inflation, technological change, and productivity increases.

2. *Cyclical.* The cyclical component is a series of irregular wavelike fluctuations or cycles of more than one year's duration due to changing economic conditions. It is the difference between the expected values of a variable (trend) and the actual values—the residual variation fluctuating around the trend.

3. *Seasonal.* Seasonal fluctuations are typically found in data classified quarterly, monthly, or weekly. Seasonal variation refers to a pattern of change that recurs regularly over time. The movement is completed within the duration of a year and repeats itself year after year.

4. *Irregular.* The irregular component is composed of fluctuations that are caused by unpredictable or nonperiodic events such as weather changes, strikes, wars, rumors of wars, elections, and the passage of legislative bills.

To study the components of a time series, the analyst must consider their mathematical relationships. The approach used most frequently is to treat the original data of a time series as a product of the components; that is, an annual series is a product of trend, cyclical, and irregular fluctuations, expressed symbolically as $T \times C \times I$, as shown in Equation 8.1. In this multiplicative composition T is measured in the units of the actual data, and the other components, C, and I, are index values.

$$Y = TCI \qquad\qquad (8.1)$$

where

Y = actual value
T = trend
C = cyclical
I = irregular

PRICE INDEX

Several of the series on production, sales, and other economic cases contain data available only in terms of dollar values. These data are affected by both the physical quantity of goods sold and their prices. Inflation and widely varying prices over time can cause analysis problems. For instance, an increased dollar volume may hide decreased sales in units caused by inflated prices. Thus frequently it is necessary to know how much of the change in dollar values represents a real change in physical quantity and how much is due to change in price because of inflation. It is desirable in these instances to express dollar values in terms of "constant dollars."

The concept of *purchasing power* is important here. The current purchasing power of $1 is defined as

$$\text{Current purchasing power of } \$1 = \frac{100}{\text{current price index}} \qquad (8.2)$$

Thus if in November 1991 the consumer price index (with 1982 as 100) reaches 150, the current purchasing power of the November 1991 consumer dollar is

$$\text{Current purchasing power of } \$1 = \frac{100}{150} = .67 \quad \text{or} \quad \$.67$$

The 1991 dollar purchased only two-thirds of the goods and services that could have been purchased with a base period (1982) dollar.

To express dollar values in terms of *constant dollars,* the following equation is used:

Deflated dollar value = (dollar value) × (purchasing power of $1)

$$(8.3)$$

Suppose that car sales rose from $300,000 in 1991 to $350,000 in 1992, while the new-car price index (1982 as base) rose from 135 to 155. Deflated sales for 1991 and 1992 would be

$$\text{Deflated 1991 sales} = (\$300,000)\left(\frac{100}{135}\right) = \$222,222$$

$$\text{Deflated 1992 sales} = (\$350,000)\left(\frac{100}{155}\right) = \$225,806$$

Note that actual dollar sales had a sizable increase of $350,000 − $300,000 = $50,000. However, deflated sales only increased by $225,806 − $222,222 = $3,584.

The purpose of deflating dollar values is to remove the effect of price changes. This adjustment is called *price deflation* or is referred to as expressing a series in terms of constant dollars.

Price deflation is the process of expressing terms in a series in constant dollars.

The deflating process is relatively simple. In it, an index number computed from the prices of commodities whose values are to be deflated is used. For example, shoe store sales should be deflated by an index of shoe prices, not by a general price index. For deflated dollar values that represent more than one type of commodity, the analyst should develop the price index by combining the appropriate price indexes together in the proper mix.

EXAMPLE 8.1

■ Mr. Burnham wishes to study the long-term growth of the Burnham Furniture Store. The long-term trend of his business should be evaluated by using the physical volume of sales. If this evaluation cannot be done, price changes reflected in dollar sales will follow no consistent pattern and will merely obscure the real growth pattern. If sales dollars are to be used, actual dollar sales need to be divided by an appropriate price index to obtain sales that are measured in constant dollars.

TABLE 8.1 Data for Example 8.1: Burnham Furniture Sales (1983–1990).

Year	Burnham Sales (Thousands)	Retail Furniture Price Index (1982 = 100)	Retail Appliance Price Index (1982 = 100)	Price Index* (1982 = 100)	Deflated Sales[†] (Thousands of 1982 dollars)
1983	42.1	111.6	105.3	109.7	38.4
1984	47.2	117.2	108.5	114.6	41.2
1985	48.4	124.2	109.8	119.9	40.4
1986	50.6	128.3	114.1	124.0	40.8
1987	55.2	136.1	117.6	130.6	42.3
1988	57.9	139.8	122.4	134.6	43.0
1989	59.8	145.7	128.3	140.5	42.6
1990	60.7	156.2	131.2	148.7	40.8

* Constructed for furniture (weight 70%) and appliance (weight 30%).

[†] Sales divided by price index times 100.

The consumer price index (CPI) is not suitable for Burnham because it contains elements such as rents, foods, and personal services not sold by the store, but some components of this index may be appropriate. Burnham is aware that 70% of sales are from furniture and 30% from appliances. He can therefore multiply the CPI retail furniture component by .70, multiply the appliance component by .30, and then add to obtain a combined price index. Table 8.1 illustrates this approach, where the computations for 1983 are

$$111.6(.70) + 105.3(.30) = 109.7$$

The sales are deflated for 1983 in terms of 1982 purchasing power.

$$\text{Deflated 1983 sales} = (42.1)\left(\frac{100}{109.7}\right) = 38.4$$

Table 8.1 shows that while actual sales gained steadily from 1983 to 1990, physical volume remained rather stable. Evidently, the sales increases were due to price markups that were generated, in turn, by the inflationary tendency of the economy. ■

TREND

Trends are long-term movements in a time series that can be described by a straight line or a curve. The basic forces producing or affecting the trend of a series are population change, price change, technological change, and productivity increases.

Population increase may cause retail sales of a community to rise each year for several years. Moreover, the sales in current dollars may have been pushed upward during the same period because of general increases in the prices of retail goods—even though the physical volume of goods sold did not change.

Technological change may cause a time series to move upward or downward. The development and improvement of the automobile, accompanied by improvements in roads, has increased car registrations. However, the automobile, produced in increasing volumes, also caused a downward trend in the production of horse-drawn wagons and buggies.

Productivity increases—which, in turn, may be due to technological change—give an upward slope to many time series. Any measure of total output, such as manufacturers' sales, is affected by changes in productivity.

Before measuring the trend of a time series, one must know the purpose for measuring it. Knowledge of the purpose guides the analyst in choice of method and the length of the time series to be used for the measurement. There are two basic purposes: to project the trend and to eliminate it from the original data.

A plot of the data is needed before one measures the trend. In trend analysis the independent variable is time. The analyst should chart the data on both arithmetic and semilogarithmic scales before choosing the method of measurement. By doing so, the analyst gets an additional guide for choosing the trend equation because the general shape is apparent. If a plot of the series indicates a straight-line movement on the arithmetic scale, the analyst will fit a straight trend line to the data. If a nonlinear trend is apparent, the appropriate trend curve can be developed. If the data are plotted on semi-logarithmic paper and a straight line seems to fit, an exponential model that indicates a constant rate of growth will be selected.

A chart of the data and a statement of purpose for measuring the trend do not always enable the analyst to make a final choice, though. Sometimes two or more trends must be computed and plotted with the original data to see which fits the time series best.

What constitutes a "best" fit is a matter of judgment. The trend that fits best is the one that does the job the analyst has to do. No method is always superior for measuring trends. Sometimes a trend drawn freehand through a time series is sufficient to reveal a picture of the general shape and direction of the series. To draw a freehand trend properly, however, the analyst must be able to recognize the major cycles and seasonal fluctuations through which the trend must pass. Sometimes this recognition is hard to achieve unless the analyst is very familiar with the particular series being analyzed. Most analysts, therefore, choose an objective method that can be stated as an equation in order to avoid the subjective decisions required for the freehand method.

The method most widely used to describe straight-line trends is called the *least squares method*. This approach computes the line that best fits a group of points mathematically in accordance with a stated criterion.[1] The trend equation is

---

[1] As discussed in Chapter 6, the least squares method minimizes the sum of the squared distances, measured in the vertical direction, from the data points to the trend line.

$$Y_R = b_0 + bX \qquad\qquad\qquad\qquad\qquad\qquad (8.4)$$

where

Y_R = predicted trend value for Y variable for selected, coded time period (X)

b_0 = value of trend when $X = 0$

b = average increase or decrease in Y_R (trend) for each increase of one period of X

X = any value of time selected

TABLE 8.2 Registration of New Passenger Cars in the United States, 1960–1988.

Year	Registrations (Millions) Y	X	Y_R	Cyclical
1960	6.577	1	7.6931	85.49
1961	5.855	2	7.7984	75.08
1962	6.939	3	7.9037	87.79
1963	7.557	4	8.0091	94.36
1964	8.065	5	8.1144	99.39
1965	9.314	6	8.2197	113.31
1966	9.009	7	8.3251	108.21
1967	8.357	8	8.4304	99.13
1968	9.404	9	8.5357	110.17
1969	9.447	10	8.6411	109.33
1970	8.388	11	8.7464	95.90
1971	9.831	12	8.8517	111.06
1972	10.409	13	8.9571	116.21
1973	11.351	14	9.0624	125.25
1974	8.701	15	9.1677	94.91
1975	8.168	16	9.2731	88.08
1976	9.752	17	9.3784	103.98
1977	10.826	18	9.4837	114.15
1978	10.946	19	9.5891	114.15
1979	10.357	20	9.6944	106.83
1980	8.761	21	9.7997	89.40
1981	8.444	22	9.9050	85.25
1982	7.754	23	10.0104	77.46
1983	8.924	24	10.1157	88.22
1984	10.118	25	10.2210	98.99
1985	10.889	26	10.3264	105.45
1986	11.140	27	10.4317	106.79
1987	10.183	28	10.5370	96.64
1988	10.398	29	10.6415	97.71

Source: Data from Department of Commerce, Survey of Current Business, 1989.

EXAMPLE 8.2

■ Data on annual registration of new passenger cars in the United States from 1960 to 1988 are shown in Table 8.2 and plotted in Figure 8.1. The values from 1960 to 1988 are used to develop the trend equation. Registrations is the Y or dependent variable and time is coded as X (1960 = 1, 1961 = 2, etc.) or the independent variable.

FIGURE 8.1 Registration Data for Example 8.2.

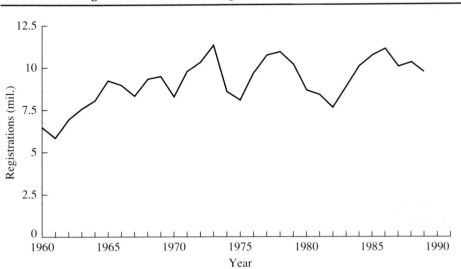

FIGURE 8.2 Trend Equation for Data of Example 8.2.

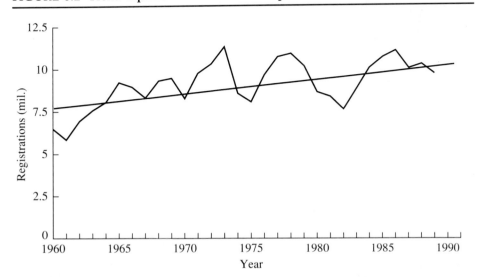

The least squares procedure, Equations 6.1 and 6.2, are used to compute the trend equation

$$Y_R = 7.5878 + .1053X$$

The r^2 is .398, which means that the time variable explains 39.8% of the variance for the new passenger car registrations variable. The estimated trend value for passenger car registrations for 1960 is 7.6931 million (7.5878 + .1053). Each year this trend is expected to increase by an average of .1053 million, or 105,300 registrations. This pattern of constant long-term growth might be attributed to the increase in the driving age population for this time period. Figure 8.2 shows the trend equation fitted to the actual data. The trend equation projects registrations to be 10,746,800 in 1989.

$$Y_R = 7.5878 + .1053X = 7.5878 + .1053(30) = 10.7468$$

Registrations of new passenger cars were actually 9,853,000 in 1989. Evidently, some other factor besides the trend must be used to forecast registrations. ■

The Minitab commands to solve Example 8.1 are

```
MTB > SET C1    *1
DATA > 6.577 5.855 7.557 8.065 9.314 9.009 8.357
DATA > 9.404 9.447 8.388 9.831 10.409 11.351 8.701
DATA > 8.168 9.752 10.826 10.946 140.357 8.761 8.444
DATA > 7.754 8.924 10.118 10.889 11.140 10.183 10.398
DATA > END
MTB > SET C2    *2
DATA > 1:29
DATA > END

MTB > REGRESS C1 1 PREDICTOR C2, RES IN C3, DHATS IN C4;    *3
SUBC > PREDICT 30.    *4
```

```
The regression equation is     *5
C1 = 7.59 + 0.105 C2
```

Predictor	Coef	Stdev	t-ratio	p
Constant	7.5878	0.4282	17.72	0.000
C2	0.10533	0.02493	4.22	0.000

s = 1.123   R-sq = 39.8%   *6   R-sq(adj) = 37.6%

Analysis of Variance

SOURCE	DF	SS	MS	F	p
Regression	1	22.522	22.522	17.85	0.000
Error	27	34.067	1.262		
Total	28	56.589			

Fit	Stdev.Fit	95% C.I.	95% P.I.
10.748 *7	0.428	(9.869, 11.626)	(8.281, 13.215)

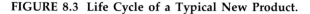

*1 The **set c1** command places the registration data in **c1**
*2 The **set c2** command generates integers from 1 to 29 and stores
    them in **c2**
*3 Subcommand **dhats** computes the estimates of Y and stores them
    in **c4**. Subcommand **res** computes the residuals and stores them
    in **c3**.
*4 Command **predict** when X is equal to 30
*5 The regression equation is C1 = 7.59 + 0.105 C2
*6 R-squared is equal to 39.8%
*7 The prediction for 1989 is 10.748

Although the least squares trend is probably used more often than
any other to describe the long-term growth of a time series, the use of
curved trends is sometimes necessary for a logical description of change. A
large variety of equations is available to compute trends for curves. Some of
the more useful trend equations include the exponential curve and the
Gompertz growth curve. A short description of these techniques follows.

Nonlinear Trend

Figure 8.3 shows that the life cycle of a typical new product is divided into
three major states: introduction, growth, and maturity and saturation. Time,
represented on the horizontal axis, can vary from days to years, depending
on the nature of the market. A linear model would not work with this type
of data. Linear models assume that a variable is increasing by a constant

FIGURE 8.3 Life Cycle of a Typical New Product.

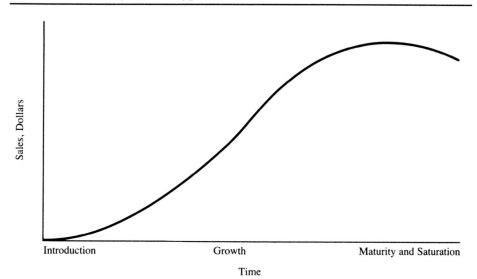

amount each time period. The growth stage of most new products appears to increase at an increasing amount or a constant rate.

When a time series starts slowly and then appears to be increasing at an increasing rate (see Figure 8.4) such that the percent difference from observation to observation is constant, and exponential trend can be fitted. The number of mutual fund salespeople in Figure 8.4 appears to be growing at a constant percentage rate instead of a constant amount. A linear trend might indicate an average growth of 8 salespeople per year. An exponential fit might indicate an average growth of 32% per year for the data of Figure 8.4. If the exponential model estimated 50 mutual fund salespeople for 1990, the increase estimated for 1991 would be 16 (55 × .32) instead of 8.

If the analyst is not careful, the exponential model can lead to very inaccurate forecasts. Notice that in Figure 8.4 the exponential model would always forecast an increasing amount for the number of mutual fund salespeople. What happens when market maturity and saturation take place and the growth rate slows down? The forecast will be higher than the actual value of the variable. Another problem involves using ordinary linear least squares to fit an exponential model. It has been argued that this type of forecast will be biased unless a variance correction is included in the formula.

Growth curves of the Gompertz or logistic type represent the tendency of many industries and product lines to grow at a declining percentage rate as they mature. If the plotted data reflect a situation where sales begin low, then as the product catches on sales "boom," and finally sales ease off as saturation is reached, the Gompertz curve might be appropriate. Figure 8.5

FIGURE 8.4 Graph of Mutual Fund Salespeople.

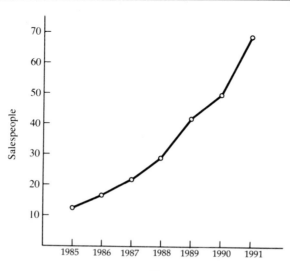

FIGURE 8.5 Gompertz Growth Curves.

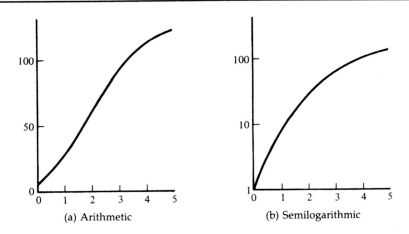

(a) Arithmetic   (b) Semilogarithmic

shows the general shape of a Gompertz growth curve plotted on both arithmetic and semilogarithmic scales. The computations for the Gompertz curve are extremely complex and are not within the scope of this text. Specialized books on time series analysis should be consulted for calculation procedures.[2]

In deciding which trend to use, one must know the purpose for computing the trend. For example, if the purpose is to obtain an estimate of expenditures for a future year, a knowledge of the basic forces producing or affecting the trend is needed. The right choice of a trend is a matter of judgment and, therefore, requires experience and common sense on the part of the analyst. The line or curve that best fits a set of data points might not make sense when projected as the trend of the future.

CYCLICAL VARIATION

The analysis of the trend of the dependent variable has direct practical value for long-term forecasting. The analysis of the cyclical component, though, is of dubious forecasting value. The cyclical component is the wavelike fluctuations or cycles of more than eight months' duration due to changing economic conditions. Economists have given extensive attention to the analysis of business cycles and their causes, but it is not within the

---

[2] For a description of the mathematical methods to fitting growth curves, see F. E. Croxton, D. J. Cowden, and B. W. Bolch, *Practical Business Statistics,* 14th ed. (Englewood Cliffs, N.J.: Prentice-Hall, 1969), pp. 332–338, or S. Makridakis and S. C. Wheelwright, *Interactive Forecasting,* Vol. 1 (Palo Alto, Calif.: Scientific Press, 1977), pp. 100–104.

scope of this text to consider the numerous theories addressing this problem.

Because both the cyclical and the irregular components of a time series are determined by the use of the residual method, they are combined for discussion purposes in this section.

The cyclical and irregular components of the time series are identified by eliminating or averaging out the effects of the trend. Because these components constitute what remains after such adjustments, the method is referred to as the *residual method.*

The specific steps included in the residual method depend on whether the analysis begins with monthly, quarterly, or annual time series data. If the data are monthly or quarterly, then the effects of both the trend and the seasonal components have to be removed. If the data are annual, then only the effects of the trend component are removed.

When annual data are used as the basis for the decomposition, no attempt is made to separate the cyclical and the irregular components. Symbolically, the decomposition of an annual time series is represented as

$$CI = \frac{Y}{T} = \frac{TCI}{T} \tag{8.5}$$

In determining the relative effect of the cyclical component in each annual value, the Y_R value is accepted as an accurate indication of trend, and the discrepancy (residual) is treated as the cyclical component.

EXAMPLE 8.3

■ The cyclical indexes for the annual registration of new passenger cars in the United States from 1960 to 1988 are presented in Table 8.2. Each cyclical relative is computed by dividing the actual number of registrations for each year (Y) by the expected number of registrations (Y_R). The trend equation, $Y_R = 7.5878 + .1053X$ is used to compute the expected trend value. This ratio is then multiplied by 100 to convert the cyclical to percentage or index number form.

For example, the cyclical value for 1960 in Table 8.2 is computed as follows (disregard rounding errors). The trend estimate for 1960 is

$$Y_R = 7.5878 + .1053(1) = 7.6931$$

The cyclical value for 1960 is

$$C = \frac{6.577}{7.6931} (100) = 85.49$$

The cyclical index shows the position of each Y value *relative* to the trend line. This position is reflected by a percentage. For example, in 1960, the Y value was 85.49% of the trend line. In 1973, Y was 125.25% of the trend line. Since the cyclical values are shown as percentages of the trend line, it can be said that the trend has been removed from the series, leaving only the cyclical component for evaluation. In 1960, new car passenger registrations were approximately 14% to 15% below what was expected based on the trend estimate. In 1973, new passenger car registrations were approximately 25% above what was expected based on the trend estimate. ■

The Minitab commands to solve Example 8.3 are as follows:

```
MTB > DIVIDE C1 BY C4, PUT INTO C5 *1
MTB > PRINT C5 *2
```

C5
0.85492	0.75079	0.87794	0.94355	0.99391	1.13313	1.08215
0.99129	1.10172	1.09327	0.95902	1.11063	1.16210	1.25254
0.94909	0.88083	1.03984	1.14154	1.14151	1.06835	0.89401
0.85249	0.77460	0.88219	0.98992	1.05448	1.06790	0.96640
0.97704						

*1 The cyclical relatives are computed by dividing the actual Y values stored in **c1** by the estimated Y values stored in **c4**. The result is stored in **c5**.
*2 The **print** command prints the contents of **c5** (cyclical relatives)

Figure 8.6 shows a cyclical chart that is developed to help analyze the cyclical component. Note that the trend equation is represented as 100% or the base line. Various patterns are easier to see on a cyclical chart. This type of chart also allows one to compare the cyclical of the variable of interest with the cyclical pattern for other variables and/or business indicators.

FIGURE 8.6 Cyclical Chart for Data of Example 8.3.

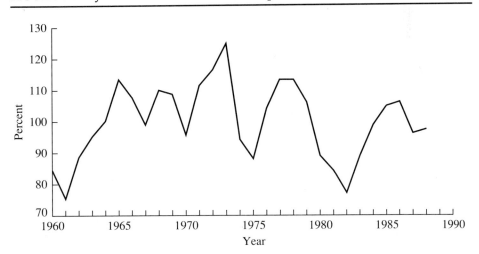

The following questions are answered by the cyclical relatives for any time series:

1. Does the series cycle?
2. If so, how extreme is the cycle?
3. Does the series follow the general state of the economy (business cycle)?

EXAMPLE 8.4

■ Figure 8.6 can be used to answer questions concerning the cyclical pattern for new passenger car registrations. Registrations were weak in the early 1960s, followed by a good period in 1965 and 1966. This good period then generally held for the years 1968 through 1979, with the exception of a weak period during 1974 and 1975. A five-year slump in registrations followed in the early 1980s. In 1985 and 1986, registrations were good, indicated by the cyclical being above the trend line. In 1987 and 1988, registrations appeared to be slipping. The cyclical pattern seems to indicate that new passenger car registrations are influenced to some extent by economic conditions. However, other factors also seem to be affecting the cyclical pattern of this variable. ■

One way to investigate cyclical patterns is through the study of business indicators. A *business indicator* is a business-related time series that is used to help assess the general state of the economy, particularly with reference to the business cycle. Many business people and economists systematically follow the movements of such statistical series to obtain economic and business information in the form of an unfolding picture that is up to date, comprehensive, relatively objective, and capable of being read and understood with a minimum expenditure of time.

Business indicators are business-related time series that are used to help assess the general state of the economy.

The most important list of statistical indicators originated during the sharp business setback of 1937–1938. The Secretary of the Treasury, Henry Morgenthau, requested the National Bureau of Economic Research (NBER) to devise a system that would signal when the setback was nearing an end. Under the leadership of Wesley Mitchell and Arthur F. Burns, NBER economists selected 21 series that from past performance promised to be fairly reliable indicators of business revival. Since then the bureau has revised the list several times. A recent list, consisting of 26 indicators, appears in Table 8.3.

TABLE 8.3 Cyclical Indicators (NBER Short List).

Leading Indicators	Roughly Coincident Indicators	Lagging Indicators
Average hourly workweek, production workers, manufacturing	GNP in current dollars	Unemployment rate, persons unemployed 15 weeks or over
Average weekly initial claims, state unemployment insurance	GNP in 1972 dollars	Business expenditures, new plant and equipment
Index of net business formation	Index of industrial production	Book value, manufacturing and trade inventories
New orders, durable goods industries	Personal income	Index of labor cost per unit of output in manufacturing
Contracts and orders, plant and equipment	Manufacturing and trade sales	Commercial and industrial loans outstanding in large commercial banks
Index of new building permits, private-housing units	Sales of retail stores	Bank rates on short-business loans
Change in book value, manufacturing and trade inventories	Employees on nonagricultural payrolls	
Index of industrial materials prices	Unemployment rate, total	
Index of stock prices, 500 common stocks		
Corporate profits after taxes (quarterly)		
Index: ratio, price to unit labor cost, manufacturing		
Change in consumer installment debt		

Source: U.S. Department of Commerce.

The NBER has found that certain statistical time series may be useful as direct indicators of cyclical expansions and contractions in business activity. After continuous study of business cycles, it has been learned that all areas of the economy do not expand simultaneously during expansions, nor do all contract concurrently during periods of contraction. A study of individual economic time series and their relation to this general cyclical movement indicates that the timing of most series conforms only loosely—

and in some series not at all—to that of the business cycle. Exceptions to this general statement, however, do exist.

The bureau has identified 26 statistical indicators—12 classified as leading, 8 as coincident, and 6 as lagging—that have proved useful as indicators of business conditions. Up-to-date figures for these series are published monthly in *Business Conditions Digest* by the U.S. Department of Commerce and weekly in *Statistical Indicator Reports* by Statistical Indicator Associates.

For the guidance of forecasters and other users, each series in the NBER list has been evaluated and scored by the bureau in terms of the following elements: (1) extent to which the series measures or represents an activity having a key role in the cyclical process, (2) statistical accuracy and dependability of the series, (3) degree of conformity of the series to historical business cycles, (4) consistency with which the series has moved in some specific phase (leading, coincident, or lagging) with cyclical movement in the economy, (5) degree of smoothness (i.e., relative absence of persistent major irregular fluctuations), and (6) timeliness of publication.[3] The series selected for the short list (Table 8.3) all have high scores and involve little duplication in coverage.

As was mentioned, three groups of indicators have been identified: those that provide advance warning of probable change in economic activity, the leading indicators; those that reflect the current performance of the economy, the coincident indicators; and those that confirm changes previously signaled, the lagging indicators.

1. *Leading indicators.* In practice, the leading series are studied to help anticipate cyclical turning points. Examples include hiring rates, construction contracts, new orders for durable goods, and formation of new business enterprises. These indicators move ahead of turns in the business cycle, primarily because decisions to expand or curtail output take time to produce influences.

2. *Coincident indicators.* The coincident series are those whose movements coincide roughly with, and provide a measure of, the current performance of economic activity. Gross national product, personal income, employment, industrial production, and wholesale prices are examples. These indicators are comprehensive in coverage and tell us whether the economy is currently experiencing a recession or a slowdown, a boom, or an inflation.

3. *Lagging indicators.* The fluctuations of these series usually follow those of the coincident indicators. Examples are long-term unemployment,

---

[3] G. H. Moore and J. Shiskin, *Indicators of Business Expansions and Contractions* (New York: National Bureau of Economic Research, 1957), pp. 8–28.

the yield on mortgage loans, labor cost per unit of output, and expenditures on new plant and equipment.

One of the major difficulties with an indicator is the determination of when it has reached a cyclical turning point. The fluctuating component of economic and business series contains short-term irregular movements in addition to cyclical ones. Thus weekly, monthly, or quarterly data plotted on a chart typically have the ragged, sawtooth appearance that was evident in Figure 8.6. Consequently, it is difficult to identify cyclical turning points near the time they occur. Remember that the turning points come into existence only as the consequence of a following decline or gain in the cyclical component. Hence several months may go by before a genuine cyclical upturn or downturn in a leading series is finally identified with any assurance.

Another problem in using the cyclical indicator approach arises because no uniformity occurs in the length of time by which a given leading indicator precedes cyclical turns in the economy. Instead, considerable variability can be noted in the lead time from cycle to cycle. Consequently, the leading indicators may signal that a recession or recovery can be expected some time in the future, but they provide less help in establishing the timing of the turn. Analysis of the coincident and lagging indicators is frequently helpful in this connection. For instance, if leading indicators have signaled a cyclical downturn, analysts will begin to look very carefully for signs of weakening in the coincident indicators. In practice, then, effective use of the cyclical indicator approach requires continuous evaluation of series in all three timing groups.

Still another difficulty with the indicators is that they occasionally give "false signals"; that is, they signal a turning point that does not materialize. Sometimes such signals are due to factors that can be identified in advance, such as a major strike, so that the signals are discounted. In other cases it has been impossible to distinguish false signals from accurate ones until after the fact.

In summary, business indicators have proved to be most useful in forecasting turning points, especially where most other methods tend to break down. Indicators have their limitations; however, over time they have performed as well as any method.

In their article entitled "Early Warning Signals for Economy," Geoffrey H. Moore and Julius Shiskin have the following to say on the usefulness of statistical indicators:[4]

> It seems clear from the record that business cycle indicators are helpful in judging the tone of current business and short-term

---

[4] G. H. Moore and J. Shiskin, "Early Warning Signals for the Economy," in *Statistics: A Guide to Business and Economics* (San Francisco: Holden-Day, 1976), p. 81.

prospects. But because of their limitations, the indicators must be used together with other data and with full awareness of the background of business and consumer confidence and expectations, governmental policies, and international events. We also must anticipate that the indicators will often be difficult to interpret, that interpretations will sometimes vary among analysts, and that the signals they give will not be correctly interpreted.

Indicators provide a sensitive and revealing picture of the ebb and flow of economic tides that a skillful analyst of the economic, political, and international scene can use to improve his chances of making a valid forecast of short-run economic trends. If the analyst is aware of their limitations and alert to the world around him, he will find the indicators useful guideposts for taking stock of the economy and its needs.

The cyclical pattern for new-car registrations is used as an example for analysis and prediction.

EXAMPLE 8.5

■ To explain the cyclical pattern of the new-car registration variable shown in Figure 8.6, several factors should be investigated. If the passenger registration variable is logically related to the economy, roughly coincident indicators that provide a measure of current performance of economic activity should provide assistance in forecasting. Many indicator series are forecast by experts, and these forecasts are often available in published sources. If such forecasts are available, and if the forecasts have a good record of reliability, they might provide a basis for forecasting new-car registrations.

Figure 8.6 clearly indicates that the car registration variable is related to the economy. When new-car registrations bottomed out in 1961, 1970, 1974–1975, and 1982, the economy was depressed. When registrations peaked in 1965, 1968, 1973, 1977 and 1978, the economy was healthy.

Another variable that might provide some forecasting assistance is the new-car price index. Logically, when prices are up, registrations should be down, and when prices are down, registrations should be up. The new-car price index is adjusted for trend to eliminate the effects of inflation and is graphed in Figure 8.7 with new-car registrations for the purpose of comparison. Figure 8.7 indicates that the two variables are inversely related. Thus knowledge of proposed price policies should help forecast new-car registrations.

The discussion so far shows how the factors that create a variation in a time series can be separated and studied individually. *Analysis* is the procedure for taking the time series apart; *synthesis* is the process of putting it back together.

To understand the new-car registration variable, the individual components are analyzed. The decomposition for the year 1988 is accomplished by determining the trend and cyclical components (see Table 8.2).

T = trend (1988) = 10.6415

C = cyclical (1988) = 97.71

FIGURE 8.7 Car Registration and New-car Price Index Cyclical Chart.

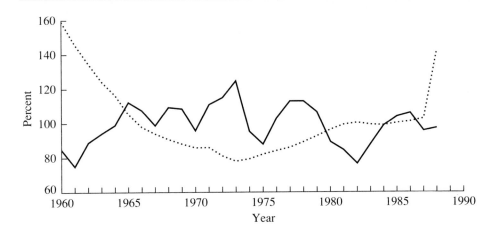

To put the series back together, the analyst uses the original multiplicative model and substitutes the appropriate components.

$$Y = TCI$$

$$Y(1988) = 10.6415 \times .9771 = 10.3978$$

The multiplicative model can also be used to estimate new-car registrations for 1989. All the analyst needs are accurate estimates for the trend and cyclical-irregular components.

The trend estimate is determined by using the appropriate trend equation, in this case $Y_R = 7.5878 + .1053X$. Since $X = 1$ represents July 1, 1960, the X-coded value for 1989 is 30. So the trend estimate for 1989 is

$$Y_R = 7.5878 + .1053(30) = 10.7468$$

Next, the cyclical relative must be estimated on a subjective basis. All the information that has been gathered concerning the cyclical pattern of new-car registrations is taken into consideration. Business indicators are studied and used whenever helpful. Leading indicators are investigated for the short-term cyclical, and if any are found, they are analyzed.

The cyclical index for new-car registrations increased slightly from 1987 to 1988 (see Figure 8.6), but the cyclical relatives for 1987 and 1988 were both less than 100. Will this pattern continue or will registrations level out or even turn downward again? How will the economy perform? What do the experts forecast for the business cycle? What are the proposed new-car pricing policies for 1989? Once these questions are answered, the analyst can choose an estimate for the cyclical relative for 1989. The most important aspect of the cyclical estimate process is for the forecaster to predict the direction correctly. If the forecaster successfully predicts whether the cyclical pattern of a particular variable will continue to increase or decrease, level off, or turn upward or downward, the forecast will be reasonably accurate. The actual value used for the estimate is not as important if the analyst gets the direction correct.

Economic indicators point to a slump in the economy in 1989. Furthermore, the new-car price index is expected to increase. For these reasons, it is decided to forecast that the cyclical relative will turn back downward. The *CI* for 1988 is 97.71 (see Table 8.2). The cyclical for 1989 is estimated to be 94 and the forecast using Equation 8.1 is

$$Y(1989) = T \times C$$
$$= 10.7468(.94) = 10.1020$$

The forecast for 1989, 10.1020, is now compared with the actual registrations of 9.853. The forecast error is

$$e_t = 9.853 - 10.1020 = -0.2490$$

The forecast overestimated registrations by 249,000. ■

It is extremely difficult to estimate the *CI* for more than a year or two into the future. Therefore any long-term forecast of such a variable is risky, at best. If the trend equation does a good job of fitting past data, a five- or ten-year projection into the future is reasonable. As long as the trend growth or decline is expected to remain consistent with past performance, an accurate forecast can be anticipated.

SEASONAL VARIATION

The analysis of trend has implications for long-term managerial planning. The analysis of the seasonal component of a time series has more immediate short-term implications. Marketing plans, for example, have to take into consideration expected seasonal patterns in consumer purchases. The identification of the seasonal component in a time series differs from trend analysis in at least two ways.

1. While the trend is determined directly from all available data, the seasonal component is determined by eliminating the other components so that only the seasonal component remains.
2. While the trend is represented by one best-fitting line, or equation, a separate seasonal value has to be computed for each month (or quarter) of the year, usually in the form of an index number. As was true for trend analysis, several methods for measuring seasonal variation have been developed; most of the seasonal index computations now used are variations of the *ratio-to-moving-average method.*

The seasonal component in a time series is measured in the form of an *index number.* The interpretation of this index number, which represents the extent of seasonal influence for a particular segment of the year, involves a comparison of the measured or expected values for that segment (month, quarter, etc.) with the overall average for all the segments of the year. Thus a seasonal index of 100 for a particular month indicates that the expected value for that month is $\frac{1}{12}$ of the total for the annual period centered at that month. A seasonal index of 125 for a different month indicates that the expected value for that month is 25% greater than $\frac{1}{12}$ of the annual total. A monthly index of 80 indicates that the expected level of activity that month is 20% less than $\frac{1}{12}$ of the total activity level for the year. Thus a monthly index number indicates the expected ups and downs in monthly or quarterly levels of activity, with effects due to trend, cyclical, and irregular components removed. Equation 8.6 shows how the seasonal component is computed.

$$S = \frac{TSCI}{TCI} \tag{8.6}$$

> *Index numbers* are percentages that show changes over time.

The ratio-to-moving-average method for measuring seasonal variation is illustrated in the next example.

EXAMPLE 8.6

■ In the analysis of new-car registrations, the monthly data for the years 1982 through 1988 are used as the basis for the analysis of the seasonal component rather than the monthly data for the entire 1960–1988 time period. One reason for this reduction in data is to simplify the computations in this illustration. Another more important reason is that if there has been any significant shift in the seasonal pattern of new-car purchases in recent years, using the entire 1960–1988 period of the seasonal analysis would result in poorer projections of expected seasonal patterns for 1989 than using the data for only 1982–1988.

Table 8.4 presents the monthly new-car registrations, in thousands, for the period from January 1982 through December 1983 to illustrate the beginning of the ratio-to-moving-average computations. The first step for monthly data is to compute a 12-month moving average (for quarterly data, a four-quarter moving average would be computed). Because all of the months of the year are included in this moving average, effects due to the seasonal component are removed, leaving only the effects due to long-term trend, cyclical, and irregular components in the moving averages.

The steps for computing seasonal indexes by the ratio-to-moving-average method are given below and shown in Table 8.4.

Step 1 Compute the 12-month moving total and place the total for January 1982 through December 1983 opposite July 1, 1982.

TABLE 8.4 Registration of New Passenger Cars: Monthly Data, in Thousands, 1982–1983.

Period	Registrations	12-month Moving Total	Two-year Moving Total	12-month Centered Moving Average	Seasonal Index
1982					
Jan.	509				
Feb.	546				
Mar.	626				
Apr.	672				
May	708				
June	717				
		7,754			
July	626 1	} 2	15,594 } 3	649.75 } 4	96.34 } 5
		7,840			
Aug.	627		15,703	654.29	95.83
		7,863			
Sept.	625		15,825	659.38	94.79
		7,962			
Oct.	655		15,980	665.83	98.37
		8,018			
Nov.	678		16,101	670.88	101.06
		8,083			
Dec.	765		16,318	679.92	112.51
		8,235			
1983					
Jan.	595		16,633	693.04	85.85
		8,398			
Feb.	569		16,942	705.92	80.60
		8,544			
Mar.	725		17,198	716.58	101.17
		8,654			
Apr.	728		17,410	725.42	100.36
		8,756			
May	773		17,535	730.63	105.80
		8,779			
June	869		17,703	737.63	117.81
		8,924			
July	789				
Aug.	773				
Sept.	735				
Oct.	757				
Nov.	701				
Dec.	910				

Step 2 So that the subsequent averages are located at the center of each month, compute a 2-year moving total.

Step 3 Since the 2-year total contains the data for 24 months (January 1982 once, February 1982–December 1982 twice, and January 1983 once), this total is centered (opposite) July 15, 1982.

$$7,754 + 7,840 = 15,594$$

Step 4 Divide the 2-year moving total by 24 in order to obtain the 12-month centered moving average.

$$\frac{15,594}{24} = 649.75$$

Step 5 The ratio to moving average is calculated by dividing the actual value for each month by the 12-month centered moving average and multiplying by 100 so that the ratio is an index number in the form of a percentage.

$$S = \frac{TSCI}{TCI} = \frac{626}{649.75}(100) = 96.34$$

Next, the average percentage ratio for each month is determined. Table 8.5 shows the use of this *modified mean method*. This approach eliminates the highest and lowest values and averages the remaining indexes.

Finally, the seasonal indexes are computed by multiplying each of the average ratios by a value so that the sum of all 12 monthly indexes is equal to exactly 1,200. Since this multiplier should be greater than 1 if the total of the averages before adjustment is less than 1,200 and smaller than 1 if the total is greater than 1,200, the multiplier is defined as

$$\text{Multiplier} = \frac{1,200}{\text{Actual total}} \qquad (8.7)$$

Table 8.6 shows the computations for the new-car registration data. The multiplier is

$$\frac{1200}{1198.46} = 1.001285$$

The final column of Table 8.6 lists the computed seasonal index values for each month, determined by making the adjustment (multiplying by 1.001285). A scan of these values shows that the seasonal peak in the number of new-car

TABLE 8.5 Computation of Modified Mean for January for Example 8.5.

85.85		Eliminate the highest (99.23)
89.33	89.33	and lowest (85.85) and average
90.17	90.17	the rest:
91.29	91.29	
92.06	92.06	$362.85 \div 4 = 90.71$
99.23	362.85	

TABLE 8.6 Summary of the Monthly Seasonal Indexes for Example 8.6.

Month	1982	1983	1984	1985	1986	1987	1988	Modified Mo. Mean	Adjusted Seasonal Index
Jan		85.85	92.06	90.17	99.23	91.29	89.33	90.71	90.8
Feb		80.60	95.43	90.68	89.53	76.66	93.57	88.60	88.7
Mar		101.17	100.78	104.88	92.31	95.55	106.26	100.60	100.7
Apr		100.36	99.94	104.08	98.54	104.79	98.66	100.76	100.9
May		105.80	104.78	100.71	100.45	97.80	101.04	101.75	101.9
Jun		117.81	109.60	101.75	111.02	113.48	113.19	111.82	112.0
Jul	96.34	105.20	106.93	103.86	102.75	106.08		104.47	104.6
Aug	95.83	101.02	100.68	100.59	99.55	105.96		100.46	100.6
Sep	94.79	94.39	102.77	120.29	128.96	110.82		107.17	107.3
Oct	98.37	96.09	97.16	106.45	106.55	94.82		99.52	99.6
Nov	101.06	87.95	94.49	90.68	81.19	83.13		89.06	89.2
Dec	112.51	113.15	95.20	92.58	102.51	104.00		103.56	103.7
								1198.46	1200.0

registrations occurs in the early summer months and that the seasonal low occurs in the months of January and February. Weather plays an important role in the explanation of the seasonal pattern of this variable. New-car registrations tend to be up in good-weather months such as June and July and down in bad-weather months such as January and February. ∎

The results of a seasonal variation analysis can be used to (1) schedule production; (2) deseasonalize sales; (3) evaluate current sales, production, and shipments; and/or (4) forecast monthly sales.

Seasonal Trend

Once the seasonal component has been identified, the next step is to compute a seasonal trend equation (monthly or quarterly trend equation). Earlier in the chapter, trend was defined as the long-term growth or decline in a time series. For this reason, the trend of a monthly or quarterly series must be consistent with its long-term growth or decline. The trend for seasonal data can be computed using one of the following approaches:

1. If long-term data are not available, the seasonal trend must be computed from the seasonal data.
2. If the trend for the seasonal data appears to be similar to the long-term growth described by the long-term trend equation, the seasonal trend can be computed from the seasonal data.
3. If monthly or quarterly data are available for the entire annual series (all 8 to 25 years), the seasonal trend equation can be computed using all these values.

4. If the long-term trend equation has already been computed, it can be mathematically converted to a seasonal trend equation and used with the available seasonal data.

EXAMPLE 8.7

■ Figure 8.2 shows the long-term trend equation for the new passenger car registration series from 1960 to 1988. The easiest way to develop a seasonal trend equation is to use the least-squares procedure on the monthly data for 1982 through 1988. This solution will work if the resulting monthly trend equation accurately reflects the long-term growth pattern presented in Figure 8.2. It appears that the slope of a monthly trend equation developed from data for 1982 through 1988 would be slightly larger than if monthly data for the entire series were used. However, since the differences are very slight, the seasonal trend equation will be computed directly from the monthly data for 1982 through 1988.

The Y variable or the monthly data for the new passenger car registration series are presented in the first column of Table 8.7. The months are coded as the independent variable X, with January 1982 represented as 1, February 1982 represented as 2, and so on. Equation 8.4 is used to compute the seasonal trend equation: $Y_R = 701.081 + 2.899X$. The rest of the trend values are shown in column 2 of Table 8.7. Note that the trend value for January 1982 is 703.980 ($701.081 + 2.899$) and the average increase each month is approximately 2.899 registrations. ■

TABLE 8.7 Calculations for the Short-Term Components.

Period		Data Y	Regression T	Seasonal Adjustment TCI	CI	C	I
1982	Jan	509	703.98	560.57	79.60		
	Feb	546	706.88	615.49	87.07		
	Mar	626	709.78	621.49	87.56	88.96	98.42
	Apr	672	712.68	666.09	93.46	90.87	102.85
	May	708	715.58	694.96	97.12	90.05	107.85
	Jun	717	718.47	640.38	89.13	89.75	99.31
	Jul	626	721.37	598.45	82.96	87.07	95.27
	Aug	627	724.27	623.34	86.06	85.66	100.47
	Sep	625	727.17	582.45	80.10	88.58	90.43
	Oct	655	730.07	657.33	90.04	92.04	97.83
	Nov	678	732.97	760.29	103.73	92.56	112.07
	Dec	765	735.87	737.77	100.26	93.84	106.84
1983	Jan	595	738.77	655.08	88.67	95.16	93.18
	Feb	569	741.67	641.42	86.48	93.73	92.27
	Mar	725	744.56	719.78	96.67	93.90	102.95
	Apr	728	747.46	721.60	96.54	96.77	99.76
	May	773	750.36	758.76	101.12	99.42	101.71
	Jun	869	753.26	776.14	103.04	100.34	102.69

continues

TABLE 8.7 Continued

Period		Data Y	Regression T	Seasonal Adjustment TCI	CI	C	I
	Jul	789	756.16	754.27	99.75	99.01	100.75
	Aug	773	759.06	768.48	101.24	98.65	102.63
	Sep	735	761.96	684.97	89.90	98.52	91.25
	Oct	757	764.86	759.70	99.33	101.35	98.01
	Nov	701	767.76	786.09	102.39	102.36	100.03
	Dec	910	770.66	877.61	113.88	107.09	106.34
1984	Jan	747	773.55	822.43	106.32	108.50	97.99
	Feb	782	776.45	881.53	113.53	109.23	103.94
	Mar	835	779.35	828.99	106.37	108.61	97.94
	Apr	837	782.25	829.64	106.06	108.38	97.86
	May	886	785.15	869.68	110.77	107.50	103.04
	Jun	928	788.05	828.83	105.18	107.57	97.78
	Jul	903	790.95	863.26	109.14	106.80	102.19
	Aug	852	793.85	847.02	106.70	105.58	101.06
	Sep	874	796.75	814.50	102.23	107.35	95.23
	Oct	834	799.64	836.97	104.67	105.23	99.46
	Nov	816	802.54	915.04	114.02	105.17	108.42
	Dec	823	805.44	793.70	98.54	106.68	92.38
1985	Jan	781	808.34	859.87	106.37	108.35	98.18
	Feb	790	811.24	890.55	109.78	108.26	101.40
	Mar	927	814.14	920.32	113.04	110.38	102.41
	Apr	936	817.04	927.77	113.55	109.15	104.04
	May	912	819.94	895.20	109.18	109.17	100.01
	Jun	923	822.84	824.37	100.19	108.78	92.10
	Jul	949	825.74	907.23	109.87	110.83	99.13
	Aug	926	828.63	920.59	111.10	112.40	98.84
	Sep	1105	831.53	1029.78	123.84	114.54	108.12
	Oct	973	834.43	976.47	117.02	112.06	104.43
	Nov	828	837.33	928.50	110.89	113.68	97.54
	Dec	849	840.23	818.78	97.45	110.82	87.93
1986	Jan	913	843.13	1005.20	119.22	107.25	111.16
	Feb	822	846.03	926.62	109.53	106.16	103.17
	Mar	848	848.93	841.89	99.17	107.75	92.04
	Apr	906	851.83	898.03	105.42	104.99	100.42
	May	918	854.72	901.09	105.42	103.83	101.53
	Jun	1012	857.62	903.86	105.39	104.59	100.77
	Jul	934	860.52	892.89	103.76	108.22	95.88
	Aug	894	863.42	888.78	102.94	109.03	94.41
	Sep	1149	866.32	1070.78	123.60	106.44	116.12
	Oct	948	869.22	951.38	109.45	105.57	103.68
	Nov	719	872.12	806.27	92.45	105.05	88.01
	Dec	902	875.02	869.89	99.41	97.50	101.96
1987	Jan	800	877.92	880.79	100.33	94.24	106.46
	Feb	671	880.81	756.40	85.88	95.76	89.68

TABLE 8.7 Continued

Period		Data Y	Regression T	Seasonal Adjustment TCI	CI	C	I
	Mar	829	883.71	823.03	93.13	94.20	98.87
	Apr	895	886.61	887.13	100.06	93.41	107.12
	May	830	889.51	814.71	91.59	95.43	95.98
	Jun	963	892.41	860.09	96.38	96.79	99.57
	Jul	899	895.31	859.43	95.99	96.53	99.44
	Aug	903	898.21	897.72	99.95	96.40	103.68
	Sep	955	901.11	889.99	98.77	94.88	104.09
	Oct	819	904.01	821.92	90.92	94.78	95.92
	Nov	718	906.91	805.15	88.78	93.47	94.98
	Dec	901	909.80	868.93	95.51	93.66	101.97
1988	Jan	774	912.70	852.16	93.37	95.34	97.93
	Feb	810	915.60	913.09	99.73	95.92	103.97
	Mar	919	918.50	912.38	99.33	95.38	104.15
	Apr	852	921.40	844.51	91.65	95.61	95.87
	May	874	924.30	857.90	92.82	93.81	98.94
	Jun	981	927.20	876.17	94.50	93.15	101.45
	Jul	883	930.10	844.14	90.76	93.48	97.09
	Aug	901	933.00	895.74	96.01	92.17	104.17
	Sep	937	935.89	873.21	93.30	91.46	102.01
	Oct	807	938.79	809.87	86.27	91.61	94.17
	Nov	764	941.69	856.73	90.98		
	Dec	896	944.59	864.10	91.48		
1989	Jan		947.49				
	Feb		950.39				
	Mar		953.29				
	Apr		956.19				
	May		959.09				
	Jun		961.99				
	Jul		964.88				
	Aug		967.78				
	Sep		970.68				
	Oct		973.58				
	Nov		976.48				
	Dec		979.38				

Trend forecast $= 701.081 + 2.899 \times$ Period

SEASONALLY ADJUSTED DATA

A large number of economic indicators appear in each issue of *The Survey of Current Business*. Many of these indicators contain *seasonally adjusted data* to enable users of the index to see patterns that are independent of seasonal variations. Removal of seasonal variations helps clarify basic strengths or weaknesses in the data. For example, new-car registrations might increase by 10% from November to December, but is this increase an indication that new-car sales are completing a banner quarter? This question can be answered more accurately if the seasonal fluctuations in new-car registrations are known. Table 8.6 indicates that a sharp increase from November to December is typical. Perhaps an adjustment for seasonal increase would demonstrate that all of the increase is due to seasonal factors.

If the original monthly values of a time series are divided by their corresponding seasonal indexes, the resulting data are said to be *deseasonalized,* or adjusted for seasonal variation. Since the resulting values still include the trend, cyclical, and irregular movements, the process of deseasonalizing data can be represented by

$$Y = TSCI \tag{8.8}$$

$$TCI = \frac{Y}{S} = \frac{TSCI}{S} \tag{8.9}$$

> *Seasonally adjusted data* result when original monthly or quarterly values of a time series are divided by their corresponding seasonal indexes.

EXAMPLE 8.8

■ Table 8.7 lists the seasonally adjusted data for new-car registrations and several short-term computations that will be discussed later in the chapter. These values were calculated by dividing the actual monthly values of Table 8.7 by the seasonal indexes of Table 8.6 and multiplying the result by 100. Because the effect of the seasonal component has been removed, the number of new-car registrations for June of each year, a high-registration month, is not markedly higher than that for February, a low-registration month. Thus the seasonally adjusted data of Table 8.7 have had the effect of the seasonal component removed but still include the effects of the trend, cyclical, and irregular components. The seasonally adjusted data (*TCI*) are shown in Table 8.7.

An example calculation for January 1982 is as follows:

$Y = 509$

$S = .908$ (Table 8.6)

$Y = TSCI$

$\dfrac{Y}{S} = TCI$

$\dfrac{509}{.908} = 560.57$ ■

SHORT-TERM CYCLICAL AND
IRREGULAR VARIATIONS

The cyclical and irregular variations can now be calculated for the short-term analysis. Since the data have been seasonally adjusted,

$$\frac{TSCI}{S} = TCI$$

these deseasonalized values can now be divided by the appropriate monthly trend values.

$$\frac{TCI}{T} = CI$$

The CI values are shown in column 4 of Table 8.7. For example, for January 1982,

$$Y = 509$$

$$S = .908 \qquad \text{(Table 8.6)}$$

$$T = 703.98 \qquad \text{(Table 8.7)}$$

$$TCI = \frac{TSCI}{S} = \frac{509}{.908} = 560.57$$

$$CI = \frac{TCI}{T} = \frac{560.57}{702.98} \, (100) = 79.6$$

After the data have been adjusted for seasonal and trend influences, the cyclical and irregular variations are analyzed. With annual data the CI is investigated as one entity; however, with monthly data the C and the I can be separated, because of the short-term effects of irregular variations. A moving average is developed to smooth out the irregularities. The computational procedure is simple and is illustrated in the next example.

EXAMPLE 8.9

■ Table 8.8 shows the computation for the five-month moving average for the data of Table 8.7.

The five-month moving averages are entered in column 5 of Table 8.7 (labeled C) and presumably reflect only the effect of the short-term cyclical component. When the cyclical column (C) in Table 8.7 is compared with the cyclical-irregular column (CI), it appears that the five-month moving average has smoothed out the irregularities of the CI column. The cyclical component (C column) rises and falls in a smooth manner and the cycle is easier to identify. The cyclical index was below 100 in 1982 and gradually rose to a high of 114.54 in September 1985. From this point the cycle of new passenger car registrations consistently dropped until it reached 91.46 in September 1988. This short-term cyclical index parallels the

**TABLE 8.8 Computational Procedure for 5-Month Moving Average for Data
of Table 8.7.**

Period (1982)	CI	5-Month Moving Total	C
Jan.	79.60		
Feb.	87.07		
Mar.	87.56	444.81	88.96
Apr.	93.46	454.34	90.87
May	97.12	450.23	90.05
Jun.	89.13		
Jul.	82.96		

long-term cyclical analyzed in Figure 8.6. if the short-term cyclical effect had been radically different from the long-term cyclical, then the monthly trend equation should have been developed by converting the long-term trend equation to be used with the monthly data. ■

Finally, the identification of the irregular component is developed in Equation 8.10 by dividing the *CI* column of Table 8.7 by the *C* column and multiplying the result by 100.

$$I = \frac{CI}{C}(100) \qquad\qquad\qquad (8.10)$$

The irregular component measures the variability of the time series after the other components have been removed. Most of the irregular component is made up of random variability. However, sometimes unpredictable events cause irregularities in a variable.

EXAMPLE 8.10

■ The last column of Table 8.7 (*I*) shows the irregular indexes for new passenger car registrations. These values were calculated by dividing the cyclical-irregular indexes in column 4 by the cyclical indexes in column 5 and multiplying the result by 100. The irregular index for March 1982 is

$$I = \frac{CI}{C}(100) = \frac{87.56}{88.96}(100) = 98.42$$

Sometimes the irregular variations in a time series can be explained. Examination of the irregular column in Table 8.7 shows that irregularities occurred in September (116.12) and November (88.01) of 1986. These irregularities were caused by wage and strike problems in the automobile industry. ■

One reason for decomposing a time series is to isolate and examine the components of the series. After the analyst is able to look at the trend, seasonal, cyclical, and irregular components of a seasonal series one at a time, insights into the patterns in the original data values may be gained. In addition to gaining knowledge from the decomposition process, the identification of individual components makes it much easier to forecast the series into the future.

SEASONAL FORECASTING

In forecasting a seasonal time series, the decomposition process is reversed. Instead of separating the series into individual components for examination, the components are recombined to develop the forecasts for future periods. The multiplicative model $Y = TSCI$ is used to develop these forecasts.

EXAMPLE 8.11

■ The short-term forecast for January 1989 for new passenger car registrations is developed using Tables 8.6 and 8.7.

1. *Trend.* The monthly trend equation estimates are shown in Table 8.7. The trend value for January 1989 was computed in the following manner. Since January 1982 was represented by $X = 1$, January 1988 is represented by $X = 85$ and the trend projection is 947.49:

$$Y_R = 701.081 + 2.899X$$
$$= 701.081 + 2.899(85)$$
$$= 947.49$$

2. *Seasonal.* The adjusted seasonal index for the month of January is found in Table 8.6 to be 90.8.

3. *Cyclical.* The cyclical index is predicted by the analyst using all the information gathered on the cyclical pattern. The analyst must answer the following questions: Was the cyclical pattern shown in Table 8.7 increasing or decreasing for the last few months of 1988? Have any leading indicators been identified? What is the economic forecast for 1989? To demonstrate the completion of this example, a cyclical index of 91 is used.

4. *Irregular.* Since most irregular fluctuations are random variations, an estimate of 100% or 1.0 is commonly used. The forecast for January 1989 is

$$Y(\text{January } 1989) = TSCI$$
$$= (947.49)(.908)(.91)(1.00)$$
$$= 782.892$$

Actual new passenger car registrations for January 1989 were 733,000. The forecast overestimated registrations by 49,892.

$$e_t = 733,000 - 782,892 = -49,892 \qquad ■$$

In actual practice, the importance of individual components dictates their use in short-term forecasting. If a variable is extremely seasonal, the seasonal variation analysis will provide important, if not complete, input into the forecasting process. If a dependable leading indicator is discovered, the short-term forecast might be totally based on it. Hence if one component dominates the analysis, it alone might provide a practical, accurate forecast.

THE CENSUS II DECOMPOSITION METHOD

One commonly utilized method of seasonally adjusting and decomposing a time series was developed by the National Bureau of Economic Research during the 1920s. Julius Shiskin is considered the prime contributor in the development of this approach. Census II has been used widely by the Bureau of the Census and other governmental agencies and is receiving increased usage by the business world. For a detailed explanation of this approach, one should consult the Bureau of the Census Technical Paper no. 15, "The X-11 Variant of the Census Method II Seasonal Adjustment Program."

The X-11 variation of the Census II approach consists of four phases. The first phase attempts to adjust the monthly time series data for trading day variations. Trading day adjustments are necessary because the number of working, or trading, days varies from year to year for a given month. In sectors such as retail sales, this factor can significantly affect the monthly sales for a given month from year to year.

The second phase of the X-11 system involves the preliminary estimates of seasonal factors and the adjustment of the series for seasonality. This phase makes a preliminary separation of the seasonality from the trend/cycle and then attempts to isolate the randomness.

The third phase refines the adjustments in order to provide more accurate seasonal factors. This step also includes the estimation of the trend, cycle and random components.

The final phase generates summary statistics that can be utilized by the analyst to determine how successfully the method has isolated the seasonal factors and to develop future estimates of the trend/cycle in the data for purposes of forecasting. The tests in this phase are based on intuitive considerations and are not statistical in a rigorous mathematical sense. For a more detailed description of the Census II method, one should refer to *Forecasting: Methods and Applications* by Makridakis, Wheelwright, and McGee.

APPLICATION TO MANAGEMENT

In recent years time series analysis has come to the forefront of statistical tools for use in forecasting future events that are intertwined with the economy in some fashion. Manufacturers are extremely interested in the boom-bust cycles of our economy as well as of foreign economies so that they can better predict demand for their products, which in turn impacts their inventory levels, employment needs, cash flows, and almost all other business activities within the firm.

The complexity of these problems is enormous. Take, for example, the problem of predicting demand for oil and its by-products. In the late 1960s the price of oil per barrel was very low, and there seemed to be an insatiable worldwide demand for gas and oil. Then came the oil price shocks of the early and mid 1970s. What would the future demand for oil be? What about prices? Firms such as Exxon and General Motors were obviously very interested in these questions. If oil prices continued to escalate logarithmically, would the demand for large cars diminish? What would be the demand for electricity? By and large, analysts predicted that the demand for energy, and therefore oil, would be very inelastic; thus prices would continue to outstrip inflation. However, these predictions did not take into account a major downswing in the business cycle of the early 1980s and the greater elasticity of consumer demand for energy than predicted. By 1980 the world began to see a glut of oil on the market and radically falling prices. It seemed hard to believe that consumers were actually benefiting once again from gasoline price wars.

Oil demand is affected not only by long-term cyclical events but also by seasonal and random events, as are most other forecasts of demand for any type of product or service. For instance, consider the service and retail industries. Business forecasters and futurists are all predicting that over the next 25 years we will see a gradual movement of employment away from manufacturing to the retail and service fields. Thus since retailing is an extremely seasonal and cyclical business and since inventory projections are critical to retailers, time series analysis will be used more widely by increasingly sophisticated retailers. Survival during periods of major competitive change like those we will be witnessing depends on being more sophisticated than one's competitor. One indication that a wider interest in using more sophisticated statistical tools is already occurring is the booming market for mini- and microcomputers in the retail field. Demand for statistical software packages is also booming.

Manufacturers will have a continued need for statistical projections of future events. What will the future inflation rate be? How will it affect the cost-of-living adjustments that may be built into a company's labor contract? How will these adjustments affect prices and demand? What is the projected pool of managerial skills for 1990? What will be the effect of the government's boom-bust spending and taxing strategies?

One of the biggest of all questions that affects almost all segments of our economy is, What will be the future population of young people? Demographers are closely watching the current fertility rate and using almost every available time series forecasting technique to try and project this trend. Very minor miscalculations will have major impacts on everything from the building of babies' toys to the financial soundness of the Social Security system. Interestingly, demographers are looking at very long-term business cycles (20 years or more per cycle) in trying to predict what this generation's population of women of childbearing age will do with regard to having children. Will they have the one or two children, as did families in the 1960s and 1970s, or will they return to having two or three, as did preceding generations? These decisions will determine the age composition of our population for the next 50 to 75 years.

Political scientists are interested in using time series analysis to study the changing patterns of government spending on defense and social welfare programs. Obviously, these trends have great impact on the future of whole industries.

Finally, one interesting microcosm of applications of time series analysis has shown up in legal fields. Lawyers are making increasing use of expert witnesses to testify about the present value of a person's or a firm's future income, the cost incurred from the loss of a job due to discrimination, or the effect on a market due to an illegal strike. These questions can often be best answered through the judicious use of time series analysis.

CHAPTER 8

GLOSSARY

Business indicators   Business indicators are business-related time series that are used to help assess the general state of the economy.

Index numbers   Index numbers are percentages that show changes over time.

Price deflation   Price deflation is the process of expressing terms in a series in constant dollars.

CHAPTER 8

KEY FORMULAS

Time series: annual data $Y = TCI$ (8.1)

Current purchasing power of $1 $\dfrac{100}{\text{Current price index}}$ (8.2)

Deflated dollar value   (Dollar value) $\times$ (Purchasing power of $1)   (8.3)

Trend equation $Y_R = b_0 + bX$ (8.4)

Cyclical-irregular component $CI = \dfrac{Y}{T} = \dfrac{TCI}{T}$ (8.5)

Seasonal component $S = \dfrac{TSCI}{TCI}$ (8.6)

Multiplier $\dfrac{1,200}{\text{Actual total}}$ (8.7)

Time series: monthly or quarterly data $\quad Y = TSCI$ $\qquad$ (8.8)

Seasonally adjusted data $\quad TCI = \dfrac{Y}{S} = \dfrac{TSCI}{S}$ $\qquad$ (8.9)

Irregular component $\quad I = \dfrac{CI}{C}$ $\qquad$ (8.10)

CHAPTER **8**

PROBLEMS

1. Explain the concept of decomposing a time series.
2. What are the components that are analyzed in the decomposition of an annual time series?
3. What are the basic forces that affect the secular trend of most variables?
4. What kind of trend model should be used in each of the following cases?
   a. The variable is increasing by a constant rate.
   b. The variable is increasing by a constant rate until it reaches saturation and levels out.
   c. The variable is increasing by a constant amount.
5. What is the basic force that affects the cyclical component of most variables?
6. Describe each of these time series established by the U.S. Department of Commerce: leading series, coincident series, lagging series.
7. What is the basic force that affects the seasonal component of most variables?
8. *Value Line* estimates of sales and earnings growth for individual companies are derived by correlating sales, earnings, and dividends to appropriate components of the National Income Accounts such as capital spending. Jason Black, an analyst for *Value Line,* is examining the trend of the capital spending variable from 1977 to 1989. The data are as follows:

Capital Spending ($ billions), 1977–1989.

Year	($ billions)	Year	($ billions)
1977	214	1984	416
1978	259	1985	443
1979	303	1986	437
1980	323	1987	443
1981	369	1988	487
1982	367	1989	512
1983	357	1990	531*

Source: *The Value Line Investment Survey* (New York: Value Line, 1988, 1990), p. 1750.

* Value Line estimate.

  a. Plot the data.
  b. Determine the appropriate trend model for the years 1977–1989.
  c. If the appropriate model is linear, compute the straight line trend model
     for the years 1977–1989.
  d. What has the average increase in capital spending per year been since
     1977?
  e. Estimate the trend value for capital spending in 1990.
  f. Compare your trend estimate with Value Line's.
  g. What factor(s) influence the trend of capital spending?

9. Jean Ito, forecaster for the Georgia Economic Development Council, has
   been asked to determine the appropriate trend model for national imports.
   The data for 1967 to 1986 are as follows:

National Imports, 1967–1986.

Year	Sales Per Share	Year	Sales Per Share
1967	332	1977	1720
1968	360	1978	2063
1969	400	1979	2408
1970	456	1980	2613
1971	556	1981	2440
1972	695	1982	2580
1973	1003	1983	3257
1974	965	1984	3453
1975	1210	1985	3654
1976	1477	1986	4062

Source: *Survey of Current Business,* 1988.

Write a memo for Jean Ito describing the appropriate trend model for
national imports.

10. This question refers to Problem 8. Analyze the cyclical component for the
    capital spending variable.
    a. Does the economy affect this cyclical component?
    b. Which component is more important, trend or cyclical?
    c. How would you forecast for 1990?

11. A large company is considering cutting back on its TV advertising in favor
    of business videos to be given to its customers. This action is being
    considered after the company president read an article in *Industry Week,*
    "Business Videos—Today's Hot Sales Weapon" (October 2, 1989, page 38).
    One thing the president would like to investigate prior to taking this action
    is the history of TV advertising in this country, especially the cyclical effect.

    Following are the total dollars spent on U.S. television advertising,
    in millions. Calculate the cyclical indexes for this annual time series.

Year	Y	Y_R
1980	11,424	11,289.1
1981	12,811	13,132.3
1982	14,566	14,975.6
1983	16,542	16,818.8
1984	19,670	18,662.0
1985	20,770	20,505.2
1986	22,585	22,348.4
1987	23,904	24,191.7
1988	25,686	26,034.9

Source: *Statistical Abstract of the United States,* various years.

Analyze the peaks and bottoms of the cyclical component in U.S. television advertising dollars. Forecast this variable for 1989.

12. Assume the following specific seasonal indexes for March based on the ratio-to-moving-average method:

    102.2   105.9   114.3   122.4   109.8   98.9

    What is the seasonal index for March using the modified mean method?

13. The expected trend value for October is $850. Assuming an October seasonal index of 112, what would be the forecast for October?

14. The following specific seasonal indexes are given for the month of December:

    75.4   86.8   96.9   72.6   80.0   85.4

    If the adjustment is 1.05, if the modified mean is used, and if the expected trend for December is $900, what is the forecast for December?

15. A large resort near Portland, Maine, has been tracking its monthly sales for several years, but has never analyzed these data. The resort computes the seasonal indexes for its monthly sales. Which of the following statements about the index are correct?
    a. The sum of the 12 monthly index numbers should be 1200.
    b. An index of 85 for May indicates that sales are 15% lower than the average monthly sales.
    c. An index of 130 for January indicates that sales are 30% above the average monthly sales.
    d. The index for any month must be between zero and 200.
    e. The average index for each of the 12 months should be 100.

16. In preparing a report for June Bancock, manager of the Kula Department Store, you include the following statistics from last year's sales. Upon seeing them, Ms. Bancock says, "This report confirms what I've been telling you; business is getting better and better." Is this statement accurate? Why or why not?

Month	Sales (thousands)	Adjusted Seasonal Index
Jan	125	51
Feb	113	50
Mar	189	87
Apr	201	93
May	206	95
Jun	241	99
Jul	230	96
Aug	245	89
Sep	271	103
Oct	291	120
Nov	320	131
Dec	419	189

Source: Kula Department Store records.

17. The quarterly sales levels of Goodyear Tire appear next. Does there appear to be a significant seasonal effect in their sales levels? Analyze this time series to get the four seasonal indexes and determine the extent of the seasonal component in Goodyear's sales.

Quarter:	1	2	3	4
1985	2292	2450	2363	2477
1986	2063	2358	2316	2366
1987	2268	2533	2479	2625
1988	2616	2793	2656	2746
1989	2643	2811	2679	2736
1990	2692			

Source: *The Value Line Investment Survey* (New York: Value Line, 1988, 1989), p. 130.

18. Following are data values that represent the monthly sales of all retail stores in the United States in billions of dollars. Analyze this series, including comments on all four components of the series.

Year:	1984	1985	1986	1987	1988	1989	1990
Jan	93.1	98.8	105.6	106.4	113.6	122.5	132.6
Feb	93.7	95.6	99.7	105.8	115.0	118.9	127.3
Mar	104.3	110.2	114.2	120.4	131.6	141.3	148.3
Apr	103.9	113.1	115.7	125.4	130.9	139.8	145.0
May	111.8	120.3	125.4	129.1	136.0	150.3	154.1
Jun	112.3	115.0	120.4	129.0	137.5	149.0	153.5
Jul	106.9	115.5	120.7	129.3	134.1	144.6	148.9
Aug	111.2	121.1	124.1	131.5	138.7	153.0	156.4
Sep	104.0	113.8	124.4	124.5	131.9	144.1	
Oct	109.6	115.8	123.8	128.3	133.8	142.3	
Nov	113.5	118.1	121.4	126.9	140.2	148.8	
Dec	132.3	138.6	152.1	157.2	171.0	176.5	

Source: *Survey of Current Business,* 1991.

19. The data in the accompanying table are for the Spokane County business activity index and the sale of houses from 1965 to 1975.

Year	Sale of Houses (Hundreds of Units)	Spokane County Business Activity Index	Year	Sale of Houses (Hundreds of Units)	Spokane County Business Activity Index
1965	32	90.0	1971	54	116.5
1966	31	95.8	1972	53	120.2
1967	38	100.0	1973	75	124.2
1968	47	105.8	1974	69	135.0
1969	58	110.0	1975	65	132.0
1970	61	113.3			

a. Calculate the cyclical-irregular relatives for both variables.
b. How confident would you be if you used the trend estimate to predict the sale of houses in Spokane for 1979?
c. How confident would you be if you used the trend estimate to predict the Spokane County business activity index for 1979?
d. Explain your answers for parts b and c.
e. Is the Spokane County business activity index of any value in forecasting the sale of houses?
f. Forecast the sale of houses in Spokane for 1976 if the cyclical-irregular index will be 95.
g. Forecast the sale of houses in Spokane for 1977 if the cyclical-irregular relative will be 102.

20. A retail store has the index of seasonal variation in sales given in the accompanying table.

Jan.	63	Jul.	80
Feb.	72	Aug.	70
Mar.	94	Sep.	103
Apr.	111	Oct.	118
May	102	Nov.	125
Jun.	106	Dec.	156

   a. The manager of the store forecasts that sales for the coming year will total $72 million. On the basis of this forecast of total sales, make a forecast of sales for each month.

   b. January sales were $3.5 million. If this is the prevailing level of sales for the remaining 11 months, what will be the total annual sales for this year?

   c. On the basis of January sales and the seasonal indexes above, what should sales be for the first quarter?

21. The index of seasonal variation given in the accompanying table reflects the changing volume of business of a mountain resort hotel that caters to the family tourist in the summer and the skiing enthusiast during the winter months. No sharp cyclical variations are expected during 1991.

Jan.	115	Jul.	150
Feb.	142	Aug.	154
Mar.	95	Sep.	90
Apr.	38	Oct.	65
May	47	Nov.	80
Jun.	125	Dec.	99

   a. If 500 tourists were at the resort in January 1991, what is a reasonable estimate for February?

   b. The monthly trend equation is $Y_R = 255 + 3X$, where $X = 1$ represents January 15, 1986. What is the seasonally adjusted forecast for January 1992?

   c. What is the average number of new tourists per month?

   d. From the trend equation and seasonal indexes, prepare a forecast for each month of 1991.

22. Select a leading indicator from the NBER's short list.

   a. Explain why this indicator leads the business cycle at cyclical turning points.

   b. Discuss this indicator's performance as a barometer of business activity in recent years.

23. What is the present position of the business cycle? Is it expanding or contracting? When will the next turning point occur?

THE SMALL ENGINE DOCTOR

"The Small Engine Doctor" was the name of a business developed by Thomas Brown. Tom Brown was a mail carrier for the U.S. Postal Service. He had been a tinkerer since childhood, always taking discarded household gadgets apart in order to understand "what made them tick." As Tom grew up and became a typical suburbanite, he acquired numerous items of lawn and garden equipment. When Tom found out about a course in small engine repair offered at a local community college, he jumped at the opportunity. Tom started small engine repair by dismantling his own equipment, overhauling it, and then reassembling it. Soon after completing the course in engine repair, he began to repair lawn mowers, rototillers, snow blowers, and other lawn and garden equipment for friends and neighbors. In the process he acquired various equipment manuals and special tools.

It was not long before Tom decided to turn his hobby into a part-time business. He placed an advertisement in a suburban shopping circular under the name of "The Small Engine Doctor." Over the last two years the business had grown enough to provide a nice supplement to his regular salary. While the growth was welcomed, as the business was about to enter its third year of operation there were a number of concerns. The business was operated out of Tom's home. The basement was partitioned into a family room, a workshop, and an office. Originally the office area was used to handle the advertising, order processing, and bookkeeping. All the engine repair was done in the workshop. Tom's policy is to stock only a limited number of parts, ordering replacement parts as they are needed. This seemed to be the only practical way of dealing with the large variety of part numbers involved in repairing engines made by the dozen or so manufacturers of lawn and garden equipment.

Spare parts had proved to be the most aggravating problem in running the business. Tom started his business by buying parts from equipment dealers. This practice had several disadvantages. First, he had to pay retail for the parts. Second, most of the time the dealer had to back-order one or more parts for any given repair job. Parts ordered from the manufacturer had lead times of anywhere from 30 to 120 days. As a result, Tom changed his policy and began to order parts directly from the factory. He found that shipping and handling charges ate into his profits, even though the part price was only 60% of retail. However, the two most important problems created by the replacement parts problem were lost sales and storage space. Tom attracted customers because of his quality service and reasonable repair charges, which were possible because of his low overhead. Unfortunately, many potential customers would go to equipment dealers rather than wait several months for repair. The most pressing problem was storage space. While a piece of equipment was waiting for spare parts, it had to be stored on the premises. It did not take long for both his workshop and his one-car garage to overflow with equipment while he was waiting for spare parts. In the second year of operation Tom actually had to suspend advertising as a tactic to limit customers due to lack of storage space.

This case study was contributed by William P. Darrow of the Towson State University, Towson, Maryland.

Tom Brown has considered stocking inventory for his third year of operation. This practice will reduce purchasing costs by making it possible to obtain quantity discounts and more favorable shipping terms. It is also hoped that it will provide much better turnaround time for the customers, improving both cash flow and sales. The risks in this strategy are uncontrolled inventory carrying costs and part obsolescence.

Before committing himself to stocking spare parts, Tom wants to have a reliable forecast for business activity in the forthcoming year. He is confident enough in his knowledge of product mix to use an aggregate forecast of customer repair orders as a basis for selectively ordering spare parts. The forecast is complicated by seasonal demand patterns and a trend toward increasing sales.

Tom plans to develop a sales forecast for the third year of operation. A sales history for the first two years is given below.

Month	1989	1990	Month	1989	1990
Jan.	5	21	Jul.	28	46
Feb.	8	20	Aug.	20	32
Mar.	10	29	Sep.	14	27
Apr.	18	32	Oct.	8	13
May	26	44	Nov.	6	11
Jun.	35	58	Dec.	26	52

QUESTIONS

1. Plot the data on a two-year time horizon, from 1989 to 1990. Connect the data points to make a scatter diagram.

2. Develop a trend line equation using linear regression, and plot the results.

3. Estimate the seasonal adjustment factors for each month by dividing the average demand for corresponding months by the average of the corresponding trend line forecasts. Plot a seasonally adjusted trend line.

4. Calculate a trend-adjusted exponential forecast using smoothing constant values of $(\alpha = .1, \beta = .1)$, $(\alpha = .25, \beta = .25)$, and $(\alpha = .5, \beta = .5)$. Plot each of the forecasts. Extrapolate the exponential forecasts through the end of year three.

5. Calculate MAD values for the two models that visually appear to give the most accurate forecasts.

6. Identify which model you would use as the basis for your business planning in 1991, and discuss why you selected that model over the others.

CASE STUDY **8.2**

WHEELER ELECTRIC RANGE

Ms. Love, an analyst for the Wheeler Electric Range Corporation, is assigned the task of forecasting corporation sales. She determines that Wheeler sales typically repre-

Marilyn Jean Love developed this time series analysis case while completing her B.A. degree at Eastern Washington University.

TABLE 8.9 Data for Wheeler Corporation: Electric Range Sales (Thousands).

Year	Sales	Year	Sales
1959	1,687	1968	2,307
1960	1,495	1969	2,342
1961	1,530	1970	2,362
1962	1,675	1971	2,714
1963	1,870	1972	3,232
1964	1,965	1973	3,430
1965	2,075	1974	2,925
1966	2,029	1975	2,014
1967	1,910		

sent 3% of nationwide electric range sales. If Love can successfully estimate sales at the national level, she will be able to forecast Wheeler Corporation sales for 1976.

Household electric ranges are not products that go out of style quickly. They are a durable good whose useful life averages between 10 and 15 years. Therefore replacement sales are very important. People who purchase ranges tend to be either first-time buyers, remodelers, or new-feature seekers. Whatever the reason for buying an electric range, sales have varied over time, and Love decides to investigate the various time series components. The nationwide electric range sales, in thousands, for 1959–1975 are presented in Table 8.9.

TREND

As shown in Figure 8.8, household electric range sales (over 2.5 kilowatts) have been growing at a fairly even amount over the past 17 years. This increased growth in sales can be attributed to many factors. One of the most important variables affecting the trend is population growth. The population of the United States has increased from approximately 180 million in 1959 to 212 million in 1975. As the population grows, the need for electric ranges also grows. The number of people in the 25–39 age bracket is of special interest because they spend the most on household appliances. The number of people in the 25–39 age bracket has been steadily increasing and is expected to grow by 23% between 1974 and 1980, as compared with a 6% expected increase in the total population.

The income level of the population has also been steadily increasing. People have been able to replace older ranges with better, more efficient ones. They have had enough income to buy new models to match new kitchen improvements, even when their old model was still in working condition.

The long-term growth movement for electric ranges is best described by the linear trend model $Y_R = 1,480.31 + 91.15X$ (origin: July, 1959; 1 unit of $X = 1$ year). There were 1,480,312 ranges sold in 1959, and the average amount of increase since then has been 91,150 per year. This trend model explains 64.7%, $r^2 = .647$, of the sales variable variance. While the linear model does accurately indicate the growth movement of electric range sales, other factors will need to be analyzed in order to forecast accurately.

FIGURE 8.8 Trend for Electric Range Sales.

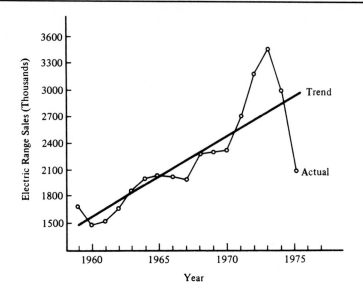

CYCLICAL AND IRREGULAR VARIATIONS

The fluctuations in the growth of electric range sales can be attributed largely to the fluctuations in the economy. The cyclical movement in the number of electric ranges sold over time is shown in Figure 8.9.

FIGURE 8.9 Cyclical Movement for Electric Range Sales.

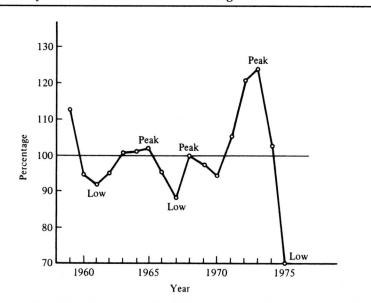

A peak time for sales was in 1965. The increasing amount of installment credit granted to those with lower incomes and the rising incomes from the healthy economy greatly increased demand for electric ranges. Kitchen remodeling was growing in popularity, and manufacturers were greeting consumers with new styles. Also, the many electric ranges bought right after World War II had come to the end of their 10- to 15-year life cycles and were ready to be replaced. In 1968 and 1973 electric range sales also peaked. In these years the economy was doing well, and there was an expanding market for mobile homes and apartments starting in 1971. The enriched demand caused electric range sales to move upward.

The low points in electric range sales usually occurred when the economy was suffering; 1969, 1970, 1974, and 1975 were time periods when the economy was depressed. A credit crunch in 1966 led to high mortgage rates, which caused housing starts to plummet in 1966, which in turn caused electric range sales to drop in 1967. Also, in 1967 electric range imports from Europe and Japan were especially high. This increase in imports together with the depressed economy decreased sales dramatically.

Figure 8.10 shows a coincidental indicator, new orders for household durables. The cyclical pattern of this indicator is related to the cyclical pattern for electric ranges sold. Knowledge of new orders for household durables might help anticipate movement in electric range sales.

The cyclical movement for new-housing starts, shown in Figure 8.11, is another indicator related to electric range sales. It tends to lead the cyclical movement for electric range sales. The low sales of 1961, 1967, and 1971 might have been forecast by the decreased number of housing units started in 1960, 1966, and 1970. In 1973 and 1974 housing starts were dropping drastically, and there was a corresponding sharp decline of electric range sales in 1974 and 1975. New-housing starts should be an effective leading indicator and should be investigated on a monthly basis.

FIGURE 8.10 Electric Range Sales Related to Manufacturers' New Orders.

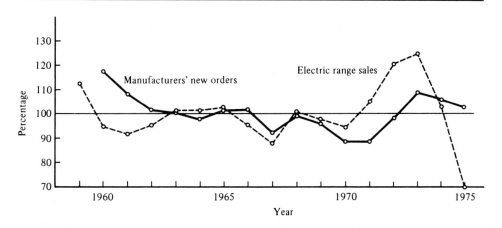

**FIGURE 8.11 Electric Range Sales Related to Number of New Housing Units
Started.**

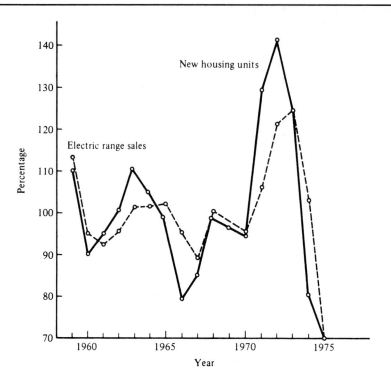

LONG-TERM FORECAST

The trend analysis, presented in Table 8.10, indicates that 3,029,900 electric ranges
are expected to be sold in 1976. Love feels that this quantity is extremely high
considering that the economy is just beginning to recover from a deep recession. In
1975 the number of housing units started dropping. The sales in 1976 can be
expected to drop below the 1975 electric range sales. Toward the end of 1975 housing
units started to increase, so Love does not expect a drastic decrease. In fact, since the
economy was expected to improve and the number of housing units started was on
the increase, Love chooses a cyclical relative index of 80 for the year 1976. Her final
forecast is

$$Y = TCI$$

$$Y(1976) = (3,029.9)(.80) = 2,423.92 \text{ thousand}$$

This figure represents a forecast of nationwide electric range sales. Love must take
3% of this estimate for her projected sales for Wheeler Corporation. Thus her
forecast for 1976 is 72,718.

TABLE 8.10 Trend Analysis and Cyclical Results for Electric Range Sales.

Year	Data	Regression	Cyclical
1959	1,687.00	1,480.31	113.96
1960	1,495.00	1,571.47	95.13
1961	1,530.00	1,662.62	92.02
1962	1,675.00	1,753.77	95.51
1963	1,870.00	1,844.92	101.36
1964	1,965.00	1,936.07	101.49
1965	2,075.00	2,027.23	102.36
1966	2,029.00	2,118.38	95.78
1967	1,910.00	2,209.53	86.44
1968	2,307.00	2,300.68	100.27
1969	2,342.00	2,391.83	97.92
1970	2,362.00	2,482.99	95.13
1971	2,714.00	2,574.14	105.43
1972	3,232.00	2,665.29	121.26
1973	3,430.00	2,756.44	124.44
1974	2,925.00	2,847.59	102.72
1975	2,014.00	2,983.74	68.53
1976		3,029.90	
1977		3,121.05	
1978		3,212.20	
1979		3,303.35	
1980		3,394.50	

Note: $Y_R = 1,480.31 + 91.15X$ (origin: July 1, 1959; 1 unit of $X = 1$ year).

SEASONAL VARIATION

Examination of the adjusted seasonal indexes in Table 8.11 shows a considerable amount of seasonal variation in the sales of electric ranges. The first-quarter sales are low mainly because house sales drop off sharply in the winter months. Leftover Christmas expenses, income taxes, car licenses, and insurance premiums all cut down on the amount people have available to spend on a major appliance. Electric range sales improve during the spring months because of numerous sales promo-

TABLE 8.11 Adjusted Seasonal Indexes for Electric Range Sales.

Jan.	92.1	Jul.	101.5
Feb.	84.8	Aug.	107.2
Mar.	97.3	Sep.	101.6
Apr.	100.5	Oct.	114.5
May	104.4	Nov.	99.6
Jun.	105.1	Dec.	91.3

tions and the improved money situation of most people. August is a good month because new housing units started in the spring are near completion and must be furnished. October is the best month because new housing units started in the summer are now completed. October is also a time when fall sales are prevalent. December is a low month because people spend on Christmas gifts and not on household appliances unless they give them as presents.

SHORT-TERM DECOMPOSITION

Table 8.12 shows an analysis of the short-term T, TCI, C, and I. The monthly trend equation $Y_R = 211.03 + .663X$ (origin: January 15, 1971; 1 unit of $X = 1$ month) is used to generate the T column. The TCI column, or seasonally adjusted data, is calculated by dividing the monthly data by the appropriate seasonal index. The C column, or cyclical variation, is computed by using a five-month moving average. Finally, the I column, or irregular, is calculated by dividing the CI column by C.

TABLE 8.12 Seasonally Adjusted Data for Wheeler Corporation.

Period	Data, Y	Regression, T	Seasonally Adjusted, TCI	CI	C	I
1971						
Jan.	163.00	211.03	176.92	83.84		
Feb.	179.00	211.66	210.99	99.68		
Mar.	224.00	212.30	230.28	108.47	97.22	111.58
Apr.	212.00	212.93	210.84	99.02	101.32	97.73
May	212.00	213.56	203.04	95.08	102.38	92.87
Jun.	235.00	214.19	223.53	104.36	102.68	101.63
Jul.	229.00	214.83	225.52	104.98	103.55	101.37
Aug.	254.00	215.46	236.95	109.97	107.60	102.21
Sep.	227.00	216.09	223.40	103.38	110.85	93.27
Oct.	286.00	216.73	249.86	115.29	113.17	101.88
Nov.	261.00	217.36	262.17	120.61	115.40	104.52
Dec.	232.00	217.99	254.11	116.57	120.31	96.89
1972						
Jan.	244.00	218.63	264.84	121.14	120.16	100.81
Feb.	238.00	219.26	280.53	127.95	120.75	105.96
Mar.	245.00	219.89	251.87	114.54	121.08	94.60
Apr.	274.00	220.52	272.50	123.57	117.70	104.99
May	273.00	221.16	261.47	118.23	115.93	101.98
Jun.	243.00	221.79	231.14	104.21	117.86	88.42
Jul.	269.00	222.42	264.91	119.10	117.61	101.27
Aug.	297.00	223.06	277.06	124.21	118.35	104.96
Sep.	278.00	223.69	273.59	122.31	124.03	98.61

TABLE 8.12 Continued

Period	Data, Y	Regression, T	Seasonally Adjusted, TCI	CI	C	I
Oct.	313.00	224.32	273.45	121.90	125.36	97.24
Nov.	297.00	224.96	298.33	132.62	127.86	103.72
Dec.	259.00	225.59	283.69	125.75	128.34	97.98
1973						
Jan.	285.00	226.22	309.35	136.74	130.54	104.76
Feb.	240.00	226.85	282.89	124.70	128.95	96.71
Mar.	294.00	227.49	302.24	132.86	129.92	102.26
Apr.	286.00	228.12	284.44	124.69	126.79	98.34
May	312.00	228.75	298.82	130.63	127.88	102.15
Jun.	292.00	229.39	277.74	121.08	125.17	96.73
Jul.	304.00	230.02	299.38	130.15	125.26	103.91
Aug.	295.00	230.65	275.20	119.31	124.07	96.17
Sep.	294.00	231.29	289.34	125.10	122.66	101.99
Oct.	331.00	231.92	289.17	124.69	118.33	105.38
Nov.	264.00	232.55	265.18	114.03	116.93	97.52
Dec.	231.00	233.18	253.02	108.51	115.54	93.91
1974						
Jan.	242.00	233.82	262.67	112.34	114.39	98.21
Feb.	235.00	234.45	277.00	118.15	114.54	103.15
Mar.	272.00	235.08	279.63	118.95	114.72	103.68
Apr.	272.00	235.72	270.51	114.76	114.25	100.45
May	270.00	236.35	258.59	109.41	111.51	98.12
Jun.	274.00	236.98	260.62	109.98	107.37	102.42
Jul.	252.00	237.62	248.17	104.44	103.45	100.95
Aug.	251.00	238.25	234.15	98.28	98.57	99.71
Sept.	231.00	238.88	227.34	95.17	92.55	102.83
Oct.	233.00	239.51	203.56	84.99	90.04	94.39
Nov.	191.00	240.15	191.85	79.89	83.43	95.76
Dec.	202.00	240.78	221.25	91.89	77.74	118.21
1975						
Jan.	145.00	241.41	157.39	65.19	73.45	88.76
Feb.	137.00	242.05	161.48	66.72	70.55	94.57
Mar.	150.00	242.68	154.21	63.54	64.34	98.76
Apr.	160.00	243.31	159.13	65.40	65.77	99.44
May	155.00	243.95	148.45	60.85	66.64	91.31
Jun.	186.00	244.58	176.92	72.34	67.52	107.13
Jul.	177.00	245.21	174.31	71.08	69.37	102.47
Aug.	179.00	245.84	166.98	67.92	71.20	95.39
Sep.	187.00	246.48	184.04	74.67	69.38	107.61
Oct.	198.00	247.11	172.98	70.00	71.40	98.05
Nov.	156.00	247.74	156.70	63.25		
Dec.	184.00	248.38	210.54	81.14		

SHORT-TERM CYCLICAL VARIATIONS

Figure 8.12 shows the cyclical variations in the monthly data for electric range sales and for the number of housing units started. The cyclical variation shows an increase between 1971 and 1973. New housing units started increased until the latter part of 1972. The increase in the number of new housing units started led the growing electric range sales by about two months. In July 1971 the electric range cyclical movement started increasing at a faster rate. This increase was due to the increase in the mobile home market during the summer months. In November 1972 the number of housing units started dropped off quickly. They rose slightly in the early part of 1973, only to drop steadily downward until February 1975. Electric range sales followed the same pattern. In the beginning of 1973 electric range sales started declining, just as the housing units started did. The decline was drastic until April 1975. However, the number of housing units started did not lead by a constant time period. It usually led by at least one or two months for upturns and downturns.

Another reason for the decline in electric range sales is the increasing amount of younger and older segments of the population eating away from home during this time period. Retirees and young marrieds with larger incomes and more free time are traveling and eating out rather than preparing food at home. In addition, fast-food and similar types of operators are catering to the average family, offering appetizing meals at a price comparable to the cost of preparing a meal at home. As a result, electric range sales decrease.

FIGURE 8.12 Monthly Cyclical Variations of Electric Range Sales and Number of New Housing Units Started.

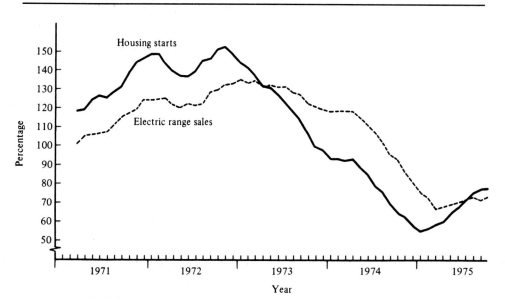

IRREGULARITIES

The irregular component in a time series helps explain random fluctuations caused by nonpredictable events. In 1971, 1972, and 1973, the irregularities in the number of household electric ranges sold are very slight (see Table 8.12, the column labeled *I*). In 1974 the high in December may have been caused by new and more attractive styles of electric ranges offered to consumers during that year. Two styles introduced were the new stay-clean oven and the space-age range control. These new styles were purchased as Christmas presents because they were practical and attractive.

SHORT-TERM FORECASTING

Love used the model $Y = TSCI$ to forecast monthly sales. The long-term trend equation is converted so that it can be used with monthly data. The monthly trend equation for Table 8.12 is $Y_R = 211.03 + .633X$ (origin: January 15, 1971; 1 unit of $X = 1$ month). The adjusted seasonal indexes and short-term forecasts for each month are presented in Table 8.13. A cyclical index is estimated for each month from knowledge of the leading indicator and past experience. Finally, the irregular index is estimated as 100 for each month since it is practically impossible to anticipate any monthly irregularities for 1976.

CONCLUSION

Love found that the cyclical variable is the most important long-term component. Thus it will be very difficult for Wheeler Corporation to forecast more than one year in the future. If the trend were the most important component, long-term projections would be possible.

TABLE 8.13 Short-Term Forecasts for Wheeler Corporation.

							Forecast	
Month	T	× S	× C	× I	=		National	Wheeler
Jan.	249.01	.921	.77	1.00			176.59	5.30
Feb.	249.64	.848	.78	1.00			165.12	4.95
Mar.	250.28	.973	.79	1.00			192.38	5.77
Apr.	250.91	1.005	.80	1.00			201.73	6.05
May	251.54	1.044	.81	1.00			212.71	6.38
Jun.	252.17	1.051	.82	1.00			217.33	6.52
Jul.	252.81	1.015	.83	1.00			212.98	6.39
Aug.	253.44	1.072	.84	1.00			228.22	6.85
Sep.	254.07	1.016	.85	1.00			219.41	6.58
Oct.	254.71	1.145	.86	1.00			250.81	7.52
Nov.	255.34	.996	.86	1.00			218.71	6.56
Dec.	255.97	.913	.87	1.00			203.32	6.10
				Totals			2,499.31	74.97

Both seasonal and cyclical variations are extremely important components for the preparation of short-term forecasts. Since housing units started usually lead electric range sales by two months, revised short-term forecasts should be prepared each month. This constant revision should improve the short-term forecasting accuracy.

QUESTIONS

1. How would you evaluate Love's analysis and conclusions?
2. Are there any additional conclusions you can reach?

CASE STUDY 8.3

GRAND COULEE DAM VISITORS

Decision Science Associates has been asked to do a feasibility study for a proposed destination resort to be built within half a mile of the Grand Coulee Dam. Paul Nosbich, company president, felt that the large number of tourists who visit the dam each year may be a significant factor in determining whether the resort should be constructed. He asked one of his employees, Mark Craze, to gather data and analyze the situation. Paul told Mark to analyze past data and forecast the number of visitors through 1990. He indicated that a monthly forecast for 1986–1987 would be extremely helpful. Mark obtained data on the number of visitors from the Grand Coulee Dam Visitors Center and provided Paul with the following report and forecasts.

TIME SERIES ANALYSIS OF VISITORS

The number of visitors who toured the Grand Coulee Dam Project from January 1969 through December 1984 was analyzed using a technique called *time series analysis.* Visitors are counted by tour guides as they enter the Visitor Center. It is important to note that the totals used do not completely reflect the number of visitors to the dam. The actual number of visitors was larger due to the fact that when the traffic flow is extremely large, the guides stop counting because of other responsibilities. It is also true that while most tourists visit the Visitors Center, not all of them do so.

Trend

Table 8.14 shows the number of visitors from 1969 through 1984. Examination of this table shows that the number of visitors has varied from 161,524 in 1980 to 617,738 in 1983. A linear regression model was developed and is shown in Figure 8.13. The trend equation is $Y_R = 267,418 + 8,363X$. The correlation between the number of visitors and time is .358, and knowledge of time allows the analyst to explain only 12.8% of the variance for the number-of-visitors variable. This regression equation indicates that the estimated number of visitors for 1969 was 267,418 and that the number has increased by an average of 8,363 per year.

TABLE 8.14 Number of Visitors Counted at the Grand Coulee Dam Visitors Center (1969–1984).

Year	Visitors	Cyclical
1969	250,265	93.6
1970	250,929	91.0
1971	321,333	113.1
1972	342,269	117.0
1973	268,528	89.3
1974	468,136	151.4
1975	390,129	123.8
1976	300,140	92.1
1977	271,140	81.1
1978	282,752	83.5
1979	244,006	70.5
1980	161,524	44.9
1981	277,134	75.4
1982	382,343	101.7
1983	617,737	160.7
1984	453,881	115.5

FIGURE 8.13 Visitors—Trend.

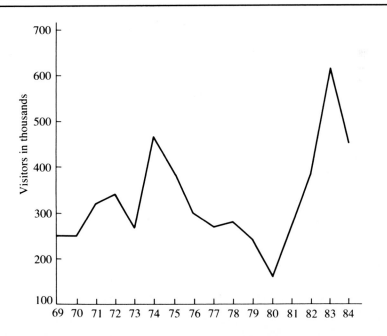

The increasing trend for the number-of-visitors variable seems to be affected mostly by population growth. The number of visitors has increased on an average of approximately 2–3% per year from 1969 to 1984. The population of Washington State has also increased by approximately 2% per year from 1970 to 1984.

Cyclical

Since time is not highly related to the number of visitors, other factors need to be identified. Cyclical relatives were calculated and are shown in Table 8.14. Figure 8.14 shows a cyclical chart for the number of visitors. The peak periods for visits were 1974 and 1983. Other above-average years were 1971, 1972, 1975, and 1984. The lowest year was 1980. Other below-average years were 1977, 1978, 1979, and 1981.

One of the major reasons why 1974 was a good year was the World's Fair that was held in Spokane, Washington. Spokane is approximately 90 miles from Grand Coulee Dam, which provided an excellent side trip for people attending the fair.

One of the major reasons why 1983 was a good year was that is was the fiftieth anniversary of Grand Coulee Dam. A well-advertised celebration was held during June, July, and August. This celebration was extremely well attended. Another reason for good attendance during 1983 was a drop in the price of gasoline.

FIGURE 8.14 Visitors—Cyclical.

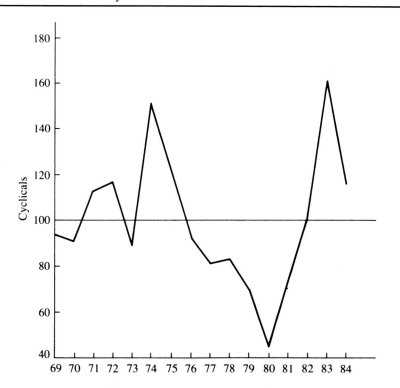

TABLE 8.15 Average National Gas Prices (1969–1984).

Year	Average Gas Price	Cyclical
1969	34.8	179.3
1970	35.7	134.1
1971	36.5	107.9
1972	36.1	88.0
1973	38.8	80.4
1974	53.2	95.9
1975	56.7	90.5
1976	59.0	84.4
1977	62.2	80.7
1978	62.6	74.2
1979	85.7	93.6
1980	123.8	125.4
1981	131.7	124.3
1982	125.2	110.6
1983	117.0	97.2
1984	117.0	91.7

FIGURE 8.15 Gas Prices—Visitors.

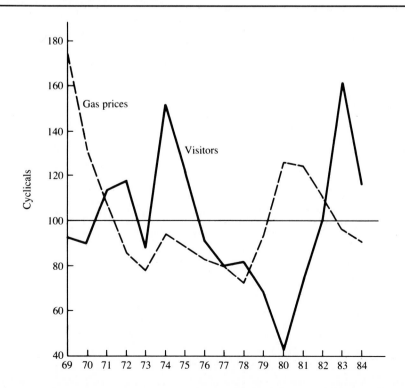

One of the major reasons why 1980 was an extremely poor year for attendance was the eruption of Mt. St. Helens in late May. Another reason for low attendance was the high price of gasoline.

Table 8.15 shows the average price of gas for 1969 through 1984 as reported by the Independent Petroleum Association of America. The cyclical relatives for gas prices are charted in Figure 8.15 along with the cyclical pattern for the number of visitors. Examination of this chart indicates a negative or inverse relationship between the price of gas and the number of visitors. When gas prices are high, the number of visitors is low, and when gas prices are down, the number of visitors is up.

Economic indicators such as gross national product (GNP) and disposable income were also compared to the cyclical pattern for the number of visitors variable. The state of the economy does not seem to have any effect on the number-of-visitors to Grand Coulee Dam.

Seasonal

Monthly data for the number of visitors was examined from January 1978 through December 1984. Table 8.16 shows that the variable was extremely seasonal. August and July are the best months, with attendance at a level that is 241% and 222% above normal. June and September are also good months, with attendance levels that are 79% and 50% above normal. The winter months (November, December, January, and February) are all approximately 90% below normal.

Weather is the key variable affecting the number of visitors to Grand Coulee Dam. The warm summer months, when people typically vacation, are tremendous

TABLE 8.16 Seasonal Variation: Calculation of Seasonal Indexes Using Percent of 12-Month Moving Average.

Month	1978	1979	1980	1981	1982	1983	1984	Modified Monthly Mean	Adjusted Seasonal Index Mean × 1.006909
Jan.		3.21	5.11	9.73	5.27	4.73	4.11	4.81	4.8
Feb.		6.51	5.77	14.48	8.43	6.86	9.15	7.74	7.8
Mar.		20.50	10.71	32.86	21.27	15.01	19.92	19.17	19.3
Apr.		33.21	27.40	32.75	28.03	17.13	25.33	28.38	28.6
May		66.57	48.15	78.78	89.10	55.67	79.57	70.15	70.6
Jun.		225.74	113.66	152.43	209.04	147.01	202.09	177.64	178.9
Jul.	343.84	312.20	228.99	301.99	320.37	419.07		319.60	321.8
Aug.	367.96	314.23	495.98	364.80	267.27	307.25		338.56	340.9
Sep.	157.22	153.45	142.84	147.10	136.37	150.75		148.53	149.6
Oct.	41.63	49.13	69.25	43.74	93.53	61.23		55.84	56.2
Nov.	11.46	10.51	19.71	15.92	14.04	11.70		13.28	13.4
Dec.	2.97	7.88	9.62	11.41	9.08	5.69		8.07	8.1
								1,191.77	1,200.0

TABLE 8.17 Number of Visitors—Random Variations.

Period	Visitors	Irregular	Period	Visitors	Irregular
1978			**1981**		
Jan.	848	—	Jul.	69,697	94.87
Feb.	1,833	—	Aug.	84,051	115.83
Mar.	3,276	73.70	Sep.	33,794	98.50
Apr.	7,760	118.64	Oct.	10,052	69.62
May	21,201	129.28	Nov.	3,734	104.13
Jun.	30,020	67.37	Dec.	2,876	123.62
Jul.	81,003	103.04	**1982**		
Aug.	86,608	115.94	Jan.	1,469	96.00
Sep.	37,040	109.87	Feb.	2,468	98.64
Oct.	9,807	90.69	Mar	6,321	99.07
Nov.	2,658	115.20	Apr.	8,678	88.22
Dec.	698	53.93	May	28,354	116.55
1979			Jun.	66,599	113.14
Jan.	752	92.45	Jul.	102,118	97.12
Feb.	1,418	103.72	Aug.	85,297	70.92
Mar.	4,218	111.12	Sep.	43,623	84.39
Apr.	6,750	108.96	Oct.	29,970	150.26
May	13,514	87.00	Nov.	4,500	88.97
Jun.	45,835	119.91	Dec.	2,947	90.74
Jul.	63,486	94.93	**1983**		
Aug.	63,825	91.58	Jan.	1,777	99.11
Sep.	30,953	112.58	Feb.	3,108	109.37
Oct.	9,792	97.22	Mar.	7,474	103.75
Nov.	2,050	88.08	Apr.	8,785	80.00
Dec.	1,413	113.24	May	28,621	92.42
1980			Jun.	75,677	93.21
Jan.	783	120.63	Jul.	215,756	135.06
Feb.	814	80.94	Aug.	158,277	87.98
Mar.	1,480	68.12	Sep.	77,694	97.33
Apr.	3,662	131.79	Oct.	31,577	118.94
May	6,457	95.66	Nov.	6,047	98.46
Jun.	15,291	71.32	Dec.	2,947	80.73
Jul.	30,922	79.47	**1984**		
Aug.	67,655	143.76	Jan.	1,934	96.36
Sep.	19,966	80.78	Feb.	3,662	120.14
Oct.	9,960	95.86	Mar.	7,507	96.31
Nov.	2,962	100.47	Apr.	9,564	81.78
Dec.	1,572	71.11	May	30,061	112.25
1981			Jun.	76,403	118.32
Jan.	1,828	120.77	Jul.	102,764	79.96
Feb.	3,052	121.98	Aug.	101,576	69.64
Mar.	7,341	113.92	Sep.	78,800	120.81
Apr.	7,505	88.26	Oct.	31,978	124.93
May	18,083	97.52	Nov.	6,266	—
Jun.	35,121	83.32	Dec.	3,366	—

attendance months, and the cold winter months, when snow, ice, and fog make it difficult to travel, are extremely weak attendance months.

Another factor that affects attendance during the summer months is a spectacular light show that begins in the middle of June and lasts until Labor Day.

Finally, the number of visitors is usually very high on holidays such as Memorial Day, July Fourth, and Labor Day, especially if they involve a three- or four-day weekend.

Irregular

The short-term irregular pattern was examined and is shown in Table 8.17. Sudden increases were observed in October 1982, July 1983, and April 1980. Sudden decreases were observed in June and December 1978; March, June, July, and December 1980; October 1981; and August 1984.

The sudden decrease that occurred in June and July of 1980 was caused by the eruption of Mt. St. Helens.

ANNUAL FORECAST

The multiplicative model $Y = TCI$ is used to develop the long-term forecast for the number of visitors to Grand Coulee Dam. This model calls for both a trend and a cyclical relative estimate. The trend is estimated using the regression equation $Y_R = 267,418 + 8,363X$. This equation seems appropriate because the population of Washington State is estimated to increase by an average of 2% through 1990. Trend estimates are provided in Table 8.18 through 1990. Next, the cyclical relative is estimated for each year. The outlook for 1985 is excellent. The effects of the large advertising campaign conducted in 1983 should still be felt. The price of gasoline is forecast to be 4% less in 1985 than in 1984.

The cyclical relative is estimated to be 120, and the forecast for 1985 is 481,471. If the price of gas stays stable, a cyclical relative of 193 is also reasonable for 1986. Vancouver, B.C., will host Expo '86, and 10 million visitors are expected to travel through Washington State. It is extremely difficult to project the cyclical

TABLE 8.18 Long-Term Forecasts of the Number of Visitors (1985–1990).

Year	Trend Estimate	Cyclical	Forecast
1985	401,226	120	481,471
1986	409,589	193	789,663
1987	417,952	115	481,262
1988	426,315	115	490,262
1989	434,678	120	521,614
1990	443,041	105	465,193

Note: The actual number of visitors will probably be larger because not all of the visitors to the dam were counted in this analysis.

TABLE 8.19 Short-Term Forecasts of the Number of Visitors (1986–1987).

Month	1986	1987
Jan.	1,948	1,905
Feb.	3,170	3,101
Mar.	7,858	7,685
Apr.	11,664	11,407
May	49,493	28,206
Jun.	120,937	71,594
Jul.	215,366	128,995
Aug.	228,208	136,879
Sep.	101,934	60,168
Oct.	40,206	22,641
Nov.	5,530	5,407
Dec.	3,349	3,274

Note: The actual number of visitors will probably be larger because not all of the visitors to the dam were counted in this analysis.

relative beyond 1986. The price of gasoline will have a major impact on the number of visitors to Grand Coulee Dam throughout the entire forecasted period.

The Winter Olympics will be held in Calgary, Canada, in the winter of 1988. While winter is not the best travel time, the Olympics should have some positive effect on the number of visitors to the Grand Coulee Dam area.

Washington State is holding its Centennial Celebration in 1989. This event should have a very positive effect on the number of visitors. Table 8.18 shows the number of visitors to Grand Coulee Dam forecast through 1990.

MONTHLY FORECASTS

The multiplicative model $Y = TSCI$ can be used to develop the short-term forecast for the number of visitors to Grand Coulee Dam. This model calls for a trend estimate, a cyclical relative estimate, and a seasonal estimate. Table 8.19 shows the short-term forecasts for 1986 and 1987.

QUESTIONS

1. Do you agree with Mark's forecasts?

2. What additional information would be important in order for Paul to decide whether to recommend that the destination resort be built?

3. Write a conclusion and recommendation section for this report.

SELECTED BIBLIOGRAPHY

Burman, J. P. "Seasonal Adjustment—A Survey." *TIMS Studies in Management Sciences* 12 (1979): 45–57.

Croxton, F. E., Cowden, D. J., and Bolch, B. W. *Practical Business Statistics.* Englewood Cliffs, N.J.: Prentice-Hall, 1969.

Makridakis, S., and Wheelwright, S. C. *Interactive Forecasting.* Palo Alto, Calif.: Scientific Press, 1977.

Makridakis, S., Wheelwright, S. C., and McGee, V. E. *Forecasting: Methods and Applications.* New York: John Wiley & Sons, 1983.

Moore, G. H., and Shiskin, J. "Indicators of Business Expansions and Contractions." New York: National Bureau of Economic Research, 1957, pp. 8–28.

Moore, G. H., and Shiskin, J. "Early Warning Signals for the Economy." In *Statistics: A Guide to Business and Economics,* J. M. Tanur et al., eds. San Francisco: Holden-Day, 1976, p. 81.

Regression of Time Series Data

I n business and economics many regression applications involve time series. The regression of monthly, quarterly, or yearly data may be carried out by using techniques described in early chapters. However, time series measures cannot be considered probability samples; instead, they are subject to trends, cycles, seasonal and irregular variations, and random fluctuations. Hence problems of interpretation often arise.

The basic regression models discussed in Chapters 6 and 7 assume that the residuals $(Y - Y_R)$ are either uncorrelated random variables or independent normal random variables. Thus the error terms are assumed to occur in a random manner. This assumption is not a valid one for most time series because the error terms tend to increase whenever a variable taken from a growing industry is related over time. Error terms get larger because the variable or variables involved tend to grow at a constant rate instead of at a constant amount. This condition is called *heteroscedasticity* and was discussed in Chapter 7.

THE PROBLEM OF HETEROSCEDASTICITY WHEN REGRESSING TIME SERIES DATA

An example is used to begin this discussion.

EXAMPLE 9.1

■ Suppose an analyst is engaged in forward planning for the Carlson Dishwasher Corporation and wishes to establish a quantitative basis for projecting future sales. Since the corporation sells regionally, a measure of disposable personal income for the region should relate closely. Table 9.1 shows sales and income for the period 1970–1990. The analyst correlates these variables and attempts to use income to forecast Carlson sales for 1991.

First, the data are plotted on an arithmetic scale, as shown in Figure 9.1. The relationship appears to be linear.

TABLE 9.1 Data for Example 9.1: Carlson Dishwasher Sales.

Year	Carlson Dishwasher Sales (Thousands of Dollars) Y	Disposable Personal Income (Millions of Dollars) X	Carlson Dishwasher Sales Lagged One Year
1970	295	273.4	—
1971	400	291.3	295
1972	390	306.9	400
1973	425	317.1	390
1974	547	336.1	425
1975	555	349.4	547
1976	620	362.9	555
1977	720	383.9	620
1978	880	402.8	720
1979	1,050	437.0	880
1980	1,290	472.2	1,050
1981	1,528	510.4	1,290
1982	1,586	544.5	1,528
1983	1,960	588.1	1,586
1984	2,118	630.4	1,960
1985	2,116	685.9	2,118
1986	2,477	742.8	2,116
1987	3,199	801.3	2,477
1988	3,702	903.1	3,199
1989	3,316	983.6	3,702
1990	2,702	1,076.7	3,316

When the data are run on an appropriate computer program, the results shown in Table 9.2 are obtained. The fit is good; 90% of the sales variable variance is explained by using the linear equation $Y_R = -792 + 4.22517X$. However, close examination of Figure 9.1 indicates that the residuals violate the constant variance assumption. The residuals are much larger as sales grow over the years. This result occurs because the variables are increasing at a constant rate.

One solution to the problem of heteroscedasticity is to express both the dependent and independent variables in constant dollars. Expressing time series variables in constant dollars (see the discussion of price deflation in Chapter 8) frequently overcomes the problem of increasing forecast errors over time. A second solution is to perform a log transformation (see the discussion in Chapter 6).

THE PROBLEM OF SERIAL CORRELATION WHEN REGRESSING TIME SERIES DATA

Another problem with time series data is their movement in cycles rather than in a purely random fashion. This phenomenon frequently causes runs

FIGURE 9.1 Linear Fit of Carlson Dishwasher Sales.

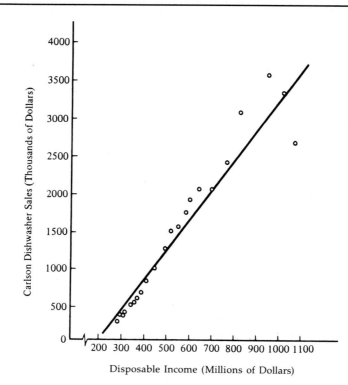

of several successive negative or positive errors in a row. An examination of Figure 9.1 illustrates this point. The first ten residuals (1970–1979) are negative, which means that the first ten estimates or predictions based on the regression equation are all too high. The next five residuals (1980–1984) are positive, which means that these predictions are too low. Each year's value is dependent on or related to that of the preceding year rather than independent of it. This fact should not surprise one. Consider, for example, a price series. If successive observations from one year to the next were indeed independent of one another, one would be living in a chaotic economy. In such a world prices would be determined like numbers drawn from a random number table. Knowledge of the price in one year would not influence the price in the next year.

Economic data ordered in a time series can seldom be regarded as a random sample. An observation on price, inventory, production, stocks, and other economic variables in a given time period is usually correlated with (dependent on) the value of the same variable in the previous time period. The term *serial correlation* is used to describe this situation (it is also called *autocorrelation*). The residuals $(Y - Y_R)$ are not independent from one

TABLE 9.2 Computer Output for Carlson Dishwasher Sales: Linear Fit.

VARIABLE NO.	MEAN	STANDARD DEVIATION	CORRELATION X VS Y	REGRESSION COEFFICIENT	STD. ERROR OF REG.COEF.	COMPUTED T VALUE
2	542.85	241.16	0.95	4.22517	0.31627	13.45

| DEPENDENT 1 | 1517.90450 | 1078.69840 | | | | |

INTERCEPT		−792		MULTIPLE CORRELATION	0.951
STD. ERROR OF ESTIMATE		341.1		R SQUARE	0.905
DURBIN-WATSON STATISTIC		0.87		CORRECTED R SQUARED	0.900

ANALYSIS OF VARIANCE FOR THE REGRESSION

SOURCES OF VARIATION	DEGREES OF FREEDOM	SUM OF SQUARES	MEAN SQUARES	F VALUE
ATTRIBUTABLE TO REGRESSION	1	21061184	21061184	181.018
DEVIATION FROM REGRESSION	19	2210624	116348	
TOTAL	20	23271808		

TABLE OF RESIDUALS

CASE NO.	Y VALUE	Y ESTIMATE	RESIDUAL
1	295	371.36	−76.36
2	400	447.53	−47.53
3	390	513.91	−123.91
4	425	557.32	−132.32
5	547	638.16	−91.16
6	555	694.76	−139.76
7	620	752.20	−132.20
8	720	841.56	−121.56
9	880	921.98	−41.98
10	1050	1067.51	−17.51
11	1290	1217.29	72.71
12	1528	1379.84	148.16
13	1586	1524.94	61.06
14	1960	1710.47	249.53
15	2118	1890.46	227.54
16	2116	2126.62	−10.62
17	2477	2368.74	108.26
18	3199	2617.67	581.33
19	3702	3050.84	651.16
20	3316	3393.38	−77.38
21	2702	3789.54	−1087.54

observation to the next. So knowledge of the error in one year helps an analyst anticipate the error in the next year.

Serial correlation exists when successive observations over time are related to each other.

The most common kind of serial correlation is first-order serial correlation in which each error term is a function of the previous time period's error term. Equation 9.1 illustrates this situation.

$$Y_t = \beta_0 + \beta X_t + \varepsilon_t \tag{9.1}$$

where ε_t depends on the value of itself one period ago or

$$\varepsilon_t = \rho\varepsilon_{t-1} + v_t \tag{9.2}$$

where

   ε_t = the error term of the equation

   ρ = the parameter (first-order serial correlation coefficient) that measures correlation between the error terms

   v_t = normally distributed independent error term

For this type of serial correlation, all that is needed is for the level of one error term (ε_{t-1}) to directly affect the level of the next error term (ε_t). The magnitude of the first-order autocorrelation coefficient (ρ) indicates the strength of the serial correlation in Equation 9.2. If ρ is zero, then there is no serial correlation, and the error terms are independent $(\varepsilon_t = v_t)$.

Consider the data illustrated in Figure 9.2, which plots a fictitious time series. The straight line is a regression line with respect to time. The serial correlation is immediately obvious. From 1979 to 1982 the error terms $(Y - Y_R)$ are all positive (the regression estimates are all too low), while from 1983 to 1990 they are negative (the regression estimates are all too high). For 1991 a negative error is anticipated. It is easy to predict the direction of each successive error term.

A major cause of positively serially correlated residuals in business and economics is a specification error such as an omitted variable or an incorrect functional form. When the time-sequenced effects of a "missing" variable are positively related, the residuals tend to be positively serially correlated in the regression equation because the effects of the missing

FIGURE 9.2 Positive Serial Correlation.

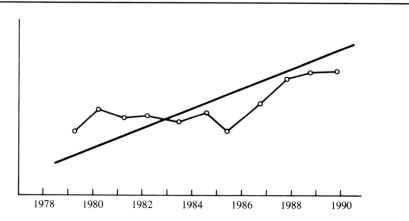

variable are included. Thus an important part of the variation of the dependent variable has not been explained.

For example, consider the new-car registration variable discussed in Chapter 8. If personal income and price are used as predictor variables, the model might explain a large portion of new-car registration variance. Unfortunately, serial correlation might be present. The model specification left out potentially key variables such as the driving-age population, which has a definite impact on auto sales and hence car registrations.

If the residuals in a regression equation are positively autocorrelated, the use of the least squares procedure poses several problems.

1. The standard error of estimate seriously underestimates the variability of the error terms.
2. The confidence intervals and tests employing the t and F distributions are no longer strictly applicable.
3. The standard error of the regression coefficient underestimates the variability of the estimated regression coefficient.

Figure 9.3 illustrates the presence of positive serial correlation in a model with a single independent variable. The residual associated with the first observation indicated by $Y - Y_R$ on the graph happens to be positive. This result leads to a series of five positive error terms and a series of four negative residuals. Notice that the estimated regression slope is less than the true slope. The least-squares-fitted regression line fits the observed data

FIGURE 9.3 Positive Serial Correlation and Least Squares Procedure.

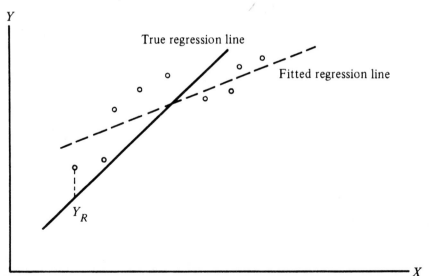

points more closely than does the true regression line. This outcome leads to an r^2 that is artificially high. Furthermore, the standard error of the estimate will be smaller than the true standard error. The success of the regression procedure will be overstated if the least squares standard error of the estimate is used to perform statistical tests.

When positive serial correlation is present and the first residual is positive (see Figure 9.3), the estimated or fitted regression line will have a slope that is underestimated (too small) and an intercept that is overestimated (too large). If the first residual is negative, the estimated or fitted regression line will have a slope that is overestimated and an intercept that is underestimated. In both cases the least squares regression line fits the observed data points more closely than does the true regression line. The problem is not bias; the problem is a large variance in the estimates. The least squares procedure is not at fault. Any other estimating procedure (such as fitting by eye) would fit the unique tilted data pattern in the same way. Techniques that may be more efficient and may improve the estimating procedure will be discussed in a later section.

DURBIN-WATSON TEST FOR SERIAL CORRELATION

One approach that is used frequently to determine if serial correlation is present is the *Durbin-Watson test*. The test involves the determination of whether the autocorrelation parameter ρ shown in Equation 9.2 is zero.

$$\varepsilon_t = \rho\varepsilon_{t-1} + v_t$$

The hypotheses to be considered are

$$H_0: \quad \rho = 0$$

$$H_1: \quad \rho > 0$$

The alternative hypothesis is $\rho > 0$ since residuals in time series applications tend to show positive correlation.

The first step in the computations is to fit the least squares regression line to the data. Next, the residuals are calculated, and the Durbin-Watson statistic is computed.

$$DW = \frac{\sum_{t=2}^{n}(e_T - e_{T-1})^2}{\sum_{t=1}^{n} e_t^2} \tag{9.3}$$

where

e_t = error or difference between point and line

e_{t-1} = error or difference between point and line for previous time period

$\sum_{t=2}^{n} (e_t - e_{t-1})^2$ = difference between present residual and previous residual, squared and summed for all observations

$\sum_{t=1}^{n} e_t^2$ = each of residuals squared and then summed.

Although an exact testing procedure is unavailable, Durbin and Watson have provided lower (L) and upper (U) bounds so that a test for serial correlation can be made after the DW value is computed. The decision rules are as follows:

1. When the Durbin-Watson statistic is larger than the upper (U) bound, the analyst concludes that the autocorrelation coefficient is equal to zero (there is no positive autocorrelation).
2. When the Durbin-Watson statistic is smaller than the lower (L) bound, the analyst concludes that the autocorrelation coefficient is greater than zero (there is positive autocorrelation).
3. When the Durbin-Watson statistic lies within the lower and upper bounds, the analyst concludes that the test is inconclusive (he or she doesn't know whether there is positive autocorrelation).[1]

The *Durbin-Watson test* is used to determine whether positive autocorrelation is present.

If $DW > U$, conclude H_0.
If $DW < L$, conclude H_1.
If DW lies within the lower and upper bounds
($L \leq DW \leq U$), conclude that the test is inconclusive.

The critical bounds for L and U are given in Appendix Table C.7. To find the appropriate L and U, the analyst needs to know the sample size, level of significance, and the number of independent variables. In the Durbin-Watson table in Appendix C, the sample size is given in the left-hand column, and the number of independent variables is determined from the top of each column. If three independent variables were used, for instance, one would look in the $p - 1 = 3$ column.

When inconclusive results are found, more observations are needed. With time series data this requirement may not be possible, so Durbin and Watson give an approximate test that requires at least 40 observations.

---

[1] J. Durbin and G. S. Watson, "Testing for Serial Correlation in Least-Squares Regression II," *Biometrika* 38 (1951): 159–178.

EXAMPLE 9.2

■ Computations showing the implementation of Equation 9.3 are demonstrated in Table 9.3. The data are from Carlson Dishwasher (Example 9.1, Table 9.1). The residuals column was taken from the computer output of Table 9.2. The computations for the other three columns for 1971 are as follows:

$$e_t - e_{t-1} = -47.53 - (-76.36) = 28.83$$

$$(e_t - e_{t-1})^2 = 28.83^2 = 831.17$$

$$e_t^2 = -47.53^2 = 2,259.1$$

The Durbin-Watson statistic is computed as

$$DW = \frac{\sum_{t=2}^{n} (e_t - e_{t-1})^2}{\sum_{t=1}^{n} e_t^2} = \frac{1,926,035.14}{2,210,641.78} = .87$$

This answer checks with the computer output of Table 9.2. Using a .01 level of significance for a sample of 21 and one independent variable, one obtains

TABLE 9.3 Durbin-Watson Calculations for Example 9.2: Carlson Dishwasher Sales.

Year	Sales, Y	Income, X	Residuals, e_t	$e_t - e_{t-1}$	$(e_t - e_{t-1})^2$	e_t^2
1970	295	273.4	−76.36	—	—	5,830.85
1971	400	291.3	−47.53	28.83	831.17	2,259.10
1972	390	306.9	−123.91	−76.38	5,833.90	15,353.69
1973	425	317.1	−132.32	−8.41	70.73	17,508.58
1974	547	336.1	−91.16	41.16	1,694.15	8,310.15
1975	555	349.4	−139.76	−48.60	2,361.96	19,532.86
1976	620	362.9	−132.20	7.56	57.15	17,476.84
1977	720	383.9	−121.56	10.64	113.21	14,776.83
1978	880	402.8	−41.98	79.58	6,332.98	1,762.32
1979	1,050	437.0	−17.51	24.47	598.78	306.60
1980	1,290	472.2	72.71	90.22	8,139.65	5,286.74
1981	1,528	510.4	148.16	75.45	5,692.70	21,951.39
1982	1,586	544.5	61.06	−87.10	7,586.41	3,728.32
1983	1,960	588.1	249.53	188.47	35,520.94	62,265.22
1984	2,118	630.4	227.54	−21.99	483.56	51,774.45
1985	2,116	685.9	−10.62	−238.16	56,720.19	112.78
1986	2,477	742.8	108.26	118.88	14,132.45	11,720.23
1987	3,199	801.3	581.33	473.07	223,795.22	337,944.57
1988	3,702	903.1	651.16	69.83	4,876.23	424,009.35
1989	3,316	983.6	−77.38	−728.54	530,770.53	5,987.66
1990	2,702	1,076.7	−1,087.54	−1,010.16	1,020,423.23	1,182,743.25
				Totals	1,926,035.14	2,210,641.78

$L = .97$

$U = 1.16$

Since $DW = .87$ falls below $L = .97$, the null hypothesis is rejected, and it is concluded that the residuals are positively autocorrelated ($\rho > 0$). ∎

Note in Table 9.3 that the adjacent error terms e and e_{t-1} tend to be of the same sign and magnitude. When positive serial correlation exists, the differences $(e - e_{t-1})$ tend to be small, leading to a small numerator in the DW statistic.

SOLUTIONS TO SERIAL CORRELATION PROBLEMS

Once serial correlation has been discovered in a regression of time series data, it is necessary to remove it before the regression equation can be evaluated for its effectiveness. The appropriate method for removing serial correlation depends on what caused it in the first place. Serial correlation can be caused by a specification error such as an omitted variable, or it can arise because the independent error terms are correlated in a correctly specified equation.

The solution to the problem of serial correlation begins with an evaluation of the model specification. Is the functional form correct? Were any important variables omitted? Are there specification errors that might have some pattern over time that could have introduced serial correlation into the residuals? Since a major cause of positively autocorrelated residuals in business is the omission of one or more key variables, the best approach to solving this problem is to find them. This technique is sometimes referred to as improving the model specification. Unfortunately, it is not always possible to use this method. The missing variable, although known to the analyst, may not be quantifiable. For example, one may suspect that business investment in future periods is related to the attitude of potential investors. However, it is difficult to quantify the variable "attitude." Nevertheless, whenever possible, the model should be specified in accordance with theoretically sound insight. The serial correlation problem will not be solved by the application of any corrective technique to a theoretically unsound model.

Only after the specification of the equation has been carefully reviewed should the possibility of an adjustment be considered. Several techniques for eliminating serial correlation will be discussed.

One approach to the elimination of serial correlation, called the regression of percentage changes, generates new variables by using the percentage changes (increase or decrease) from period to period. The Carlson Dishwasher data shown in Table 9.1 are used to demonstrate this generation of new variables. The amount by which Y changed from 1970 to 1971 was 105. As a percentage of the previous values of Y (295) this change represents a percentage increase of $105/295 = .356$ or 35.6%. This value is the new dependent variable for period 2 (1971). Since the actual values of the variables are not used, serial correlation will be eliminated. Unfortunately, the percentage changes of the independent variable might not do a good job of explaining the percentage changes of the dependent variable.

A second approach to the elimination of serial correlation, the creation of an autoregressive model, generates a new predictor variable by using the Y variable lagged one or more periods. In the Carlson Dishwasher example the predictor variable for 1971 is the sales for 1970 (295).

Another approach to the elimination of serial correlation, called first differencing, generates new variables that use the actual differences (increase or decrease) from period to period. Again the Carlson Dishwasher data shown in Table 9.1 are used. The amount by which Y changed from 1970 to 1971 was 105. This value is the new dependent variable for period 2 (1971). The first differences approach assumes that the relationship between the error terms measured by the autocorrelation coefficient is 1.

The iterative approach to the elimination of serial correlation also generates new variables that use the actual differences (increase or decrease) from period to period. The iterative approach estimates the autocorrelation coefficient or relationship between error terms.

An example of each approach to the elimination of serial correlation is presented next.

Model Specification Error (Omitting a Variable)

Example 9.3 shows how the problem of a missing variable can be solved.

TABLE 9.4 Data for Example 9.3: Billings Corporation Sales.

Year	Sales (Millions)	Year	Sales (Millions)
1973	8.0	1983	16.4
1974	8.2	1984	17.8
1975	8.5	1985	18.6
1976	9.2	1986	20.0
1977	10.2	1987	21.9
1978	11.4	1988	24.9
1979	12.8	1989	27.3
1981	13.6	1990	29.1
1982	14.6		

EXAMPLE 9.3

■ The Billings Corporation wishes to develop a forecasting model for the projection of future sales. Since the corporation has outlets regionwide, disposable personal income on a regionwide basis is chosen as a possible predictor variable. Table 9.4 shows Billings sales for 1973–1990. Disposable personal income data were shown in Table 9.1.

    The Minitab commands to solve this example are as follows:

```
MTB > READ 'BILLINGS.DAT' C1-C2  *1
      17 ROWS READ

  ROW     C1        C2

    1     8.0      336.1
    2     8.2      349.4
    3     8.5      362.9
    4     9.2      383.9
    .     .        .
```

```
MTB > NAME C1 'SALES' C2 'INCOME'
MTB > REGRESS C1 1 PREDICTOR C2, RES IN C3, DHATS IN C4;  *2
SUBC> RESIDUALS C5;  *3
SUBC> DW.  *4
```

```
The regression equation is
SALES = - 1.50 + 0.0292 INCOME

Predictor          Coef        Stdev      t-ratio         p
Constant        -1.5046       0.3290        -4.57     0.000
INCOME        0.0291916    0.0005129        56.92     0.000

s = 0.4767       R-sq = 99.5%      R-sq(adj) = 99.5%

Analysis of Variance

SOURCE          DF          SS          MS          F          p
Regression       1       736.15      736.15     3239.89     0.000
Error           15         3.41        0.23
Total           16       739.56

Unusual Observations
Obs.   INCOME     SALES       Fit Stdev.Fit  Residual    St.Resid
 17      1077    29.100    29.926      0.270     -0.826      -2.10R

R denotes an obs. with a large st. resid.
```

```
Durbin-Watson statistic = 0.72    *5
```

```
MTB > NAME C4 'ESTIMATE' C5 'RESIDUAL'
MTB > PRINT C1 C2 C4 C5
```

ROW	SALES	INCOME	ESTIMATE	RESIDUAL
1	8.0	336.1	8.3067	−0.30671
2	8.2	349.4	8.6949	−0.49495
3	8.5	362.9	9.0890	−0.58904
4	9.2	383.9	9.7020	−0.50206
5	10.2	402.8	10.2538	−0.05378
6	11.4	437.0	11.2521	0.14786
7	12.8	472.2	12.2797	0.52032
8	13.6	510.4	13.3948	0.20520
9	14.6	544.5	14.3902	0.20977
10	16.4	588.1	15.6630	0.73701
11	17.8	630.4	16.8978	0.90222
12	18.6	685.9	18.5179	0.08209
13	20.0	742.8	20.1789	−0.17892
14	21.9	801.3	21.8866	0.01337
15	24.9	903.1	24.8583	0.04166
16	27.3	983.6	27.2083	0.09175
17	29.1	1076.7	29.9260	−0.82599

MTB > STOP

---

[1] The **read** command places the Billings data in **c1** and **c2**
[2] Command **res** computes the standardized residuals and stores
them in **c3**. Command **dhats** computes the estimates of Y and
stores them in **c4**.
[3] Command **residuals** subtacts the estimates **c4** from the actual
observed observations **c1**
[4] Command **dw** computes the Durbin-Watson statistic
[5] The output for the Durbin-Watson statistic

Using a .01 level of significance for a sample of 17 and one independent
variable, one obtains

$L = .87$

$U = 1.10$

The Durbin-Watson statistic of .72 indicates that positive autocorrelation exists
(.72 < .87). Evidently, one or more key variables are missing from the model. An
important part of the variation of the sales variable has not been explained. This
result is true even though the Minitab output indicates that disposable income is
explaining 99.5% of the sales variable variance.

The best solution to this dilemma is to search for the missing variable or
variables. The unemployment rate is added to the model, and the results of the
computer run are presented next.

MTB > READ 'BILLINGS.DAT' C1-C3   [1]
   17 ROWS READ

ROW	C1	C2	C3
1	8.0	336.1	5.5
2	8.2	349.4	5.5
3	8.5	362.9	6.7
4	9.2	383.9	5.5
.	.	.	

continues

Continued

```
MTB > NAME C1 'SALES' C2 'INCOME' C3 'UNEMP'
MTB > REGRESS C1 2 PREDITORS C2 C3, RES IN C4, DHATS C5;  *2
SUBC> RESIDUALS C6;  *3
SUBC> DW.  *4

The regression equation is
SALES = - 0.014 + 0.0297 INCOME - 0.350 UNEMP

Predictor         Coef         Stdev      t-ratio          p
Constant       -0.0140        0.2498        -0.06      0.956
INCOME       0.0297492     0.0002480       119.96      0.000
UNEMP         -0.34987       0.04656         -7.51      0.000

s = 0.2199       R-sq = 99.9%      R-sq(adj) = 99.9%

Analysis of Variance

SOURCE        DF          SS          MS          F          p
Regression     2       738.88      369.44    7637.92      0.000
Error         14         0.68        0.05
Total         16       739.56

SOURCE        DF       SEQ SS
INCOME         1       736.15
UNEMP          1         2.73

Unusual Observations
Obs.   INCOME     SALES      Fit Stdev.Fit  Residual    St.Resid
 17     1077    29.1000    29.0430    0.1713    0.0570        0.41 X

X denotes an obs. whose X value gives it large influence.
```

```
┌─────────────────────────────────────────────┐
│  Durbin-Watson statistic = 1.98              │     *5
└─────────────────────────────────────────────┘
```

```
MTB > NAME C5 'ESTIMATE' C6 'RESIDUAL'
MTB > PRINT C1 C2 C3 C5 C6

ROW   SALES   INCOME   UNEMP   ESTIMATE    RESIDUAL

  1     8.0    336.1     5.5     8.0604   -0.060394
  2     8.2    349.4     5.5     8.4561   -0.256058
  3     8.5    362.9     6.7     8.4378    0.062171
  4     9.2    383.9     5.5     9.4824   -0.282405
  5    10.2    402.8     5.7     9.9747    0.225310
  6    11.4    437.0     5.2    11.1670    0.232953
  7    12.8    472.2     4.5    12.4591    0.340875
  8    13.6    510.4     3.8    13.8405   -0.240452
  9    14.6    544.5     3.8    14.8549   -0.254899
 10    16.4    588.1     3.6    16.2219    0.178064
 11    17.8    630.4     3.5    17.5153    0.284685
 12    18.6    685.9     4.9    18.6766   -0.076576
 13    20.0    742.8     5.9    20.0194   -0.019434
 14    21.9    801.3     5.6    21.8647    0.035278
 15    24.9    903.1     4.9    25.1381   -0.238096
 16    27.3    983.6     5.6    27.2880    0.012003
 17    29.1   1076.7     8.5    29.0430    0.056976

MTB > STOP
```

*1 The **read** command places the Billings data in **c1, c2,** and **c3**
*2 Command **res** computes the standardized residuals and stores
   them in **c4.** Command **dhats** computes the estimates of Y and
   stores them in **c5.**
*3 Command **residuals** subtacts the estimates **c5** from the actual
   observed observations **c1**
*4 Command **dw** computes the Durbin-Watson statistic
*5 The output for the Durbin-Watson statistic

Using a .01 level of significance for a sample of 17 and two independent variables, one obtains

$L = .77$

$U = 1.25$

The Durbin-Watson statistic of 1.98 indicates that the autocorrelation problem $(1.98 > 1.25)$ has been eliminated.

The regression equation $Y_R = -.014 + .03X_2 - .35X_3$ can be used to estimate Billings Corporation's sales with the knowledge that the error terms are independent. Expert estimates of disposable personal income ($1,185 million) and the unemployment rate (7.8%) for the region are used in order to forecast Billings sales for 1991 of $32.8 million.

$$Y_R = -.014 + .03(1,185.0) - .35(7.8) = 32.8 \qquad \blacksquare$$

REGRESSION OF PERCENTAGE CHANGES

Example 9.4 shows how to use the method of regression of percentage changes to correct for serial correlation.

EXAMPLE 9.4

■ Fred Gardner is engaged in forecasting Sears Roebuck sales in thousands of dollars for the western region. He has chosen disposable personal income for the region as his independent variable. Table 9.5 shows Sears sales and disposable income for the period 1970–1990.

The Minitab commands to run these data are as follows:

```
MTB > READ 'SEARS.DAT' C1-C2
      21 ROWS READ
```

ROW	C1	C2
1	3307	273.4
2	3556	291.3
3	3601	306.9
4	3721	317.1

. . .

```
MTB > REGRESS C1 1 PREDICTOR C2;
SUBC> DW.
```

The regression equation is
C1 = - 524 + 14.0 C2

Predictor	Coef	Stdev	t-ratio	p
Constant	-524.3	188.4	-2.78	0.012
C2	14.0496	0.3185	44.11	0.000

s = 343.5   R-sq = 99.0%   R-sq(adj) = 99.0%

Analysis of Variance

SOURCE	DF	SS	MS	F	p
Regression	1	229603712	229603712	1945.86	0.000
Error	19	2241929	117996		
Total	20	231845648			

Durbin-Watson statistic = 0.63

The MINITAB output indicates that Fred can explain 99% of
the Sears sales variance for the western region through the
knowledge of its relationship with disposable income for the
western region. However, the Durbin-Watson statistic is .63.
At the .01 significance level for a sample of 20 and one
independent variable the test statistics are

          L = .95
          U = 1.15

The Durbin-Watson statistic indicates positive serial
correlation (.63 < .95).

In an attempt to eliminate the relationship among residuals,
a regression line is fitted to the percentage changes from
year to year rather than to the actual data. MINITAB is used
to perform these computations. First, the differences are
computed for the two variables and stored in columns C3 and
C4.

```
MTB > DIFFERENCES 1 FOR C1, STORE IN C3
MTB > DIFFERENCES 1 FOR C2, STORE IN C4
```

   Next, each of the variables are lagged and stored in C5 and
   C6.

```
MTB > LAG 1 DATA IN C1, PUT IN C5
MTB > LAG 1 DATA IN C2, PUT IN C6
```

The differences for Sears sales which are stored in C3 are
divided by Sears sales lagged one period to compute the
percentage change from the previous year. This result is
stored in C7. The differences for disposable income which
are stored in C4 are divided by disposable income lagged one
period to compute the percentage change from the previous
year. This result is stored in C8.

```
MTB > DIVIDE C3 BY C5, STORE IN C7
MTB > DIVIDE C4 BY C6, STORE IN C8
```

Next, the results of each of the columns is printed.

MTB > PRINT C1-C8

ROW	C1	C2	C3	C4	C5	C6	C7	C8
1	3307	273.4	*	*	*	*	*	*
2	3556	291.3	249	17.900	3307	273.4	0.075295	0.065472
3	3601	306.9	45	15.600	3556	291.3	0.012655	0.053553
4	3721	317.1	120	10.200	3601	306.9	0.033324	0.033236
5	4036	336.1	315	19.000	3721	317.1	0.084655	0.059918
6	4134	349.4	98	13.300	4036	336.1	0.024281	0.039572
7	4268	362.9	134	13.500	4134	349.4	0.032414	0.038638
8	4578	383.9	310	21.000	4268	362.9	0.072634	0.057867
9	5093	402.8	515	18.900	4578	383.9	0.112495	0.049232
10	5716	437.0	623	34.200	5093	402.8	0.122325	0.084906
11	6357	472.2	641	35.200	5716	437.0	0.112141	0.080549
12	6769	510.4	412	38.200	6357	472.2	0.064810	0.080898
13	7296	544.5	527	34.100	6769	510.4	0.077855	0.066810
14	8178	588.1	882	43.600	7296	544.5	0.120888	0.080073
15	8844	630.4	666	42.300	8178	588.1	0.081438	0.071927
16	9251	685.9	407	55.500	8844	630.4	0.046020	0.088039
17	10006	742.8	755	56.900	9251	685.9	0.081613	0.082957
18	11200	801.3	1194	58.500	10006	742.8	0.119328	0.078756
19	12500	903.1	1300	101.800	11200	801.3	0.116071	0.127044
20	13101	983.6	601	80.500	12500	903.1	0.048080	0.089137
21	13640	1076.7	539	93.100	13101	983.6	0.041142	0.094652

Finally, the percentage changes for disposable income (C8) is
used to predict the percentage change in Sears sales (C7).
Since percentage changes are being used instead of actual
values, the regression is run without using a constant or Y-
intercept.

MTB > NAME C7 'SALES' C8 'INCOME'
MTB > REGRESS C7 1 PREDICTOR C8;
SUBC> NOCONSTANT;

SUBC> DW.

The regression equation is
SEARS = 1.01 INCOME

20 cases used 1 cases contain missing values

Predictor	Coef	Stdev	t-ratio	p
Noconstant				
INCOME	1.01297	0.09616	10.53	0.000

s = 0.03201
Analysis of Variance

SOURCE	DF	SS	MS	F	p
Regression	1	0.11375	0.11375	110.98	0.000
Error	19	0.01947	0.00102		
Total	20	0.13322			

Durbin-Watson statistic = 1.27

TABLE 9.5 Data for Example 9.4: Sears Sales, U.S. Disposable Income, and
Unemployment Rate (1970–1990).

Year	Sears Sales, Y	Disposable Income, X_2	Unemployment Rate (%), X_3	Percent Change from Previous Year		
				ΔY	ΔX_2	ΔX_3
1970	3,307	273.4	4.4	—	—	—
1971	3,556	291.3	4.1	7.5	6.5	−6.8
1972	3,601	306.9	4.3	1.3	5.4	4.9
1973	3,721	317.1	6.8	3.3	3.3	58.1
1974	4,036	336.1	5.5	8.5	6.0	−19.1
1975	4,134	349.4	5.5	2.4	4.0	.0
1976	4,268	362.9	6.7	3.2	5.7	21.8
1977	4,578	383.9	5.5	7.3	5.8	−17.9
1978	5,093	402.8	5.7	11.2	6.3	3.6
1979	5,716	437.0	5.2	12.2	8.5	−8.8
1980	6,357	472.2	4.5	11.2	8.1	−13.5
1981	6,769	510.4	3.8	6.5	8.1	−15.6
1982	7,296	544.5	3.8	7.8	6.7	.0
1983	8,178	588.1	3.6	12.1	8.0	−5.3
1984	8,844	630.4	3.5	8.1	7.2	−2.8
1985	9,251	685.9	4.9	4.6	8.8	40.0
1986	10,006	742.8	5.9	8.2	8.3	20.4
1987	11,200	801.3	5.6	11.9	7.9	−5.1
1988	12,500	903.1	4.9	11.6	12.7	−12.5
1989	13,101	983.6	5.6	4.6	8.9	14.3
1990	13,640	1,076.7	8.5	4.0	9.5	51.8

The plotted residuals are more randomly distributed, as indicated by the Durbin-Watson statistic of 1.27 (1.27 > 1.15). The various standard errors computed for these percentage changes ($s_{y.x}$, s_b) are more valid than those computed from the original values. This result does not mean, of course, that the forecast itself is necessarily more accurate.

At this point Fred can turn to his knowledge of multiple regression for help. If the changes in Sears sales are related simultaneously to other variables that affect sales, the estimation accuracy should improve. For example, change in unemployment rate (see Table 9.5) is introduced into the model. Table 9.6 shows the computer output results. The Durbin-Watson statistic has improved to 1.82. Thus no autocorrelation problem is apparent.

Fred now faces the dilemma of whether to add more independent variables to the model. However, whenever a new variable is added to the model, in order to forecast, one must use expert estimates of that variable. It seems possible that the accuracy of the forecast will be decreased by this procedure.

REGRESSION OF TIME SERIES DATA 355

TABLE 9.6 Computer Output for Percentage Change from Previous Year of Sears Sales, Disposable Income, and Unemployment Rate.

```
The regression equation is
SEARS = 1.05 INCOME - 0.0694 UNEMP

20 cases used 1 cases contain missing values

Predictor       Coef        Stdev      t-ratio       p
Noconstant
INCOME        1.05230      0.08739     12.04      0.000
UNEMP        -0.06942      0.02874     -2.42      0.027

s = 0.02859
Analysis of Variance

SOURCE          DF         SS          MS         F         p
Regression       2      0.118511    0.059255    72.52     0.000
Error           18      0.014708    0.000817
Total           20      0.133219

SOURCE          DF       SEQ SS
INCOME           1      0.113745
UNEMP            1      0.004766

Durbin-Watson statistic = 1.82
```

If the analyst decides to use the model demonstrated in Table 9.6, expert estimates of both disposable personal income and the unemployment rate will need to be acquired. The forecasting procedure is shown below and in Table 9.7.

1. Estimate disposable personal income for 1991.

2. Estimate unemployment rate for 1991.

3. $(1,185.0 - 1,076.7) = 108.3$, and

$$\frac{108.3}{1,076.7} = 10.1\%$$

TABLE 9.7 Forecasting Procedure for Sears Sales.

Year	Y	X_2	X_3	X_4 ΔY	X_5 ΔX_2	X_6 ΔX_3
1990	13,640	1,076.7	8.5	4.0	9.5	51.8
1991	15,164[6]	1,185.0[1]	7.8[2]	11.174[5]	10.1[3]	−8.2[4]

Note: Superscript numbers refer to steps in the text.

4. $(7.8 - 8.5) = -.7$, and

$$\frac{-.7}{8.5} = -8.2\%$$

5. Sears $= 1.05(\text{income}) - 0.0694(\text{unemployment})$
   $= 1.05(10.1) - 0.0694(-8.2)$
   $= 11.174\%$ estimated change or percentage increase in Sears sales

6. $Y(1991) = Y(1990) \times \Delta Y(1991) + Y(1990)$
   $= 13,640 \times .11174 + 13,640$
   $= 1,524 + 13,640$
   $= 15,164$, forecast of Sears sales for the western region

The estimate of Sears sales for 1991 is \$15,164. The various standard errors computed for this multiple regression model are valid and can be used to develop confidence intervals. If more accuracy is desired, one can introduce other important variables (population, number of stores, consumption expenditures, and price index) into the model. ∎

Autoregressive Models

One way to solve the serial correlation problem is to take advantage of the correlation between adjacent observations. This method is referred to as an *autoregressive model.* The dependent variable is lagged one or more periods and is used as an independent variable. For instance, in the Carlson Dishwasher sales, Y_T is lagged one period and is used along with personal income as an independent variable. This model is written

$$\hat{Y}_t = b_0 + b_2 X_2 + b_3 X_3 \qquad (9.4)$$

where $X_3 = Y_{t-1}$.

An *autoregressive model* expresses a forecast as a function of previous values of that time series.

EXAMPLE 9.5

∎ The data for the model in Equation 9.4 are presented in Table 9.1. Note that one year of data is lost since Carlson sales for 1969 are not known. The sample size is 20 instead of 21.

The results of running this multiple regression model are presented in Table 9.8. The Durbin-Watson statistic has improved to 1.92. However, this Durbin-Watson statistic should not be used when a lagged dependent variable appears as an

TABLE 9.8 Computer Output for Carlson Dishwasher Sales: Autoregressive Model.

VARIABLE NO.	MEAN	STANDARD DEVIATION	CORRELATION X VS Y	REGRESSION COEFFICIENT	STD. ERROR OF REG.COEF.	COMPUTED T VALUE
2	2.709	0.179	0.96792	-0.370	0.40752	-0.91
3	3.041	0.348	0.98769	1.127	0.20928	5.38

DEPENDENT		
1	3.089	0.331

INTERCEPT	0.666	MULTIPLE CORRELATION	0.98826
STD. ERROR OF ESTIMATE	0.05346	R SQUARE	0.97665
DURBIN-WATSON STATISIC	1.91897	CORRECTED R SQUARED	0.97390

ANALYSIS OF VARIANCE FOR THE REGRESSION

SOURCES OF VARIATION	DEGREES OF FREEDOM	SUM OF SQUARES	MEAN SQUARES	F VALUE
ATTRIBUTABLE TO REGRESSION	2	2.032	1.016	355.544
DEVIATION FROM REGRESSION	17	0.049	0.003	
TOTAL	19	2.081		

CORRELATION MATRIX: 3 BY 3

VAR.	1	2	3
1	1.000	0.968	0.988
2	0.968	1.000	0.986
3	0.988	0.986	1.000

TABLE OF RESIDUALS

CASE NO.	Y VALUE	Y ESTIMATE	RESIDUAL
1	2.60206	2.53630	0.06576
2	2.59106	2.67722	-0.08616
3	2.62839	2.65926	-0.03087
4	2.73799	2.69196	0.04603
5	2.74429	2.80920	-0.06491
6	2.79239	2.81021	-0.01782
7	2.85733	2.85536	0.00197
8	2.94448	2.92081	0.02368
9	3.02119	3.00590	0.01529
10	3.11059	3.07987	0.03072
11	3.18412	3.16809	0.01603
12	3.20030	3.24054	-0.04024
13	3.29226	3.24639	0.04587
14	3.32592	3.33883	-0.01290
15	3.32551	3.36319	-0.03768
16	3.39393	3.34992	0.04400
17	3.50501	3.41481	0.09020
18	3.56844	3.52075	0.04769
19	3.52022	3.57848	-0.05826
20	3.43168	3.51006	-0.07837

independent variable because it tends to be biased upward. Instead, the Durbin h statistic should be used to test for serially correlated residuals.[2]

The estimate of Carlson Dishwasher sales for 1991 is $2,607,000.

$$Y_{1991} = .666 - .37X_2 + 1.127X_3$$

---

[2] J. Johnston, *Econometric Methods,* 2nd ed. (New York: McGraw-Hill, 1972).

where $X_3 = Y_{1990}$. So,[3]

$$Y_{1991} = .666 - .37(1,185) + 1.127(2,702) = 2,607$$

A check of the correlation matrix in Table 9.8 leads to the conclusion that collinearity might be a problem. The high interrelationship between the independent variables, $r_{23} = .986$, indicates that they are probably explaining the same dependent variable variance. The collinearity problem becomes obvious when the regression coefficient for the disposable personal income variable is analyzed, $b_2 = -.37$. Since the income variable shows a high positive relationship with sales, $r_{12} = .968$, the regression coefficient is not meaningful. The model might be improved if the only independent variable were Carlson Dishwasher sales lagged one period. This model would involve an autoregressive model of order 1 and will be explained in the discussion of Box-Jenkins techniques in Chapter 10. ∎

Generalized Least Squares

One way to solve autocorrelation problems is to develop a model that recognizes the relationship among the residuals in some appropriate fashion. Originally each data point was represented by Equation 9.1, that is,

$$Y_t = \beta_0 + \beta X_t + \varepsilon_t$$

A new model needs to be created that recognizes that the error term (ε_t) consists of a fraction of the previous error term plus some random effect. In Equation 9.2 the error term was written

$$\varepsilon_t = \rho\varepsilon_{t-1} + v_t$$

or

$$v_t = \varepsilon_t - \rho\varepsilon_{t-1}$$

where

ρ = correlation between residuals

v_t = random error

$v_t = \varepsilon_t$ when $\rho = 0$

The new model becomes

$$Y_t = \beta_0 + \beta X_t + \rho\varepsilon_{t-1} + v_t \tag{9.5}$$

If the residuals are unrelated and ρ is equal to zero, the result is Equation 9.1, that is,

---

[3] Estimate of disposable personal income for 1991 is $1,185.

$$Y_t = \beta_0 + \beta X_t + \rho \varepsilon_{t-1} + v_t$$
$$= \beta_0 + \beta X_t + 0\varepsilon_{t-1} + v_t$$
$$= \beta_0 + \beta X_t + v_t$$
$$= \beta_0 + \beta X_t + \varepsilon_t \qquad \text{when } v_t = \varepsilon_t$$

If the error terms are related and ρ is greater than zero, it is desirable to recognize the related structure of the error terms.

If ρ is known, then generalized differencing can be used to adjust the least squares regression procedure so that the error terms are independent. To describe this procedure, one utilizes the fact that the linear model, Equation 9.1, holds for all time periods. In particular,

$$Y_{t-1} = \beta_0 + \beta X_{t-1} + \varepsilon_{t-1} \tag{9.6}$$

Now the equation can be transformed by multiplying Equation 9.6 by ρ and by subtracting it from Equation 9.1.

$$Y_t = \beta_0 + \beta X_t + \varepsilon_t \qquad \text{[Eq. 9.1]}$$
$$\rho(Y_{t-1}) = \rho\beta_0 + \rho\beta X_{t-1} + \rho\varepsilon_{t-1} \qquad \text{[}\rho \times \text{Eq. 9.6]}$$
$$Y_t - \rho(Y_{t-1}) = (\beta_0 - \rho\beta_0) + (\beta X_t - \rho\beta X_{t-1}) + (\varepsilon_t - \rho\varepsilon_{t-1}) \qquad \text{[subtract]}$$
$$Y'_t = \beta_0(1 - \rho) + \beta X'_t + v_t \tag{9.7}$$

The transformed equation has an error process that is independently distributed with a mean equal to zero and a constant variance. Thus ordinary least squares regression applied to Equation 9.7 will yield valid estimates of regression parameters. Remember, the variables have been transformed to

$$Y'_t = Y_t - \rho Y_{t-1}$$
$$X'_t = X_t - \rho X_{t-1}$$

Equation 9.7 can be rewritten as

$$Y'_t = \beta'_0 + \beta X'_t + v_t \tag{9.8}$$

Equation 9.8 is called a generalized least squares version of Equation 9.7, where

1. The error term is not serially correlated.
2. The regression coefficient β is the same as the regression coefficient of the original serially correlated equation, Equation 9.1.

First Differences

One commonly used estimation procedure, known as *first differencing,* assumes that ρ is equal to 1. If $\rho = 1$, the transformed model in Equation 9.7 becomes

$$Y'_t = \beta_0(1 - \rho) + \beta X'_t + \varepsilon_t$$
$$= \beta_0(1 - 1) + \beta X'_t + \varepsilon_t = \beta X'_t + \varepsilon_t \qquad (9.9)$$

Therefore the regression coefficient β can be estimated by using the least squares method for regression through the origin with the transformed variables

$$Y'_t = Y_t - \rho Y_{t-1}$$
$$X'_t = X_t - \rho X_{t-1}$$

Note that these transformed variables are first differences. This approach is effective in a variety of applications.

EXAMPLE 9.6

■ Table 9.9 contains the transformed variables Y'_t and X'_t based on the first-differences transformation for Sears sales. The table also contains the computations for estimating the linear regression through the origin. Notice that the estimated regression coefficient, $b = .0117$, is similar to that obtained with ordinary least squares applied to the original variables, $b = .014$. However, the standard error of the regression coefficient, $s_b = .00114$, is considerably higher than $s_b = .00032$. The new standard error of the regression coefficient, $s_b = .00114$, is probably more accurate. The original standard error, $s_b = .00034$, for ordinary least squares applied to the original variables is likely to understate the true standard error due to autocorrelation.

The Minitab commands to solve this problem are as follows:

```
MTB > READ 'SEARS.DAT' C1 C2
      21 ROWS READ

  ROW      C1         C2

    1      3307      273.4
    2      3556      291.3
    3      3601      306.9
    4      3721      317.1
      .   .   .

MTB > DIFFERENCES 1 FOR C1, STORE IN C3
MTB > DIFFERENCES 1 FOR C2, STORE IN C4
MTB > NAME C3 'SEARS' C4 'INCOME'
MTB > REGRESS C3 1 PREDICTOR C4;
SUBC> NOCONSTANT.

The regression equation is
SEARS = 0.0117 INCOME
```

```
20 cases used 1 cases contain missing values

Predictor      Coef       Stdev      t-ratio         p
Noconstant
INCOME       0.011747    0.001154     10.18       0.000

s = 0.2479
Analysis of Variance

SOURCE        DF         SS          MS         F           p
Regression     1       6.3696      6.3696     103.62      0.000
Error         19       1.1679      0.0615
Total         20       7.5375
```
■

TABLE 9.9 Data for Example 9.6: First Differences for Sears Sales Computations of Linear Regression Through Origin.

Year	Sales, Y (000)	Disposable Income, X	Y_t'	X_t'	$X_t'Y_t'$	$(X_t')^2$	$(Y_t' - bX_t')^2$
1970	3.307	273.4					
1971	3.556	291.3	.249	17.9	4.5	320.4	.0016
1972	3.601	306.9	.045	15.6	.7	243.4	.0189
1973	3.721	317.1	.120	10.2	1.2	104.0	.0000
1974	4.036	336.1	.315	19.0	6.0	361.0	.0086
1975	4.134	349.4	.098	13.3	1.3	176.9	.0033
1976	4.268	362.9	.134	13.5	1.8	182.3	.0006
1977	4.578	383.9	.310	21.0	6.5	441.0	.0041
1978	5.093	402.8	.515	18.9	9.7	357.2	.0864
1979	5.716	437.0	.623	34.2	21.3	1,169.6	.0497
1980	6.357	472.2	.641	35.2	22.6	1,239.0	.0525
1981	6.769	510.4	.412	38.2	15.7	1,459.2	.0012
1982	7.296	544.5	.527	34.1	18.0	1,162.8	.0164
1983	8.178	588.1	.882	43.6	38.5	1,901.0	.1383
1984	8.844	630.4	.666	42.3	28.2	1,789.3	.0293
1985	9.251	685.9	.407	55.5	22.6	3,080.3	.0587
1986	10.006	742.8	.755	56.9	43.0	3,237.6	.0080
1987	11.200	801.3	1.194	58.5	69.8	3,422.3	.2596
1988	12.500	903.1	1.300	101.8	132.3	10,363.2	.0119
1989	13.101	983.6	.601	80.5	48.4	6,480.3	.1162
1990	13.640	1,076.7	.539	93.1	50.2	8,667.6	.3028
				Totals	542.3	46,158.4	1.1681

$$b = \frac{\Sigma X_t'Y_t'}{\Sigma (X_t')^2} = \frac{542.3}{46,158.4} = .0117$$

$$s_b^2 = \frac{\Sigma (Y_t' - bX_t')^2/(n-1)}{\Sigma (X_t')^2} = \frac{1.1681/19}{46,158.4} = \frac{.0614789}{46,158.4} = .0000013$$

$$s_b = .00114$$

Iterative Approach

The iterative approach also involves the transformation of the original variables that were shown in Equation 9.8.

$$Y'_t = Y_t - \rho Y_{t-1}$$
$$X'_t = X_t - \rho X_{t-1}$$

The process is based on the transformed model, Equation 9.7, which can be solved with ordinary least squares methods. Unfortunately, the transformed model

$$Y'_t = \beta_0(1 - \rho) + \beta X'_t + \varepsilon_t$$

cannot be used directly because the autocorrelation parameter ρ needed to obtain the transformed variables in Equation 9.8 is unknown. However, techniques to estimate ρ have been developed. Several approaches are discussed in *Econometric Models and Economic Forecasts* by Pindyck and Rubinfeld.[4] These approaches generally utilize the notion that ρ is a correlation coefficient associated with errors of adjacent time periods. The iterative approach does not always work, because the autocorrelation parameter ρ tends to be underestimated.

One of the more popular procedures for estimating ρ in the presence of first-order serial correlation was developed by Cochrane and Orcutt. This iterative procedure produces successive estimates of ρ until further iteration results in little change.

The initial estimate of ρ is derived from the residuals using Equation 9.10.

$$\hat{\rho} = \frac{\sum_{t=2}^{n} e_t e_{t-1}}{\sum_{t=2}^{n} e_{t-1}^2} \tag{9.10}$$

The value $\hat{\rho}$ is substituted for ρ in Equation 9.7, forming

$$Y'_t = \beta_0(1 - \hat{\rho}) + \beta X'_t + v_t \tag{9.11}$$

Equation 9.11 is now solved using ordinary least squares. A second estimate of ρ is determined using the same procedure:

---

[4] R. S. Pindyck and D. L. Rubinfeld, *Econometric Models and Economic Forecasts* (New York: McGraw-Hill, 1976), pp. 108–113.

$$\hat{\rho} = \frac{\displaystyle\sum_{t=2}^{n} \hat{v}_t \hat{v}_{t-1}}{\displaystyle\sum_{t=2}^{n} \hat{v}_{t-1}^2} \tag{9.12}$$

where the $\hat{v}_t$s are the residuals from the ordinary least squares fit. The second estimate of ρ is compared to the first estimate, and if these two values are reasonably close, the second estimate is used. If not, another iteration is made.

EXAMPLE 9.7

■ The Minitab output shows the results of using the independent variable personal income to predict Sears sales with the ordinary least squares approach. If the Sears data is run in thousands of dollars, the prediction equation is

$$Y_R = -.524 + .014X$$

where

$$s_b = .0003185$$

$$t = 44.1$$

$$r^2 = .99$$

$$DW = .63$$

If generalized least squares (using the Cochrane-Orcutt method) is used, the result is

$$Y_R = 2.34 + .010933X$$

where

$$s_b = .00137$$

$$t = 7.96$$

$$r^2 = .78$$

$$\hat{\rho} = .936$$

The output for this example is shown in the TSP Example at the end of the chapter. Note that the final estimate of ρ is .936, which means that Y was actually run as $Y_t' = Y_t - .936Y_{t-1}$ and X as $X_t' = X_t - .936X_{t-1}$. When the generalized least squares equation is compared to the ordinary least squares equation, the t-score has decreased. This result makes sense since one of the consequences of serial correlation is that ordinary least squares underestimates the standard error of the regression coefficient. Indeed, one reason for adjusting for serial correlation is to avoid making mistakes of inference because of t-scores that are too high. Finally, serial correlation does not cause any bias in the estimate of the regression coefficient; however, the amount that any given estimate is likely to differ from the true β is increased. The generalized least squares solution (.010933) provided approximately the same result as the ordinary least squares method (.014). ∎

When regression analysis is applied to time series data, the residuals are frequently correlated. Since regression analysis assumes that residuals are independent, problems arise. The term *serial correlation* describes this situation. The r^2 for a model containing serial correlation is artificially high; furthermore, the standard error seriously underestimates the variability of the residuals, and the regression coefficients become quite inefficient.

A major cause of autocorrelated residuals is the omission of one or more key variables. This omission usually means that an important part of the dependent variable variation has not been explained. When the time-sequenced effects of a missing variable are positively related, the residuals are autocorrelated because they include the effects of the missing variable. The best solution to this problem is to search for the missing variable to include in the model.

APPLICATION TO MANAGEMENT

The applications described in Chapter 8 are also appropriate for this chapter. However, the techniques described in this chapter permit the analyst to detect and correct for the problem of autocorrelation. Therefore, the ability of management to deal with time series data becomes more robust. The net result is that management can deal with a far greater variety of time-dependent data and feel confident that the predictions are sound. Areas where these techniques are particularly helpful include the following:

Sales forecasting   Stock and bond price projections
Raw materials cost projections   New-product penetration projections
Personnel needs estimates   Advertising-sales relationship studies
Inventory control

None of the above applications is new or something that could not be dealt with before. Rather, the tools being used to make the projections are more sophisticated and should provide more reliable and valid answers. Specifically, solutions have been found to the problem of autocorrelation that usually accompanies the regression of a time series dependent variable.

CHAPTER **9**

GLOSSARY

Autoregressive model   An autoregressive model expresses a forecast as a function of previous values of that time series.

Serial correlation   Serial correlation exists when successive observations over time are related to each other.

KEY FORMULAS

Ordinary least squares linear model $Y_t = \beta_0 + \beta X_t + \varepsilon_t$ (9.1)

First-order serial correlation $\varepsilon_t = \rho \varepsilon_{t-1} + v_t$ (9.2)

Durbin-Watson statistics $DW = \dfrac{\displaystyle\sum_{t=2}^{n} (e_t - e_{t-1})^2}{\displaystyle\sum_{t=1}^{n} e_t^2}$ (9.3)

Autoregressive model $\hat{Y}_t = b_0 + b_2 X_2 + b_3 Y_{t-1}$ (9.4)

First-order serial correlation $Y_t = \beta_0 + \beta X_t + \rho \varepsilon_{t-1} + v_t$ (9.5)

Ordinary least squares linear model: previous time period

$\quad Y_{t-1} = \beta_0 + \beta X_{t-1} + \varepsilon_{t-1}$ (9.6)

Transformed ordinary least squares linear model

$\quad Y_t' = \beta_0(1 - \rho) + \beta X_t' + v_t$ (9.7)

Generalized least squares $Y_t' = \beta_0' + \beta X_t' + v_t$ (9.8)

First difference model $Y_t' = \beta X_t' + \varepsilon_t$ (9.9)

Cochrane-Orcutt: initial estimate of ρ $\hat{\rho} = \dfrac{\displaystyle\sum_{t=2}^{n} e_t e_{t-1}}{\displaystyle\sum_{t=2}^{n} e_{t-1}^2}$ (9.10)

Cochrane-Orcutt: linear model $Y_t' = \beta_0(1 - \hat{\rho}) + \beta X_t' + v_t$ (9.11)

Cochrane-Orcutt: second estimate of ρ $\hat{\hat{\rho}} = \dfrac{\displaystyle\sum_{t=2}^{n} \hat{v}_t \hat{v}_{t-1}}{\displaystyle\sum_{t=2}^{n} \hat{v}_{t-1}^2}$ (9.12)

Standardized coefficients $\beta = b\left(\dfrac{s}{s_y}\right)$ (9.13)

PROBLEMS

1. Why is serial correlation a problem when time series data are analyzed?
2. What is the major cause of serial correlation?
3. Which underlying assumption is violated most frequently when time series variables are analyzed?

4. Which statistic is used to detect serial correlation?

5. You test a series of 32 observations with two independent variables at the .01 significance level, and the calculated Durbin-Watson statistic is equal to 1.0. What is your conclusion?

6. You test a series of 61 observations with one independent variable at the .05 significance level, and the calculated Durbin-Watson statistic is equal to 1.6. What is your conclusion?

7. How is the problem of serial correlation eliminated?

8. How does an autoregressive model work?

9. How do the first difference and iterative techniques for solving serial correlation differ?

10. Tamson Russell, an economist working for the government, is trying to determine the demand function for passenger car motor fuel in the United States. Tamson developed a model that used the actual price of a gallon of regular gasoline to predict motor fuel consumed per year. She was only able to explain 72.8% of the variance with this model. Tamson has decided to add a variable representing the population of the United States to the model. Determine whether serial correlation is a problem. The data are as follows:

Year	Motor Fuel Consumed by Cars (Billions of Gallons) Y	Price of Gasoline X_2	Population of U.S. (Millions) X_3
1973	78.8	.39	211.9
1974	75.1	.53	213.9
1975	76.4	.57	216.0
1976	79.7	.59	218.0
1977	80.4	.62	220.2
1978	81.7	.63	222.6
1979	77.1	.86	225.1
1980	71.9	1.19	227.7
1981	71.0	1.31	230.1
1982	70.1	1.22	232.5
1983	69.9	1.16	234.8
1984	68.7	1.13	237.0
1985	69.3	1.12	239.3
1986	71.4	.86	241.6
1987	71.0	.90	243.9

Source: *Statistical Abstract of the United States,* various years.

11. Decision Science Associates has been asked to do a feasibility study for a proposed destination resort to be located within half a mile of the Grand Coulee Dam. Mark Craze is not happy with the regression model that used the price of a regular gallon of gasoline to predict the number of visitors to the Grand Coulee Dam Visitors Center. After plotting the data on a scatter diagram, Mark decides to use a dummy variable to represent significant celebrations in the general area. Mark uses a 1 to represent a celebration and a zero to represent no celebration. Note that the 1 in 1974 represents the Expo 74 World's Fair celebrated in Spokane, Washington, the 1 in 1983 represents the celebration of the fiftieth anniversary of the construction of Grand Coulee Dam, and the 1 in 1986 represents the World's Fair held in Vancouver, Canada. Mark also decides to use time as a predictor variable.

   Write a report for Mark to present to his boss. Indicate whether serial correlation is a problem. Also, indicate what additional information would be important in deciding whether to recommend that the destination resort be built.

Year	Number of Visitors Y	Time X_2	Price of Gasoline X_3	Celebration X_4
1973	268,528	1	.39	0
1974	468,136	2	.53	1
1975	390,129	3	.57	0
1976	300,140	4	.59	0
1977	271,140	5	.62	0
1978	282,752	6	.63	0
1979	244,006	7	.86	0
1980	161,524	8	1.19	0
1981	277,134	9	1.31	0
1982	382,343	10	1.22	0
1983	617,737	11	1.16	1
1984	453,881	12	1.13	0
1985	471,417	13	.86	0
1986	654,147	14	.90	1

Sources: Grand Coulee Dam Visitors Center and *Statistical Abstract of the United States,* 1988.

12. Jim Jackson, a rate analyst for the Washington Water Power Company, is preparing for a rate case and needs to forecast electric residential revenue for 1990. Jim decides to investigate three potential predictor variables: residential use per kilowatt hour (kWh), residential charge per kWh (cents/kWh), and number of residential electric customers. He collects data from 1968 to 1989. The data are as follows:

Year	Revenue (Millions) Y	Use per kWh X_2	Charge (Cents/kWh) X_3	Number of Customers X_4
1968	19.3	10,413	1.33	139,881
1969	20.4	11,129	1.29	142,806
1970	20.9	11,361	1.25	146,616
1971	21.9	11,960	1.21	151,640
1972	23.4	12,498	1.19	157,205
1973	24.5	12,667	1.19	162,328
1974	25.8	12,857	1.21	166,558
1975	30.5	13,843	1.29	170,317
1976	33.3	14,223	1.33	175,536
1977	37.2	14,427	1.42	181,553
1978	42.5	14,878	1.52	188,325
1979	48.8	15,763	1.59	194,237
1980	55.4	15,130	1.84	198,847
1981	64.3	14,697	2.17	201,465
1982	78.9	15,221	2.55	203,444
1983	86.5	14,166	2.97	205,533
1984	114.6	14,854	3.70	208,574
1985	129.7	14,997	4.10	210,811
1986	126.1	13,674	4.34	212,865
1987	132.0	13,062	4.71	214,479
1988	138.1	13,284	4.82	215,610
1989	141.2	13,531	4.81	217,164

Source: "Financial and Operating Supplement," *Washington Water Power Annual Report,* various years.

Jim testified before the Idaho Rate Commission and was asked if serial correlation was a problem. He didn't know the answer and has asked you to write a response to the commission's question.

13. Paul Raymond, president of Washington Water Power, is worried about the possibility of a takeover attempt and the fact that the number of common shareholders has been decreasing since 1983. He instructs you to study the number of common shareholders since 1968 and forecast for 1990. You decide to investigate three potential predictor variables: earnings per share (common), dividends per share (common), and payout ratio. You collect the data from 1968 to 1989 as shown on the following page.

a. Run these data on the computer and find the best prediction model.
b. Is serial correlation a problem in this model?
c. If serial correlation is a problem, write a memo to Paul that discusses various solutions to the autocorrelation problem and includes your final recommendation.

Year	Common Shareholders Y	Earnings per Share X_2	Dividends per Share X_3	Payout Ratio X_4
1968	26,472	1.68	1.21	72
1969	28,770	1.70	1.28	73
1970	29,681	1.80	1.32	73
1971	30,481	1.86	1.36	72
1972	30,111	1.96	1.39	71
1973	31,052	2.02	1.44	71
1974	30,845	2.11	1.49	71
1975	32,012	2.42	1.53	63
1976	32,846	2.79	1.65	55
1977	32,909	2.38	1.76	74
1978	34,593	2.95	1.94	61
1979	34,359	2.78	2.08	75
1980	36,161	2.33	2.16	93
1981	38,892	3.29	2.28	69
1982	46,278	3.17	2.40	76
1983	47,672	3.02	2.48	82
1984	45,462	2.46	2.48	101
1985	45,599	3.03	2.48	82
1986	41,368	2.06	2.48	120
1987	38,686	2.31	2.48	107
1988	37,072	2.54	2.48	98
1989	36,968	2.70	2.48	92

Source: "Financial and Operating Supplement," *Washington Water Power Annual Report,* various years.

14. Thompson Airlines has determined that 5% of the total number of U.S. domestic airline passengers fly on Thompson planes. Because of this relationship, you are given the task of forecasting the number of passengers who will fly on Thompson Airlines in 1965. The data are presented in the accompanying table.

Year	Number of Passengers (Millions)	Year	Number of Passengers (Millions)	Year	Number of Passengers (Millions)	Year	Number of Passengers (Millions)
1952	22.8	1958	39.5	1964	61.9	1970	117.2
1953	26.1	1959	45.4	1965	69.9	1971	124.9
1954	29.4	1960	46.3	1966	79.9	1972	136.6
1955	34.5	1961	45.8	1967	96.3	1973	144.8
1956	37.6	1962	48.0	1968	109.0	1974	147.9
1957	40.3	1963	54.6	1969	116.0		

    a. Develop a time series regression model, using time as the independent variable and the number of passengers as the dependent variable.

    b. Are the error terms for this model dispersed in a uniform manner?

    c. Transform the number of passengers variable so that the error terms will be uniformly dispersed.

    d. Run a computer program for the transformed model developed in part c.

    e. Are the error terms independent for the model run in part d?

    f. If the error terms are dependent, what problems are involved with using this model?

    g. Estimate the number of Thompson Airlines passengers for 1975.

15. Thomas Furniture Company concludes that production scheduling can be improved by developing an accurate method of predicting quarterly sales. The company analyst, Mr. Estes, decides to investigate the relationship between housing construction permits and furniture sales in the Springfield area. Estes feels that permits will lead sales by one or two quarters. In addition, he wonders if seasons affect furniture sales. Estes decides to consider another independent variable:

$$X_3 = \begin{cases} 0 & \text{if first or second quarter sales} \\ 1 & \text{if third or fourth quarter sales} \end{cases}$$

The data are given in the accompanying table.

Year	Quarter	Sales (Thousands), Y	Permits, X_2	Year	Quarter	Sales (Thousands), Y	Permits, X_2
1986	3		19	1989	1	120	72
	4		3		2	150	31
1987	1	120	35		3	660	19
	2	80	11		4	270	14
	3	400	11	1990	1	200	75
	4	200	16		2	280	41
1988	1	75	32		3	800	17
	2	120	10		4	320	10
	3	270	12				
	4	155	21				

    a. Develop a regression model that uses housing construction permits as the predictor variable.

    b. Test this model for autocorrelation.

    c. Develop a regression model that uses both permits and the seasonal effect.

    d. Is the multiple regression model better than the simple regression model? (Test at the .05 significance level.)

e. Does your best model contain an autocorrelation problem? If so, how might it be corrected?

f. Forecast Thomas Furniture Company sales for 1991 by the quarter.

16. The data in the accompanying table show seasonally adjusted quarterly sales for Dickson Corporation and for the entire industry for the most recent 20 quarters.

Year	Quarter	Dickson Sales (Thousands), Y	Industry Sales (Millions), X_2	Year	Quarter	Dickson Sales (Thousands), Y	Industry Sales (Millions), X_2
1986	1	83.8	31.8	1988	3	98.2	37.1
	2	85.6	32.5		4	97.2	36.6
	3	87.8	33.2	1989	1	100.1	37.6
	4	86.1	32.4		2	102.6	38.3
1987	1	89.6	33.8		3	105.4	39.3
	2	91.0	34.3		4	107.9	40.2
	3	93.9	35.3	1990	1	110.1	41.1
	4	94.6	35.7		2	111.1	41.4
1988	1	96.4	36.4		3	110.1	41.1
	2	96.0	36.3		4	111.1	41.4

a. Fit the linear regression model, obtain the residuals, and plot them against time. What do you find?

b. Calculate the Durbin-Watson statistic, and determine whether autocorrelation exists.

c. Estimate the regression coefficient b_2 by the first differences approach.

d. Estimate the standard error of the regression coefficient by the first differences approach.

e. Are your estimates using the first differences approach more accurate?

17. A study is done in an attempt to relate personal savings and personal income (in billions of dollars) for the time period 1935–1954. The data are presented in the accompanying table.

Year	Personal Savings, Y	Personal Income, X	Year	Personal Savings, Y	Personal Income, X	Year	Personal Savings, Y	Personal Income, X
1935	2	60	1942	28	123	1949	9	207
1936	4	69	1943	33	151	1950	13	279
1937	4	74	1944	37	165	1951	18	257
1938	1	68	1945	30	171	1952	19	273
1939	3	73	1946	15	179	1953	20	288
1940	4	78	1947	7	191	1954	19	290
1941	11	96	1948	13	210			

a. Evaluate the simple regression model where personal income is used to predict personal savings. Specifically, (1) test the regression coefficient for significance ($\alpha = .01$); (2) test the personal income variable's contribution to the prediction of personal savings, using the F test ($\alpha = .01$); (3) test for autocorrelation. How can the model be improved?

b. Develop a dummy variable X_3 for war years. Let $X_3 = 0$ for peacetime and $X_3 = 1$ for wartime. The war years are considered to be 1941–1945. Run a computer program for this multiple regression model, and evaluate the results. Specifically, (1) test to determine whether knowledge of war years makes a significant contribution to the prediction of personal savings ($\alpha = .01$); (2) test for autocorrelation. Is the multiple regression model better than the simple regression model?

18. Use the Cochrane-Orcutt method to correct for serial correlation in the Carlson Dishwasher Corporation data of Example 9.1.

19. Use the Cochrane-Orcutt method to correct for serial correlation in the Billings Corporation data of Example 9.3.

CASE STUDY 9.1

COMPANY OF YOUR CHOICE

As mentioned several times in this chapter, the many variables in every company measured every year, quarter, and month are vital measurements of a company's health. For each of these, there may be several other variables that are highly correlated and might provide valuable insights and forecasting power.

The purpose of this case is to simulate the identification of an important time series variable for a company of your choice and to then analyze the patterns in the data using autocorrelation analysis. In addition, you can use a regression analysis computer program to see if a good prediction equation can be found.

QUESTIONS

1. Identify a company or organization that interests you. The company can be a local or national company that has published records, including the measurement of time series variables.

2. Identify a key variable for your chosen company and record its values for several years, quarters, or months.

3. Either by hand or with a computer, calculate several autocorrelation coefficients and plot them on a correlogram.

4. Based on the correlogram pattern, describe the patterns in your time series.

5. Compute Y lagged and first differences for your data, compute the autocorrelation coefficients, plot them on a correlogram and describe the resulting patterns.

6. Identify several potential predictor variables that you think might be correlated with the dependent variable. You can use company records along with other data sources in this process.

7. Run the data on a regression analysis computer program and obtain a correlation matrix. Assemble several predictor variable combinations that you think might be successful and run a regression analysis for each. See if you can find a good prediction equation for your dependent variable.

8. Check your model to make sure that serial correlation is not a problem.

CASE STUDY 9.2

BUSINESS ACTIVITY INDEX FOR SPOKANE COUNTY

Prior to 1973 Spokane County, Washington, had no up-to-date measurement of general business activity. What is happening in this area as a whole, however, affects every local business, government agency, and individual. Plans and policies made by an economic unit would be incomplete without some reliable knowledge about the recent performance of the economy of which the unit is a component part. A Spokane business activity index should serve as a vital input in the formulation of strategies and decisions in private as well as in public organizations.

A business activity index is an indicator of the relative changes in overall business conditions within a specified region. At the national level the gross national product (by the Department of Commerce) and the industrial production index (by the Federal Reserve Board) are generally considered excellent indicators. Each of these series is based on thousands of pieces of information—the collecting, editing, and computing of which are costly and time-consuming undertakings. For a local area such as Spokane County, Washington, a simplified version, capable of providing reasonably accurate and current information at moderate cost, is most desirable.

Multiple regression is commonly used to construct a business activity index. There are three essential questions with which the construction of such an index must deal.

- What are the components of the index?
- Do these components adequately represent the changes in overall business conditions?
- What weight should be assigned to each of the chosen components?

Answers to these questions can be obtained through regression analysis.

Dr. Shik Chun Young, professor of economics at Eastern Washington University, is attempting to develop a business activity index for Spokane County. Young selects personal income as the independent variable. At the county level personal income is judged as the best available indicator of local business conditions. Personal income measures the total income received by households before personal taxes are paid. Since productive activities are typically remunerated by monetary means, personal income may, indeed, be viewed as a reasonable proxy for the general economic performance. Why then is it necessary to construct another index if personal income can serve as a good business activity indicator? Unfortunately, personal income data at the county level are estimated by the U.S. Department of Commerce on an annual basis and are released 16 months too late. Consequently, these data are of little use for short-term planning. Young's task is to establish an up-to-date business activity index.

The independent variables are drawn from those local data that are readily available on a monthly basis. Currently, about 50 series of such monthly data are available and range from employment, bank activities, and real estate transactions to electricity consumption. If each series were to be included in the regression analysis, the effort would yield low productivity because only a handful of these series would be statistically significant. Therefore some knowledge of the relationship between personal income and the available data is necessary in order to determine which series are to be included in the regression equation. From Young's knowledge of the Spokane economy, the following 10 series are selected:

X_2, total employment

X_3, manufacturing employment

X_4, construction employment

X_5, wholesale and retail trade employment

X_6, service employment

X_7, bank debits

X_8, bank demand deposits

X_9, building permits issued

X_{10}, real estate mortgages

X_{11}, total electricity consumption

The first step in the analysis is to run the model,

$$Y_R = b_0 + b_2 X_2 + b_3 X_3 + \cdots + b_{11} X_{11}$$

where

Y = personal income

b_0 = Y intercept

$b_2, b_3, \ldots, b_{11}$ = coefficients of respective independent variables

The total corrected R^2 is .96, which means that the 10 variables used together explain 96% of the variance in the dependent variable, personal income. However, other regression statistics indicate problems. First, of these 10 independent variables only 3 have a computed t value significant at the .05 level, namely, total employment, service employment, and total bank debits. Second, the correlation matrix shows a high degree of interdependence among several of the independent variables—multicollinearity. For example, the total employment and bank debits have a correlation coefficient of .88; total electricity consumption and the bank demand deposits, .76; and building permits issued and real estate mortgages, .68. Third, autocorrelation, as indicated by a Durbin-Watson statistic of .91, is present. This phenomenon is rather common in time series data where each observation is not independent of the other observations in the same series.

Since one of the basic concepts in statistical inference is the randomness of the observations, Young chooses to deal with the autocorrelation problem first. He adopts the first difference method to minimize the interdependence among the observations in each of the time series. The 10 independent variables are now measured by the difference between the periods rather than by the absolute value of each period. So that the sets of data can be distinguished, a new designation for the independent variables is used.

ΔX_2, change in total employment

ΔX_3, change in manufacturing employment

ΔX_4, change in construction employment

ΔX_5, change in wholesale and retail trade employment

ΔX_6, change in service employment

ΔX_7, change in bank debits

ΔX_8, change in demand deposits

ΔX_9, change in building permits issued

ΔX_{10}, change in real estate mortgages

ΔX_{11}, change in total electricity consumption

The regression equation becomes

$$\Delta Y_R = b_0 + b_2 \Delta X_2 + b_3 \Delta X_3 + \cdots + b_{11} \Delta X_{11}$$

where

ΔY = change in personal income

b_0 = Y intercept

$b_2, b_3, \ldots, b_{11}$ = regression coefficients of respective independent variables

A regression run using this equation, based on the first difference data, produces a Durbin-Watson statistic of 1.71. It indicates that no serious autocorrelation remains.

The next step is to determine which of the 10 variables are significant predictors of the dependent variable. A variety of possible combinations of the 10 are regressed against the Y in order to select the best equation. The criteria used in the selection are as follows:

A satisfactorily high corrected R^2

Low correlation coefficients among the independent variables

Each of the independent variable's regression coefficient being significant at the .05 level

After careful scrutiny of the regression results, Young finds that the equation that contains ΔX_5, ΔX_6, and ΔX_{11} as independent variables best meets the above criteria.

However, Young reasons that (in addition to commercial and industrial uses) total electricity consumption includes residential consumption, which should not have a significant relation to business activity in the near term. To test this hypothesis, Young subdivides the total electricity consumption into four variables: ΔX_{12}, change in residential electricity use; ΔX_{13}, change in commercial electricity use; ΔX_{14}, change in industrial electricity use; and ΔX_{15}, change in commercial and industrial use. Each of these four variables, combined with ΔX_5 and ΔX_6, are used to produce the four new regression equations (see Table 9.10).

TABLE 9.10 Young's Regression Equations and Variables.

Equation	Independent Variables	Dependent Variable
A	$\Delta X_5, \Delta X_6, \Delta X_{12}$	ΔY
B	$\Delta X_5, \Delta X_6, \Delta X_{13}$	ΔY
C	$\Delta X_5, \Delta X_6, \Delta X_{14}$	ΔY
D	$\Delta X_5, \Delta X_6, \Delta X_{15}$	ΔY

Statistical analysis indicates that equation D is the best. As compared with the earlier equation that contains ΔX_5, ΔX_6, and ΔX_{11} as independent variables, equation A is the only one that shows a deterioration in statistical significance. This result confirms Young's notion that commercial and industrial electricity use are better predictors of personal income than total electricity use, which includes residential electricity use.

Therefore, equation D is selected as the final regression equation, and the results are

$$\Delta Y = -1.86 + 17.10\,\Delta X_5 + 23.01\,\Delta X_6 + .007\,\Delta X_{15}$$
$$ (4.07) \qquad (56.1) \qquad\; (.002)$$

$$N = 15 \qquad R_C^2 = .835$$

$$DW = 1.769 \qquad F = 26.26$$

The figures in parentheses below the regression coefficients are the standard errors of estimation of the coefficients, all significant at the .05 level. The t values of the coefficients are 4.10, 4.20, and 2.97 for ΔX_5, ΔX_6, and ΔX_{15}, respectively. The R_C^2 indicates that nearly 84% of the variance in change in personal income is explained by the three independent variables. The DW statistic shows that autocorrelation is not a problem. In addition, the correlation coefficient matrix of Table 9.11 demonstrates a low level of interdependence among the three independent variables.

For index construction purposes the independent variables in the final regression equation become the index components. The weights of the components can be determined from the regression coefficients. (Recall that the regression coefficient represents the average change in the dependent variable for a one-unit increase in the independent variable.) However, since the variables in the regres-

TABLE 9.11 Correlation Coefficient Matrix.

	ΔX_5	ΔX_6	ΔX_{15}
ΔX_5	1.000	.452	.113
ΔX_6	.452	1.000	.122
ΔX_{15}	.113	.122	1.000

sion equation do not have the same unit of measurement (for example, ΔY is measured in thousands of dollars and ΔX_{15} in thousands of kilowatt-hours), the regression coefficients must be transformed into relative terms. This transformation is accomplished by computing their β coefficients.

$$\beta = b\left(\frac{s}{s_y}\right) \tag{9.13}$$

where

$\quad b$ = the independent variable's regression coefficient

$\quad s$ = the independent variable's standard deviation

$\quad s_y$ = the dependent variable's standard deviation

The values of all these statistics are typically available from the regression computer output. Hence the standardized coefficients of the three independent variables are

$$\beta_5 = .4959 \qquad \frac{.4959}{1.2811} = .3871$$

$$\beta_6 = .4833 \qquad \frac{.4833}{1.2811} = .3772$$

$$\beta_{15} = \underline{.3019} \qquad \frac{.3019}{1.2811} = .2357$$

$$\text{Total} \quad 1.2811$$

Finally, because the sum of the weights in an index must be 100%, the standardized coefficients are normalized.

Component	Weight
ΔX_5	.3871
ΔX_6	.3772
ΔX_{15}	.2357
Total	1.0000

After the components and their respective weights have been determined, the index can be obtained by the following steps:

Step 1. Compute the percentage change of each component since the base period.

Step 2. Multiply the percentage change by the appropriate weight.

Step 3. Sum the weighted percentage changes obtained in Step 2.

The completed Spokane County activity index is compared with the U.S. GNP, in constant dollars (1967 = 100), in Figure 9.4.

FIGURE 9.4 Spokane County Business Activity Index and U.S. GNP, in Constant Dollars (1967 = 100).

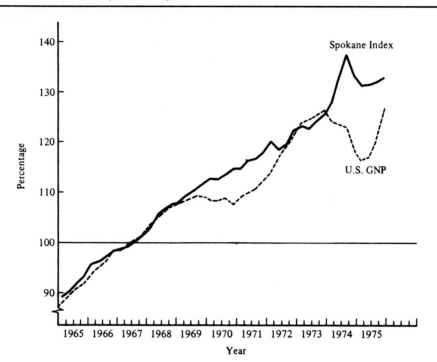

QUESTIONS

1. Young chose to solve the autocorrelation problem first. Would it have been better to eliminate multicollinearity first and then tackle autocorrelation?

2. How does the small sample size affect the analysis?

3. Should the regression done on the first differences have been through the origin?

4. Is there any potential for the use of lagged data?

5. What conclusions can be drawn from a comparison of the Spokane County business activity index and the GNP?

TSP EXAMPLE

A statistical package frequently used by economists that runs on both mainframe and microcomputers is TSP. TSP allows the user to run many techniques commonly used in the econometrics area.

TSP will be demonstrated in this section to illustrate the use of statistical software packages for solving a serial correlation problem using the Cochrane-Orcutt method.

THE PROBLEM

In Example 9.7 disposable personal income was used to predict Sears sales. Serial correlation was a problem, so the Cochrane-Orcutt method was used to provide a valid model.

The TSP Solution

The command file to run the data of Example 9.7 (see your instructor about the information you need to run TSP on your particular computer system) is

```
         PROGRAM
LINE ****************************************************************
    1    NAME SEARS 'SEARS';
    1    FREQ A;
    2    SMPL 1,21;
    3    LOAD SALES;
    3    3.307, 3.556, 3.601, 3.721, 4.036, 4.134, 4.268, 4.578, 5.093,
    3    5.716, 6.357, 6.769, 7.296, 8.178, 8.844, 9.251, 10.006, 11.2,
    3    12.5, 13.101, 13.640;
    4    LOAD INCOME;
    4    273.4, 291.3, 306.9, 317.1, 336.1, 349.4, 362.9, 383.9, 402.8,
    4    437, 472.2, 510.4, 544.5, 588.1, 630.4, 685.9, 742.8, 801.3,
    4    903.1, 983.6, 1076.7;
    5    AR1 (PRINT, METHOD=CORC) SALES C INCOME;
    6    END;
                          EXECUTION
****************************************************************************
```

After execution, the TSP output for the Sears sales data is as follows:

```
         EQUATION   1
         ************
         FIRST-ORDER SERIAL CORRELATION OF THE ERROR
         COCHRANE-ORCUTT ITERATIVE TECHNIQUE
    MEAN OF DEPENDENT VARIABLE =       7.29225
            STANDARD DEVIATION =       3.37732
    DEPENDENT VARIABLE: SALES

                                       OPTIONS FOR THIS ROUTINE
                                       ************************
    FAIR     = TRUE        MAXIT  = 20            METHOD  = CORC
    PRINT    = TRUE        RMAX   = 0.90000       RMIN    = -0.90000
    RSTART   = 0           RSTEP  = 0.10000       TOL     = 0.00500
    TSCS     = FALSE       UNNORM = FALSE         WEIGHT  =
        INITIAL ESTIMATE
          SSR =    2.2419
          PARAMETER ESTIMATES:
    -.5243     0.1405E-01
    CONVERGENCE ACHIEVED AFTER    7 ITERATIONS

    ITERATION          RHO           STD ERROR OF EQN
    *********          ***           ****************
         1           0.815355          0.248105
         2           0.870710          0.244495
         3           0.897917          0.242975
         4           0.913437          0.242195
         5           0.923445          0.241729
         6           0.930504          0.241421
         7           0.935808          0.241201
         FINAL VALUE OF RHO =    0.935808
    STANDARD ERROR OF RHO =    0.788240E-01
       T-STATISTIC FOR RHO =   11.8721
```

continues

Continued

```
                    STATISTICS BASED ON RHO-TRANSFORMED VARIABLES
                    ********************************************
                    SUM OF SQUARED RESIDUALS =       1.04720
              STANDARD ERROR OF THE REGRESSION =     0.241201
                    MEAN OF DEPENDENT VARIABLE =     0.951593
                           STANDARD DEVIATION =      0.499369
                                    R-SQUARED =      0.778978
                           ADJUSTED R-SQUARED =      0.766699
              F-STATISTIC(    1,     18) =            63.4400
    DURBIN-WATSON STATISTIC (ADJ. FOR  0 GAPS) =      1.0813
                       NUMBER OF OBSERVATIONS =      20
                                    ESTIMATED         STANDARD
         VARIABLE                   COEFFICIENT         ERROR        T-STATISTIC
         C                           2.340258        1.778342        1.315977
         INCOME                      0.1093294E-01   0.1372636E-02   7.964924
```

CHAPTER **9**

SELECTED BIBLIOGRAPHY

Cochrane, D., and Orcutt, G. N. "Application of Least Squares to Relationships Containing Autocorrelated Error Terms." *Journal of the American Statistical Association* 44 (1949): 32–61.

Durbin, J., and Watson, G. S. "Testing for Serial Correlation in Least-Squares Regression II." *Biometrika* 38 (1951): 159–178.

Johnston, J. *Econometric Methods,* 2nd ed. New York: McGraw-Hill, 1972.

King, J. L., and Bessler, D. A. "A Comparison of Multivariate Forecasting Procedures for Economic Time Series." *International Journal of Forecasting* 1 (1) (1985): 5–24.

Lesser, C. E. V. "A Survey of Econometrics." *Journal of the Royal Statistical Society,* Series A, 34 (1968): 530–566.

Makridakis, S., Wheelwright, S. C., and McGee, V. E. *Forecasting: Methods and Applications.* New York: John Wiley & Sons, 1983.

Pindyck, R. S., and Rubinfeld, D. L. *Econometric Models and Economic Forecasts.* New York: McGraw-Hill, 1976, pp. 108–113.

Young, R. M. "Forecasting with an Econometric Model: The Issue of Judgemental Adjustment." *Journal of Forecasting* 1 (2) (1982): 189–204.

The Box-Jenkins (ARIMA) Methodology

T he exponential smoothing (Chapter 5), correlation and regression analysis (Chapters 6–7), and time series analysis decomposition (Chapter 8) approaches to forecasting assume that the values of a series being forecast are statistically independent of or not related to each other. In Chapters 6 and 7 linear regression equations were used to forecast the dependent variable by substituting values of the independent variable(s) into the regression equation and calculating a predicted value for Y.

This chapter deals with a class of models that can produce forecasts based on a synthesis of historical patterns in data. Autoregressive integrated moving-average (ARIMA) models are a specialized class of linear filtering techniques that completely ignore independent variables in making forecasts. ARIMA is a highly refined curve-fitting device that uses current and past values of the dependent variable to produce accurate short-term forecasts. An example of such forecasts is stock market price predictions created by brokerage analysts that are based entirely on past patterns of movement of the stock prices.

The ARIMA methodology is appropriate if the observations of a time series are statistically dependent on or related to each other. This chapter discusses analysis and the Box-Jenkins methods.

BOX-JENKINS TECHNIQUE

The *Box-Jenkins method* of forecasting is different from most methods. This technique does *not* assume any particular pattern in the historical data of the series to be forecast. It uses an iterative approach of identifying a possible useful model from a general class of models. The chosen model is then checked against the historical data to see whether it accurately describes the series. The model fits well if the residuals between the forecasting model and the historical data points are small, randomly distributed, and independent. If the specified model is *not* satisfactory, the process is repeated by using another model designed to improve on the original one. This process is repeated until a satisfactory model is found. Figure 10.1 illustrates the approach.

FIGURE 10.1 Flow Diagram of Box-Jenkins Method.

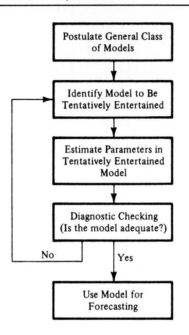

Source: G. P. Box and G. M. Jenkins, *Time Series Analysis Forecasting and Control* (San Francisco: Holden-Day, 1970), p. 19. Reprinted with permission.

A general class of Box-Jenkins models for a stationary time series is the ARIMA, or autoregressive integrated moving-average, models. Remember that a stationary time series is one whose average value is not changing over time. This group of models includes the AR models with only autoregressive terms, the MA models with only moving-average terms, and the ARIMA models with both autoregressive and moving-average terms. The Box-Jenkins methodology allows the analyst to select the model that best fits the data.

Selection of an appropriate model can be made by comparing the distributions of autocorrelation coefficients of the time series being fitted with the theoretical distributions for the various models. Theoretical distributions for the autocorrelation coefficients for some of the more common ARIMA models are shown in Figures 10.2, 10.3, and 10.4.

> The *Box-Jenkins techniques* apply autoregressive and moving-average methods to time series forecasting problems.

FIGURE 10.2 Autocorrelation and Partial Autocorrelation Coefficients of AR(1) and AR(2) Models.

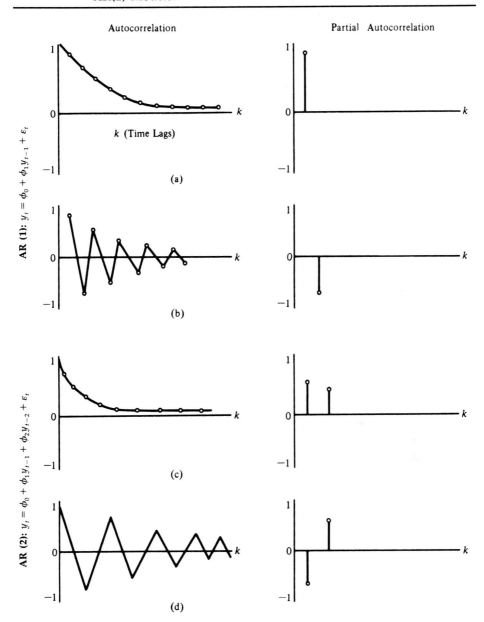

In selecting a model, remember that the distributions shown are theoretical distributions and that it is highly unlikely that the autocorrelations of actual data will be exactly identical to any of the theoretical

FIGURE 10.3 Autocorrelation and Partial Autocorrelation Coefficients of MA(1) and MA(2) Models.

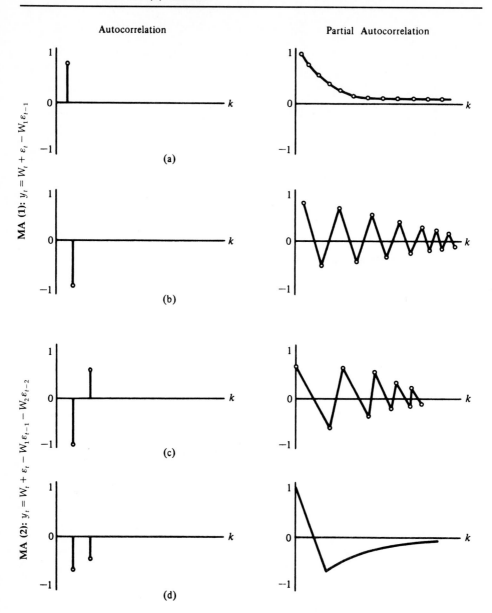

distributions. However, you should be able to adequately match most time series data through trial and error, and as you gain experience, the task becomes much easier.

FIGURE 10.4 Autocorrelation and Partial Autocorrelation Coefficients of a Mixed ARIMA(1, 1) Model.

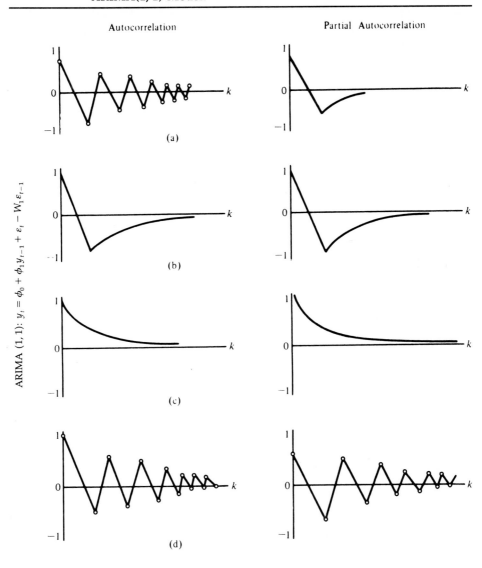

PARTIAL AUTOCORRELATIONS

Initially, the analyst may not be aware of the appropriate order of the autoregressive process to fit to a time series. This same type of problem was faced when deciding on the number of independent variables to include in a multiple regression model. *Partial autocorrelations* are used to help identify an appropriate ARIMA model for forecasting. They allow the analyst to identify the degree of relationship between current values of a variable and earlier values of the same variable, while holding the effects of all other variables (time lags) constant.

A discussion of the derivation of partial autocorrelations is beyond the scope of this text.[1] Instead, this section will concentrate on the fairly mechanical manner in which they are applied to each group of models.

Autoregressive Model

An autoregressive model takes the form

$$y_t = \phi_0 + \phi_1 y_{t-1} + \phi_2 y_{t-2} + \cdots + \phi_p y_{t-p} + \varepsilon_t \qquad (10.1)$$

where

y_t = dependent variable

$y_{t-1}, y_{t-2}, y_{t-p}$ = independent variables that are dependent variables lagged specific time periods

$\phi_0, \phi_1, \phi_2, \phi_p$ = regression coefficients

ε_t = residual term that represents random events not explained by model

Equation 9.4 introduced autoregressive models. However, Equation 10.1 differs in several important ways. In Equation 9.4 the regression coefficients are estimated by using the linear least squares method. In Equation 10.1 the regression coefficients are found by using a nonlinear least squares method.

The nonlinear least squares method generally uses an iterative solution technique to calculate the parameters rather than using direct computation. Preliminary estimates are used as starting points; then these estimates are systematically improved until optimal values are found. Furthermore, the variance for Equation 10.1 is calculated in a different manner that takes into account the fact that the independent variables are correlated with each other. Finally, Equation 10.1 may or may not contain a constant term. No constant term is used when the dependent variable values (the ys) are expressed as deviations from their mean ($y' = y - \bar{y}$).

Figure 10.2 shows the equations of an AR model of order 1, AR(1) model, and an AR model of order 2, AR(2) model. Terms can be added to represent an AR(p) model, where p is the number of past observations to be included in the forecast of the next period. Figures 10.2(a) and (b) illustrate the behavior of the theoretical autocorrelation and partial autocorrelation functions for an AR(1) model. Notice how differently the autocorrelation and partial autocorrelation functions behave. The autocorrela-

---

[1] For a discussion of partial autocorrelations, refer to G. Box and G. Jenkins, *Time Series Analysis: Forecasting and Control* (San Francisco: Holden-Day, 1976).

tion coefficients trail off to zero gradually, while the partial autocorrelation coefficients drop to zero after the first time lag. Figures 10.2(c) and (d) show an AR(2) model. Again, the autocorrelation coefficients trail off to zero, while the partial autocorrelation coefficients drop to zero after the second time lag. This type of pattern will generally hold for any AR(p) model. However, it must be remembered that sample autocorrelation functions are going to differ from these theoretical functions because of sampling variation.

EXAMPLE 10.1

■ An example of the use of an AR(2) model for forecasting is shown in Table 10.1. Assume that sales are shown for the last five periods of a series containing 100 observations. The AR(2) model is chosen, and the Box-Jenkins computer program computes regression coefficients of $B_1 = .59$ and $B_2 = .40$. The forecast for period T_t without using a constant in the equation is

$$\hat{y}_t = \phi_1 y_{t-1} + \phi_2 y_{t-2}$$
$$= .59(250) + .40(240) = 243.5$$ ■

Unfortunately, not all data series can be handled with autoregressive models. For this reason the Box-Jenkins approach also considers the moving-average (MA) model.

TABLE 10.1 Forecasting with an Autoregressive Model: Example 10.1.

Period	Values	Forecast Values	Residual ε_t
$t-5$	240	238.3	1.7
$t-4$	230	240.1	-10.1
$t-3$	225	231.7	-6.7
$t-2$	240	224.8	$+15.2$
$t-1$	250	231.6	$+18.4$
t		243.5	

Moving-Average Models

A moving-average model takes the form

$$\hat{y}_t = w_0 + \varepsilon_t - w_1\varepsilon_{t-1} - w_2\varepsilon_{t-2} + \cdots + w_q\varepsilon_{t-q} \tag{10.2}$$

where

y_t = dependent variable
w_0, w_1, w_2, w_q = weights

ε_t = residual or error

$\varepsilon_{t-1}, \varepsilon_{t-2}, \varepsilon_{t-q}$ = previous values of residuals

Equation 10.2 is similar to Equation 10.1 except that the dependent variable y_t depends on previous values of the residuals rather than on the variable itself. Moving-average (MA) models provide forecasts of y_t based on a linear combination of past errors, whereas autoregressive (AR) models express y_t as a linear function of some number of actual past values of y_t. It is customary to show the weights with negative coefficients, even though the weights can be either positive or negative. The sum of $w_1 + w_2 + \cdots + w_q$ does not need to equal 1, and the values of w_1 are *not* "moving" with new observations, as they are with the moving-average computation in Chapter 5. Note that the average level μ of an MA(q) series is equal to the constant term, w_0, in the model since $E(\varepsilon_t) = 0$ for all values of t. The name *moving average* may seem misleading since the model is actually similar to exponential smoothing.

Figure 10.3 shows the equations of an MA model of order 1, MA(1) model, and an MA(2) model. Terms can be added to represent an MA(q) model, where q is the number of past error terms to be included in the forecast of the next period. Figures 10.3(a) and (b) also illustrate the behavior of the theoretical autocorrelation coefficients of the MA(1) model. Note how fortunate it is that the autocorrelation and partial autocorrelation functions of AR and MA models behave very differently. The autocorrelation coefficients for the MA(1) model drop to zero after the first time lag, while the partial autocorrelation coefficients trail off to zero gradually. Furthermore, the autocorrelation coefficients for the MA(2) model will drop to zero after the second time lag, while the partials trail off gradually [see Figures 10.3(c) and (d)]. Again, it must be mentioned that sample autocorrelation functions are going to differ from these theoretical functions because of sampling variation.

EXAMPLE 10.2

■ An example of the use of an MA(2) model for forecasting is shown by using the error terms presented in Table 10.1. If the Box-Jenkins program computes the values of w as $w_1 = -.9$ and $w_2 = .35$, then

$$\hat{y}_t = w_0 - w_1 \varepsilon_{t-1} - w_2 \varepsilon_{t-2}$$
$$= 237 - (-.9)(18.4) - (.35)(15.2) = 248.2 \qquad ■$$

Autoregressive Moving-Average Models

In addition to AR and MA models, the two can be mixed, providing a third class of general models called ARIMA. Equations 10.1 and 10.2 are combined, forming

$$y_t = \phi_0 + \phi_1 y_{t-1} + \phi_z y_{t-2} + \cdots + \phi_p y_{t-p} + \varepsilon_t - w_1 \varepsilon_{t-1}$$
$$- w_2 \varepsilon_{t-2} - \cdots - w_q \varepsilon_{t-q} \qquad\qquad\qquad (10.3)$$

ARIMA (p, q) models use combinations of past values and past errors and offer a potential for fitting models that could not be adequately fitted by using an AR or an MA model separately.

Figure 10.4 shows the equation of an ARIMA(1,1) model and the behavior of the theoretical autocorrelation and partial autocorrelation coefficients.

A significant difference between the Box-Jenkins methodology and previous methods is that Box-Jenkins does not make assumptions about the number of terms or the relative weights to be assigned to the terms. The analyst selects the appropriate model, including the number of terms; then the program calculates the coefficients, using a nonlinear least squares method. Forecasts for future periods can then be made, and confidence intervals can be constructed for these estimates.

APPLYING THE METHODOLOGY

As shown in Figure 10.1, the Box-Jenkins approach involves three separate stages. These stages are model identification, model estimation and testing, and model application.

Stage 1: Model Identification

1. The first step in model identification is to determine whether the series is stationary, that is, whether the mean value is changing over time.

If the series is not stationary, it can generally be converted to a stationary series by the method of differencing. The analyst specifies the degree of differencing, and the Box-Jenkins algorithm converts the data into a stationary series and then performs subsequent computations by using the converted data.

2. Once a stationary series has been obtained, the analyst must identify the form of the model to be used.

This step is accomplished by comparing the autocorrelation and partial-autocorrelation coefficients of the data to be fitted with the corresponding distributions for the various ARIMA models. The theoretical distributions for some of the more common ARIMA models are shown in Figures 10.2, 10.3, and 10.4 for help in selecting an appropriate model.

As can be seen, each model has a unique set of autocorrelations and partial autocorrelations, and the analyst should be able to match the corresponding coefficients of the data to one of the theoretical distributions.

Although it generally will not be possible to match data exactly with the theoretical distributions, tests can be done during stage 2 to determine whether the model is adequate. Then an alternative model can be tried if the first model is unsatisfactory. After a little practice, the analyst should become more adept at identifying an adequate model.

In general, the analyst should identify the autocorrelations that drop off exponentially to zero. If the autocorrelations trail off exponentially to zero, an AR process is indicated; if the partial autocorrelations trail off, an MA process is indicated; and if both trail off, a mixed ARIMA process is indicated. By counting the number of autocorrelation and partial autocorrelation coefficients that are significantly different from zero, the analyst can determine the order of the MA and/or AR processes.

Stage 2: Model Estimation and Testing of Model Adequacy

1. Once a tentative model has been selected, the parameters for that model must be estimated.

    For example, suppose an ARIMA(1, 1) model has been selected. The mathematical form and forecast formula for the model are, respectively,

    $$y_t = \phi_0 + \phi_1 y_{t-1} + \varepsilon_t - w_1 \varepsilon_{t-1}$$

    and

    $$\hat{y} = \phi_0 + \phi_1 y_{t-1} - w_1 \varepsilon_{t-1}$$

    To use the forecast equation, the analyst must calculate values for ϕ_1 and w_1. These calculations are done by the Box-Jenkins computer program, using the minimum mean squared error as the criterion for selecting the optimal values.

    Assume that values for ϕ_1 and w_1 have been computed to be .25 and .5. The tentative forecast model is now

    $$\hat{y}_t = .25y_{t-1} - .5\varepsilon_{t-1}$$

2. Before using the model for forecasting, the analyst much check it for adequacy.

This step is done by checking the error terms, $\varepsilon_t = y_t - \hat{y}_t$, to be sure they are random. This check can be done by checking the autocorrelations of the error terms to be sure they are not significantly different from zero. If a few low-order or seasonal lags are significantly different from zero, then the model is inadequate. The analyst should return to stage 1, step 2, select an alternative model, and then continue the analysis.

The model can also be checked for adequacy by doing a chi-square (χ^2) test, known as the Box-Pierce Q statistic, on the autocorrelations of the residuals. The test statistic is

$$Q = (N - d) \sum_{k=1}^{m} r_k^2 \qquad (10.4)$$

which is approximately distributed as a chi-square distribution with $k - p - q$ degrees of freedom. In this equation

N = length of time series

k = first k autocorrelations being checked

m = maximum number of lags checked

r_k = sample autocorrelation function of the kth residual term

d = degree of differencing to obtain a stationary series

If the calculated value of Q is larger than the χ^2 for $k - p - q$ degrees of freedom, then the model should be considered inadequate. The analyst should return to stage 1, step 2, select an alternative model, and continue the analysis until a satisfactory model has been found.

Neither of these two tests for adequacy should be considered the final word, but they should generally be used together, along with considerable judgment on the analyst's part. If some large deviations can be adequately explained by unusual circumstances, for example, these deviations may be ignored if the rest of the model is deemed adequate.

It is possible that two or more models may be judged to be approximately equal, yet none of the models may be an exact fit for the data. In this case the principle of parsimony should prevail, and the simpler model should be chosen.

Stage 3: Forecasting with the Model

1. Once an adequate model has been found, forecasts for one period or several periods into the future can be made.

Confidence intervals can also be constructed about these estimates. In general, the further into the future the forecast is, the larger the confidence interval will be. These forecasts and confidence intervals are computed by the Box-Jenkins program at the analyst's request.

2. As more data become available, the same model can be used to revise forecasts by choosing another time origin.

3. If the series appears to be changing over time, the model parameters may need to be recalculated, or an entirely new model may have to be developed.

If small differences in forecast errors are noticed, they may indicate that the parameters need to be recalculated, and the analyst should return to stage 2, step 1. When large differences are noticed in the size of the forecast errors, they may indicate that an entirely new model is needed, and the analyst should return to stage 1, step 2, or even stage 1, step 1, and repeat the process of fitting a new model to the time series.

EXAMPLE 10.3

■ The Cameron Consulting Corporation specializes in portfolio investment services. Lynn Stephens, the company analyst, was assigned the task of developing more sophisticated techniques for forecasting Dow-Jones averages. Lynn had recently attended a workshop on Box-Jenkins methodology and decided to try the technique on the Transportation Index. Table 10.2 represents 55 daily closing averages of the Transportation Index during the summer months of 1978.

FIGURE 10.5 Daily Closing Averages of the Transportation Index, Summer 1978.

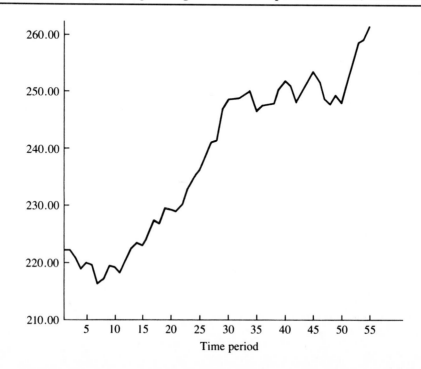

TABLE 10.2 Daily Closing Averages of the Transportation Index, Summer 1978.

Time Period	Closing Average	Time Period	Closing Average	Time Period	Closing Average	Time Period	Closing Average
1	222.34	15	223.07	29	246.74	43	249.76
2	222.24	16	225.36	30	248.73	44	251.66
3	222.17	17	227.60	31	248.83	45	253.41
4	218.88	18	226.82	32	248.78	46	252.04
5	220.05	19	229.69	33	249.61	47	248.78
6	219.61	20	229.30	34	249.90	48	247.76
7	216.40	21	228.96	35	246.45	49	249.27
8	217.33	22	229.99	36	247.57	50	247.95
9	219.69	23	233.05	37	247.76	51	251.41
10	219.32	24	235.00	38	247.81	52	254.67
11	218.25	25	236.17	39	250.68	53	258.62
12	220.30	26	238.31	40	251.80	54	259.25
13	222.54	27	241.14	41	251.07	55	261.49
14	223.56	28	241.48	42	248.05		

FIGURE 10.6 Autocorrelations of Raw Data from Table 10.2.

Time Lags		Autocorrelations
24		−.23
23		−.19
22		−.15
21		−.10
20		−.05
19		−.01
18		.04
17		.09
16		.15
15		.22
14		.28
13		.33
12		.38
11		.44
10		.51
9		.56
8		.61
7		.66
6		.71
5		.75
4		.80
3		.85
2		.90
1		.95

Lynn began the analysis by looking at a plot of the data shown in Figure 10.5. There appeared to be a trend in the data. Her first step in identifying a tentative model was to look at the autocorrelations of the data shown in Figure 10.6. When Lynn observed that the first 12 autocorrelations appeared to be trailing off to zero, she recognized that her original observation was correct and that these data points did have a trend and should be differenced. Lynn took the upward tendency in the data into account by applying nonseasonal differencing.

The plot of the autocorrelations of the differenced series presented in Figure 10.7 showed that the data were stationary. However, no pattern appears to exist. An examination of the partial autocorrelations confirms the absence of a pattern. Evidently, only a trend exists in the Transportation Index data. Box-Jenkins methodology can be used to model the data; however, other methods would be less costly and possibly more accurate. ■

The following notation is frequently used with Box-Jenkins techniques. A model is identified as ARIMA(p, d, q), where p is the order for

FIGURE 10.7 Autocorrelations of Nonseasonal Differenced Data from Table 10.2.

Time Lags		Autocorrelations
24	• | * •	.06
23	• * | •	−.15
22	• * | •	−.08
21	• * | •	−.10
20	• * | •	−.09
19	* | •	−.25
18	* | •	−.27
17	• *| •	−.06
16	• * | •	−.09
15	• * •	.02
14	• | * •	.09
13	• * •	−.01
12	• *| •	−.04
11	• *| •	−.04
10	• | * •	.07
9	• * | •	−.20
8	• * | •	−.09
7	• | * •	.11
6	• * | •	−.09
5	• * | •	−.11
4	• | * •	.14
3	• | * •	.09
2	• *| •	−.04
1	• | * •	.19

```
  | | | | | | | | | | | | | | | | | | | | | |
 -1                  0                  +1
```

the autoregressive term, d is the level of differencing, and q is the order for the moving average term. Actually, when no differencing takes place, the appropriate model is ARMA(p, q). The appropriate model for the Transportation Index data might have zero-order autoregressive and moving-average terms and first differenced data: ARIMA(0, 1, 0).

The estimate of the overall constant is .725. Examination of the residual autocorrelation function showed the model to be adequate. Lynn confirmed this observation by testing the chi-square statistic. The calculated chi-square value is smaller than the value from the table for 17 degrees of freedom at the .05 significance level ($17.06 < 27.6$).

Normally the ys are expressed as deviations from their mean ($y' = y - \bar{y}$); however, when a constant term is used, the actual Y values are modeled.

The forecasting model with a constant term is

$$\hat{y}_t = .725 + y_{t-1}$$

The forecasts for periods 56 and 57 are

$$\hat{y}_{56} = .725 + 261.49$$

$$\hat{y}_{56} = 262.22$$

and

$$\hat{y}_{57} = .725 + 262.22$$

$$\hat{y}_{57} = 262.94$$

Note that the forecast is increasing by .725 each time period.

Lynn decided that the marginally high autocorrelation (.19) at lag 1 in Figure 10.7 indicated the need to try an ARIMA(0, 1, 1) model. Note that in Box-Jenkins methodology the simplest model is always run first. Again, examination of the residual autocorrelation function showed the model to be adequate. Lynn again tested the chi-square statistic. The calculated chi-square value is smaller than the tabulated value for 15 degrees of freedom at the .05 significance level ($13.8 < 25.0$).

The Minitab commands to solve this example are as follows:

```
MTB > READ 'TRANS1.DAT' C1
     55 ROWS READ

C1
   222.34    222.24    221.17    218.88     .    .    .
```

continues

Continued

```
MTB > ACF C1  *1

ACF of C1
                 -1.0 -0.8 -0.6 -0.4 -0.2  0.0  0.2  0.4  0.6  0.8  1.0
                  +----+----+----+----+----+----+----+----+----+----+
     1    0.951                            XXXXXXXXXXXXXXXXXXXXXXXXXX
     2    0.900                            XXXXXXXXXXXXXXXXXXXXXXXXX
     3    0.847                            XXXXXXXXXXXXXXXXXXXXXXXX
     4    0.795                            XXXXXXXXXXXXXXXXXXXXXXX
     5    0.748                            XXXXXXXXXXXXXXXXXXXXX
     6    0.707                            XXXXXXXXXXXXXXXXXXXX
     7    0.658                            XXXXXXXXXXXXXXXXXX
     8    0.609                            XXXXXXXXXXXXXXXXX
     9    0.561                            XXXXXXXXXXXXXXXX
    10    0.505                            XXXXXXXXXXXXXX
    11    0.440                            XXXXXXXXXXXX
    12    0.381                            XXXXXXXXXXX
    13    0.328                            XXXXXXXXX
    14    0.277                            XXXXXXXX
    15    0.215                            XXXXX
    16    0.152                            XXXXX
    17    0.093                            XXX

MTB > DIFFERENCE C1, STORE IN C2  *2
```

*1 Command **acf** computes the autocorrelation coefficients for
   the transportation data in **c1**
*2 Command **differences** takes the first differences of the **c1**
   column and stores them in **c2**

```
MTB > PRINT C1-C2

    ROW        C1          C2

     1      222.34           *
     2      222.24     -0.09999
     3      221.17     -1.07001
     4      218.88     -2.28999
     5      220.05      1.17000
     6      219.61     -0.44000
     7      216.40     -3.21001
     8      217.33      0.93001
     9      219.69      2.36000
    10      219.32     -0.37000
    11      218.25     -1.07001
    12      220.30      2.05000
    13      222.54      2.23999
    14      223.56      1.02000
    15      223.07     -0.48999
    16      225.36      2.28999
    17      227.60      2.24001
    18      226.82     -0.78000
    19      229.69      2.87000
    20      229.30     -0.39000
    21      228.96     -0.34000
    22      229.99      1.03000
    23      233.05      3.06000
    24      235.00      1.95000
```

```
        25     236.17     1.17000
        26     238.31     2.14000
        27     241.14     2.83000
        28     241.48     0.34000
        29     246.74     5.26001
        30     248.73     1.98999
        31     248.83     0.10001
        32     248.78    -0.05000
        33     249.61     0.83000
        34     249.90     0.28999
        35     246.45    -3.45000
        36     247.57     1.12001
        37     247.76     0.18999
        38     247.81     0.05000
        39     250.68     2.87000
        40     251.80     1.12001
        41     251.07    -0.73000
        42     248.05    -3.02000
        43     249.76     1.70999
        44     251.66     1.90001
        45     253.41     1.75000
        46     252.04    -1.37001
        47     248.78    -3.25999
        48     247.76    -1.02000
        49     249.27     1.51001
        50     247.95    -1.32001
        51     251.41     3.46001
        52     254.67     3.25999
        53     258.62     3.95000
        54     259.25     0.63000
        55     261.49     2.23999
```

MTB > ACF C2 *3

ACF of C2

```
           -1.0 -0.8 -0.6 -0.4 -0.2  0.0  0.2  0.4  0.6  0.8  1.0
            +----+----+----+----+----+----+----+----+----+----+
    1    0.185                          XXXXXX
    2   -0.044                        XX
    3    0.093                          XXX
    4    0.136                          XXXX
    5   -0.110                      XXXX
    6   -0.095                       XXX
    7    0.110                          XXXX
    8   -0.088                       XXX
    9   -0.196                    XXXXXX
   10    0.069                          XXX
   11   -0.042                        XX
   12   -0.044                        XX
   13   -0.009                         X
   14    0.095                          XXX
   15    0.025                         XX
   16   -0.086                       XXX
   17   -0.056                        XX
```

MTB > PACF C2 *4

continues

Continued

```
PACF of C2

              -1.0 -0.8 -0.6 -0.4 -0.2  0.0  0.2  0.4  0.6  0.8  1.0
              +----+----+----+----+----+----+----+----+----+----+
   1   0.185                            XXXXXX
   2  -0.081                          XXX
   3   0.121                            XXXX
   4   0.094                            XXX
   5  -0.151                        XXXXX
   6  -0.038                          XX
   7   0.108                            XXXX
   8  -0.148                        XXXXX
   9  -0.104                        XXXX
  10   0.125                            XXXX
  11  -0.149                        XXXXX
  12   0.080                            XXX
  13   0.009                            X
  14   0.006                            X
  15   0.054                            XX
  16  -0.082                          XXX
  17  -0.118                        XXXX
```

*3 Command **acf** computes the autocorrelation coefficients for
   the first differenced data in **c2**
*4 Command **pacf** computes the partial autocorrelation coefficients
   for the first differenced data in **c2**

   Now the appropriate ARIMA model is tried. The previous analysis
indicated that the first difference data was a random walk with an upward
drift. The appropriate Minitab commands are as follows:

```
MTB > ARIMA(0 1 0)C1;  *5
SUBC> CONSTANT;  *6
SUBC> FORECAST 3 DAYS AHEAD STORE IN C3, & CONF LIMITS
CONT>  IN C4 C5.  *7

Estimates at each iteration
Iteration        SSE      Parameters
     0        191.847      0.825
     1        191.308      0.730
     2        191.307      0.725
     3        191.307      0.725

Relative change in each estimate less than  0.0010

Final Estimates of Parameters
```

Type | Estimate | *8 St. Dev. | t-ratio | *9
Constant | 0.7248 | 0.2581 | 2.81 |

```
Differencing: 1 regular difference
No. of obs.:  Original series 55, after differencing 54
Residuals:    SS = 191.307  (backforecasts excluded)

              MS =   3.610    *10  DF = 53
```

```
Modified Box-Pierce chisquare statistic
Lag              12            24              36              48
Chisquare     9.5(DF=12)   27.0(DF=24)    33.7(DF=36)    49.8(DF=48)


Forecasts from period 55
                              95 Percent Limits
   Period      Forecast        Lower          Upper        Actual
     56        262.215        258.490        265.939
     57        262.940        257.672        268.207
     58        263.664        257.213        270.115
```

*5 Command **arima(0 1 0)** runs a model with no ar or ma term
    on the first differenced data
*6 Subcommand **constant** indicates that the model should be
    run with a constant term
*7 Subcommand **forecast** stores 3 forecasts in **c3** and places
    confidence limits in **c4** and **c5**
*8 The output shows that the final estimate of the constant
    parameter is .7248
*9 The output shows that the t ratio for this parameter is 2.81
*10 The output shows that the MSE equals 3.61

Now the first-order moving average model is tried. The Minitab
commands are the following:

```
MTB > ARIMA(0 1 1)C1;
SUBC> CONSTANT.

Estimates at each iteration
Iteration        SSE       Parameters
    0         200.915     0.100      0.825
    1         188.362    -0.050      0.787
    2         183.584    -0.190      0.741
    3         183.383    -0.219      0.731
    4         183.377    -0.224      0.730
    5         183.377    -0.225      0.729
    6         183.377    -0.226      0.730
Relative change in each estimate less than   0.0010

Final Estimates of Parameters
Type        Estimate     St. Dev.   t-ratio
MA    1      -0.2256       0.1366     -1.65
Constant     0.7296       0.3132      2.33

Differencing: 1 regular difference
No. of obs.:  Original series 55, after differencing 54
Residuals:    SS = 183.359  (backforecasts excluded)
              MS =    3.526  DF = 52

Modified Box-Pierce chisquare statistic
Lag              12            24              36              48
Chisquare     9.6(DF=11)   23.7(DF=23)    29.6(DF=35)    42.4(DF=47)
```

Note that the t ratio for the MA(1) term is not significant when tested
at the .01 significance level. For this reason and also because it is simpler,

the model with zero-order autoregressive and moving average terms is considered best.

EXAMPLE 10.4

■ The analyst for Atron Corporation, Jim White, had a time series of readings for a process that needed to be forecast. The data are shown in Table 10.3. The readings are plotted in Figure 10.8. Jim believed that the Box-Jenkins methodology might work best for these data.

TABLE 10.3 Readings for Atron Process.

60.0	99.0	75.0	79.5	61.5	88.5	72.0	90.0
81.0	25.5	78.0	64.5	81.0	51.0	66.0	78.0
72.0	93.0	66.0	99.0	76.5	85.5	73.5	87.0
78.0	75.0	97.5	72.0	84.0	58.5	66.0	99.0
61.5	57.0	60.0	78.0	57.0	90.0	73.5	72.0
78.0	88.5	97.5	63.0	84.0	60.0	103.5	
57.0	76.5	61.5	66.0	73.5	78.0	60.0	
84.0	82.5	96.0	84.0	78.0	66.0	81.0	
72.0	72.0	79.5	66.0	49.5	97.5	87.0	
67.5	76.5	72.0	87.0	78.0	64.5	73.5	

FIGURE 10.8 Readings for Atron Process.

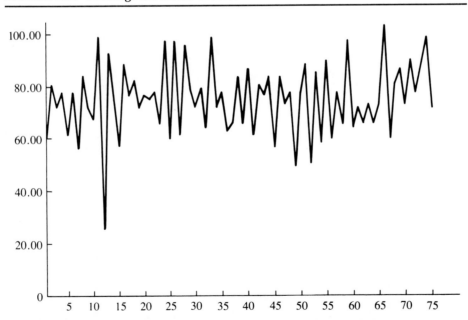

Jim began the first step in identifying a tentative model by looking at the autocorrelations of the data shown in Figure 10.9 to determine whether the series is stationary. The autocorrelations for low lags die down rapidly toward zero, so Jim concluded that the time series is stationary.

The first two sample autocorrelation coefficients ($-.53$ and $.28$) are significant at the 95% level since they lie outside the range.

$$0 \pm 1.96\left(\frac{1}{\sqrt{75}}\right)$$

$$0 \pm 1.96(.115)$$

$$0 \pm .225$$

The sample autocorrelation coefficient at lag 21 ($-.32$) is also significant, but this result is probably due to a ripple occurring in large lags.

FIGURE 10.9 Autocorrelations of Raw Data from Table 10.3.

Time Lags		Autocorrelations
24		.08
23		−.19
22		.20
21		−.32
20		.18
19		−.20
18		.11
17		−.09
16		−.12
15		.22
14		−.23
13		.19
12		−.19
11		.16
10		−.15
9		.07
8		−.04
7		.15
6		−.14
5		.14
4		.01
3		−.04
2		.28
1		−.53

−1   0   +1

FIGURE 10.10 Partial Autocorrelations of Raw Data from Table 10.3.

Time Lags		Autocorrelations
23	• * | •	−.09
22	• *| •	−.07
21	* | •	−.23
20	• * •	−.01
19	• * | •	−.09
18	• *| •	−.06
17	• * | •	−.13
16	• | * •	.04
15	• | * •	.12
14	• * | •	−.14
13	• | * •	.06
12	• * | •	−.14
11	• * •	−.01
10	• * | •	−.18
9	• | * •	.08
8	• | * •	.06
7	• | * •	.03
6	• * •	.00
5	• | * •	.19
4	• | * •	.07
3	• | * •	.15
2	• * •	.00
1	* • | •	−.53

```
  | |  | | |  | | |  | | |  | | |  | | |  | | |
 −1                 0                +1
```

From the sample partial autocorrelation coefficients shown in Figure 10.10, Jim saw that the first is significant, but none of the other partial autocorrelations approach significance.

Two models are suggested by this examination of the autocorrelation coefficients and partial autocorrelation coefficients. The partial at lag 2 is zero (see Figure 10.10). The meaning of this partial is the key to which model will function best. Since the partials at lags 3, 4, and 5 are not close to zero, Jim feels that the partial autocorrelation coefficient of zero at lag 2 probably occurred due to chance sampling error. If the partials are actually trailing off to zero, then an MA(2) model is suggested by the two significant autocorrelation coefficients at lags 1 and 2 in Figure 10.9. However, if the partial autocorrelations have really dropped off to zero at lag 2, then an AR(1) process might be appropriate.

Minitab will be used to analyze the data using both models. Note that, since the dependent variable values have not been expressed as deviations from their mean, a constant term is included in the models. If the data had been differenced, no constant term would be used. The Minitab commands are as follows:

```
MTB > READ 'ATRON.DAT' C1
      75 ROWS READ

C1
    60.0     81.0     72.0     78.0     .    .    .

MTB > ACF C1

ACF of C1

            -1.0 -0.8 -0.6 -0.4 -0.2  0.0  0.2  0.4  0.6  0.8  1.0
            +----+----+----+----+----+----+----+----+----+----+
     1 -0.528              XXXXXXXXXXXXXX
     2  0.282                            XXXXXXX
     3 -0.038                          XX
     4  0.008                          X
     5  0.144                          XXXXX
     6 -0.137                      XXXX
     7  0.147                          XXXXX
     8 -0.036                        XX
     9  0.068                          XXX
    10 -0.150                      XXXXX
    11  0.158                          XXXXX
    12 -0.189                     XXXXXX
    13  0.187                          XXXXXX
    14 -0.234                   XXXXXXX
    15  0.221                          XXXXXXX
    16 -0.120                      XXXX
    17 -0.086                       XXX
    18  0.105                          XXXX

MTB > PACF C1

PACF of C1

            -1.0 -0.8 -0.6 -0.4 -0.2  0.0  0.2  0.4  0.6  0.8  1.0
            +----+----+----+----+----+----+----+----+----+----+
     1 -0.528              XXXXXXXXXXXXXX
     2  0.003                          X
     3  0.155                          XXXXX
     4  0.065                          XXX
     5  0.189                          XXXXXX
     6  0.002                          X
     7  0.026                          XX
     8  0.060                          XXX
     9  0.084                          XXX
    10 -0.184                     XXXXXX
    11 -0.009                         X
    12 -0.143                      XXXXX
    13  0.057                          XX
    14 -0.135                      XXXX
    15  0.123                          XXXX
    16  0.038                          XX
    17 -0.129                      XXXX
    18 -0.055                        XX
```

continues

Continued

The MINITAB commands to try the MA(2) model are

```
MTB > ARIMA(0 0 2)C1;  *1
SUBC> CONSTANT;
SUBC> FORECAST 3 PERIODS AHEAD STORE IN C3, & CONF LIMITS
CONT> IN C4 AND C5
```

```
Estimates at each iteration
Iteration        SSE        Parameters
    7          9786.2    0.567   -0.356   75.410
Relative change in each estimate less than  0.0010
```

Final Estimates of Parameters

Type		Estimate		St. Dev.	t-ratio	
MA	1	0.5667		0.1107	5.12	*3
MA	2	-0.3560	*2	0.1146	-3.11	
Constant		75.410		1.061	71.08	
Mean		75.410		1.061		

```
No. of obs.:  75
Residuals:    SS = 9724.97  (backforecasts excluded)
              MS =  135.07   DF = 72
```

```
Modified Box-Pierce chisquare statistic
Lag              12              24              36              48
Chisquare    7.0(DF=10)    23.8(DF=22)    31.8(DF=34)    46.9(DF=46)
```

```
Forecasts from period 75
                          95 Percent Limits
Period     Forecast      Lower       Upper        Actual
  76        80.648      57.864      103.431
  77        78.169      51.982      104.356
  78        75.410      47.996      102.825
```

```
MTB > STOP
```

*1 Command arima(0 0 2) runs a MA(2) model.
*2 The output shows the parameter estimates for the two
   moving average terms
*3 The output shows the t-ratios for these two terms

The MINITAB commands to try the AR(1) model are

```
MTB > ARIMA(1 0 0)C1;  *4
SUBC> CONSTANT.
```

```
Estimates at each iteration
Iteration        SSE        Parameters
    7         10113.5    -0.538   115.842
Relative change in each estimate less than  0.0010
```

```
Final Estimates of Parameters
Type      Estimate    St. Dev.   t-ratio
AR   1    -0.5379     0.0986     -5.46
Constant  115.842     1.356      85.44
Mean      75.3267     0.8816
```

```
No. of obs.:   75
Residuals:     SS = 10065.2   (backforecasts excluded)
               MS =    137.9  DF = 73

Modified Box-Pierce chisquare statistic
Lag                    12            24            36            48
Chisquare     9.3(DF=11)   29.9(DF=23)   37.3(DF=35)   58.3(DF=47)

Forecasts from period 75
                              95 Percent Limits
Period        Forecast        Lower        Upper
  76           77.116        54.097      100.135
  77           74.364        48.226      100.502
  78           75.844        48.871      102.817
```

*4 Command arima(1 0 0) runs a AR(1) model.

Both models appear to be adequate. The t ratios for both parameters of the MA(2) model are significant at the .01 level. The parameter for the AR(1) model is significant at the .01 significance level. The modified Box-Pierce chi square statistic is also significant for all lags given. This test shows that the residuals are not significantly different from zero. The MSE for both models is similar. Therefore, since the AR(1) model has only one parameter versus two for the MA(2), it is probably the best choice because it is the simpler of the two models. The parameters estimated for the model are 115.84 for the constant and $-.5379$ for the autoregressive parameter.

The residual autocorrelation coefficients are shown in Figure 10.11. Only one coefficient is significant, and it could easily have occurred by chance. Jim confirmed this observation by testing the chi-square statistic for 25 time lags. The calculated chi-square value is less than the tabulated value for 23 degrees of freedom at the .05 significance level $(30.31 < 35.2)$. The model is deemed adequate. ∎

The AR(1) forecasting model with a constant term is

$$\hat{y}_t = 115.84 + (-.5379)y_{t-1}$$

The forecast for period 76 is

$$\hat{y}_{76} = 115.84 + (-.5379)(72)$$
$$\hat{y}_{76} = 77.11$$

The forecast for period 77 is

$$\hat{y}_{77} = 115.84 + (-.5379)(77.11)$$
$$\hat{y}_{77} = 74.36$$

FIGURE 10.11 Residual Autocorrelation Coefficients for AR(1) Model Fitted with a Constant Term.

Time Lags		Autocorrelations
25	• *│ •	−.07
24	• *│ •	−.07
23	• * │ •	−.11
22	• *│ •	−.03
21	* • │ •	−.28
20	• *│ •	−.06
19	• * │ •	−.14
18	• *│ •	−.02
17	• * │ •	−.15
16	• * │ •	−.11
15	• │ * •	.14
14	• * │ •	−.15
13	• │* •	.04
12	• * │ •	−.10
11	• *│ •	−.03
10	• *│ •	−.07
9	• *│ •	−.03
8	• │ * •	.10
7	• │ * •	.14
6	• *│ •	−.06
5	• │ * •	.16
4	• │ * •	.09
3	• │ * •	.15
2	• │ * •	.09
1	• * •	.00

```
    │ │ │ │ │ │ │ │ │ │ │ │ │ │ │ │ │ │ │ │ │ │
   −1                      0                      +1
```

EXAMPLE 10.5

■ Jim White was pleased with the results of his forecast for the time series of readings for the process shown in Table 10.3. He decided to use the Box-Jenkins methodology to attempt to forecast the errors in a manufacturing quality control process under his control. The data are shown in Table 10.4 and are plotted in Figure 10.12.

Jim began the first step in identifying a tentative model by looking at the autocorrelations of the data shown in Figure 10.13 to determine whether the series is stationary. Only one autocorrelation is significantly different from zero at the 95% significance level, so Jim concluded that the time series is stationary.

Figure 10.13 shows that only the first sample autocorrelation coefficient (−.49) is significant at the 95% level. An MA(1) model is suggested since the autocorrelation coefficients cut off after lag 1.

FIGURE 10.12 Errors for Atron Quality Control.

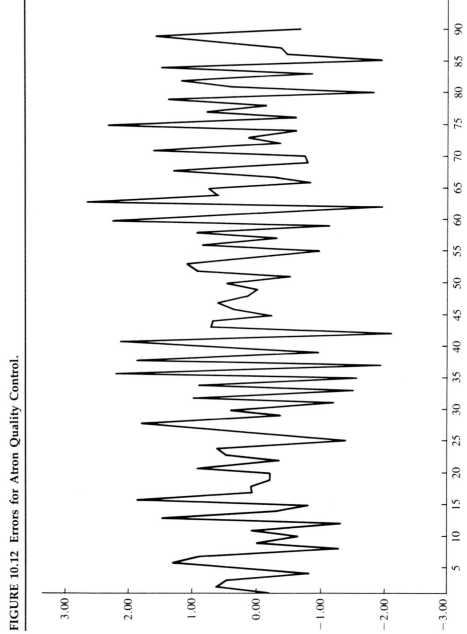

TABLE 10.4 Errors for Atron Quality Control.

−.23	−.2	−1.93	−.97	.1
.63	−.21	1.87	.83	−.62
.48	.91	−.97	−.33	2.27
−.83	−.36	.46	.91	−.62
−.03	.48	2.12	−1.13	.74
1.31	.61	−2.11	2.22	−.16
.86	−1.38	.7	.8	1.34
−1.28	−.04	.69	−1.95	−1.83
0	.9	−.24	2.61	.31
−.63	1.79	.34	.59	1.13
.08	−.37	.6	.71	−.87
−1.3	.4	.15	−.84	1.45
1.48	−1.19	−.02	−.11	−1.95
−.28	.98	.46	1.27	−.51
−.79	−1.51	−.54	−.8	−.41
1.86	.9	.89	−.76	.49
.07	−1.56	1.07	1.58	1.54
.09	2.18	.2	−.38	−.96

FIGURE 10.13 Autocorrelations of Raw Data from Table 10.4.

Time Lags		Autocorrelations
24	• * •	.00
23	• * •	−.02
22	• | * •	.03
21	• *| •	−.04
20	• | * •	.03
19	• *| •	−.03
18	• * •	−.02
17	• | * •	.04
16	• *| •	−.05
15	• * •	.01
14	• | * •	.05
13	• *| •	−.03
12	• * •	−.02
11	• | * •	.12
10	• * •	.02
9	•* | •	−.16
8	• * •	.02
7	• | * •	.15
6	•* | •	−.13
5	• * •	−.01
4	• | * •	.07
3	• *| •	−.06
2	• | * •	.09
1	* • | •	−.49

```
     |  |  |  |  |  |  |  |  |  |  |  |  |  |  |  |  |  |  |  |  | |
       −1                         0                        +1
```

FIGURE 10.14 Partial Autocorrelations of Raw Data from Table 10.4.

Time Lags		Autocorrelations
23	• * •	.01
22	• *| •	−.04
21	• * •	.00
20	• | * •	.03
19	• * | •	−.12
18	• * •	−.02
17	• | * •	.09
16	• * •	−.02
15	• |* •	.03
14	• | * •	.10
13	• |* •	.05
12	• |* •	.07
11	• |* •	.05
10	•* | •	−.16
9	•* | •	−.13
8	• | * •	.12
7	• * •	.00
6	•* | •	−.15
5	• |* •	.03
4	• * •	−.01
3	•* | •	−.14
2	* | •	−.20
1	* • | •	−.49

```
      │ │ │ │ │ │ │ │ │ │ │ │ │ │ │ │ │ │ │ │ │ │
     −1                 0                +1
```

From the sample partial autocorrelation coefficients shown in Figure 10.14, Jim saw that the first and second partial autocorrelations are significant. This pattern resembles that of a process in which the theoretical partials tail off toward zero, again suggesting an MA(1) model. Next, Jim used Minitab to estimate the parameters for the model.

```
MTB > ARIMA(0 0 1)C1,C5; *1
SUBC> CONSTANT;
SUBC> FORECAST 3 C2, C3 C4.

Estimates at each iteration
Iteration          SSE      Parameters
    6          74.3130    0.588    0.153
Relative change in each estimate less than  0.0010

Final Estimates of Parameters
Type      Estimate    St. Dev.   t-ratio
MA   1      0.5880     0.0862      6.82
Constant   0.15256    0.04012      3.80
Mean       0.15256    0.04012
```

continues

Continued

```
No. of obs.:   90
Residuals:     SS = 74.3056   (backforecasts excluded)
               MS =  0.8444   DF = 88
```

```
Modified Box-Pierce chisquare statistic
Lag                 12              24              36              48
Chisquare    9.1(DF=11)    10.9(DF=23)    17.2(DF=35)    31.3(DF=47)
```

```
Forecasts from period 90
                              95 Percent Limits
Period      Forecast        Lower         Upper        Actual
  91        0.27810       -1.52331       2.07952
  92        0.15256       -1.93716       2.24227
  93        0.15256       -1.93716       2.24227
```

[*1] Command arima(0 0 1) runs a MA(1) model for the data in **c1** and stores the residuals in **c5**

FIGURE 10.15 Residual Autocorrelation Coefficients for MA(1) Model.

Time Lags		Autocorrelations
30	• | * •	.04
29	• * •	.01
28	• * •	.02
27	• | * •	.05
26	• *| •	−.03
25	• | *	.19
24	• | * •	.11
23	• |* •	.07
22	• | * •	.09
21	• |* •	.04
20	• | * •	.08
19	• |* •	.04
18	• |* •	.05
17	• | * •	.09
16	• |* •	.04
15	• | * •	.11
14	• | *•	.15
13	• | * •	.09
12	• | * •	.12
11	• | •*	.23
10	• | * •	.09
9	• * | •	−.09
8	• | * •	.08
7	• | *	.19
6	• * •	−.02
5	• |* •	.05
4	• | *•	.13
3	• |* •	.04
2	• | * •	.10
1	• * | •	−.08

```
  | | | | | | | | | | | | | | | | | | | | | |
 −1                      0                    +1
```

The parameter for the MA(1) is estimated to be .588 and the constant is .15256. The t ratios are significant for both. The residual autocorrelation coefficients for this model were stored in column 5. An examination of the autocorrelation coefficients of these residuals is shown in Figure 10.15 and indicates that they are random. This observation was confirmed by testing the modified Box-Pierce chi square statistic for various lags.

The MA(1) forecasting model is

$$\hat{y}_t = .15256 - (.588)e_{t-1}$$

$$\hat{y}_{91} = .15256 - (.588)(-.21353) = .27816$$

Note that the forecast for period 92 is the constant .15256 since the error for period 91 is not known. ■

EXAMPLE 10.6

■ The analyst for Atron Corporation, Jim White, was happy with the Box-Jenkins forecasting procedure for the errors in the manufacturing quality control process discussed in Example 10.5. Jim met his old friend Ed Jones at a conference and told him about his success. Ed had a similar application and decided to give Box-Jenkins a try. The data are shown in Table 10.5. Figure 10.16 shows a plot of the data.

Ed began the first step in identifying a tentative model by looking at the autocorrelations of the data shown in Figure 10.17 to determine whether the series is

FIGURE 10.16 Errors for Ed Jones' Quality Control.

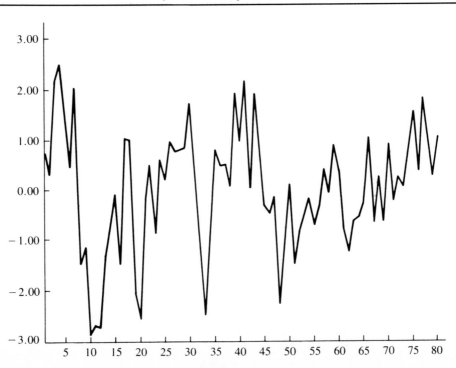

TABLE 10.5 Errors for Ed Jones' Quality Control.

.77	1.04	−2.46	−.73	−.23
.33	1.02	−.37	.10	1.05
2.15	−2.03	.80	−1.47	−.66
2.50	−2.54	.49	−.89	.25
1.36	−.23	.50	−.53	−.63
.48	.49	.07	−.20	.91
2.05	−.87	1.92	−.70	−.21
−1.46	.61	1.00	−.27	.24
−1.13	.20	2.16	.39	.05
−2.85	.98	.04	−.07	.85
−2.67	.78	1.91	.89	1.55
−2.71	.80	.43	.37	.40
−1.30	.86	−.32	−.75	1.82
−.88	1.72	−.48	−1.24	.81
−.07	.15	−.13	−.62	.28
−1.47	−1.15	−2.26	−.54	1.06

FIGURE 10.17 Autocorrelations of Raw Data from Table 10.5.

Time Lags		Autocorrelations
24	• * | •	−.08
23	• | * •	.03
22	• * •	−.01
21	• * •	−.02
20	• * | •	−.09
19	• * | •	−.10
18	• * | •	−.13
17	• * | •	−.09
16	* | •	−.18
15	• * | •	−.10
14	• * •	.00
13	• | * •	.04
12	• *| •	−.04
11	• *| •	−.03
10	• *| •	−.07
9	• * | •	−.10
8	* | •	−.19
7	* | •	−.22
6	• * | •	−.16
5	• * | •	−.13
4	• | *•	.13
3	• | *	.19
2	• | • *	.35
1	• | • *	.49

```
   | | | | | | | | | | | | | | | | | | | | |
  −1              0                +1
```

stationary. The autocorrelations for low lags die down toward zero after the third lag, so Ed concluded that the time series is stationary.

The first two sample autocorrelation coefficients (.49 and .35) are significant at the 95% level since they lie outside the range.

$$0 \pm 1.96\left(\frac{1}{\sqrt{80}}\right)$$

$$0 \pm 1.96(.112)$$

$$0 \pm .219$$

The sample autocorrelation coefficients at lag 7 ($-.22$) is also significant, but this result is probably due to chance. The autocorrelation coefficients trail off to zero, suggesting an AR model.

From the sample partial autocorrelation coefficients shown in Figure 10.18, Ed saw that the first is significant. Since the partial autocorrelations drop off to zero after the first time lag and the autocorrelation coefficients can be considered to trail off exponentially to zero, an AR(1) process is indicated. However, the partial autocorrelation for the second lag is .14, which could indicate that the partials are

FIGURE 10.18 Partial Autocorrelations of Raw Data from Table 10.5.

Time Lags		Autocorrelations
23	• * | •	−.03
22	• * | •	−.04
21	• * | •	−.03
20	• * | •	−.04
19	• * •	.02
18	• * | •	−.03
17	• | * •	.06
16	• * | •	−.10
15	• * | •	−.17
14	• * | •	−.03
13	• | * •	.03
12	• * | •	−.10
11	• * •	.00
10	• * | •	−.04
9	• | * •	.13
8	• * •	−.01
7	• * | •	−.07
6	• * | •	−.05
5	* • | •	−.27
4	• * •	.01
3	• * | •	−.03
2	• | * •	.14
1	• | • *	.49

```
  | | | | | | | | | | | | | | | | | | | | | |
 −1                     0                   +1
```

trailing off exponentially to zero. Since there is this possibility, an ARIMA$(1, 0, 1)$ model could also be tested.

Next, Ed used a Box-Jenkins computer program to estimate the parameter(s) for the model. Since the dependent variable values have not been expressed as deviations from their mean, a constant term would normally be included in the model. However, since the mean of y is extremely small (close to zero) compared with the standard deviation, no constant term is included in this model. The parameter for the AR(1) model is estimated to be .50084. An examination of the residual autocorrelation coefficients shown in Figure 10.19 indicates that they are random, with a sum of the squared residuals equal to 1.1. Ed confirmed this observation by testing the chi-square statistic for 26 time lags. The calculated chi-square value is less than the tabulated value for $(k - p - q = 26 - 1 - 0 = 25)$ 25 degrees of freedom at the .05 significance level ($17.43 < 37.6$). The model is deemed adequate. ∎

FIGURE 10.19 Residual Autocorrelation Coefficients for AR(1) Model.

Time Lags		Autocorrelations
26	• * | •	−.10
25	• | * •	.06
24	• * | •	−.11
23	• | * •	.11
22	• * •	−.02
21	• | * •	.03
20	• *| •	−.07
19	• *| •	−.03
18	• * | •	−.08
17	• | * •	.05
16	* | •	−.18
15	• *| •	−.03
14	• | * •	.03
13	• | * •	.10
12	• * | •	−.09
11	• | * •	.04
10	• *| •	−.04
9	• * •	.01
8	• * | •	−.10
7	• * | •	−.12
6	• *| •	−.04
5	* | •	−.19
4	• | *	.18
3	• * •	.00
2	• | * •	.11
1	• *| •	−.07

```
| | | | | | | | | | | | | | | | | | | |
    −1              0              +1
```

The ARIMA(1, 0, 0) forecasting model is

$$\hat{y}_t = .50084 y_{t-1}$$

The forecasts for periods 81 and 82 are

$$\hat{y}_{81} = (.50084)(1.06) \qquad \text{and} \qquad \hat{y}_{82} = (.50084)(.53)$$
$$\hat{y}_{81} = .53 \qquad\qquad\qquad\qquad \hat{y}_{82} = .265$$

EXAMPLE 10.7

■ The analyst for the ISC Corporation, Jill Blake, needed to find a method for forecasting the closing offerings of ISC stock. The data are shown in Table 10.6. Jill believed that the Box-Jenkins methodology might work best for these data. Figure 10.20 shows a plot of the data.

FIGURE 10.20 Closing Stocks for ISC Corporation.

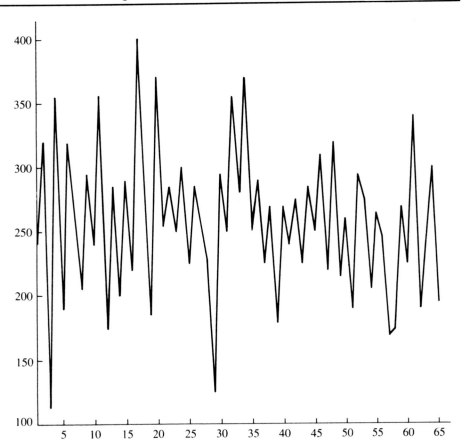

TABLE 10.6 Closing Stocks for ISC Corporation.

235	200	250	270	275
320	290	225	240	205
115	220	125	275	265
355	400	295	225	245
190	275	250	285	170
320	185	355	250	175
275	370	280	310	270
205	255	370	220	225
295	285	250	320	340
240	250	290	215	190
355	300	225	260	250
175	225	270	190	300
285	285	180	295	195

FIGURE 10.21 Autocorrelations of Raw Data from Table 10.6.

Time Lags		Autocorrelations
21		.01
20		−.01
19		−.07
18		.03
17		−.10
16		.13
15		.02
14		.03
13		.09
12		−.11
11		.14
10		−.02
9		.04
8		−.08
7		.02
6		.01
5		−.18
4		.11
3		−.20
2		.33
1		−.40

−1   0   +1

Jill began the first step in identifying a tentative model by looking at the autocorrelations of the data shown in Figure 10.21 to determine whether the series is stationary. The autocorrelations for low lags die down rapidly toward zero, so Jill concluded that the time series is stationary.

The first two sample autocorrelation coefficients ($-.40$ and $.33$) are significant at the 95% level, and the rest appear to trail off exponentially to zero.

From the sample partial autocorrelation coefficients shown in Figure 10.22, Jill saw that the first is significant and the second very close. However, the third lag cuts off to zero. Since the partial autocorrelations drop off to zero after the second time lag and the autocorrelation coefficients can be considered to trail off exponentially to zero, an AR(2) process should be considered.

Next, Jill used a Box-Jenkins computer program to estimate the parameter(s) for the model. Since the dependent variable values have not been expressed as deviations from their mean, a constant term should be included in the model. The parameters estimated for the AR(1) model are 361.47 for the overall constant and $-.40152$ for the autoregressive parameter. None of the residual autocorrelation coefficients are significantly different from zero, and the sum of the squared residuals equals 2,851.4. The model appears to be adequate. Jill confirms this observation by testing the chi-square statistic for 24 time lags. The calculated chi-square is less than the tabulated value for 22 degrees of freedom at the .05 significance level ($16.45 < 33.92$).

FIGURE 10.22 Partial Autocorrelations of Raw Data from Table 10.6.

Time Lags		Autocorrelations
19	• | * •	.04
18	• * | •	−.12
17	• *| •	−.03
16	• | * •	.21
15	• | * •	.08
14	• | * •	.13
13	• *| •	−.04
12	• *| •	−.03
11	• | * •	.14
10	• * •	.01
9	• *| •	−.04
8	• *| •	−.06
7	• |* •	.07
6	• * | •	−.13
5	• * | •	−.14
4	• *| •	−.03
3	• * •	−.02
2	• | * •	.21
1	* • | •	−.40

$$-1 \qquad\qquad 0 \qquad\qquad +1$$

Next, Jill used the computer program to estimate the parameters for the ARIMA(2, 0, 0) model. The parameters are estimated to be $-.32218$ and $.20809$ with an overall constant equal to 286.48. None of the residual autocorrelation coefficients are significantly different from zero, and the sum of the squared residuals equals 2,719.9. This model also appears to be adequate. Jill confirmed this observation by testing the chi-square statistic for 24 time lags. The calculated chi-square value is less than the tabulated value for 21 degrees of freedom at the .05 significance level $(13.76 < 32.67)$. Since the sum of the squared residuals is considerably lower, the ARIMA(2, 0, 0) model should be used. ■

The ARIMA(2, 0, 0) forecasting model is

$$\hat{y}_t = 268.48 + (-.32218)y_{t-1} + .20809y_{t-2}$$

The forecasts for periods 66 and 67 are

$$\hat{y}_{66} = 268.48 + (-.32218)(195) + .20809(300) = 268.08$$

$$\hat{y}_{67} = 268.48 + (-.32218)(268.08) + .20809(195) = 222.69$$

A SEASONAL ANALYSIS

Seasonal patterns add more difficulty to forecasting with Box-Jenkins models because in addition to the period-to-period pattern there is a longer, repetitive pattern occurring every Lth period, where L is the length of seasonality. To estimate the seasonal pattern, seasonal parameters must be

TABLE 10.7 Sales of the Keytron Corporation.

1,736.8	1,627.6	1,895.4	1,768.0	2,191.8	2,035.8	2,056.6
1,297.4	1,575.6	1,822.6	1,840.8	2,202.2	2,152.8	2,340.0
559.0	1,682.2	2,054.0	1,804.4	2,449.2	1,708.2	2,033.2
1,455.6	1,710.8	1,544.4	2,007.2	2,090.4	806.0	2,288.0
1,526.2	1,853.8	600.6	2,067.0	2,184.0	2,028.0	2,275.0
1,419.6	1,788.8	1,604.2	2,048.8	2,267.2	2,236.0	2,581.8
1,484.6	1,822.4	1,796.6	2,314.0	1,705.6	2,028.0	2,540.2
1,651.0	1,838.2	1,822.6	2,072.2	962.0	2,100.8	2,519.4
1,661.4	1,635.4	1,835.6	1,952.6	1,929.2	2,327.0	2,267.2
1,851.2	618.8	1,944.8	2,134.6	2,202.2	2,225.6	2,615.6
1,617.2	1,593.8	2,009.8	1,799.2	1,903.2	2,321.8	2,163.2
1,614.6	1,898.0	2,116.4	756.6	2,337.4	2,275.0	899.6
1,757.6	1,911.0	1,994.2	1,890.2	2,022.8	2,171.0	2,210.0
1,302.6	1,695.2	1,895.4	2,256.8	2,225.6	2,431.0	2,376.4
572.0	1,757.6	1,947.4	2,111.2	2,441.4	2,165.8	2,259.4
1,458.6	1,944.8	1,770.6	2,080.0	2,113.8	780.0	2,584.4
1,567.8	2,108.6	626.6				

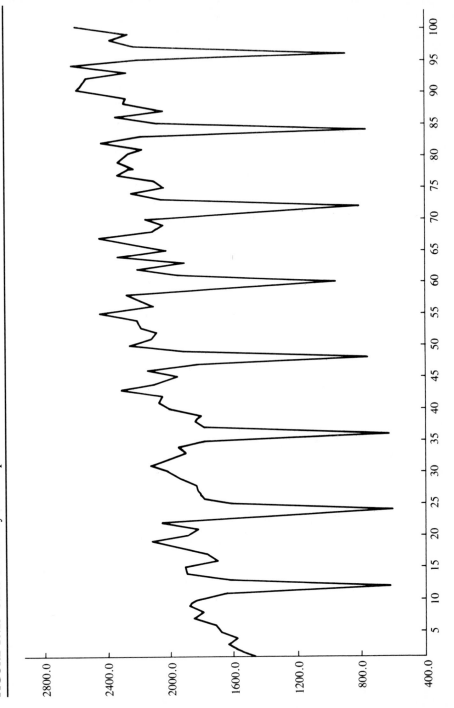

FIGURE 10.23 Sales of the Keytron Corporation.

included in the model. As in the nonseasonal models, they can be either autoregressive or moving-average processes. Seasonal models will not be covered in this text; however, Example 10.8 will provide an indication of how a seasonal application is solved.

EXAMPLE 10.8

■ Kathy Fisher has been given the responsibility for forecasting sales for Keytron Corporation. The company started over 10 years ago, and Kathy was able to find 115 months of sales data. The data begin in January 1981 and are shown in Table 10.7. Kathy examined the plotted data in Figure 10.23 and decided to try the Box-Jenkins methodology.

FIGURE 10.24 Autocorrelations of Raw Data from Table 10.7.

Time Lags		Autocorrelations
30	• *| •	−.06
29	• * | •	−.10
28	• *| •	−.03
27	• | * •	.05
26	• * •	.00
25	• | • *	.24
24	• | • *	.64
23	• | • *	.23
22	• | * •	.03
21	• | * •	.10
20	• | * •	.04
19	• *| •	−.05
18	• * •	−.01
17	• *| •	−.03
16	• | * •	.04
15	• | * •	.12
14	• | * •	.07
13	• | • *	.32
12	• | • *	.79
11	• | • *	.33
10	• | * •	.11
9	• | *	.21
8	• | * •	.13
7	• | * •	.03
6	• | * •	.06
5	• | * •	.04
4	• | * •	.13
3	• | • *	.23
2	• | * •	.15
1	• | • *	.43

$$-1 \qquad\qquad 0 \qquad\qquad +1$$

Kathy began the first step in identifying a tentative model by looking at the autocorrelations of the data shown in Figure 10.24 to determine whether the series is stationary. The data are not stationary in their original form. Several autocorrelations are significantly different from zero (lags 1, 3, 9, 11, 12, 13, 23, 24, and 25). A slight trend pattern is indicated because all but five of the autocorrelations are positive. Kathy decided to first-difference the data.

Figure 10.25 shows the autocorrelations for the first differences of the original data. The slight trend pattern has been removed. Stationarity has been achieved on a period-to-period basis. However, there are very large autocorrelations at lags 12, 24, and 36. Kathy concluded that there is a trend between successive seasonal periods (separated by a time lag of 12 months). If the autocorrelation coefficient had

FIGURE 10.25 Autocorrelations of First Difference of Data from Table 10.7.

Time Lags		Autocorrelations
30	• *| •	−.06
29	• * | •	−.10
28	• *| •	−.03
27	• |* •	.05
26	• * •	.00
25	• | •*	.24
24	• | • *	.64
23	• | •*	.23
22	• |* •	.03
21	• | * •	.10
20	• |* •	.04
19	• *| •	−.05
18	• * •	−.01
17	• *| •	−.03
16	• |* •	.04
15	• | * •	.12
14	• |* •	.07
13	• | • *	.32
12	• | • *	.79
11	• | • *	.33
10	• | * •	.11
9	• | *	.21
8	• | *•	.13
7	• |* •	.03
6	• |* •	.06
5	• |* •	.04
4	• | *•	.13
3	• | •*	.23
2	• | *•	.15
1	• | • *	.43

| \| \| \| \| \| \| \| \| \| \| \| \| \| \| \| \| \| \| \| \| \| |
| −1 | 0 | +1 |

dropped off to zero at lag 24, she would have concluded that the first-differenced data were stationary.

     Long-term differences (differences whose length is 12 periods apart) are used to eliminate the trend for lags 12, 24, and 36. Figure 10.26 shows the autocorrelations for the data first-differenced and long-differenced (separated by a time lag of 12 months.) Only the autocorrelations at time lags 1, 11, 12, and 13 are significantly different from zero. The rest of the autocorrelation coefficients are randomly dispersed around zero, and the series appears to be stationary.

     Kathy examined the autocorrelations in Figure 10.26 and the partial autocorrelations in Figure 10.27 to identify the appropriate model. She concentrated on the nonseasonal pattern first. Figure 10.26 shows that the autocorrelations drop off to zero after the first significant coefficient at time lag 1 (−.55). Figure 10.27 shows an exponential decay of the nonseasonal partial autocorrelations indicating an IMA(1) model for the nonseasonal pattern.

FIGURE 10.26 Autocorrelations for One Short and One Long Difference for Data from Table 10.7.

Time Lags		Autocorrelations
26	• | * •	.13
25	• * | •	−.11
24	• |* •	.05
23	• *| •	−.05
22	• |* •	.06
21	• *| •	−.03
20	• * •	−.02
19	• |* •	.04
18	• * | •	−.09
17	• | * •	.14
16	• *| •	−.07
15	• * •	−.02
14	• *| •	−.05
13	• | • *	.29
12	* • | •	−.45
11	• | •*	.25
10	• *| •	−.03
9	• |* •	.04
8	• *| •	−.07
7	• |* •	.06
6	• |* •	.03
5	• * | •	−.09
4	• * •	.02
3	• |* •	.05
2	• |* •	.04
1	* • | •	−.55

        −1   0   +1

FIGURE 10.27 Partial Autocorrelations for One Short and One Long Difference for Data from Table 10.7.

Time Lags		Autocorrelations
25	• * | •	−.13
24	• * | •	−.04
23	• | *	.18
22	• * | •	−.06
21	• * | •	−.13
20	• * | •	−.08
19	• * •	.02
18	• * | •	−.09
17	• * | •	−.03
16	• * | •	−.11
15	• * •	.01
14	• * | •	−.06
13	• * | •	−.07
12	• * | •	−.12
11	• | • *	.37
10	• * | •	−.06
9	• * •	−.02
8	• * | •	−.07
7	• * | •	−.06
6	• * | •	−.16
5	• * | •	−.13
4	• * | •	−.06
3	* | •	−.21
2	* • | •	−.38
1	* • | •	−.55

```
| | | | | | | | | | | | | | | | | | | | |
-1                    0                    +1
```

Now Kathy examined the seasonal pattern. Figure 10.26 shows that the autocorrelations drop off to zero (.05 at time lag 24) after the first significant coefficient at time lag 12 (−.45). Figure 10.27 shows an exponential decay of the seasonal partial autocorrelation, indicating an IMA(1) model for the seasonal pattern. It would have been desirable to examine the coefficients for lags 36, 48, and 60, but it was not possible.

Next, Kathy used a Box-Jenkins computer program to estimate the parameter(s) for the model. The parameters for the ARIMA$(0, 1, 1)(0, 1, 1)$ model are estimated to be .77948 and .61031. An examination of the residual autocorrelation coefficients shown in Figure 10.28 indicates that they are random. Kathy confirmed this observation by testing the chi-square statistic for 34 time lags. The calculated chi-square value is less than the tabulated value at the .05 significance level (11.82 < 43.8). The model is deemed adequate. ∎

FIGURE 10.28 Residual Autocorrelation Coefficients for ARIMA Model (0, 1, 1)(0, 1, 1).

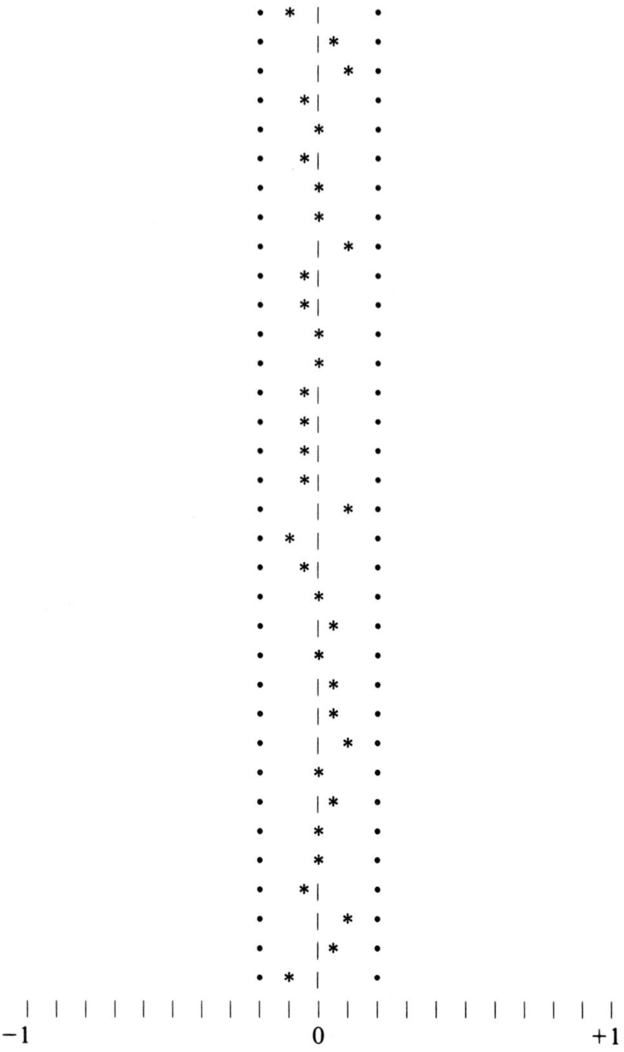

Time Lags		Autocorrelations
34	• * | •	−.08
33	• |* •	.04
32	• | * •	.12
31	• *| •	−.03
30	• * •	−.02
29	• *| •	−.04
28	• * •	.00
27	• * •	−.02
26	• | * •	.09
25	• *| •	−.05
24	• *| •	−.04
23	• * •	−.01
22	• * •	−.02
21	• *| •	−.05
20	• *| •	−.03
19	• *| •	−.05
18	• *| •	−.06
17	• | * •	.10
16	• * | •	−.10
15	• *| •	−.03
14	• * •	−.01
13	• |* •	.03
12	• * •	−.01
11	• |* •	.04
10	• |* •	.05
9	• | * •	.12
8	• * •	.00
7	• |* •	.07
6	• * •	.01
5	• * •	−.01
4	• *| •	−.03
3	• | * •	.10
2	• |* •	.03
1	• * | •	−.09

```
   |  |  |  |  |  |  |  |  |  |  |  |  |  |  |  |  |  |  |  |
  −1                    0                   +1
```

The ARIMA(0, 1, 1)(0, 1, 1) forecasting model is

$$\hat{y}_t = y_{t-1} + y_{t-2} - y_{t-13} + \varepsilon_t - .77948e_{t-1} - .61031e_{t-12} + .47572e_{t-13}$$

$$\hat{y}_{116} = y_{115} + y_{104} - y_{103} + e_{116} - .77948e_{115} - .61031e_{104} + .47572e_{103}$$

The forecast for period 116 is

$$\hat{y}_{116} = 2{,}584.4 + 2{,}275 - 2{,}288 - .77948(181.48)$$

$$- .61031(-36.43) + .47572(34.35)$$

$$\hat{y}_{116} = 2{,}468.5$$

The forecast for period 117 is

$$\hat{y}_{117} = 2{,}599.8$$

The Box-Jenkins approach to time series analysis is a very powerful tool for providing more accurate short-range forecasts. It combines the strengths of both the autoregressive and the moving-average methods without making assumptions about the number of terms in the forecast equation or the interrelationships among their coefficients. Also, a statistical test is provided for determining the adequacy of the fitted model, as well as a means of constructing confidence intervals about the forecasts.

However, the Box-Jenkins approach is not without disadvantages. Some of these disadvantages are as follows.

1. A relatively large amount of data is required. It should be recognized that if the data are seasonal, such as yearly seasonal data, then monthly observations for one year generally constitute 1 data point and not 12. Makridakis and colleagues estimate minimum data requirements for reliable use of the Box-Jenkins method to be 72 data points, assuming a seasonal pattern of 12 months' duration. In many cases of this type sufficient historical data for reliable use of the Box-Jenkins method are simply not available, and some other time series method should be used.

The Box-Jenkins method is generally considered to be applicable when the data occur over a relatively short period of time. Some of the applications appropriate for this method would be analysis of stock prices on a daily or weekly basis and data from a chemical or manufacturing process where samples can be taken often.

2. There are no easy ways to update the parameters of the model as new data become available, as there are in direct smoothing models. The model has to be periodically completely refitted, or, worse, a new model must be developed.

3. The building of a satisfactory model requires a high investment in the analyst's time and other resources. The costs of model development, computer run time, and storage requirements are substantially higher for

Box-Jenkins models than for the more traditional techniques such as smoothing.[2]

APPLICATION TO MANAGEMENT

Forecasts are one of the most important inputs managers develop to aid them in the decision-making process. Virtually every important operating decision depends to some extent on a forecast. Inventory accumulation is related to the forecast of expected demand; the production department has to schedule employment needs and raw materials orders for the next month or two; the finance department must arrange short-term financing for the next quarter; the personnel department must determine hiring and layoff requirements. The list of forecasting applications is quite lengthy.

Executives are keenly aware of the importance of forecasting. Indeed, a great deal of time is spent studying trends in economic and political affairs and how events might affect demand for products and/or services. One issue of interest is the importance executives place on quantitative forecasting methods versus their own opinions. This issue is especially sensitive when events that have a significant impact on demand are involved. One problem with quantitative forecasting methods is that they depend on historical data. For this reason they are probably least effective in calling the turn that often results in sharply higher or lower demand. The computer has aided managers in automating sensitivity to sharp changes in demand through adaptive systems and causal models.

One type of problem that business managers frequently face is the need to prepare short-term forecasts for a number of different items. A typical example is the manager who must schedule production on the basis of some forecast of demand for several hundred different products in a product line. The techniques that are used most frequently in this situation are referred to as smoothing methods.

Exponential smoothing is a popular technique for short-run forecasting. Its major advantages are low cost and simplicity. It is usually not as accurate as more sophisticated methods, such as autoregressive techniques. However, when forecasts are needed for inventory systems containing

---

[2] For a summary of the relative computer and analyst time requirements, minimum data requirements, applications, and so on, for various forecasting methods, refer to S. Makridakis *et al.*, "An Interactive Forecasting System," *American Statistician,* vol. 28 (1974), p. 157. For a summary of some disadvantages of the Box-Jenkins methodology, refer to D. C. Montgomery and L. A. Johnson, *Forecasting and Time Series Analysis* (New York: McGraw-Hill, 1976). Use levels for various demand forecasting techniques in the process industries is shown in S. G. Taylor, "The APICS Process Industry Survey: Implications for Education and Research," *Proceedings and Abstracts of the American Institute for Decision Sciences Eighth Annual Meeting, Western Regional Conference, 1979,* pp. 202–204.

thousands of items, smoothing methods are often the only reasonable approach.

Time series analysis depends on the assumption that there are regular and repeating components interacting to produce a total series. The analyst's task is to examine and identify each of these components. Once forecasters know something about each of the parts, they are in a better position to say something about the expected value of the total series in some future period. Time series techniques are appropriate for forecasting variables that fluctuate in some stable pattern over time.

Autoregressive models are employed with economic variables in order to account for correlations between adjacent observations in a time series.

The adaptive-filtering technique is both simple and economical. It provides the unique characteristic of automatically adjusting parameters. It is clearly more powerful than smoothing methods, but it is also more complicated. Adaptive filtering fills a gap in existing forecasting techniques because it can effectively handle any data pattern.

The Box-Jenkins approach is a very powerful tool for providing more accurate short-range forecasts. It is generally considered to be more applicable when the data occur over a relatively short period of time. Managers must be aware that building a satisfactory model with the Box-Jenkins technique requires a high investment in the analyst's time and a firm's computer resources.

Appropriate applications for Box-Jenkins methodology are the analysis of stock prices on a daily basis or the analysis of data from chemical or manufacturing processes where samples can be taken often. Box-Jenkins methodology has also been used to

Estimate a change in price structure in the U.S. telephone industry

Investigate the relationship among ammonia concentration, flow rate, and temperature in rivers

Analyze the competition between rail and airline routes

Forecast employment

Analyze a large number of energy time series for a utility company

Analyze the effect of promotions on the sales of consumer products

Forecast different categories of assurance

CHAPTER **10**

GLOSSARY

Box-Jenkins techniques The Box-Jenkins techniques apply autoregressive and moving-average methods to time series forecasting problems.

KEY FORMULAS

Box-Jenkins: autoregressive model

$$y_t = \phi_0 + \phi_1 y_{t-1} + \phi_2 y_{t-2} + \cdots + \phi_p y_{t-p} + \varepsilon_t \tag{10.1}$$

Box-Jenkins: moving average model

$$y_t = w_0 + \varepsilon_t - w_1 \varepsilon_{t-1} - w_2 \varepsilon_{t-2} + \cdots + w_q \varepsilon_{t-q} \tag{10.2}$$

Box-Jenkins: ARIMA model

$$
\begin{aligned}
y_t = \phi_0 + \phi_1 y_{t-1} + \phi_2 y_{t-2} + \cdots + \phi_p y_{t-p} + \varepsilon_t - w_1 \varepsilon_{t-1} \\
- w_2 \varepsilon_{t-2} - \cdots - w_q \varepsilon_{t-q}
\end{aligned}
\tag{10.3}
$$

Box-Pierce Q statistic $\quad Q = (N - d) \sum_{k=1}^{m} r_k^2$ $\tag{10.4}$

PROBLEMS

1. **a.** For a sample of 100 observations of random data, calculate a 95% confidence interval for the autocorrelation coefficients.
    b. If all the autocorrelation coefficients are within the interval and show no particular pattern, what conclusion can be drawn?
    c. If the first five autocorrelation coefficients are significantly different from zero and the pattern gradually trails to zero, what conclusion can be drawn?
    d. If r_4, r_8, and r_{12} are significantly different from zero, what conclusion can be drawn?

2. Suppose the following time series model has been fitted to historical data and has been checked and found to be an adequate model.

    $$y_t = 35 + e_t + .25e_{t-1} - .3e_{t-2}$$

    The first four observations are $y_1 = 32.5$, $y_2 = 36.6$, $y_3 = 33.3$, and $y_4 = 31.9$. Compute forecasts for periods 5, 6, and 7 from origin 4. Let e_{t-1} and e_{t-2} equal 0 for period 1.

3. A time series model has been fitted to historical data, yielding

    $$y_t = 50 + .45y_{t-1} + e_t$$

    Suppose at time $t = 50$ the observation is $y_{50} = 100$.

   a. Determine forecasts for periods 51, 52, and 53 from origin 50.

   b. Suppose the observed value of y_{51} is 90. Revise the forecasts for periods 52 and 53.

   c. Suppose the estimate of the variance of the error term $(\hat{\sigma}^2)$ is 1.2. Compute a 95% confidence interval about the estimate for period 51.

4. Fill in the missing information in the accompanying table, indicating whether the theoretical distributions of autocorrelations and partial auto-correlations trail off or drop off for these models.

Model	Autocorrelations	Partial-Autocorrelations
AR		
MA		
ARIMA		

5. Given the accompanying graphs of the autocorrelations and partial auto-correlations of the original data for some time series, identify a potential model for each.

6. After an MA(1) model is fit to the first differences for 24 observations of a time series, the autocorrelations of the first 10 residuals are as shown in the accompanying figure.

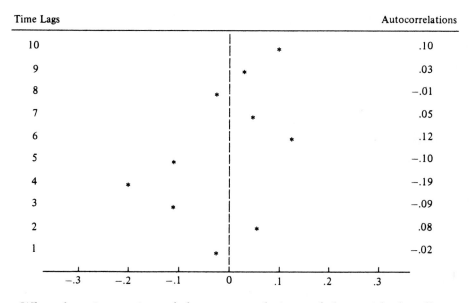

Time Lags	Autocorrelations
10	.10
9	.03
8	−.01
7	.05
6	.12
5	−.10
4	−.19
3	−.09
2	.08
1	−.02

−.3　−.2　−.1　0　.1　.2　.3

   a. What does inspection of the autocorrelations of the residuals tell you about the adequacy of the model?

   b. Calculate the chi-square statistic for these data, and test to see whether the model is adequate on the basis of the chi-square test.

Figure for Problem 5a.

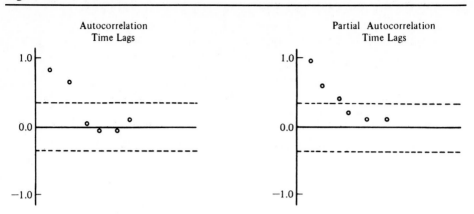

Figure for Problem 5b.

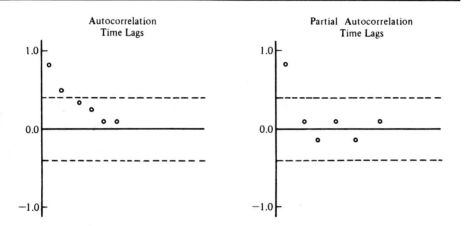

Figure for Problem 5c.

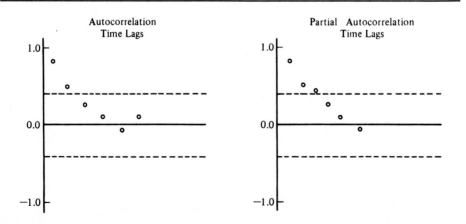

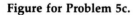

7. Chips Bakery has been having trouble forecasting the demand for its special high-fiber bread and would like your assistance. Data for the weekly demand, and the autocorrelations of the raw data and the various differences, are shown in the accompanying tables.

Table 1 for Problem 7: Weekly Sales Demand (Thousands) for High-Fiber Bread.

Week	Demand	Week	Demand	Week	Demand	Week	Demand
1	22.46	14	30.21	27	39.29	40	47.31
2	20.27	15	30.09	28	39.61	41	50.08
3	20.97	16	33.04	29	41.02	42	50.25
4	23.68	17	31.21	30	42.52	43	49.00
5	23.25	18	32.44	31	40.83	44	49.97
6	23.48	19	34.73	32	42.15	45	52.52
7	24.81	20	34.92	33	43.91	46	53.39
8	25.44	21	33.37	34	45.67	47	52.37
9	24.88	22	36.91	35	44.53	48	54.06
10	27.38	23	37.75	36	45.23	49	54.88
11	27.74	24	35.46	37	46.35	50	54.82
12	28.96	25	38.48	38	46.28	51	56.23
13	28.48	26	37.72	39	46.70	52	57.54

Table 2 for Problem 7: Autocorrelation Function of the Raw Data.

Time Lag	Autocorrelation	Time Lag	Autocorrelation
1	.94	7	.59
2	.88	8	.53
3	.82	9	.48
4	.77	10	.43
5	.71	11	.38
6	.65	12	.32

Table 3 for Problem 7: Autocorrelation Function of the First-Differenced Series.

Time Lag	Autocorrelation	Time Lag	Autocorrelation
1	−.40	7	.20
2	−.29	8	−.03
3	.17	9	−.03
4	.21	10	−.23
5	−.22	11	.21
6	−.05	12	.14

Table 4 for Problem 7: Autocorrelation Function of the Second-Differenced Series.

Time Lag	Autocorrelation	Time Lag	Autocorrelation
1	−.53	7	.16
2	−.10	8	−.05
3	.11	9	.06
4	.18	10	−.23
5	−.20	11	.16
6	−.04	12	.13

  a. Inspect the plots and suggest an appropriate model for forecasting weekly sales demand. How did you decide on this model?

  b. What is the equation for forecasting weekly sales demand for the high-fiber bread?

  c. Perform the necessary diagnostic tests to determine whether the chosen model is adequate or not.

  d. Using the Box-Jenkins program, forecast the demand for the next 4 weeks starting with week 53, and construct 95% confidence intervals about these forecasts.

8. The data in the accompanying table are weekly stock quotations for IBM stock.

Period		IBM	Period		IBM	Period		IBM	Period		IBM
Jan.	6	267	Apr.	7	241	Jul.	7	258	Oct.	6	279
	13	267		14	244		14	259		13	287
	20	268		21	254		21	268		20	276
	27	264		28	262		28	276		27	273
Feb.	3	263	May	5	261	Aug.	4	285	Nov.	3	270
	10	260		12	265		11	288		10	264
	17	256		19	261		18	295		17	261
	24	256		26	261		25	297		24	268
Mar.	2	252	Jun.	2	257	Sep.	1	292	Dec.	1	270
	10	245		9	268		8	299		8	276
	17	243		16	270		15	294		15	274
	24	240		23	266		22	284		22	284
	31	238		30	259		29	277		29	304

  a. Obtain plots of the data, autocorrelations, and partial autocorrelations by using the Box-Jenkins program; then use this information to suggest an appropriate forecast model(s).

  b. Is the series stationary? What correction would you recommend if the data are nonstationary?

c. Use the Box-Jenkins program to calculate improved parameter values.

d. Perform diagnostic tests to determine whether the model is adequate.

e. After a satisfactory model has been found, make forecasts for January for the first week of the next year.

9. The data in the accompanying table are closing stock quotations for the DEF Corporation for 150 days. Determine the appropriate Box-Jenkins model and forecast 5 days into the future. How accurate is your forecast?

Period	DEF	Period	DEF	Period	DEF
1	136.0000	36	136.8000	71	138.4000
2	132.8000	37	140.8000	72	139.2000
3	130.4000	38	141.6000	73	141.6000
4	128.8000	39	139.2000	74	134.4000
5	136.8000	40	142.4000	75	135.2000
6	135.2000	41	140.8000	76	136.0000
7	134.4000	42	140.0000	77	135.2000
8	139.2000	43	132.0000	78	136.0000
9	136.8000	44	142.4000	79	132.8000
10	136.0000	45	138.4000	80	133.6000
11	133.6000	46	138.4000	81	134.4000
12	139.2000	47	136.8000	82	133.6000
13	137.6000	48	139.2000	83	131.2000
14	139.2000	49	135.2000	84	132.0000
15	139.2000	50	138.4000	85	131.2000
16	136.0000	51	140.8000	86	132.8000
17	138.4000	52	135.2000	87	132.0000
18	137.6000	53	133.6000	88	133.6000
19	139.2000	54	134.4000	89	131.2000
20	134.4000	55	134.4000	90	131.2000
21	136.8000	56	137.6000	91	129.6000
22	139.2000	57	134.4000	92	131.2000
23	139.2000	58	140.8000	93	130.4000
24	140.0000	59	137.6000	94	131.2000
25	139.2000	60	132.8000	95	136.0000
26	140.8000	61	136.8000	96	135.2000
27	139.2000	62	135.2000	97	136.8000
28	138.4000	63	132.8000	98	136.8000
29	136.0000	64	144.0000	99	133.6000
30	142.4000	65	137.6000	100	135.2000
31	140.0000	66	138.4000	101	136.0000
32	144.8000	67	136.0000	102	137.6000
33	140.0000	68	135.2000	103	131.2000
34	139.2000	69	138.4000	104	136.0000
35	139.2000	70	134.4000	105	136.0000

continues

Continued

Period	DEF	Period	DEF	Period	DEF
106	133.6000	121	135.2000	136	132.0000
107	129.6000	122	136.8000	137	133.6000
108	132.8000	123	134.4000	138	134.4000
109	135.2000	124	136.0000	139	133.6000
110	132.0000	125	137.6000	140	133.6000
111	132.8000	126	138.4000	141	132.8000
112	132.8000	127	137.6000	142	132.0000
113	136.0000	128	138.4000	143	136.0000
114	136.8000	129	137.6000	144	133.6000
115	136.8000	130	137.6000	145	133.6000
116	133.6000	131	140.0000	146	135.2000
117	134.4000	132	135.2000	147	139.2000
118	130.4000	133	135.2000	148	136.8000
119	132.8000	134	135.2000	149	136.0000
120	134.4000	135	136.0000	150	134.4000

10. The data in the accompanying table are the number of weekly automobile accidents for the years 1984 and 1985. Determine the appropriate Box-Jenkins model and forecast accidents for the 91st week. How accurate is your forecast?

Period	Observation	Period	Observation	Period	Observation
1	101.0000	19	20.0000	37	62.0000
2	84.0000	20	23.0000	38	57.0000
3	54.0000	21	30.0000	39	46.0000
4	39.0000	22	50.0000	40	40.0000
5	26.0000	23	61.0000	41	32.0000
6	40.0000	24	59.0000	42	23.0000
7	99.0000	25	64.0000	43	20.0000
8	148.0000	26	58.0000	44	18.0000
9	147.0000	27	44.0000	45	24.0000
10	134.0000	28	26.0000	46	33.0000
11	106.0000	29	24.0000	47	52.0000
12	83.0000	30	18.0000	48	66.0000
13	76.0000	31	16.0000	49	78.0000
14	63.0000	32	17.0000	50	83.0000
15	57.0000	33	21.0000	51	87.0000
16	37.0000	34	28.0000	52	64.0000
17	32.0000	35	30.0000	53	44.0000
18	22.0000	36	51.0000	54	24.0000

Period	Observation	Period	Observation	Period	Observation
55	29.0000	67	78.0000	79	71.0000
56	73.0000	68	114.0000	80	110.0000
57	138.0000	69	140.0000	81	112.0000
58	154.0000	70	112.0000	82	93.0000
59	119.0000	71	82.0000	83	75.0000
60	102.0000	72	80.0000	84	60.0000
61	79.0000	73	70.0000	85	63.0000
62	53.0000	74	55.0000	86	46.0000
63	40.0000	75	37.0000	87	32.0000
64	27.0000	76	23.0000	88	23.0000
65	31.0000	77	20.0000	89	53.0000
66	56.0000	78	39.0000	90	90.0000

11. Use Box-Jenkins methodology to model the U.S. retail sales data presented in Case Study 4.1.

RESTAURANT SALES

This case refers to the data and situation for the restaurant sales case in Chapter 7.

Jim Price has now completed a course in forecasting and is anxious to apply the Box-Jenkins methodology to the restaurant sales data. These data, shown in Table 10.8(a), begin with the week ending Sunday, January 4, 1981 and continue through the week ending Sunday, December 26, 1982. Table 10.8(b) contains new data for the week ending January 2, 1983 through the week ending October 30, 1983.

TABLE 10.8(a) Restaurant Sales: Old Data.

Week Ending	Sales	Week Ending	Sales	Week Ending	Sales
1/4/81	$1,688	3/22/81	$5,188	6/7/81	$3,399
1/11/81	2,514	3/29/81	5,944	6/14/81	3,376
1/18/81	5,843	4/5/81	5,842	6/21/81	3,627
1/25/81	4,912	4/12/81	6,589	6/28/81	4,201
2/1/81	5,133	4/19/81	5,447	7/5/81	3,515
2/8/81	4,563	4/26/81	7,548	7/12/81	3,645
2/15/81	5,416	5/3/81	6,403	7/19/81	3,416
2/22/81	6,416	5/10/81	4,103	7/26/81	3,565
3/1/81	5,879	5/17/81	6,594	8/2/81	2,428
3/8/81	3,460	5/24/81	5,742	8/9/81	3,292
3/15/81	4,517	5/31/81	3,714	8/16/81	3,460

TABLE 10.8(a) Restaurant Sales: Old Data.

Week Ending	Sales	Week Ending	Sales	Week Ending	Sales
8/23/81	$6,212	2/7/82	$5,328	7/25/82	$3,614
8/30/81	6,057	2/14/82	5,014	8/1/82	3,722
9/6/81	5,739	2/21/82	4,986	8/8/82	4,307
9/13/81	5,560	2/28/82	5,213	8/15/82	3,322
9/20/81	5,335	3/7/82	4,807	8/22/82	5,962
9/27/81	5,305	3/14/82	3,964	8/29/82	6,784
10/4/81	5,364	3/21/82	5,201	9/5/82	6,069
10/11/81	5,511	3/28/82	4,863	9/12/82	5,897
10/18/81	5,698	4/4/82	5,019	9/19/82	5,916
10/25/81	5,382	4/11/82	4,868	9/26/82	4,998
11/1/81	5,629	4/18/82	5,777	10/3/82	5,111
11/8/81	5,617	4/25/82	6,543	10/10/82	5,612
11/15/81	5,742	5/2/82	6,352	10/17/82	5,906
11/22/81	3,747	5/9/82	5,837	10/24/82	6,010
11/29/81	4,159	5/16/82	7,162	10/31/82	5,937
12/6/81	4,853	5/23/82	4,997	11/7/82	6,004
12/13/81	5,607	5/30/82	4,063	11/14/82	5,959
12/20/81	3,946	6/6/82	3,942	11/21/82	4,223
12/27/81	1,919	6/13/82	4,011	11/28/82	4,679
1/3/82	1,898	6/20/82	3,999	12/5/82	5,307
1/10/82	1,870	6/27/82	4,794	12/12/82	6,101
1/17/82	3,962	7/4/82	4,956	12/19/82	6,896
1/24/82	5,973	7/11/82	3,885	12/26/82	2,214
1/31/82	5,009	7/18/82	4,209		

TABLE 10.8(b) Restaurant Sales: New Data.

Week Ending	Sales	Week Ending	Sales	Week Ending	Sales
1/2/83	$2,431	4/17/83	$6,357	7/31/83	$3,558
1/9/83	2,796	4/24/83	7,273	8/7/83	3,791
1/16/83	4,432	5/1/83	8,678	8/14/83	3,946
1/23/83	5,714	5/8/83	7,418	8/21/83	3,054
1/30/83	5,324	5/15/83	10,388	8/28/83	6,893
2/6/83	5,011	5/22/83	4,940	9/4/83	8,037
2/13/83	5,336	5/29/83	4,195	9/11/83	6,884
2/20/83	4,999	6/5/83	3,895	9/18/83	7,143
2/27/83	5,340	6/12/83	3,762	9/25/83	8,318
3/6/83	5,009	6/19/83	3,739	10/2/83	6,871
3/13/83	5,590	6/26/83	3,975	10/9/83	6,514
3/20/83	3,308	7/3/83	4,634	10/16/83	6,656
3/27/83	6,558	7/10/83	4,891	10/23/83	6,484
4/3/83	4,991	7/17/83	3,463	10/30/83	6,125
4/10/83	6,952	7/24/83	3,536		

QUESTIONS

1. What is the appropriate Box-Jenkins model to use on the original data?

2. What are your forecasts for the first four weeks of January 1983?

3. How do these forecasts compare with actual sales?

4. How does your Box-Jenkins model compare to the regression models used in Chapter 7?

5. Would you use the same Box-Jenkins model if the new data were combined with the old data?

CASE STUDY **10.2**

DAILY DEMAND FOR TROUT TAGS

To conserve natural resources and provide recreation for its citizens and tourists, the State of Missouri operates 15 trout management areas. The Missouri Department of Conservation rears approximately 3 million trout annually. After 15 months these trout are released in lakes and streams. Four of the larger operations are "trout parks" having spring-fed streams stocked daily during a season that lasts from March 1 through October 31 (245 days). This case describes the development and application of a model for forecasting daily demand for trout at the state's largest trout park, Bennett Spring.[3] The model has been used by the hatchery manager for the daily planning of fish releases. The results of its use during the 1979 season are discussed below.

To fish at Missouri trout parks, a person must have a license and purchase a daily trout tag for $1.50. This tag entitles a fisherman to a limit of 5 trout per day. Each of Missouri's four trout parks has a manager responsible for forecasting the sales of tags so that an appropriate number of trout can be released. To acclimate them to the stream and the shock of transportation and handling, trout are released the night before the next day's fishing period. The policy of the Department of Conservation is to release, on the average, 2.25 fish per tag sold. Yet, only forecasts of the number of tags sold are available when fish are released. Consequently, the quality of fishing on any day is dependent on the accuracy of the forecast. If not enough fish are released, the quality and quantity of fishing declines. While a decline in fishermen might not seem a serious problem, hatchery revenues and the local economy are very much dependent on the fisherman/tourist trade. In contrast, if too many fish are released, operating costs will become excessive.

Before trout are released in the evening, the current day's sale of tags is known. This information is used by the hatchery manager to make a one-day-ahead forecast. As one might expect, the sale of tags is seasonal with respect to both the day of the week and the month of the year. Figures 10.29(a) and (b) illustrate the demands for tags in 1977 and 1978. Note the high degree of association between the two series. By using these data, a forecasting model is developed.

This case study was contributed by Stephen A. De Lurgio, University of Missouri, Kansas City.

[3] Stephen A. De Lurgio, "Forecasting Daily Demand at a State Trout Park Using ARIMA/Box-Jenkins Methodology," *Proceedings of the American Institute for Decision Sciences Conference—1980,* Las Vegas, Nev., pp. 237–239.

FIGURE 10.29 Tags Sold in 1977 and 1978 by Day.

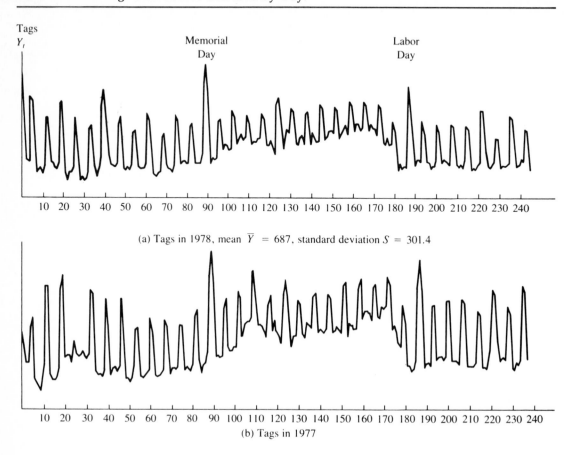

(a) Tags in 1978, mean $\overline{Y}$ = 687, standard deviation S = 301.4

(b) Tags in 1977

MODEL IDENTIFICATION

The plots of Figures 10.29(a) and (b) reveal a daily as well as an annual seasonality [i.e., the sales on a given day of the week, period t, is highly correlated with that of the same day (not date) last year, that is $t - 364$]. This high correlation from week to week and year to year suggests three possible approaches to modeling the series: (1) models with weekly seasonal parameters (e.g., 7 day differencing or seasonal indexes), (2) those with annual differencing and parameters (e.g., 364-day differencing or parameters), and (3) some combination of (1) and (2).

To model the stochastic process of a time series, it is necessary to have a series that is stationary in the level and variance. Stationarity in level is achieved through differencing and stationarity in variance, through the use of power transformations (e.g., logarithms and exponentiation). Figures 10.30(a) and (b) illustrate the autocorrelation values and patterns for the 1978 sale of tags. As shown there, the series does have a pronounced 7-day seasonality; in fact, the series is nonstationary with respect to 7-day lags. Therefore, 7-day differencing is necessary to achieve stationarity. While not illustrated here, the autocorrelations at lags 364 and 728

FIGURE 10.30(a) Autocorrelation Values for Original Series.

```
AUTOCORRELATION FUNCTION                    245 OBSERVATIONS
DATA - BENNET SPRINGS DAILY DATA 1978
DIFFERENCING - ORIGINAL SERIES IS YOUR DATA.
                  DIFFERENCES BELOW ARE OF ORDER    1

ORIGINAL SERIES
MEAN OF THE SERIES =0.63993E+03
ST. DEV. OF SERIES =0.30138E+03
NUMBER OF OBSERVATIONS =    245

   1-  7      0.56    0.06   -0.04   -0.05    0.01    0.43    0.76
   ST.E.      0.06    0.08    0.08    0.08    0.08    0.08    0.09

   8- 14      0.42    0.01   -0.05   -0.04    0.03    0.40    0.70
   ST.E.      0.11    0.12    0.12    0.12    0.12    0.12    0.13

  15- 21      0.38    0.00   -0.05   -0.04    0.01    0.36    0.64
   ST.E.      0.14    0.14    0.14    0.14    0.14    0.14    0.15

  22- 28      0.33   -0.04   -0.10   -0.10   -0.05    0.31    0.60
   ST.E.      0.16    0.16    0.16    0.16    0.16    0.16    0.16

  29- 35      0.29   -0.08   -0.13   -0.12   -0.07    0.27    0.56
   ST.E.      0.17    0.18    0.18    0.18    0.18    0.18    0.18

  36- 42      0.26   -0.10   -0.16   -0.16   -0.12    0.19    0.46
   ST.E.      0.19    0.19    0.19    0.19    0.19    0.19    0.19

  43- 49      0.19   -0.12   -0.17   -0.16   -0.11    0.18    0.43
   ST.E.      0.19    0.19    0.19    0.20    0.20    0.20    0.20

  50          0.18
   ST.E.      0.20

MEAN DIVIDED BY ST. ERROR = 0.33235E+02

TO TEST WHETHER THIS SERIES IS WHITE NOISE, THE VALUE
0.10935E+04 SHOULD BE COMPARED WITH A CHI-SQUARE VARIABLE
WITH  50 DEGREES OF FREEDOM

DIFFERENCE  1
MEAN OF THE SERIES =-.96311E+00
ST. DEV. OF SERIES =0.28340E+03
NUMBER OF OBSERVATIONS =    244

   1-  7      0.07   -0.45   -0.10   -0.09   -0.40    0.09    0.77
   ST.E.      0.06    0.06    0.08    0.08    0.08    0.09    0.09

   8- 14      0.07   -0.38   -0.07   -0.08   -0.35    0.08    0.70
   ST.E.      0.11    0.11    0.12    0.12    0.12    0.12    0.12

  15- 21      0.06   -0.36   -0.06   -0.06   -0.33    0.07    0.68
   ST.E.      0.14    0.14    0.14    0.14    0.14    0.14    0.14

  22- 28      0.06   -0.34   -0.07   -0.06   -0.37    0.08    0.69
   ST.E.      0.16    0.16    0.16    0.16    0.16    0.16    0.16

  29- 35      0.06   -0.34   -0.07   -0.05   -0.34    0.06    0.67
   ST.E.      0.18    0.18    0.18    0.18    0.18    0.18    0.18

  36- 42      0.07   -0.33   -0.07   -0.05   -0.31    0.04    0.61
   ST.E.      0.19    0.19    0.19    0.19    0.19    0.20    0.20

  43- 49      0.06   -0.29   -0.07   -0.04   -0.29    0.05    0.57
   ST.E.      0.20    0.20    0.20    0.20    0.20    0.21    0.21

  50          0.06
   ST.E.      0.21

MEAN DIVIDED BY ST. ERROR = 0.53086E-01

TO TEST WHETHER THIS SERIES IS WHITE NOISE, THE VALUE
0.12280E+04 SHOULD BE COMPARED WITH A CHI-SQUARE VARIABLE
WITH  50 DEGREES OF FREEDOM
```

FIGURE 10.30(b) Autocorrelation Patterns for Original Series.

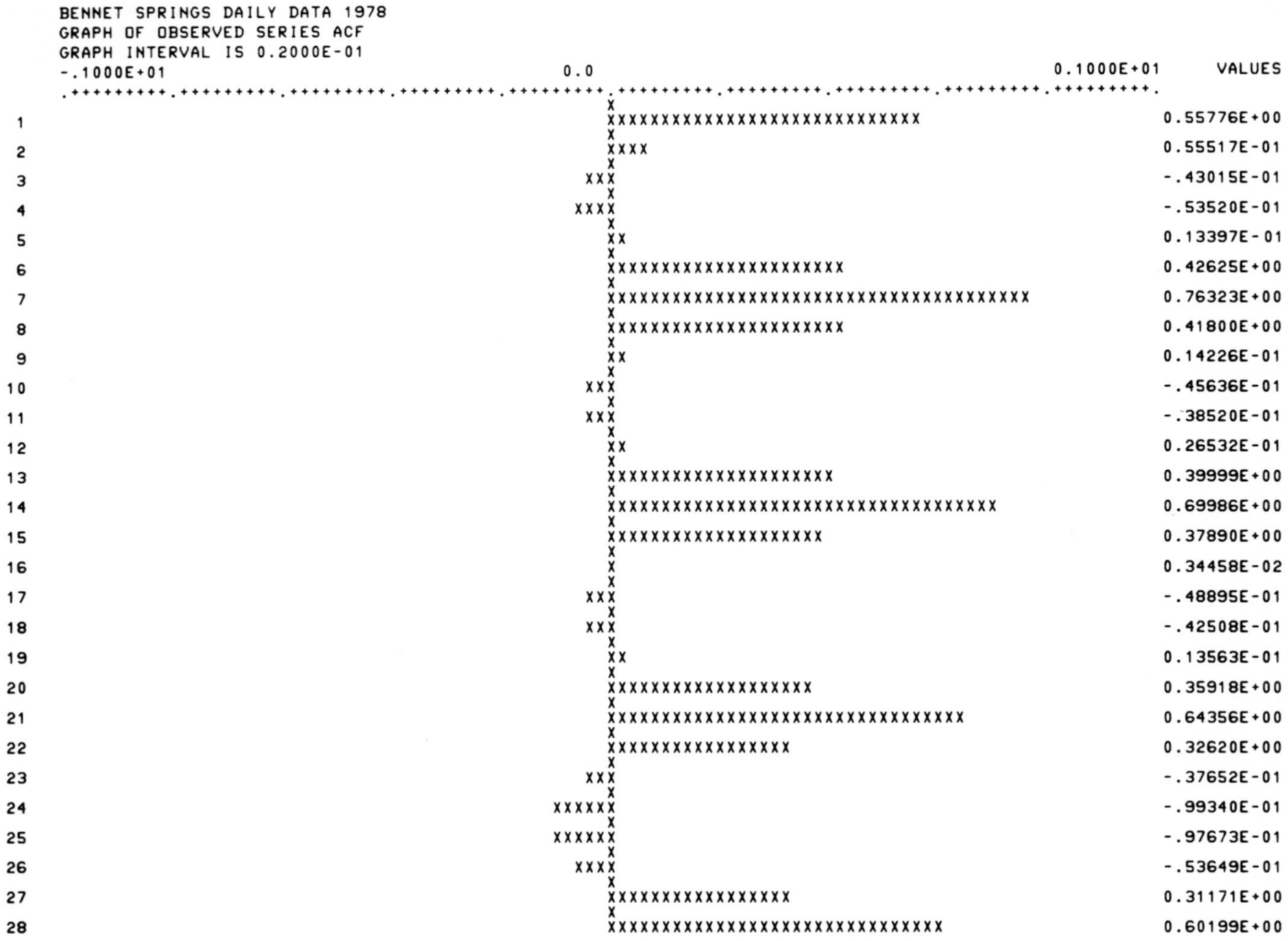
BENNET SPRINGS DAILY DATA 1978
GRAPH OF OBSERVED SERIES ACF
GRAPH INTERVAL IS 0.2000E-01
-.1000E+01
0.0
0.1000E+01
VALUES
1 0.55776E+00
2 0.55517E-01
3 -.43015E-01
4 -.53520E-01
5 0.13397E-01
6 0.42625E+00
7 0.76323E+00
8 0.41800E+00
9 0.14226E-01
10 -.45636E-01
11 -.38520E-01
12 0.26532E-01
13 0.39999E+00
14 0.69986E+00
15 0.37890E+00
16 0.34458E-02
17 -.48895E-01
18 -.42508E-01
19 0.13563E-01
20 0.35918E+00
21 0.64356E+00
22 0.32620E+00
23 -.37652E-01
24 -.99340E-01
25 -.97673E-01
26 -.53649E-01
27 0.31171E+00
28 0.60199E+00

confirmed that the series is nonstationary with respect to 364-day lags. Therefore, 364-day differencing is an alternative way to achieve stationarity. Because taking either 7 or 364 differences yields a stationary series, it is not necessary to take both 7 and 364 differences. That is, two alternative approaches to modeling the series exist: model the stochastic behavior using 7-day differences, or model the annual differences, but not both.

Because the annually differenced series yielded the best model, only the annually differenced models will be developed here. The effectiveness of annually differencing is fairly evident in the association of the (a) and (b) plots of Figure 10.29. This association is confirmed by the high coefficient of determination (R^2) for Z.

$$Z_t = y_t - y_{t-364}$$

The standard deviation of the daily tag sales for 1978 is 301.4, while the standard deviation of annually differenced series (Z_t) is 116.7. Therefore, the coefficient of determination is

$$R^2 = 1 - \frac{(y_t - y_{t-364})^2/(n-1)}{(y_t - \bar{y}_t)^2/(n-1)}$$

$$= 1 - \frac{85^2}{301.4^2} = 92\%$$

While entertaining potential models, it was evident that there are at least two different series represented by the 245-day season. Figure 10.31 illustrates the plot of annual differences (Z_t). As shown there, the demand in the first 60 days of the year is much more variable than later in the year. This greater variability is, in part, the result of higher weather variability in the months of March and April. Temperatures are lower and more variable, while rain and snowfall are higher during this period. Also, in the spring, relatively more anglers come from the immediate vicinity of the state park, while in the summer, more fishermen are tourists from nearby cities and states. The number of extreme observations during March and April confounds model identification; consequently, it was decided to study two models, one for the 60 days of spring and the other for the 185 days of summer. Next, the summer model will be discussed. The spring model is briefly discussed later.

Figure 10.32 illustrates the autocorrelation functions (ACFs) and partial autocorrelation functions (PACFs) for the annually differenced series of the summer months. As shown there, the autocorrelation pattern confirms that the series is stationary with respect to level (i.e. the ACFs die out rapidly). The exponential decline of the autocorrelations of lags 1 through 5 is indicative of a first-order autoregressive process. To confirm this identification, consider the PACF patterns shown in Figure 10.33. The PACFs of a first-order autoregressive model should have a single peak at lag 1. Figure 10.39 does show a single peak at 1. None of the other lags has a statistically significant PACF. Therefore, this identification appears to be correct.

Annual differences have been taken of the original series to achieve stationarity. If the mean of these differences (Z_t) is statistically different from zero, then the series has been experiencing a trend; in contrast, if the mean of the differenced series is not statistically different from zero, then the series has been experiencing a

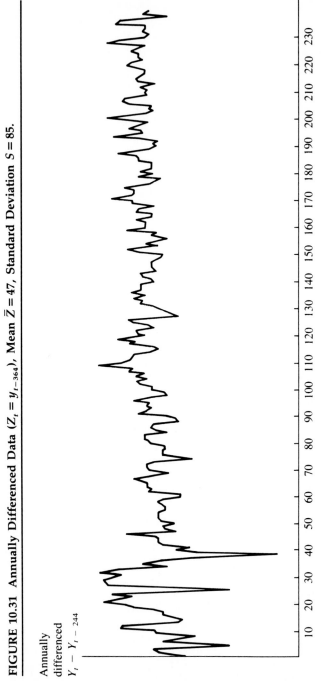

FIGURE 10.31 Annually Differenced Data ($Z_t = y_{t-364}$), Mean $\bar{Z} = 47$, Standard Deviation $S = 85$.

Annually
differenced
$Y_t - Y_{t-244}$

183 OBSERVATIONS

AUTOCORRELATION FUNCTION
DATA - BENNET SPRINGS YEARLY DIFFERENCED DATA
DIFFERENCING - ORIGINAL SERIES IS YOUR DATA.
          DIFFERENCES BELOW ARE OF ORDER   1

ORIGINAL SERIES
MEAN OF THE SERIES =0.47246E+02
ST.DEV. OF SERIES =0.84706E+02
NUMBER OF OBSERVATIONS =   183

```
 1- 7   0.49   0.22   0.17   0.16   0.12   0.17   0.16
ST.E.   0.07   0.09   0.09   0.09   0.10   0.10   0.10
 8-14   0.15   0.11   0.10   0.04   0.12   0.19   0.17
ST.E.   0.10   0.10   0.10   0.10   0.10   0.10   0.10
15-21   0.13   0.06   0.04  -0.07  -0.05  -0.02  -0.04
ST.E.   0.11   0.11   0.11   0.11   0.11   0.11   0.11
22-28  -0.03  -0.02  -0.01   0.02   0.08   0.15   0.11
ST.E.   0.11   0.11   0.11   0.11   0.11   0.11   0.11
29-35   0.05  -0.04  -0.10  -0.10  -0.09   0.00   0.01
ST.E.   0.11   0.11   0.11   0.11   0.11   0.11   0.11
36-42  -0.10  -0.06  -0.07  -0.09  -0.05   0.02   0.01
ST.E.   0.11   0.11   0.11   0.11   0.11   0.11   0.11
43-49  -0.10  -0.17  -0.11  -0.10  -0.05  -0.02   0.10
ST.E.   0.11   0.11   0.11   0.12   0.12   0.12   0.12
50      0.10
ST.E.   0.12
```

MEAN DIVIDED BY ST. ERROR = 0.75453E+01

TO TEST WHETHER THIS SERIES IS WHITE NOISE, THE VALUE   0.13752E+03
SHOULD BE COMPARED WITH A CHI-SQUARE VARIABLE WITH 50 DEGREES OF FREEDOM

GRAPH OF OBSERVED SERIES ACF
GRAPH INTERVAL IS 0.2000E-01

```
     -.1000E+01                           0.0                           0.1000E+01      VALUES
      .++++++++.++++++++.++++++++.++++++++.++++++++.++++++++.++++++++.++++++++.++++++++.
                                          X
 1                                        XXXXXXXXXXXXXXXXXXXXXXXXXXX                    0.49088E+00
 2                                        XXXXXXXXXXX                                    0.21950E+00
 3                                        XXXXXXXXX                                      0.16585E+00
 4                                        XXXXXXXXX                                      0.16362E+00
 5                                        XXXXXXX                                        0.12050E+00
 6                                        XXXXXXXXX                                      0.16733E+00
 7                                        XXXXXXXXX                                      0.15930E+00
 8                                        XXXXXXXX                                       0.14695E+00
 9                                        XXXXXX                                         0.11335E+00
10                                        XXXXXX                                         0.10092E+00
11                                        XXX                                           0.40855E-01
12                                        XXXXXXX                                        0.11918E+00
13                                        XXXXXXXXXX                                     0.18523E+00
14                                        XXXXXXXXXX                                     0.17087E+00
15                                        XXXXXXX                                        0.12816E+00
16                                        XXXX                                           0.64959E-01
```

443

FIGURE 10.33 Partial Autocorrelations for Annually Differenced Series.

PARTIAL AUTOCORRELATIONS   183 OBSERVATIONS

DATA - BENNET SPRINGS YEARLY DIFFERENCED DATA
DIFFERENCING - ORIGINAL SERIES IS YOUR DATA.
           DIFFERENCES BELOW ARE OF ORDER   1

ORIGINAL SERIES
MEAN OF THE SERIES =0.47246E+02
ST.DEV. OF SERIES =0.84706E+02
NUMBER OF OBSERVATIONS =   183

1- 7	0.49	-0.03	0.09	0.07	0.01	0.12	0.02
8- 14	0.05	0.00	0.02	-0.05	0.12	0.08	0.03
15- 21	0.02	-0.06	-0.11	-0.05	-0.04	-0.01	-0.04
22- 28	-0.02	0.02	0.02	0.05	0.09	0.11	-0.01
29- 35	-0.01	-0.08	-0.07	-0.04	-0.05	0.08	-0.03
36- 42	-0.13	0.06	-0.07	-0.05	0.00	0.02	0.01
43- 49	-0.10	-0.06	0.12	-0.01	0.05	0.05	0.18
50	0.03						

BENNET SPRINGS YEARLY DIFFERENCED DATA
GRAPH OF OBSERVED SERIES PACF
GRAPH INTERVAL IS 0.2000E-01

	VALUES
1	0.49088E+00
2	-.28271E-01
3	0.90889E-01
4	0.67994E-01
5	0.56142E-02
6	0.12271E+00
7	0.22506E-01
8	0.49187E-01
9	0.41294E-02
10	0.17691E-01
11	-.51217E-01
12	0.12201E+00
13	0.83580E-01
14	0.25146E-01
15	0.15836E-01
16	-.60585E-01
17	-.10534E+00
18	-.53679E-01
19	-.41861E-01
20	-.79435E-02
21	-.43159E-01

444

seasonal drift. A statistical significance test is performed on the annually differenced series. As shown in Figure 10.32, the mean of the annually differenced series (Z_t) is 47.246 with a standard deviation of 84.7. This mean is 7.54 standard errors away from the no-trend mean of zero.

$$Z = \frac{47.24 - .0}{\dfrac{84.7}{\sqrt{183}}}$$

$$= 7.54$$

Consequently, the tentative model that has been identified is a first-order autoregressive process of an annually differenced series that appears to possess a trend:

$$Z_t = \phi_1 Z_{t-1} + \phi_0 + \varepsilon_t$$

$$y_t - y_{t-364} = \phi_1(y_{t-1} - y_{t-365}) + \phi_0 + \varepsilon_t$$

where

ϕ_1 = the first-order autoregressive parameter

ϕ_0 = a trend parameter

ε_t = the error in fitting the model

ESTIMATION

By using the Pack[4] programs, the statistics and 95% parameter confidence intervals of Table 10.9 were estimated.

The estimated model (hereafter referred to as model 1) is

$$y_t - y_{t-364} = .4969(y_{t-1} - y_{t-365}) + 49.7 + \varepsilon_t$$

TABLE 10.9 Statistics and Parameters of Model 1.

Parameter	Value	95% Percent Confidence Level	
		Lower Limit	Upper Limit
ϕ_1	.4969	.3666	.6272
ϕ_0	49.7	26.41	70.17

Residual standard error of $\varepsilon_t = 74.22$
Number of residuals $= 182$

[4] David J. Pack, *A Computer Program for the Analysis of Time Series Models Using the Box-Jenkins Philosophy* (Hatboro, Pa: Automatic Forecasting Systems, 1978).

If this model is written in forecasting form, it is intuitively appealing and insightful.

$$\hat{y}_t = y_{t-364} + .4969(y_{t-1} - y_{t-365}) + 49.7$$

The forecasted demand in period t is equal to the demand for the same day last year plus .4969 times the annual change in demand experienced in period $t-1$ plus an annual increase (trend) of 49.7. This result appears to be very logical considering the type of seasonality of the series.

DIAGNOSTICS

The Box-Jenkins ARIMA modeling procedure is iterative. After identifying and estimating a model, the analyst is obligated to diagnose the model using well-defined statistical tests. These tests include (1) a statistical test of model parameters, (2) analysis of the ACFs and PACFs of the residuals, (3) a chi-square goodness-of-fit test on the autocorrelation coefficients, and (4) an analysis of the plot of residuals to further confirm randomness and stationarity in level and variance. If any of these tests indicates an inadequate model, then a new model is identified, estimated, and diagnosed. Let us perform these tests on model 1.

Diagnostic Tests

Statistical Test of Model Parameters

Because the 95% confidence intervals of Table 10.9 do not include zero, both parameters of this model are statistically different from zero. Consequently, the model appears to be adequate with respect to individual parameters.

The ACFs and PACFs of the Residual

The ACFs of the residuals of the model are given in Figure 10.34. As shown there, the ACFs at low and long lags are all statistically insignificant (i.e., have been shown not to be statistically significantly different from zero). There are no ACFs that are more than two standard errors from zero. Therefore, the series appears to be white noise. The PACFs, while not shown, also confirm this conclusion.

Incidentally, recognize that in a plot of 50 ACFs from a white noise series that some ACFs would be expected to be more than two standard errors away from zero just because of random chance. For this series, if a single peak were to occur at lags 1, 2, 3, 7, or 14, one might be concerned because it would be an indication that the residuals might not be white noise and therefore that the model would be inadequate. Yet, if a few peaks occurred at other lags, one would infer that they were a consequence of random error. The structure of the model and series guides us in deciding whether a large ACF is a matter of concern.

Chi-Square Goodness-of-Fit Test

It was confirmed above that no individual peak was more than two standard errors away from zero. Yet, one can have several statistically insignificant peaks that are,

FIGURE 10.34 Autocorrelations for Residuals of Model 1.

```
AUTOCORRELATION FUNCTION                       182 OBSERVATIONS

DATA - THE ESTIMATED RESIDUALS - MODEL 1

ORIGINAL SERIES
MEAN OF THE SERIES =0.43597E-04
ST. DEV. OF SERIES =0.73815E+02
NUMBER OF OBSERVATIONS =   182
    1-  7     0.02   -0.07    0.02    0.08   -0.02    0.09    0.06
    ST.E.     0.07    0.07    0.07    0.07    0.08    0.08    0.08

    8- 14     0.05    0.03    0.08   -0.08    0.04    0.12    0.07
    ST.E.     0.08    0.08    0.08    0.08    0.08    0.08    0.08

   15- 21     0.05    0.05   -0.05   -0.05   -0.03    0.03   -0.02
    ST.E.     0.08    0.08    0.08    0.08    0.08    0.08    0.08

   22- 28    -0.02   -0.01   -0.02   -0.01    0.03    0.11    0.05
    ST.E.     0.08    0.08    0.08    0.08    0.08    0.08    0.08

   29- 35     0.04   -0.03   -0.06   -0.05   -0.08    0.06    0.07
    ST.E.     0.08    0.08    0.08    0.08    0.08    0.08    0.08

   36- 42    -0.13    0.01   -0.01   -0.06   -0.03    0.05    0.07
    ST.E.     0.08    0.08    0.08    0.08    0.08    0.08    0.08

   43- 49    -0.06   -0.14    0.02   -0.07    0.01   -0.06    0.11
    ST.E.     0.08    0.08    0.09    0.09    0.09    0.09    0.09

   50         0.08
    ST.E.     0.09

MEAN DIVIDED BY ST. ERROR = 0.79678E-05

TO TEST WHETHER THIS SERIES IS WHITE NOISE, THE VALUE
0.30010E+02 SHOULD BE COMPARED WITH A CHI-SQUARE VARIABLE
WITH  43 DEGREES OF FREEDOM
```

individually, consistent with the white noise assumption, but collectively these peaks are a strong indication of nonrandom (nonwhite noise) behavior. The two standard error test may not detect such nonrandomness. Fortunately, a chi-square goodness-of-fit test is available to test the significance of a group of autocorrelations. As shown in Figure 10.34, the chi-square value for ACFs is 30.00 at 43 degrees of freedom. This value is not statistically significantly different from zero. That is, the chi-square value for 43 degrees of freedom from a white noise model has somewhere between a 90% and 95% chance of having a value greater than or equal to 30.00. Alternatively, at 40 degrees of freedom, a chi-square value would have to exceed 51.8 before a .10 level of significance is reached. Consequently, the series has been shown not to be significantly different from white noise.

A Plot of Residuals

Because it is not insightful for these data, a plot of residuals is not illustrated. The visual analysis of residual plots is a very important step in diagnosing any forecasting model. The plot of residuals for this model is consistent with the white noise hypothesis.

FORECAST ACCURACY

The strength of ARIMA building methods is their ability to model the underlying stochastic process of the series. When this stochastic process remains stable into the future, very accurate forecasts can be obtained. Let us explore the forecast accuracy of the model as well as compare its forecast with those of management.

Table 10.10 illustrates the forecast accuracies of the model and the manager using a one-period-ahead forecast during 1979. The first forecast (May) was made using the parameters fitted to 1977–1978 data. The mean of the residuals ε_t and the residual standard error are obtained from a one-period-ahead forecast (e.g., forecast May 13 knowing May 12's demand). After all of May's data have been realized, parameters are reestimated using the differenced series of May–October 1978 through May 1979 data. Forecasts are then made for June, and the procedure is repeated. As shown in Table 10.10, the model was quite accurate; in fact, it was as accurate in forecasting four months of the 1979 season (RSE = 76.6) as it was in fitting 1978 data (RSE = 74.22).

As shown in Table 10.10, if the manager had used model 1 instead of his subjective estimates, his forecast would have been slightly more accurate. He would have experienced a mean error closer to zero and a lower RSE. Yet there is little difference between the manager's and the model's forecasts because the manager uses the same data as the model in arriving at his forecast. That is, he compares period $t - 1$ with period $t - 365$ and adjusts period $t - 364$ to arrive at the forecast for period t. While the differences between the manager's forecasts and those of the model are not great, the effectiveness and parsimony of the model are quite evident.

IMPLEMENTATION

Model 1 is very easy to implement. The data necessary to forecast demand have been kept routinely for five years prior to 1979. In the latter part of 1979 the manager used the forecasts of model 1 with his own estimates to yield tomorrow's expected demand. Approximately every four weeks the parameters of the model were updated through use of the Pack programs.

As shown in Table 10.9, the parameters of the model have varied little. If parameters were reestimated only once a year, the accuracy of the forecast would be affected only very slightly.

TABLE 10.10 Adaptive (Rolling) Forecast for 1979.

Month	Model 1 Parameters		Model 1 Forecast		Manager's Forecast	
	W_0	B_1	$\bar{\varepsilon}_t$	RSE	$\bar{\varepsilon}_t$	RSE
May	42.6	.5373	−9.3	89.9	−20.8	81.8
Jun.	38.9	.5067	9.8	66.8	−7.5	84.2
Jul.	35.7	.5033	−9.1	90.3	−12.7	76.0
Aug.	37.5	.4623	10.0	59.4	−27.7	77.0
		Mean	.5	76.6	−17.2	80.0

SUMMARY AND CONCLUSIONS

The purpose of modeling is to provide an operating manager with a parsimonious model. As shown here, the procedures of Box and Jenkins do represent an effective approach in this application. Through use of the model, the accuracy and ease with which forecasts are made can be improved. The manager has found the ARIMA model useful and easy to implement. That these models perform slightly better than an experienced manager is evidence of their effectiveness in improving the practice of forecasting. It is doubtful that other methods of forecasting would have converged as quickly on so simple and accurate a model as the ARIMA procedures.

APPENDIX—EARLY SPRING MODELS

For this series and geographical location, the influences of weather on tag sales was much greater in the first 60–90 days of the series than in the summer months. A number of methods including multivariate ARIMA and multiple regression using temperature and rainfall data were used to forecast the demand for trout tags during March, April, and May. While statistically adequate models were identified, their error statistics (i.e., accuracy) were either inferior to those of the manager or, if they were more accurate, were so complex as to make them undesirable alternatives for operating personnel. These models are still under investigation at this time.

QUESTIONS

1. Given the following actual demands, forecast the demand for period t using model 1.

$$y_{t-1} = 700$$
$$y_{t-364} = 732$$
$$y_{t-365} = 670$$

2. Discuss the reasons why the manager's forecasts are nearly as accurate as those of the model during the summer period, and why his forecast might be much more accurate during the early spring season.

3. Write out model 1 in forecasting form for two-period-ahead forecasts.

4. The sale of tags is highly seasonal. Identify as many underlying causes of this seasonality as you believe relevant.

5. For these data, why do you think the annually differenced models perform significantly better than the seven-period models (i.e, those modeling the seven-day seasonality)?

6. In calculating 20 ACFs for a white noise series, what is the probability that one or more ACFs would be more than two standard errors away from the hypothetical value of zero?

SELECTED BIBLIOGRAPHY

Box, G., and Jenkins, G. *Time Series Analysis: Forecasting and Control.* San Francisco: Holden-Day, 1976.

De Lurgio, S. A. "Forecasting Daily Demand at a State Trout Park Using ARIMA/ Box-Jenkins Methodology." *Proceedings of the American Institute for Decision Sciences Conference, 1980,* Las Vegas, Nev., pp. 237–239.

Jenkins, G., and McLeod, G. *Case Studies in Time Analysis.* Lancaster, UK: Gwilym Jenkins & Partners Ltd., 1982.

Libert, G. "The M-Competition with a Fully Automatic Box-Jenkins Procedure." *Journal of Forecasting* 3 (3) (1984): 325–328.

Lusk, E. J., and Neves, J. S. "A Comparative ARIMA Analysis of the 111 Series of the Makridakis Competition." *Journal of Forecasting* 3 (3) (1984): 329–332.

Makridakis, S., and Wheelwright, S. C. *Interactive Forecasting.* Palo Alto, Calif.: Scientific Press, 1977.

Makridakis, S., et al. "An Interactive Forecasting System." *American Statistician* 28 (1974): 153–158.

Montgomery, D. S., and Johnson, L. A. *Forecasting and Time Series Analysis.* New York: McGraw-Hill, 1976.

O'Donovan, T. M. *Short Term Forecasting: An Introduction to the Box-Jenkins Approach.* New York: John Wiley & Sons, 1983.

Pack, D. J. "In Defense of ARIMA Modeling." *International Journal of forecasting* 6 (2) (1990): 211–218.

Quenouille, M. H. "The Joint Distribution of Serial Correlation Coefficients." *Annuals of Mathematical Statistics* 20 (1949): 561–571.

11

Judgmental Elements in Forecasting

T he forecasting techniques covered in this book all involve the manipulation of historical data to produce predictions or forecasts of important variables of interest. The discussions in previous chapters were concerned with complex data analyses and implied that the forecaster's judgment was not involved. In fact, the use of good judgment is an essential component of all good forecasting techniques. Good judgment is required in deciding on the data that are relevant to the problem and in interpreting the results of the data analysis process and sometimes constitutes a major portion of the analysis itself.

In Chapter 3, methods of identifying and collecting relevant forecasting data were described. This chapter discusses some of the important forecasting elements that are adjuncts or substitutions for the methodical manipulation of such historical data. In addition, several elements involving the management of the forecasting process are described.

JUDGMENTAL FORECASTING

There are many forecasting situations where only the analysis of historical data is used to generate the final forecast; the judgment or opinion of the analyst is not injected into the process. This book is concerned primarily with such forecasting techniques and, as a result, with short- and intermediate-term forecasts. Such forecasts are the essential concern of most levels of management in an organization and are associated with most of the critical decisions that must be made.

These forecasting procedures rely on the manipulation of historical data and assume a past and a future that are indistinguishable except for the specific variables identified as affecting the likelihood of future outcomes. This assumption precludes a substantive shift in the technological base of the society, an assumption that many recent developments suggest is erroneous. Consider, for example, the introduction and proliferation of high-speed, inexpensive personal computers.

In some forecasting situations, the data analysis process is supplemented by the analyst after considering the unusual circumstances of the situation, or after recognizing that past history is not an accurate predictor of the future. The amount of judgment injected into the forecasting process tends to increase as the historical data are few in number or are judged to be partially irrelevant. In the extreme case, it may be the analyst's opinion that there are no historical data that are directly relevant to the forecasting process. Under these conditions, forecasts based purely on the opinions of "experts" are used to formulate the forecast or scenario for the future.

Interestingly, research has shown that when historical data are available, the modification of the forecasts produced by analytical methods tends to reduce the accuracy of the forecasts.[1] This fact may be attributed to some bias on the part of the forecaster, possibly because of a tendency to be overly optimistic or to underestimate future uncertainty. It has also been shown that using a judgment component in the forecasting process tends to increase the forecasting cost.[2]

When there is little or no relevant historical data available to assist in the forecasting process, judgment must be relied on if forecasts or predictions about the future are desired. Since such situations often arise, especially for top management, techniques have been developed to improve the accuracy of such forecasts by utilizing the available executive judgment to the best advantage. The use of these techniques is worthy of consideration since executives frequently consider their own judgment superior to other methods of predicting the future. As Makridakis states, "People prefer making forecasts judgmentally. They believe that their knowledge of the product, market, and customers as well as their insight and inside information gives them a unique ability to forecast judgmentally."[3]

Following are several questions, each of which suggests the use of imagination and "brainstorming" rather than complete reliance on the collection and manipulation of historical data. For each of these questions, one of the forecasting techniques discussed in this chapter may provide a company's management team with valuable insights into its firm's future operating environment.

- What will be the age distribution of the United States in the year 2025?
- To what extent will U.S. citizens work in the home 25 years from now?
- What cities will be the major population and business centers in 20 years?
- What is the likelihood of a major war by the year 2050?

---

[1] S. Makridakis, "The Art and Science of Forecasting," *International Journal of Forecasting,* Vol. 2 (1986), p. 45.

[2] *Ibid.*

[3] *Ibid.,* p. 63.

- To what extent will the United States depend on other countries for the manufacture of key consumer items?
- To what extent will shopping from the home using television and computers be popular in 20 years?
- What kinds of recreation will occupy U.S. citizens in the year 2025?
- How much leisure time will the average U.S. citizen have during the next century?
- Will the United States begin pulling back from its commitments around the globe over the next 25 years? If so, in what ways will this affect U.S. business?

The techniques discussed in this chapter are sometimes called *judgmental forecasting* methods since judgment is the primary or sole component of the process. Some of them are also referred to as *technological forecasting* methods since they frequently deal with projecting the effects of technology changes into the uncertain future. The remainder of this chapter outlines some of the commonly used forecasting methods where the judgment of the forecaster is the primary ingredient.[4]

Growth Curves

The growth curve forecasting method concentrates on the long-term changes in a variable of interest and projects this variable into the future without regard to the technology that might bring about the predicted changes. The cost per computer transaction, for example, might be projected into the next century based on the past history of this variable. The technology that is necessary to produce the projected changes is not considered in this process.

The cost per mile of automobile travel might be projected similarly, as might automobile usage by the American population. Again, the technology involved in producing the cars and fuel needed for the predicted changes is not considered.

Since growth curve projections usually involve long-term forecasts, various curved relationships between time and the variable of interest are generally used. The exponential curve is often the basis for growth curve projections since this curve involves ever-decreasing improvements over time.

Even though inaccuracies may be expected when using growth curves to predict the future, this method can be of great benefit to management since it concentrates attention on the long-term aspects of a

---

[4] For an organized outline of many forecasting methods including judgment forecasting, see David M. Georgoff and Robert G. Murdick, "Manager's Guide to Forecasting," *Harvard Business Review,* Vol. 1 (January–February 1986), pp. 110–120.

company's business. Growth curves are typically used by top management, often in executive retreat or "think tank" sessions.

The Delphi Method

When experts are gathered in a single meeting location and asked about the future, group dynamics can sometimes distort the process and result in a consensus that may not be carefully thought out by all participants. The Delphi method, first used by an Air-Force-funded RAND Corporation project in the 1950s, attempts to remove the group dynamic aspect from the deliberations of the forecasters. In the first round of the method, the experts reply in writing to the questions posed by the investigating team. The team then summarizes the comments of the participants and mails them back. Participants are then able to read the reactions of the others and to either defend their original views or modify them based on the views of others.

This process continues through two or three rounds until the investigators are satisfied that many viewpoints have been developed and carefully considered. Participants may then be invited to meet together to share and debate their viewpoints. At the conclusion of this process, the investigating team may have a very good viewpoint on the future and can begin to plan their organization's posture accordingly.

Variations on the Delphi method include the elimination of the group conference at the end of the written process. It may be extremely difficult to gather several noted experts for a meeting, and so the process can be concluded after two or three written rounds.

Another variation is the "real-time" Delphi method where the experts are in the same location but are kept apart during the written phase. Each expert receives feedback on the viewpoints of others within a few minutes; in this way, many written rounds are possible before the experts are assembled for the discussion phase.

Another variation involves the use of real-time computers connected by telephone. The written phase can be conducted in a short period of time even though the participants are in different locations. A follow-up conference using computers or telephones can be used to conclude the process.

The advantage of the Delphi method is that noted experts can be asked to carefully consider the subject of interest and to reply thoughtfully to the viewpoints of others without the interference of group dynamics. The result, if the process is carefully handled, may be a good consensus of the future along with several alternative scenarios.[5]

---

[5] See the following for a detailed description of the Delphi method: Frederick J. Parente and Janet K. Anderson-Parente, "Delphi Inquiry Systems," in *Judgmental Forecasting*, George Wright and Peter Ayton, eds. (New York: John Wiley & Sons, 1987), pp. 129–156.

Scenario Writing

Scenario writing involves defining the particulars of an uncertain future by writing a "script" for the environment of an organization over many years in the future. New technology, population shifts, and changing consumer demands are among the factors that are considered and woven into this speculation to provoke the thinking of top management.

A most likely scenario is usually written along with one or more less likely, but possible, scenarios. By considering the posture of the company for each of these possible future environments, top management of the company is in a better position to react to actual business environment changes as they occur and to recognize the long-range implications of subtle changes that might otherwise go unnoticed. In this way, the organization is in a better position to maintain its long-term profitability rather than concentrate on short-term profits and ignore the changing technological environment in which it operates.

The scenario writing process is oftentimes followed by a discussion phase, sometimes by a group other than the one that developed the scenarios. Discussion among the groups can then be used to defend and modify viewpoints so that a solid consensus and alternative scenarios are developed. For example, scenarios might be developed by a company's planning staff and then discussed by the top management team. Even if none of the scenarios is subsequently proven to be true, this process encourages the long-range thinking of the top management team and better prepares it to recognize and react to important environmental changes.

COMBINING FORECASTS

A developing branch of forecasting study involves the combination of two or more forecasting methods to produce the final forecasts. An issue of the *International Journal of Forecasting* (Volume 5, Number 4, 1989) contained a special section on this new technique. Portions of the abstracts of three articles in this issue illustrate the developing nature of combining forecasts:

> Research from over 200 studies demonstrates that combining forecasts produces consistent but modest gains in accuracy. However, this research does not define well the conditions under which combining is most effective nor how methods should be combined in each situation.[6]

> The amount of research on combining forecasts is substantial. Yet, relatively little is known about when and how managers combine

---

[6] J. Scott Armstrong, "Combining Forecasts: The End of the Beginning or the Beginning of the End?" *International Journal of Forecasting*, Vol. 5, No. 4 (1989), pp. 585–592.

forecasts. Important managerial issues that require further study include managerial adjustment of quantitative forecasts, the use of expert systems in combining forecasts, and analyses of the costs of combining forecasts.[7]

Considerable literature has accumulated over the years regarding the combination of forecasts. The primary conclusion of this line of research is that forecast accuracy can be substantially improved through the combination of multiple individual forecasts.... This paper provides a review and annotated bibliography of that literature....[8]

In the coming years, further research will likely be conducted on the advantages of combining forecasts, along with the techniques for doing so. The objective of such combinations will be to develop accurate forecasts that are cost effective.

SUMMARY OF JUDGMENTAL FORECASTING

The danger in using most of the forecasting methods discussed in this text is that they involve the manipulation of historical data to generate the forecast. This practice is a valid procedure if the forecast is for the near-term future but becomes increasingly suspect as the length of the forecasting horizon increases. The methods discussed in this chapter are valuable additions to the forecaster's arsenal when the particular concern of top management, the long-term prediction of the company's environment, is being considered.

Several authors have fascinated the general public with their speculations about the long-term trends currently evident in our society and the future that they portend. Among the more provocative are:

Alvin Toffler, *Future Shock* (New York: Random House, 1970)

Alvin Toffler, *The Third Wave* (New York: Bantam Books, 1980)

John Naisbitt, *Megatrends* (New York: Warner Books, 1982)

John Naisbitt and Patricia Aburdene, *Megatrends 2000* (New York: William Morrow, 1990)

These authors have a unique ability to speculate about the future in provocative ways. The specific forecasting requirements of a business,

---

[7] Essam Mahoud, "Combining Forecasts: Some Managerial Issues," *International Journal of Forecasting,* Vol. 5, No. 4 (1989), pp. 599–600.

[8] Robert T. Clemen, "Combining Forecasts: A Review and Annotated Bibliography," *International Journal of Forecasting,* Vol. 5, No. 4 (1989), pp. 559–583.

however, require more formal procedures that yield plausible projections of the long-range makeup of its competitive environment. This chapter is concerned with some of the methods that can be used to formulate such projections.

OTHER JUDGMENTAL ELEMENTS IN FORECASTING

There are a number of techniques that have been developed to assist decision makers in the process of weighing information about the uncertain future and making the best possible decisions. These techniques are frequently discussed in textbooks and journal articles under the general heading of "decision making" or sometimes "decision making under uncertainty." When managers are faced with the task of making decisions in the face of uncertainty, their ability to forecast becomes a critical element in the decision-making process.

When the analysis of historical data has been completed, a judgment must be made by the decision maker regarding alterations in the firm's course of action. In other words, the analyst must weave the results of the forecasting process into the firm's existing decision-making procedures. A few of the elements of decision theory that are often relevant at this stage of the process are briefly discussed here.

The concept of *expected value* is frequently used by decision makers, either explicitly or implicitly. This concept involves calculating the average value that a random numerical variable will assume over many trials. In Table 11.1, a discrete random variable X is displayed in a probability distribution; every possible value that X can assume is shown along with the probability of each.

> The *expected value* of a discrete random variable is the average value that the random variable assumes over a large number of observations.

TABLE 11.1 Probability Distribution for Expected Value.

X	$P(X)$
1	.10
2	.20
3	.25
4	.30
5	.15
	$\overline{1.00}$

Notice that the sum of the probabilities in Table 11.1 is 1.00, or 100%, which means that every possible value that X can assume has been identified. Suppose that in Table 11.1 X represents the number of new major contracts that a firm will sign during the next fiscal year. The question that is answered by the expected value is: How many new orders can be expected, on the average, if the probability distribution of Table 11.1 is valid? Equation 11.1 is used to calculate the expected value of a probability distribution such as the one shown in Table 11.1.

$$E(X) = \Sigma \ X[P(X)] \hspace{5cm} \textbf{(11.1)}$$

where

$E(X)$ = expected value
X = values that the random variable can assume
$P(X)$ = probability of each X occurring

The expected value of Table 11.1 can be calculated using Equation 11.1 as follows:

$$E(X) = 1(.10) + 2(.20) + 3(.25) + 4(.30) + 5(.15)$$
$$= 3.2$$

The expected value of the probability distribution shown in Table 11.1 is 3.2. If X in this example represents the number of new major contracts for the coming fiscal year, it could be said that, on average, if this same distribution were repeated many times, 3.2 new contracts would be signed. Notice that the value 3.2 is not possible in any one year; only integer values $(1, 2, 3, 4, 5)$ are possible. Nevertheless, the value 3.2 represents the *average* value of the distribution over many trials. Decision makers are frequently interested in such expected values and use them as their best guesses for critical numerical variables in planning for the uncertain future.

Utility theory concepts are used by every decision maker on a daily basis for both personal decisions and organization decisions. Yet few people realize that utility theory has been studied formally and that the decision-making process can be improved by its usage. Utility theory formally recognizes that dollar amounts cannot be judged simply by looking at their values. The impact of various dollar amounts on the firm must be considered as well.

Consider Tables 11.1 and 11.2. In Table 11.1, the expected value was calculated to be 3.2. The expected value of Table 11.2 is also 3.2, calculated using Equation 11.1 as follows:

$$E(X) = -10(.15) + -5(.10) + 0(.25) + 1(.25) + 19.8(.25)$$
$$= 3.2$$

TABLE 11.2 Probability Distribution for Utility Theory.

X	P(X)
−10	.15
−5	.10
0	.25
1	.25
19.8	.25
	1.00

Now suppose the X values in both Table 11.1 and Table 11.2 represent the possible net profits for a large company in millions of dollars. The company's management team must decide whether they wish to embark on the project reflected by the possible profits of Table 11.1, or whether they would prefer the profit picture reflected in Table 11.2. If the expected value concept alone were being used, the two projects would be identical in appeal since they have the same expected value, $3.2 million.

However, notice the vast difference between the two tables in terms of risk and payoffs. In Table 11.1, it is impossible to incur a loss. Even in the worst possible state, a positive profit of $1 million will occur. On the other hand, the largest possible profit is only $5 million. In Table 11.2, there are distinct possibilities of losing a lot of money. On the other hand, a large profit of $19.8 million is possible. A conservative firm might choose the venture reflected in Table 11.1, while an aggressive company might choose the profit/loss picture shown in Table 11.2. Utility theory procedures enable decision makers to formally reflect their attitudes toward different amounts of money in the decision-making process.

Decision theory formally addresses the elements that comprise the decision-making function of business leaders. Expected values and utility theory are often woven into this more general consideration of decision making. As well, the *tree diagram* is used to help the decision maker visualize a complex situation and to make rational decisions. Such a decision tree diagram is shown in Figure 11.1.

Figure 11.1 reflects the uncertainty that exists about the nature of future sales and incorporates the decision about whether to build a new plant or repair the old one. The problem is that if the company knew that high demand would result, it would be better off building the new plant; on the other hand, if it knew that low demand would result, profits would be higher if it repaired the old plant. Even in this simple example, the benefit of the tree diagram can be seen: it enables the decision maker to see the various choices available, to identify those uncertainties beyond the firm's control, and to explicitly determine costs, profits, and the probabilities of future events. In more complicated situations, the benefits of the tree diagram and formal decision theory are even more evident.

FIGURE 11.1 Tree Diagram.

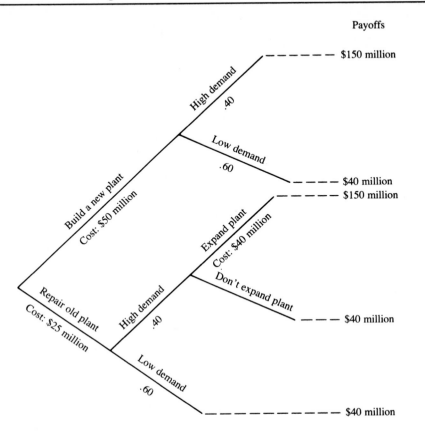

Payoffs

A statistical concept designed to revise preliminary probabilities on the basis of sample evidence is *Bayes' theorem*. This concept is often applicable in situations where estimates of the probabilities of unknown future events are determined and then modified after collecting sample evidence. An example is the test market concept used by many manufacturers of consumer products. Such a company might estimate the probability of public acceptance of a new product as being quite high. However, before risking the millions of dollars that a national campaign requires, a test market might be undertaken in areas the company regards as good representative markets. The results of the test market are then used to modify the original estimates of product success, and a decision about introducing the product nationally is made.

Figure 11.2 reflects a specific application of Bayes' theorem in a test market situation. Management of a large consumer products company needs to decide whether to introduce a new product nationally. They estimate that their new product has a 50% chance of high sales in the national market. They are considering the use of a test market to determine

FIGURE 11.2 Bayes' Decision for New Product Introduction.

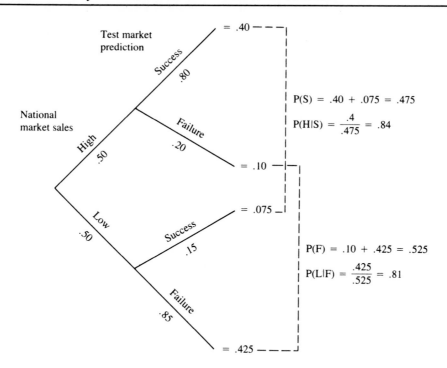

whether they can do a better job of forecasting high or low sales of the new product. Figure 11.2 shows a decision tree of the test market outcomes.

Past experience shows that when a new product was introduced and high sales were achieved, the test market successfully predicted these high sales 80% of the time. Past experience also shows that when a new product was introduced and low sales were achieved, the test market successfully predicted low sales 85% of the time. Bayes' theorem can be used to compute the probability of the new product being successful in the national market under different test market conditions. Figure 11.2 shows the computation of the two probabilities of particular interest.[9]

- If the test market predicts success, there is an 84% chance the product will have high sales nationally.
- If the test market predicts failure, there is an 81% chance the product will have low sales nationally.

---

[9] The general statement of Bayes' theorem for n events $A_1, A_2, \ldots, A_n$ is

$$P(A_1 \mid B) = \frac{P(A_1)P(B \mid A_1)}{P(A_1)P(B \mid A_1) + P(A_2)P(B \mid A_2) + \cdots + P(A_n)P(B \mid A_n)}$$

In this example, a test market would help management decide whether or not to introduce the new product nationally. The test market accuracy is sufficient to change the probability of high sales from the pretest value of 50% to either 84% (success) or 81% (failure); these probabilities were calculated using Bayes' Theorem. The decision about product introduction will be much easier to make than it would have been without the test market since the probability of success will change significantly from the pretest value of 50%.

The formal statistical procedure for modifying prior probabilities on the basis of new evidence is incorporated in Bayes' law. A discussion of this procedure can be found in books on business statistics, statistical inference, and structured decision making.[10]

MANAGING THE FORECASTING PROCESS

Chapter 1 introduced the subject of forecasting with suggestions about its usefulness within the modern organization. The need for forecasting stems from the necessity for modern organizations to make timely decisions in the face of uncertainty. This process of making educated guesses about the uncertain future (forecasting) involves a rational process of extending historical data and experiences into the future. Now, with the benefit of the intervening chapters covering numerous forecasting techniques, it is possible to review the basic notions of Chapter 1 using these techniques to illustrate the important points made there.

The Forecasting Process

One key point discussed in Chapter 1 is the importance of using good management judgment along with quantitative techniques in developing good forecasts. Good management judgment is indeed important and can now be illustrated using several of the forecasting techniques discussed in the previous chapters. A judicious mixture of quantitative techniques with common sense is always necessary if forecasts are to be accurate, understood, and used by the firm's decision makers.

Time series analysis (decomposition) is a good example of a technique involving the necessity of using sound judgment along with an analysis of past history. Past unit sales history might be forecast by a company using a time series analysis program that uses monthly data and yields an analysis of trend, cyclical variation, seasonal variation, and irregular movements. A recomposition of these four factors into future months would involve considerable judgment as to the future course of the

---

[10] See, for example, John E. Hanke and Arthur G. Reitsch, *Understanding Business Statistics* (Homewood, Ill.: Richard D. Irwin, Inc., 1991), Chapter 19.

cyclical and irregular elements and, if these elements were well formulated, would produce a usable forecast of unit sales.

Regression analysis involves the necessity of using judgment along with statistical analysis whenever forecasting takes place. If a multiple regression were conducted using employee job performance rating as the dependent variable and two variables—entry test score and age—as predictor variables, an R-squared value of 75% might be obtained. In addition, the t values for the predictor variables might both be significant along with the regression F value. The forecaster is then tempted to measure the two predictor variables on each job applicant and use them to predict job performance. However, three additional questions need to be considered. First, is the 75% explained variation sufficient for forecasting purposes? Perhaps intuitive judgment on the desirability of hiring a person is a superior method, or perhaps more precision in the forecasting process is needed and other predictor variables should be sought. Second, can it be assumed that future job applicants are essentially identical to those sampled in the regression study? If they differ in any substantive way, the forecasting model may not be valid. Finally, is the cost of the forecasting process justified in terms of benefit received? The company test may be expensive, especially if purchased from an outside testing agency, and must be justified by the benefits of the forecast.

The Box-Jenkins techniques discussed in this text illustrate a common problem in forecasting discussed in Chapter 1. These procedures are often superior forecasting methods, producing lower forecasting errors in many complex situations. Their disadvantage is that some sophistication is required on the part of the user. If the process that generates the forecasts is totally mysterious to the decision maker, the forecasts may be disregarded in the management of the organization regardless of their precision.

The chi-square tests discussed in this book illustrate the extension of data analysis into nonnumerical data areas. People's opinions are often the input for these techniques and allow organizations to probe the reactions of the public toward new products, advertising campaigns, or company images. There are many other statistical techniques designed for qualitative data, but the chi-square tests are commonly used to analyze such data, especially in data tabulation software programs now widely available for personal computers.

Regression of time series data is a common occurrence in organizations where tracking important measures of performance on a weekly, monthly, or quarterly basis is conducted. As autocorrelation is a common problem in such studies, an understanding of this condition and its cure becomes vital if the results of such analyses are to be valid in the decision-making process. Unfortunately, such understanding is often lacking; this shortcoming has become an increasing problem with the advent of inexpensive regression analysis software.

The short-, medium-, and long-term aspects of forecasting tech-

TABLE 11.3 Forecasting Models.

Method	Description	Applications	Cost	Computer Necessary?	Chapter
Casual Forecasting Models					
Regression analysis	Explanatory forecasting; assumes a cause-and-effect relationship between the input to a system and its output	Short- and medium-range forecasting of existing products and services; marketing strategies, production, personnel hiring, and facility planning	Medium	Usually	6
Multiple regression	Explanatory forecasting; assumes a cause-and-effect relationship between more than one input to a system and its output	Same as above	Medium	Yes	7
Time Series Forecasting Models					
Decomposition method	Explanatory forecasting; assumes a cause-and-effect relationship between time and the output of a system; the system is decomposed into its components	Medium-range forecasting for new plant and equipment planning, financing, new-product development, and new methods of assembly; short-range forecasting for personnel, advertising, inventory, financing, and production planning	Medium	No, but usually used	8

Moving averages	To eliminate random-ness in a time series; forecast based on projection from time series data smoothed by a moving average	Short-range forecasts for operations such as inventory, scheduling, control, pricing, and timing special promo-tions; used to compute both the seasonal and cyclical components for the short-term decom-position method	Low	No	5 and 8
Exponential smoothing	Similar to moving averages but values weighted exponentially, giving more weight to most recent data	Short-range forecasts for operations such as inventory, scheduling, control, pricing, and timing special promotions	Low	Yes	5
Autoregressive models	Employed with economic variables to account for relationships between adjacent observations in a time series	Short- and medium-range forecasting for economic data ordered in a time series; price, inventory, production, stocks and sales	Medium	Yes	9 and 10
Box-Jenkins techniques	Does not assume any particular pattern in the historical data of the series to be fore-cast; uses an iterative approach of identi-fying a possibly useful model from a general class of models	Same as above	High	Yes	10

niques as they relate to different levels of management in a firm can be illustrated with time series analysis and technological forecasting. First- and second-line management in a firm might be interested in a time series analysis of monthly unit sales with data collected over the past four years. By using judgment regarding the future of the cyclical component of this series, sales might be forecasted for the next fiscal year and used to schedule monthly production for the factory. Mid-level managers might use the same time series program to analyze annual unit sales data over the past eight years and forecast it for five years into the future. In this case, the cyclical component might be ignored in an attempt to plan capital expenditure needs for the factory during this five-year period. At the same time, top management might be engaged in technological forecasting using the Delphi method along with scenario writing. Their purpose would be to evaluate the company's current position in the market and to search for technology or societal changes that would threaten its market niche over the next 20 years, or offer it opportunities not evident in day-to-day operations.

The data analysis techniques discussed in this book are summarized in Table 11.3. This table provides descriptions, describes applications, estimates cost levels, and indicates whether computer capabilities are necessary for the implementation of each technique. Each technique is also referenced to the chapters where it is discussed.

MONITORING FORECASTS

Collecting data and selecting an acceptable forecasting technique are only the first steps in an effective, ongoing forecasting process. Several steps in the forecasting process have been described in this book, with the emphasis on learning the techniques commonly employed in the actual forecasting. The key steps in the forecasting process are summarized in Figure 11.3.

The collection and examination of appropriate historical data were described earlier in this book (Chapters 3 and 4), along with considerations in selecting a forecasting technique or model. As suggested by Figure 11.3, the next step is usually to forecast past historical periods whose actual values are known. The resulting errors can be summarized in several ways, as discussed in Chapter 4, and this process is continued until a technique with a sufficient cost-benefit ratio is found. The model is then used to forecast future periods, and the results are incorporated into the firm's decision-making process.

From time to time it is necessary to pause in the forecasting process and reconsider the procedures being used. The usual steps are as follows:

1. The oldest historical values in the data being used by the forecasting technique are discarded and the most recent actual values are added to the data bank.

FIGURE 11.3 Forecasting Process.

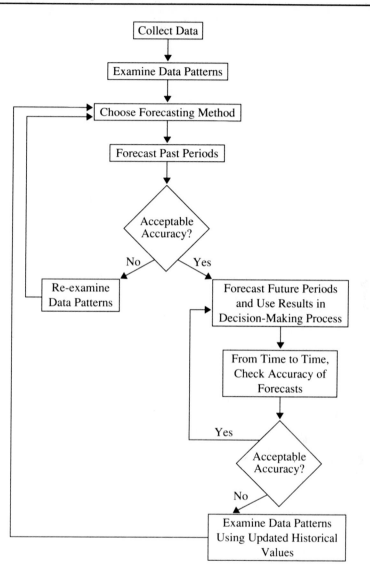

2. Following this data update, the parameters used in the forecasting model are recalculated. For example, the optimum value(s) of the weighting constant(s) used in exponential smoothing may shift, possibly considerably, when more recent data values are added. Or the coefficients in a regression analysis can change when different data values are fitted with an equation.

3. The forecasting model with new parameters is examined for adequate accuracy. If this accuracy is judged to be sufficient, the model is then used as before until the next update period. If forecasting accuracy is deemed inadequate or marginal, the patterns in the new data can be examined with the possibility of choosing a new forecasting procedure. This process continues until the accuracy of the chosen model, as judged by the accuracy of forecasting past historical periods, is judged to be adequate.

The above process is summarized in the flow diagram of Figure 11.3 and constitutes the kind of feedback loop commonly found in system designs of all types.

Forecasts are sometimes monitored constantly using a tracking signal, a concept discussed in Chapter 5 following the material on simple exponential smoothing. The idea is to establish limits within which the errors generated by the forecasts are expected to fall if the forecasting process is adequate. As long as the errors fall within these acceptable limits, the forecasting process continues. As soon as an error falls outside the acceptable range, management attention is focused on the forecasting process, and the updating and revision steps outlined above are undertaken. This concept is illustrated in Example 11.1.

EXAMPLE 11.1

■ Sue Bradley is responsible for forecasting the monthly dollar sales of her company. A forecasting model has been chosen by Sue that has an error rate acceptable to her managers. Specifically, the standard error of this forecasting process is $935; that is, the forecast and actual values of monthly dollar sales are typically $935 apart.

Sue assumes that forecast errors are normally distributed with a mean of zero and a standard deviation of $935. She makes this assumption after examining a plot of past forecasting errors and finds that they follow a bell-shaped curve about zero. Using a 95% confidence level, she then establishes the following limits within which she expects the forecast error of each month to fall:

$$0 \pm (1.96)(935)$$

$$0 \pm 1,833$$

So Sue expects each monthly forecast to be within $1,833 of the actual value for the month, with 95% confidence. If it is, the forecasting procedure will continue without her attention. But if the error should be greater than $1,833, she will examine both the parameters in her chosen forecasting technique and even consider using another technique.

To monitor the forecasting errors more easily, Sue designs a chart to track them. Over the course of several months, Sue finds two plots that cause her to closely examine her forecasting procedures. The first, shown in Figure 11.4, shows forecasting errors that appear to be randomly distributed, until the most recent

FIGURE 11.4 Data Error Plot.

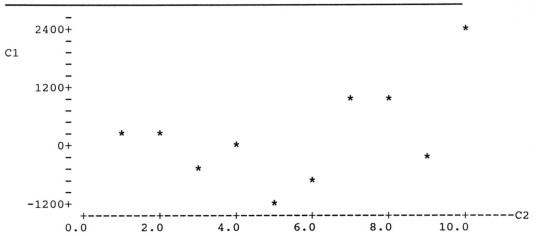

period. This out-of-tolerance error leads Sue to update the parameters in her forecasting model, after updating her data base by adding recent values and discarding the same number of older values. Some time later, a second error plot, Figure 11.5, again causes Sue to look at her forecasting process. Although none of the errors has exceeded her tolerance limits, Sue notes that recent errors do not appear to be randomly distributed. In fact, the errors are increasing in the positive direction, and it is obvious that they will soon be out of control. Sue updates her data base and, after carefully examining the data patterns, chooses a new forecasting technique. ■

FIGURE 11.5 Data Error Plot.

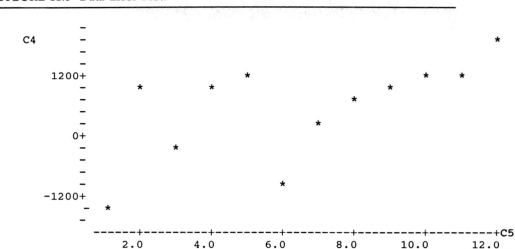

FORECASTING STEPS REVIEWED

In Chapter 1, the point was made several times that sound judgment must be constantly exercised along with quantitative analysis if useful and accurate forecasting is to take place. Several questions were listed that should be raised if management of the forecasting process is to be properly conducted. They are repeated here.

- Why is a forecast needed?
- Who will use the forecast, and what are their specific requirements?
- What level of detail or aggregation is required, and what is the proper time horizon?
- What data are available, and will the data be sufficient to generate the needed forecast?
- What will the forecast cost?
- How accurate can the forecast be expected to be?
- Will the forecast be made in time to help the decision-making process?
- Does the forecaster clearly understand how the forecast will be used in the organization?
- Is a feedback process available to evaluate the forecast after it is made and adjust the forecasting process accordingly?

When the above questions have been properly addressed and answered, the actual forecasting process can begin. Chapter 1 listed the steps followed in such a process.

Data collection
Data reduction or condensation
Model building
Model extrapolation (the actual forecast)

To this list of steps might be added another: feedback after the forecasting process is underway to determine if sufficient accuracy has been obtained and if management is finding the forecast useful and cost effective in the decision-making process.

While the primary concern of this book has been with model building or selection of the appropriate forecasting method, it is the authors' hope that the importance of managing the forecasting process has been emphasized as well. The questions listed above are important in all forecasting situations and must be addressed if useful results are to be obtained. We especially recommend study of the cases at the end of this chapter. They are designed to emphasize the judgmental aspects of forecasting.

FORECASTING RESPONSIBILITY

The location of the forecasting process within a firm varies depending on the size of the firm, the importance attached to formal forecasting, and the nature of the firm's management style. The forecasting responsibility falls somewhere on the continuum between a separate forecasting department, and forecasting within small management units without reference to other efforts within the firm.

Forecasting staffs are more common in large organizations than in small ones. Large firms can afford to hire the expertise needed for sophisticated forecasting and can equip their staffs with modern computing and software capabilities. The advantage of such a centralized effort is that such expertise is available to all units of the organization. The disadvantage is that coordination between the forecasting staff and line managers is often quite difficult to achieve. The forecasting staff may find itself spending more time negotiating with users and explaining its role than in actual forecasting.

At the other extreme is the location of the forecasting process within each unit of the firm without coordination or cooperation across units. The advantage of this process is that there is no misunderstanding between those forecasting and those using the forecasts: they are the same persons. Forecasts generated under these conditions tend to be accepted and used in the decision-making process. The disadvantage is that sophistication, and therefore forecasting accuracy, may be difficult to achieve because computing and software needs cannot be spread across many users. It is usually difficult to persuade top management to acquire hardware and software when they know it exists in other locations in the company.

Many organizations attempt to locate the responsibility for forecasting midway between the extremes mentioned above. A small staff of forecasters may be assigned to subunits within the firm to service the needs of several functional areas. The task of such a forecasting staff involves proper coordination with clients as well as generating accurate forecasts. Sometimes this forecasting responsibility is combined with other staff functions such as statistical support or computing support.

The advent of inexpensive small computers and forecasting software has tended to move the forecasting function downward in the organization. It is now possible for managers to have access to sophisticated forecasting tools at a fraction of the cost of such capability five or ten years ago. However, the knowledge required to properly use this capability does not come with the hardware or software package; the need to understand the proper use of forecasting techniques has increased as the computing capability has moved out of the hands of the "experts" into those of the users in an organization.

FORECASTING COSTS

Computing hardware and software are the obvious costs involved with creating forecasts. But additional costs are involved that may not be as obvious due to the expenditure of company personnel time as well as money. The time of salaried persons spent in gathering data for the forecasting process, monitoring the process, and interpreting the results must be considered a cost of forecasting. Such cost must be balanced against benefits received if rational decisions regarding the usefulness of the resulting forecasts are to be reached.

An alternative to producing forecasts internally is to use consultants for this purpose. This practice is especially appealing if the need for a forecast involves a one-time requirement rather than an ongoing one. Also, a forecasting requirement beyond the technical capability of company personnel suggests the use of professional consultants. Such outside hiring of forecasting assistance makes the identification of cost an easy matter.

SELLING MANAGEMENT ON FORECASTING

Several factors are important considerations if the forecasts generated within a firm are to become important aspects of the decision-making process. First, it must be recognized that effective managers are interested in practical and useful results. In general, forecasts must meet the needs of such managers; they must provide answers to the series of questions posed earlier in this chapter.

Second, forecasts must be accurate enough to be useful. Good managers will not stay with a forecasting process long, regardless of its sophistication, if accurate results are not generated.

Finally the cost-benefit capabilities of all good managers must be recognized in the forecasting process. The ability to analyze situations in terms of cost incurred versus benefit received is the keystone of an effective management process and must be recognized by the forecasting staff. This situation often creates difficulties between the forecaster and the user. The forecaster must always keep in mind that the end result of the forecasting process is to produce a product whose benefit to the management process exceeds the cost of producing it.

FORECASTING AND THE MIS SYSTEM

The management information systems of modern firms have increased in sophistication and usefulness in recent years. Their primary benefit to the forecasting process involves their enormous capability to collect and record data throughout the organization. The forecaster must resist the temptation to collect data for the forecasting models being used if such data have already been collected and recorded in the company's MIS system.

Reliance on existing data banks is important even if the available data are not in precisely the format or time sequence desired by the forecaster. Modifications in the forecasting model or in the available data should be considered before abandoning the MIS system data in favor of collecting new data. This advice presumes, of course, that the data collection process involves a considerable time expenditure. If the data needed for a forecasting model are easy to obtain in the correct format, this would be preferable to using precollected data that are not in the proper form or that are out of date.

An additional advantage of using data available on the company's MIS system is that the forecasting process then becomes a component of this system. As such, it enters the distribution and decision-making network already established by the system and may become more readily incorporated into the company's decision-making process. This situation is in contrast to a forecasting procedure that attempts to infiltrate the decision-making procedures already in use by company managers.

THE FUTURE OF FORECASTING

An mentioned in Chapter 1, forecasting continues to gain in importance in modern organizations due to the increasing complexity of the business world along with the availability of lower cost and more powerful computing equipment and software. The continuing competition in the small computer and software areas is obvious to everyone; less obvious may be the long-term trends that slowly change the makeup of the business scene and that exert subtle but powerful pressures on the ways businesspeople operate.

Consider some of the "megatrends" identified by Naisbitt in his book by that title.[11] These forces have particular importance to the business world and bring to mind the need for forecasting using modern equipment and software.

> Industrial to information society
> National to world economy
> Short- to long-term thinking
> Centralization to decentralization
> Either/or to multiple options

The above trends underline the importance of continuing management development on the part of businesspeople who must deal with the

---

[11] John Naisbitt, *Megatrends* (New York: Warner Books, 1982).

complex issues facing their firms over the next several years. In particular, they emphasize the necessity of developing more and more sophisticated methods of dealing with the uncertainties of future events. They emphasize, in other words, the growing importance of combining good judgment and sophisticated data-manipulative methods into sound business forecasting.

As Naisbitt's trends, or some combination of them, begin to unfold across the business scene, the ability of business leaders to react quickly and profitably to changing events is brought into sharper focus. The basic business question "What will happen next?" will assume even greater importance; it is with this question that business forecasting is concerned.

CHAPTER **11**

GLOSSARY

Expected value   The expected value of a discrete random variable is the average value that the random variable assumes over a large number of observations.

CHAPTER **11**

KEY FORMULA

Expected value formula $E(X) = \Sigma\ X[P(X)]$ **(11.1)**

CASE STUDY **11.1**

BOUNDARY ELECTRONICS

Boundary Electronics is a large supplier of electronic products for home use. Among its largest sellers are home video recorders and satellite television systems. Because the company's business has grown so rapidly, Guy Preston, Boundary's president, is concerned that a change in market conditions could alter its sales pattern.

In asking his managers about the future of the company, Guy has discovered two things. First, most of his managers are too busy thinking about the day-to-day problems of meeting growing demand to give much thought to the long-range future. Second, such opinions as they do have vary considerably from quite optimistic to quite pessimistic. As president of the company, Guy feels he has an obligation to seriously consider the future environment of his company.

After thinking about this matter, Guy plans a Saturday retreat for the six members of his top management team. He rents a meeting room in a local hotel and arranges for lunch and coffee breaks for the day. When the team meets Saturday morning, he introduces the topic of the day and then instructs each person to prepare a one- or two-page description of the company's operating environment over the next 20 years for each of the following situations:

1. The company's environment will continue essentially as it is now. Products demanded by the market will be modifications of current products, and no new technology will intervene.
2. Major technological changes will render the company's current line of products obsolete. New products will have to be developed to meet the leisure demands of the American population.
3. Between these two extremes, what is the most likely scenario for the company's operating environment?

Guy allows one hour for each team member to develop the scenarios for each of these three situations. During this hour, Guy thinks about the rest of the day and what will develop. He hopes that there will be some provocative ideas developed by his managers and that subsequent discussions will prove lively and interesting. In addition to gaining ideas for his own use, Guy hopes that the day's exercise will help his managers look beyond the company's immediate problems and opportunities and give them a more long-range view of the company.

QUESTIONS

1. What process do you think Guy should use after the hour's writing activities have been completed?
2. Is there some other approach that Guy might have tried, given his objectives?
3. Do you think Guy will accomplish his objectives with the Saturday meeting?

CASE STUDY **11.2**

GOLDEN GARDENS RESTAURANT

Sue and Bill Golden have decided to open a restaurant in a city in the midwest. They have spent over a year researching the area and visiting medium- to high-price restaurants. They definitely believe that there is room for another restaurant and have found a good site that is available at a good price.

In addition, they have contacts with a number of first-class chefs and believe they can attract one of them to their new restaurant. Their inquiries with local bankers have convinced them that financing will be readily available, given their own financial resources and their expertise in the restaurant business.

The only thing still troubling the Goldens is the atmosphere or motif for their restaurant. They have already conducted a series of three focus groups with area residents who eat out regularly, and no consensus on this matter emerged. They have talked about the matter considerably between themselves but now believe some other opinions would be valuable.

After reading about some of the techniques used in judgment forecasting, they believe some of them might help them decide on the atmosphere for their new restaurant. They have identified a number of their friends and associates in other cities who would be willing to help them but are not certain how to utilize their talents.

QUESTIONS

1. What method would you suggest to the Goldens in utilizing the expertise of their friends to decide on the atmosphere and motif for their new restaurant?

2. Are there any other methods they have overlooked in trying to research this matter?

CASE STUDY **11.3**

BUSBY ASSOCIATES

Jill Tilson is a recent graduate of a university business school and has taken a job with Busby Associates, a large exporter of farm equipment. Busby's president noticed a forecasting course on Jill's resume during the hiring-in process and has decided to start Jill's employment with a forecasting project that has been discussed many times by Busby's top managers.

Busby's president believes there is a strong relationship between the company's export sales and the national figures for exports. The national figures are readily available from government sources, so Jill's project is to forecast a good, representative export variable. If this effort is successful, Busby's president believes the company will have a powerful tool for forecasting its own export sales.

Jill locates the most recent copy of the *Survey of Current Business* in a local library and records the quarterly figures for consumer goods exports in billions of dollars. She believes this variable is a good representative of total national exports. Anticipating the possibility of forecasting using regression analysis, she also records values for other variables she thinks might possibly correlate well with this dependent variable. She ends up with values for four variables for 14 quarters.

She then computes three additional variables from her dependent variable values: change in Y, percent change in Y, and Y lagged one period. So, as she begins to think about various ways to forecast her variable, she has collected the data shown in Table 11.4.

Jill keys her data into a computer program that performs regression analysis and computes the correlation matrix for her seven variables. After examining this matrix, she chooses three regressions with one predictor variable and six regressions with two predictor variables. She then runs these regressions and chooses the one she considers best: it uses one predictor (Y lagged one period) with the following results:

$$r \text{ squared} = .98389, \quad t = 25.9, \quad F = 671.6, \quad \text{Durbin-Watson} = 2.18$$

The Durbin-Watson table Jill is using starts at $n = 15$ and her sample size is only 13. So she interpolates the DW critical values and estimates that the upper limit for the autocorrelation test is 1.35. Since her DW statistic is 2.18, she easily concludes that no autocorrelation is present in her regression. She believes she has found a good predictor variable (Y lagged one period).

Jill realizes that her sample size is rather small: 13 quarters. She returns to the *Survey of Current Business* to collect more data points and is disappointed to find that during the years she is interested in the definition of her dependent variable

TABLE 11.4 Quarterly Time Series Data.

Time Period	Variable						
	1	2	3	4	5	6	7
1987							
1	18.2	128.3	306.2	110.0	—	—	—
2	19.8	45.8	311.6	109.7	1.6	8.79	18.2
3	20.9	66.1	320.7	109.9	1.1	5.56	19.8
4	22.1	129.7	324.2	109.7	1.2	5.74	20.9
1988							
1	24.0	136.4	331.0	109.4	1.9	8.60	22.1
2	26.0	140.7	337.3	110.5	2.0	8.33	24.0
3	27.7	156.9	342.6	110.6	1.7	6.54	26.0
4	29.7	148.5	352.6	110.9	2.0	7.22	27.7
1989							
1	33.6	189.8	351.5	113.4	3.9	13.13	29.7
2	35.0	168.9	357.6	112.4	1.4	4.17	33.6
3	35.0	154.5	365.2	111.9	0.0	0.00	35.0
4	38.0	174.1	366.3	111.0	3.0	8.57	35.0
1990							
1	40.7	191.3	369.1	111.9	2.7	7.11	38.0
2	42.0	201.2	370.0[a]	112.1	1.3	3.19	40.7

[a] Estimated.

Variable key:
  1: Consumer goods, exports, billions of dollars
  2: Gross personal saving, billions of dollars
  3: National income, retail trade, billions of dollars
  4: Fixed weight price indexes for national defense purchases, military equipment, 1982 = 100
  5: Change in dependent variable from previous period
  6: Percent change in dependent variable from previous period
  7: Dependent variable lagged one period

Source for variables 1 through 4: *Survey of Current Business,* Vol. 70, No. 7 (July 1990), U.S. Department of Commerce.

changed, resulting in an inconsistent time series. That is, the series takes a jump upward halfway through the late 1980s period that she is studying.

Jill points out this problem to her boss, and it is agreed that total merchandise exports can be used as the dependent variable instead of consumer goods exports. Jill finds that this variable remains consistent through several issues of the *Survey of Current Business* and that several years of data can be collected. She collects the data shown in Table 11.5, lags the data one period, and again runs a regression analysis using Y lagged one period as the predictor variable.

This time she again finds good statistics in her regression printout, except for the Durbin-Watson statistic. This value is .96 and she must conclude that autocorre-

TABLE 11.5 Quarterly Time Series Data: Total Merchandise Exports (Billions of Dollars).

	Time Period	Y	Y Lagged One Period
1984	1	219.3	—
	2	223.1	219.3
	3	225.9	223.1
	4	228.0	225.9
1985	1	225.0	228.0
	2	221.6	225.0
	3	218.0	221.6
	4	218.6	218.0
1986	1	220.7	218.6
	2	221.4	220.7
	3	225.7	221.4
	4	230.4	225.7
1987	1	234.5	230.4
	2	246.6	234.5
	3	261.6	246.6
	4	281.3	261.6
1988	1	306.7	281.3
	2	319.2	306.7
	3	327.9	319.2
	4	342.8	327.9
1989	1	360.6	342.8
	2	373.2	360.6
	3	367.3	373.2
	4	378.7	367.3
1990	1	394.2	378.7
	2	394.4	394.2

Source: *Survey of Current Business,* various issues.

lation is present, since this value is below the lower table value for the Durbin-Watson test. She tries additional runs by adding the period number and the change in Y as additional predictor variables. But she is unable to find a Durbin-Watson statistic high enough for her to conclude that the autocorrelation has been removed. Jill decides to look at other forecasting techniques to forecast her new dependent variable: total merchandise exports. She will use the time series data shown in the Y column of Table 11.5.

Among the computer software available at Busby's is Sibyl/Runner, a forecasting program that performs a variety of forecasting methods. Jill prepares her data for use with this program and begins working her way through several forecasting routines. Among these is a procedure that plots the raw data. The quarterly plot of total merchandise exports for the years 1984 through the second quarter of 1990 is shown in Figure 11.6.

FIGURE 11.6 Plot of Quarterly Data Values: Total Merchandise Exports, First Quarter of 1984 to Second Quarter of 1990.

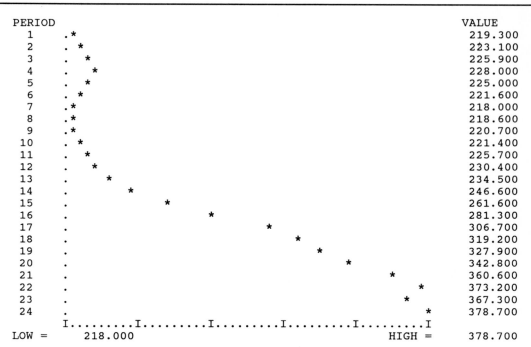

```
 PERIOD                                                          VALUE
    1    . *                                                   219.300
    2    .  *                                                  223.100
    3    .    *                                                225.900
    4    .      *                                              228.000
    5    .    *                                                225.000
    6    .  *                                                  221.600
    7    .*                                                    218.000
    8    .*                                                    218.600
    9    .*                                                    220.700
   10    .  *                                                  221.400
   11    .    *                                                225.700
   12    .      *                                              230.400
   13    .         *                                           234.500
   14    .            *                                        246.600
   15    .                *                                    261.600
   16    .                    *                                281.300
   17    .                         *                           306.700
   18    .                            *                        319.200
   19    .                              *                      327.900
   20    .                                 *                   342.800
   21    .                                    *                360.600
   22    .                                       *             373.200
   23    .                                      *              367.300
   24    .                                          *          378.700
         I.........I.........I.........I.........I.........I
 LOW  =       218.000                          HIGH  =        378.700
```

After studying Figure 11.6, Jill decides to use only the last 16 data points in her forecasting effort. She reasons that, beginning with period 9, the series has shown a relatively steady increase, whereas before that period it exhibited an increase and decline. The Sibyl/Runner program warns her about using a low number of data points (16), but continues after she ignores this warning.

She begins her analysis by calling for the Sibyl routine of the program, using only the last 16 data points. The first analysis produced by the program indicates that there is some pattern to the data, but that there is no seasonality. The program uses several forecasting methods to forecast the sample values and prints a table showing the forecast errors as percentages for each method and each period.

After studying these forecast errors, Jill chooses three forecasting techniques for further analysis. The three she chooses have the lowest percentage forecasting errors and are

Simple exponential smoothing

Brown's exponential smoothing, which can accommodate a trend in the data

Quadratic exponential smoothing, which allows for a curved trend line through the data

She then calls for forecasts of her data using each technique, with the following results:

Technique	Mean Square Error	Optimum Smoothing Constant
Simple exponential	185.5	.999
Brown's exponential	81.0	.722
Quadratic exponential	87.7	.485

Jill notes that the optimum smoothing constant using simple exponential smoothing is almost 1.00 (.999). Apparently, in order to track through the data in an optimum fashion, the program is basically using one data value to predict the next. This is equivalent to using the simple naive method to forecast.

Since Brown's exponential smoothing produced the lowest mean square error, Jill thinks she should use that method. She examines the printout for this method further and finds that the mean absolute percentage error (MAPE) is 2.39% and the mean percentage error (MPE) or bias is .34%. Jill considers these values satisfactory and decides to use Brown's exponential smoothing to forecast future values.

Using her chosen method, she asks for forecasts for the next four periods beyond the end of her data. The forecast values are as follows:

Period	Forecast
17	401.27
18	407.30
19	413.34
20	419.38

Jill realizes that, with each passing quarter, a new actual value of total merchandise exports will be available and the forecasts for future periods can be updated.

Jill then meets with her boss to discuss her results. She indicates that she thinks she has a good way to forecast the national variable, total merchandise exports, using exponential smoothing with trend adjustments. Her boss asks her to explain this method, which she does. Her next assignment is to use actual data to verify the hunch of Busby's president: that Busby's exports are well correlated with national exports. If she can establish this linkage, Busby will have a good forecasting method for its exports and can use the forecasts to plan future operations.

QUESTIONS

1. Jill has not considered combining the forecasts generated by the three methods she analyzed. How would she go about doing so? What would be the advantages and disadvantages of such action?

2. The optimum smoothing constant used by Brown's exponential smoothing is .722. As new data come in over the next few quarters, Jill should probably rerun her data to see if this value changes. How often do you think she should do this?

3. It is possible that the choice of forecasting method could shift to another technique as new quarterly data are added to the data base. Should Jill rerun her entire analysis once in a while to check this? How often should this be done?

CASE STUDY **11.4**

METROPOLITAN MORTGAGE

INTRODUCTION

J & H Research Service was asked to conduct a market feasibility study for the proposed redevelopment of the Harbor View Marina in Garfield Bay. Metropolitan Mortgage & Securities Company, Inc., financed the construction of the marina in 1983; however, it was only operational for a six-month period in 1984. The lake property was repossessed by Metropolitan in 1986, and it is Metropolitan's goal to sell this property in the most profitable manner. J & H Research identified three selling options, which are discussed in the next section.

OPTIONS AVAILABLE TO METROPOLITAN

1. Metropolitan can sell the subject property as is for an estimated price of $400,000 to $600,000. This estimated range for the selling price is based on an appraiser's report dated August 25, 1986, deterioration of the property since that time, and market conditions as indicated by the selling prices of marinas within the competitive market area during the past few years.

2. Metropolitan can sell the subject property after renovation of docks and the addition of a floating breakwater for an estimated price of $800,000 to $1 million. The estimated cost of renovating the docks and adding a floating breakwater is $170,000. This estimated range for the selling price is based on an interview with a potential buyer and on the selling prices of marinas within the competitive market area during the past few years.

3. Metropolitan can sell the subject property in the year in which reasonable occupancy of the marina is achieved for an estimated price of $1,100,000 to $1,400,000. This approach would include the renovation of docks, addition of a floating breakwater, and the addition of a $15,000 crane and sling. The estimated selling price is based on appraisals using the income approach with a capitalization rate of 10%.

This case was contributed by Mark Craze and Alex Cameron, professors at Eastern Washington University, Cheney, Washington.

ANALYSIS OF OPTIONS

Analysis of the three options faced by Metropolitan Mortgage is complicated for the following two reasons: (1) the range of possible selling prices each option might realize and (2) the timing differences of cash flows resulting from the selection of each option. J & H Research decides that an accurate analysis will involve converting the range of selling prices and other costs under each option to a single dollar amount that is stated in today's dollars.

Expected Value

Expected value analysis was used to compute a point estimate for the selling price of the marina under the various options considered. This process involved multiplying a given price by its probability of occurrence. The price probabilities were estimated by commercial property brokers who knew the marina and the competitive market area in which it was located.

Option 1

Option 1 is to sell the property as is. While the subject property has a high replacement cost, its low market value is a result of an ineffective floating breakwater that cannot diminish the impact of six-foot waves caused by winter storms blowing from the south directly into Garfield Bay. The property would be extremely difficult to sell because of its deteriorated condition and the ineffective floating breakwater. Table 11.6 shows the possible selling prices along with their probability of realization for development of option 1.

Option 2

Option 2 is to sell the subject property after renovation of docks and the addition of a floating breakwater. Northern Idaho boater registration levels and high-boat-slip utilization rates suggest sufficient demand for boat slips on the northern portion of Pend Oreille Lake to justify an additional marina in Garfield Bay. Of the 588 boat slips available, 522 were occupied (utilization rate of 90%). These factors account for the increased market value of the property after renovation of docks and addition of a floating breakwater. Table 11.7 shows the possible selling prices along with their probability of realization.

TABLE 11.6 Expected Values for Option 1.

Price, X	Probability, P(X)	X[P(X)]
$400,000	.40	$160,000
500,000	.40	200,000
600,000	.20	120,000
	Expected value =	$480,000

TABLE 11.7 Expected Values for Option 2.

Price, X	Probability, P(X)	X[P(X)]
$ 480,000*	.10[†]	$ 48,000
800,000	.50	400,000
900,000	.30	270,000
1,000,000	.10	100,000
	Expected value =	$818,000

* Based on the expected value for an unimproved marina calculated in Table 11.4.

[†] Based on a 10% estimated probability that the breakwater will not work.

Option 3

Option 3 involves selling the marina in the year in which reasonable occupancy is achieved. This approach would require the renovation of docks, the addition of a floating breakwater, and the addition of a crane and sling to hoist boats in and out of the water. Table 11.8 shows the possible selling prices along with their probability of realization.

This analysis of expected values results in a single selling price for Harbor View Marina under each of the three options examined. The analysis is incomplete because the timing differences and costs required to realize the expected values have been ignored. Present value concepts are now utilized in complete the analysis of the three options.

Present Values

Most investments produce revenues in future time periods. Present value indicates how much the prospect of future income is worth today after taking into account the time value of money. The time value of money states that a dollar today is worth more than a dollar tomorrow, because the dollar today can be invested now and earns interest immediately. The net present value of an investment is calculated by

TABLE 11.8 Expected Values for Option 3.

Price, X	Probability, P(X)	X[P(X)]
$1,100,000	.50	$ 550,000
1,250,000	.30	375,000
1,400,000	.20	280,000
	Expected value =	$1,205,000

subtracting the initial cost of the investment required from the present value of future cash flows. Investment alternatives with the greatest net present values are most desirable.

Discount factors can be obtained from a present value table. To identify the proper discount factor, simply select an interest rate and the time period in which the cash flow takes place. The intersection of the row and column contains the discount factor.

Option 1

This section analyzes option 1 based on net present value. Table 11.9 uses the expected values from Table 11.6 to show the economic impact of this option. The depreciation tax shield shows the reduction in income tax liability that results from claiming depreciation as an expense for tax purposes. The amount of the tax shield in this example was calculated based on straight-line depreciation[12] and an effective tax rate of 34%. The discount rate used was 10%.

Option 2

This section analyzes option 2 based on net present value. Table 11.10 uses the expected values from Table 11.7 to show the economic impact of this option. The depreciation tax shield is calculated based on straight-line depreciation and an effective tax rate of 34%. The discount rate used was 10%. Cash flow of $3,300 is based on an estimated occupancy rate of 5% for open slips during 1988. Costs for breakwater construction and dock renovation were based on engineering estimates.

Option 3

The next sections analyze the projected income for the proposed marina for a five-year period and show a present value analysis based on projected cash flow for the five-year period.

TABLE 11.9 Net Present Values for Option 1.

	1988
Depreciation tax shield	$ 5,437
Expected value from sale	480,000
Total cash flow	485,437
Discount factor, 1 year @ 10%	.909
Present value of expected cash flows	$441,262
Required investment	0
NPV	$441,262

---

[12] In practice, ACRS depreciation would be used to gain the most favorable tax treatment. Sufficient information was not available for such treatment. The decision outcome was not affected.

TABLE 11.10 Net Present Values for Option 2.

	1988
Net income cash flow	$ 3,300
Depreciation tax shield	12,047
Expected value from sale	818,000
Less:	
Engineering fees	25,000
Total cash flow	$808,347
Discount factor, 1 year @ 10%	.909
Present value of expected cash flows	$734,787
Less:	
Breakwater	100,000
Dock renovation	70,000
	170,000
NPV of expected cash flows	$564,787

Projected Income

Table 11.11 shows the projected income analysis for the proposed marina for the years ended March 31, 1994. The assumptions made for this analysis were as follows:

Revenue Assumptions

1. The marina will contain 220 slips, half covered and half open.
2. Covered slips will rent for $750 on a yearly basis, and open slips will rent for $300 based on a seven-month season.
3. An occupancy rate of 88%, half covered and half open, will be achieved by April 1, 1994.
4. Launch charges for hoisting boats out of the water are estimated at $15 at an annual usage of 2.5 times occupancy.
5. Fuel sales estimates are based on an average use of 50 hours per boat, consumption of 5 gallons per hour, and an average price of $1.20 per gallon.
6. Lease income will accrue from the repair shop, store, and office/apartments.

Five-Year Present Value Analysis

Table 11.12 shows the present value of projected cash flows for the proposed marina for the five-year period ended March 31, 1994.

TABLE 11.11 Projected Harbor View Marina Statement of Operations, Year Ended March 31, 1994.

Year: Occupancy Rate:	1988 5%	1989 18%	1990 36%	1991 54%	1992 72%	1993 88%
Revenues:						
Moorage	$ 5,775	$20,790	$41,580	$62,370	$83,160	$101,640
Launch charges	413	1,485	2,970	4,455	5,940	7,260
Fuel sales	3,300	11,880	23,760	35,640	47,520	58,080
Lease income	22,000	22,000	22,000	22,000	25,000	25,000
Total revenues	31,488	56,155	90,310	124,465	161,620	191,980
Variable Costs						
Gas	$ 2,805	$10,098	$20,196	$30,291	$40,392	$ 49,368
Maintenance	231	832	1,663	2,495	3,326	4,066
Administration	144	520	1,040	1,559	2,079	2,541
Total variable costs	3,180	11,450	22,899	34,348	45,797	55,975
Contribution margin	28,308	44,705	67,411	90,117	115,823	136,005
Fixed Costs						
Management fees	$	$22,500	$22,500	$22,500	$22,500	$ 22,500
Advertising		7,500	7,500	10,000	10,000	10,000
Maintenance		6,500	6,500	8,500	8,500	8,500
Insurance	$15,000	15,000	15,000	15,000	15,000	15,000
Taxes	8,400	8,400	8,400	8,400	8,400	8,400
Total fixed costs	23,400	59,900	59,900	64,400	64,400	64,400
Net Income	$ 4,908	($15,195)	$ 7,511	$25,717	$51,423	$ 71,605

TABLE 11.12 Net Present Values for Option 3.

	1988	1989	1990	1991	1992	1993
Net income cash flow	$ 4,908	−$15,195	$ 7,511	$25,717	$51,423	$ 71,605
Depreciation tax shield	12,047	12,047	12,047	12,047	12,047	12,047
Engineering fees	−25,000					
Expected value from sale						1,205,000
Total cash flow	−$8,045	−$3,148	$19,558	$37,764	$63,470	$1,288,652
Discount factors @ 10%	.909	.826	.751	.683	.621	.564
Present value	$ 7,313	−$2,600	$14,688	$25,793	$39,415	$ 726,800

PV of return	$811,409
Less: Breakwater	100,000
Dock renovation	70,000
Crane & sling	15,000
Slip coverage	55,000
Engineering fee	25,000
	265,000
NPV of expected cash flows	$546,409

CONCLUSIONS

Option 1 is a desirable approach because it provides the simplest solution to Metropolitan's problem. The property should be sold as is, provided a minimum selling price of $? (net of sales expenses) can be obtained. Below this value, option 2 is preferable.

Under option 2 the docks should be renovated and a floating breakwater installed. Below a minimum selling price of $? for option 1, the increase in the fair market value gained with option 2 exceeds the cost of the proposed improvements. It should be noted that there is a slight risk that the new floating breakwater will not be functional. If the breakwater is operational, the property should be sold with these additional improvements provided a minimum selling price of $? (net of sales expenses) can be obtained. Below this value, option 3 is preferable.

QUESTIONS

1. Judgment was used to acquire quantitative estimates. List a few examples.

2. Under what circumstances should option 1 be chosen?

3. Under what circumstances should option 2 be chosen?

4. Under what circumstances should option 3 be chosen?

5. Write a recommendation in memo form for Metropolitan Mortgage using your analysis of questions 2–4.

CHAPTER 11

SELECTED BIBLIOGRAPHY

Adams, F. G. *The Business Forecasting Revolution*. New York: Oxford University Press, 1986.

Georgoff, D. M., and Mardick, R. G. "Manager's Guide to Forecasting." *Harvard Business Review* 1 (1986): 110–120.

Hogarth, R. M., and Makridakis, S. "Forecasting and Planning: An Evaluation." *Management Science* 27 (2) (February 1981): 115–138.

Makridakis, S. "The Art and Science of Forecasting." *International Journal of Forecasting* 2 (1986): 15–39.

Reid, R. A. "The Forecasting Process: Guidelines for the MIS Manager." *Journal of Systems Management* (November 1986): 33–37.

Wright, G., and Ayton, P., eds. *Judgmental Forecasting*. New York: John Wiley & Sons, 1987.

APPENDIXES

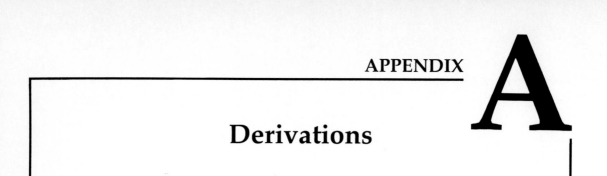

APPENDIX

A

Derivations

Correlation Derivation

$$r = \frac{\Sigma\, Z_X Z_Y}{N} = \Sigma\, \frac{[(X - \mu_X)/\sigma_X][(Y - \mu_Y)/\sigma_Y]}{N}$$

$$= \frac{\Sigma\,(X - \mu_X)(Y - \mu_Y)}{\sqrt{(\Sigma\, X^2/N) - (\Sigma\, X/N)^2}\,\sqrt{[(\Sigma\, Y^2/N) - (\Sigma\, Y/N)^2]/N}}$$

$$= \frac{\Sigma\,(X - \mu_X)(Y - \mu_Y)}{\sqrt{[N\,\Sigma\, X^2 - (\Sigma\, X)^2]/N^2}\,\sqrt{[N\,\Sigma\, Y^2 - (\Sigma\, Y)^2]/(N^2/N)}}$$

$$= \frac{N\,\Sigma\,(X - \mu_X)(Y - \mu_Y)}{\sqrt{N\,\Sigma\, X^2 - (\Sigma\, X)^2}\,\sqrt{N\,\Sigma\, Y^2 - (\Sigma\, Y)^2}}$$

$$= \frac{N\,\Sigma\,(XY - Y\mu_X - X\mu_Y + \mu_X\mu_Y)}{\sqrt{N\,\Sigma\, X^2 - (\Sigma\, X)^2}\,\sqrt{N\,\Sigma\, Y^2 - (\Sigma\, Y)^2}}$$

$$= \frac{N[\Sigma\, XY - (\Sigma\, X\,\Sigma\, Y/N) - (\Sigma\, X\,\Sigma\, Y/N) + N(\Sigma\, X/N)(\Sigma\, Y/N)]}{\sqrt{N\,\Sigma\, X^2 - (\Sigma\, X)^2}\,\sqrt{N\,\Sigma\, Y^2 - (\Sigma\, Y)^2}}$$

$$= \frac{N[\Sigma\, XY - (\Sigma\, X\,\Sigma\, Y/N) - (\Sigma\, X\,\Sigma\, Y/N) + (\Sigma\, X\,\Sigma\, Y/N)]}{\sqrt{N\,\Sigma\, X^2 - (\Sigma\, X)^2}\,\sqrt{N\,\Sigma\, Y^2 - (\Sigma\, Y)^2}}$$

$$= \frac{N[\Sigma\, XY - (\Sigma\, X\,\Sigma\, Y/N)]}{\sqrt{N\,\Sigma\, X^2 - (\Sigma\, X)^2}\,\sqrt{N\,\Sigma\, Y^2 - (\Sigma\, Y)^2}}$$

$$= \frac{N\,\Sigma\, XY - \Sigma\, X\,\Sigma\, Y}{\sqrt{N\,\Sigma\, X^2 - (\Sigma\, X)^2}\,\sqrt{N\,\Sigma\, Y^2 - (\Sigma\, Y)^2}}$$

Least Squares Derivation

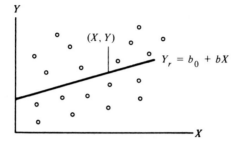

$$d = Y - Y_r$$
$$= Y - (b_0 + bX)$$
$$d^2 = [Y - (b_0 + bX)]^2$$
$$\Sigma d^2 = \Sigma [Y - (b_0 + bX)]^2$$
$$= \Sigma (Y - b_0 - bX)^2$$

Partial Derivatives

$$\frac{\delta \Sigma}{\delta b} = 2 \Sigma (Y - bX - b_0)(-X) \qquad \frac{\delta \Sigma}{\delta b_0} = 2 \Sigma (Y - bX - b_0)(-1)$$

$$= 2 \Sigma (-XY + bX^2 + b_0 X) \qquad\qquad = 2 \Sigma (-Y + bX + b_0)$$

To obtain minimums, set partials = 0

$$\frac{\delta \Sigma}{\delta b} = 0: \quad 2 \Sigma (-XY + bX^2 + b_0 X) = 0 \qquad \frac{\delta \Sigma}{\delta b_0} = 0: \quad 2 \Sigma (-Y + bX + b_0) = 0$$

$$\Sigma (-XY + bX^2 + b_0 X) = 0 \qquad\qquad \Sigma (-Y + bX + b_0) = 0$$

$$-\Sigma XY + b_0 \Sigma X + bX^2 = 0 \qquad\qquad -\Sigma Y + Nb_0 + b \Sigma X = 0$$

Find a b_0 and b such that Σd^2 is a minimum

$$b_0 \Sigma X + b \Sigma X^2 = \Sigma XY \qquad \times N$$
$$Nb_0 + b \Sigma X = \Sigma Y \qquad \times \Sigma X$$
$$Nb_0 \Sigma X + Nb \Sigma X2^2 = N \Sigma XY$$
$$\underline{Nb_0 \Sigma X + b(\Sigma X)^2 = \Sigma X \Sigma Y \qquad \text{subtract}}$$
$$Nb \Sigma X^2 - b(\Sigma X)^2 = N \Sigma XY - \Sigma X \Sigma Y$$
$$b[N \Sigma X^2 - (\Sigma X)^2] = N \Sigma XY - \Sigma X \Sigma Y$$
$$b = \frac{N \Sigma XY - \Sigma X \Sigma Y}{N \Sigma X^2 - (\Sigma X)^2} \qquad \text{slope formula}$$
$$Nb_0 + b \Sigma X = \Sigma Y$$
$$Nb_0 = \Sigma Y - b \Sigma X$$
$$b_0 = \frac{\Sigma Y}{N} - \frac{b \Sigma X}{N} = \bar{Y} - b\bar{X} \qquad Y \text{ intercept formula}$$

Ratio or
Semilogarithmic Graphs

M any types of problems are encountered where a graph with an arithmetic vertical scale does not prove useful.

As a typical example of such a situation, consider the case of the Alexander Furniture Company. This concern has been manufacturing a line of furniture that we will call product line A. In 1968 it began producing an additional line of furniture, product line B, that differed from the old line in both style and price range. Sales of both lines had been increasing during the period 1978–1982, as shown in Figure B.1. This graph, which utilizes an

FIGURE B.1 Sales of Two Product Lines by Alexander Furniture Company, 1978–1982; Arithmetic Line Graph.

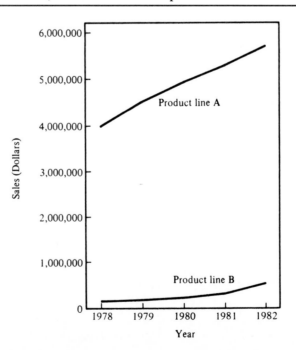

arithmetic vertical scale, conveys the distinct impression that product line A performed much better during this period than product line B. Such an impression arises because the *absolute* increase in sales of product line A was much greater than that of product line B, and therefore the curve for line A climbs more steeply on the chart.

The company's management had no expectations that the sales volume of the new line would match that of the established one as yet, nor that the increases in sales of the new line would equal or surpass those of the established line. Hence interest did not center on a comparison of the *absolute* sales or of the *absolute* increases as much as on a comparison of the *relative* increases in the sales of both lines. Specifically, the question was asked whether sales of line B were increasing more rapidly than those of line A. This question can be answered by calculating link relatives of sales for each product line and plotting them on arithmetic graph paper. A graph with a ratio or logarithmic scale also will answer the question—and without any intermediate calculations.

Before continuing the discussion relating to the Alexander Furniture Company, we will discuss the characteristics of a ratio or logarithmic scale.

RATIO OR LOGARITHMIC SCALE

Figure B.2 shows a graph in which the horizontal, or time, scale is a conventional arithmetic scale. The vertical scale, however, is a *ratio* or *logarithmic scale*—that is, a scale in which equal intervals represent equal differences in the logarithms of numbers. Such a graph is called a *ratio* or *semilogarithmic graph*.

Note the graduated spacing of the thick marks on the vertical scale. Two sets of numbers are shown on the vertical scale. The inner numbers, consisting of 1, 2, and so on, are not part of the scale proper but are guide numbers found on semilogarithmic graph paper. Ordinarily, these guide numbers are not reproduced with the graph, but we include them here to show how a ratio scale is set up.

The bottom guide number is 1 and serves as the starting point of the scale. Any positive scale number other than zero may be placed here. In the case of the Alexander Furniture Company the smallest sales volume was $135,000; hence it is most convenient to begin the baseline of the scale with $100,000. While we may begin with any positive value at the baseline other than zero, it usually is easiest to start with 1, 10, or some multiple of 10 since the major horizontal divisions marked by ticks will then represent round numbers. Opposite guide number 2 we place the value that is twice that of the baseline, or $200,000. Similarly, we write $300,000 corresponding to guide number 3, and so on. The guide number 1 that follows number 9 is assigned a value ten times that of the baseline; in the present case it is given a value of $1,000,000. Note that the vertical distances between the guide numbers, which have been getting smaller up to this point, now

FIGURE B.2 Sales of Two Product Lines by Alexander Furniture Company, 1978–1982; Ratio or Semilogarithmic Line Graph.

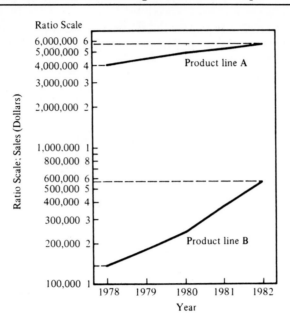

become larger. In fact, the same sequence of graduations is starting all over again. Each full sequence of graduations is called a *cycle*. In labeling the next cycle, we proceed as before. We must write $2,000,000 corresponding to the guide number 2 in the second cycle, since this number is twice the value of the base of the second cycle. Note that the top of the first cycle has now become the base of the second one. Proceeding in this manner, we fill in the vertical scale in Figure B.2. Note that the second cycle is not complete, since there is no need to carry the scale to $1,000,000.

Ratio or semilogarithmic graph paper is available in one, two, three, or even more cycles. The number of cycles needed depends, of course, on the range of the data. Should a series be plotted in which the largest value is eight times the smallest, one-cycle paper would usually be used, since we know that the top of a cycle has a value ten times as great as that of the baseline. On the other hand, a series whose largest value is, say, twelve times the smallest would require semilogarithmic graph paper with at least two cycles.

Once the vertical scale has been labeled, the plotting of the series proceeds in the usual manner. Semilogarithmic graph paper generally shows grid lines between the guide numbers on the vertical scale to aid in the plotting. If, say, there are 20 spaces between guide numbers 1 and 2 on the graph paper used to plot Figure B.2, each of the spaces would represent $5,000 in the first cycle and $50,000 in the second cycle. These additional grid lines on the vertical scale enable one to plot the data quite accurately.

INTERPRETATION OF RATIO OR LOGARITHMIC SCALE

Having considered the mechanics of labeling the vertical scale and plotting points, we now discuss ways of interpreting a semilogarithmic graph. First, compare the distance on the vertical scale of Figure B.2 between $100,000 and $300,000 and between $300,000 and $900,000. Note that in each instance the same distance has been covered on the vertical scale, despite the fact that the first case represents an increase of $200,000, while the second represents an increase of $600,000. Note also that the *relative* increase in each case is the same, namely 200%. If the vertical distance for any other case in which there is a 200% increase is measured, it will be found that the distance required for a 200% increase on the vertical scale of Figure B.2 is always the same.

In general, the ratio scale has the following important characteristics:

- Equal percentage changes require equal vertical distances on the ratio scale.
- The greater the relative change, the larger is the vertical distance required.

We now return to our discussion of the sales of product lines A and B of the Alexander Furniture Company. In Figure B.2, horizontal dashed lines have been superimposed on the graph to aid in comparing the vertical distances required to portray the increase in sales between 1978 and 1982 for each of the two product lines. Since the vertical distance is greater for product line B than for product line A, we conclude that the newer product line experienced a greater *relative* increase in sales between these two years.

The measurement of vertical distance in this way is not necessary in order to interpret the ratio graph. Note from Figure B.2 that the curve for product line B is steeper than that for product line A, since the curve for B has to cover a larger vertical distance during the same time period. Hence we simply say the following:

- The steeper the curve on a ratio chart, the larger is the percentage change.

This result means that we need only compare the slopes of the curves to draw conclusions about relative changes. If the two lines in Figure B.2 had been parallel, equal rates of change would have been indicated, of course, because two parallel straight lines have the same slope.

In addition to comparing relative changes between two periods in several series on a ratio graph, we also can study relative changes from period to period in any given series. For instance, Figure B.3(a) presents a ratio graph in which the series is represented by a straight line. It is at once evident that the percentage increase from period to period in this series is a

FIGURE B.3 Examples of Different Patterns on Ratio Paper.

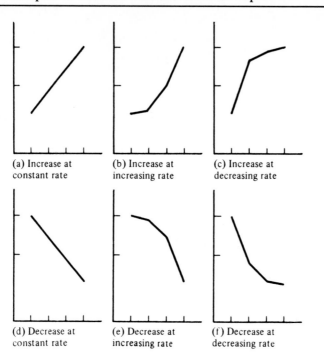

(a) Increase at
constant rate

(b) Increase at
increasing rate

(c) Increase at
decreasing rate

(d) Decrease at
constant rate

(e) Decrease at
increasing rate

(f) Decrease at
decreasing rate

constant one, because a straight line has a constant slope. While a straight line on an arithmetic chart indicates a constant *amount* of change, a straight line on a ratio chart indicates a constant *rate* of change.

Figure B.3(b) presents on a ratio graph a series whose rate of increase is becoming greater and greater as each successive point is plotted. This result is known because the curve becomes steeper and steeper. In short, we state that this series is increasing at an increasing rate.

Similarly, we can readily see that the series in Figure B.3(c) is increasing at a decreasing rate because the curve is becoming less and less steep. Figure B.3(d) presents a series that is decreasing at a constant rate, while Figures B.3(e) and (f) present two series that are decreasing at increasing and decreasing rates, respectively.

Let us now interpret Figure B.2 more fully. While the sales of both product lines have been increasing, sales of the new product line have been increasing more rapidly. Indeed, sales of product line B have been increasing at an increasing rate, while sales of product line A have been increasing at a decreasing rate. Thus while sales of the new product line are still far less than those of the established line, and while the *absolute* increases in sales of the new line are far less than those of the established one, the ratio graph shows that the new product line has been catching on. Thus the ratio graph provides ready answers to management's questions about the *relative* increases in sales of the two product lines.

Tables

TABLE C.1 Individual Terms of the Binomial Distribution.

n	x	.05	.10	.15	.20	.25	.30	.35	.40	.45	.50	.55	.60	.65	.70	.75	.80	.85	.90	.95
1	0	.9500	.9000	.8500	.8000	.7500	.7000	.6500	.6000	.5500	.5000	.4500	.4000	.3500	.3000	.2500	.2000	.1500	.1000	.0500
	1	.0500	.1000	.1500	.2000	.2500	.3000	.3500	.4000	.4500	.5000	.5500	.6000	.6500	.7000	.7500	.8000	.8500	.9000	.9500
2	0	.9025	.8100	.7225	.6400	.5625	.4900	.4225	.3600	.3025	.2500	.2025	.1600	.1225	.0900	.0625	.0400	.0225	.0100	.0025
	1	.0950	.1800	.2550	.3200	.3750	.4200	.4550	.4800	.4950	.5000	.4950	.4800	.4550	.4200	.3750	.3200	.2550	.1800	.0950
	2	.0025	.0100	.0225	.0400	.0625	.0900	.1225	.1600	.2025	.2500	.3025	.3600	.4225	.4900	.5625	.6400	.7225	.8100	.9025
3	0	.8574	.7290	.6141	.5120	.4219	.3430	.2746	.2160	.1664	.1250	.0911	.0640	.0429	.0270	.0156	.0080	.0034	.0010	.0001
	1	.1354	.2430	.3251	.3840	.4219	.4410	.4436	.4320	.4084	.3750	.3341	.2880	.2389	.1890	.1406	.0960	.0574	.0270	.0071
	2	.0071	.0270	.0574	.0960	.1406	.1890	.2389	.2880	.3341	.3750	.4084	.4320	.4436	.4410	.4219	.3840	.3251	.2430	.1354
	3	.0001	.0010	.0034	.0080	.0156	.0270	.0429	.0640	.0911	.1250	.1664	.2160	.2746	.3430	.4219	.5120	.6141	.7290	.8574
4	0	.8145	.6561	.5220	.4096	.3164	.2401	.1785	.1296	.0915	.0625	.0410	.0256	.0150	.0081	.0039	.0016	.0005	.0001	.0000
	1	.1715	.2916	.3685	.4096	.4219	.4116	.3845	.3456	.2995	.2500	.2005	.1536	.1115	.0756	.0469	.0256	.0115	.0036	.0005
	2	.0135	.0486	.0975	.1536	.2109	.2646	.3105	.3456	.3675	.3750	.3675	.3456	.3105	.2646	.2109	.1536	.0975	.0486	.0135
	3	.0005	.0036	.0115	.0256	.0469	.0756	.1115	.1536	.2005	.2500	.2995	.3456	.3845	.4116	.4219	.4096	.3685	.2916	.1715
	4	.0000	.0001	.0005	.0016	.0039	.0081	.0150	.0256	.0410	.0625	.0915	.1296	.1785	.2401	.3164	.4096	.5220	.6561	.8145
5	0	.7738	.5905	.4437	.3277	.2373	.1681	.1160	.0778	.0503	.0313	.0185	.0102	.0053	.0024	.0010	.0003	.0001	.0000	.0000
	1	.2036	.3281	.3915	.4096	.3955	.3602	.3124	.2592	.2059	.1563	.1128	.0768	.0488	.0284	.0146	.0064	.0022	.0004	.0000
	2	.0214	.0729	.1382	.2048	.2637	.3087	.3364	.3456	.3369	.3125	.2757	.2304	.1811	.1323	.0879	.0512	.0244	.0081	.0011
	3	.0011	.0081	.0244	.0512	.0879	.1323	.1811	.2304	.2757	.3125	.3369	.3456	.3364	.3087	.2637	.2048	.1382	.0729	.0214
	4	.0000	.0004	.0022	.0064	.0146	.0283	.0488	.0768	.1128	.1562	.2059	.2592	.3124	.3602	.3955	.4096	.3915	.3281	.2036
	5	.0000	.0000	.0001	.0003	.0010	.0024	.0053	.0102	.0185	.0312	.0503	.0778	.1160	.1681	.2373	.3277	.4437	.5905	.7738
6	0	.7351	.5314	.3771	.2621	.1780	.1176	.0754	.0467	.0277	.0156	.0083	.0041	.0018	.0007	.0002	.0001	.0000	.0000	.0000
	1	.2321	.3543	.3993	.3932	.3560	.3025	.2437	.1866	.1359	.0938	.0609	.0369	.0205	.0102	.0044	.0015	.0004	.0001	.0000
	2	.0305	.0984	.1762	.2458	.2966	.3241	.3280	.3110	.2780	.2344	.1861	.1382	.0951	.0595	.0330	.0154	.0055	.0012	.0001
	3	.0021	.0146	.0415	.0819	.1318	.1852	.2355	.2765	.3032	.3125	.3032	.2765	.2355	.1852	.1318	.0819	.0415	.0146	.0021
	4	.0001	.0012	.0055	.0154	.0330	.0595	.0951	.1382	.1861	.2344	.2780	.3110	.3280	.3241	.2966	.2458	.1762	.0984	.0305
	5	.0000	.0001	.0004	.0015	.0044	.0102	.0205	.0369	.0609	.0938	.1359	.1866	.2437	.3025	.3560	.3932	.3993	.3543	.2321
	6	.0000	.0000	.0000	.0001	.0002	.0007	.0018	.0041	.0083	.0156	.0277	.0467	.0754	.1176	.1780	.2621	.3771	.5314	.7351
7	0	.6983	.4783	.3206	.2097	.1335	.0824	.0490	.0280	.0152	.0078	.0037	.0016	.0006	.0002	.0001	.0000	.0000	.0000	.0000
	1	.2573	.3720	.3960	.3670	.3115	.2471	.1848	.1306	.0872	.0547	.0320	.0172	.0084	.0036	.0013	.0004	.0001	.0000	.0000
	2	.0406	.1240	.2097	.2753	.3115	.3177	.2985	.2613	.2140	.1641	.1172	.0774	.0466	.0250	.0115	.0043	.0012	.0002	.0000
	3	.0036	.0230	.0617	.1147	.1730	.2269	.2679	.2903	.2918	.2734	.2388	.1935	.1442	.0972	.0577	.0287	.0109	.0026	.0002
	4	.0002	.0026	.0109	.0287	.0577	.0972	.1442	.1935	.2388	.2734	.2918	.2903	.2679	.2269	.1730	.1147	.0617	.0230	.0036
	5	.0000	.0002	.0012	.0043	.0115	.0250	.0466	.0774	.1172	.1641	.2140	.2613	.2985	.3177	.3115	.2753	.2097	.1240	.0406
	6	.0000	.0000	.0001	.0004	.0013	.0036	.0084	.0172	.0320	.0547	.0872	.1306	.1848	.2471	.3115	.3670	.3960	.3720	.2573
	7	.0000	.0000	.0000	.0000	.0001	.0002	.0006	.0016	.0037	.0078	.0152	.0280	.0490	.0824	.1335	.2097	.3206	.4783	.6983
8	0	.6634	.4305	.2725	.1678	.1001	.0576	.0319	.0168	.0084	.0039	.0017	.0007	.0002	.0001	.0000	.0000	.0000	.0000	.0000
	1	.2793	.3826	.3847	.3355	.2670	.1977	.1373	.0896	.0548	.0313	.0164	.0079	.0033	.0012	.0004	.0001	.0000	.0000	.0000
	2	.0515	.1488	.2376	.2936	.3115	.2965	.2587	.2090	.1569	.1094	.0703	.0413	.0217	.0100	.0038	.0011	.0002	.0000	.0000
	3	.0054	.0331	.0839	.1468	.2076	.2541	.2786	.2787	.2568	.2188	.1719	.1239	.0808	.0467	.0231	.0092	.0026	.0004	.0000
	4	.0004	.0046	.0185	.0459	.0865	.1361	.1875	.2322	.2627	.2734	.2627	.2322	.1875	.1361	.0865	.0459	.0185	.0046	.0004
	5	.0000	.0004	.0026	.0092	.0231	.0467	.0808	.1239	.1719	.2188	.2568	.2787	.2786	.2541	.2076	.1468	.0839	.0331	.0054
	6	.0000	.0000	.0002	.0011	.0038	.0100	.0217	.0413	.0703	.1094	.1569	.2090	.2587	.2965	.3115	.2936	.2376	.1488	.0515
	7	.0000	.0000	.0000	.0001	.0004	.0012	.0033	.0079	.0164	.0313	.0548	.0896	.1373	.1977	.2670	.3355	.3847	.3826	.2793
	8	.0000	.0000	.0000	.0000	.0000	.0001	.0002	.0007	.0017	.0039	.0084	.0168	.0319	.0576	.1001	.1678	.2725	.4305	.6634

Binomial probability table (individual terms). Each value is $P(X = x)$ for the given n and p.

n = 9

x	.05	.10	.15	.20	.25	.30	.35	.40	.45	.50	.55	.60	.65	.70	.75	.80	.85	.90	.95
0	.6302	.3874	.2316	.1342	.0751	.0404	.0207	.0101	.0046	.0020	.0008	.0003	.0001	.0000	.0000	.0000	.0000	.0000	.0000
1	.2985	.3874	.3679	.3020	.2253	.1556	.1004	.0605	.0339	.0176	.0083	.0035	.0013	.0004	.0001	.0000	.0000	.0000	.0000
2	.0629	.1722	.2597	.3020	.3003	.2668	.2162	.1612	.1110	.0703	.0407	.0212	.0098	.0039	.0012	.0003	.0000	.0000	.0000
3	.0077	.0446	.1069	.1762	.2336	.2668	.2716	.2508	.2119	.1641	.1160	.0743	.0424	.0210	.0087	.0028	.0006	.0001	.0000
4	.0006	.0074	.0283	.0661	.1168	.1715	.2194	.2508	.2600	.2461	.2128	.1672	.1181	.0735	.0389	.0165	.0050	.0008	.0000
5	.0000	.0008	.0050	.0165	.0389	.0735	.1181	.1672	.2128	.2461	.2600	.2508	.2194	.1715	.1168	.0661	.0283	.0074	.0006
6	.0000	.0001	.0006	.0028	.0087	.0210	.0424	.0743	.1160	.1641	.2119	.2508	.2716	.2668	.2336	.1762	.1069	.0446	.0077
7	.0000	.0000	.0000	.0003	.0012	.0039	.0098	.0212	.0407	.0703	.1110	.1612	.2162	.2668	.3003	.3020	.2597	.1722	.0629
8	.0000	.0000	.0000	.0000	.0001	.0004	.0013	.0035	.0083	.0176	.0339	.0605	.1004	.1556	.2253	.3020	.3679	.3874	.2985
9	.0000	.0000	.0000	.0000	.0000	.0000	.0001	.0003	.0008	.0020	.0046	.0101	.0207	.0404	.0751	.1342	.2316	.3874	.6302

n = 10

x	.05	.10	.15	.20	.25	.30	.35	.40	.45	.50	.55	.60	.65	.70	.75	.80	.85	.90	.95
0	.5987	.3487	.1969	.1074	.0563	.0282	.0135	.0060	.0025	.0010	.0003	.0001	.0000	.0000	.0000	.0000	.0000	.0000	.0000
1	.3151	.3874	.3474	.2684	.1877	.1211	.0725	.0403	.0207	.0098	.0042	.0016	.0005	.0001	.0000	.0000	.0000	.0000	.0000
2	.0746	.1937	.2759	.3020	.2816	.2335	.1757	.1209	.0763	.0439	.0229	.0106	.0043	.0014	.0004	.0001	.0000	.0000	.0000
3	.0105	.0574	.1298	.2013	.2503	.2668	.2522	.2150	.1665	.1172	.0746	.0425	.0212	.0090	.0031	.0008	.0001	.0000	.0000
4	.0010	.0112	.0401	.0881	.1460	.2001	.2377	.2508	.2384	.2051	.1596	.1115	.0689	.0368	.0162	.0055	.0012	.0001	.0000
5	.0001	.0015	.0085	.0264	.0584	.1029	.1536	.2007	.2340	.2461	.2340	.2007	.1536	.1029	.0584	.0264	.0085	.0015	.0001
6	.0000	.0001	.0012	.0055	.0162	.0368	.0689	.1115	.1596	.2051	.2384	.2508	.2377	.2001	.1460	.0881	.0401	.0112	.0010
7	.0000	.0000	.0001	.0008	.0031	.0090	.0212	.0425	.0746	.1172	.1665	.2150	.2522	.2668	.2503	.2013	.1298	.0574	.0105
8	.0000	.0000	.0000	.0001	.0004	.0014	.0043	.0106	.0229	.0439	.0763	.1209	.1757	.2335	.2816	.3020	.2759	.1937	.0746
9	.0000	.0000	.0000	.0000	.0000	.0001	.0005	.0016	.0042	.0098	.0207	.0403	.0725	.1211	.1877	.2684	.3474	.3874	.3151
10	.0000	.0000	.0000	.0000	.0000	.0000	.0000	.0001	.0003	.0010	.0025	.0060	.0135	.0282	.0563	.1074	.1969	.3487	.5987

n = 11

x	.05	.10	.15	.20	.25	.30	.35	.40	.45	.50	.55	.60	.65	.70	.75	.80	.85	.90	.95
0	.5688	.3138	.1673	.0859	.0422	.0198	.0088	.0036	.0014	.0005	.0002	.0000	.0000	.0000	.0000	.0000	.0000	.0000	.0000
1	.3293	.3835	.3248	.2362	.1549	.0932	.0518	.0266	.0125	.0054	.0021	.0007	.0002	.0000	.0000	.0000	.0000	.0000	.0000
2	.0867	.2131	.2866	.2953	.2581	.1998	.1395	.0887	.0513	.0269	.0126	.0052	.0018	.0005	.0001	.0000	.0000	.0000	.0000
3	.0137	.0710	.1517	.2215	.2581	.2568	.2254	.1774	.1259	.0806	.0462	.0234	.0102	.0037	.0011	.0002	.0000	.0000	.0000
4	.0014	.0158	.0536	.1107	.1721	.2201	.2428	.2365	.2060	.1611	.1128	.0701	.0379	.0173	.0064	.0017	.0003	.0000	.0000
5	.0001	.0025	.0132	.0388	.0803	.1321	.1830	.2207	.2360	.2256	.1931	.1471	.0985	.0566	.0268	.0097	.0023	.0003	.0000
6	.0000	.0003	.0023	.0097	.0268	.0566	.0985	.1471	.1931	.2256	.2360	.2207	.1830	.1321	.0803	.0388	.0132	.0025	.0001
7	.0000	.0000	.0003	.0017	.0064	.0173	.0379	.0701	.1128	.1611	.2060	.2365	.2428	.2201	.1721	.1107	.0536	.0158	.0014
8	.0000	.0000	.0000	.0002	.0011	.0037	.0102	.0234	.0462	.0806	.1259	.1774	.2254	.2568	.2581	.2215	.1517	.0710	.0137
9	.0000	.0000	.0000	.0000	.0001	.0005	.0018	.0052	.0126	.0269	.0513	.0887	.1395	.1998	.2581	.2953	.2866	.2131	.0867
10	.0000	.0000	.0000	.0000	.0000	.0000	.0002	.0007	.0021	.0054	.0125	.0266	.0518	.0932	.1549	.2362	.3248	.3835	.3293
11	.0000	.0000	.0000	.0000	.0000	.0000	.0000	.0000	.0002	.0005	.0014	.0036	.0088	.0198	.0422	.0859	.1673	.3138	.5688

n = 12

x	.05	.10	.15	.20	.25	.30	.35	.40	.45	.50	.55	.60	.65	.70	.75	.80	.85	.90	.95
0	.5404	.2824	.1422	.0687	.0317	.0138	.0057	.0022	.0008	.0002	.0001	.0000	.0000	.0000	.0000	.0000	.0000	.0000	.0000
1	.3413	.3766	.3012	.2062	.1267	.0712	.0368	.0174	.0075	.0029	.0010	.0003	.0001	.0000	.0000	.0000	.0000	.0000	.0000
2	.0988	.2301	.2924	.2835	.2323	.1678	.1088	.0639	.0339	.0161	.0068	.0025	.0008	.0002	.0000	.0000	.0000	.0000	.0000
3	.0173	.0852	.1720	.2362	.2581	.2397	.1954	.1419	.0923	.0537	.0277	.0125	.0048	.0015	.0004	.0001	.0000	.0000	.0000
4	.0021	.0213	.0683	.1329	.1936	.2311	.2367	.2128	.1700	.1208	.0762	.0420	.0199	.0078	.0024	.0005	.0001	.0000	.0000
5	.0002	.0038	.0193	.0532	.1032	.1585	.2039	.2270	.2225	.1934	.1489	.1009	.0591	.0291	.0115	.0033	.0006	.0000	.0000
6	.0000	.0005	.0040	.0155	.0401	.0792	.1281	.1766	.2124	.2256	.2124	.1766	.1281	.0792	.0401	.0155	.0040	.0005	.0000
7	.0000	.0000	.0006	.0033	.0115	.0291	.0591	.1009	.1489	.1934	.2225	.2270	.2039	.1585	.1032	.0532	.0193	.0038	.0002
8	.0000	.0000	.0001	.0005	.0024	.0078	.0199	.0420	.0762	.1208	.1700	.2128	.2367	.2311	.1936	.1329	.0683	.0213	.0021
9	.0000	.0000	.0000	.0001	.0004	.0015	.0048	.0125	.0277	.0537	.0923	.1419	.1954	.2397	.2581	.2362	.1720	.0852	.0173
10	.0000	.0000	.0000	.0000	.0000	.0002	.0008	.0025	.0068	.0161	.0339	.0639	.1088	.1678	.2323	.2835	.2924	.2301	.0988
11	.0000	.0000	.0000	.0000	.0000	.0000	.0001	.0003	.0010	.0029	.0075	.0174	.0368	.0712	.1267	.2062	.3012	.3766	.3413
12	.0000	.0000	.0000	.0000	.0000	.0000	.0000	.0000	.0001	.0002	.0008	.0022	.0057	.0138	.0317	.0687	.1422	.2824	.5404

Source: Table A, pages 464–466 in *Business Statistics: Concepts and Applications* by William J. Stevenson. Copyright © 1978 by William J. Stevenson. Reprinted by permission of Harper & Row, Publishers. Inc.

TABLE C.2 Table of Areas for Standard Normal Probability Distribution.

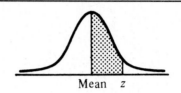

Mean   z

For z = 1.93, shaded area is .4732 out of total area of 1.

z	.00	.01	.02	.03	.04	.05	.06	.07	.08	.09
0.0	.0000	.0040	.0080	.0120	.0160	.0199	.0239	.0279	.0319	.0359
0.1	.0398	.0438	.0478	.0517	.0557	.0596	.0636	.0675	.0714	.0753
0.2	.0793	.0832	.0871	.0910	.0948	.0987	.1026	.1064	.1103	.1141
0.3	.1179	.1217	.1255	.1293	.1331	.1368	.1406	.1443	.1480	.1517
0.4	.1554	.1591	.1628	.1664	.1700	.1736	.1772	.1808	.1844	.1879
0.5	.1915	.1950	.1985	.2019	.2054	.2088	.2123	.2157	.2190	.2224
0.6	.2257	.2291	.2324	.2357	.2389	.2422	.2454	.2486	.2518	.2549
0.7	.2580	.2612	.2642	.2673	.2704	.2734	.2764	.2794	.2823	.2852
0.8	.2881	.2910	.2939	.2967	.2995	.3023	.3051	.3078	.3106	.3133
0.9	.3159	.3186	.3212	.3238	.3264	.3289	.3315	.3340	.3365	.3389
1.0	.3413	.3438	.3461	.3485	.3508	.3531	.3554	.3577	.3599	.3621
1.1	.3643	.3665	.3686	.3708	.3729	.3749	.3770	.3790	.3810	.3830
1.2	.3849	.3869	.3888	.3907	.3925	.3944	.3962	.3980	.3997	.4015
1.3	.4032	.4049	.4066	.4082	.4099	.4115	.4131	.4147	.4162	.4177
1.4	.4192	.4207	.4222	.4236	.4251	.4265	.4279	.4292	.4306	.4319
1.5	.4332	.4345	.4357	.4370	.4382	.4394	.4406	.4418	.4429	.4441
1.6	.4452	.4463	.4474	.4484	.4495	.4505	.4515	.4525	.4535	.4545
1.7	.4554	.4564	.4573	.4582	.4591	.4599	.4608	.4616	.4625	.4633
1.8	.4641	.4649	.4656	.4664	.4671	.4678	.4686	.4693	.4699	.4706
1.9	.4713	.4719	.4726	.4732	.4738	.4744	.4750	.4756	.4761	.4767
2.0	.4772	.4778	.4783	.4788	.4793	.4798	.4803	.4808	.4812	.4817
2.1	.4821	.4826	.4830	.4834	.4838	.4842	.4846	.4850	.4854	.4857
2.2	.4861	.4864	.4868	.4871	.4875	.4878	.4881	.4884	.4887	.4890
2.3	4893	.4896	.4898	.4901	.4904	.4906	.4909	.4911	.4913	.4916
2.4	.4918	.4920	.4922	.4925	.4927	.4929	.4931	.4932	.4934	.4936
2.5	.4938	.4940	.4941	.4943	.4945	.4946	.4948	.4949	.4951	.4952
2.6	.4953	.4955	.4956	.4957	.4959	.4960	.4961	.4962	.4963	.4964
2.7	.4965	.4966	.4967	.4968	.4969	.4970	.4971	.4972	.4973	.4974
2.8	.4974	.4975	.4976	.4977	.4977	.4978	.4979	.4979	.4980	.4981
2.9	.4981	.4982	.4982	.4983	.4984	.4984	.4985	.4985	.4986	.4986
3.0	.49865	.4987	.4987	.4988	.4988	.4989	.4989	.4989	.4990	.4990
4.0	.4999683									

TABLE C.3 Critical Values of *t*.

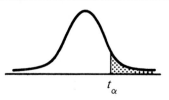

t_α

df	$t_{.100}$	$t_{.050}$	$t_{.025}$	$t_{.010}$	$t_{.005}$
1	3.078	6.314	12.706	31.821	63.657
2	1.886	2.920	4.303	6.965	9.925
3	1.638	2.353	3.182	4.541	5.841
4	1.533	2.132	2.776	3.747	4.604
5	1.476	2.015	2.571	3.365	4.032
6	1.440	1.943	2.447	3.143	3.707
7	1.415	1.895	2.365	2.998	3.499
8	1.397	1.860	2.306	2.896	3.355
9	1.383	1.833	2.262	2.821	3.250
10	1.372	1.812	2.228	2.764	3.169
11	1.363	1.796	2.201	2.718	3.106
12	1.356	1.782	2.179	2.681	3.055
13	1.350	1.771	2.160	2.650	3.012
14	1.345	1.761	2.145	2.624	2.977
15	1.341	1.753	2.131	2.602	2.947
16	1.337	1.746	2.120	2.583	2.921
17	1.333	1.740	2.110	2.567	2.898
18	1.330	1.734	2.101	2.552	2.878
19	1.328	1.729	2.093	2.539	2.861
20	1.325	1.725	2.086	2.528	2.845
21	1.323	1.721	2.080	2.518	2.831
22	1.321	1.717	2.074	2.508	2.819
23	1.319	1.714	2.069	2.500	2.807
24	1.318	1.711	2.064	2.492	2.797
25	1.316	1.708	2.060	2.485	2.787
26	1.315	1.706	2.056	2.479	2.779
27	1.314	1.703	2.052	2.473	2.771
28	1.313	1.701	2.048	2.467	2.763
29	1.311	1.699	2.045	2.462	2.756
inf.	1.282	1.645	1.960	2.326	2.576

Source: "Table of Percentage Points of the *t*-Distribution." Computed by Maxine Merrington, *Biometrika,* vol. 32 (1941), p. 300. Reproduced by permission of Professor D. V. Lindley.

TABLE C.4 Critical Values of Chi Square.

df	$\chi^2_{.995}$	$\chi^2_{.990}$	$\chi^2_{.975}$	$\chi^2_{.950}$	$\chi^2_{.900}$
1	0.0000393	0.0001571	0.0009821	0.0039321	0.0157908
2	0.0100251	0.0201007	0.0506356	0.102587	0.210720
3	0.0717212	0.114832	0.215795	0.351846	0.584375
4	0.206990	0.297110	0.484419	0.710721	1.063623
5	0.411740	0.554300	0.831211	1.145476	1.61031
6	0.675727	0.872085	1.237347	1.63539	2.20413
7	0.989265	1.239043	1.68987	2.16735	2.83311
8	1.344419	1.646482	2.17973	2.73264	3.48954
9	1.734926	2.087912	2.70039	3.32511	4.168216
10	2.15585	2.55821	3.24697	3.94030	4.86518
11	2.60321	3.05347	3.81575	4.57481	5.57779
12	3.07382	3.57056	4.40379	5.22603	6.30380
13	3.56503	4.10691	5.00874	5.89186	7.04150
14	4.07468	4.66043	5.62872	6.57063	7.78953
15	4.60094	5.22935	6.26214	7.26094	8.54675
16	5.14224	5.81221	6.90766	7.96164	9.31223
17	5.69724	6.40776	7.56418	8.67176	10.0852
18	6.26481	7.01491	8.23075	9.39046	10.8649
19	6.84398	7.63273	8.90655	10.1170	11.6509
20	7.43386	8.26040	9.59083	10.8508	12.4426
21	8.03366	8.89720	10.28293	11.5913	13.2396
22	8.64272	9.54249	10.9823	12.3380	14.0415
23	9.26042	10.19567	11.6885	13.0905	14.8479
24	9.88623	10.8564	12.4011	13.8484	15.6587
25	10.5197	11.5240	13.1197	14.6114	16.4734
26	11.1603	12.1981	13.8439	15.3791	17.2919
27	11.8076	12.8786	14.5733	16.1513	18.1138
28	12.4613	13.5648	15.3079	16.9279	18.9302
29	13.1211	14.2565	16.0471	17.7083	19.7677
30	13.7867	14.9535	16.7908	18.4926	20.5992
40	20.7065	22.1643	24.4331	26.5093	29.0505
50	27.9907	29.7067	32.3574	34.7642	37.6886
60	35.5347	37.4848	40.4817	43.1879	46.4589
70	43.2752	45.4418	48.7576	51.7393	55.3290
80	51.1720	53.5400	57.1532	60.3915	64.2778
90	59.1963	61.7541	65.6466	69.1260	73.2912
100	67.3276	70.0648	74.2219	77.9295	82.3581

continues

TABLE C.4 Concluded.

df	$\chi^2_{.100}$	$\chi^2_{.050}$	$\chi^2_{.025}$	$\chi^2_{.010}$	$\chi^2_{.005}$
1	2.70554	3.84146	5.02389	6.63490	7.87944
2	4.60517	5.99147	7.37776	9.21034	10.5966
3	6.25139	7.81473	9.34840	11.3449	12.8381
4	7.77944	9.48773	11.1433	13.2767	14.8602
5	9.23635	11.0705	12.8325	15.0863	16.7496
6	10.6446	12.5916	14.4494	16.8119	18.5476
7	12.0170	14.0671	16.0128	18.4753	20.2777
8	13.3616	15.5073	17.5346	20.0902	21.9550
9	14.6837	16.9190	19.0228	21.6660	23.5893
10	15.9871	18.3070	20.4831	23.2093	25.1882
11	17.2750	19.6751	21.9200	24.7250	26.7569
12	18.5494	21.0261	23.3367	26.2170	28.2995
13	19.8119	22.3621	24.7356	27.6883	29.8194
14	21.0642	23.6848	26.1190	29.1413	31.3193
15	22.3072	24.9958	27.4884	30.5779	32.8013
16	23.5418	26.2962	28.8454	31.9999	34.2672
17	24.7690	27.5871	30.1910	33.4087	35.7185
18	25.9894	28.8693	31.5264	34.8053	37.1564
19	27.2036	30.1435	32.8523	36.1908	38.5822
20	28.4120	31.4104	34.1696	37.5662	39.9968
21	29.6151	32.6705	35.4789	38.9321	41.4010
22	30.8133	33.9244	36.7807	40.2894	42.7956
23	32.0069	35.1725	38.0757	41.6384	44.1813
24	33.1963	36.4151	39.3641	42.9798	45.5585
25	34.3816	37.6525	40.6465	44.3141	46.9278
26	35.5631	38.8852	41.9232	45.6417	48.2899
27	36.7412	40.1133	43.1944	46.9630	49.6449
28	37.9159	41.3372	44.4607	48.2782	50.9933
29	39.0875	42.5569	45.7222	49.5879	52.3356
30	40.2560	43.7729	46.9792	50.8922	53.6720
40	51.8050	55.7585	59.3417	63.6907	66.7659
50	63.1671	67.5048	71.4202	76.1539	79.4900
60	74.3970	79.0819	83.2976	88.3794	91.9517
70	85.5271	90.5312	95.0231	100.425	104.215
80	96.5782	101.879	106.629	112.329	116.321
90	107.565	113.145	118.136	124.116	128.299
100	118.498	124.342	129.561	135.807	140.169

Source: "Tables of the Percentage Points of the χ^2-Distribution," Biometrika, vol. 32 (1941), pp. 188–189, by Catherine M. Thompson. Reproduced by permission of Professor D. V. Lindley.

TABLE C.5 Table of Random Digits.

43732	52254	51717	24199	14995	28638	94266	95896	97286	93363
29127	93840	32774	55120	65026	42329	24853	20025	76811	81401
24907	74544	66673	00700	66710	66969	74990	20032	21995	06036
27618	67022	10133	91336	55075	03262	96546	49329	25175	18575
76254	64180	39786	34653	87041	62316	40460	13053	81241	04385
62416	36939	55843	27845	49480	77704	47938	49743	45798	81296
31941	66753	21574	01290	78304	10121	25145	44925	96389	02748
48769	40172	91480	49345	40787	26343	44517	27111	69002	07130
19841	14663	09283	61166	78039	33309	94009	13456	49850	07814
95278	45022	96058	47206	45136	06897	13029	98610	47895	29255
11681	17274	17775	70451	22664	67014	88052	07139	86031	41752
19662	09277	24043	30468	25419	44660	52122	77683	89932	61867
38220	45565	14942	08320	43174	92076	52890	98982	51549	24199
74342	90018	21144	33405	63152	95923	77259	09132	55290	49080
36330	30763	76197	40481	45306	40321	67829	49329	59366	84654
55667	24316	35987	50597	08340	19788	50319	57122	43216	85841
97044	03505	01390	48719	77194	08143	85905	95243	18460	81857
10801	41372	68587	75813	97859	89824	00856	68893	89724	13555
62086	15756	82269	62301	54394	88005	69419	92167	81404	27619
82969	15207	17095	99636	32773	53706	01064	71431	60025	76456
92689	66288	41679	28175	43057	31307	79854	99889	65340	67466
82257	95475	34860	82583	88431	28935	87509	20727	37989	73978
03500	89229	23013	34269	86323	82028	09026	03845	47049	09033
49935	10627	06590	00319	21022	67060	97351	83563	49386	68421
90394	48453	98568	59114	67484	92490	15912	17007	06152	46270
46528	28504	62341	69676	36687	62032	57678	78816	59456	60820
61139	84737	07313	96815	80079	28473	00893	54263	84568	89126
72052	17047	82703	98378	61551	52642	01676	82279	78996	97089
96412	05437	41920	79190	96446	75572	86149	04486	64642	99840
38542	80332	61559	51540	27508	77623	52532	76913	03934	25756
13240	10094	36445	78755	02259	79075	86304	44848	05617	19112
73520	51141	98860	57952	91325	24661	21656	40584	88869	66593
80523	22661	47316	22278	41056	46455	72563	09140	32256	48198
46746	30636	21103	65113	40794	62196	72234	26648	48913	34334
93786	00483	52986	55922	30830	40750	63223	63371	65047	20933
16286	09146	89517	87223	79385	41937	91686	50357	70316	09026
46721	17036	59388	17337	96097	60336	81050	02307	69823	10816
52053	30051	42444	54844	77985	70091	60464	79822	63536	15688
67526	93477	21244	58252	75052	19270	62520	47603	61385	25861
77360	06067	93429	68336	45621	75564	73052	00972	10065	97831
46689	76298	22771	73816	08640	77702	13451	51694	53359	83400
01401	68433	58746	01648	68134	22848	67255	66420	70730	78826
53605	54676	09068	58018	61071	32171	47150	68624	56213	75608
01524	52265	96518	45107	36343	93236	84759	25889	43255	98284
12742	23345	74617	19338	29434	91944	62796	37134	18666	31430

TABLE C.6 Table of _F_ Distribution.

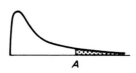

For example, the _F_ scale value for $\delta_2 = 3$, $\delta_1 = 10$ corresponding to area .01 in right tail is 6.55.

_F_ value corresponding to area .05 in right tail in lightface type.
_F_ value corresponding to area .01 in right tail in boldface type.

δ_1, Denominator Degrees of Freedom	δ_2, Numerator Degrees of Freedom									
	1	2	3	4	5	6	7	8	9	10
1	161	200	216	225	230	234	237	239	241	242
	4,052	4,999	5,403	5,625	5,764	5,859	5,928	5,981	6,022	6,056
2	18.51	19.00	19.16	19.25	19.30	19.33	19.36	19.37	19.38	19.39
	98.49	99.00	99.17	99.25	99.30	99.33	99.36	99.37	99.39	99.40
3	10.13	9.55	9.28	9.12	9.01	8.94	8.88	8.84	8.81	8.78
	34.12	30.82	29.46	28.71	28.24	27.91	27.67	27.49	27.34	27.23
4	7.71	6.94	6.59	6.39	6.26	6.16	6.09	6.04	6.00	5.96
	21.20	18.00	16.69	15.98	15.52	15.21	14.98	14.80	14.66	14.54
5	6.61	5.79	5.41	5.19	5.05	4.95	4.88	4.82	4.78	4.74
	16.26	13.27	12.06	11.39	10.97	10.67	10.45	10.29	10.15	10.05
6	5.99	5.14	4.76	4.53	4.39	4.28	4.21	4.15	4.10	4.06
	13.74	10.92	9.78	9.15	8.75	8.47	8.26	8.10	7.98	7.87
7	5.59	4.74	4.35	4.12	3.97	3.87	3.79	3.73	3.68	3.63
	12.25	9.55	8.45	7.85	7.46	7.19	7.00	6.84	6.71	6.62
8	5.32	4.46	4.07	3.84	3.69	3.58	3.50	3.44	3.39	3.34
	11.26	8.65	7.59	7.01	6.63	6.37	6.19	6.03	5.91	5.82
9	5.12	4.26	3.86	3.63	3.48	3.37	3.29	3.23	3.18	3.13
	10.56	8.02	6.99	6.42	6.06	5.80	5.62	5.47	5.35	5.26
10	4.96	4.10	3.71	3.48	3.33	3.22	3.14	3.07	3.02	2.97
	10.04	7.56	6.55	5.99	5.64	5.39	5.21	5.06	4.95	4.85
11	4.84	3.98	3.59	3.36	3.20	3.09	3.01	2.95	2.90	2.86
	9.65	7.20	6.22	5.67	5.32	5.07	4.88	4.74	4.63	4.54
12	4.75	3.88	3.49	3.26	3.11	3.00	2.92	2.85	2.80	2.76
	9.33	6.93	5.95	5.41	5.06	4.82	4.65	4.50	4.39	4.30
13	4.67	3.80	3.41	3.18	3.02	2.92	2.84	2.77	2.72	2.67
	9.07	6.70	5.74	5.20	4.86	4.62	4.44	4.30	4.19	4.10
14	4.60	3.74	3.34	3.11	2.96	2.85	2.77	2.70	2.65	2.60
	8.86	6.51	5.56	5.03	4.69	4.46	4.28	4.14	4.03	3.94
15	4.54	3.68	3.29	3.06	2.90	2.79	2.70	2.64	2.59	2.55
	8.68	6.36	5.42	4.89	4.56	4.32	4.14	4.00	3.89	3.80
16	4.49	3.63	3.24	3.01	2.85	2.74	2.66	2.59	2.54	2.49
	8.53	6.23	5.29	4.77	4.44	4.20	4.03	3.89	3.78	3.69

TABLE C.6 Concluded.

δ_1, Denominator Degrees of Freedom	δ_2, Numerator Degrees of Freedom									
	1	2	3	4	5	6	7	8	9	10
17	4.45	3.59	3.20	2.96	2.81	2.70	2.62	2.55	2.50	2.45
	8.40	6.11	5.18	4.67	4.34	4.10	3.93	3.79	3.68	3.59
18	4.41	3.55	3.16	2.93	2.77	2.66	2.58	2.51	2.46	2.41
	8.28	6.01	5.09	4.58	4.25	4.01	3.85	3.71	3.60	3.51
19	4.38	3.52	3.13	2.90	2.74	2.63	2.55	2.48	2.43	2.38
	8.18	5.93	5.01	4.50	4.17	3.94	3.77	3.63	3.52	3.43
20	4.35	3.49	3.10	2.87	2.71	2.60	2.52	2.45	2.40	2.35
	8.10	5.85	4.94	4.43	4.10	3.87	3.71	3.56	3.45	3.37
21	4.32	3.47	3.07	2.84	2.68	2.57	2.49	2.42	2.37	2.32
	8.02	5.78	4.87	4.37	4.04	3.81	3.65	3.51	3.40	3.31
22	4.30	3.44	3.05	2.82	2.66	2.55	2.47	2.40	2.35	2.30
	7.94	5.72	4.82	4.31	3.99	3.76	3.59	3.45	3.35	3.26
23	4.28	3.42	3.03	2.80	2.64	2.53	2.45	2.38	2.32	2.28
	7.88	5.66	4.76	4.26	3.94	3.71	3.54	3.41	3.30	3.21
24	4.26	3.40	3.01	2.78	2.62	2.51	2.43	2.36	2.30	2.26
	7.82	5.61	4.72	4.22	3.90	3.67	3.50	3.36	3.25	3.17
25	4.24	3.38	2.99	2.76	2.60	2.49	2.41	2.34	2.28	2.24
	7.77	5.57	4.68	4.18	3.86	3.63	3.46	3.32	3.21	3.13

Source: Abridged by permission from *Statistical Methods*, 7th ed., by George W. Snedecor and William C. Cochran. Copyright © 1980 by the Iowa State University Press, Ames, Iowa.

TABLE C.7 Durbin–Watson Test Bounds.

Level of Significance $\alpha = .05$

n	$p-1=1$		$p-1=2$		$p-1=3$		$p-1=4$		$p-1=5$	
	d_L	d_U	d_L	d_U	d_L	d_U	d_L	d_U	d_L	d_U
15	1.08	1.36	0.95	1.54	0.82	1.75	0.69	1.97	0.56	2.21
16	1.10	1.37	0.98	1.54	0.86	1.73	0.74	1.93	0.62	2.15
17	1.13	1.38	1.02	1.54	0.90	1.71	0.78	1.90	0.67	2.10
18	1.16	1.39	1.05	1.53	0.93	1.69	0.82	1.87	0.71	2.06
19	1.18	1.40	1.08	1.53	0.97	1.68	0.86	1.85	0.75	2.02
20	1.20	1.41	1.10	1.54	1.00	1.68	0.90	1.83	0.79	1.99
21	1.22	1.42	1.13	1.54	1.03	1.67	0.93	1.81	0.83	1.96
22	1.24	1.43	1.15	1.54	1.05	1.66	0.96	1.80	0.86	1.94
23	1.26	1.44	1.17	1.54	1.08	1.66	0.99	1.79	0.90	1.92
24	1.27	1.45	1.19	1.55	1.10	1.66	1.01	1.78	0.93	1.90
25	1.29	1.45	1.21	1.55	1.12	1.66	1.04	1.77	0.95	1.89
26	1.30	1.46	1.22	1.55	1.14	1.65	1.06	1.76	0.98	1.88
27	1.32	1.47	1.24	1.56	1.16	1.65	1.08	1.76	1.01	1.86
28	1.33	1.48	1.26	1.56	1.18	1.65	1.10	1.75	1.03	1.85
29	1.34	1.48	1.27	1.56	1.20	1.65	1.12	1.74	1.05	1.84
30	1.35	1.49	1.28	1.57	1.21	1.65	1.14	1.74	1.07	1.83
31	1.36	1.50	1.30	1.57	1.23	1.65	1.16	1.74	1.09	1.83
32	1.37	1.50	1.31	1.57	1.24	1.65	1.18	1.73	1.11	1.82
33	1.38	1.51	1.32	1.58	1.26	1.65	1.19	1.73	1.13	1.81
34	1.39	1.51	1.33	1.58	1.27	1.65	1.21	1.73	1.15	1.81
35	1.40	1.52	1.34	1.58	1.28	1.65	1.22	1.73	1.16	1.80
36	1.41	1.52	1.35	1.59	1.29	1.65	1.24	1.73	1.18	1.80
37	1.42	1.53	1.36	1.59	1.31	1.66	1.25	1.72	1.19	1.80
38	1.43	1.54	1.37	1.59	1.32	1.66	1.26	1.72	1.21	1.79
39	1.43	1.54	1.38	1.60	1.33	1.66	1.27	1.72	1.22	1.79
40	1.44	1.54	1.39	1.60	1.34	1.66	1.29	1.72	1.23	1.79
45	1.48	1.57	1.43	1.62	1.38	1.67	1.34	1.72	1.29	1.78
50	1.50	1.59	1.46	1.63	1.42	1.67	1.38	1.72	1.34	1.77
55	1.53	1.60	1.49	1.64	1.45	1.68	1.41	1.72	1.38	1.77
60	1.55	1.62	1.51	1.65	1.48	1.69	1.44	1.73	1.41	1.77
65	1.57	1.63	1.54	1.66	1.50	1.70	1.47	1.73	1.44	1.77
70	1.58	1.64	1.55	1.67	1.52	1.70	1.49	1.74	1.46	1.77
75	1.60	1.65	1.57	1.68	1.54	1.71	1.51	1.74	1.49	1.77
80	1.61	1.66	1.59	1.69	1.56	1.72	1.53	1.74	1.51	1.77
85	1.62	1.67	1.60	1.70	1.57	1.72	1.55	1.75	1.52	1.77
90	1.63	1.68	1.61	1.70	1.59	1.73	1.57	1.75	1.54	1.78
95	1.64	1.69	1.62	1.71	1.60	1.73	1.58	1.75	1.56	1.78
100	1.65	1.69	1.63	1.72	1.61	1.74	1.59	1.76	1.57	1.78

TABLE C.7 Concluded.

Level of Significance $\alpha = .01$

n	$p - 1 = 1$ d_L	d_U	$p - 1 = 2$ d_L	d_U	$p - 1 = 3$ d_L	d_U	$p - 1 = 4$ d_L	d_U	$p - 1 = 5$ d_L	d_U
15	0.81	1.07	0.70	1.25	0.59	1.46	0.49	1.70	0.39	1.96
16	0.84	1.09	0.74	1.25	0.63	1.44	0.53	1.66	0.44	1.90
17	0.87	1.10	0.77	1.25	0.67	1.43	0.57	1.63	0.48	1.85
18	0.90	1.12	0.80	1.26	0.71	1.42	0.61	1.60	0.52	1.80
19	0.93	1.13	0.83	1.26	0.74	1.41	0.65	1.58	0.56	1.77
20	0.95	1.15	0.86	1.27	0.77	1.41	0.68	1.57	0.60	1.74
21	0.97	1.16	0.89	1.27	0.80	1.41	0.72	1.55	0.63	1.71
22	1.00	1.17	0.91	1.28	0.83	1.40	0.75	1.54	0.66	1.69
23	1.02	1.19	0.94	1.29	0.86	1.40	0.77	1.53	0.70	1.67
24	1.04	1.20	0.96	1.30	0.88	1.41	0.80	1.53	0.72	1.66
25	1.05	1.21	0.98	1.30	0.90	1.41	0.83	1.52	0.75	1.65
26	1.07	1.22	1.00	1.31	0.93	1.41	0.85	1.52	0.78	1.64
27	1.09	1.23	1.02	1.32	0.95	1.41	0.88	1.51	0.81	1.63
28	1.10	1.24	1.04	1.32	0.97	1.41	0.90	1.51	0.83	1.62
29	1.12	1.25	1.05	1.33	0.99	1.42	0.92	1.51	0.85	1.61
30	1.13	1.26	1.07	1.34	1.01	1.42	0.94	1.51	0.88	1.61
31	1.15	1.27	1.08	1.34	1.02	1.42	0.96	1.51	0.90	1.60
32	1.16	1.28	1.10	1.35	1.04	1.43	0.98	1.51	0.92	1.60
33	1.17	1.29	1.11	1.36	1.05	1.43	1.00	1.51	0.94	1.59
34	1.18	1.30	1.13	1.36	1.07	1.43	1.01	1.51	0.95	1.59
35	1.19	1.31	1.14	1.37	1.08	1.44	1.03	1.51	0.97	1.59
36	1.21	1.32	1.15	1.38	1.10	1.44	1.04	1.51	0.99	1.59
37	1.22	1.32	1.16	1.38	1.11	1.45	1.06	1.51	1.00	1.59
38	1.23	1.33	1.18	1.39	1.12	1.45	1.07	1.52	1.02	1.58
39	1.24	1.34	1.19	1.39	1.14	1.45	1.09	1.52	1.03	1.58
40	1.25	1.34	1.20	1.40	1.15	1.46	1.10	1.52	1.05	1.58
45	1.29	1.38	1.24	1.42	1.20	1.48	1.16	1.53	1.11	1.58
50	1.32	1.40	1.28	1.45	1.24	1.49	1.20	1.54	1.16	1.59
55	1.36	1.43	1.32	1.47	1.28	1.51	1.25	1.55	1.21	1.59
60	1.38	1.45	1.35	1.48	1.32	1.52	1.28	1.56	1.25	1.60
65	1.41	1.47	1.38	1.50	1.35	1.53	1.31	1.57	1.28	1.61
70	1.43	1.49	1.40	1.52	1.37	1.55	1.34	1.58	1.31	1.61
75	1.45	1.50	1.42	1.53	1.39	1.56	1.37	1.59	1.34	1.62
80	1.47	1.52	1.44	1.54	1.42	1.57	1.39	1.60	1.36	1.62
85	1.48	1.53	1.46	1.55	1.43	1.58	1.41	1.60	1.39	1.63
90	1.50	1.54	1.47	1.56	1.45	1.59	1.43	1.61	1.41	1.64
95	1.51	1.55	1.49	1.57	1.47	1.60	1.45	1.62	1.42	1.64
100	1.52	1.56	1.50	1.58	1.48	1.60	1.46	1.63	1.44	1.65

Source: Reprinted, with permission, from J. Durbin and G. S. Watson, "Testing for Serial Correlation in Least Squares Regression—II," *Biometrika,* vol. 38 (1951), pp. 159–178.

Data for Case Study 7.1

14.75	0.00	0.00	2.01	12.57	10.00	20.50
14.50	0.00	0.00	2.53	12.57	10.00	20.00
14.13	1.00	0.00	2.10	12.57	10.00	20.00
14.63	0.00	1.00	4.13	12.14	30.00	20.00
14.00	1.00	0.00	2.10	12.57	10.00	20.00
13.38	0.00	1.00	3.97	12.57	10.00	20.00
14.57	0.00	1.00	3.27	12.14	30.00	20.00
13.88	1.00	0.00	3.50	13.19	10.00	19.50
15.38	0.00	0.00	2.85	13.19	10.00	19.50
15.63	0.00	0.00	1.81	13.12	10.00	18.50
15.88	1.00	0.00	2.72	12.69	30.00	18.50
15.00	1.00	0.00	2.43	13.12	10.00	18.00
16.13	0.00	0.00	3.27	12.69	30.00	18.00
15.25	0.00	1.00	3.13	12.69	30.00	17.50
16.00	0.00	0.00	2.55	13.68	10.00	17.00
16.25	0.00	0.00	2.08	13.68	10.00	17.50
17.38	0.00	0.00	2.12	13.20	30.00	17.50
16.35	1.00	0.00	3.40	14.10	10.00	19.00
17.00	1.00	0.00	2.63	13.60	30.00	19.00
16.00	0.00	1.00	2.61	14.10	10.00	19.50
16.63	1.00	0.00	2.06	14.10	10.00	19.50
16.38	0.00	0.00	2.08	14.10	10.00	20.00
16.75	1.00	0.00	2.09	13.60	30.00	20.00
15.13	0.00	1.00	4.29	12.69	30.00	20.00
16.00	1.00	0.00	2.50	12.96	30.00	20.00
14.50	0.00	1.00	3.32	13.47	10.00	20.00
16.25	0.00	0.00	2.95	12.96	30.00	20.00
16.88	0.00	0.00	1.85	14.28	10.00	20.50
17.38	0.00	0.00	1.55	13.59	30.00	20.50
16.00	0.00	1.00	3.33	14.28	10.00	20.50
16.75	1.00	0.00	2.77	14.94	10.00	20.50
17.13	0.00	0.00	2.18	14.94	10.00	20.50
17.50	0.00	1.00	4.21	14.67	30.00	20.50
17.00	1.00	0.00	2.66	15.32	10.00	19.50
16.75	0.00	1.00	3.58	15.32	10.00	19.50
17.20	0.00	1.00	2.96	15.32	10.00	19.50
18.75	0.00	0.00	1.93	15.32	10.00	19.50
17.50	0.00	1.00	2.57	14.68	30.00	19.00

17.50	0.00	0.00	3.18	15.15	10.00	18.00
18.00	0.00	0.00	1.93	15.15	10.00	18.00
15.63	0.00	0.00	2.20	13.39	10.00	17.00
14.75	1.00	0.00	2.21	13.39	10.00	17.00
15.25	0.00	1.00	3.24	13.35	30.00	16.50
15.75	1.00	0.00	2.35	13.35	30.00	16.50
15.25	1.00	0.00	2.11	13.39	10.00	16.50
15.75	1.00	0.00	2.80	13.35	30.00	16.50
15.63	0.00	0.00	1.95	13.39	10.00	16.50
16.13	0.00	0.00	2.80	13.39	10.00	16.50
15.75	1.00	0.00	4.00	13.35	30.00	16.00
16.13	0.00	0.00	2.81	13.50	10.00	15.80
16.25	1.00	0.00	3.38	13.50	30.00	15.80
16.00	0.00	0.00	2.57	13.50	10.00	15.80
15.88	0.00	1.00	3.96	13.50	30.00	15.80
16.50	1.00	0.00	2.67	13.50	30.00	15.80
16.38	1.00	0.00	3.05	13.50	30.00	15.80
12.50	1.00	0.00	2.36	10.60	30.00	15.30
12.25	1.00	0.00	2.54	10.60	30.00	15.30
14.25	1.00	0.00	2.20	12.13	30.00	15.30
15.00	1.00	0.00	3.03	12.13	30.00	15.80
15.25	1.00	0.00	3.24	12.13	30.00	16.50
16.00	0.00	0.00	1.95	12.34	30.00	17.80
14.88	1.00	0.00	2.86	12.34	30.00	17.80
14.75	1.00	0.00	2.64	12.34	30.00	19.00
15.50	1.00	0.00	2.23	11.40	30.00	20.00
13.75	1.00	0.00	2.24	11.40	30.00	19.50
11.30	1.00	0.00	3.24	11.36	30.00	17.50
12.38	1.00	0.00	1.95	11.36	30.00	17.50
12.15	1.00	0.00	2.32	11.36	30.00	14.50
11.75	1.00	0.00	2.45	9.81	30.00	13.00
12.38	1.00	0.00	1.88	9.81	30.00	13.00
12.63	0.00	0.00	1.76	9.81	30.00	13.00
11.13	1.00	0.00	1.99	9.81	30.00	12.50
11.38	0.00	0.00	2.20	9.78	10.00	12.50
11.88	1.00	0.00	2.14	9.81	30.00	12.00
11.75	1.00	0.00	2.61	9.81	30.00	12.00
13.63	0.00	0.00	1.84	10.24	30.00	11.00
13.88	0.00	0.00	1.62	11.00	30.00	11.00
13.00	1.00	0.00	3.56	11.00	30.00	11.00
12.00	1.00	0.00	2.65	11.10	10.00	11.00
13.13	1.00	0.00	2.65	11.00	30.00	11.00
14.27	0.00	0.00	1.80	11.34	30.00	12.30
14.63	0.00	0.00	1.69	11.34	30.00	12.30
15.25	0.00	0.00	1.88	11.34	30.00	12.20
14.25	1.00	0.00	2.77	11.34	30.00	12.30
13.52	1.00	0.00	2.22	11.75	10.00	13.50
14.63	1.00	0.00	2.42	11.59	30.00	13.50
14.75	0.00	0.00	1.77	11.39	30.00	13.50
14.00	0.00	0.00	2.22	11.75	10.00	13.50
14.50	0.00	0.00	2.99	11.59	30.00	13.50
14.25	0.00	0.00	2.22	11.75	10.00	13.50
14.63	0.00	0.00	1.93	11.75	10.00	14.50
13.30	1.00	0.00	3.35	12.68	10.00	15.50
14.50	0.00	0.00	2.21	12.68	10.00	17.00

E

Data Sets and Database

This appendix contains seven time series data sets and eight financial variables measured on each of 266 U.S. corporations in a recent year.[1]

---

[1] We are indebted to Dr. Lynn Stephens of Eastern Washington University for providing these data values.

APPENDIX E   DATA SETS

	Foreign Travel U.S., Citizen Departures (Thousands)	Production on Farms Case of Eggs (Millions)
1961	2,020	173.4
	2,292	176.6
	2,588	176.4
	2,841	181.2
	3,341	182.5
1966	3,814	184.7
	4,334	194.8
	4,820	192.5
	5,767	191.5
	6,499	190.1
1971	7,059	193.6
	8,312	192.3
	8,758	183.5
	8,306	182.3
	8,177	179.5
1976	7,755	179.2
	8,330	179.5
	9,245	186.5
	9,939	192.3
	9,971	193.6
1981	9,978	194.0
	10,275	193.7
	12,258	189.4
	13,909	189.5
	14,768	190.0
1986	14,357	190.0
	16,425	193.2
	17,209	193.0
1989	17,403	186.4

Household Major Appliances, Industry Shipments, Freezers (Thousands).

Year:	1983	1984	1985	1986	1987	1988	1989	1990
Jan	100	109	110	90	84	91	93	99
Feb	97	100	73	77	82	89	94	80
Mar	115	94	88	80	105	82	90	88
Apr	111	97	90	99	97	108	93	90
May	113	118	112	106	106	112	111	103
Jun	136	134	136	140	136	126	116	126
Jul	148	153	149	159	137	156	129	155
Aug	134	133	131	122	138	152	144	136
Sep	117	106	108	110	109	128	123	123
Oct	92	87	100	94	87	110	95	101
Nov	78	80	66	72	93	99	84	90
Dec	82	70	75	72	86	94	90	96

Beer Production (Millions of Barrels).

Year:	1983	1984	1985	1986	1987	1988	1989	1990
Jan	14.77	14.15	15.50	15.71	15.60	15.80	15.88	16.46
Feb	14.53	14.75	14.55	15.21	15.63	15.85	15.29	15.74
Mar	16.78	17.72	16.76	16.51	17.66	17.12	17.57	17.97
Apr	18.42	16.81	17.97	17.99	17.42	17.73	17.30	17.47
May	18.17	18.74	18.86	18.67	17.44	18.31	18.40	18.10
Jun	18.47	18.47	18.23	18.65	18.58	18.58	18.75	18.58
Jul	18.50	19.12	18.59	18.33	18.09	18.17	18.28	18.21
Aug	18.27	17.59	17.71	17.06	16.81	17.72	18.35	
Sep	15.71	14.58	14.54	15.26	15.82	15.45	15.28	
Oct	15.41	15.14	14.36	15.62	15.50	15.61	15.82	
Nov	13.62	13.06	13.12	13.53	13.81	14.02	14.78	
Dec	12.46	12.89	13.13	13.97	13.69	13.22	13.45	

New Prescriptions (Thousands).

Year:	1984	1985	1986	1987	1988	1989	1990
Jan	154	200	223	346	518	613	628
Feb	96	118	104	261	404	392	308
Mar	73	90	107	224	300	273	324
Apr	49	79	85	141	210	322	248
May	36	78	75	148	196	189	272
Jun	59	91	99	145	186	257	634
Jul	95	167	135	223	247	324	299
Aug	169	169	121	272	343	404	424
Sep	210	289	335	445	464	677	548
Oct	278	347	460	560	680	858	372
Nov	298	375	488	612	711	895	876
Dec	245	203	326	467	610	664	676

Seattle, Washington, Daily Bus Ridership for 146 Days on the Pike Street Route.

350	339	351	364	369	331	340	346	340	341	357	398	381	367	383	375
353	361	375	371	373	366	382	406	429	403	429	425	427	409	402	409
419	404	429	463	428	449	444	474	467	463	432	453	462	456	474	514
489	475	492	525	527	533	527	526	522	513	564	599	572	587	599	601
611	620	579	582	592	581	630	638	663	631	645	682	601	595	521	521
516	496	538	575	537	534	542	547	538	540	526	548	555	545	594	643
625	616	640	625	637	634	621	654	641	649	662	699	672	704	700	711
715	718	652	664	695	704	733	716	772	712	732	755	761	748	748	750
744	731	782	810	777	816	840	872	868	811	810	762	634	626	649	697
657	549														

Data are read across the table.

Monthly Occupancy Statistics for Motel Nine.

Year:	1981	1982	1983	1984	1985	1986	1987	1988	1989	1990
Jan	563	635	647	676	748	795	843	778	895	875
Feb	599	639	658	748	773	788	847	856	856	993
Mar	669	712	713	811	814	890	942	939	893	977
Apr	598	622	688	729	767	797	804	813	875	969
May	580	621	724	701	729	751	840	783	835	872
Jun	668	676	707	790	749	821	872	828	935	1006
Jul	499	501	629	594	681	692	656	657	833	832
Aug	215	220	238	231	241	291	370	310	300	346
Sep	556	561	613	617	680	727	742	780	791	850
Oct	587	603	730	691	708	868	847	860	900	914
Nov	546	626	735	701	694	812	732	780	782	869
Dec	571	606	652	706	772	800	899	808	880	994

DATABASE.

Company Number	Sales (Millions)	Employees (Thousands)	Capital Expenditures (Millions)	Intangibles Expenditures (Millions)	Cost of Goods Sold (Millions)	Labor and Related Expense (Millions)	Advertising Expense (Millions)	Research and Development Expense (Millions)
1	3221.8008	42.0000	147.9000	30.6000	2285.2007	599.7998	118.3000	28.0000
2	1690.6001	20.9050	93.0000	29.1000	1057.2002	343.2000	114.9000	8.9000
3	2197.2764	39.0000	66.8670	55.8600	1387.0679	661.3997	95.5680	11.1820
4	2357.8206	23.3000	59.5560	69.6080	1743.7952	25.6320	51.9170	8.5000
5	8129.0000	35.0000	297.0000	29.0000	7423.0000	1178.0000	12.8000	9.2530
6	11851.0000	23.0000	394.0000	20.0000	10942.0000	2556.0000	11.6530	14.6000
7	323.8606	3.9000	2.5900	4.2880	233.5300	22.8350	3.5290	30.7320
8	660.4856	8.3780	10.9840	3.3720	582.2649	25.6250	44.9990	64.8730
9	4351.1601	50.9120	102.7080	217.0920	4156.8671	12.8360	66.2640	8.7790
10	958.8357	5.5000	16.6010	29.5900	874.1287	19.5000	112.3860	18.3650
11	3802.5581	39.6000	206.1020	157.3520	2997.2703	518.0000	139.7290	16.4130
12	2576.0464	22.6000	50.6690	45.0790	1885.9053	349.4910	48.8170	9.5000
13	106.0160	28.0000	1.3120	42.0000	84.6590	35.5550	22.9370	8.7330
14	5669.8945	46.8810	103.0000	31.1000	4424.3007	785.0000	141.3000	18.5000
15	319.6570	2.8940	4.5770	2.2090	246.6980	42.8370	87.0000	1.1000
16	511.7217	10.1000	19.5600	27.0000	286.2288	48.9990	1.8700	23.6520
17	884.6189	22.8010	58.0940	33.0000	467.4436	36.5000	16.0350	29.6320
18	166.3750	2.3000	3.9510	5.2890	111.0310	31.0000	4.0230	38.5420
19	59.1310	18.0000	1.1400	14.5000	43.7430	26.3210	90.3250	56.9820
20	136.6970	3.1000	2.0090	18.4930	105.3300	15.8880	46.3000	8.6330
21	767.8799	8.1000	37.4250	18.0560	519.3948	112.1350	21.8470	2.7860
22	61.3280	1.1390	1.3880	26.3250	35.2020	17.3140	2.4270	88.5230
23	445.6387	5.8000	18.9780	12.6000	213.2880	12.1000	62.8060	1.4600
24	2259.6316	16.0270	228.7270	27.3350	1696.3772	421.8057	116.5990	9.6000
25	624.8040	8.7000	86.4030	2.8080	408.4707	168.0200	33.4700	9.4440
26	329.9578	4.0000	14.9460	8.3710	225.0410	20.9850	12.9790	32.0000
27	308.7327	2.1070	14.8080	43.5920	239.1300	36.5000	18.1220	1.8510
28	598.9507	5.0000	39.7150	27.8920	481.9436	45.0000	39.8230	.7500
29	172.7920	1.5760	1.6590	23.5420	118.7090	48.2000	7.9090	26.3330
30	910.8406	7.0000	14.4610	5.5880	677.2527	7.0000	58.2130	1.8000
31	142.1830	1.6000	5.5880	72.5190	126.9660	1.6000	2.7310	57.2710

continues

DATABASE Continued.

Company Number	Sales (Millions)	Employees (Thousands)	Capital Expenditures (Millions)	Intangibles Expenditures (Millions)	Cost of Goods Sold (Millions)	Labor and Related Expense (Millions)	Advertising Expense (Millions)	Research and Development Expense (Millions)
32	425.0828	6.8330	72.5190	31.8030	256.2837	6.8330	12.1440	44.1550
33	4337.9140	36.1000	306.0220	101.4290	2344.1631	36.1000	270.2576	16.1100
34	271.0076	2.0780	27.1230	6.5030	134.3790	35.7730	20.2540	87.4830
35	209.4520	2.9980	14.4690	14.6060	176.4890	2.0780	1.8970	714.9990
36	62.4180	3.8000	3.7390	7.6680	34.4700	2.9980	44.0500	121.3300
37	4300.0000	95.5000	412.2886	157.6030	2108.5503	5.1000	257.6807	11.6440
38	390.6829	5.1000	30.8480	10.8550	225.1080	6.3000	18.3780	33.4770
39	270.0127	6.3000	40.0340	22.4540	189.8000	2.0000	4.9080	43.7430
40	97.9660	2.0000	6.9940	5.2500	64.5920	31.9700	2.5900	18.9700
41	66.4090	12.5261	3.7570	1.0090	57.2310	33.2000	59.1300	14.9460
42	56.5550	3.9000	1.6240	6.9940	44.0550	53.5000	19.5600	1.6590
43	3267.9551	31.9790	502.0398	45.6140	2517.7566	754.8977	3.9510	57.7210
44	2745.7439	43.9680	251.0340	16.1110	1638.7969	45.0000	161.2000	108.1480
45	2609.0000	33.2000	248.0001	10.0000	1874.0000	564.0000	18.0000	83.0000
46	1677.6016	11.6440	284.6089	87.4830	1185.9717	24.4530	6.4840	36.1310
47	6887.6210	53.5000	1075.1719	84.0390	4721.9570	1375.7996	44.0700	231.4690
48	10584.1990	132.1400	714.2002	22.6000	7353.5000	3204.2688	93.4000	377.1001
49	2912.7644	45.8540	195.2680	45.6430	2189.5293	879.6548	14.9460	66.0560
50	4309.5820	66.8000	275.3079	67.3120	2913.9036	993.3997	1.6590	40.5470
51	1946.4766	24.4530	121.3300	6.2920	1403.4976	546.0508	35.2020	40.0810
52	9254.1171	151.2000	1431.0906	121.3300	6187.7851	2125.2012	95.9510	334.8057
53	5018.6914	62.8510	479.8997	1.6240	3478.0989	1318.0999	9.2530	144.3000
54	1510.7798	15.3000	207.9320	63.5190	1157.2117	13.9700	27.6660	39.7150
55	1560.0750	22.7000	162.5190	61.9380	1188.9126	18.4340	19.3190	24.7010
56	2794.0000	37.4000	256.0999	7.3000	1928.4988	780.7996	18.3650	70.1000
57	921.3689	13.9700	61.9380	18.4340	597.7700	45.1640	19.2020	22.6500
58	1253.5430	13.0580	66.4310	13.9700	806.6758	236.5000	32.0000	48.6510
59	1328.1138	13.1160	201.1960	31.2730	851.8938	1.1550	31.2730	33.5620
60	1314.6299	27.3460	36.9330	43.0750	569.7327	6.4690	174.4610	42.1160
61	7869.6914	113.3710	687.7998	90.2000	5580.5976	1931.5005	76.5000	155.9000
62	73.0550	7.8240	26.5680	20.6650	38.9980	22.8990	43.0750	99.8430
63	108.5090	87.4350	5.6630	37.3860	77.1740	36.9990	90.2000	1.6500

64	1422.4507	16.5000	100.4700	69.8820	1060.5420	305.7000	6.3970	25.4520
65	87.4350	7.6550	8.5150	15.3750	51.3970	11.3940	69.8820	2.7200
66	7.8240	9.5280	26.6950	7.7640	6.7860	20.5720	4.2100	52.1780
67	868.7107	15.3400	42.4040	1.2120	686.0518	200.4850	10.4000	22.7240
68	137.3950	2.8750	14.1080	9.7470	112.2350	30.7620	83.1580	1.9000
69	753.8848	6.5480	24.2870	4.2120	596.5076	13.4000	88.8250	6.4200
70	1445.0166	27.0030	84.1490	99.9080	786.8777	1.9360	39.8650	76.1870
71	3062.6316	49.6190	67.6310	83.1580	1446.5227	668.9910	243.0450	74.5240
72	2450.4285	32.6000	81.9220	88.8250	906.9639	6.7120	423.2698	90.5730
73	141.2580	1.3040	4.5050	6.7300	95.1540	3.7000	9.9040	9.7580
74	6.8030	5.1000	9.5230	1.4590	2.3980	12.2490	.7230	11.9490
75	1852.0896	25.4000	89.5500	57.7900	672.7947	4.5070	28.4910	148.0770
76	365.7217	4.9030	17.0620	16.7160	217.5420	3.4720	6.730	11.8950
77	1981.4397	28.7000	155.8530	141.2700	668.7720	634.0596	55.2940	161.3500
78	2362.1326	40.7000	110.1000	99.8430	1055.4187	11.3940	75.7000	113.1280
79	357.0696	5.5500	12.6430	52.1780	141.2700	2.1130	36.8860	18.9510
80	220.3790	3.7000	10.7860	9.7580	67.1220	20.5720	7.1610	6.2610
81	1082.4927	17.9000	51.3360	52.1780	310.7820	315.8997	114.9660	65.6910
82	848.3799	17.1000	41.2990	11.9490	386.0066	16.0000	40.6150	61.6940
83	1112.0386	16.5890	74.5790	44.6610	378.7710	7.3000	91.2150	77.3130
84	1515.8816	37.0000	108.0460	52.3290	758.5320	469.9229	74.5950	61.8300
85	1328.5508	19.9200	44.6810	6.2850	566.2200	323.7090	36.9560	115.5890
86	2878.4956	58.0000	182.2670	348.1426	1247.2339	1.1500	391.6277	85.3970
87	4312.0507	56.6000	169.2950	66.9970	2672.3262	6.4600	260.3870	37.6540
88	54.3250	37.3860	1.0660	2.8130	26.5960	4.7670	0.7520	44.6610
89	122.9470	57.1720	13.7480	7.5620	94.6720	17.6580	1.4590	3.8670
90	2014.7056	31.0000	74.7910	74.7910	700.4778	503.6768	45.0900	21.1460
91	969.8328	18.5170	40.8340	54.2710	448.5286	9.4450	91.2690	8.5670
92	45.3670	8.3500	1.6430	7.0670	15.7310	2.1230	5.1820	52.3290
93	255.1320	3.3000	10.6420	20.2520	131.6750	12.2220	42.5670	6.2850
94	1710.4700	31.7000	91.5640	54.7540	752.5889	530.2456	239.9010	42.0600
95	365.8809	3.4800	20.0140	6.7300	177.5500	25.8740	16.7100	23.7910
96	33.2650	2.0870	1.5120	4.4840	19.7100	19.7100	1.1550	2.8890
97	53.7460	.5250	2.0870	42.2810	16.1820	16.1800	7.6770	19.7100
98	52.8760	1.1420	2.4190	1.2160	27.1500	27.1500	6.4690	16.1820
99	9.6630	2.4190	12.7460	7.9670	5.6960	5.6950	0.4570	27.1500
100	1451.6687	29.0000	86.6820	97.2690	505.8267	36.1200	137.7250	30.7620
101	321.3638	4.9110	13.1180	11.0840	268.0159	57.2600	1.1110	13.4000
102	156.4580	2.3500	4.5670	3.8620	114.1930	6.4800	4.7670	5.6960

continues

DATABASE Continued.

Company Number	Sales (Millions)	Employees (Thousands)	Capital Expenditures (Millions)	Intangibles Expenditures (Millions)	Cost of Goods Sold (Millions)	Labor and Related Expense (Millions)	Advertising Expense (Millions)	Research and Development Expense (Millions)
103	52.1870	.8650	1.5100	20.6490	36.5130	59.3250	18.0150	1.9360
104	447.2100	7.7670	12.7460	41.7940	280.3218	26.8120	9.4400	505.8267
105	86.8170	1.1000	1.2810	19.3850	57.2600	26.6950	2.1230	1.3420
106	1132.3499	18.0150	16.8570	1.6970	785.0718	36.9240	25.8740	6.7120
107	217.4120	3.2000	4.4840	10.5440	142.6020	57.5790	3.2520	3.7000
108	7.7640	86.6820	1.2810	7.2210	6.4800	9.5280	20.8580	268.0159
109	1581.8760	20.8580	142.2810	5.8820	1280.1670	359.0999	1.1000	12.2490
110	201.4650	1.1000	7.9670	1.3370	169.2630	57.5700	7.4000	114.1930
111	198.9010	.9110	9.7470	.4290	164.1940	73.9670	1.8400	36.5130
112	1497.0076	7.4000	131.9400	6.0210	1098.2969	99.4080	5.1000	280.3280
113	153.2290	1.8400	11.0840	3.4390	59.2350	9.2800	8.3500	4.5070
114	367.9246	5.1000	20.6490	11.2110	230.1690	73.9670	1.2110	11.3940
115	494.4136	8.3500	19.3850	3.1490	342.9849	6.4490	3.8030	2.1000
116	52.4550	1.2120	7.2210	7.0620	26.8120	4.7670	4.0510	57.2600
117	37.3860	.8200	1.3370	44.3730	26.6950	9.4400	5.6000	785.0718
118	57.7120	13.1190	3.4390	.7160	36.9240	2.1230	7.5620	.9510
119	586.4766	3.8030	44.3730	34.2780	391.3706	25.8740	2.8100	20.5720
120	476.2078	4.0510	34.2780	30.2360	244.7830	99.9080	5.8820	16.0000
121	15.3570	4.5671	16.8570	53.2830	9.5280	29.0000	6.0200	142.6020
122	393.6016	5.6000	30.2360	2.8890	265.3079	9.2800	11.2110	7.3000
123	4701.1210	7.5620	353.2830	48.6920	3707.6846	4.9110	3.1490	6.4800
124	1167.8340	2.8100	48.6920	8.4580	1017.6038	2.3500	7.0620	59.2350
125	12298.3980	50.7000	1221.8008	10.4000	9285.7109	1016.5000	13.116	64.6000
126	439.4727	1.9020	65.1100	39.8650	263.8108	51.1480	27.3460	31.2730
127	29127.0030	108.7000	1897.0005	9.9040	20032.0000	78.7700	16.5000	86.0000
128	1993.6624	8.0000	43.4190	45.7820	1755.5662	3.5730	31.1370	43.0750
129	4660.8945	18.1000	636.1238	28.4900	3675.6895	440.7996	3.4000	11.6000
130	976.4578	8.8280	14.8590	55.2940	879.3516	91.8000	15.3440	90.2000
131	3834.9324	6.6610	316.7156	68.2690	3557.4734	7.4050	2.8250	69.8820
132	9535.7382	42.7800	1107.3838	75.7000	7075.1875	971.0000	6.5480	29.7730
133	657.7776	1.2640	56.1460	36.8860	565.0176	14.4700	27.0030	4.2120
134	100.4570	43.0750	44.0680	7.1610	72.7830	22.0310	49.6110	83.1580

135	60334.5110	130.0000	4186.9296	40.6150	45999.0070	3405.0000	32.6000	290.0000
136	2150.0000	90.2110	311.7000	91.2150	1460.7996	57.4030	1.3040	25.1000
137	18069.0000	58.3000	1680.0000	74.5900	13442.0000	1345.0000	25.4000	88.8250
138	109.7380	69.8870	32.2560	36.9560	97.0130	2.5200	4.9030	6.7300
139	592.7710	3.2520	123.7680	3.8770	420.3206	67.3300	28.7000	1.4590
140	4642.3945	14.3280	353.5999	33.5620	4085.0989	324.0000	40.7000	25.0000
141	2072.4412	11.1480	270.1846	42.1160	1640.8118	1.2400	5.5500	4.9810
142	4509.3828	13.3540	502.2720	1.6500	2838.0845	236.4540	2.0370	12.8000
143	34736.0030	207.7000	1760.7100	2.7200	26053.9060	20.9400	3.7000	16.7160
144	1191.0337	4.2070	255.6150	1.9000	865.6477	82.6730	.2670	99.8430
145	312.7300	4.2120	76.5000	6.4200	452.4130	17.0050	17.9000	52.1780
146	1553.1077	9.1500	343.9539	23.6410	988.8760	185.6600	12.5840	9.7580
147	6997.7734	30.0080	956.1719	11.2330	4886.8125	720.5000	17.1000	58.2460
148	513.1880	5.1420	41.9800	41.9800	375.3599	25.0200	11.3330	11.9490
149	28085.0030	94.8000	2913.0000	32.5600	20632.0000	2344.0000	89.0000	231.0000
150	11062.8980	34.9740	1774.3904	43.0250	8259.7656	1051.0000	16.5890	114.0000
151	23232.4060	37.5750	1049.6729	90.2110	19964.6050	994.0000	37.0000	89.7370
152	14961.5000	47.0110	1744.0364	69.8870	10046.0000	1126.7310	19.9200	80.3250
153	5197.7070	24.1450	762.2510	4.2120	3336.7566	431.9976	7.7130	15.0520
154	7428.2343	33.7210	601.1216	6.7310	5714.3085	9.7320	58.0000	21.0000
155	28607.5030	67.8410	1344.3777	10.4000	24787.6050	1572.7996	56.6000	52.0000
156	87.6100	6.7310	12.7120	39.8650	74.5510	31.5580	31.0000	44.6610
157	1165.6736	3.5310	26.6780	9.9040	1035.7129	6.6000	18.5170	2.4490
158	567.3650	1.5420	97.4910	28.9400	480.5110	23.5230	3.3000	52.3290
159	5954.9414	16.2970	732.0000	55.9240	4540.4609	444.8997	31.7000	18.5000
160	368.0940	2.3150	15.0860	2.7160	319.4939	10.6050	3.4800	6.2850
161	751.7327	6.2550	51.1060	13.5380	606.8318	3.5230	6.8000	9.9000
162	895.4087	10.9000	145.5140	9.3840	681.9656	26.3250	39.0000	30.6000
163	1063.2908	16.1790	51.1480	25.7670	746.2820	12.6000	16.6980	14.6320
164	1306.0867	19.3970	78.7700	2.7490	1021.4856	435.2998	23.3000	13.2830
165	140.4440	1.9190	3.5730	55.8600	122.3210	27.3350	35.0000	29.1000
166	4357.2812	52.1400	110.4470	12.0830	3540.9612	1235.0000	3.9000	55.8600
167	263.9048	3.7000	7.4050	27.2080	203.3440	2.8080	8.3780	3.2500
168	6184.8945	94.5000	398.2000	69.6080	5224.0000	2550.0000	50.9120	37.1000
169	257.6509	3.3640	14.4730	7.5700	190.4190	8.3710	5.5000	69.6080
170	50.5150	52.5350	29.1000	29.0000	18.0560	43.5920	39.6000	29.0000
171	419.6470	4.3020	22.0310	20.0000	341.5906	135.6000	22.6000	20.0000
172	1227.4490	20.0000	57.4030	4.2880	999.7520	27.8920	28.0000	9.0000
173	779.3450	8.8000	22.0670	3.3700	678.4258	229.1270	46.8810	4.2880

continues

DATABASE Continued.

Company Number	Sales (Millions)	Employees (Thousands)	Capital Expenditures (Millions)	Intangibles Expenditures (Millions)	Cost of Goods Sold (Millions)	Labor and Related Expense (Millions)	Advertising Expense (Millions)	Research and Development Expense (Millions)
174	72.1760	1.3000	2.5210	29.5900	50.9650	24.8290	2.8940	3.3700
175	3248.0076	36.0620	263.6167	19.4460	2710.3455	974.3379	10.1000	29.5900
176	921.1270	12.6590	67.3340	10.5250	771.0059	23.5420	22.8010	157.3520
177	711.9827	12.5120	133.3850	45.0790	653.8069	351.4700	2.3000	45.0790
178	72.4110	1.0250	1.2400	42.0000	60.0820	93.0000	18.0000	42.0000
179	297.5686	4.1520	20.9420	.8990	248.7160	123.1000	3.1000	31.1000
180	677.8489	6.0700	17.0050	31.1000	613.3047	169.2570	8.1000	2.2090
181	582.6238	1.4000	25.0290	2.2090	474.3450	66.8670	1.1390	27.0000
182	3750.4109	38.1700	120.8280	27.0000	3240.7886	1132.6216	5.8000	33.0000
183	88.8070	2.3330	9.7320	7.2110	66.6540	59.5500	16.0270	5.2890
184	306.9397	2.8000	31.5880	33.0000	220.4980	2.5900	8.7000	14.5000
185	331.7366	5.2000	6.6000	11.0250	295.3848	10.9840	4.0000	18.4930
186	546.9500	8.9000	23.5230	5.2890	439.0479	16.0010	2.1000	18.0560
187	7.5910	30.6000		14.5000	5.0480	50.6690	5.0000	26.3250
188	3479.4573	41.3940	170.3720	18.4930	3100.5391	1177.5999	1.5760	15.0500
189	485.6138	6.6580	58.6750	3.5250	335.3318	42.0000	93.0000	1.4320
190	123.2280	2.0450	10.6050	5.2550	96.6630	20.9000	66.8670	12.6000
191	488.2327	4.6500	20.4800	1.1111	402.8457	402.8400	77.0101	22.2426
192	100.7820	1.7030	2.4430	1.6800	88.7960	4.0000	21.0000	28.3032
193	165.7970	4.7660	3.2790	88.0003	120.1080	2.0000	4.0008	18.2022
194	274.8440	3.5500	21.7900	2.9530	213.1860	3.0000	3.7521	24.2628
195	11049.5000	166.8480	667.7998	55.5000	9955.3984	4485.1953	22.0007	52.5000
196	1154.8477	14.4190	32.2360	4.0800	1037.4727	424.4556	21.1234	30.3234
197	578.7107	11.4920	26.3000	8.0141	433.8230	1.0111	12.3456	5.3300
198	124.5440	1.8000	4.6280	1.9850	101.5300	23.6630	78.9101	36.3840
199	3711.2029	63.4000	303.3838	4.5720	2729.9280	22.0222	91.0111	33.0000
200	124.8600	2.0000	5.2240	2.3200	79.7770	51.0000	21.3141	2.6500
201	2466.0000	26.8650	161.7000	2.0202	2028.7996	18.4021	3.2000	14.9000
202	2829.2991	36.2000	156.8000	27.1000	2261.0000	930.2000	51.1617	25.2000
203	814.8196	14.8000	48.5520	16.0111	622.9507	204.9000	18.1920	1.4150
204	4051.7996	46.0000	349.5999	2.6000	3036.5999	1215.2996	21.2223	56.6000
205	67.0390	28.0000	3.5010	2.5170	54.9070	66.5620	24.2526	42.4446

206	240.5670	4.0000	5.5670	1.3220	184.1350	61.6900	2.5860	3.0470
207	45.2140	2.0000	1.4110	18.1010	38.0970	62.3201	27.2829	48.5052
208	69.9520	81.0000	33.3333	8.0033	65.4570	52.3302	30.3132	54.5658
209	54.5490	1.1270	1.7720	17.7200	42.5990	42.4444	33.3435	60.6264
210	317.4480	5.7840	12.6650	11.0330	254.1990	80.1010	36.3738	66.6870
211	847.9927	24.0000	85.0240	19.7930	664.9578	34.1021	39.4041	10.4000
212	467.9546	4.8450	13.1650	2.3810	400.5806	4.0999	42.4344	1.0011
213	126.6750	14.0007	7.7490	14.1441	109.6830	50.6410	45.4647	1.0022
214	85.7290	49.0000	2.1610	49.4949	72.8400	9.9901	48.4950	1.0033
215	680.7666	8.2200	19.2340	77.7878	578.8528	9.8175	51.5253	1.3090
216	211.3230	1.5670	4.8350	15.6180	171.4130	65.0000	54.5556	1.8201
217	254.3030	3.1000	2.7620	2.3570	205.8410	42.4381	57.5859	2.0880
218	1396.8108	29.4160	79.9820	28.2626	1000.2886	3.8107	16.1580	3.4510
219	3981.0000	52.9000	188.3000	70.3000	3120.5999	1085.7996	75.8000	37.5000
220	3943.0990	56.5320	259.5000	49.9000	3352.3008	1275.7002	60.6162	42.3000
221	1260.2349	17.2880	103.0320	11.4810	1055.9436	12.0000	63.6465	2.1133
222	973.2527	9.8850	25.4530	5.5580	848.7227	4.0877	66.6768	3.3210
223	19.9060	18.0002	5.6666	1.4100	16.5170	3.3876	69.7071	4.2242
224	66.8260	1.3200	6.1110	88.1388	48.9480	4.5222	72.7374	5.6210
225	178.7460	2.1980	5.5430	138.0000	138.5690	43.4350	75.7677	6.2155
226	26.7510	1.0560	8.8888	211.0113	17.9930	18.1111	78.7980	7.2102
227	20.5750	43.1111	7.7777	82.1003	13.9720	14.2222	81.8283	8.9712
228	51.5960	18.5216	1.6940	1.1620	38.8190	88.9922	81.0077	24.2601
229	106.1150	2.6000	4.6850	9.9210	64.0500	12.4243	77.0222	23.2810
230	8.5160	14.2421	12.0818	12.1402	5.9500	7.8246	22.4443	24.8588
231	308.8916	5.7000	15.8370	13.1402	144.7340	42.4444	47.8877	2.7060
232	753.8069	16.8750	37.4620	3.6210	491.1160	210.0050	16.4370	4.9340
233	41.2960	1.1080	2.5820	12.1213	28.1320	81.8118	12.5456	24.5293
234	145.6840	3.4190	13.3250	1.0087	105.1630	51.7100	51.8196	1.8480
235	51.3130	1.0000	1.5700	8.0025	35.9730	43.4400	21.4231	59.6085
236	21.4070	12.5358	18.7842	5.5554	12.9550	12.8888	37.8286	64.8821
237	585.6597	8.2000	56.0530	80.9960	359.8350	77.9999	13.6920	8.9610
238	516.7239	10.3000	17.9320	9.3610	376.4170	1.1007	5.6670	5.6000
239	316.8147	7.0000	3.9360	12.1314	267.2456	2.0008	86.8686	76.7686
240	509.7000	10.0000	27.0360	15.1617	375.3457	179.9240	85.8686	3.6080
241	341.3887	7.1270	7.1570	8.1819	287.6907	9.0007	86.8888	86.7795
242	33.0660	1.0872	1.9540	9.2021	24.0720	12.7210	83.1111	95.9594

continues

DATABASE Concluded.

Company Number	Sales (Millions)	Employees (Thousands)	Capital Expenditures (Millions)	Intangibles Expenditures (Millions)	Cost of Goods Sold (Millions)	Labor and Related Expense (Millions)	Advertising Expense (Millions)	Research and Development Expense (Millions)
243	200.5920	4.0000	5.3320	20.0290	153.5480	7.6660	82.2222	94.9388
244	184.5810	4.0500	7.2780	10.3570	142.7160	8.7770	22.6665	1.0790
245	217.7520	4.0880	7.3840	10.1146	179.1020	78.3910	44.6621	89.9012
246	386.8118	7.4040	18.4880	47.1213	302.5586	2.9990	18.1716	3.8620
247	69.1530	12.1212	1.6190	48.1415	54.4310	11.3410	15.1413	13.8125
248	81.4650	1.6220	4.1890	16.4950	70.5080	4.4555	12.1110	47.8552
249	329.5518	6.0040	12.2520	8.0540	269.6377	12.1417	9.8765	51.9185
250	36.3870	133.0000	12.7246	51.5355	27.7690	21.8283	4.3210	54.3321
251	344.7937	7.5000	24.7400	57.5982	205.0610	92.9395	8.1234	4.8200
252	22.8030	84.1000	2.1060	83.4952	10.6830	96.9899	5.6788	43.8388
253	196.3030	5.4660	5.9730	99.9242	142.1520	97.9294	12.4582	2.2710
254	31.5660	13.7124	8.1264	10.1115	22.3750	95.0092	14.5220	66.7274
255	108.8580	1.7000	1.2870	92.4445	45.9130	92.6666	1.4330	53.5422
256	83.6260	1.2320	4.1220	55.6677	45.0950	92.5555	13.5620	22.5673
257	390.8726	6.1660	17.3310	40.5880	296.8577	58.2130	18.0000	10.0000
258	363.9839	7.0160	11.2700	11.5610	234.6320	2.7310	6.4860	86.0000
259	52.2620	.4420	5.1030	1.1500	43.5110	12.1440	44.0700	16.0000
260	228.6110	5.6500	1.8370	41.5600	161.4700	20.5400	14.9460	3.0730
261	60.8250	1.5000	1.4910	45.3100	41.6820	1.8970	1.6590	30.7300
262	16.6890	40.5000	57.6000	9.8540	9.8450	18.3700	35.2020	63.5300
263	39.8290	62.1000	3.9900	1.5610	32.6580	4.9080	9.2530	30.0000
264	28.9020	93.4000	1.1040	36.5000	23.1410	2.5900	18.3650	10.0000
265	8.7410	27.0000	55.6000	32.1400	6.3700	59.3100	27.6600	56.6660
266	61.9446	7.0000	35.0470	43.2000	432.3777	160.6660	19.2020	6.3530

Index